Yearbook of International Humanitarian Law

Volume 14

For further volumes:
http://www.springer.com/series/8912

Michael N. Schmitt
General Editor

Louise Arimatsu
Managing Editor

Yearbook of International Humanitarian Law Volume 14, 2011

T·M·C·ASSER PRESS

CAMBRIDGE
UNIVERSITY PRESS

Springer

General Editor
Michael N. Schmitt
CNWS-ILD
United States Naval War College
Newport, RI
USA

Managing Editor
Louise Arimatsu
Chatham House
The Royal Institute of International Affairs
London
UK

Cover Photo: Arab Spring; photo ANP/AFP

ISBN 978-90-6704-854-5 ISBN 978-90-6704-855-2 (eBook)
DOI 10.1007/978-90-6704-855-2

This Volume is also available as a journal product through Cambridge University Press. In addition to the electronic version published on www.springerlink, the Yearbook is also available online through the Cambridge Journals Online service.
Published by T.M.C. Asser press, The Hague, The Netherlands www.asserpress.nl
Produced and distributed for T.M.C. Asser press by Springer-Verlag Berlin Heidelberg

Printed on acid-free paper

Springer is part of Springer Science+Business Media (www.springer.com)

Editors' Note

In order to make the Correspondents' Reports more timely and widely accessible, the Editors are pleased to announce that these Reports will henceforth be available online at www.asser.nl/YIHL/correspondentsreports. This brings the added benefit of making them fully searchable, thereby more easily serving the needs of scholars and practitioners.

The editors wish to extend a special thanks to Hemeeni Mistry for her assistance in the production of this volume.

Contents

Part I Articles

Part II Current Developments

Part IV Documentation

Abbreviations

AALCO	Asian-African Legal Consultative Organization
Abl.	Amtsblatt
AC	Appeal Cases
ACTR	Australian Capital Territory Reports
AD	Annual Digest of Public International Law Cases
Adelaide LR	Adelaide Law Review
ADF	Australian Defence Force
AFDI	Annuairefrançais de droit international
AFRC	Armed Forces Revolutionary Council (Sierra Leone)
African HRLJ	African Human Rights Law Journal
African JI & CL	African Journal of International and Comparative Law
African YIHL	African Yearbook on International Humanitarian Law
Air Force LR	Air Force Law Review
Air LR	Air Law Review
Airpower J	Airpower Journal
Air Univ. Rev.	Air University Review
AJCL	American Journal of Comparative Law
AJIL	American Journal of International Law
AJLP	Australian Journal of Legal Philosophy
Albany LR	Albany Law Review
All ER	All England Law Reports
ALR	Australian Law Reports
Amer. Crim. LR	American Criminal Law Review
Amer. Univ. JIL & Pol.	American University Journal of International Law and Policy

Amer. Univ. ILJ	American University International Law Journal
Amer. Univ. ILR	American University International Law Review
Amer. Univ. LR	American University Law Review
AMISOM	African Union Mission to Somalia
ANA	Afghanistan National Army
AP	Additional Protocol
AP	Associated Press
APL(s)	Anti-personnel landmine(s)
ARABSAT	Arab Satellite Communications Organization
Arizona JI & CL	Arizona Journal of International and Comparative Law
Army Law.	The Army Lawyer
ASEAN	Association of South East Asian Nations
ASF	African Standby Force
ASIL Proc.	American Society of International Law Proceedings
ATCA	Alien Tort Claims Act (USA)
ATT	Arms Trade Treaty
AU	African Union
AMIB	African Union Mission in Burundi
AMIS	African Union Mission in Sudan
AMISOM	African Union Mission in Somalia
Australian YIL	Australian Yearbook of International Law
Austrian JPIL	Austrian Journal for Public International Law
Austrian Rev. Int. & Eur. L	Austrian Revue of International and European Law
AVM	Anti-vehicle landmine
Berkeley JIL	Berkeley Journal of International Law
B.O.	Boletín Oficial de la República Argentina
BGBl	Bundesgesetzblatt
BGH	Bundesgerichtshof
Boston Univ. ILJ	Boston University International Law Journal
Boston College Int. & Comp. LR	Boston College International and Comparative Law Review
Brooklyn JIL	Brooklyn Journal of International Law
BTF	Balkans Task Force
BverfGE	Bundesverfassungsgericht
BYIL	British Yearbook of International Law

California LR	California Law Review
Calif. Western ILJ	California Western International Law Journal
Can. JL & Jur.	Canadian Journal of Law and Jurisprudence
Canadian YIL	Canadian Yearbook of International Law
CardozoLR	Cardozo Law Review
Case Western Reserve JIL	Case Western Reserve Journal of International Law
Catholic Univ. LR	Catholic University Law Review
CCW	Convention on Certain Conventional Weapons
CD	Conference on Disarmament
CDF	Civil Defence Forces (Sierra Leone)
CENTCOM	Central Command
Chicago JIL	Chicago Journal of International Law
Chinese JIL	Chinese Journal of International Law
CHR (UN)	Centre for Human Rights
CIA	Central Intelligence Agency
CICC	Coalition for the International Criminal Court
CICR	Comité International de la Croix Rouge
CID	Criminal Investigation Division
CIS	Commonwealth of Independent States
CIVPOL	Civilian Police
CLA	Chief Legal Advisor
CLJ	Criminal Law Journal
CLR	Commonwealth Law Reports
CMAC	Court Martial Appeal Court
Cmnd.	Command Paper
Columbia HRLR	Columbia Human Rights Law Review
Columbia JTL	Columbia Journal of Transnational Law
Columbia LR	Columbia Law Review
Connecticut JIL	Connecticut Journal of International Law
Cornell ILJ	Cornell International Law Journal
Cr. App. R	Criminal Appeals Reports
CRC	Convention on the Rights of the Child
Criminal LF	Criminal Law Forum
Criminal LR	Criminal Law Review
CSP	Conference of States Parties
CTBT	Comprehensive Test Ban Treaty
CTED	Counter-Terrorism Committee Executive Directorate
CTS	Commonwealth Treaty Series
CWC	Chemical Weapons Convention

DalhousieLJ	Dalhousie Law Journal
Denver JIL & Pol.	Denver Journal of International Law and Policy
DLR	Dominion Law Reports
DMU	Detainee Management Unit
DoD	Department of Defense (USA)
Drake LR	Drake Law Review
DRC	Democratic Republic of Congo
Duke JCIL	Duke Journal of Comparative and International Law
ECCAS	Economic Community of Central African States
ECCC	Extraordinary Chambers in the Courts of Cambodia
ECHR Rep.	European Convention on Human Rights Reports
ECHR	European Convention on Human Rights
ECOMOG	ECOWAS Cease-Fire Monitoring Group
ECOSOC	United Nations Economic and Social Council
ECOWAS	Economic Community of West African States
ECtHR	European Court on Human Rights
EECC	Eritrea-Ethiopia Claims Commission
EHRR	European Human Rights Reports
Emory ILR	Emory International Law Review
EJIL	European Journal of International Law
ERW	Explosive Remnants of War
EU	European Union
Eur. Ct. HR	European Court of Human Rights
EUFOR	European Union Force
Eur. Comm. HR	European Commission of Human Rights
Eur. J Crime, Crim. L & Crim. Jus.	European Journal of Crime, Criminal Law and Criminal Justice
Ex D	Exchequer Digest
F	Federal
F Supp.	Federal Supplement
FARDC	Armed Forces of the Democratic Republic of the Congo
FCJ	Federal Court of Justice (Canada)
FCR	Federal Court Reports
FDC	Force Detention Centre
FDTL	East Timorese Defence Force
Fed. Reg.	Federal Register (United States)

Fed. Rep.	Federal Reporter
Finnish YIL	Finnish Yearbook of International Law
FNI	Front des Nationalistes et Intégrationistes (Congo)
Fordham ILJ	Fordham International Law Journal
Fordham LR	Fordham Law Review
FPLC	Forces Patriotiques pour la Libérationdu Congo
FRETILIN	Frente Revolucionaria Timor Lest Independence
FRPI	Force de Résistance Patriotique en Ituri (Congo)
FRY	Federal Republic of Yugoslavia
FYROM	Former Yugoslav Republic of Macedonia
GA	General Assembly (United Nations)
GAOR	General Assembly Official Records
GA Res.	General Assembly Resolution (United Nations)
GC	Geneva Conventions
Georgetown Int. Environ. LR	Georgetown International Environmental Law Review
Georgetown JIL	Georgetown Journal of International Law
Georgia JI & Comp. L	Georgia Journal of International and Comparative Law
German LJ	German Law Journal
GR2P	Global Responsibility to Protect
GWILR	The George Washington International Law Review
GWJIL and Econ.	The George Washington Journal of International Law and Economics
GU	Gazzetta Ufficiale (Italian Official Gazette)
GYIL	German Yearbook of International Law
Hague YIL	Hague Yearbook of International Law
Harvard ILJ	Harvard International Law Journal
Harvard JHR	Harvard Journal of Human Rights
Harvard JL & Pub. Pol.	Harvard Journal of Law & Public Policy
Harvard JOL	Harvard Journal on Legislation
Harvard LR	Harvard Law Review
Harvard NSJ	Harvard National Security Journal
HCJ	High Court of Justice
HRLJ	Human Rights Law Journal
HRLR	Human Rights Law Review
HRQ	Human Rights Quarterly

I/A Court HR	Inter-American Court of Human Rights
I/A Comm. HR	Inter-American Commission on Human Rights
I/A YBHR	Inter-American Yearbook on Human Rights
ICA	International Council on Archives
ICBL	International Campaign to Ban Landmines
ICBS	International Committee of the Blue Shield
ICC	International Criminal Court
ICCPR	International Covenant on Civil and Political Rights
ICCROM	International Centre for the Study of the Preservation and Restoration of Cultural Property
ICISS	International Commission on Intervention and State Sovereignty
ICJ	International Court of Justice
ICJ Rep.	International Court of Justice Reports
ICLR	International Criminal Law Review
ICLQ	International and Comparative Law Quarterly
ICOM	International Council of Museums
ICOMOS	International Council on Monuments and Sites
ICRC	International Committee of the Red Cross
ICRtoP	International Coalition for the Responsibility to Protect
ICTR	International Criminal Tribunal for Rwanda
ICTY	International Criminal Tribunal for the former Yugoslavia
IDR	International Defense Review
IFLA	International Federation of Library Association and Institutions
IFOR	Implementation Force
IHL	International Humanitarian Law
IJLM	International Journal of Legal Medicine
IJRL	International Journal of Refugee Law
ILASJI & Comp. L	ILAS Journal of International and Comparative Law
ILC	International Law Commission
ILC Yearbook	Yearbook of the International Law Commission
ILM	International Legal Materials
ILR	International Law Reports

IMO	International Maritime Organization
IMT	International Military Tribunal (in Nuremberg)
IMTFE	International Military Tribunal for the Far East (in Tokyo)
Indian JIL	Indian Journal of International Law
Indiana I & Comp. LR	Indiana International & Comparative Law Review
INTELSAT	International Telecommunications Satellite Organization
Int. LF	International Law Forum
INTERFET	International Force in East Timor
IRA	Irish Republican Army
Iran-US CTR	Iran-United States Claims Tribunal Reports
IRRC	International Review of the Red Cross
ISAF	International Security Assistance Force
Israel LR	Israel Law Review
Israel YB	Israel Yearbook
Israel YB HR	Israel Yearbook on Human Rights
IYIL	Italian Yearbook of International Law
JAMA	Journal of the American Medical Association
J Armed Conflict L	Journal of Armed Conflict Law
JCSL	Journal of Conflict and Security Law
JICL	Journal of International and Comparative Law
JIL & Prac.	Journal of International Law and Practice
J Int. Criminal Justice	Journal of International Criminal Justice
JPI	Judicial Police Inspectors
J Trans. L & Pol.	Journal of Transnational Law & Policy
J Trauma	The Journal of Trauma
KFOR	Kosovo Force
KLA	Kosovo Liberation Army
LAS	League of Arab States
Leiden JIL	Leiden Journal of International Law
LNTS	League of Nations Treaty Series
LOAC	Law of Armed Conflict
Loy. LA I & CLJ	Loyola of Los Angeles International and Comparative Law Journal
Loyola I & CLJ	Loyola International and Comparative Law Journal
LQR	Law Quarterly Review

Maryland JIL & T	Maryland Journal of International Law and Trade
MCC	Military Criminal Code
Melbourne JIL	Melbourne Journal of International Law
Melbourne Univ. LR	Melbourne University Law Review
Michigan JIL	Michigan Journal of International Law
Michigan LR	Michigan Law Review
Mil. LR	Military Law Review
MINURCAT	United Nations Mission in the Central African Republic and Chad
MINURSO	United Nations Mission for the Referendum in Western Sahara
MINUSTAH	United Nations Stabilization Mission in Haiti
MLR	Modern Law Review
MNF	Multinational Force
MonashLR	Monash Law Review
MoniteurBelge	Belgian Official Parliamentary Journal
MONUC	United Nations Mission in the Democratic Republic of Congo
Moscow JIL	Moscow Journal of International Law
MPYBUNL	Max Planck Yearbook of United Nations Law
MPYIL	Max Planck Yearbook of International Law
MRT	Militair Rechtelijk Tijdschrift
NATO	North Atlantic Treaty Organisation
Naval LR	Naval Law Review
NCOs	Non-Commissioned Officers
Nebraska LR	Nebraska Law Review
New England LR	New England Law Review
NGO	Non-Governmental Organisation
NILR	Netherlands International Law Review
NJ	Nederlandse Jurisprudentie
NLA	Albanian National Liberation Army
NLR	Naval Law Review
Nordic JIL	Nordic Journal of International Law
North Carolina LR	North Carolina Law Review
Northwestern JIHR	Northwestern Journal of International Human Rights
Northwestern Univ. LR	Northwestern University Law Review
Notre Dame JL	Notre Dame Journal of Law
Notre Dame LR	Notre Dame Law Review
NPC	New Penal Code

NQHR	Netherlands Quarterly of Human Rights
NYIL	Netherlands Yearbook of International Law
NY Univ. JIL & Pol.	New York University Journal of International Law and Politics
NY Univ. LR	New York University Law Review
NZLR	New Zealand Law Review
ÖAD	Österreichische Außenpolitische Dokumentation
OAS	Organization of American States
OECS	Organization of Eastern Caribbean States
OEF	Operation Enduring Freedom (Afghanistan)
OIF	Operation Iraqi Freedom
ONU	Organisation des Nations Unies
ONUB	United Nations Operation in Burundi
ONUC	United Nations Operation in the Congo
OPCW	Organisation for the Prohibition of Chemical Weapons
OSA	Operational Support Arrangement
OTP	Office of the Prosecutor (of the ICTR and/or ICTY)
Palestine YIL	Palestine Yearbook of International Law
PCIJ	Permanent Court of Justice
PD	Probate Division, English Law Reports
Penn. State ILR	Pennsylvania State International Law Review
PKF	Peace Keeping Force
PMG	Peace Monitoring Group
POC	Protection of Civilians
POW	Prisoner of War
Proc. ASIL	Proceedings of the American Society of International Law
QB	Queen's Bench
RBDI	Revue Belgededroit international
RDI	Rivista di dirittointernazionale
RDPC	Revue de droit pénal et decriminologie
Recueil des Cours	Collected Courses of the Hague Academy of International Law
RGDIP	Revue générale de droit international public
RIAA	Reports of International Arbitral Awards
RICR	Revue International de la Croix Rouge
RPF	Rwandan Patriotic Front

RQDI	Revue QuébécoisedeDroit International
RSC	Rules of the Supreme Court
RSCDPC	Revue de science criminelle et de droit pénal comparé
RSDIE	Revue Suissededroit international et de droit européen
RSK	Republic of Serbian Krajina
RUF	Revolutionary United Front (Sierra Leone)
Rutgers LR	Rutgers Law Review
R2P-RtoP	Responsibility to Protect
SADC	South African Development Community
San Diego LR	San Diego Law Review
SASC	South African Security Council
Saskatchewan LR	Saskatchewan Law Review
SC	Security Council
SC CTC	Security Council's Counter-Terrorism Committee
SCOR	Security Council Official Records
SC Res.	Security Council Resolution
SCR	Supreme Court Reports
S. Ct.	Supreme Court Reporter (United States)
SCU	Serious Crimes Unit
SFOR	Stabilization Force
SFRY	Socialist Federal Republic of Yugoslavia
SG	Secretary-General
SIPRI	Stockholm International Peace Research Institute
SOFA	Status of Force Agreement
South African YIL	South African Yearbook of International Law
South Texas LR	South Texas Law Review
Stanford JIL	Stanford Journal of International Law
Stanford JIR	Stanford Journal of International Relations
Stanford LR	Stanford Law Review
Syracuse JIL & Com.	Syracuse Journal of International Law & Commerce
SZIER	Schweizerische Zeitschrift für internationales und europäisches Recht
Tel Aviv Univ. LR	Tel Aviv University Law Review
Temple LR	Temple Law Review
Tennessee LR	Tennessee Law Review
Texas ILJ	Texas International Law Journal
Texas LR	Texas Law Review

TFG	Transitional Federal Government (Somalia)
TIAS	Treaties and other International Acts Series
Tilburg For. LR	Tilburg Foreign Law Review
TLPS	Timorese Police Force
Transn. L & Contemp. Probs.	Transnational Law and Contemporary Problems
TRC Report	Truth and Reconciliation Commission Report (South African)
Tulane JI & Comp. L	Tulane Journal of International & Comparative Law
Tulsa J Comp. & IL	Tulsa Journal of Comparative and International Law
TVF	Trust Fund for Victims
UCLALR	University of California Los Angeles Law Review
UN	United Nations
UNAKRT	United Nations Assistance to the Khmer Rouge Trial
UNAMA	United Nations Assistance Mission in Afghanistan
UNAMET	United Nations Mission in East Timor
UNAMI	United Nations Assistance Mission for Iraq
UNAMID	United Nations/ African Union Hybrid Operation in Darfur
UNAMIR	United Nations Assistance Mission for Rwanda
UNAMSIL	United Nations Mission in Sierra Leone
UNCHR	United Nations Commission on Human Rights
UNCHS	United Nations Centre for Human Settlements
UNCIVPOL	United Nations Civilian Police
UNCTAD	United Nations Conference on Trade and Development
UN Doc.	United Nations Documents Series
UNDOF	United Nations Disengagement Observer Force
UNDP	United Nations Development Programme
UNEF	United Nations Emergency Force (in the Sinai)
UNEP	United Nations Environment Programme

UNESCO	United Nations Educational, Scientific and Cultural Organisation
UNFICYP	United Nations Force in Cyprus
UNGCI	United Nations Guards Contingent in Iraq
UNHCR	United Nations High Commissioner for Refugees
UNHFOR	United Nations Human Rights Field Office in Rwanda
UNICEF	United Nations (International) Children's (Emergency) Fund
UNIDIR	United Nations Institute for Disarmament Research
UNIFEM	United Nations Development Fund for Women
UNIFIL	United Nations Interim Force in Lebanon
UNIIMOG	United Nations Iran/Iraq Military Observer Group
UNIKOM	United Nations Iraq/Kuwait Observer Mission
UNIPSIL	United Nations Integrated Peacebuilding Office in Sierra Leone
UNITAF	United Nations Unified Task Force
UNITAF	United Nations Task Force (in Somalia)
UNMEE	United Nations Mission in Ethiopia and Eritrea
UNMIL	United Nations Mission in Liberia
UNMIN	United Nations Mission in Nepal
UNMIS	United Nations Mission in Sudan
UNMIT	United Nations Mission in Timor-Leste
UNOCI	United Nations Operations in Côte d'Ivoire
UNOMIG	United Nations Observer Mission in Georgia
UNOMSIL	United Nations Observer Mission in Sierra Leone
UNOSOM	United Nations Operation in Somalia
UNPF	United Nations Peacekeeping Force
UNPOS	United Nations Political Office for Somalia
UNPROFOR	United Nations Protection Force (in Bosnia and Herzegovina)
UNTAC	United Nations Transitional Authority in Cambodia
UNTAET	United Nations Transitional Authority in East Timor
UNTS	United Nations Treaty Series
UNWCC	United Nations War Crimes Commission

Univ. Calif. Davis LR	University of California Davis Law Review
Univ. Chicago LR	University of Chicago Law Review
Univ. Miami I & Comp. LR	University of Miami International & Comparative Law Review
Univ. Pa. J Const. L	University of Pennsylvania Journal of Constitutional Law
Univ. Pitt. LR	University of Pittsburgh Law Review
Univ. Richmond LR	University of Richmond Law Review
USAFAJLS	United States Air Force Academy Journal of Legal Studies
Vanderbilt JTL	Vanderbilt Journal of Transnational Law
VCLT	Vienna Convention on the Law of Treaties
Vermont LR	Vermont Law Review
Virginia JIL	Virginia Journal of International Law
Virginia LR	Virginia Law Review
VWU	Victims and Witness Unit of the Registry (Congo)
Wake Forest LR	Wake Forest Law Review
WBR	Wound Ballistics Review
WCR	War Crimes Reports
WHO	World Health Organisation
Whittier LR	Whittier Law Review
Wisconsin ILJ	Wisconsin International Law Journal
WLR	Weekly Law Reports
Yale HR & Dev. LJ	Yale Human Rights & Development Law Journal
Yale JIL	Yale Journal of International Law
Yale LJ	Yale Law Journal
YbEur. Conv. HR	Yearbook of the European Convention of Human Rights
YbILC	Yearbook of the International Law Commission
YIHL	Yearbook of International Humanitarian Law
Yug. Rev. IL	Yugoslav Review of International Law
ZaöRV	Zeitschrift für ausländisches öffentliches Recht und Völkerrecht
ZöR	Zeitschrift für öffentliches Recht

Part I
Articles

Chapter 1
Evaluating the Use of Force During the Arab Spring

Annyssa Bellal and Louise Doswald-Beck

Contents

1.1 Introduction

When, on 17 December 2010, Mohamed Bouazizi, a 26-year old, set himself on fire as a desperate act of protest in Sidi Bouzid, Tunisia, he did not know that he was going to spark a historical movement of political revolutions that would sweep through the nations bordering the Mediterranean Sea. The 'Arab Spring', which in the spring of 2011 touched Tunisia, Egypt, Bahrain, Libya, and most recently

A. Bellal (✉) · L. Doswald-Beck
Geneva Academy of International Humanitarian Law and Human Rights (the Academy), Geneva, Switzerland
e-mail: annyssa.bellal@graduateinstitute.ch

L. Doswald-Beck
The Graduate Institute of International and Development Studies, Geneva, Switzerland
e-mail: louise.doswaldbeck@graduateinstitute.ch

M.N. Schmitt and L. Arimatsu (eds.), *Yearbook of International Humanitarian Law Volume 14, 2011*, DOI: 10.1007/978-90-6704-855-2_1,

Syria, among other countries, has so far led to mixed results in terms of regime change.[1] Whereas in Tunisia and Egypt, autocratic leaders relinquished power relatively quickly and with limited bloodshed, in Libya, Bahrain, Yemen and Syria protests were, and still are in the latter three of these countries, harshly repressed over the course of several weeks and months leading to thousands of people being killed or wounded. Of course, each of these revolutions has different political, social, and historical backgrounds. It is almost trite to note that power structures in Egypt or Libya are not the same, nor are, for example, the characteristics of society in Syria or Bahrain. This helps to explain the difference between the types of revolution that have taken place. Nevertheless the common aspiration that has pushed huge numbers of ordinary citizens to risk their lives, namely, to achieve freedom by bringing to an end longstanding despotic governments, unites all these cases. The courage of those who have risked all to secure change and those of many others who are still confronting death and torture for exercising their right to peaceful protest, has attracted widespread admiration.

The legal questions raised by the Arab Spring are almost as numerous and as complex as the scenarios that occurred. In Libya, for instance, the late Colonel Qaddafi, in response to civil protests in the east of the country, launched armed attacks against protesters, and then later plunged the country into an armed conflict of a non-international character with groups that became organised and armed, thereby triggering the application of international humanitarian law (IHL). This had the paradoxical consequence under IHL of allowing the Libyan government to use force against persons participating directly in hostilities, who could also be tried for having taken up arms against the regime. In Syria, at the time of the writing of the present article, the movement of civil protest has largely been engaged in an unarmed struggle despite the continued use of force and violence by the regime. There have been recent statements, however, that the degree of violence could now have reached that of a non-international armed conflict.[2]

The evaluation of the use of force in such contexts needs to start with an analysis of the right to protest under international law and to its regulation. May a government use force to limit or control mass protest, and if so, what is its scope? In particular, what does public international law have to say, if anything, about *armed* civil resistance against oppressive political regimes? Can a State commit the equivalent of aggression against its own people and, were this the case, is there a collective right to self-defence for a population in danger? Would this change the applicable law?

We will discuss these issues from different angles. After a summary of facts and applicable law, the article will review human rights law applicable to civil protest.

---

[1] Countries concerned are, albeit to a different extent: Algeria, Bahrain, Egypt, Iran, Iraq, Israel, Jordan, Kuwait, Lebanon, Libya, Morocco, Palestine, Saudi Arabia, Syria, Tunisia, the United Arab Emirates, and Yemen. For an interesting time line of the events, see, for example—Blight et al. 2011.

[2] Bakri 2011, citing a statement made by the UN High Commissioner for Human Rights.

We next examine whether there is, under international law, the right of a population to rebel against an oppressive government, what force may be lawfully used in such circumstances and whether protesters can resort to self-defence. Finally, we will discuss whether any of the above considerations make any difference to the IHL applicable to a non-international conflict arising from organised armed resistance in response to the force used by the government.

1.2 Summary of Facts and Applicable Law

At the time of the writing of this article, among the 'Arab Spring' countries where civil protest took place, Yemen was, and still is, in a situation of armed conflict; Syria may be entering such a situation; and an armed conflict took place in Libya from March to October 2011.

Before the popular uprising, Yemen was already in situation of armed conflict which began in 2000, and was opposing government forces and Huthi rebels in the Sa'ad region.[3] A conflict between Al Qaeda elements present in Yemen against Yemeni and US forces has also been on going for several years.[4] Civil unrest, however, started in January 2011. Following the wave of protest in Tunisia, mass street demonstrations called for the resignation of President Ali Abdullah Saleh. Finally, after months of protests, President Saleh signed an agreement on 23 November 2011, immediately transferring power to his vice-president.[5] It seems clear that human rights law standards on law enforcement restricting the use of force during demonstrations would apply in that case, and that the application of IHL be limited to the zone of conflict in the Sa'ad region and in situations of combat against Al Qaeda.[6]

Libyan protesters took to the streets in February 2011. After the brutal repression of the demonstration by the Qaddafi regime, which was condemned by

[3] Human Rights Watch 2008, and Geneva Academy of International Humanitarian Law and Human Rights, Rule of Law in Armed Conflicts Project: Country Profile, Yemen, available at http://www.adh-geneva.ch/RULAC/current_conflict.php?id_state=234.

[4] See the assessment of the Council for Foreign Policy on Al Qaeda in Yemen, Council on Foreign Policy 2011.

[5] New York Times (2011).

[6] Thus for example, in the context of Afghanistan, Denmark took the view that where its soldiers are in direct combat with the Taliban in Helmand province, such actions are regulated by international humanitarian law on non-international armed conflict. Where, however, its soldiers are patrolling 'the more peaceful areas north of Helmand' and they 'detain a person outside the framework outside of the armed conflict', it is human rights law that is applicable. Text cited in Stigall et al. 2009, p. 1379; See also Casey-Maslen 2013, who underlines that a same conclusion must be implied regarding the legality of the use of weapons other than as a method of warfare, or in riot control situations.

the international community,[7] an insurgency started to organise, took control of the eastern part of the country and announced that it had formed 'a national council.'[8] On 17 March 2011, acting under Chapter VII of the UN Charter, the Security Council authorized the use of 'all necessary measures' to protect civilians in Libya.[9] By late February 2011, Libya was in a situation of a non international armed conflict and from mid-March it was engaged in an international armed conflict governed by IHL with the States participating militarily in the implementation of the measures to protect civilians, including a no-fly zone, authorised by UN Security Council resolution 1973, fighting against the Libyan regime.[10] Common Article 3, as well as Additional Protocol II, to which Libya is a party, applied to the simultaneous non-international armed conflict between the rebels and the regime. It is also worth noting that Libya did not derogate from any of the provisions in the International Covenant on Civil and Political Rights (ICCPR); accordingly, all of these rights applied throughout the country. However, heavy fighting rather than protest took place in the country until the death of Qaddafi on 20 October 2011.[11] In its report, the International Commission of Inquiry for Libya, which was established by the UN Human Rights Council in February 2011, examined the excessive use of force by the Libya government during the demonstrations. The applicable law was the ICCPR and the Code of Conduct for Law Enforcement Officials and the Basic Principles on the Use of Force and Firearms by Law Enforcement Officials. The Commission concluded that there was:

> sufficient evidence to suggest that the Government forces engaged in excessive use of force against demonstrators, at least in the early days of the protests, leading to significant deaths and injuries. The nature of injuries inflicted in several locations (with high proportions shot in the head or upper body) is indicative of "shoot to kill" operations. From the common style of response in many parts of the country, it would appear likely that the forces were given orders to engage in the harsh crackdown of demonstrators. Such actions represented a serious breach of a range of rights under the ICCPR including the right to life, the right to security of person, as well as freedom of assembly and freedom of expression. In relation to the latter days of protests as the situation escalated, more investigation would be required to assess the security forces' use of force, in particular

---

[7] The United Nations Human Rights Council ordered inquiries into abuses and suspended Libya from its membership. It was the first time a country was suspended from membership to the Council following serious human rights violations—UN News Centre 2011a.

[8] Geneva Academy of International Humanitarian Law and Human Rights, Rule of Law in Armed Conflicts Project: Country Profile: Libya, available at http://www.adh-geneva.ch/RULAC/current_conflict.php?id_state=128.

[9] UNSC Res. 1973, 17 March 2011, para 4—UN News Centre 2011b.

[10] See the UN Human Rights Council, Report of the International Commission of Inquiry to investigate all alleged violations of international human rights law in the Libyan Arab Jamahiriya, 1st June 2011a, A/HRC/17/44, available at http://www2.ohchr.org/english/bodies/hrcouncil/docs/17session/A.HRC.17.44_AUV.pdf, para 40 (Accessed 13 December 2011) ('Hereinafter 'UN Human Rights Council Libya Report').

[11] The Guardian 2011b.

more detail concerning the actions taken by demonstrators in these days in order to assess the response by Government authorities.[12]

Civil unrest reached Syria in March 2011. The regime of Al-Assad violently repressed the peaceful protests and, according to the UN, more than 4,000 people were killed between March and the end of November.[13] As of November 2011, there have been reports of soldiers deserting the official army to join protesters[14] and the political opposition has met with the UK's foreign secretary. It may be the case, therefore, that an organised armed opposition group fighting governmental forces has formed in Syria and the country is on the brink of a non-international armed conflict. Until that is established, however, international human rights law, including the provision on the use of force and arbitrary killings, regulates the situation. That being said, the legal situation in Syria regarding use of force would probably become more complex if defected soldiers were to use force in defence of civilians, as was reported in the news.[15] The report of the Independent International Commission of Inquiry on the Syrian Arab Republic established by the UN Human Rights Council based itself on Syria's human rights obligations under human rights treaty law to report excessive use of force and extrajudicial executions, arbitrary detentions, enforced disappearances, torture and other forms of ill-treatment, violation of children rights, displacement and restriction of movement and violations of economic and social rights.[16] The Commission also noted that it was 'concerned that the armed violence in the Syrian Arab Republic risks rising to the level of an "internal armed conflict" under international law.' It also noted that it believed crimes against humanity had been committed by the Syrian military and security forces, irrespective of the existence of an armed conflict and the application of IHL.[17]

1.3 The Human Rights Dimension of Civil Protest

Civil protest has always been perceived as being a potential risk for the State and for society as a whole. This is because of the inherently political dimension of acts of protest which can lead to changes in government (freedom of association and assembly, for example, include the right to form political parties) and therefore

---

[12] UN Human Rights Council Libya Report, n. 10, para 99.

[13] The Guardian 2011c; Bakri 2011.

[14] Haaretz 2011.

[15] See France 24 2011.

[16] UN Human Rights Council, Report of the Independent International Commission of Inquiry on the Syrian Arab Republic, 23 November 2011b, UN doc. A/HRC/S-17/Add.1, available at http://www2.ohchr.org/english/bodies/hrcouncil/specialsession/17/docs/A-HRC-S-17-2-Add1.pdf.

[17] *Id*, paras 97–100.

predictably, 'authoritarian States of each ideological kind are paranoid about assemblies of their subjects.'[18] Protest can also endanger democratically established structures (adopted legislation can be challenged on the streets) but, in addition, represents a risk to the human rights of others, in particular, property rights and the right to physical integrity and security. This potentially 'explosive' character of protest has been acknowledged in international human rights law, notably through the possibility to restrict, in certain circumstances, the exercise of that right.

International human rights law does not recognize *per se* a 'right to protest', but it is, however, covered both by the right to freedom of expression and the right to freedom of assembly, two of the oldest human rights protected by law. The First Amendment of the American Constitution of 1791, for instance, guarantees a 'right of the people peaceably to assemble', while the 1789 French *Declaration of the Rights of Man and of the Citizen* recognizes that '(t)he free communication of ideas and opinions is one of the most precious of the rights of man.'[19] In contemporary international law, freedom of expression and freedom of assembly are protected by a wide range of international instruments.[20]

In addition to the historical origins of the freedom of expression and of assembly, their longstanding protection at both national and international levels, bears some significance on their status under customary international law. It is not the place here to elaborate more on this issue, but it suffices to note that government statements made during the Arab Spring could constitute an *opinio juris* with regard to the customary nature of these freedoms. One can quote, for instance, the US Secretary of State, Hillary Clinton, on the Syrian events: 'The Syrian people, like people everywhere, have the inherent right to exercise their universal freedoms, including peaceful assembly, expression, and speech.'[21]

For the purpose of this article, we will focus on the right to freedom of assembly and its scope. Article 21 of the ICCPR states the following:

> The right of peaceful assembly shall be recognized. No restrictions may be placed on the exercise of this right other than those imposed in conformity with the law and which are necessary in a democratic society in the interests of national security or public safety, public order (order public), the protection of public health or morals or the protection of the rights and freedoms of others.

---

[18] Weiss 2011, para 1.

[19] Ibid., para 2.

[20] Articles 19–20 of the Universal Declaration of Human Rights (UDHR), Articles 19 and 21 of the International Covenant on Civil and Political Rights (ICCPR), Articles 10–11 of the European Convention of Human Rights (ECHR), Articles 13 and 15 of the American Convention of Human Rights (ACHR), Articles 9 and 11 of the African Charter on Human and Peoples Rights (AfCHPR), and Articles 24 and 32 of the Arab Charter on Human Rights (ArCHHR).

[21] Clinton HR (2011) Press Statement: Violence in Syria, US Department of State, 6 May 2011, available at http://www.state.gov/secretary/rm/2011/05/162843.htm (Accessed 13 December 2011).

Three elements must be noted here: only *peaceful* assembly is protected, and it comprises a *negative* as well as a *positive* obligation for the State.

Case law[22] and a literal reading of the texts have shown that 'peaceful' should be understood as meaning 'without arms',[23] the 'absence of violence', or 'without uproar disturbance of the use of arms.'[24] A protest is not peaceful if protesters carry weapons even if they do not use them (except for 'protective' objects such as helmets).[25] If the right to assembly must be exercised peacefully in order to be protected, States Parties to the ICCPR have nevertheless the obligation 'to prevent a peaceful assembly from leading to riots due to provocation or use of force by the security forces or by private parties (individual extremists, counter-demonstrators, or 'agents provocateurs'), because the organisers and the peaceful participants would thereby lose their human rights protection.'[26] A demonstration that turns violent may be prohibited or dispersed without the need to observe the conditions laid down in Article 21. However, it needs to be noted that because the right of peaceful assembly rests with the individual, it is that individual's intention and behaviour that matters; in other words, if others become violent, the police are not thereby entitled to arrest and charge those remaining non-violent.[27]

The negative duty entails an obligation upon the State not to interfere in the exercise of freedom of assembly. Thus, participants must be able to hold a demonstration without fear of being subjected to physical violence. States also have a positive obligation to ensure that freedom of peaceful assembly can be exercised (an obligation to organise traffic to provide police protection against clashes, as well as a public space to meet).[28]

Article 21 of the ICCPR stipulates the standard limitations on the freedoms protected in the Covenant: they must be imposed in conformity with the law, serve one of the listed purposes (national security or public safety, public order, the protection of public health or morals, or the protection of the rights and freedoms

22 See, *Stankov and the United Macedonian Organisation Llinden v Bulgaria*, nos. 29221/95 and 29225/95, ECHR 2001; and *United Macedonia Organization Llinden and Others v Bulgaria*, Case no. 59491/00 ECHR, 2006, in which the Court recognized that a hostile environment, while requiring preventive measures of protection, does not preclude per se the exercise of freedom of assembly. See also Weiss, para 19.

23 Article 15 ACHR.

24 Manfred 2005, p. 374.

25 Weiss 2011, para 7; Clapham and Marks 2005, p. 279.

26 Manfred 2005, p. 376.

27 *Ezelin v. France*, no. 21/1990/212/274 ECHR, 1991, paras 40–41. Also, Doswald-Beck 2011, p. 412.

28 Weiss 2011, para 8; see also *Plattform 'Ärte für das Leben' v. Austria*, no.10126/82 ECHR 1988: 'genuine, effective freedom of peaceful assembly cannot, therefore, be reduced to a mere duty on the part of the State not to interfere: a purely negative conception would not be compatible with the object and purpose of Article 11. Like Article 8, Article 11 sometimes requires positive measures to be taken, even in the sphere of relations between individuals, if need be', para 32.

of others)[29] and be necessary in a democratic society for attaining this purpose. In that respect, an important body of case law deals with the requirement of prior notification as a lawful restriction to peaceful assembly. Case law from the treaty bodies shows that notification, or even authorisation, may be required for demonstrations so that the authorities may organise the necessary security measures. Such requirements may not, in practice, amount to a prohibition. Restrictions may be allowed, provided that they can be shown to be necessary for one of the legitimate aims; in other words, such restrictions may not be arbitrary or unreasonable. On the other hand, the requirement of unreasonable notifications or authorisations prior to a demonstration, which in practice would make it impossible to hold it, would be considered a violation of the right of freedom of assembly and speech.[30]

Finally, freedom of peaceful assembly can be theoretically derogated from in time of emergency "to the extent strictly required by the exigencies of the situation" (Article 4, ICCPR). In this context, the Human Rights Committee has considered that the 'possibility of restricting certain Covenant rights under the terms of, for instance [...] freedom of assembly (Article 21) is generally sufficient during such situations and no derogation from the provisions in question would be justified by the exigency of the situation.'[31] In other words, derogations to freedom of assembly even in times of public emergency would not normally be considered "strictly required by the exigencies of the situation" and would therefore be unlawful, given that States already have the possibility to limit this right under the conditions imposed by Article 21.

At this stage, one can note that international human rights law has recognized the right to peaceful assembly as one of the core elements of democratic entitlements. This freedom is the rule and not the exception. Even though it can be limited, case law has shown that the restrictions must be interpreted narrowly. Hence, although States have the possibility to restrict the exercise of peaceful assembly under certain circumstances, human rights law makes it clear that the people are the final holder of sovereignty, even if protest ultimately leads to a change of government.

---

29 For example, war propaganda could be limited for reasons of national security (but only in serious cases of political or military threats to the entire nation); public morals would require that an assembly in a cemetery could be forbidden and finally, respect for the freedoms of others, such as the right to property or reputation, would justify in some cases that freedom of assembly be limited. See White and Ovey 2010, pp. 453–461; De Schutter 2009, pp. 288–322; Boyle 2010, pp. 450–461.

30 See, e.g. UNHRCte, *Velechkin v. Belarus,* Com. 1022/2001, 23 November 2005, paras 7.2–7.3; AComHPR, *Amnesty International and others v. Sudan*, Coms. 48/90 et al., 15 November 1999, para 82; *Oya Ataman v. Turkey*, no. 74552/01 ECHR 2006, para 37; Doswald-Beck 2011, pp. 440–443.

31 Human Rights Committee, General Comment n. 29, on State of Emergency (Article 4), CCPR/C/21/Rev1/Add.11, 31 August 2011, para 5.

1.4 Is There a Right to Rebellion?

If most of the revolutions that have occurred or are still occurring in the Arab world in 2011 have been manifestations of peaceful protest, which were subsequently repressed by the governing regimes, it remains interesting to briefly reflect upon the legality of the use of force by the people against the government in certain situations and, in particular, against oppressive regimes.

One possible source that some might cite is the right of self-determination as expressly mentioned in Articles 1(2) and 55 of the UN Charter and in Article 1 of both the ICCPR and the International Covenant on Economic, Social and Cultural Rights (CESCR). However, the Arab Spring revolutions are not technically self-determination movements as the notion of self-determination has been normally applied to peoples under colonial rule or military occupation. It suffices to note here that, although the legality of the use of force in order to achieve decolonisation has been historically discussed among scholars, the UN Charter does not itself authorize the use of force for self-determination: 'the dominant view in the community of nations denies a right of secession by force. This implies that the sovereignty of States remain the highest priority.'[32] On the other hand, international law does not positively prohibit the use of force by non-State actors. A possible use of force to achieve self-determination is, for example, contemplated in the *1970 Declaration on Principles of International Law concerning Friendly Relations and Cooperation among States in Accordance with the Charter of the United Nations.* The Declaration reaffirms that 'Every State has the duty to refrain from any forcible action which deprives peoples (…) of their right to self-determination and freedom and independence. In their actions against and resistance to, such forcible action in pursuit of the exercise of their right to self-determination, such peoples are entitled to seek and receive support in accordance with the purpose and principles of the Charter.' Hence as noted by Ben Saul, 'liberation movements have no legal right to use force to secure self-determination, but they do not breach international law by using force (defensively) against its forcible denial.'[33]

The same point could be made with regard to rebellions. The 'right to rebel' has been the subject of much debate in both the legal and philosophical literature. For some scholars, a right to rebel, individual as well as collective, must exist to ensure the respect for and remedy to other fundamental human rights: 'the right to rebel (…) must be a secondary rather than a primary right. It exists only when a wrong has been committed. Its point is to provide remedy in the vent of the violation on a large scale of primary rights like the right to freedom from arbitrary arrest.'[34] A right to rebel against an oppressive government does exist in the constitutions of some states in the United States (including New Hampshire, Pennsylvania, and

---

32 Doehring 2002, p. 61; Saul 2008, p. 10; Crawford 2001, p. 42.

33 Saul, p. 10.

34 Honoré 1988, p. 38.

Delaware, but not in the US Constitution).[35] More notably, Article 20(4) of the Constitution of the German Federal Republic authorizes citizens to exercise a right to resistance against attempts to destroy the democratic constitutional order (and not to change the regime).[36]

At the international level, the preamble of the Universal Declaration of Human Rights would give some credit to this interpretation when it states that 'whereas it is essential, if man is not to be compelled to have recourse, as a last resource, to rebellion against tyranny and oppression, that human rights should be protected by the rule of law…'. However, although there was much discussion among delegations during the drafting of the Universal Declaration, a right to rebel against tyranny was not listed as a protected right in the final text, as it was feared it could be abused to undermine genuinely democratic governments or might lead to political destabilisation.[37]

Nor was a right to armed rebellion against tyranny included in subsequent human rights treaties and, as we saw, only peaceful protest is protected. As the European Court of Human Rights made clear in its judgment in *Yazar and other v. Turkey*, the purpose of allowing a plurality of views to be expressed is to enable democratic debate and not to force a change of government to take place through the use of armed violence.[38] The provision of abuse of rights present in human rights treaties constitutes another qualification of the right to protest. Article 5(1) of the ICCPR states that: 'Nothing in the present Covenant may be interpreted as implying for any State, group or person any right to engage in any activity or perform any act aimed at the destruction of any of the rights and freedoms recognized herein or at their limitation to a greater extent than is provided for in the present Covenant.' An *armed* protest would most probably lead to violations of other persons' human rights (to life or security or property rights) and could constitute in that sense an abuse of rights. On the other hand, human rights treaties specify that their purpose is to protect democracy so that recourse to violence in self-defence against unlawful force used by an autocratic government against protesters could be seen as not involving an abuse of rights.

As international law does not expressly confer a right to rebel, 'there are no correlative duties on affected States not to suppress or criminalize rebellions.'[39] International human rights law hence allows a State to use lethal force, provided the conditions of necessity and proportionality are respected, 'in action taken for the purpose of quelling a riot or insurrection.' (ECHR, Article 2(2)). We will return to this point later.

It is clear, therefore, that international law does not positively grant the right to rebel. As noted by one author, 'sovereign states can hardly be expected as a matter

---

[35] Ibid., p. 42.

[36] Ibid, p. 43.

[37] Morsink 1999, p. 312.

[38] *Yazar and others v. Turkey*, Nos. 22723/93, 22724/93 and 22725/93 ECHR 2002-II, para 57.

[39] Saul 2008, p. 21; see also Crawford 2001, pp. 48–49.

of course to grant their subjects a right to secede or rebel.'[40] However, it is equally true that for time immemorial many recognised governments have come into being through rebellion, and this continues to be the case. It is therefore quite clear that international law does not positively prohibit such rebellion. The situation is, by analogy, similar to the use of spies in international conflict: the use of spies by a State is not a violation of international law, but a capturing State may punish such spies under its national law. In other words, the right to punish under national law does not thereby mean that the punished action is a violation of international law.

This is precisely the rationale for not applying counter-terrorism treaties to armed conflicts. The definition of a terrorist act, in such treaties, is typically the use of violence in order to force the government to do something. An example of such exclusion is the following:

> The activities of armed forces during an armed conflict, as those terms are understood under international humanitarian law, which are governed by that law, are not governed by this Convention...[41]

The purpose of excluding the "armed forces" in "an armed conflict" is to cover groups, not associated with the government, that are fighting in a non-international armed conflict. Although such fighters may be punished by the government of the State concerned, until now starting an armed rebellion has not been seen as an international crime. Indeed, members of quite a few governments began their life as insurrectionists and it would be a very strange situation if they were to carry the label of "terrorist" or "international criminal" for the rest of their days. Such a result also presents the danger of repressing the right to protest. As noted by Ben Saul:

> Unless non-state armed forces in internal conflicts (...) are excluded from an international crime of terrorism, there is an acute danger of internationally legitimising State repression of internal dissidence.[42]

This result would also contradict the IHL rule that encourages an amnesty for those actions that do not amount to war crimes, and many peace treaties adopted after non-international armed conflicts include such amnesties.[43]

---

[40] Honoré 1988, p. 42.

[41] International Convention on the Suppression of Terrorist Bombing, 1997, Article 19; also International Convention on the Suppression of Acts of Nuclear Terrorism, 2005, Article 4 § 2. The 1979 International Convention against the Taking of Hostages specifies, in Article 12, that it does not apply to any hostage-taking occurring in a situation covered by the 1949 Geneva Conventions or their Additional Protocols.

[42] Saul 2008, p. 24.

[43] See Protocol Additional to the Geneva Conventions of 12 August 1949, and Relating to the Protection of Victims of Non-International Armed Conflicts (Protocol II)(AP2), Article 6 § 5; Rule 159 and commentary thereto of the ICRC Customary law study: Henckaerts and Doswald-Beck 2005, pp. 611–612.

In conclusion, therefore, international law neither allows nor prohibits rebellions. It does, however, regulate what force may be used by governments, a point to which we will now turn.

1.5 State Responses to Protests and the Use of Force

During the Arab Spring, but also more broadly in other parts of the world where mass protest happens, arbitrary killings are not the only serious violations that take place. Torture, enforced disappearances, arbitrary arrest, and prolonged unlawful detention are part of the many violations that can and do occur during protest.[44] In this article, however, we will concentrate on the use of force.

A typical articulation of the legal regime applicable to the use of force has been that human rights law governs a law enforcement regime whereas IHL governs the conduct of hostilities. This is an oversimplification. Although it is certainly true that IHL cannot be relevant unless there is an armed conflict (or military occupation), and that without such a situation only human rights law is applicable, the evaluation of the lawfulness of any particular use of force will depend on the degree of control over territory or over a person in both human rights law and humanitarian law.

It should be noted from the outset that excessive use of force during protest does not only occur in oppressive regimes. In Europe or the USA, there has been a rise in recent years of public protest, fuelled in part by anti-globalisation movements. This led, for example, to the massive anti-globalisation demonstrations in Seattle in 1999.[45] Demonstrations have since been held regularly for each of the G8, World Trade Organization, World Bank and International Monetary Fund meetings. More recently, the Occupy Wall Street movement in the USA has attracted worldwide attention. Those different demonstrations have sometimes been met with tough police responses,[46] causing injury to, and even on occasion the death of, a number of protesters.[47]

---

[44] See, for example, Human Rights Watch 2011b.

[45] Clapham and Marks 2005, p. 271.

[46] See, for example, Wolf 2011.

[47] On 20 July 2001, during an anti-G8 demonstration in Genoa, Carlo Giuliani, 23, was shot in the head during violent clashes between police and militant radicals. His family complained to the ECtHR of a violation of Article 2 (right to life). In a decision issued in March 2011, the Court found that the policeman who fired the fatal shot had "acted in the honest belief that his own life and physical integrity and those of his colleagues were in danger from the attack to which they were being subjected" and found no violation of the right to life of C. Giuliani by the police officer; *Giuliani and Gaggio v. Italy* [GC], no. 23458/02 ECHR, 2011, para 189. In 2009, Anti-G20 demonstrations took place in London where serious allegation of mistreatment and abusive use of force were made against law enforcement officials, notably after the death of a passer-by, Ian Tomlinson, BBC News 2011a. See also Mead 2010 for a recent study on peaceful protest in the UK.

The human right to life, which is protected by treaty law[48] and is part of customary international law, is not an absolute right in that there are circumstances in which a State can legally use potentially lethal force. The use of lethal force by the State takes into account the different interests and obligations at stake. Therefore, while States have the obligation to respect and ensure the exercise of the right to peaceful assembly, they also have the obligation to maintain public order and to protect the rights and freedom of others.

In a situation outside armed conflict, and also in a situation of occupation which is relatively "peaceful", it is generally accepted that the law enforcement standard will be relevant. Human rights law will evaluate the use of force more strictly in such a context than during hostilities, and the same is true for the interpretation of an occupying State's duties to ensure security in the case of demonstrations and other unrest not amounting to military hostilities by the occupied population.[49] It may also be pointed out that IHL does not allow the use of deadly force against people that are in the adversary's power. This is not only evident from the prohibition of attacking a soldier *hors de combat*, but also from the rules regulating the treatment of prisoners of war and civilian internees which would not allow the use of deadly force against demonstrating prisoners.[50] Indeed, deaths in detention have to be investigated and a suspected guilty perpetrator prosecuted.[51]

In the specific context of protest and peaceful assembly, the right to life under human rights law concerns the life of protesters, of the people not participating in the protest, but also the life of policemen or other law enforcement officers.

The ECHR states specifically when the deprivation of life can be considered as not arbitrary:

> Deprivation of life shall not be regarded as inflicted in contravention of this article when it results from the use of force which is no more than absolutely necessary
> (a) in defence of any person from unlawful violence;
> (b) in order to effect a lawful arrest or to prevent the escape of a person lawfully detained;
> (c) in action taken for the purpose of quelling a riot or insurrection.[52]

---

[48] ICCPR, Article 6(1); ACHR, Article 4(1); and Arab Charter on Human Rights 2004 (ArCHR), Article 5(2).

[49] To this effect, see, University Centre for International Humanitarian Law (2005) Expert Meeting on the Right to Life in Armed Conflicts and Situations of Occupation, 1–2 September 2005, available at www.adh-geneva.ch/docs/expert-meetings/2005/3rapport_droit_vie.pdf, p. 23. Although not stated, the understanding was that this was the most appropriate way to ensure public order and safety as required by Article 43 of the Hague Regulations.

[50] An example of the need to avoid, if at all possible, the use of force is to be found in Article 42 of the Third Geneva Convention which provides that the use of weapons against escaping prisoners of war is an extreme measure that must be preceded by warnings.

[51] Third Geneva Convention, Article 121; Fourth Geneva Convention Article 131.

[52] The term 'insurrection' should be understood as referring to 'non international armed conflict', see Doswald-Beck 2011, p. 193.

Apart from the different provisions on the right to life stipulated in human rights treaties, the most significant document relating to the protection of life during law-enforcement operations is the *Basic Principles on the Use of Force and Firearms by Law Enforcement Officials.*[53] A footnote to this document specifies that '[i]n countries where police powers are exercised by military authorities, whether uniformed or not, or by State security forces, the definition of law enforcement officials shall be regarded as including officers of such services.' Principle 8 of this document states that '[e]xceptional circumstances such as internal political instability or any other public emergency may not be invoked to justify any departure from these basic principles.'

Although it is true that this document is not a treaty and therefore not formally binding, it can be said to reflect a widespread understanding of what level of force would be appropriate or not for such operations. The UN Human Rights Committee, in its Concluding Observations to States Parties' reports, has frequently stated that States should ensure that their legislation and practice conform to this document and the document has also been referred to by other treaty bodies as an important reference in their analysis of the right to life.

The document as a whole stresses the need to avoid a disproportionate use of force and that 'force and firearms' may only be used 'if other means remain ineffective or without any promise of achieving the intended result.' The actual use of firearms is regulated in Principle 9 which reads as follows:

> Law enforcement officials shall not use firearms against persons except in self-defence or defence of others against the imminent threat of death or serious injury, to prevent the perpetration of a particularly serious crime involving grave threat to life, to arrest a person presenting such danger and resisting their authority, or to prevent his or her escape, and only when less extreme means are insufficient to achieve these objectives. In any event, intentional lethal use of firearms may only be made when strictly unavoidable in order to protect life.

Policing violent demonstrations is a context where the principle of necessity and proportionality of force apply. The UN Basic Principles simply state that:

> In the dispersal of violent assemblies, law enforcement officials may use firearms only when less dangerous means are not practicable and only to the minimum extent necessary. Law enforcement officials shall not use firearms in such cases, except under the conditions stipulated in principle 9.[54]

The regional treaties have interpreted the right to life in the context of demonstrations and riots in the same manner, including in cases where such demonstrations took place in the context of occupation or armed conflict.

In the case of *Solomou and Others v.Turkey,* which concerned the shooting of a protester by Turkish troops in the buffer zone between occupied and southern

---

[53] Adopted by the 8th United Nations Congress on the Prevention of Crime and the Treatment of Offenders, Cuba, 1990; See also the Code of Conduct for Law Enforcement Officials adopted by the General Assembly Resolution 34/169 of 17 December 1979.

[54] UN *Basic Principles on the Use of Force and Firearms*, Principle 10.

Cyprus, the European Court stressed that the use of any specific act of force will only be acceptable if it is aimed at calming or dispersing a violent demonstration or riot.[55] The use of live bullets was found to be a violation in the case of *Güleç v. Turkey*. This concerned an illegal and violent pro-PKK demonstration, taking place in south-eastern Turkey (which could be classified as experiencing armed conflict, even if this has always been denied by the government). In response to serious acts of violence, which damaged property and injured some police, the security officers sent reinforcements in the form of armoured vehicles. One of these fired a machine gun into the crowd, resulting in deaths. The European Court accepted that force may be used, under Article 2, para 2 (c), to suppress a riot or insurrection, but then stressed that a balance must be struck between the aim pursued and the means employed to achieve it. The Court criticised in particular the lack of preparation of the authorities to deal with such demonstrations. This region was already experiencing violence and the police should have been equipped with non-lethal means to disperse the protesters.[56]

The use of law-enforcement criteria to evaluate the use of force in the context of a riot, even when the country is experiencing a non-international armed conflict, is illustrated in the Inter-American Court of Human Rights case of *Neira Alegrìa* et al. *v. Peru*. This case concerned the use of force to suppress an armed riot in a prison. During the raid, 111 inmates died and 34 were injured. The pavilion where the rioters were was demolished by the Peruvian Navy and it would seem that many of the dead had been killed by being crushed under the collapsed structure. No effort had been made to find and rescue any who might still have been alive. The Court suspected that the confrontation was in the nature of a political one.[57] It found that although the detainees were highly dangerous and were armed, the amount of force was disproportionate and held that the persons concerned had been arbitrarily deprived of their life by the Peruvian forces.[58] Although the case concerned an armed confrontation between the Peruvian government and alleged

---

[55] *Solomou and Others v. Turkey*, no. 36832/97 ECHR, 2008, paras 75–78. This may be compared with the ECtHR case of *Guiliani and Gaggio v. Italy*, where, during a violent demonstration an injured police officer used a firearm in genuine personal self-defence against imminent likely death at the hands demonstrator; the circumstances were such that this was his only option. The organisation of the demonstration was found to be adequate in the circumstances: *Giuliani and Gaggio v. Italy*, no. 23458/02 ECHR, 2010, paras 183–194 and 252–262.

[56] *Güleç v. Turkey*, no. 54/1997/838/1044 ECHR, 1998, para 71. A similar point was made by the African Commission in a case concerning the death of two students during a demonstration. It specified that even when the demonstrations are not authorised, those responsible for public order must use adequate means to cause the barest minimum of damage AComHPR, *Mouvement Burkinabé des Droits de l'Homme et des Peuples v. Burkina Faso*, Com. 204/97, 7 May 2001, para 43.

[57] IACtHR, *Neira Alegrìa et al. v. Peru*, Judgment, 19 January 1995, paras 74–75.

[58] IACtHR, *Neira Alegrìa et al. v. Peru*, Judgment, 19 January 1995, para 76.

members of the guerrilla group *Shining Path*, the principle of proportionality[59] was applied in a law-enforcement manner because the events took place in a prison and the use of such heavy weaponry by the security forces was excessive.

In the light of these cases it is evident that using live bullets against unarmed protesters, such as has been the case in Bahrain Egypt, Syria, and Tunisia, is in flagrant violation of these principles.[60]

But let us note finally that the use of firearms against protesters or any other use of deadly force is not the only way that life or physical integrity during the Arab Spring has been threatened. Certain so-called 'non-lethal weapons' notably tear gas, and rubber bullets have also sometimes led to fatalities.[61] Tear gas and pepper spray are qualified as chemical weapons and although their use as a method of warfare is forbidden by the *1993 Chemical Weapons Convention,* they can still be used for 'law enforcement including domestic riot control purposes.'[62] In Tunisia, during the 'jasmine revolution', it has been reported that the use of tear gas led to a number of deaths of as a result of either the effects of the gas or following the trauma caused by the firing of tear gas canisters.[63] Hence, because of their possible deadly effects, the legislation, training and modalities for the use of tear gas is crucial to prevent deaths, as required by the positive obligation to respect the right

---

59 In law-enforcement the principle of proportionality is applied to all aspects of an operation, including the degree of violence inflicted against people using force. This is unlike the conduct of hostilities under IHL, where proportionality is applied to evaluate the likely extent of collateral injuries and damage compared with the expected military advantage obtained from an attack against a valid military target.

60 See, for example, the Report of the Bahrain Independent Commission of Inquiry (available at http://files.bici.org.bh/BICIreportEN.pdf) which reported 12 cases of death caused by the use of a shotgun and a firearm, pp. 223–232. Other persons died because of acts of torture, p. 214.

61 See for a legal assessment of non-lethal weapons under human rights law, Casey-Maslen 2013. Rubber bullets have also caused deaths. The relatively old case of *Kathleen Stewart v. United Kingdom* concerned the death of a young boy by a plastic baton round fired by the army in Northern Ireland during a violent demonstration. The case was declared inadmissible on the basis that the weapon was not shown to be as dangerous as alleged and, more to the point, the boy was only hit because the soldier's aim was disturbed at the moment of discharge: *Kathleen Stewart v. United Kingdom* (Admissibility), no. 10092/82 EComHR, 1984, paras 28 and 29. The Report of the Independent Commission on policing for Northern Ireland noted that '[s]ince 1981, a total of 41,657 [of plastic baton rounds] have been discharged by the police, and 14,572 by the army. 11 deaths have been attributed to PBRs since 1981 (and 5 before that), and 615 injuries. The most recent fatality was in 1989, but the issue of PBRs remains highly controversial' see Report of the Independent Commission on policing for Northern Ireland ("The Patten Report") September 1999, available at http://cain.ulst.ac.uk/issues/police/patten/patten99.pdf, para 9.12, p. 54.

62 Article 2, para 9, 1993 Chemical Weapons Convention.

63 Human Rights Watch has reported the death of a 7 year old baby who died of a teargas-related cause, Human Rights Watch 2011a. On 17 January 2011, a French journalist, Luca Mebrouk Dolega who was covering the events in Tunisia, died following trauma caused by the firing of a tear gas canister which hit him in the face. See The Guardian 2011a.

to life.[64] The same is true for new technologies, which also need to be carefully evaluated and any use properly regulated.[65]

In conclusion, if we look at the conditions laid down by international law for the policing of demonstrations, the deadly use of force against protesters is almost never justified. If a person is not a direct threat to the life of other persons, or if other less lethal methods were possible to apprehend dangerous persons, case law systematically finds a violation of the right to life.[66]

This means that, under human rights law, governments do not have the right to create a non-international armed conflict. This conclusion is supported by the reaction of the international community to violence inflicted on protesters in Libya, Syria and Yemen. In the case of Libya, the UN Security Council not only deplored the "repression of peaceful protesters" and underlined "the need to respect the freedoms of peaceful assembly and of expression", but also demanded "an immediate end to the violence" and called for "steps to fulfil the legitimate demands of the population."[67] This resolution was followed by the suspension of Libya from the Human Rights Council on 1 March 2011.[68] Security Council resolution 1973, that adopted the no-fly zone, similarly referred to the "legitimate demands of the Libyan people" and the need for "dialogue to lead to the political reforms necessary to find a peaceful and sustainable solution."[69] United Nations resolutions on Syria[70] and Yemen[71] also condemned government attacks on peaceful protesters and insisted on the need for a peaceful settlement.

The effect of human rights law is that governments are positively prohibited from creating a non-international conflict, whereas, as we have seen above, international law traditionally neither allows nor prohibits a rebellion. It is interesting to consider, therefore, whether there could be, by analogy to Articles 2 (4) and Article 51 of the UN Charter, a right for protesters to resort to self-defence in case of excessive use of force by law enforcement officers. The question is not without importance, not only from the point of view of 'just war' theory, but also

---

64 Doswald-Beck 2011, pp. 162 and 165–167.

65 Doswald-Beck 2011, p. 171.

66 See e.g. *McCann and others v. United Kingdom* [GC], no.18984/91 ECHR 1995; *Nachova and others v. Bulgaria* [GC], no. 43577/98 ECHR 2005; *Erdogan and Others v. Turkey*, no. 19807/92 ECHR 2006; *Güleç v. Turkey*, n. 56; UNHRCte, *Guerrero v. Columbia*, Com. 45/1979, 31 March 1982, paras 13.2–13.3.

67 UNSC Res. 1970, 26 February 2011, UN DOC S/RES.1970 preambular paras 2 and 10, and operative para 1.

68 UNGA, General Assembly Suspends Libya from Human Rights Council, 1 March 2011, GA/11050 available at http://www.un.org/News/Press/docs/2011/ga11050.doc.htm (Accessed 13 December 2011).

69 UNSC Res. 1973, 17 March 2011, UN DOC S/RES.1973, operative para 2.

70 UN Human Rights Council, The Human Rights Situation in the Syrian Arab Republic, 2 December 2011, A/HRC/RES/S-18/1; UNGA Third Committee, Situation of Human Rights in the Syrian Arab Republic, A/C.3/66/L.57/Rev.1, Adopted by the Third Committee on 22 November 2011.

71 UNSC Res. 2014, 21 October 2011, UN DOC S/RES.2014, operative paras 2–5.

because it could perhaps have consequences for the *jus in bello* applicable to non-international armed conflict. This issue will be treated in the following section.

1.6 Do Protesters Have a Right to Individual or Collective Self-Defence Against a Government That Uses Excessive Force?

What comes to mind when one thinks of cases of collective self-defence in the context of the Arab Spring, is the particular situation that prevailed in Libya. By using excessive force against peaceful protesters, Colonel Qaddafi and his agents were not only in violation of basic human rights rules, but have also allegedly committed crimes against humanity. The understandable reaction of the Libyan people was to resort to force against the illegal actions of the government. Was the organisation of a rebellion in that case a legal act of self-defence?

Article 51 of the UN Charter reaffirms the right to self-defence for States (and international organisations established by states) and for recognized self-determination movements.[72] Indeed, even if the monopoly of violence that resides in the State has been challenged on moral grounds, the traditional approach has been that 'international law considers the use of force by non-State actors (outside armed conflict) largely as an internal affair, subject to basic human rights obligations. There is no right to collective 'self-defence' by sub-States communities.'[73] Ben Saul pleads for the recognition of a group's right to self-defence which is closer to 'individual self-defence.' He notes that a State policy of genocide or violent persecution, even if it does not amount to a military armed attack, is 'clearly serious enough to trigger group self-defence. Whether conduct is necessary in self-defence should be based on a strict and objective assessment, leaving no room for discretion by the group itself, just as these requirements apply to State actors.'[74]

The right for an *individual* to use violence in his or her self-defence in case of a threat to life, including during a demonstration, is a general principle of criminal law.[75] Thus, the 1998 Rome Statute excludes criminal responsibility when '[t]he person acts reasonably to defend himself or herself or another person (…) against an imminent and unlawful use of force in a manner proportionate to the degree of danger to the person of the other person.' However, there does not seem to be significant State practice authorising self-defence beyond this individual protection. It appears to be generally understood that 'self-defence does not confer a license to use violence in a strategic way in protest at a generalized policy of State

[72] Saul 2008, p. 52; Cassese 1996, p. 197; Benjamin 2009.

[73] Saul 2008, p. 54.

[74] Saul 2008, p. 55.

[75] *Prosecutor v Kordic and Cerkez*, Judgment, Trial Chamber (IT-95-14/2-T) 26 February 2001, para 449.

oppression.'[76] An exception to this was the case of Libya where the air campaign by NATO States unambiguously assisted the rebels. This was made possible by Security Council resolution 1973 which authorised the use of force "to protect civilians and civilian populated areas under threat of attack in the Libyan Jamahiriya, including Benghazi."[77] The specific reference to Benghazi, the hub of the rebellion, revealed the international community's implicit support of the rebels.[78] Moreover, it was somewhat unrealistic to imagine that in practice it would be possible to protect civilians without attacking the Government's forces. Nevertheless, such positive military help to the rebels led some States, in particular Russia and China, to adopt a far more reticent position in the case of the resolutions concerning Syria and Yemen later in the same year.

In the case of Syria, Russia and China voted against resolutions primarily on the basis that they could lead to outside military interference. As explained by the representative of China when voting against the Human Rights Council resolution of 2 December, "United Nations Member States should not use force or the threat of the use of force to solve differences or undermine the territorial integrity of a country." Like the representative of Russia, China stressed the need for "national reconciliation and dialogue."[79]

The resolution adopted by the Security Council in relation to Yemen is even more blatant in its desire to avoid giving an impression of a positive right to rebel using force. After strongly condemning the excessive use of force against peaceful protesters by the Yemeni authorities, it also condemned "the use of force and human rights abuses perpetrated by other actors."[80] Additionally it demanded that "all sides immediately reject the use of violence to achieve political goals" specifying that it was essential to achieve "political transition" through a peaceful "political settlement."[81]

It is, of course, the standard rule that IHL applies in non-international conflicts equally to both sides. The intention, when drafting common Article 3 of the 1949 Geneva Conventions, was to try to copy the same equality principle as in the case of IHL applicable to international conflicts. The reality is that this is not quite true. Although behaviour that would be a violation of IHL is described in the same way

---

[76] Saul 2008; p. 37.

[77] UNSC Res. 1973, n. 69, operative para 4.

[78] Support for rebels in Libya is not the only example, of course, of States actively helping rebels, despite this being contrary to classical international law. NATO military involvement in the insurgency of Kosovo rebels against the Serbian government in 1999 springs to mind. However, unlike Libya, both this involvement, and all the others, did not have the permission of a UN Security Council resolution.

[79] UN Human Rights Council, Human Rights Council Concludes Special Session on Situation of Human Rights in the Syrian Arab Republic, 2 December 2011, available at www.ohchr.org/en/NewsEvents/Pages/DisplayNews.aspx?NewsID=11680&LangID=E (Accessed 13 December 2011).

[80] UNSC Res. 2014, n. 71, para 2. The resolution was adopted unanimously.

[81] UNSC Res. 2014, n. 71, paras 3 and 4.

for all parties to a non-international conflict, the status of parties is not the same. The government does have more obligations than rebels because it is also bound by international human rights law, whereas it is still controversial as to whether the same is true for rebels.[82] There is also no combatant immunity in non-international conflicts, as any insurgent can be put on trial in national courts for the mere fact of having participated in hostilities.[83] However, the same cannot be done by the rebels. In other words, the absence of combatant immunity (i.e. non-entitlement to prisoner-of-war status) in such conflicts undermines, in reality, the principle of equality.

The lack of rebel immunity from national prosecution appears unreasonable in cases where the government unlawfully started the conflict. It would also amount to an abuse of rights in that the State would benefit from a right on the basis of its own wrong. Is there any indication that international community responses to such unlawful violence have had any effect on the traditional right to prosecute any rebel? So far the answer does not seem to be in the affirmative. The resolutions condemning the violent suppression of the protests in Syria refer to human rights violations such as arbitrary executions, the excessive use of force, arbitrary detention, forced disappearances and torture,[84] but do not mention any requirement to avoid arresting protesters using force, even in self-defence. Indeed, the Security Council resolution on Yemen appears to positively condone the traditional rule by stating that "all those responsible for violence, human rights violations and abuses should be held accountable."[85] This reference was probably required to achieve unanimity, in particular in the light of Russia's complaint that the Human Rights Council's resolution on Syria did not take into account "serious crimes committed by anti-government forces."[86]

Nevertheless, it is worth considering whether the international community should call for an exception in cases of violence in the form of individual or even collective self-defence. The present situation in non-international conflicts is the equivalent of punishing a State for exercising its right to self-defence against the unlawful aggression of another State. This would be manifestly absurd in an inter-State context. Total freedom for a government to treat its citizens as it wishes has

---

[82] There have been an increasing number of UN General Assembly and Security Council resolutions calling on rebel groups to respect both IHL and human rights, see Doswald-Beck 2011, pp. 120–121. The International Commission of Inquiry on Libya also examined the alleged human rights violations committed by the NTC, see UN Human Rights Council Libya Report, n. 10, para 72.

[83] However, Protocol I recognizes self-determination struggles as international armed conflicts, where forces of the parties to these conflicts will be recognized as combatants. AP I, Article 1(4), Article 44 (3). So far, however, Article 1 (4) of API has remained theoretical.

[84] UN Human Rights Council, n. 70, operative para 2; UNGA Third Committee, n. 70, operative para 1.

[85] UNSC Res. 2014, n. 71, operative para 2.

[86] Explanation of negative vote by the representative of the Russian Federation after adoption of the Human Rights Council's resolution on 2 December 2011.

long since disappeared and the reaction to the violence in Syria, even by the Arab League which imposed sanctions, shows that attitudes are changing.[87] In particular, the old refrain of "interfering in internal affairs" has been conspicuously absent in international discussions to the Arab Spring uprisings. When considering the applicable IHL rules, it might be objected that the positive entitlements in this body of law, e.g. to attack military objectives, etc. do have the effect of enabling an aggressor to benefit from its own wrong. To some degree this is true. However, in international armed conflicts, in addition to remaining responsible for the aggression, IHL does at least spare combatants from being tried for criminal offences associated with having taken part in hostilities,[88] i.e. through POW entitlement for both sides. Although there can be no hope of introducing the equivalent for all non-international conflicts, as there is such a strong objection to this idea, it should be remembered that the objection stems from the reasonable notion that no government wishes to automatically grant immunity from prosecution to people that start an armed rebellion.

1.7 Deprivation of Life During Hostilities: Does Human Rights Law Arrive at a Different Result from IHL?

This is not the place to go into the details of the complex question of the relationship between international human rights law and IHL in general terms. It is, however, worth reflecting briefly on the legal framework regarding the use of force and the holding of demonstrations when a situation in a country has attained that of an armed conflict, in particular with regard to the situation of the Arab Spring.

The International Court of Justice has confirmed on several occasions that human rights law continues to apply in armed conflict, alongside IHL.[89] In its Advisory Opinion on the *Legality of the Threat or Use of Nuclear Weapons*, it specified that an evaluation of what amounts to an arbitrary deprivation of life under human rights law during hostilities falls to be determined by IHL, as the relevant *lex specialis*.[90] In that case, of course, the ICJ was required to give an opinion *in abstracto* on the use of a certain weapon. In the case of *Congo v. Uganda*, however, it simply found violations of both IHL and the human right to

---

87 See BBC News 2011b; See also The Arab League Resolution of 28 November 2011 that adopted sanctions against Syria: http://www.arableagueonline.org.

88 For example, murder, assault, unlawful possession of weapons etc.

89 *Legality of the Threat or Use of Nuclear Weapons,* Advisory Opinion (1996) ICJ Rep 226, para 25; *Legal Consequences of the Construction of a Wall in the Occupied Palestinian Territory*, Advisory Opinion, (2004) ICJ Rep 136, para 106; *Armed Activities on the Territory of the* Congo (DRC v Uganda) Merits Judgment (2005) ICJ Rep 168, para 216.

90 *Legality of the Threat or Use of Nuclear Weapons*, n. 89, para 25.

life under Article 6 of the ICCPR as a result of murders in occupied territory, without specifying that it interpreted Article 6 in the light of IHL.[91]

As we have seen above, in cases where the government has control over persons or territory, the use of force is to be considered in the context of the law-enforcement model i.e. unless a person is a direct threat to life, and if he or she can be arrested, then the use of potentially lethal force will not be "absolutely necessary" and would therefore be arbitrary. The law-enforcement model also presupposes the use, by police or other security forces, of primarily non-lethal methods of restoring order. In a situation which has degenerated into a non-international armed conflict, as was the case in Libya, and now probably in Syria, it is evident that both IHL and human rights law apply.[92] A situation of armed hostilities is in most cases one where the government does not have sufficient control to be able to use the law-enforcement model.[93]

With the exception of defining when a civilian takes a direct part in hostilities, IHL rules are sufficiently clear and well-known as to not necessitate summarising them here. However, what is less obvious is how human rights law deals with the right to life during hostilities. The International Court of Justice has the ability to choose whether it wishes to apply IHL rules or human rights rules in any particular situation. However, this is not the case for human rights treaty bodies. Their mandate derives from the human rights treaties to which they are attached and they have no choice but to apply the rules within those treaties. In general terms, these treaty bodies have in practice applied their own treaty provisions and for the most part have not analysed what IHL would have said, unless it is to support the conclusion it would have arrived at in any event.[94]

The treaty body which has had to rule on active hostilities in a non-international armed conflict is the European Court of Human Rights. It has heard a number of cases relating to the conflicts in south-eastern Turkey and Chechnya. In both cases, the government had not accepted the existence of an armed conflict, but this is irrelevant to the application of human rights law. Although Arab countries are not party to the ECHR, the relevant provisions of the other applicable human rights treaties state that no one may be "arbitrarily deprived" of life,[95] and, in practice, the interpretation of the right to life by all the human rights treaty bodies is essentially the same.[96]

---

91 *Case concerning Armed Activities on the Territory of the Congo*, n. 87, para 219.

92 As with all the other situations of non-international conflicts, the UNSC resolutions on Libya insisted that the authorities respect of both IHL and human rights law: UNSC Res. 1970, n.66, operative para 2(a); UNSC Res. 1973, n.68, operative para 3.

93 The fact that the ICJ's dictum in *Nuclear Weapons* Advisory Opinion cannot be interpreted as applying to all deprivations of the right to life and that even in situations of armed conflict the law-enforcement model is more appropriate in certain circumstances is supported by Sassòli and Olson 2008, p. 613.

94 See generally Doswald-Beck 2011, pp. 108–117; Abresch 2005.

95 ICCPR, Article 6 para 1; AfChHPR, Article 4; ArCHR, Article 5 § 2.

96 Doswald-Beck 2011, pp. 161–188.

As explained above, Article 2 para 2 of the ECHR specifies that force may only be used by government authorities if it is "absolutely necessary" to achieve one or more of the aims listed. For our purposes, the most relevant aim would be "action lawfully taken for the purpose of quelling a riot or insurrection."[97] Another possibility could be "in defence of any person from unlawful violence."[98]

The applicants in the hostilities cases brought before the European Court were relatives of deceased persons that were themselves not actively using force. The version of events put forward by the applicants was contested by the government in each case and therefore the Court was forced to make a conclusion based on uncontested facts and whatever seemed the most plausible version of events. The cases also depended to some extent on the pleadings of the parties.

The first test in evaluating the lawful use of force by the government is whether it met one of the aims required under Article 2 para 2. In the cases concerning Chechnya, the Russian government argued that its use of force was necessary under sub-para 2 (a) i.e. in defence of a person from unlawful violence. In the case of *Isayeva, Yusopova and Bazayeva v. Russia,* the Court began with the claim that government fighter planes were shot at by a rebel truck. After analysis of the facts available to it, the Court discounted this version of events and went on as follows:

> In the absence of corroborated evidence that any unlawful violence was threatened or likely, the Court retains certain doubts as to whether the aim can at all be said to be applicable. However, given the context of the conflict in Chechnya at the relevant time, the Court will assume...that the military reasonably considered that there was an attack or a risk of attack from illegal insurgents, and that the air strike was a legitimate response to that attack.[99]

The second part of this statement implies that Article 2, sub-para 2 (a) does not require the pilots to have been acting in immediate and personal self-defence, but that it is enough that rebel violence was likely. This approach was confirmed, and indeed extended, in the other case decided on the same day, namely, that of *Isayeva v. Russia.* The government in that case argued on the more general basis that the situation in Katyr-Yurt at the time (i.e. the capture of the village by rebel fighters) rendered the use of force necessary:

> The Court accepts that the situation that existed in Chechnya at the relevant time called for exceptional measures by the State in order to regain control over the Republic and to suppress the illegal armed insurgency. Given the context of the conflict in Chechnya at the relevant time, those measures could presumably include the deployment of army units equipped with combat weapons, including military aviation and artillery. The presence of a very large group of armed fighters in Katyr-Yurt, and their active resistance to the law-enforcement bodies, which are not disputed by the parties, may have justified use of lethal force by the agents of the State, thus bringing the situation within paragraph 2 of Article 2.[100]

---

97 ECHR, Article 2 para 2 (c).

98 ECHR, Article 2 para 2 (a).

99 *Isayeva, Yusopova and Bazayeva v. Russia*, no. 57947-49/00 ECHR, 2005, para 181.

100 *Isayeva v. Russia*, n. 99, § 180. Also, to the same effect, *Khatsiyeva and others v. Russia*, no. 5108/02 ECHR 2008, para 134.

It would be interesting to see if the same approach would be taken by a human rights treaty body in a case similar to that of Libya or Syria, namely, where the government itself created the problem. In the Chechen cases, as well as those concerning south-eastern Turkey, the non-international conflicts originated with the rebel movements. It may be that in cases where the government began the conflict, the treaty body would be less ready to accept the general aim of suppressing an insurgency, but would consider the aim met in specific instances where its forces are being attacked.[101] Whatever the answer to this particular point, what is clear is that the law-enforcement model requiring non-lethal methods of control is not required by human rights law when evaluating a possible violation of the right to life during hostilities. In other words, active fighters are not protected during hostilities, unlike protesters during a demonstration.[102]

The next stage of analysis is whether the force used was not more than "absolutely necessary" to achieve the valid aim. The first significant case in this regard was that of *Ergi v. Turkey* which concerned the death of the applicant's sister during an operation by Turkish security forces near a village. The Court concentrated on the planning and the conduct of the operation and in so doing used language that is virtually identical to that of precautions in attack required by IHL:

> ...[t]he responsibility of the State is not confined to circumstances where there is significant evidence that misdirected fire from agents of the State has killed a civilian. It may also be engaged where they fail to take all feasible precautions in the choice of means and methods of a security operation mounted against an opposing group with a view to avoiding and, in any event, minimising, incidental loss of civilian life.[103]

In the circumstances of the case, the villagers were put at considerable risk of being caught in cross-fire between the security forces, positioned south of the village, and the PKK "terrorists" who had approached from the north or north-

---

[101] As was the case, e.g. in *Özkan and others v. Turkey*, in which the European court accepted that security forces were fired on by PKK rebels so that the use of force met the valid aim of defence against lawful use of force: *Özkan and others v. Turkey*, no. 21689/93 ECHR 2004, para 298.

[102] The same conclusion is drawn from these cases by Melzer 2008, pp. 392, 393. Mention may also be made of an oral statement made by Wilder Tayler (presently Secretary-General of the International Commission of Jurists) during one of the ICRC's expert meetings on Direct Participation in Hostilities. Whilst he was working for Human Rights Watch in New York in the 1990s, a rebel fighter from Peru had tried to complain to the Inter-American Commission of Human Rights of a violation of the right to life of his comrades during a shoot-out between government forces and insurgents. He had asserted that the government forces should have waited after spotting the insurgents and offered that the insurgents surrender. The answer by both the Commission and Human Rights Watch was that there was no possibility of such a case being considered by a human rights body (this statement is not recorded in the ICRC's publication of the meetings, but is reproduced here with the express permission of its author).

[103] *Ergi v. Turkey,* no. 23818/94 ECHR 1998-IV, para 79. The second sentence is almost identical to Article 57 para 2 (a)(ii) of the Protocol Additional to the Geneva Conventions of 12 August 1949, and Relating to the Protection of Victims of International Armed Conflicts (Protocol I) (API) 1977.

west. Given the lack of evidence of any precautions being taken by the government to protect the villagers, the Court found a violation of Article 2.

A lack of sufficient precautions before the attack was also the reason for finding a violation of the right to life in two Chechen cases. The case of *Isayeva, Yusopova and Bazayeva v. Russia* concerned the bombing of a convoy of civilians trying to leave Grozny via a "humanitarian corridor" in order to escape the fighting. Two planes circled over the convoy and fired several missiles at it, resulting in deaths and injuries. The government stated that the pilots were on a mission to prevent supplies and personnel of the rebel fighters being brought to Grozny by heavy transport. The government also argued that the civilian vehicles appeared on the road only after the rockets had been fired and that the fighters were deliberately using the convoy as a human shield. The applicants contested this version of events stating that only civilian vehicles were present.

The case of *Isayeva v. Russia* similarly involved deaths and injuries of civilians trying to escape fighting. Shortly after Chechen fighters entered the village of Katyr-Yurt bombing began by Russian forces. According to the applicant, a number of families, including her own, began to leave the village as soon as there was a lull in shelling because the military had apparently granted safe passage to the village's residents. While on the road, the vehicles were bombed. The government version was that their troops had offered safe exit routes to the civilians of the village but many were prevented from leaving by the fighters. Once the residents who were able to do so had left, the air force and artillery struck the village on the basis of incoming intelligence information on where the rebel fighters were placed.

In the case of *Isayeva, Yusopova and Bazayeva v. Russia,* the pilots in question had not been notified of the humanitarian corridor. They could only communicate with an air controller at a centre from which he could not see the road and could not be involved in any independent evaluation of the targets. The Court stressed that all this placed the civilians at a very high risk of been seen as suitable targets by the pilots.[104] Many witnesses also submitted that the attacks lasted for several hours and it had been established that the pilots circled the area several times at altitudes ranging from 2000 to only 200 metres. The European Court was able to make use of the conclusion of the domestic investigation which stated that each plane fired 12 S-24 non-guided air-to-ground missiles and that each missile created several thousand pieces of shrapnel and its impact exceeded 300 metres. The Court made its evaluation of "absolutely necessary" on the basis of whether the use of such weapons, as well as their timing and context, was proportional to the military aim being sought. The finding was in the negative:

> ...the Court does not accept that the operation...was planned and executed with the requisite care for the lives of the civilian population.[105]

[104] *Isayeva v. Russia*, n. 99, paras 187–189.

[105] Ibid. para 199.

The situation in the case of *Isayeva v. Russia* was somewhat different in that the authorities knew in advance that the rebel fighters were likely to enter the village of Katyr-Yurt and therefore the military operation was not spontaneous.[106] The main issue the Court considered was whether appropriate precautions had been taken:

> The Court regards it as evident that when the military considered the deployment of aviation equipped with heavy combat weapons within the boundaries of a populated area, they also should have considered the dangers that such methods invariably entail. There is however no evidence to conclude that such considerations played a significant part in the planning…there is no evidence that at the planning stage of the operation any serious calculations were made about the evacuation of civilians, such as ensuring that they were informed of the attack beforehand, how long such an evacuation would take, what routes evacuees were supposed to take, what kind of precautions were in place to ensure safety, what steps were to be taken to assist the vulnerable and infirm etc.
>
> …The planes…carried heavy free-falling high-explosion aviation bombs…with a damage radius exceeding 1,000 metres [which were] used against targets both in the centre and on the edges of the village.[107]

Not surprisingly, the Court came to the same conclusion as the previous case, i.e. the operation had been carried out without the requisite care for the civilian population and that therefore it failed the proportionality test of Article 2 para 2. The Court concluded as follows:

> Even when faced with a situation where, as the Government submit, the population of the village had been held hostage by a large group of well-equipped and well-trained fighters, the primary aim of the operation should be to protect lives from unlawful violence. The massive use of indiscriminate weapons stands in flagrant contrast with this aim and cannot be considered compatible with the standard of care prerequisite to an operation of this kind involving the use of lethal force by State agents.[108]

These cases indicate that the Court in practice uses IHL required precautions in attack for its evaluation of "absolutely necessary", without direct reference to IHL as such. These cases also show that not taking the required precautions to avoid or at least minimize civilian losses amounts to a violation of the right to life.

It could be asserted, as does Melzer,[109] that these cases show that the result is identical with that if the IHL hostilities paradigm were used. This would be the case if IHL were interpreted strictly, namely, that an attack would be unlawful if precautions were not taken to avoid or minimize damage. The extent to which IHL

[106] Rebel fighters had been lured out of Grozny with information of a safe passage and when moving south were attacked by Russian government forces. Those entering the village were part of this rebel group: *Isayeva v. Russia*, n. 99, paras 12–15.

[107] *Isayeva v. Russia*, n. 99, paras 189–190.

[108] *Isayeva v. Russia*, n. 99, para 191.

[109] Melzer 2008, pp. 392, 393.

tolerates collateral deaths and injuries, however, remains problematic.[110] In this regard, only an attack that violates the rule that such casualties must not be excessive in relation to the value of the military objective attacked is defined as 'indiscriminate.'[111] IHL requires "feasible precautions" to avoid or minimise incidental civilian casualties and damage, but the question is whether this is necessary to ensure that such incidental effects are not excessive (i.e. disproportionate to the military advantage), or whether the precautions are an additional independent requirement. In other words, even if there is no excessive incidental damage, will there still be a violation of IHL if such damage could have been minimised further by a better respect of the required precautions in attack? A discussion during an expert meeting on this subject did not reach an agreement to this effect.[112] A less protective interpretation may be understandable where a war crime needs to be proved, but in other cases the stricter IHL interpretation, which would be in keeping with the human rights approach would be more protective of the civilian population. The IHL rule that allows a certain amount of collateral damage is non-existent as such in human rights law. The case of *Ahmet Özkan and Others v. Turkey*, in which a violation was not found because "only" one civilian injury occurred during a military operation, should not be taken to mean that "non-excessive" incidental injuries are therefore lawful in human rights law. Rather, this fact was used as evidence by the European Court to arrive at the conclusion that the use of force by the security forces was not more than "absolutely necessary" for repelling an attack against them, i.e. that the security forces must have taken the necessary care.[113]

Another very important point in a non-international armed conflict is the need to ensure that only armed fighters are targeted. This point arose in the case of *Khatsiyeva and Others v. Russia*. The case concerned the attack on six men by a Russian military helicopter in Ingushetia, near the border with Chechnya. The Russian government was carrying out a "counter-terrorism" operation in that area to catch insurgents and "prevent further criminal activity",[114] because a government helicopter had been earlier shot down near there. The government argued that the pilots saw the men carrying light machine guns who "could have belonged to illegal armed groups,"[115] whereas the applicants insisted that they were unarmed

[110] The two provisions are to be found in Additional Protocol I, Article 57(2) (ii) and (iii), respectively. They are also reflected in Rules 17 and 18 of the ICRC *Customary Law Study*—Henckaerts and Doswald-Beck 2005.

[111] API, Article 51(5) (b).

[112] Expert meeting held by the then University Centre for International Humanitarian Law (now the Geneva Academy of International Humanitarian Law and Human Rights) on "Targeting Military Objectives" 12 May 2005, Report, pp. 13, 14, www.adh-geneva.ch/docs/expert-meetings/2005/1rapport_objectif_militaire.pdf.

[113] *Ahmet Özkan and Others v. Turkey*, no. 21689/93 ECHR 2004, paras 305, 306.

[114] *Khatsiyeva and Others v. Russia*, n. 100.

[115] Ibid. § 126.

and were in fact cutting grass.[116] The European Court found that in the 15 minutes between the time that the pilots reported to the command centre the existence of these men and the order to fire on them, it was "highly doubtful that the authorities in command established the identity of the [men]" in particular as no further details had been requested from the pilots.[117] There was no indication that even if the men were carrying such arms, they could have posed a threat to the helicopter.[118] In these circumstances the Court found that there had been insufficient care in assessing the situation so that, even if they had been carrying arms, the use of force was not absolutely necessary for the aims stated in Article 2 para 2 (a) or (b).[119] The question remains whether it would have made sense if the Russian government had argued the aim provided by Article 2 para 2 (c), i.e. to suppress an insurrection. Even if it had expressly done so, the lack of proper identification should still have been a major problem.

One IHL approach would allow the attack on sight of any suspected members of a rebel group in non-international armed conflicts, and this would be at odds with the judgment of the European Court in this case. Another interpretation by IHL specialists is that such an attack is not possible unless people are actually using force at the time.[120] This approach is more protective and more in keeping with the judgment in the *Khatsiyeva* case. When considering the situation in Syria, this issue is particularly significant. The government has argued that the protesters are in fact armed groups illegally using force, whereas this is contested. On the other hand, some military personnel that defected to the protesters' side have admitted to using force, but supposedly to protect the protesters. Whatever the real facts may be, the issue of correct identification becomes crucial if the unrest in Syria does become a non-international armed conflict. The ICRC's Interpretative Guidance on the Notion of Direct Participation in Hostilities specifies that only fighters of armed groups lose their protection from attack, as well as those actively involved in hostilities at any particular time.[121] The danger of simplistically applying the same distinction in non-international conflicts, between armed forces and civilians which applies to international conflicts, has been well explained by Sassòli and Olson:

---

116 Ibid. § 116.

117 Ibid. § 136.

118 Ibid. § 126.

119 Ibid. §§ 137, 138. It may be noted that, in keeping with its approach in earlier cases, the violation of the right to life was found with regard to the use of lethal force against all six men, even though only two died.

120 This is usually interpreted as including persons manifestly about to use force or having just done so. The ICRC Interpretative Guidance, Recommendation VI, describes it as "measures preparatory to the execution of a specific act of direct participation in hostilities, as well as the deployment to and return from the location of its execution."

121 ICRC Interpretative Guidance, Recommendations II, IV and V. Fighters in armed groups are referred to as those having a continuous combat function.

> Many non-international armed conflicts are fought against or between groups that are not well structured. It is much more difficult to determine who belongs to an armed group then who belongs to government armed forces. The positive humanitarian law of armed conflicts does not even explicitly prescribe…that fighters must distinguish themselves from the civilian population. Individuals join and quit armed groups in an informal way…Claiming that fighters may be shot at on sight may therefore put many civilians in danger, whether they are sympathisers of the group, members of the 'political wing', belong to the same ethnic group or simply happen to be in the wrong place at the wrong time.[122]

It would be particularly inappropriate to interpret IHL in a way that would allow attacks to all persons associated with an armed group when many such persons in Syria have not themselves been fighters but rather protesters who were illegally shot at by the government, thereby provoking the need for fighters to come to their defence. Recommendation IX of the ICRC's Interpretative Guidance, which specifies that lethal force must not be used if in a particular circumstance this is not militarily necessary is particularly apposite here. This recommendation remains controversial among IHL specialists,[123] which is, in these authors' view, unfortunate. The recommendation was influenced by human rights law that prohibits the killing of rebels in circumstances where they can be easily captured (or arrested to use human rights language).[124] However, this is not contrary to the spirit or even letter of IHL which provides, for example, in Article 41 of Additional Protocol I that a person may not be attacked if "he is in the power of an adverse Party."[125] The situation of unrest in the Arab Spring, in particular Yemen and Syria, is likely to remain a mixed one of protest, force in self-defence and fighting. Given that much of the fighting has been illegally provoked by the government, it is suggested that IHL be interpreted in a way that is the most protective of the civilian population, which is the way that human rights law has been applied to hostilities during armed conflict.

Finally, an important issue is that of investigation into killings that may amount to a violation. Like human rights treaties, a duty of investigation for deaths caused by security forces is not spelled out in IHL treaties, but as the UN Special Rapporteur on Extrajudicial, Summary or Arbitrary Executions has observed, a *bona*

---

122 Sassòli and Olson 2008, p. 609.

123 ICRC Intepretative Guidance, Footnote 212.

124 See, e.g. UNHRCte, *Guerrero v. Columbia*, Com. 45/1979, 31 March 1982. The case concerned the killing of suspected Colombian rebels at point-blank range whilst they were arriving, unarmed, at a house in which the authorities thought they were holding a hostage (which was not the case). No attempt at arrest had been made.

125 Article 41 of Protocol I additional to the Geneva Conventions describes when a person is considered to be *hors de combat*. The provision quoted is in para 2(a) of Article 41. The other two subparagraphs of this provision include a person who has surrendered or has been rendered unconscious, or is incapacitated by wounds or sickness. The phrase in sub-para (a) must therefore refer to something else. This is supported in the case of non-international conflicts by Article 3 common to the 1949 Geneva Conventions which prohibits attacks on members of armed forces who have laid down their arms and those placed *hors de combat* by sickness, wounds, detention or *any other cause* (emphasis added).

fide interpretation of IHL must come to the same conclusion, i.e. any suspected violation of IHL needs to be properly investigated for the same reasons as those stated by the human rights treaty bodies. Otherwise, as he pointed out, how can war crimes be prosecuted if suspected violations are not investigated using the same transparency and impartiality criteria as that spelled out by human rights treaty bodies?[126]

1.8 Conclusion in the Context of the Arab Spring

The right to protest through peaceful assembly is a fundamental human right. The events that have and still are taking place in several Arab countries bring both hope and despair at the same time. Hope that the people are sovereign and can decide their political destiny; despair that the price for liberty has been so high.

This brief overview of the applicable law to the use of force in those situations, and the international community's reaction to the events in the Arab Spring, show that irrespective of the degree of violence used by the government to oppress its people, the traditional rule remains that there is no legal right to rebel. The reaction to Libya's rebellion seems to remain an exception. On the other hand, there is insufficient evidence to assert that rebellion is actively prohibited in *international* law, as opposed to national law.

International law does impose strict conditions to the use of force when dealing with protest or riots. The conditions of necessity and proportionality and the requirement to take all preventive measures in order to avoid using lethal force makes it almost impossible for a State to legally justify the use of live ammunition or deadly force during protest. If it does so, not only will law enforcement agents commit serious violations of the human right to life, but if the use of firearms against protesters is massive and systematic, they and their leaders may face international criminal responsibility for crimes against humanity. All of this means that a government is prohibited from creating a non-international armed conflict.

If, as a response to the use of lethal force by the government, protesters have organised themselves as an armed group and if the level of violence is sufficiently intensive, IHL will apply, irrespective of which party started the conflict. As is the case with international armed conflict, *jus in bello* is not dependent on *jus ad bellum* in a non-international armed conflict and it seems both reaffirmed and reasonable that this legal situation should remain in place. Human rights law has in practice been applied to active hostilities during non-international armed conflict. Notions of IHL have been borrowed when interpreting what is justified and "absolutely necessary" in these contexts, but the interpretation corresponds to what would be quite a strict interpretation of IHL i.e. one that would be most protective of the civilian population. However, even in armed conflict situations, it

[126] Alston 2006, paras 33–43.

is the law-enforcement model that is required both by human rights law and by IHL when the actual situation being regulated is not one of armed hostilities. It is also crucial that notions of direct participation in hostilities do not in practice affect peaceful protesters and others that are not a threat to life.

In particular it is submitted that further thought should be given to the traditional rule allowing governments to prosecute insurrectionists. Although any idea of POW status in non-international armed conflicts is at present a non-starter, as there is firm opposition to the idea by most, if not all, governments, an exception should be considered in the case of people that use force in self-defence when governments use excessive violence against protesters. Saul would go one step further:

> There is a powerful argument that rebel violence against oppressive states, while respecting IHL constraints, should be lawfully justified in international law—by conferring combatant immunity.[127]

Even if this is impracticable at the moment, it would at least seem reasonable that in cases where the government began the conflict, the international community should prevent it from abusing its right to prosecute those that reacted to the government's unlawful violence. It is all very well for the international community to insist that disputes between a government and its people be limited to peaceful means, but when it is the government that flatly refuses to do this, then what is a people realistically expected to do?

Whatever the future direction of the law, it remains crucial, as a lesson learned from the civil protest movement in the Arab countries, that the responsibility of State agents who unlawfully repress peaceful protest is clearly established and that victims and their families receive adequate reparation.[128] Perhaps only then can the message be heard that lawful acts of protest do not have to be exercised at the price of one's life under modern international human rights law.

References

Abresch W (2005) A human rights law of internal armed conflict: the European court of human rights in Chechnya. Eur J Int Law 16:741–767

Alston P (2006) Report to the Human Rights Commission. UN Doc. E/CN.4/2006/53

Bakri N (2011) United Nations says unrest in Syria amounts to civil war. New York Times (1 December 2011). Available at http://www.nytimes.com/2011/12/02/world/middleeast/united-nations-says-syrian-unrest-amounts-to-civil-war.html?_r=1&scp=1&sq=syria%20civil%20war&st=cse. Accessed 1 Dec 2011

[127] Saul 2008, p. 26.

[128] Such a call was made by Human Rights Watch in Tunisia, but it does not seem to have been listened to by the transitional authorities at that time nor by the elected government today. HRW, Tunisia: Hold Police Accountable for shootings, http://www.hrw.org, January 29, 2011.

BBC News (2011a) Ian Tomlinson unlawfully killed by PC at G20 protests. BBC News (3 May 2011). Available at http://www.bbc.co.uk/news/uk-13268633. Accessed 13 Dec 2011

BBC News (2011b) Syria is facing a new Arab League deadline to accept proposals to allow observers into the strife-torn country. BBC News (4 Dec 2011). Available at www.bbc.co.uk/news/mobile/world-middle-east-16021738. Accessed 13 Dec 2011

Benjamin C (2009) Occupation, resistance & the law was armed resistance to the occupation of Iraq justified under International Law? Doctoral thesis, University of Melbourne

Blight G, Pulham S, Torpey P (2011) Arab spring: an interactive timeline of Middle East Protests. The Guardian (18 Novemb 2011). Available at http://www.guardian.co.uk/world/interactive/2011/mar/22/middle-east-protest-interactive-timeline. Accessed 1 Dec 2011

Boyle K (2010) Thought, expression, association, and assembly. In: Moeckli et al (ed) International Human Rights Law. OUP, Oxford

Casey-Maslen S (2013) Weapons under International Human Rights Law. Cambridge University Press, Cambridge (forthcoming)

Cassese A (1996) Self-determination of peoples. CUP, Cambridge

Clapham A, Marks S (2005) International Human Rights Lexicon. Oxford University Press, Oxford

Council on Foreign Policy (2011) Backgrouder: Al-Qaeda in the Arabian Peninsula (AQAP) (updated 7 Dec 2011). Available at http://www.cfr.org/yemen/al-qaeda-arabian-peninsula-aqap/p9369#p7. Accessed 13 Dec 2011

Crawford J (2001) The right of self-determination in International Law: its development and future. In: Alston P (ed) Peoples'rights. OUP, Oxford, pp 7–42

De Schutter O (2009) International Human Rights Law. Cambridge University Press, Cambridge

Doehring K (2002) Self determination. In: Simma B (ed) The charter of the United Nations: a commentary, 2nd edn. OUP, Oxford

Doswald-Beck L (2011) Human rights in times of conflict and terrorism. OUP, Oxford

France 24 (2011) Free Syrian Army forms military council to oust Assad France 24 (16 November 2011). Available at http://www.france24.com/en/20111116-free-syrian-army-forms-military-council-oust-assad. Accessed 13 Dec 2011

Haaretz (2011) Over 10,000 soldiers have deserted Syria Army, says high ranking defector (1 October 2011). Available at www.haaretz.com/news/middle-east/over-10-000-soldiers-have-deserted-syria-army-says-high-ranking-defector-1.387494. Accessed 1 Dec 2011

Henckaerts J-M, Doswald-Beck L (2005) Customary International Humanitarian Law, vol I. Cambridge University Press, Cambridge

Honoré T (1988) The right to rebel. Oxf J Leg Stud 8:34–54

Human Rights Watch (2008) Disappearances and arbitrary arrests in the armed conflict with Huthi rebels in Yemen. www.hrw.org/en/reports/2008/10/24/disappearances-and-arbitrary-arrests-armed-conflict-huthi-rebels-yemen-0. Accessed 1 Dec 2011

Human Rights Watch (2011a) Tunisia: hold police accountable for shootings, tranitional government should open an investigation (29 January 2011). Available at www.hrw.org/en/2011/01/29/tunisia-hold-police-accountable-shootings. Accessed 13 Dec 2011

Human Rights Watch (2011b) We live as in war: crackdown on protesters in the Governorate of Homs, in Syria. Available at www.hrw.org/reports/2011/11/11/we-live-war-0. Accessed 1 December 2011

Manfred N (2005) UN covenant on civil and political rights: CCPR commentary, 2nd rev. ed. Engel, Kehl am Rhein

Mead D (2010) The new law of peaceful protest: rights and regulation in the Human Rights Act era. Hart Publishing, Portland

Melzer N (2008) Targeted killing in international law. Oxford University Press, Oxford

Morsink J (1999) The universal declaration of human rights: origins, drafting, and intent. University of Pennsylvania Press, Phildelphia, Pennsylvania

New York Times (2011) Yemen—Protests 2011. Available at http://topics.nytimes.com/top/news/international/countriesandterritories/yemen/index.html?scp=3&sq=yemen%20arab%20spring&st=cse. Accessed 1 Dec 2011

Sassòli M, Olson L (2008) The relationship between international humanitarian and human rights law where it matters: admissible killings and internment of fighters in non-international armed conflicts. Int Rev Red Cross 90:599

Saul B (2008) Defending 'terrorism': justifications and excuses for terrorism in International Criminal Law. N08/122 Legal Studies Research Paper. http://ssrn.com/abstract=1291584. Accessed 1 Dec 2011

Stigall D, Blakesley C, Jenks C (2009) Human rights and military decisions: counterinsurgency and trends in the law of international armed conflict. William S Boyd School of Law, University of Nevada. Available at www.scholars.law.unlv.ed/cgi/viewcontent.cgi?article=10028&context=facpub. Accessed 1 Dec 2011

The Guardian (2011a) French photographer dies after being hit by police teargas canister in Tunisia. The Guardian (16 January 2011). Available at www.guardian.co.uk/world/2011/jan/16/french-photographer-dies-tunisia-protests. Accessed 1 Dec 2011

The Guardian (2011b) Gaddafi killed as Sirte falls—blog. Guardian News (20 October 2011). Available at http://www.guardian.co.uk/world/middle-east-live/2011/oct/20/gaddafi-killed-sirte-falls-live. Accessed 13 Dec 2011

The Guardian (2011c) Syria on brink of civil war, says UN—video. The Guardian (2 December 2011). Available at http://www.guardian.co.uk/world/video/2011/dec/02/syria-civil-war-un-video. Accessed 13 Dec 2011

UN Human Rights Council (2011a) Report of the International Commission of Inquiry to investigate all alleged violations of international human rights law in the Libyan Arab Jamahiriya, A/HRC/17/44

UN Human Rights Council (2011b) Report of the Independent International Commission of Inquiry on the Syrian Arab Republic—A/HRC/S-17/Add.1

UN News Centre (2011a) UN rights council recommends suspending Libya, orders inquiry into abuses (25 Febr 2011). Available at http://www.un.org/apps/news/story.asp?NewsID=37626&Cr=Libya&Cr1. Accessed 13 Dec 2011

UN News Centre (2011b) Security Council authorizes 'all necessary measures' to protect civilians in Libya (17 March 2011). Available at http://www.un.org/apps/news/story.asp?NewsID=37808&Cr=libya&Cr1=. Accessed on 13 December 2011

Weiss N (2011) Assembly, freedom of, international protection. Max Planck Encyclopaedia of Public International Law. www.mprpil.com. Accessed 1 Dec 2011

White R, Ovey C (2010) White & Ovey: European convention on human rights, 5th edn. OUP, Oxford

Wolf N (2011) The shocking truth about the crackdown on occupy. The Guardian (25 November 2011). Available at http://www.guardian.co.uk/commentisfree/cifamerica/2011/nov/25/shocking-truth-about-crackdown-occupy?CMP=NECNETTXT766. Accessed on 27 November 2011

Chapter 2
Beyond the Grave Breaches Regime: The Duty to Investigate Alleged Violations of International Law Governing Armed Conflicts

Amichai Cohen and Yuval Shany

Contents

We would like to thank Noa Amirav and Ido Rosenzweig for their research assistance.

A. Cohen (✉)
Faculty of Law, Ono Academic College, Kiryat Ono, Israel
e-mail: amichai.cohen@gmail.com

A. Cohen · Y. Shany
Israel Democracy Institute, Jerusalem, Israel

Y. Shany
Hersch Lauterpacht Chair in Public International Law, Hebrew University, Jerusalem, Israel
e-mail: shany.yuval@gmail.com

M.N. Schmitt and L. Arimatsu (eds.), *Yearbook of International Humanitarian Law Volume 14, 2011*, DOI: 10.1007/978-90-6704-855-2_2,

2.1 Introduction

The observation that international humanitarian law (IHL) does not need more rules, but rather better enforcement mechanisms has become somewhat of a universally accepted mantra, as well as a call for action.[1] Indeed, the last quarter of a century has witnessed considerable progress in the strengthening of IHL enforcement procedures: new international criminal courts with jurisdiction over certain IHL issues have been established[2]; universal and other forms of criminal jurisdiction have been exercised by a growing number of states during and in the aftermath of numerous armed conflicts[3]; and military lawyering has been expanded in scope and deepened in reach in many national militaries.[4] In addition, it has become widely-accepted that international human rights law (IHRL) continues to apply in situation of armed conflict, at least with regard to persons situated under the effective control of the relevant states.[5] As a result, IHRL courts and committees have increasingly asserted their authority over armed conflicts.[6]

Given the clear potential for the involvement of military personnel in violations of the rules applicable in armed conflicts, on the one hand, and the capabilities of militaries for exercising effective control over soldiers, on the other hand, it is only natural that military legal institutions are deemed to be an important, if not the most important, line of defense against violations of international law perpetrated

---

[1] See e.g., ICRC 2007, p. 721 ("in the ICRC's view, the main cause of suffering during armed conflicts and of violations of IHL remains the failure to implement existing norms—whether owing to an absence of political will or to another reason—rather than a lack of rules or their inadequacy").

[2] Mackenzie et al. 2010, Chapter 3.

[3] Example: The International Criminal Court for Former Yugoslavia (ICTY); The International Criminal Court for Rwanda (ICTR).

[4] See e.g., Newton 2007, Dickinson 2010.

[5] See e.g., Ben-Naftali 2011, p. 3.

[6] Example: Abresch 2005, Byron 2007.

during armed conflicts.[7] Arguably, a robust system of military investigations and prosecutions may prevent future violations (*inter alia,* through generating deterrence and removing repeat offenders from the battlefield), and punish those who have committed them in the past. Such a system can also help in identifying organizational and procedural deficiencies that may have permitted IHL violations to take place to begin with.

The increased focus on the structures and procedures of military investigative mechanisms—reflected in part in the growing scrutiny of such mechanisms by judicial bodies applying human rights standards[8]—has led many militaries to reevaluate the manner in which they investigate allegations of international law violations occurring during armed conflict. Thus, a number of legal and institutional reforms have been launched in recent years—Canada established new investigative bodies in 1997[9] and Australia followed suit in 2007[10]; the UK in 2006 adopted a new Armed Forces Act[11]; and the US issued new Directives on investigations in 2011. Furthermore, almost a 100 countries have created national IHL committees to supervise their implementation efforts[12]; and in other countries, such as Israel, a robust public debate has revolved around the proper scope and nature of the duty to investigate military acts (an official commission and inquiry, as well as the national Supreme Court, have reviewed the matter in Israel).[13]

Notwithstanding these developments, there remain fundamental questions about the duty to investigate violations of international law applicable in situations of armed conflict. For example, what should be the investigative trigger and how and

---

[7] Example: Article 82 of the First Additional Protocol (Protocol Additional to the Geneva Conventions of 12 August 1949, and Relating to the Protection of Victims of International Armed Conflicts, 8 June 1977, 1125 UNTS 3) (AP I) requires militaries to "ensure that legal advisers are available, when necessary, to advise military commanders at the appropriate level on the application of the Conventions and this Protocol and on the appropriate instruction to be given to the armed forces on this subject."

[8] See e.g., *Isayeva, Yusopova and Bazayeva v. Russia,* Judgment of 24 February 2005, no. 57947-49/00 ECHR, 2005; *Issa v. Turkey,* Judgment of 16 Nov.2004, no. 31821/96 ECHR 2004; *Al Skeini v. UK,* Grand Chamber, Judgment of 7 July 2011, no.55721/07 ECHR 2011.

[9] National Defence Act, R.S.C. 1985, c. N-5 (Can.).

[10] Defence Act 1903 (2006 amendments) Defense Instructions 2007 available at: http://www.defence.gov.au/fr/Policy/ga67_02.pdf. Some parts of the 2006 act were challenged before the High Court of Australia. On 29 August 2009 the High Court of Australia ruled that the newly created Australian Military Court was unconstitutional: Lane v. Morrison [2009] HCA 29 (26 August 2009).

[11] UK Armed Forces Act 2006.

[12] http://www.icrc.org/eng/resources/documents/misc/table-national-committees.htm.

[13] See HCJ 9594/03 *B'Tselem and Association for Civil Rights in Israel v. Military Advocate General,* Judgment of 21 August 2011 (in Hebrew); http://www.turkel-committee.gov.il/index.html. The Mandate of the Turkel commission includes, *inter alia,* review of the question whether the military investigation mechanisms addressing complaints and allegations regarding violations of the laws of war meet Israel's international obligations.

to what extent are human rights principles governing criminal investigations during peacetime transposable to the military context? What is the relationship between the duty to undertake criminal investigations and to engage in other fact-finding exercises? And how do principles of military necessity and proportionality affect the scope and contents of any duty to investigate? As will be shown below, state practice on these issues diverges, and it has been argued that for some questions no international standards exist at all.[14] Furthermore, a few of these questions seem to have escaped, by and large, the attention of judges and commentators, although their practical importance may be significant.

The purpose of the present article is to critically evaluate the contemporary international law obligation to investigate military conduct in times of conflict and to identify relevant normative trends. In a nutshell, we argue that the traditional focus on the Geneva grave breaches regime in the context of military investigations is misplaced. The duty to investigate is far broader encompassing alleged violation of many other norms of IHL and IHRL and engaging the responsibility of both military and civilian officials. It is also more diverse in its objective and richer in its methods than sometimes has been assumed. Thus, for example, some allegations would justify a criminal investigative response whereas others may merit alternative reactions, such as disciplinary proceedings, civil proceedings or some other fact-finding process. What is more, some of these responses are primarily geared towards ensuring personal accountability for past deeds, while others are more concerned with improving future practices. Nevertheless, we are of the view that all reactions to alleged violations, as well as the mechanism for selecting between them, should be governed by IHRL principles (such as independence, impartiality, promptness and transparency), although their manner of application to battlefield investigations would necessitate adjustment.

Section 2.2 of the article (after this introduction) discusses the breadth of the duty to investigate. It shows that the duty extends far beyond the grave breaches regimes and discusses, in that context, the necessary triggering mechanisms. Section 2.3 discusses the main legal standards governing military investigations—genuineness, effectiveness, independence and impartiality, promptness and transparency. Section 2.4 addresses trends in international legislation and state practice concerning the maintenance of independence under the challenging conditions featured in many military investigations. Section 2.5 explains the reasons supporting the move away from criminal enforcement in some cases and sketches a possible solution to some of the practical problems identified in this article—the establishment of a permanent commission of inquiry for evaluating IHL compliance in military operations. Section 2.6 concludes.

---

14 Schmitt 2011.

2.2 What Should Be Investigated?

2.2.1 The Non-Exclusive Nature of the Grave Breaches Regime Under IHL

There is little question that states must investigate serious allegations of war crimes committed by individuals subject to their jurisdiction with a view to ascertaining the criminal responsibility of the suspected perpetrators. This rule, found in the grave breaches provisions of the Geneva Conventions,[15] is also supported by the jurisprudence of human rights courts on violations of the right to life and the prohibition against torture, stipulating a second order "effective remedy" obligation to respond through criminal investigation and prosecution to serious IHRL violations by state agents as well as other perpetrators.[16] Even so, the claim sometimes made, explicitly or implicitly, that the military is required under international law to investigate *only* allegations of grave breaches[17] appears to us erroneous for the following reasons.

First, the grave breaches provisions of the Geneva Conventions entail much more than a duty to investigate and prosecute soldiers accused of committing war crimes. They also contain the following obligations: (1) to enact suitable criminal legislation[18]; (2) not to absolve perpetrators of grave breaches from legal responsibility[19]; and, most significantly, (3) to search and prosecute (or extradite) any individual—regardless of his or her nationality—that allegedly committed grave breaches.[20] Hence, the main effect of the grave breaches provisions appears to be the *internationalization* of war crimes (a process further enhanced by the inclusion of grave breaches provisions in the statutes of international criminal tribunals—including the International Criminal Court (ICC)).[21] The claim that the

---

[15] Geneva Convention for the Amelioration of the Condition of the Wounded and Sick in Armed Forces in the Field, 12 August 1949, Article 49, 75 UNTS 31 (GC-I); Geneva Convention for the Amelioration of the Condition of Wounded, Sick and Shipwrecked Members of Armed Forces at Sea of August 12, 1949, Article 50, 75 UNTS 85 (GC-II); Geneva Convention Relative to the Treatment of Prisoners of War of August 12, 1949, Article 129, 75 UNTS 135 (GC-III); Geneva Convention Relative to the Protection of Civilian Persons in Times of War of August 12, 1949, Article 146, 75 UNTS 287 (GC-IV); AP-I, Article 85.

[16] See e.g., *Velasquez Rodriguez v. Honduras*, Judgment of July 29, 1988, Inter-Am.Ct.H.R. (Ser. C) No. 4 (1988), at para 176.

[17] Schmitt 2011.

[18] GC I, Article 49; GC II, Article 50; GC III, Article 129; GC IV, Article 146, AP-I, Article 85(5).

[19] Ibid.

[20] Ibid.

[21] Statute of the International Criminal Tribunal for Former Yugoslavia, 25 May 1993, Article 2, UN Doc. S/RES/827 (1993)(ICTY Statute); Statute for the International Criminal Tribunal for Rwanda, 8 Nov. 1994, Article 4, UN Doc. S/RES/955 (1994)(ICTR Statute); Statute of the International Criminal Court, 17 July 1998, Article 8(2)(a), 2187 UNTS 90 (ICC Statute).

state's duty to investigate and prosecute violations committed by its own military is co-extensive with its obligations to exercise criminal jurisdiction over any crime committed by any person, anywhere in the world, is not dictated by either the terms of the grave breaches provision nor by their internal logic. In fact, the opposite seems to be true. Alongside the specific obligation to suppress grave breaches through a particularly aggressive criminal law response (formal legislation, no exoneration, universal jurisdiction—subject to the *aut dedere aut judicare* principle) the Conventions require states to address through appropriate means *other* violations of the Convention. As explained below, we are of the opinion that such appropriate means may entail, in certain circumstances, criminal investigations and prosecutions.

The proposition that the Geneva Conventions and their Additional Protocols impose a broad duty to investigate going beyond situations in which grave breaches have been allegedly committed is borne out by a close reading of the terms of the grave breaches provisions themselves, and is supported by the parallel language used in the First Additional Protocol.

All four grave breaches provisions contain the following language:

> Each High Contracting Party shall take measures necessary for the *suppression* of all acts contrary to the provisions of the present Convention other than the grave breaches defined in the following Article.[22] (emphasis added)

Thus, alongside the specific obligations to exercise criminal jurisdiction under the grave breaches regime, the Conventions introduce a general obligation of taking measures necessary for suppression of other violations (in the original French text—*prendra les mesures nécessaires pour faire cesser les actes contraires aux dispositions de la présente Convention*). Indeed, the Pictet Commentary to the Geneva Conventions clarifies that the drafters did not intend the grave breaches regime to limit the general duty to investigate and prosecute (which covers all violations of the Conventions):

> Article 29 of the 1929 Convention called for the punishment of 'all' acts contrary to the provisions of the Convention, and there could be no question of the Diplomatic Conference of 1949 not going as far as in 1929.... It is thus clear that 'all' breaches of the present Convention should be repressed by national legislation. At the very least, the Contracting Powers, having arranged for the repression of the various grave breaches and fixed an appropriate penalty for each, must include a general clause in their national legislative enactments, providing for the punishment of other breaches of the Convention. Furthermore, under the present paragraph the authorities of the Contracting Parties should issue instructions in accordance with the Convention to all their subordinates, and arrange for judicial or disciplinary proceedings to be taken in all cases of failure to comply with such instructions.[23]

---

[22] GC I, Article 49; GC II, Article 50; GC III, Article 129; GC IV Article 146.

[23] Pictet 1958, vol. I at pp. 367–368. Pictet also notes that there is a certain overlap between the obligation to investigate and prosecute other violations, and the specific duty to repress abuses of the emblem, specified in Article 54 of the First Geneva Convention. Like the grave breaches regime, Article 54 does not exhaust the obligations of the member states in the field of norm enforcement.

In the same vein, Article 86(1) of the First Additional Protocol provides that:

> The High Contracting Parties and the Parties to the conflict shall repress grave breaches, and take measures necessary to suppress *all other breaches*, of the Conventions or of this Protocol which result from a failure to act when under a duty to do so. (emphasis added)

Although the duty to suppress other breaches under Article 86(1) appears to be limited to omission-type violations, this must be understood in light of the duty imposed on military commanders in Article 87 to prevent all violations of the Conventions and the Protocol by persons subject to their control.[24] Hence, the combination of Articles 86 and 87 establishes a general duty to suppress all violations—certainly going far beyond the grave breaches regime.

Developments in international criminal law in the 1990s, involving the expansion of war crimes beyond the grave breaches specified in the Geneva Conventions and the First Additional Protocol, underscore the non-exclusivity of the grave breaches regime as a basis for criminal prosecutions under international law: The International Criminal Tribunal for the Former Yugoslavia (ICTY) has been authorized to prosecute violations of the laws and customs of war other that grave breaches of the Geneva Conventions[25]—a mandate that was interpreted by the Appeals Chamber as encompassing " any serious offence against international humanitarian law" not covered by the other provisions in the Statute (referring to grave breaches, crimes against humanity and genocide).[26] A similar mandate going beyond the grave breaches regime can be found in, for instance, the statutes of the International Criminal Tribunal for Rwanda (ICTR), the Special Court for Sierra Leone (SCSL) and the ICC.[27] The trend towards enumerating lists of international crimes subject to the jurisdiction of international courts that go beyond the grave breaches regime implies *a fortiori* that national legal systems should also treat these other serious violations as justifying a criminal response. This is especially so given the rising expectation that international criminal courts

---

[24] AP 1, Article 87(1) reads: "The High Contracting Parties and the Parties to the conflict shall require military commanders, with respect to members of the armed forces under their command and other persons under their control, to prevent and, where necessary, to suppress and to report to competent authorities breaches of the Conventions and of this Protocol."

[25] ICTY Statute, Article 3.

[26] ICTY, *Prosecutor v Dusko Tadić*, Decision on the Defence Motion for Interlocutory Appeal on Jurisdiction, Appeals Chamber I (IT-94-1-AR72) 2nd October 1995, para 91.

[27] ICTR Statute, Article 4 ("The International Tribunal for Rwanda shall have the power to prosecute persons committing or ordering to be committed serious violations of Article 3 common to the Geneva Conventions of 12 August 1949 for the Protection of War Victims, and of Additional Protocol II thereto of 8 June 1977"); Statute of the Special Court for Sierra Leone, 16 Jan. 2002, Articles 3, 4, http://www.sc-sl.org/LinkClick.aspx?fileticket=uClnd1MJeEw%3d&tabid=176 (SCSL Statute)(authorizing the court to try individuals who committed serious violations of common Article 3, and the Second Additional Protocol to the Geneva Conventions, as well as three other serious violations of IHL); ICC Statute, Article 8(2)(b)–(e).

adhere to the principle of complementarity thereby leaving the bulk of investigations and prosecutions in the hands of national authorities.[28]

The need to investigate serious violations of international humanitarian law beyond the grave breaches regime is further supported by three key principles embraced in the Geneva Conventions and Additional Protocols: (1) The general duty to ensure respect of the Conventions (or principle of effectiveness),[29] (2) the command responsibility doctrine,[30] and (3) the precautionary obligations of the parties to the conflict.[31] It is also supported, though less clearly, by the duty to respond to allegations of violations made by the other party to the conflict.[32]

2.2.1.1 Ensuring Respect for IHL

Common Article 1 to the four Geneva Conventions requires the Contracting Parties to "respect and to ensure respect for the present Convention[s] in all circumstances"; similar provisions can be found in the First Additional Protocol.[33] According to the Pictet Commentary this entails, *inter* alia, a duty to supervise the execution of the Conventions,[34] a point with which the commenters of the Additional Protocols concur.[35] The duty to ensure respect for IHL was deemed by the ICRC Study to constitute part of customary international law.[36]

Investigation of serious violations of IHL can be viewed as an indispensible means by which to effectively carry out the duty to ensure respect for IHL. As is well known, the International Military Tribunal in Nuremberg was of the view that criminal prosecutions are an essential strategy for enforcing international law obligations: "Crimes against international law are committed by men, not by abstract entities, and only by punishing individuals who commit such crimes can the provisions of international law be enforced."[37] Indeed, criminal investigations and prosecutions may promote respect for IHL through increased deterrence and the physical removal of offenders from the battlefield. Other considerations, including learning from operational misdeeds in order to avoid future violations

---

[28] On the issue of complementarity, see Holmes 1999, Danner 2003, p. 526.

[29] GC I, Article 1; GC II, Article 1; GC III, Article 1; GC IV, Article 1.

[30] AP-I, Article 87, ICC Statute, Article 28.

[31] Example: AP-I, Articles 57, 58.

[32] AP-I, Article 89.

[33] AP1, Article 1(1).

[34] Pictet 1958, vol I, at 26 ("It would not, for example, be enough for a State to give orders or directives to a few civilian or military authorities, leaving it to them to arrange as they pleased for the details of their execution. It is for the State to supervise their execution").

[35] Sandoz et al. (1987), Article 1, para 41. See also AP 1, Article 80(1).

[36] Henckaerts and Doswald-Beck 2005, Rule 139, p. 495.

[37] Judgment of the International Military Tribunal at Nuremberg, 30 Sept.–1 Oct. 1946, I Trial of the Major War Criminals before the International Military Tribunal (1947) 223.

and the second-order obligation to satisfy victims of violations,[38] also militate in favor of an expansive duty to investigate as an effective method to ensure respect for IHL.

As will be explained below, since the duty to ensure respect is relative in nature—circumscribed, *inter alia,* by resource constraints—states may legitimately decide, at times, to implement the duty to ensure respect through the pursuit of non-criminal avenues of investigation (such as disciplinary proceedings or fact-finding inquiries). In fact, we will claim that non-criminal investigations are sometimes more conducive to ensuring future compliance with IHL than criminal proceedings. Hence, notwithstanding the *Nuremberg dicta,* the duty to ensure respect for IHL does not mandate a duty to launch a criminal investigation for each and every alleged violation of IHL. However, at least for serious violations, there ought to be a strong presumption in favor of investigation entailing both legal accountability for past events and forward-looking pressure to prevent future unlawful acts (or omissions).

2.2.1.2 Command Responsibility

Another source for a broad duty to investigate IHL violations can be found in the institution of command responsibility, specified in Articles 86, 87 of the First Additional Protocol and accepted now, by and large, as part of customary international law.[39] The command responsibility doctrine requires military commanders to "to prevent and, where necessary, to suppress and to report to competent authorities breaches of the Conventions and of this Protocol"[40] Whereas considerable attention has been afforded in the legal literature and the case law of international criminal tribunals to the criminal law implications of dereliction on the part of commanders to prevent or punish war crimes (in particular, following the introduction of a superior responsibility in Article 28 of the ICC Statute),[41] far less attention has been given to the duty to investigate and prosecute imposed on military commanders in connection with violations not amounting to grave breaches For our purpose, it is clear that the broad duty to prevent and suppress—encompassing *all* breaches of the Geneva Conventions and the First Additional Protocol—implies a concomitant obligation on the state party

[38] Hague Convention concerning the Laws and Customs of War on Land, 18 October 1907, Article 3, 3 Martens Nouveau Recueil (ser. 3) 461 (Hague Convention/Regulations); International Covenant on Civil and Political Rights, 16 Dec. 1966, Article 2(3), 999 U.N.T.S. 171 (ICCPR).

[39] Henckaerts and Doswald-Beck 2005, Rule 153 p. 558.

[40] AP I, Article 87(1).

[41] Shany and Michaeli 2002; Ronen 2010, pp. 313–356; ICTY, *Prosecutor v Zejnil Delalić, Zdravko Mucić, Hazim Delić, and Esad Landžo* ("*Čelebići*"), Judgment of the Appeals Chamber (IT-96-21-T) 20th February 2001, pp. 54–104; ICTY, *Prosecutor v. Sefer Halilović,* Judgment of the Appeals Chamber (IT-01-48-A)16 October 2007.

to conduct criminal or disciplinary investigations and prosecutions in appropriate cases.

Once a violation of the Convention and/or First Additional Protocol is expected to occur or has already occurred, military commanders are required to take active steps to prevent and suppress the said violations. Article 87(3) explicitly provides that the duty to suppress involves, "where appropriate, to initiate disciplinary or penal action against violators thereof." In other words, with regard to violations of IHL other than grave breaches, military commanders are expected to resort to one of following responses: criminal measures, disciplinary measures, or—where appropriate—other measures not necessarily entailing individual responsibility; such measures are to be taken by the commander herself or by other competent authorities.[42]

In any event, the investigation of alleged violations is integral to the carrying out of the commander's duty to prevent and suppress. This is because investigation of past violations would allow the commander to make an informed decision as to what would be, under the circumstances, the appropriate response to the alleged violation[43]; such an investigation may also facilitate changes in the conduct of the military unit in question that would prevent future violations.

2.2.1.3 The Principle of Precaution

The broad duty to investigate violations can also be anchored in the precautionary obligations of the parties to the conflicts. Article 57(1) of the First Additional Protocol prescribes that "[i]n the conduct of military operations, constant care shall be taken to spare the civilian population, civilians and civilian objects." In the same vein, Article 57 (2)(a)(ii) of the First Additional Protocol provides that the parties should "take all feasible precautions in the choice of means and methods of attack with a view to avoiding, and in any event to minimizing, incidental loss of civilian life, injury to civilians and damage to civilian objects." Both obligations are closely related to the "least injurious means" prong of the

---

[42] See e.g., ICTY, *Prosecutor v. Ljube Boškoski and Johan Tarčulovski,* Judgment of the Trial Chamber (IT-04-83-T) 10 July 2008 ("A superior's duty to punish the perpetrators of a crime may encompass an obligation to conduct an effective investigation with a view to establishing the facts. The obligation to investigate translates into an obligation on the part of the superior to take active steps to ensure that the perpetrators will be punished. To that end, the superior may exercise his own powers of sanction, or if he lacks such powers, report the perpetrators to the competent authorities. It has been held in the jurisprudence of the Tribunal that civilian superiors, who may lack the disciplinary or sanctioning powers of military commanders, may discharge their obligation to punish by reporting to the competent authorities whenever a crime has been committed if these reports are likely to trigger an investigation or initiate disciplinary or criminal proceedings").

[43] See Sandoz et al. (1987), Article 87, para 3560 ("[The commanders'] role obliges them to be constantly informed of the way in which their subordinates carry out the tasks entrusted them, and to take the necessary measures for this purpose").

proportionality test—that is, the requirement that parties select among all possible measures that similarly advance their military goals those measures that cause the least humanitarian harm. Investigation of past incidents in which harm has occurred is arguably part of the "constant care" which parties are expected to demonstrate in order to assess on an ongoing basis the proportionate nature of the methods and means of warfare they employ. In other words, monitoring the effects of military actions through investigation of possible violations arguably constitutes a "feasible precaution" against excessive harm.

The Israeli Supreme Court, which relies heavily on the principle of proportionality in its major decisions on IHL, has identified an obligation to investigate targeted killing operations, apparently in the context of a harm mitigation rationale:

> [A]fter an attack on a civilian suspected of taking an active part, at such time, in hostilities, a thorough investigation regarding the precision of the identification of the target and the circumstances of the attack upon him is to be performed (retroactively). That investigation must be independent … In appropriate cases it is appropriate to pay compensation as a result of harm caused to an innocent civilian.[44]

2.2.1.4 Duty to Address Request for an Inquiry

Finally, one may link the duty to investigate alleged violations of IHL, albeit tenuously, to the duty to accommodate requests for an inquiry made by another party to the conflict and/or to pay compensation for violations.[45] Arguably, allegations of violations raised by one party to a conflict require the other party to consider, in good faith, the need to initiate an investigation into the allegations.[46] Similarly, the duty to compensate victims of violations may imply an antecedent duty to investigate alleged violations. However, practice explicitly involving these provisions is virtually non-existent thus, weakening the force of the proposed interpretative constructions[47]

[44] *The Public Committee Against Torture in Israel v. Gov't of Israel,* Judgment of 14 Dec. 2006, H.C.J. 769/02, available at http://elyon1.court.gov.il/files_eng/02/690/007/a34/02007690.a34.pdf, at para 40.

[45] See e.g., AP 1, Article 91 ("A Party to the conflict which violates the provisions of the Conventions or of this Protocol shall, if the case demands, be liable to pay compensation. It shall be responsible for all acts committed by persons forming part of its armed forces"); GC 3, Article 132 ("At the request of a Party to the conflict, an enquiry shall be instituted, in a manner to be decided between the interested Parties, concerning any alleged violation of the Convention"); Hague Convention, Article 3 ("A belligerent party which violates the provisions of the said Regulations shall, if the case demands, be liable to pay compensation. It shall be responsible for all acts committed by persons forming part of its armed forces").

[46] For the general obligation to carry out treaty obligations in good faith, see Vienna Convention on the Law of Treaties, 23 May 1969, Article 26, 1155 UNTS 331 (VCLT).

[47] VCLT, Article 31(3)(b).

In sum, there is considerable support in the central instruments comprising IHL for the proposition that states are required to investigate grave breaches, as well as other violations of IHL. This broad proposition is supported not only in legal texts but also by policy considerations since the close relationship between investigation of past violations and the need to prevent future violations renders investigation a key strategy for the effective implementation of IHL. Moreover, given the possible inter-connectedness between grave breaches and other violations (e.g., denial of POW status may facilitate the torture of detainees), investigating one category of violations may assist also in suppressing violations belonging to the other category as well. Finally, the duty to investigate all IHL violations may be independently supported by the need to satisfy victims and afford them with remedies.

At the same time, the broader aspects of the duty to investigate identified here are more flexible in nature than those appertaining to the narrower duty to investigate allegations of grave breaches. Whereas the latter implies universal jurisdiction and a duty to employ criminal law tools, the former is more localized in scope and may entail a choice of investigation technique (criminal, disciplinary, civil measures and/or fact-finding inquiry). Furthermore, even if there had been only a relative legal obligation to prosecute all violations (grave breaches and non-grave breaches) the more serious nature of grave breaches would have implies greater expectations for a stronger response to such breaches than to other IHL violations. Thus, the absence of a general legal duty to opt for a criminal response in cases of violations not constituting grave breaches is reflective both of the state of IHL and the expected correlation between the seriousness of the violation and the harshness of the response thereto.

2.2.2 Human Rights Law as a Complementary Source of the Duty to Investigate

There is increased acceptance that IHRL continues to apply in times of armed conflict in a manner which affords protection to individuals from the states to whose jurisdiction they are subject.[48] Although there is no full consensus on the matter, the overwhelming body of legal opinion points today in the direction of the view that IHRL may apply extraterritorially to military operations conducted in foreign territories, provided that certain areas or individuals are brought under the

[48] ICCPR, Article 2(1), European Convention for the Protection of Human Rights and Fundamental Freedoms, 4 Nov. 1950, Article 1, ETS 5 (ECHR). The continued applicability of human rights law during wartime was confirmed by the International Court of Justice in its Nuclear Weapons advisory opinion, as well as in the subsequent Wall and Armed Activities (Congo) cases. *Legality of the Threat or Use of Nuclear Weapons*, Advisory Opinion (1996) ICJ Rep 226, 240; *Legal Consequences of the Construction of a Wall in the Occupied Palestinian Territory*, Advisory Opinion, (2004) ICJ Rep 136, 178; *Armed Activities on the Territory of the Congo (DRC v Uganda)* Merits Judgment (2005) ICJ Rep 168, pp. 243–244.

effective control of the military in question.[49] Since, the International Court of Justice has indicated that in situations of parallel applicability of IHL and IHRL the former typically serves as *lex specialis,* IHRL norms on the duty to investigate ought to be understood primarily as gap fillers, regulating issues not addressed by IHL, or as interpretive tools, shaping the contents and manner of application of IHL.[50]

Under IHRL, states are placed under two relevant sets of obligations. Whereas the duty to respect human rights imposes on states negative obligations, the duty to protect victims (sometimes couched in language prescribing a duty to secure or ensure human rights)[51] requires states, *inter alia,* to embrace positive measures designed to prevent the infringement of individual rights. As noted before, the investigation of past violations may fulfill an important preventive function and could thus be regarded as a necessary positive measure of protection. Indeed, General Comment 31 of the Human Rights Committee, which purports to restate the law in the field, provides that:

> There may be circumstances in which a failure to ensure Covenant rights as required by article 2 would give rise to violations by States Parties of those rights, as a result of States Parties' permitting or failing to take appropriate measures or to exercise due diligence to prevent, punish, *investigate* or redress the harm caused by such acts by private persons or entities.[52] (emphasis added)

In addition, the duty to provide effective remedy to victims of violations has been understood to contain a 'second order' obligation to offer legal or administrative remedies in response to past violations. Here too, investigations serve as the antechamber for dispensation of remedies.[53]

In any event, like its IHL counterpart, the duty to investigate under IHRL is an obligation of a relative nature and correlates to the seriousness of the violation and the circumstances under which it may have occurred. For example, ECHR case law on the duty to institute criminal investigations has focused almost exclusively on violations of the most fundamental human rights standards—Articles 2, 3 and 5

---

49 For a comprehensive discussion of the extraterritorial application of human rights law, see Milanovic 2011; Lubell 2010.

50 Ben-Naftali and Shany 2004, p. 17, Prud'homme 2007.

51 ICCPR, Article 2(1), ECHR, Article 1.

52 Human Rights Committee, General Comment 31: Nature of the General Legal Obligation Imposed on States Parties to the Covenant, UN Doc. CCPR/C/21/Rev.1/Add.13 (2004), at para 8.

53 Ibid, at para 15 ("A failure by a State Party to investigate allegations of violations could in and of itself give rise to a separate breach of the Covenant. Cessation of an ongoing violation is an essential element of the right to an effective remedy"). See also *Kaya v Turkey,* Judgment of 28 March 2000, no.225335/93 ECHR 2000, at para 124 ("Article 13 requires, in addition to the payment of compensation where appropriate, a thorough and effective investigation capable of leading to the identification and punishment of those responsible for the deprivation of life and including effective access for the complainant to the investigation procedure").

of the European Convention (the right to life, the prohibition against torture and the right to liberty).[54] Furthermore, in difficult circumstances, such as conflict situations, full investigations may be impracticable either because of objective battlefield conditions or because of other pressing needs taking priority over investigations.

Indeed, a recent fact-finding committee (headed by Christian Tomuschat) appointed by the Human Rights Council to examine, *inter alia,* Israeli and Palestinian investigations in the aftermath of the 2008–2009 conflict in Gaza has stated as follows:

> [T]here are constraints during armed conflict that do impede investigations. For example, not every death during an armed conflict can be effectively investigated[55]

Such constraints may justify in some cases—at least those featuring relatively minor harms—either no criminal investigation or even of any form of investigation. The same constraints may also explain, even in those cases where investigation has been initiated, the resort to sub-optimal investigative measures.[56]

The upshot of this analysis is that IHRL provides an independent basis for a duty to investigate harms to individuals occurring during armed conflicts. Given the breadth of the scope of rights covered by human rights treaties, which exceed in some important areas the protections afforded by IHL (for example, with respect to freedom of movement), some harmful conduct not covered by the IHL duty to investigate would nonetheless be covered by the parallel duty under IHRL. It therefore appears that, to the extent that they also compromise IHRL norms, violations of IHL norms other than grave breaches should be investigated also by virtue of IHRL; it is also clear that some violations not covered at all by IHL should nonetheless be investigated under IHRL.

In addition, to the extent that IHRL introduces more demanding investigation standards, these may supplement the requirements found in IHL unless the latter requirements are deemed as *lex specialis,* or if there are overriding considerations (such as military necessity) that pull in specific cases in the direction of partial application of human rights standards. In the next Part of this article we discuss and largely reject the *lex specialis* argument as far as it pertains to investigation requirements; we acknowledge, however, the need to engage in constant balancing between the duty to investigate and battlefield conditions.

---

54 *Kaya v. Turkey* (*supra* n.53); *Isayeva v. Russia, supra* n.8; *Jordan v. United Kingdom,* Judgment of 4 August 2001, no.24746/94 ECHR 2001. For a rare example of a judgment finding a duty to investigate case involving another Convention right, see *Gündem v Turkey*, Judgment of 16 March 2000, no.23144/93 ECHR 2000, at para 71 (state violated duty to investigate attacks against a newspaper, violating thereby freedom of expression).

55 Tomuschat report 2010, para 32.

56 Ibid.

2.2.3 Triggering Mechanisms

Although violations of IHL and IHRL applicable in conflict situations result in a relative duty to investigate, as with other positive obligations, such a duty should be carried out with due diligence, i.e., in accordance with the legal requirements of reasonableness or appropriateness.[57] The relativity of the duty to investigate implies not only that states should prioritize serious violations over less grave ones; it also suggests that they should prioritize investigating credible allegations or reasonable suspicions over those that lack credibility or unreasonable ones. As a practical matter, militaries cannot be expected to spend precious time and resources in order to investigate far-fetched or highly dubious allegations. Indeed, the European Court of Human Rights (ECtHR) in its case law on the duty to investigate allegations of disappearances and torture has established an "arguable claim"[58] or a "credible assertion" of a violation[59] as the relevant triggers for investigations into alleged violations.

Still, one may posit that, at least as a matter of *lex ferenda,* some correlation ought to exist between the gravity of the alleged or suspected violation and the triggering requirements.[60] Hence, allegations or suspicions pertaining to the most serious violations of law may require investigation even on the basis of less than fully credible allegations or well-founded suspicions. A lowering of the threshold in potentially serious cases not only ensures a higher level of humanitarian protection, it also increases the prospect that less serious violations are effectively addressed. This is because evidence, which cannot sustain allegations of serious violations (e.g., premeditated killings), may nonetheless sustain allegations of a less serious nature (e.g., negligent killings). As a result, an incident featuring serious consequences in questionable circumstances, such as unexpected loss of life or wanton harm to property without a clear justification, may warrant an investigation even if no evidence of wrongdoing is initially available.

One may find some support for this last proposition in the ECtHR's holding that every killing perpetrated by government forces must be investigated even if no

---

[57] Koivurova 2008.

[58] See e.g., *Assenov v. Bulgaria*, Judgment of 28 October 1998, no. 80/1997/874/1086 ECHR 1998-VIII, para 102; *Ilhan v Turkey*, Grand Chamber, Judgment of 27 June 2000, no. 22277/93 ECHR 2000-VII, para 97; *Cyprus v Turkey,* Grand Chamber, Judgment of 10 May 2001, no. 25781/94 ECHR 2001, para 132.

[59] See e.g., *Labita v. Italy*, Grand Chamber, Judgment of 6 April 2000, no. 26772/95 ECHR 2000-IV, para 131; *Khashiyev v. Russia*, Judgment of 24 February 2005, nos. 57942/00 and 57945/00 ECHR, para 177.

[60] Any serious violation of the right to life requires investigation, even in cases of armed conflicts: Human Rights Committee, General Comment 31 (2004), at para 18; *Isayeva v. Russia* (*supra* n.8), paras 209–212; *Las Palmeras v. Colombia*, I/A CHR Judgment of 6 Dec. 2001, para 65; Watkin 2004, pp. 17–20.

prima facie indication of illegality is shown,[61] whereas other violations of the right to life—not directly implicating the government—need to be supported by "credible allegations" of wrongfulness or involve "suspicious circumstances."[62] Although this line of decisions does not necessarily apply as a matter of *lex lata* to battlefield conditions (where conducting an investigation after every act of killing may be impractical),[63] it does support the view that a lower threshold should be established when the most serious of violations—extrajudicial killings by governments—may have occurred.

In any event, it is clear that the duty to investigate can be triggered on the basis of suspicious circumstances, in the absence of any formal complaint or allegation.[64] It is also clear that the duty encompasses both acts and omissions of direct perpetrators as well as accomplices and also extends to relevant military or civilian superiors.[65]

2.2.4 State Practice

The broad duty to investigate described above finds some, though not full, support in actual state practice. This picture of partial compliance is characteristic of areas of law in which slow changing practices often lag behind faster moving normative developments (as for example in the recent evolution of IHRL into battlefield investigations). Partial compliance can also be explained by the weakness of IHL's enforcement machinery, which exacts limited pressure on militaries to introduce legal reforms in response to new legal standards. This lag in compliance is exacerbated by the tendency of militaries to view with some apprehension the introduction of new and onerous legal obligations that would be costly to meet and potentially limit policy options.[66]

Still, one may observe trends in actual state practice which point in the normative direction identified in this article. For example, the recent UK Armed Forces Act of 2006 introduces a two-layer duty to investigate: (1) A strong obligation on commanding officers to refer serious crimes (including, as specified in

[61] See e.g., *Kaya v Turkey, supra* n. 53, para 91.

[62] See e.g., *Silih v Slovenia*, Grand Chamber, Judgment of 9 April 2009, no.71463/01 ECHR 2009, para 157, and para 4 of the joint dissenting opinion of Judge Bratza and Judge Turmen.

[63] UN Report 2010, para 29.

[64] See e.g., *Al Skeini v UK, supra* n.8, para 165 ("What form of investigation will achieve the purposes of Article 2 may vary depending on the circumstances. However, whatever mode is employed, the authorities must act of their own motion once the matter has come to their attention. They cannot leave it to the initiative of the next-of-kin either to lodge a formal complaint or to take responsibility for the conduct of any investigative procedures").

[65] ICTY, *Prosecutor v. Sefer Halilović*, Judgment of the Trial Chamber (IT-01-48-T) 16 November 2005.

[66] Jochnik and Normand 1994.

Schedule 2 of the Act, grave breaches of the Geneva Conventions)[67] to service police investigation; and (2) a weaker obligation to investigate, as appropriate, other service offences (with or without the involvement of the service police). The UK Act introduces a test of reasonableness according to which an obligation to investigate is triggered if the relevant allegations or circumstances "would indicate to a reasonable person that [an offence] has or may have been committed by a relevant person."[68]

US military law does not contain a two-level obligation similar to that found in UK law. Still, the relevant 2006 Department of Defense Directive (DODD 2311.01E) introduces a putative duty to investigate that goes well beyond the grave breaches regime. Section 3.2 of the DODD broadly defines "reportable incident" in the following terms: "A possible, suspected, or alleged violation of the law of war, for which there is credible information, or conduct during military operations other than war that would constitute a violation of the law of war if it occurred during an armed conflict."[69] Note, that the duty to report incidents arises in the face of allegations or suspicions suggesting *any* violation of the law of war (i.e., not only grave breaches).[70] In addition, the evidentiary threshold identified in the Directive is quite low—credible information suggesting a *possible* violation of IHL.

Australian military procedures seem to set an even lower threshold for opening some form of preliminary examination into legally questionable situations. Defence Instructions (General) Admin 67-2 of 2007 provides that a "Quick Assessment" be conducted by a service member who is free, to the maximum extent feasible, from bias or conflict of interest. Whether such an assessment is required is subject to the common sense judgment of the relevant commanders or supervisors following "an occurrence, which can be any significant incident, allegation or problem, which comes to the attention of the commander/supervisor."[71] In the same vein, a 2010 amendment to the Australian Defence Instructions (General) Admin 45-2 defines a "notifiable incident," potentially setting in motion military investigation procedures, to include *inter alia* (1) an incident giving rise to a reasonable suspicion that an offence was committed under the Australian Defence Force Discipline Act 1982 (except minor offences), Australian criminal law or the criminal law of another country, where the incident involves Defence personnel, property or premises[72]; (2) any case involving "the death, serious injury or disappearance of non-Defence personnel [excluding non-detained enemy combatants], involving any Defence activity, property or premises (even where

[67] UK Armed Forces Act 2006, Schedule 2, section 12(t).

[68] UK Armed Forces Act 2006, sections 113(2), 115(2).

[69] Department of Defence Directive 2311.01E, May 9, 2006, section 3.2 (US).

[70] Schmitt 2011, p. 70.

[71] Defence Instructions (General) Admin 67-2, 7 Aug. 2007, at para 8 (Austl.).

[72] Defence Instructions (General) Admin 45-2, Amdt No 1, 26 March 2010, at para 6(a), (b) (Austl.).

there may be no reasonable suspicion of an offence having been committed)"[73]; and (3) "an incident deemed by commanders or managers to be serious, sensitive or urgent not covered by the definitions above. As a guide, these incidents are events that may bring Defence into disrepute; attract media or Parliamentary attention; or may adversely affect the efficiency of Defence."[74]

The combined effect of the different tracks for initiating investigation under Australian military law ensures that incidents giving rise to reasonable suspicions of an IHL or IHRL violation or serious incidents even raising such a possibility will be investigated by some inquiry mechanism. Of course, this broad triggering system goes well beyond the grave breaches regime. In fact, it goes even beyond the duty to investigate just IHL violations as identified in the previous section. It also supports the position that a movement may be occurring towards lowering the evidentiary requirements for opening investigation in all cases involving serious consequences.

Canadian military procedures are also generally consistent with some aspects of a broad duty to investigate violations of the laws applicable to armed conflict situations. The 2003 Joint Doctrine Manual published by the Office of the Judge Advocate-General requires commanders, in language mirroring Article 87(3) of the First Additional Protocol, to initiate disciplinary or penal proceedings if they become aware that one of their subordinates violated the laws of armed conflict.[75] Furthermore, the Manual lists as war crimes, mandating criminal investigation and prosecution, violations of a number of laws of armed conflict provisions other than the grave breaches clauses of the Geneva Convention and the First Additional Protocol.[76] In addition, a 1999 amendment to the Queen's Regulations and Orders for the Canadian Forces provides that a preliminary criminal investigation should be initiated whenever (1) a complaint (of a non-frivolous or vexatious nature) has been made that a service offence has been committed; or (2) when there are other reasons to believe that a service offence was committed.[77] The broad scope of service offences under Canadian military law[78] ensures that many violations of IHL and IHRL applicable to situations of armed conflict would be subject to a duty to investigate.

Finally, it may be noted that the Israeli Supreme Court has recently issued a short decision, rejecting a petition brought by a number of Israeli NGOs against what they considered to be excessively rigid triggering criteria applied by the

---

73 Ibid, at para 6(e).

74 Ibid, at para 6(f).

75 Office of the Judge Advocate-General, Joint Doctrine Manual: Law of Armed Conflict at the Operational and Tactical Levels, B-GJ-005-104/FP-021 (2003), section 1504.

76 Ibid, at section 1609.

77 Queen's Regulations and Orders for the Canadian Forces, P.C. 1999-1305 of 8 July 1999, section 106.02.

78 See e.g., National Defence Act, R.S.C., 1985, N-5, section 77(d)(destruction of property), section 92 (disgraceful conduct), section 124 (negligent performance of duties), section 130 (offences punishable by ordinary law).

investigation authorities of the IDF.[79] The Court noted that while the case was pending, new triggering criteria had been introduced by the IDF, mandating the opening of a criminal investigation in each lethal incident involving IDF service members in the West Bank (except cases clearly qualifying as combat actions, where the decision to open a criminal investigation would depend on the findings of a preliminary inquiry). According to the Court, this change in policy has rendered the petition moot. Still, the Court did formulate a general triggering standard that delineates the scope of the duty to launch a criminal investigation under Israeli law in cases involving loss of life (both in times of peace and at time of war). Such a duty now arises whenever death may have resulted from an unlawful conduct[80]—a test potentially covering both violations of IHL and IHRL. The Court also held that the inability to pursue a criminal investigation does not relieve the state of its obligation to identify some other avenue of redress, including a change in policy or financial compensation. Thus, non-criminal investigations may be required in certain circumstances not involving the loss of life and/or indications of illegality.

2.2.5 Interim Conclusions

In sum, we find clear indications in recent doctrine, as well as in recent state practice, that the duty to investigate goes well beyond the grave breaches regimes and encompasses both criminal and non-criminal responses to violations of international law applicable in situations of armed conflict. This development appears to be supported by weighty policy considerations. While grave breaches most certainly need to be investigated, prosecuted and punished, many if not most IHL and IHRL violations occurring during situations of armed conflicts—especially involving the regular armed forces of "rule of law" countries—do not qualify as grave breaches. Yet, although negligent designation of military targets, reckless endangerment of enemy civilians or skewed proportionality analysis may not qualify always as a war crime (or proven to be committed with criminal intent), such acts or omissions may be systemic in nature and reflective of an official governmental policy. It cannot be ruled out that the harm to humanitarian interests caused by these chronic lower-level violations may far outweigh the harm caused by grave breaches *per se*.

Consequently, when discussing the strengthening of IHL and IHRL enforcement mechanisms, our focus should not be exclusively directed at the grave breaches regimes; instead, we should also look closely at how national institutions are handling the bulk of other IHL and IHRL alleged violations. This may include less dramatic responses to violations than criminal investigations, such as

[79] *B'Telem v. Military Advocate General, supra* n. 13.
[80] Ibid, at para 10.

disciplinary measures, civil proceedings and fact-finding inquiries. As will be shown below, it is with respect to this latter category of more moderate responses that IHRL can particularly enrich and reinvigorate IHL.

2.3 Investigation Standards Governing All Forms of Investigation

Even if states were to agree that investigations are indeed required in a specific instance, the question which then arises pertains to the form of the investigation. What form should an investigation into allegations or suspicions of IHL or IHRL violations take? The purpose of this part of the article is to identify the *minimum* requirements for investigation under IHL and IHRL. As no IHL treaty directly addresses the issue at hand, we first direct our attention to sources of IHL which indirectly regulate it. We then examine the relevant contents of the duty to investigate as developed under IHRL. Finally, we comment on the practices of some states engaged in the investigation of allegations or suspicions of IHL or IHRL violations. The examination of law and practice may enable us to inject some concrete contents into the somewhat abstract duty to investigate.

2.3.1 Standards of Investigation Under IHL

No IHL treaty text explicitly addresses the requirements for a proper investigation into allegations or suspicions of IHL violations. However, the doctrine of command responsibility under IHL may introduce implicit obligations that can assist us in specifying the contents of the IHL duty to investigate.

As mentioned earlier, the doctrine of command responsibility requires commanders to suppress all violations of IHL, a duty which is interpreted as requiring investigations where appropriate. Under this doctrine commanders are required to investigate (or refer to the competent investigation authorities) violations of IHL committed by their subordinates with a view to identifying past IHL violations and suppressing future violations. In those cases where criminal sanctions are required (i.e. grave breaches of the Geneva Conventions and other serious violations) the purpose of the investigation is also to facilitate punishing the perpetrators of these violations.

The case law of international criminal tribunals on command (or superior) responsibility throws some light on the principles that govern these investigation objectives. In the ICTY *Boskoski and Turcalovski* case, the duty of commanders to punish their subordinates who committed IHL violations was understood to encompass: "an obligation to conduct an *effective* investigation with a view to establishing the facts" (emphasis added).[81] The decision does not specify,

[81] ICTY, *Prosecutor v. Ljube Boškoski and Johan Tarčulovski, supra* n. 42, at para 418.

however, what elements are integral to an effective fact-finding process. In the same vein, the ICC Pre-Trial Chamber in *Bemba* opined that the measures taken by the superior in response to IHL violations must be "necessary and reasonable."[82] Again, the Court did not define what would constitute necessary and reasonable measures of investigation and punishment; it merely noted that the application of this standard that must be assessed "*in concreto*"[83]—i.e., on a case-by-case basis.

The following segments try to offer some concrete contents to the general standards of effectiveness, necessity and reasonableness identified by the ICTY and ICC. Arguably, such contents can be derived from the ICC Statute (by way of analogy), the internal logic of the duty to investigate, IHRL and state practice.

2.3.2 Standards of Investigation Under the ICC Statute

As already mentioned, the ICC may try cases involving violations of certain IHL norms.[84] However, the Court's jurisdiction is limited by the principle of complementarity, which bars the ICC from investigating and prosecuting cases properly investigated by relevant states. Arguably, investigative acts deemed proper by the ICC for the purpose of satisfying the requirements of complementarity could be viewed as effective, necessary and reasonable also for the purpose of the satisfying the duty to investigate under IHL. At the same time, it may well be the case that national legal systems are required to adopt higher standards of investigation than the minimum requirements found in the ICC Statute. According to this view, assumption of jurisdiction by the ICC *in lieu* of national legal system can be understood as a reaction only to serious deviation from the standards of investigation. Under both alternatives, however, failure to meet the standards for a proper investigation identified in the ICC Statute would suggest that the duty to investigate was not properly carried out.

According to Article 17(1)(a) of the ICC Statute, the Prosecutor cannot initiate a case if:

> The case is being investigated or prosecuted by a State which has jurisdiction over it, unless the State is unwilling or unable genuinely to carry out the investigation or prosecution.

The meaning of "genuine" is explained in subsection (2) of the same article:

> (a) The proceedings were or are being undertaken or the national decision was made for the purpose of shielding the person concerned from criminal responsibility for crimes within the jurisdiction of the Court referred to in Article 5;

---

[82] ICC, *Prosecutor v Jean Pierre Bemba*, Decision Pursuant to Article 61(7)(a) and (b) of the Rome Statute on the Charges of the Prosecutor Against Jean-Pierre Bemba Gombo, Pre-Trial Chamber II (ICC-01/05-01/08-424) 15 June 2009, para 440.

[83] Ibid, para 443.

[84] ICC Statute, Article 8.

(b) There has been an unjustified delay in the proceedings which in the circumstances is inconsistent with intent to bring the person concerned to justice;
(c) The proceedings were not or are not being conducted independently or impartially, and they were or are being conducted in a manner which, in the circumstances, is inconsistent with an intent to bring the person concerned to justice.

From the above text it is clear that, *at the minimum,* a "genuine" investigation for complementarity purposes should be *bona fide* in nature, prompt, independent and impartial. We discuss below all of these notions.

2.3.3 The Internal Logic of the Duty to Investigate

The application of the aforementioned requirements for a proper investigation—good faith, promptness, independence and impartiality, is also supported by the internal logic of the duty to investigate and legitimacy considerations. As we already mentioned, a principle objective of the duty to investigate is to prevent future IHL violations by punishing the perpetrators of past violations. It is difficult, if not impossible, to conceive of an effective and legitimate manner in which the duty to investigate can be carried which lacks good faith, independence and impartiality or reasonable promptness. An investigation that fails to genuinely strive to ascertain the truth and to hold accountable wrongdoers would not be effective or legitimate; an investigation which is not independent and impartial might not be *bona fide* in nature and is unlikely to be effective and legitimate; finally, a slow investigative process raises concerns about its genuineness (as suggested in Article 17(2)(b) of the ICC Statute), and may be ineffective in identifying past violations (due to the loss of evidence and fading memory) and prevent future violations. It is not surprising in light of inter-connectedness of the various requirements for a proper investigation that some of the most influential military manuals allude explicitly or implicitly to some or all of these requirements.[85]

2.3.4 The Contents of the Duty to Investigate Under International Human Rights Law

The above survey reveals that the duty to investigate violations is indeed part of IHL. It also establishes that certain general principles pertaining to the manner in which this duty ought to be executed can be deduced from IHL, the ICC Statute and the duty's internal logic. Still, further development of these general principles is necessary in order to enable us to flesh out a concrete set of practices that

85 See e.g., Bill and Marsh 2010, p. 36.

militaries would be expected to follow. Otherwise, the compliance pull attendant to the duty to investigate is likely to remain relatively low.[86]

It is against this background that the more developed norms relating to the duty to investigate found under IHRL should be considered. The invocation of IHRL standards can be justified not only as a particularly persuasive analogy based on the substantive proximity between the situations regulated by IHL and IHLR (a second order obligation imposed on governments in response to harm to protected individuals or individual interests by government agents); it is also supported by the co-application of IHRL and IHL in many (though not all) armed conflict situations.

Still, the different degrees of 'fit' between IHL and IHRL and conflict situations underlie the preferred status of IHL as *lex specialis* under international law,[87] with the pride of place it affords the principle of military necessity. As a result, the application of the duty to investigate under IHRL should be viewed as *lex generalis* that can be modified in light of the relevant rules and principles of IHL; in the same vein, actual battlefield conditions may require adjustments to conflict situations of the manner in which human rights violations are normally investigated.[88]

Still, we understand the *lex specialis/lex generalis* relationship between the IHL and IHRL duties to investigate as implying that IHRL norms on the duty to investigate should apply in armed conflict, as in all other cases involving human rights violations, *as long as there are no compelling reasons to modify their manner of application*. These compelling reasons may derive from the rules of IHL (e.g., the permissibility of certain targeting decisions under IHL may obviate the need to investigate them under IHRL), the difference between the formulas employed by IHL and IHRL in cases involving balancing between military necessity and humanitarian interests (e.g., the greater tolerance for collateral damage under IHL or the lesser weight IHL attributes to transparency in military matters), or practical problems in conducting battlefield investigations.

In those cases of parallel applicability, the more developed rules of investigation under IHRL can serve to complement the more general principles found in IHL; but even when IHRL is not applicable, its norms may offer an important source for inspiration in interpreting the general principles of IHL on the duty to investigate. In both cases, however, IHRL standards should be invoked carefully,

---

[86] On the relationship between compliance and norm-specificity, see Franck 1990, p. 62.

[87] *Nuclear Weapons, supra* n.48, p. 240.

[88] As Schmitt puts it: "Evidence may have been destroyed during the hostilities, civilian witnesses may have become refugees or internally displaced persons, military witnesses may be deployed elsewhere or be engaged in combat, territory where the offense occurred may be under enemy control, forensic and other investigative tools may be unavailable on or near the battlefield, military police may be occupied by other duties such as prisoner of war handling, legal advisers may be providing conduct of hostilities advice, judicial bodies may be distant from the theatre of operations, communications may be degraded, travel may be hazardous, and so forth"—Schmitt 2011, at p. 54.

respecting the normative and circumstantial differences between the two legal branches. Furthermore, as in other instances, the exact content of the duty to investigate must be examined in light of the specific circumstances ruling at the relevant time and place.[89]

2.3.4.1 Specific Duties in International Human Rights Law

The substance of the duty to investigate under in IHRL appears in two principal sources. The first source is a variety of soft law instruments, which purport to apply universally; the second is the rich jurisprudence of the ECtHR on this issue.

Soft Law Sources

In 2005 the UN General Assembly adopted by consensus a set of "Basic Principles and Guidelines on the Right to Remedy and Reparations for Victims of Violations of International Human Rights and Serious violations of International Humanitarian Law."[90] According to this instrument, the duty to investigate must be exercised in a manner that is effective, prompt, impartial and thorough. Interestingly enough, the 2005 Principles purport to cover investigations under IHRL, as well as under IHL. Other UN resolutions have identified effectiveness, independence, impartiality and promptness as the core principles of the duty to investigate under IHRL.[91]

The principles governing the duty to investigate under IHRL appear to have become generally accepted and the 2009 report of the UN Fact Finding Mission on the Gaza Conflict (the Goldstone Report) termed them "universal principles" of investigation.[92]

---

[89] In the *Blaskic* case, the Appeal Chamber of the ICTY stated that: "The Appeals Chamber considers that [...] a determination of the necessary and reasonable measures that a commander is required to take in order to prevent or punish the commission of crimes, is dependent on the circumstances surrounding each particular situation"—ICTY, *Prosecutor v. Tihomir Blaškić,* Judgment of the Appeals Chamber (IT-95-14-A) 29 July 2004, para 417.

[90] The Basic Principles and Guidelines on the Right to Remedy and Reparations for Victims of Violations of International Human Rights and Serious violations of International Humanitarian Law, 16 Dec. 2005, UN Doc. A/RES/60/147 (2006).

[91] Principles on the Effective Prevention and Investigation of Extrajudicial, Arbitrary and Summary Executions, 24 May 1989 (Economic and Social Council Resolution 1989/65, annex); Principles on the Effective Investigation and Documentation of Torture and Other Cruel, Inhuman or Degrading Treatment or Punishment, 4 Dec. 2000 (General Assembly Resolution 55/89, annex).

[92] Goldstone Report 2009, para 1814. Schmitt 2011.

ECtHR Jurisprudence

The most elaborate discussion of the specific contents of the duty to investigate under IHRL, and its applicability to armed conflict situations, can be found in the rich jurisprudence of the ECtHR. The European Court issued in recent years a number of judgments addressing situations that may qualify as armed conflicts, including the Russian operations in Chechnya,[93] British operations in Iraq[94] and Turkish attempts to curb Kurdish activity in its South-Eastern border with Iraq.[95] In all of these cases, the court applied certain IHRL norms (found in the European Convention on Human Rights (ECHR)), while noting that the situation before it is not one of ordinary law enforcement. While not explicitly discussing the applicability of IHL norms, the Court was clearly aware of the need to attenuate the contents of the relevant IHRL obligations in light of the realities of armed conflict situations.

For instance, in its seminal *Isayeva* judgment (2005),[96] the ECtHR laid down the basic principles of investigation under the ECHR (which mirrors in large parts of its contents other IHRL instruments, such as the International Covenant on Civil and Political rights (ICCPR)). According to the Court, any investigation must include the following criteria: independence, effectiveness, promptness, and some degree of public scrutiny. The Court refined these four criteria in its post-*Isayeva* jurisprudence,[97] including in the *Al Skeini* judgment.[98] Since the *Al Skeini* case dealt with events that took place in Iraq during its occupation by the US-UK led coalition, the Court directly addressed in its judgment the relationship between IHL and IHRL[99]:

---

[93] Abresch 2005.

[94] Example: *Al Jedda v. UK,* Grand Chamber, Judgment of 7 July 2011, no.27021/08 ECHR 2011.

[95] Example: *Issa v. Tureky, supra* n.8.

[96] *Isayeva v. Russia, supra* n.8, at 836: "For an investigation into alleged unlawful killing by State agents to be effective, it may generally be regarded as necessary for the persons responsible for and carrying out the investigation to be independent from those implicated in the events. This means not only a lack of hierarchical or institutional connection but also a practical independence. The investigation must also be effective in the sense that it is capable of leading to a determination of whether the force used in such cases was or was not justified in the circumstances... and to the identification and punishment of those responsible... A requirement of promptness and reasonable expedition is implicit in this context. For the same reasons, there must be a sufficient element of public scrutiny of the investigation or its results to secure accountability in practice as well as in theory. The degree of public scrutiny required may well vary from case to case. In all cases, however, the victim's next-of-kin must be involved in the procedure to the extent necessary to safeguard his or her legitimate interests."

[97] See e.g., *Bazorkina v. Russia*, Judgment of 27 July 2006, no.69481/01 ECHR 2006, para 117–119; *Abuyeva v Russia,* Judgment of 2 December 2010, no.27065/05 ECHR 2010, para 204–216.

[98] *Al Skeini v. UK, supra* n.8.

[99] Ibid, at para 90–93.

> The Court has held that the procedural obligation under Article 2 continues to apply in difficult security conditions, including in a context of armed conflict ... It is clear that where the death to be investigated under Article 2 occurs in circumstances of generalised violence, armed conflict or insurgency, obstacles may be placed in the way of investigators and, ... concrete constraints may compel the use of less effective measures of investigation or may cause an investigation to be delayed. Nonetheless, the obligation under Article 2 to safeguard life entails that, even in difficult security conditions, all reasonable steps must be taken to ensure that an effective, independent investigation is conducted into alleged breaches of the right to life.[100]

Above and beyond the general principles of investigation, the ECtHR developed the more specific contents of each and every one of these principles. The following segment will introduce, in brief, the main components of the ECtHR's jurisprudence on the different requirements of a proper investigation.

Effectiveness

In several of its decisions, the ECtHR noted that the most important component of a proper investigation is its effectiveness.[101] In the *Al Skeini* judgment, it expanded on this issue:

> [T]he investigation must be effective in the sense that it is capable of leading to a determination of whether the force used was or was not justified in the circumstances and to the identification and punishment of those responsible. **This is not an obligation of result, but of means. The authorities must take the reasonable steps available to them to secure the evidence concerning the incident,** including *inter alia* eye-witness testimony, forensic evidence and, where appropriate, an autopsy which provides a complete and accurate record of injury and an objective analysis of clinical findings, including the cause of death. Any deficiency in the investigation which undermines its ability to establish the cause of death or the person or persons responsible will risk falling foul of this standard.[102]

Independence

In addition to effectiveness, the Court emphasized in its case law the need for an independent investigation. Again, it address the matter in its *Al Skeini* judgment:

> For an investigation into alleged unlawful killing by State agents to be effective, it is necessary for the persons responsible for and carrying out the investigation to be independent from those implicated in the events. This means not only a lack of hierarchical or institutional connection but also a practical independence.[103]

---

[100] *Al Skeini, supra* n.8, para 164.

[101] See *Ahmet Özkan v. Turkey,* Judgment of 6 April 2004, no.21689/93 ECHR 2004, para 312; *Isayeva, supra* n.8, para 212 and the cases cited therein.

[102] *Al Skeini, supra* n.8, para 166.

[103] Ibid, at para 167.

In assessing the actual independence of the investigation in the specific cases discussed in the *Al Skeini* case, the Court found that the British authorities in Iraq failed to comply with their obligation to conduct an independent investigation. This is because the commanding officer on the ground had the power to initiate the investigation, or to terminate it (even when it was initiated by the Special Investigation Branch).[104]

Promptness

Promptness is another important component of the duty to investigate under IHRL identified by the ECtHR. Although, the Court recognized in its *Al Skeini* judgment that a prompt investigation may encounter serious difficulties during the armed conflict itself, it emphasized the need to proceed with it at reasonable speed:

> A requirement of promptness and reasonable expedition is implicit in this context. While there may be obstacles or difficulties which prevent progress in an investigation in a particular situation, a prompt response by the authorities in investigating a use of lethal force may generally be regarded as essential in maintaining public confidence in their adherence to the rule of law and in preventing any appearance of collusion in or tolerance of unlawful acts.[105]

Transparency and Public Confidence

A number of ECtHR decisions have insisted that investigations be, as far as possible, transparent.[106] Like promptness, the quest for public confidence appears to be a key consideration in favor of a transparency requirement. For example, in *Özkan v. Turkey* (2004), the Court held that:

> For the same reasons [maintaining public confidence—AC & YS] there must be a sufficient element of public scrutiny of the investigation or its results to secure accountability in practice as well as in theory. The degree of public scrutiny required may well vary from case to case. In all cases, however, the victim's next-of-kin must be involved in the procedure to the extent necessary to safeguard his or her legitimate interests[107]

The principle of transparency illustrates the need to evaluate the manner in which proper investigation principles derived from IHRL can apply to armed conflicts. Phillip Alston, while serving as the UN Rapporteur of Extrajudicial, Summary or Arbitrary Executions, laid down what he assessed to be the major principles of international law regarding the investigation of targeted killing operations, including the need for transparency:

---

[104] Ibid, at para 172.

[105] Ibid, at para 167.

[106] See e.g., *McKerr v. United Kingdom.*, Judgment of 4 May 2001, no. 29993/95 ECHR 2001-III, para 148; *Güleç v. Turkey*, Judgment of 27 July 1998, no. 21593/93 ECHR 1998-IV, at para 82; *Oğur v. Turkey*, Judgment of 20 May 1999, no. 21594/93 ECHR1999-III, para 92. *Özkan v. Turkey* (*supra* n. 101) paras 85–90 and 309–320 and 326–330.

[107] *Ahmet Özkan v. Turkey*, *supra* n. 101, para 314.

> [W]ithout disclosure of the legal rationale as well as the bases for the selection of specific targets (consistent with genuine security needs), States are operating in an accountability vacuum. It is not possible for the international community to verify the legality of a killing, to confirm the authenticity or otherwise of intelligence relied upon, or to ensure that unlawful targeted killings do not result in impunity. The fact that there is no one-size-fits-all formula for such disclosure does not absolve States of the need to adopt explicit policies[108]

This call for transparency in operational investigations is problematic to the extent it suggests that states should publicly divulge the intelligence on which they relied for specific military actions, or even to provide specific operational guidelines (e.g., under what precise circumstances it will resort to targeted killings). Such a position appears to strongly conflict, at times, with military necessity interests and is unlikely to be heeded to by many, if not most militaries around the world. Still, as we suggest below, the problem of public scrutiny can be partly addressed in a different way—through independent mechanisms of oversight operating within the state concerned.

The above quotations from decisions of the ECtHR represent only a small sample of that body's rich jurisprudence on the duty to investigate under the ECHR. At a more general level it appears as if the principles of effectiveness, independence, promptness and public scrutiny identified by the Court are all premised on the position that an appropriate investigation must attract public confidence and enjoy a degree of perceived legitimacy. Public scrutiny helps to ensure the genuineness and effectiveness of the investigation and to ascertain that the investigative acts taken are necessary and reasonable; the need to protect the perceived legitimacy of the investigation by maintaining its independence and impartiality supports the same genuineness and effectiveness requirements, which ensure, in turn, the past and future oriented objectives of IHL investigations. Thus, at the end of the day, the principles underlying IHRL investigations are largely compatible with the objectives of the duty to investigate under IHL, though the precise manner of application of these principles may vary across the different legal regimes.[109]

2.4 How States Maintain in Practice the Independence and Impartiality of Their Systems of Military Investigations

As we have seen, the ECtHR has described what a proper system of investigations—applicable to all situations including armed conflict—should look like, focusing on conditions of effectiveness, independence, promptness and public scrutiny. The issue of independence (and impartiality) deserves, however, special

---

[108] Alston Report 2010, p. 27.

[109] Cf. *Al Skeini, supra* n. 8, para 163: "The essential purpose of such an investigation is to secure the effective implementation of the domestic laws safeguarding the right to life and, in those cases involving State agents or bodies, to ensure their accountability for deaths occurring under their responsibility."

attention in the context of military investigations. True, the ECtHR has stated that any form of investigation which is subject to the same chain of command as the operation itself is illegitimate and contrary to the requirements of a proper investigation.[110] However, the application of such a standard is fraught with difficulties given the autonomy traditionally afforded by many national jurisdictions to military investigation systems and the dual role of military commanders as legal subjects and law-enforcers (vis-a-vis their subordinates), a state of affairs which stands in potential tension with requirements of independence and impartiality. As a result, questions of great practical importance—such as the precise relationship between civil and military investigations, the role of civilian courts in monitoring military investigation, and the exact features of the military institutions conducting the investigation—all merit further discussion.

Given the paucity of international judicial practice that reviewed such matters and the virtual non-existence of relevant treaty standards, actual state practice may serve as a convenient point of departure for studying possible modalities for implementing the requirements of independence and impartiality to investigations of military operations. Of course, state practice may serve as a source of international law obligations or the interpretation thereof.[111] Yet, identifying customary international law governing battlefield investigations requires proof that state practices derive out of conviction that international law obligates them to behave in specific ways (*opinio juris*).[112]

Since states investigate alleged violations of IHL on the basis of their own specific laws (and not international law sources), and since there exist a variety of investigative methods, Michael Schmitt concluded that state behavior cannot, in most cases, provide the basis for obligations under customary international law. We take a somewhat different position on the matter. In our view, international law does not consist only of hard and fast rules found in treaties or custom (or general principles of law); it also consists of general interpretive principles derived from treaty law, customary law or even domestic laws. Thus, even when states behave in divergent ways, common principles may be extracted from their practices and the general direction in which their practices develop may affect the manner in which existing norms are construed.

Applying this general position to the duty to investigate under IHL and IHRL we may offer the following three observations: **First**, to the extent that general principles of investigation law, such as effectiveness, independence, promptness and public scrutiny are reflected in state conduct they may constitute general principles of law respected by civilized nations, and represent, as such, a distinct source of international law.[113] **Second**, the resort to criminal or disciplinary

[110] Ibid, at para 167.

[111] Statute of the International Court of Justice, 26 June 1945, Article 38(1)(b)(ICJ Statute): VCLT, Article 31(3)(b).

[112] *SS Lotus* (France v Turkey), 1927 PCIJ (ser. A) No. 10.

[113] ICJ Statute, Article 38(1)(c).

measures to address IHL and IHRL violations lie at the border between domestic and international law. Thus, it is difficult to neatly distinguish between the domestic law and international law sources of the duty to investigate; instead, the two bodies of law appear to mutually reinforce one another. Thus, although Schmitt is right in observing that the specific details of national investigation procedures are regulated by domestic law, such laws can also be understood as the means through which states carry out their relevant international law obligations. **Third**, the ways in which states carry out their obligations to investigate can be indicative of developments in international law. Such developments may further underscore the emergence of general principles of international law which would further direct future practices at the national level.

2.4.1 State Practice Suggestive of Robust Independence Standards

2.4.1.1 The Continental Approach

One possible approach towards protecting the independence of investigations into military operations and avoiding the conflict of interests attendant to the dual role of the military as a potential law-breaker and law-enforcer, is to apply the regular rules governing domestic law violations also to violations of international law in military circumstances.[114] This seems to be the approach embraced by the German legal system, where ordinary criminal procedures also control violations of the laws of war and all other military matters.[115] Under this approach, which is also applicable in France and the Netherlands,[116] there is no separate system of military investigations and the prosecution of crimes committed by military personnel is carried out by civilian prosecutors.

Note that even in those continental systems, such as Belgium,[117] in which a designated military prosecutor for military offenses does exist, the holder of that office usually operates in complete separation from the military chain of command. Moreover, continental countries, such as Denmark or Poland, that subject military prosecutors to a certain institutional hierarchy, ensure that they are subordinate to civilian officials in the Ministry of Defense or other government institutions and not to uniformed officers.[118]

---

[114] The following material regarding the Continental systems is based on the compilation by Georg Nolte, *European Military Court Systems* (Nolte and Krieger 2003)—a comparative review of all European military laws. The citations below are specifically to Chapter 2 "Comparison of European Military Law Systems" by Georg Nolte and Heike Krieger (ibid, at pp. 23–182).

[115] Ibid, pp. 168, 169.

[116] Ibid, p. 168.

[117] Ibid, p. 169.

[118] Ibid, p. 168.

2.4.1.2 Common Law Jurisdictions

The principles of independence and impartiality are becoming also more pronounced in the context of military investigations undertaken by states following common law systems. Following several notable instances of IHL and IHRL violations, several common law countries reformed their military criminal prosecution and investigation procedures with the intention of better reflecting the principles of independence and impartiality. Perhaps the most conspicuous of these changes is the noticeable tendency to detach the investigation of military operations from the military chain of command and to prefer military police investigations to traditional investigations orchestrated by unit commanders on the ground.

Canada

Following a scandalous incident in Somalia, in which Canadian soldiers were involved in the killing of civilians,[119] Canada reformed its system of military investigations and created the Canadian Forces National Investigation Service (CFNIS). All allegations of serious crimes (and all war crimes fall under that category)[120] must be transferred immediately to the CFNIS which is under the direct authority of the Provost Marshal and not controlled by the commander of the unit involved. In cases where the CFNIS investigation is alleged to have been inadequate, a complaint may be filed with an independent quasi-judicial body, the Military Police Complaint Commission (MPCC), which is headed by a civilian. This body has the authority to review the investigation and issue recommendations, including the reopening of the investigation.[121] The MPCC can deal with two kinds of complaints: "adequacy complaints"—brought by external bodies against an MP investigation, and "intervention complaints" brought by investigators if they feel that external intervention is hampering the investigation.[122]

These combined solutions, independence from the chain of command and reliance on a non-military external review commission, form the basis of the independence and impartiality of the Canadian military system of investigations. The military chain of command can no longer control the opening or halting of an investigation; nor is it responsible for the conduct of investigation. On the other hand, any external interference in the operations of the independent investigative bodies might be reviewed by a civil non-military commission.

A further aspect of the independence of the Canadian military investigation system is the role of the prosecuting authority. The prosecution of cases is handled

---

[119] See Bercuson 2010, pp. 159–169.

[120] See Canadian Forces National Investigation Service 2009.

[121] National Defence Act, Article 250.

[122] For general information on the MPCC see: http://www.mpcc-cppm.gc.ca/index-eng.aspx.

by the Canadian Military Prosecution Service (CMPS) which is nominally part of the office of the Judge Advocate General (JAG) of the Canadian Forces but, in effect, enjoys substantial independence. This independence manifests itself in three ways. First, the director of military prosecution, which heads the office of the CMPS, is appointed by the Minister of Defense for a fixed term. Second, instructions from the JAG to the Director of Military Prosecutions must be made public; and third, there are clear guidelines as to the permissible communication between military prosecutors and legal advisors assigned to military units.[123]

Australia

The Australian system has also undergone several changes in recent years, especially following a report issued by the Australian Parliament in 2005 which criticized the adequacy of the military system of investigations.[124] Since further reforms are currently in the legislative pipeline, the system is still in flux. Nevertheless, following a recent decision of the Australian Supreme Court, the essential contours of the new system have already emerged and parts of it have already been applied to the Australian Defence Forces (ADF).

Perhaps the most noticeable characteristic of the Australian system of investigation is its heavy reliance on monitoring bodies which are essentially civilian or directly controlled by civilian authorities. The primary investigative authority is the ADF Investigative Service which is responsible for investigating all serious crimes (including all war crimes).[125] This service is independent from the regular military chain of command and is under the command of the Australian Provost Marshal, who is appointed by the Chief of Staff. ADF legal services that carry responsibility for the prosecution of crimes are under the command of a civilian prosecutor who heads the service. In addition, the organizational command of the military disciplinary system is in the hands of the Judge Advocate General—a civilian Federal judge who is appointed to the post for a term of 7 years. Finally, the Military Inspector General (another official operating outside the military chain of command) has authority to review the operation of the military system.

It is important to note that recent war crimes legislation adopted in Australia, following its accession to the ICC, might allow for the civil prosecution of certain

---

[123] Director of Military Prosecutions, Policy Directive no. 009/00: Communications with Legal Advisors (updated on March 18, 2009). The role of this directive is:

To permit those communication that provide "the required degree of coordination but do not impact on the independence of the Prosecutor and the exercise of prosecutorial discretion." Ibid, Article 2. Available at: http://www.forces.gc.ca/jag/publications/cmps-scpm/policy-politiques-009-eng.asp.

[124] Foreign Affairs, Defence and Trade References Committee, The Effectiveness of Australia's Military Justice System (June, 2005).

[125] Department of Defence Instructions (*supra* n. 72).

violations of IHL.[126] Although no prosecutions have yet been carried out in accordance with the new war crimes legislation, this development clearly increases the potential for civilian involvement in the investigation of military operations.

United Kingdom

The United Kingdom's system is similar to the Australian in several respects. First, the Special Investigative Service is independent of the regular military chain of command and has independent authority to initiate military investigation. Moreover, although many investigations are initiated on the authority of the commanding officer, holders of that office no longer possess the authority to halt investigations. In addition, it is notable that the prosecuting service of the UK is headed by a civilian.

There are, however, several additional and unique features of the UK investigative procedure which merit a short discussion. First, UK courts have been willing in recent years to embroil themselves in assessing the adequacy of military investigations. In recent years the courts have issued opinions regarding the *Al Skeini* case,[127] *Al Jedda* Case,[128] the *Baha Mousa* inquiry (which originated from the *Al Skeini* case)[129] and others. This willingness on the part of UK courts to review military investigations is an additional form of review which contributes to the independence of the military system.

Second, one could mention the ability of individual cabinet members and of the cabinet as a whole to form independent investigation bodies. Several such investigations have been initiated in the UK in recent years, the most notable of which being the Iraq Historic Allegation Team (IHAT) established with a mandate to "investigate allegations of abuse of Iraqi citizens by British Service personnel."[130] Interestingly enough, the Court of Appeal recently struck down the IHAT investigation mechanism, declaring it as not independent because some members of the IHAT team were also members of the Royal Military Police (RMP). The RMP, the Court emphasized, was potentially a subject of the investigation and hence the investigation could not be said to be independent.[131]

The examples cited above suggest a trend in the practices of three important common law systems of military investigations. This trend aligns these systems

[126] International Criminal Court (Consequential Amendments) Act 2002 (Austl.).

[127] *Al Skeini v. Secretary of State for Defence* [2007] UKHL 26.

[128] *R (on the application of Al-Jedda) (FC) v. Secretary of State for Defence* [2007] UKHL 58, 12 December 2007).

[129] http://www.bahamousainquiry.org.

[130] http://www.mod.uk/DefenceInternet/DefenceNews/DefencePolicyAndBusiness/IraqHistoricAllegationsTeamStartsWork.htm.

[131] *Mousa v. Secretary of State* [2011] EWCA Civ 1334.

more closely to the continental way of thinking about the independence of investigations of compliance by the military with its IHL and IHRL obligations and suggest increasing support in state practice for the need to ensure the independence of military investigations through removing investigative bodies from the chain of command, involving civilians in the administration and monitoring of military investigations, and subjecting investigations to civilian review institutions, such as courts and commissions of inquiry.

In the *Mousa* decision, cited above, the Court of Appeal explained the reasons for this shift in emphasis:

> One of the essential functions of independence is to ensure public confidence and, in this context, perception is important.[132]

Thus, independence is an important part of maintaining public trust in military investigation and persons who conduct an investigation into military conduct should be as detached as possible from any institution which could be viewed as responsible for the investigated violation. While such practices do not constitute in themselves an international custom, they do suggest a movement in international practice towards more robust standards of independence and impartiality in military investigations.

2.4.2 State Practice Standing in Tension with the Principle of Independence

The above analysis of the investigative practices adopted in various countries is not intended to suggest that the procedures used in each reviewed country are perfectly compatible with the principles governing proper investigations. To the contrary, certain specific aspects of military investigation employed by some armed forces appear to us to be inadequate when juxtaposed against the principles of independence and impartiality.

2.4.2.1 Operational De-Briefing

Operational de-briefings are investigations conducted by the same unit implicated in the alleged violated through investigators who belong to the same chain of command as the suspects. These procedures are not carried out with the intention of initiating criminal prosecution; rather, they are military tools for assessing the quality of operational activity and for lesson learning. While no doubt useful from

132 Ibid, at para 35.

a military point of view, operational debriefings may pose a significant problem to the effectiveness and legitimacy of criminal investigation since they are conducted by the same service members that may have been responsible for the violation in question (as direct perpetrators, accomplices or incurring command responsibility). Hence, they cannot satisfy the requirements of independence and impartiality.[133]

It is not surprising that some militaries have adopted procedures designed to limit the use of operational de-briefings in serious cases and to minimize their harmful effects when used. Hence, some military laws provide that criminal investigations would take precedence over operational debriefings,[134] and some even go further and require their suspension in cases suitable for a criminal investigation.[135]

2.4.2.2 Limited Exercise of Jurisdiction by Civilian Courts

Another problem related to the independence of military investigations is the tendency of civilian courts not to assert their jurisdiction over the conduct of such investigations. This reluctance is sometimes explained by reference to the view that military investigations are a matter of policy and, as a result, are situated in an area of law over which judicial monitoring should be minimal.[136] This is reinforced by a set of legal doctrines limiting the involvement of domestic courts in reviewing military operations conducted outside the relevant state's territory.[137] The upshot of this reluctance to supervise military investigations is that militaries have a smaller incentive to conform their practices to high standards of investigative conduct (including, independence and impartiality); furthermore, the absence of a credible threat of external judicial review makes it more difficult for military investigators to resist organizational pressures and conflicts.

---

[133] Operational debriefings may suffer from other relevant quality deficiencies: First, they are performed by members of the military who are not professional investigators. This adversely affects the quality of the investigation, especially if the scene of the crime is not adequately preserved. Second, the process also allows suspects to coordinate their testimony and to find out what evidence was gathered. Hence, it might be said that the continued use of debriefing when there exists a *prime facie* need for a full criminal investigation is problematic, and might cause a violations of the duty to conduct a proper investigation.

[134] See e.g., Department of Defence Directive 2311.01E, May 9, 2006, section 4.5 (US).

[135] See e.g., Defence Instructions (General) Admin 67-2, 7 Aug. 2007, Annex C (Austl.).

[136] For an analysis of the different views regarding National Court's involvement in national security matters see: Benvenisti 2008, p. 241.

[137] See e.g., *Banković v. Belgium,* Judgment of 12 Dec. 2001, no.52207/99 ECHR 2001, para 59 (ECHR does not apply to extra-territorial air attacks). These limits were eroded, but revoked in *Issa v. Turkey, supra* n.8; *Al Skeini v. UK, supra* n.8.

2.4.3 The Recent Israeli Debate Over the Independence and Impartiality of Its System of Military Investigations

The debate in Israel concerning the independence and impartiality of its military investigations system, generated by the follow-up reports of the HRC to the Goldstone Report and by the Turkel Committee (a public committee formed after the 2010 Gaza Flotilla incident), are valuable to the present article as they demonstrate an attempt by a legal system to reevaluate the independence and impartiality of its responses to alleged IHL and IHRL violations perpetrated by its armed forces on the battlefield. At the heart of the debate currently taking place in Israel lies the extensive use of operational debriefings, the delicate position of IDF military lawyers and the limited civilian control over military investigations. All of these aspects of the IDF military investigation system appear to be out of step with developments taking place in some other military and stand in tension with the requirements of independence and impartiality of military investigations.

2.4.3.1 Operational Debriefing

Israel's experience with using operational debriefings has changed over the years. Since 2001 operational debriefings have become, in effect, part of the investigation procedures applied by the IDF; such fact-finding inquiries have been routinely opened by the military following military operations resulting in one or more civilian deaths (in the absence of evidence showing the perpetration of a crime). Thus, such procedures serve as *de facto* substitutes for criminal investigations (up until 2000—the year in which violent hostilities broke between Israelis and Palestinians—criminal investigations were the automatic reaction to civilian deaths). In his testimony before the Turkel commission, examining Israel's military investigation system, the IDF Military Attorney General (MAG) stated that information disclosed by the operational de-briefings may lead him to open a full-fledged criminal investigation.[138]

We are of the view that operational debriefings—to the extent that they are conducted by officers of the same unit involved in the allegedly unlawful military operation—fail to meet international standards of independence and impartiality required from proper investigations. While there is no prohibition against conducting lessons-learnt exercises in parallel to proper investigations (which should be effective, independent, impartial, prompt and subject to some form of public scrutiny), more attention must be given to the potential conflict between the needs of the investigation and the conduct of operational debriefings. The latter should be prioritized in our view only in exceptional cases where overriding concerns of

[138] The information in this part is based on the submissions of the IDF MAG to the Turkel Commission (on file with authors).

military necessity require the postponement of independent and impartial investigations.

2.4.3.2 The Delicate Position of IDF Military Lawyers

Although the IDF MAG, the most senior lawyer in the Israeli military, is nominally independent in his decisions, he is appointed jointly by the Chief of the IDF General Staff (CGS) and the Minister of Defense. In addition, his term of office is not defined and recent MAG's have been promoted (to the rank of Major General) during their term of office. Naturally, this raises some concerns regarding the independence of their office when conducting investigations that may implicate the highest ranks in the military and government.

An additional problem afflicting the Israel system of military investigations involves the dual capacity of the MAG as both the chief legal advisor of the military and the head of military prosecutions (and in effect also the head of military investigations).[139] This highly centralized system creates the appearance of partiality: the MAG is responsible both for giving operational advice with respect to military operations and for conducting investigations which sometimes involve operations which followed the same advice.[140]

2.4.3.3 Limited Civilian Controls over IDF Military Investigations

The aforementioned independence and impartiality shortcomings may be somewhat offset by the involvement of civilian officials—the office of the State Attorney General and the Israeli Supreme Court—in important decisions regarding investigations and prosecutions. Still, it is questionable whether the Attorney General's office possesses sufficient expertise in international law in order to effectively monitor the MAG and his subordinates. As for the Supreme Court, it has shown interest in almost all aspects of national security[141] including military investigations. However, the main thrust of the court's jurisprudence has been in

---

[139] In his written and oral testimonies before the Turkel Commission, the MAG emphasized the fact that he is involved personally, or through subordinates, in all important MP investigations through the system of "operational investigative unit" at the MAG's headquarters.

[140] Criticism on the multiple roles of the MAG has been voiced by the UN Report 2010, at para 53 ("In spite of the structural guarantees of independence built into the military justice system, the dual responsibilities of the MAG, in the specific context of these investigations, raise concerns of a lack of impartiality. The MAG is legal adviser to the Chief of Staff and other military authorities. Yet, at the same time, he is the supervisor of disciplinary law in the military. Although the combination of the advisory and supervisory functions in one office does not automatically lead to a conflict of interest or a lack of impartiality, the situation is complicated in the present case by the fact that many of the allegations of serious violations of IHL and IHRL in the FFM report directly link to the advice he provided").

[141] Cohen and Cohen 2011.

support of an institutional solution that would *not* require a case-by-case review by the Supreme Court of military investigations but, rather, be based on other forms of independent inquiry. Up until now, only a few independent mechanisms of inquiry have been established by the Israeli government—mostly on an *ad hoc* basis—and with limited jurisdiction.

2.4.4 Interim Conclusions

The survey of law and practice above points at the emergence of legal standards governing proper investigations into military operations in which IHL and/or IHRL norms may have been violated. Such principles include requirements of effectiveness, genuineness, promptness, independence and impartiality, and public scrutiny. The application of these principles may be subject, however, to specific IHL provisions including military necessity interests and to battlefield conditions. But even here, we have identified increased willingness by some military legal systems to review existing procedures in order to minimize tensions between traditional military practices and the principles of proper investigation. Such a review has led to increased resort to investigation conducted by individuals and institutions located outside the chain of command, a growing involvement of civilians in the process and stronger mechanisms of judicial review. Even a country such as Israel that has not embraced fully such reforms is at present in the process of considering them.

2.5 Operationalizing a Broad Duty to Investigate: Reconciling Tensions Between Different Investigation Tracks

In the *Al Skeini* case, the ECtHR pointed out that:

> Civil proceedings, which are undertaken on the initiative of the next-of-kin, not the authorities, and which do not involve the identification or punishment of any alleged perpetrator, cannot be taken into account in the assessment of the State's compliance with its procedural obligations under Article 2 of the Convention. Moreover, the procedural obligation of the State under Article 2 cannot be satisfied merely by awarding damages.[142]

This *dicta* reflects a strong preference for criminal law as the main vehicle for addressing serious violations of IHL and IHRL. Still, once it is accepted that a duty to investigate arises beyond the grave breaches regime covering less serious violations of IHL and IHRL, a more nuanced position on the role of criminal investigation may be considered, Furthermore, modalities for ensuring the application of the principles of proper investigation across the board of investigation mechanisms need to be developed.

---

142 *Al Skeini v. UK, supra* n.8.

In this part of the paper we wish to stress that *in some specific cases,* criminal investigation does not constitute the sole avenue open to states wishing to satisfy the duty to investigate violations of IHL and IHRL. In so doing, we shall take issue with the position that only criminal investigations satisfy the conditions of independence, impartiality, effectiveness, promptness and public scrutiny.

In actuality, many, if not most, criminal investigations do not end in prosecution or conviction—an outcome which may be less indicative of institutional sloppiness or bad faith and more to do with the inherent difficulties of establishing individual guilt in battlefield conditions. Under these circumstances, one may seriously question whether criminal investigations are the most *effective* investigative technique available to militaries.[143] In fact, the experience of states such as the UK and Israel suggests that non-criminal investigations, which satisfy the requirements of international law, are sometimes more *effective* than criminal ones.

In order to understand when criminal investigations may represent a suboptimal response to certain IHL and IHRL violations, it may be useful to identify some of the problems associated with *criminal* investigations. We shall then discuss the pros and cons of a few alternative mechanisms that may better fulfill, under certain circumstances, the broad duty to investigate.

2.5.1 Problems with the Criminal Investigation of IHL and IHRL Violations

Criminal investigations of IHL and IHRL violations confront enormous obstacles in all military conflicts, regardless of their precise nature and intensity. Such obstacles may render suboptimal a criminal response to certain violations occurring under battlefield conditions.

2.5.1.1 Clarity and Certainty of IHL

One problem confronting investigators and prosecutors endeavoring to apply criminal law to IHL violations involves the application of the principle of legality in situations of legal uncertainty. Although historically, the Laws of Armed

143 According to the information discussed in the *Al Skeini, supra* n.8—out of 200 investigation opened by the SIB regarding UK operations in Iraq, relating to suspected law violations leading to a death of civilians, only four were transferred to prosecutors with a recommendation to indict. Of these three were indeed brought to trial, in no case was there a conviction for murder or manslaughter. In Israel the situation is quite similar. Of almost 50 criminal investigations opened by The MAG Department of the IDF after "Operation Cast Lead" in Gaza (Dec. 2008–Jan. 2009), only a few were brought to trial, and conviction were handed in two (2) cases—one of which deal with looting, and the other with endangering a civilian. See: Ministry of Foreign Affairs 2010.

Conflict (LOAC) were associated with clear rules (reflective to a considerable degree with the combatants' self-interest),[144] the move *from rules to standards*[145] reduced legal certainty, and thus created serious problems for criminal enforcement—a process which assumes the existence of pre-existing and well defined legal prohibitions. Perhaps the best known example is the proportionality principle, which leaves unanswered many questions that can only be resolved, if at all, at the law-application stage.[146] As the special report to the prosecutor of ICTY regarding the NATO campaign in Yugoslavia pointed out when explaining the recommendation not to initiate criminal proceedings against NATO service members for excessive collateral damage: "[i]t is much easier to formulate the principle of proportionality in general terms than it is to apply it to a particular set of circumstances."[147]

Without going into further detail, it is quite clear that this apparent shift in IHL complicated the possibility for establishing beyond reasonable doubt the criminal nature of the *actus reus* and *mens rea* of military operations leading to what is often unforeseen collateral damage. Such proof of guilt is rendered particularly difficult to attain when battlefield conditions hinder evidence gathering, and in situations where the investigated incidents involve the activities of groups of individuals, whose distinct contribution to the alleged violation is hard to isolate. It is therefore not surprising that international criminal courts tend to avoid dealing with the application of the principle of proportionality.[148] Arguably, the criminal enforcement under battlefield conditions of many IHRL norms, which also reflect equilibrium between competing values and interests subject to a proportionality analysis, raises similar challenges.

2.5.1.2 Legal Advice and Criminal Prosecutions

Another important problem associated with the use criminal law as a tool for suppressing violations of IHL is, perhaps paradoxically, the increased tendency of many militaries to resort to operational legal advice. The obligation to employ legal advisors was first mentioned in the First Additional Protocol to the Geneva Conventions. Article 82 to the Protocol states that:

> The High Contracting Parties at all times, and the Parties to the conflict in time of armed conflict, shall ensure that legal advisers are available, when necessary, to advise military commanders at the appropriate level on the application of the Conventions and this Protocol and on the appropriate instruction to be given to the armed forces on this subject.[149]

---

[144] Jochnik and Normand 1994.

[145] Cohen 2008.

[146] For a general survey of the proportionality principle in *jus in bello* see Gardam 1993, p. 391.

[147] NATO Bombing Review Committee Report 2000.

[148] Cohen 2009, p. 35.

[149] AP-I, Article 82.

According to the Commentary to the Protocol, legal advisors should be available at the level of the division, or even of the brigade, if the brigade operates independently.[150] Over time, many militaries developed operational legal advisory services for their armed forces meeting to a large extent the standards identified in the Protocol and its Commentary.[151]

There are several good reasons why armed forces should seek legal advice. Most obviously, the extensive reliance on legal advisors supports a culture of legality and internalizes international law norms into the operations of the armed forces.[152] Still, it might prove to be very problematic to prosecute commanders and other military personnel who follow the legal advice that they receive, as basic principles of criminal law render it difficult to convict a person who followed the advice of his or her lawyers. Although legal advice cannot serve as a defense in circumstances where the violation of law was clear in nature,[153] the increased ambiguity of modern IHL and IHRL norms renders it increasingly unlikely that clear violations would be committed in a manner exposing the service-member in question or his or her lawyer to criminal proceedings. Hence, operational legal advice may shield, in effect, military service members acting on such advice from criminal responsibility.

2.5.1.3 Reluctance to Prosecute

Another problem associated with criminal prosecutions for violations of IHL and IHRL by the military is the reluctance of states to prosecute persons who acted in their name, often pursuant to superior orders. It is important in this regard to draw a bright line separating violations of international law which are also violations of internal military codes and order from violations of international law committed as part of official military policy.[154] While militaries occasionally prosecute low-ranked soldiers for unauthorized violations, prosecutions of high-ranked officers responsible for promulgating allegedly criminal policies or orders (or of low-ranked soldiers that followed them) are much less common. It follows that the main added value of international criminal law is to force the state to do precisely

[150] This conforms to the current American military doctrine see Army Field Manual 27-100 (1991) 1-9, g. (pp. 5, 6).

[151] Military manuals which contain such obligations include those of Australia, Belgium, Cameroon, Canada, France, Germany, Hungary, Italy, Netherlands, Nigeria, Russia, Spain, Sweden and the US. Many of the states which have not joined the additional protocol have also declared that they possess this service—e.g., India, Sri Lanka, Turkey, and Israel. In fact, the ICRC Study on Customary International had declared the existence of the legal advisors service as customary in nature. Henckaerts and Doswald-Beck 2005, p. 500.

[152] Cohen 2011.

[153] Bowker 2005, p. 183.

[154] Cohen 2005; Ben Ari and Cohen 2010.

that which is most reluctnat to do—to prosecute high level officers for devising and implementing official state policy that runs contrary to international law.

The tendency of the state not to prosecute for serious violations of IHL and IHRL is facilitated, in part, by the above-mentioned lack of enthusiasm by domestic courts to involve themselves in matters of national security. Hence, both military and civilian legal institutions might under-enforce IHL and IHLR against perpetrators of 'official' violations. Note that even when military trials do take place, they often result in acquittals or the imposition of relatively modest levels of punishment for crimes committed by one's own soldiers against enemy soldiers or civilians.[155]

As much as we object to this sad state of affairs, this situation must be taken into account when considering the entire gamut of responses to IHL and IHRL violations. To be sure, we are not claiming that the criminal venue is an inadequate response to war crimes or other serious violations of international law. Domestic criminal prosecutions, even on a small scale and with relatively light punishments, may have an important symbolic effect and generate real deterrence.[156] Still, it is questionable whether an exclusive focus on criminal law is always an effective means for enforcing IHL and IHRL. Instead, we propose in the next segment that a greater role in the enforcement of IHL and IHRL should be assigned to independent commissions of inquiry.

[155] There were only three criminal cases in the UK regarding the operations in Iraq, and in all cases the convictions did not concern manslaughter or murder, but lesser offences (*supra* note 143). In Israel, military courts convicted Israeli soldiers during the *second intifada* of relatively minor offences, such as "behavior unbecoming." See e.g., Ben Naftali and Zamir 2009. In the aftermath of the Abu Ghraib prison scandal, 11 US soldiers were convicted on charges of abuse of prisoners and negligent performance of duty. No one was convicted of murder or manslaughter (although several Iraqi prisoners died while in custody). No officer was convicted in charges relating to the actual abuse. The highest rank of a soldier convicted in relations to the actual abuse was a Staff Sergeant. In Canada a similar pattern took place: in the *Belet Huen* incident in Somalia, out of the 9 persons charged, four were officers. All were either acquitted of all charges (two cases) or convicted for negligent performance of duty. Three soldiers at the ranks of Private and Sergeant were convicted of second degree murder, and sentenced to up to 5 years in jail, of which they served a maximum of 1 year.

[156] For example, the legal proceedings that took place in the US following the *My Lai* massacre in Vietnam produced a lasting effect on the US military despite the relatively minor results of the trials,. See generally Lippman 1993, Similarly, an Israeli criminal conviction in the case of *Malinki* (Kaffar Kasem case, 1958), instilled in the IDF the principle of the duty to disobey a blatantly unlawful order, notwithstanding the light punishment imposed. Military Court case no. 3/57(central command) *Military Prosecutor v. Malinki*, District Court Case 17, 90 (p. 21-3-214) (1958).

2.5.2 *The Use of Non-Criminal Accountability Mechanisms: Independent Commissions*

One possible non-criminal response to allegations or suspicions of violations of IHL and IHLR can be found in the form of commissions of inquiry. Such commissions are composed of independent and impartial reviewers and are authorized to ascertain the events that led to the alleged violation and issue policy and other recommendations. Such recommendations may lead to the revision of military practices and can include certain sanctions (such as demotion or dismissal of officers) or remedies (such as compensation to victims).[157] In certain cases, the factual record of commissions of inquiry may serve as the basis for follow-up legal proceedings including criminal prosecution of suspected criminals. Arguably, some commissions—especially composed of experts in military law and doctrine—are better placed than courts in reviewing systemic problems involving IHL violations and in facilitating policy reforms.[158]

Recent examples of commission of inquiry include the 'Somalia Commission' appointed by the Government of Canada in order to investigate the misconduct of members of the Canadian Airborne Regiment at Belet Huen in south central Somalia in 1993[159]; the enquiry conducted by the Dutch Institute for War Documentation into the responsibility of Netherlands forces for the Srebrenica massacre of 1995 in Bosnia and Herzegovina[160]; and the Chilcot Inquiry established by the British government to consider the UK's involvement in Iraq from mid-2001 to July 2009.[161] In Israel, the Supreme Court recommended that an independent commission examine allegations of illegality concerning targeted killing operations[162] (one *ad hoc* commission reviewed the legality of one specific targeted killing attack from 2002 resulting in extensive collateral damage)[163]; in

---

[157] Ronen 2009.

[158] In a recent case the Israeli Supreme Court stressed this point. While rejecting a petition to open criminal investigation regarding Israeli operations in the Gaza strip in 2004, it noted that the Israeli system provides for alternative methods of investigation where, as in that case, criminal investigations are inappropriate. See HCJ 3292/07 *Adallah v. Attorney General* (unpublished decision of 8 December 2011)("The petitioners before us ask for a conduct of a criminal investigation. In the circumstances before us, the tool of criminal investigation is inappropriate and does not properly respond to the problematic issues raised in this case, first and foremost for reasons based on the character of criminal law") (unofficial translation).

[159] The Somalia Commission of Inquiry 1997.

[160] http://www.srebrenica-project.com/index.php?option=com_content&view=article&id=140:niod-report&catid=12:2009-01-25-02-01-02.

[161] http://www.iraqinquiry.org.uk/about.aspx

[162] *The Public Committee Against Torture in Israel v. Gov't of Israel, supra* n.44.

[163] On July 22, 2002 a targeted killing operation took place against Saleh Shehadeh, a leading Hamas operative. In addition to Shehadeh himself, his wife and daughter, 14 other people were killed. Following a recommendation of the Israeli Supreme Court, an independent commission was formed to investigate possible violations of law in the incident. The commission, headed by

addition, a committee was established in 2010 to review the legality of IDF operations against the Gaza flotilla (the Turkel Commission).[164] The US has also resorted to commissions of inquiry to review the propriety of certain military or intelligence operations. Thus, a commission was established in the aftermath of the Abu Ghraib prison scandal[165]; another commission led by a former Secretary of Defense reviewed the entire detention operations of the US[166]; and yet another committee reviewed the responsibility of lawyers who authorized aggressive investigation techniques.[167]

Although commissions of inquiry may meet the general requirements of a proper investigation, this form of response nevertheless remains open to several objections. One key concern is that governments may manipulate the commission's mandate or composition in order to deflect responsibility or avoid it altogether. Hence, a critical assessment of the effectiveness and independence of each commission is warranted.

One possible fix to the threat of governmental manipulation of the composition of commissions of inquiry may be found in entrusting their investigative tasks in the hands of permanent investigative bodies that would operate beside, or as part of, national humanitarian law commissions[168] or human rights institutions.[169] The structure of such permanent Humanitarian Law Commissions (HLC) should conform, as much as possible, to the Paris Principles governing the operation of national human rights institutions,[170] which call *inter alia* for independence, adequate resources and representation of civil society.

Note that the permanency of HLCs addresses not only several independence and impartiality concerns, but also some effectiveness concerns: over time,

(Footnote 163 continued)
retired Supreme Court justice Tova Strassberg Cohen, the report concluded that there were no criminal violations of IHL in the incident, but made several recommendations as for the future use of targeted killings—Strassberg—Cohen Commission 2011.

164 The Turkel Commission 2011.

165 Article 15-6 investigation of the 800th Military Police Brigade (Tagoba Report) June 2004, available at: http://news.findlaw.com/hdocs/docs/iraq/tagubarpt.html#ThR1.13.

166 Schlesinger Report 2004.

167 The Office of Professional Responsibility report 2009.

168 National Humanitarian Law Committees' (NHLC's) now exist in 93 countries. Their functions vary from country to country, but frequently extend to: monitoring decisions taken by national security agencies; coordinating between different government agencies regarding the implementation of IHL; disseminating IHL material; proposing legislation that conforms with IHL; and reviewing international treaties and developments. For a description of NHLC's see: http://www.icrc.org/eng/war-and-law/ihl-domestic-law/natrional-committees/index.jsp.

169 National Human Rights Institutions (NHRIs) or Commissions, currently operate in more than a hundred countries. Their precise powers and functions vary from one case to another. In some places, they adjudicate complaints against the executive and its various agencies regarding violations of human rights, including at times violations committed by the military (e.g., as in the case of Uganda). Livingstone 1999, Lee Wetzel 2007.

170 G.A Res. 48/134, December 20, 1993.

permanent investigative bodies can accumulate considerable expertise in handling problems relating to IHL and IHRL compliance in military operations. In addition, the establishment of a permanent HLC may signal greater commitment on the part of the state in question to international law[171]—a signal which may entail reputational dividends, as well as decrease the prospects of intervention by international judicial bodies in that state's military investigation system.

If established, an HLC could monitor the propriety of criminal or disciplinary investigations conducted by the military; but, more importantly, it could also engage in policy review—i.e., reviewing *ex post* whether a specific policy or operation was conducted in accordance with international law and issuing recommendations for future military actions. Such recommendations may clarify for the military some of the more complex norms it is required to implement. HLC reports may also lead to the award of compensation by law or *ex gratia* payments to individuals harmed in military operations.[172] In order to fulfill these functions, HLCs need to be invested with genuine investigative powers (e.g., the power to require witnesses to appear before them, to receive any document it seeks, and to gather information *in situs*).

One important advantage that may appertain to a permanent HLC concerns the aforementioned tension between the military need for secrecy and the principle of public scrutiny. By entrusting an independent commission with powers of monitoring and investigating military operations and inquiries, some degree of accountability and transparency is maintained; at the same time, the commission would be expected to protect the confidentiality of sensitive intelligence and testimonies. So, unlike courts, permanent HLCs may deal with systemic issues—not just individual cases—and may do so in a more flexible and, at times, more confidential manner. Still, courts ought to retain the power to monitor the propriety of the commissions and their operations.[173]

2.6 Conclusion

In this article we reviewed the international duty upon states to investigate alleged violations of international law occurring during armed conflicts. We found that international standards for the conduct of a proper investigation in international law require a genuine process that is effective, independent and impartial, prompt and subject to public scrutiny. We also pointed out that the current trend in

[171] For the importance of signaling to the effectiveness of international law obligations see: Guzman 2008.

[172] For a general call for compensation in all collateral damage cases, see Ronen 2009.

[173] The Ali Mousa decision issued by the UK High Court of Justice in December 2010, exercises this precise function with relation to the IHAT. In its decision, the court reviewed the independence and impartiality of the IHAT, which it declared to be sufficiently independent. *Ali Zaki Mousa v. Secretary of Defence* [2010] EWHC 3304 (admin).

national investigation practices is towards a greater degree of independence and civilian control over military investigation bodies.

In addition, we are of the view that military investigation systems should not maintain an exclusive focus on criminal investigations of grave breaches of IHL. This is because international law requires states to suppress *all* breaches of IHL and IHRL. Furthermore, suppression of violations through criminal investigation and prosecution is not always the most effective response to alleged violations. Instead, international law sources as well as state practice support resort to other possibilities including permanent commissions of inquiry, which can, if built properly, satisfy under certain circumstances international law's requirements for a proper investigation.

References

Abresch W (2005) A Human Rights Law of Internal Armed Conflicts: The European Court of Human Rights in Chechnya. Eur J Int Law 16:741

Alston Report (2010) Report of the special rapporteur on extrajudicial, summary or arbitrary executions, Philip Alston Addendum: study on targeted killings, UN Doc A/HRC/14/24/Add.6 (28 May 2010)

Ben Ari E, Cohen A (2010) (unpublished paper, on file with authors) The application of International Humanitarian Law by the Israel Defence Forces: a legal and organizational analysis

Ben Naftali O (2011) Introduction International Humanitarian Law and International Human Rights Law—Pas De Deux. In: Ben-Naftali O (ed) International Humanitarian Law and International Human Rights Law. Oxford University Press, Oxford

Ben-Naftali O, Shany Y (2004) Living in denial: the application of human rights in the occupied territories. Israel Law Rev 37:17

Ben-Naftali O, Zamir N (2009) Whose conduct unbecoming? The shooting of a handcuffed blindfolded demonstrator. J Int Crim Justice 7:155

Benvenisti E (2008) Reclaiming democracy: the strategic uses of foreign and international law by national courts. Am J Int Law 102:241

Bercuson DJ (2010) Up from the ashes: the re-professionalization of the Canadian forces after the 'Somalia Affair'. In: Cohen Stuart A (ed) The new citizen armies. Routledge, London

Bill B, Marsh J (eds) (2010) International and Operational Law Department. Operational Law Handbook. Available at http://www.loc.gov/rr/frd/Military_Law/pdf/operational-law-handbook_2010.pdf

Bowker DW (2005) Unwise counsel: the war on terrorism and the criminal mistreatment of detainees in U.S. custody. In: Greenberg KJ (ed) The torture debate in America. Cambridge University Press, Cambridge

Byron C (2007) A blurring of the boundaries: the application of International Humanitarian Law by human rights bodies. Va J Int Law 47:839

Canadian Forces National Investigation Service (2009) Annual report (Novemb 2009). Available at http://www.vcds.forces.gc.ca/cfpm-gpfc/cfp-ggp/nis-sne/ar-ra/2008/doc/nisar-snera-2008-eng.pdf

Cohen A (2005) Administering the territories: an inquiry into the application of IHL in the territories. Israel Law Rev 38(3):24

Cohen A (2008) Rules and standards in the application of International Humanitarian Law. Israel Law Rev 41:41

Cohen A (2009) The principle of proportionality in the context of operation cast lead: institutional perspectives. Rutgers Law Rec 35:23
Cohen A (2011) Legal operational advice in the IDF. Conn J Int Law 26:367
Cohen A, Cohen SA (2011) Israel's National Security Law: political dynamics and historical development. Routledge, London
Dickinson LA (2010) Military lawyers on the battlefield: an empirical account of International Law compliance. Am J Int Law 104:1
Danner MA (2003) Enhancing the legitimacy and accountability of prosecutorial discretion at the International Criminal Court. Am J Int Law 97:510
Franck TM (1990) The power of legitimacy among nations. Oxford University Press, Oxford
Gardam JG (1993) Proportionality and force in International Law. Am J Int Law 87:391
Goldstone Report (2009) UN fact-finding mission on the Gaza conflict (25 Sept 2009). UN Doc. A/HRC/12/48
Guzman AT (2008) How International Law works? A rational choice theory. Oxford University Press, Oxford
Henckaerts J-M, Doswald-Beck L (2005) Customary International Humanitarian Law (vol 1). Cambridge University Press, Cambridge
Holmes JT (1999) The principle of complementarity. In: Lee RS (ed) The International Criminal Court: the making of the Rome Statute. Kluwer International, The Hague
ICRC (2007) International Humanitarian Law and the challenges of contemporary armed conflicts. Int Rev ICRC 89:719
Israel Law Review (2007) Special issue: the parallel applicability of International Humanitarian Law and International Human Rights Law. Israel Law Rev 40:307
Jochnick C, Normand R (1994) The legitimization of violence: a critical history of the laws of war. Harv Int Law J 35:49
Koivurova T (2008) Due diligence. In: Rüdiger W (ed) (online edn.) Max Planck Encyclopedia of Public International Law. Oxford University Press, Oxford
Lee Wetzel A (2007) Post-conflict national human rights institutions: emerging models from Northern Ireland and Bosnia & Herzegovina. Columbia J Eur Law 13:427
Lippman M (1993) The My Lai massacres and the Vietnam war. S-Diego Justice J 1:295
Livingstone S (1999) The Northern Ireland Human Rights Commission. Fordham Int Law J 22:1465
Lubell N (2010) Extraterritorial use of force against non-state actors. Oxford University Press, Oxford
Mackenzie R et al (eds) (2010) Manual on international courts and tribunals. Oxford University Press, Oxford
Milanovic M (2011) Extraterritorial application of human rights treaties: law, principles and policy. Oxford University Press, Oxford
Ministry of Foreign Affairs (2010) Second report on the status of investigations of alleged violations of international law during "Operation Cast Lead" undertaken by the Israel Defense Forces (July 2010). Available at http://www.mfa.gov.il/NR/rdonlyres/1483B296-7439-4217-933C653CD19CE859/0/GazaUpdateJuly2010.pdf
NATO Bombing Review Committee (2000) Final report to the prosecutor by the committee established to review the NATO bombing campaign against the Federal Republic of Yugoslavia. ILM 39:1257
Newton M (2007) Modern military necessity: the role and relevance of military lawyers. Roger Williams Univ Law Rev 12:877
Nolte G, Krieger H (2003) Comparison of European military law systems. In: Nolte G (ed) European military court system. De Gruyter Recht, Berlin
Office of Professional Responsibility (2009) Investigation into the office of legal counsel's memoranda concerning issues related to the Central Intelligence Agency's use of "enhanced interrogations techniques" on suspected terrorists (29 July 2009). Available at http://judiciary.house.gov/issues/issues_OPRReport.html

Pictet JS (ed) (1958) Commentary on the IV Geneva Convention relative to the protection of civilian persons in time of war of 12 August 1949. International Committee of the Red Cross, Geneva
Prud'homme N (2007) Lex Specialis: oversimplifying a more complex and multifaceted relationship? Israel Law Rev 40:356
Ronen Y (2009) Avoid or compensate? liability for incidental injury to civilians inflicted during armed conflict. Vanderbilt J Transnatl Law 42:181
Ronen Y (2010) Superior responsibility of civilians for international crimes committed in civilian settings. Vanderbilt J Transnl Law 43:313
Sandoz Y et al (eds) (1987) Commentary on the additional protocols of 8 June 1977 to the Geneva conventions of 12 August 1949 International Committee of the Red Cross. Martinus Nijhof Publishers, Geneva
Schlesinger Panel (2004) Final report of the independent panel to review DOD detention (August 2004). Available at http://www.au.af.mil/au/awc/awcgate/dod/d20040824finalreport.pdf
Schmitt MN (2011) Investigating violations of international law in armed conflicts. Harv Natl Secur J 2:31
Shany Y, Michaeli K (2002) The Sharon case: revisiting the doctrine of command responsibility. N Y Univ J Int Law Politics 34:797
Strasberg—Cohen Commission (2011) Report of the Special Investigatory Commission (27 Feb 2011). Available in Hebrew at http://www.pmo.gov.il/PMO/Communication/Spokesman/2011/02/spokeshchade270211.htm
The Somalia Commission of Inquiry (Canada) (1997) Final report (2 July 1997). Available at http://www.dnd.ca/somalia/somaliae.htm
The Turkel Commission (2011) The public commission to examine the maritime incident of 31 May 2010: report part 1 (January 2011). Available at http://www.turkel-committee.gov.il/files/wordocs//8707200211english.pdf. Last Accessed 30 Dec 2011
Tomuschat Report (2010) Report of the committee of independent experts in International Humanitarian and Human Rights Laws to monitor and assess any domestic, legal or other proceedings undertaken by both the Government of Israel and the Palestinian side, in the light of General Assembly resolution 64/254, including the independence, effectiveness, genuineness of these investigations and their conformity with international standards, UN Doc. A/HRC/15/50 (2010) http://unispal.un.org/UNISPAL.NSF/0/B07AE44EC3B4F211852577A5004C709B
Watkin K (2004) Controlling the use of force: a role for human rights norms in contemporary armed conflict. Am J Int Law 98:1

Chapter 3
Domestic Investigation of Suspected Law of Armed Conflict Violations: United States Procedures, Policies, and Practices

Sean Watts

Contents

3.1 Introduction

The Israeli interception of a flotilla of civilian ships bound for Gaza in May of 2010 fueled ongoing questions about the content, efficacy, and adequacy of the law of armed conflict (LOAC). Debate focused quickly concerning fundamental substantive legal issues such as proportionality, humanitarian assistance, treatment during detention, and even the overall legal character of the hostile relationship between Israel and Hamas. Public reactions revealed, at once, misconceptions of and dissatisfaction with the legal regime applicable to the operation. Given the highly political context of Gaza itself and the longstanding Israeli naval blockade, it is unsurprising that the substantive legal gap between the Israeli Defense Forces and their critics remains wide. Publication of the legal analysis and conclusions of

S. Watts (✉)
Creighton University Law School, Omaha, NE, USA
e-mail: seanwatts@creighton.edu

S. Watts
Department of Law, United States Military Academy,
United States Army Reserve, West Point, NY, USA

M.N. Schmitt and L. Arimatsu (eds.), *Yearbook of International Humanitarian Law Volume 14, 2011*, DOI: 10.1007/978-90-6704-855-2_3,

a commission of three Israeli jurists aided by international legal observers and consultants appears to have done little to quell dissent.[1]

Quickly, however, debate spread beyond mere doctrinal matters of LOAC interpretation and application. Critics have begun to devote significant attention to the procedural aspects of the Israel investigative response as well.[2] In particular, some have questioned the adequacy of what was in most respects a domestic inquiry. Such criticism echoes concerns expressed by an earlier United Nations inquiry into Israeli military operations in Gaza between December 2008 and January 2009.[3] Both events highlight interesting questions concerning the extent and nature of States' obligations to investigate potential law of armed conflict violations. Crucial questions include the degree of independence and neutrality required and whether domestic, internal military investigations can ever suffice to address what are alleged breaches of international legal obligations. Still deeper methodological and interpretive inquiries surely loom as well. For instance, to what extent does international law regulate the processes of investigations of potential LOAC violations? Or better yet, to what extent to do *States* regard investigative procedure as an issue committed to LOAC or international law more generally?

An examination of all the forces behind the addition of procedural to substantive scrutiny of LOAC investigations is beyond the scope of this brief Comment. However, surely future discussions and analyses will profit from thorough understandings of the domestic legal investigative procedures of the major and frequent participants in present armed conflicts and the use of force. This Comment will briefly outline the investigative procedures available under current United States domestic law for suspected LOAC violations. Formal and informal procedures available under both civil and military justice systems will be explored.

[1] The Public Commission to Examine the Maritime Incident of 31 May 2010, The Turkel Commission Report, Part 1, (Jan. 2011) available at http://turkel-committee.gov.il/content-107.html.

[2] Doyle 2010 (criticizing lack of international enquiry into the Gaza Flotilla incident). Amnesty International Middle East and North Africa Programme Director Malcolm Smart said, "The investigations undertaken by Israel fail to meet international standards of independence, impartiality, transparency, promptness and effectiveness. The Israeli military is investigating itself and in no way can this be adequate in obtaining the truth and ensuring justice for the victims." Amnesty International argued, "the military investigations also preclude the possibility of examining decisions taken by civilian officials, who are also alleged to be responsible for serious violations."—see Amnesty International 2010.

[3] United Nations Human Rights Council, *Report of the United Nations Fact Finding Mission on the Gaza Conflict*, 15 September 2009, A/HRC/12/48. Known for its lead author, Richard Goldstone, the Goldstone report proved critical of Israeli domestic responses to alleged law of armed conflict violations. The report observed, "the system put in place by Israel, and described above, to deal with allegations of serious wrongdoing by armed forces personnel does not comply with all those principles." *Id.* at para 1612. The report also concluded, that the failure of Israel to open prompt, independent and impartial criminal investigations even after 6 months have elapsed constitute a violation of its obligation to genuinely investigate allegations of war crimes and other crimes, and other serious violations of international law." *Id.* at para 1620.

Investigative jurisdiction is often tied to prosecutorial jurisdiction and thus aspects of the latter will be presented to the extent required to understand the former. Special attention will be given to evidence that U.S. investigative procedures, policies, and protocols are influenced by or are functions of perceived international legal obligations. This Comment concludes by offering a few brief observations concerning the U.S. system and the likely direction of future scrutiny.

3.2 The United States LOAC Investigation System

The United States system of investigative and prosecutorial jurisdiction over LOAC violations is split between the federal civil and military sectors. United States civilian and military authorities have concurrent jurisdiction to investigate and prosecute most alleged LOAC violations. Generally speaking, the U.S. military has primary jurisdiction to investigate and prosecute LOAC violations by persons affiliated with the armed forces and captured enemies. The military uses both administrative and criminal systems to process alleged LOAC violations. The U.S. civilian criminal justice system supplements the military system with respect to LOAC violations and is the primary system for civilians without military or enemy affiliation. The civilian system, through several executive branch agencies, investigates and prosecutes LOAC violations by civilians and persons not subject to the U.S. military criminal justice system. Agreements between U.S. federal agencies and the military clarify the operation of concurrent jurisdiction over LOAC violations.

In some circumstances, inquiries into LOAC violations gain political and popular support. The United States Congress has authority to exercise oversight over some Executive Branch functions.[4] For instance, Congress enjoys the power to "make Rules for the Government and Regulation of land and naval Forces."[5] The Supreme Court of the United States has also recognized the authority of Congress's oversight function in both the Senate and the House.[6] Congress has adopted statutes and rules requiring its bodies to engage in specific forms of oversight. For instance U.S. code provides, "Each standing committee of the Senate and the House of Representatives shall review and study, on a continuing basis, the application, administration, and execution of those laws, or parts of laws, the subject matter of which is within the jurisdiction of that committee."[7]

---

[4] Kaiser 2006.

[5] U.S. Const., art. I, § 8, cl. 14. *See also*, *Id.* cls 10–13, 15.

[6] *See McGrain v. Daugherty*, 273 U.S. 135, 174 (1927) (stating that inquiry is a necessary and essential legislative function); *Watkins v. United States*, 354 U.S. 178, 187 (1957) (stating, "The power of the Congress to conduct investigations is inherent in the legislative process. That power is broad. It encompasses inquiries concerning the administration of existing law as well as proposed or possibly needed statutes.... But broad as is this power of inquiry, it is not unlimited.").

[7] 2 U.S.C. § 190d.

The form of oversight varies between bodies of Congress. The Senate Armed Services Committee, for example, has no specific rule requiring oversight. The House, however, requires its committees to oversee the areas within their jurisdiction.[8] Recently, the House Armed Services Committee of the 110th Congress stated, "the military tribunals and the detainees at Guantanamo Bay and elsewhere raise a number of critical issues that fall within the jurisdiction of the committee."[9] Additionally the Committee stated it would "conduct thorough oversight of, among other things, the possible implications of members of the armed services in alleged incidents of detainee abuse."[10] The specific language used by the 110th Congress was changed in the oversight plans for the 111th Congress, stating that it would "take other necessary actions and conduct related oversight."[11]

Congressional inquiries into war crimes accusations draw from such oversight authority but have been used only rarely.[12] Congressional oversight of alleged U.S. war crimes at My Lai and Abu Ghraib mark two examples of such investigations.[13] War crimes investigations by Congress are often highly politicized. As two scholars argue, political climate and individual agendas often play determinative roles.[14] Although it is foreseeable that concerns of inappropriate influence such as disruption of military investigations or taint panel (jury) pools could result from Congressional investigations, the My Lai and the Abu Graib hearings did not perceive significant barriers to criminal prosecution in either case. Thus Congressional inquiries are generally not regarded as barriers to concurrent administrative or criminal investigations conducted by executive branch agencies.

Unlike an increasing body of States, the United States has generally not been receptive to international intervention in or conduct of LOAC investigations. The U.S. is not a State Party to the 1977 Additional Protocol I to the 1949 Geneva

---

[8] Rules of the United States House of Representatives. Rule X, cl. 2(b)(2).

[9] U.S. House of Representatives, House Armed Services Comm., Oversight Plan for the 110th Congress, available at: http://armedservices.house.gov/oversight110.shtml.

[10] *Id.*

[11] U.S. House of Representatives, House Armed Services Comm., Oversight Plan for the 111th Congress, available at: http://armedservices.house.gov/oversight_plan.shtml.

[12] United States Senate, Committee on Armed Services, *Inquiry into the Treatment of Detainees in U.S. Custody* (November 20, 2008), available at http://documents.nytimes.com/report-by-the-senate-armed-services-committee-on-detainee-treatment. See U.S. House of Representatives, House Armed Services Comm., *Oversight Plan for the 110th U.S. Congress*, available at http://armedservices.hous.gov/oversight110.shtml. Brenner 2010.

[13] Brenner 2010, p. 4.

[14] *Id.* at 92. See also Fowler and Hill (2006) stating ideological polarization can extend to relations with the executive branch and that sophisticated political parties can use various means to claim success.

Conventions.[15] Thus it is also not a party to that Protocol's optional international LOAC investigative provision.[16]

The U.S. has also not consented to standing jurisdiction before any regional human rights tribunal to investigate LOAC violations. The U.S. is a member of the Organization of American States but is not a Party to that body's human rights instrument, the American Convention on Human Rights.[17] Nor is the U.S. subject to the jurisdiction of the Inter-American Court of Human Rights.

In November 2005, however, the Inter-American Commission on Human Rights extended precautionary measures concerning U.S. detention operations at the Naval Base at Guantanamo Bay, Cuba.[18] The Commission requested the U.S. investigate and prosecute alleged instances of torture and mistreatment of detainees. Specifically, the Commission expressed concern that investigations to date had been internal to the military, calling into question impartiality.[19] In 2006, the Commission issued a resolution calling on the U.S. to close the Guantanamo Bay detention facility.[20] The U.S responded that the Commission lacked jurisdiction over the U.S. and also contended that the law of war rather than human rights law was the legal regime applicable to detention operations at Guantanamo.[21]

3.2.1 Federal Civilian Criminal Investigative Authority

The U.S. primary federal civilian investigative agency is the Federal Bureau of Investigation (FBI). The FBI derives its general investigative authority from statutory provisions stating, "the Attorney General may appoint officials to detect

[15] Protocol Additional to the Geneva Conventions of 12 August 1949, and Relating to the Protection of Victims of International Armed Conflicts, 1977, 1125 U.N.T.S. 3 [hereinafter 1977 Additional Protocol I].

[16] *Id.* art. 90. Of the Protocol's 171 States parties, 72 are States parties to the article 90 investigative regime. International Committee of the Red Cross, *State Parties to the Following International Humanitarian Law and Other Related Treaties as of 6-Dec-2011*, available at http://www.icrc.org/ihl.

[17] American Convention on Human Rights, 1144 UNTS 123, November 22, 1969. The U.S. has signed but not ratified the American Convention. *See* Organization of American States, Department of International Law, Multilateral Treaties, available at http://www.oas.org/juridico/english/sigs/b-32.html.

[18] See Center for Constitutional Rights, *Inter-American Commission on Human Rights Extends Precautionary Measures on Guantanamo Detainees,* available at http://ccrjustice.org/newsroom/press-releases/inter-american-commission-human-rights-extends-precautionary-measures-guant%C3%A1.

[19] See *id.*

[20] Inter-American Commission on Human Rights, Resolution No. 2/06, available at http://www.cidh.oas.org/resolutions/resolution2.06.htm.

[21] State Department Digest of U.S. Practice in International Law 935-36 (2007) available at http://www.state.gov/documents/organization/147120.pdf.

and prosecute crimes against the United States."[22] A statutory source of supervisory control over the investigative functions of the FBI identifies the Attorney General as an advisor, approving regulations proposed by the Director of the FBI.[23] The Attorney General also oversees various regulations on the FBI, including, but not limited to, the regulation of investigatory techniques employed by the FBI during domestic operations.[24] An *Attorney General's Guide for Domestic Operations* indicates appropriate forms of investigative techniques.[25]

In addition to the power to investigate, the FBI also has statutory authority to arrest.[26] The DoJ has interpreted this provision as granting broad investigative authority,[27] permitting the FBI to investigate all crimes against the United States, including LOAC violations except where Congress has specifically assigned the responsibility to investigate to another exclusive agency.[28] The DoJ has also determined that the FBI's investigative and arrest authority extends to extraterritorial investigations and arrests, affirming its power to investigate and arrest persons for violations of customary international law.[29] The DoJ justified this position by citing various examples where Congress has extended FBI jurisdiction extraterritorially.[30] The DoJ identified Congressional intent to extend the FBI's extraterritorial authority based on the its role as the chief enforcement unit for the statutes to which Congress extended authority abroad.[31] The DoJ has consistently held the position that the FBI's investigative power derives from a delegation of investigative authority from the Attorney General.[32] The opinion's weight is reflected in the Government's Code of Federal Regulations which states the duties and responsibilities of the FBI including to "[i]nvestigate violations of the laws … of the United States and collect evidence in cases in which the United States is or

---

22 28 U.S.C § 533(1).

23 *Id.* at (4)(a).

24 The Attorney General's Guidelines For Domestic FBI Operations (2006), available at http://www.ignet.gov/pande/standards/prgexhibitg1.pdf.

25 *Id.*

26 18 U.S.C § 3052 (emphasis added).

27 *United States v. Marzani*, 71 F. Supp. 615, 617 (D.D.C. 1947), aff'd, 168 F.2d 133 (D.C. Cir.), aff'd, 335 U.S. 895 (1948) (per curiam).

28 *Delegation of the Attorney General's Authority to Investigate Credit Card Fraud*, 7 U.S. Op. Off. Legal Counsel 172 (1983).

29 *Authority of the Federal Bureau of Investigation to Override International Law in Extraterritorial Law Enforcement Activities*, 13 U.S. Op. Off. Legal Counsel 163 (1989) [hereinafter *Authority to Override International Law*].

30 See e.g., 18 U.S.C § 844(i) (enacting penalties for destruction of property used in foreign commerce); 18 U.S.C § 1116(c) (implementing Convention on the Prevention and Punishment of Crimes Against Internationally Protected Persons); 18 U.S.C § 1472(l) (enacting penalties for carrying weapons or explosives aboard aircraft).

31 See *Authority to Override International Law*, supra n. 29.

32 See *FBI Authority to Investigate Violations of Subtitle E of Title 26 or 18 U.S.C. Sections 921–930*, 20 U.S. Op. Off. Legal Counsel 242 (1996); *Authority to Override International Law*, supra note 29.

may be a party in interest, except in cases in which such responsibility is by statute or otherwise exclusively assigned to another investigative agency."[33] Suspected violations of LOAC, especially those executed by domestic law easily fall within such investigative authority.

The DoJ and DoD have concluded an agreement concerning investigative practices. Memorandum of Understanding 938 states the FBI will yield its duty to investigative to the authority of the military justice system.[34] Military authorities investigate crimes occurring on military installations, other than corruption.[35] Additionally federal crimes by service members that occur off military installations fall under military investigative jurisdiction unless the crime alleged is an offense not normally tried by court-martial.[36] If the alleged crime is "reasonably believed" to be a federal crime "not normally tried by court-martial" then DoD refers the case to DoJ for investigation and prosecution.[37] This provision seems to indicate that following a referral the FBI retains investigative authority to search for a violation of federal law, per its statutory authority.[38]

The increased use of private security contractors (PSCs) has drawn attention to the means available to investigate and prosecute suspected LOAC violations by PSCs. Generally, civilian government actors are subject to several specific statutes providing for prosecution under United States law. First, a recent amendment to the Uniform Code of Military Justice (UCMJ) permits trial of civilians accompanying the armed forces, not only in wartime, but also in "a contingency operation[s]."[39] The amendment could be used to investigate and prosecute civilian government actors' violations of LOAC.

A recent memorandum provides guidance concerning operation of the UCMJ amendments against civilian personnel.[40] Other violations of the UCMJ by government actors not amounting to war crimes could also be investigated under the amendment. It is likely the scope of government actors covered would be broad.

---

[33] 28 C.F.R. § 0.85(a) (1995) (emphasis added).

[34] Dep't of Defense Memorandum of Understanding 938, Memorandum of Understanding between the Departments of Justice and Defense Relating to the Investigation and Prosecution of Certain Crimes, Aug. 1984, *available at* http://www.justice.gov/usao/eousa/foia_reading_room/usam/title9/crm00938.htm.

[35] *Id.* at para (2).

[36] *Id.* at para (3)(b).

[37] *Id.*

[38] *Id. See also* 28 C.F.R § 0.85.

[39] 10 U.S.C. § 802(a)(10) as amended by The National Defense Authorization Act of 2007. The Act defines a "contingency operation" as a military operation designated by the Secretary of Defense as one in which participant are or may become involved in military actions, operations, or hostilities or that results in an order preventing active duty service members from separating from service. 10 U.S.C. § 101(a)(13).

[40] Department of Defense, Office of General Counsel, Directive-Type Memorandum 09-015, *Policy and Procedures Applicable to DoD and United States Coast Guard Civilian Personnel Subject to Uniform Code of Military Justice Jurisdiction in Time of Declared War or Contingency Operation.* (February 16, 2010 with change 1 dated Aug. 19 2010).

The key interpretive point regards the term "accompanying the force." To date, the amendments have not been used to investigate and prosecute any persons directly employed with the U.S. government. The legislative record, however, shows Congress clearly had PSCs in mind when drafting the amendment. The military recently prosecuted a civilian, Canadian-Iraqi interpreter for aggravated assault in Iraq under these provisions.[41] The constitutionality of these provisions remains in doubt, however.

Second, PSC violations of LOAC may be investigated and prosecuted under the Military Extraterritorial Jurisdiction Act of 2000 (MEJA). The Act covers conduct committed outside the United States punishable by more than a year by the members of or persons accompanying the armed forces.[42] Congress amended MEJA in 2004 to include private security and military contractors more broadly.

In addition to MOU 938, discussed above, the DoJ has released statements from then Deputy Attorney General of the Criminal Division indicating that the FBI generally will not have lead investigative authority, in instances where MEJA is concerned.[43] The DoJ concludes that the FBI will likely not have lead investigatory status because most MEJA cases are initially investigated overseas by DoD or the Department of State.[44] The DoJ has concluded that the FBI "may participate in certain investigations" if the investigation is particularly "complex or serious."[45] The DoJ position indicates a general policy to yield investigative authority to the military even in instances of non-LOAC violations.

Two cases relating to war crimes allegations in Iraq surfaced under MEJA, both involving members of the armed forces discharged prior to discovery of their offenses. Although not involving PSCs, the cases illustrate how relevant statutory schemes might operate against PSCs. First, a former Marine, Jose Luis Nazario, Jr., was indicted in June 2007 for killing four unnamed civilians in Fallujah, Iraq.[46] At trial, prosecutors presented testimony from former military personnel, as well

---

41 *United States v. Ali*, Docket No. Army 20080559 (June 22, 2008). In March 2010, the Army TJAG directed the Army Court of Criminal Appeal to determine whether the court-martial had subject matter and personal jurisdiction in the case. See The United States Army Judge Advocate General's School, *Criminal Law Deskbook*, D-15 (2011) [hereinafter Army Criminal Law Deskbook].

42 18 U.S.C. § 3261 (2000): "Whoever engages in conduct outside the United States that would constitute an offense punishable by imprisonment for more than 1 year if the conduct had been engaged in within the special maritime and territorial jurisdiction of the United States (1) while employed by or accompanying the Armed Forces outside the United States; or (2) while a member of the Armed Forces subject to chapter 47 of title 10 (the Uniform Code of Military Justice), shall be punished as provided for that offense.

43 Department of Justice 2008.

44 *Id.*

45 *Id.*

46 Indictment, *United States v. Nazario*, CR07-00127-SGL, (September 4, 2007), available at http://www.haguejusticeportal.net/Docs/NLP/US/Nazario_Indictment_4-9-2007.pdf.

as polygraph evidence.[47] Nazario was ultimately acquitted, causing significant debate in the United States and abroad regarding the effectiveness of the civilian courts in response to military crimes.[48]

Federal prosecutors also used MEJA to investigate and bring charges against a former soldier, Steven Green, for the alleged rape and murder of an Iraqi girl and her family.[49] Green was tried in the federal Western District of Kentucky, in civilian court, because, like Nazario, he had been previously administratively discharged from the military as a matter of routine. On May 21, 2009, Green was convicted of rape, conspiracy, and multiple counts of murder.[50] On September 4, 2009, the court sentenced Green to five consecutive life sentences, without the possibility of parole.[51] Interestingly, Green's sentence may be significantly longer than it would have been under the military justice system.[52]

Third, the reach of several federal statutes extends to U.S. nationals at U.S. facilities overseas that qualify as part of the U.S Special Maritime and Territorial Jurisdiction (SMTJ).[53] This category has been interpreted to include a wide variety of installations, such as safehouses used for detention and interrogation, prisons owned by foreign nations used by the United States, residences occupied by United States personnel foreign countries, and compounds used by United States international agencies.[54] Use of SMTJ has declined with the amendments made to MEJA in 2004, however, recent case law demonstrates how the United States could employ the statute.[55]

A recent case illustrates how far-reaching, in geographic and jurisdictional terms, SMTJ investigations might be. In 2003, David Passaro, a CIA contractor at

---

[47] See generally The Hague Justice Portal, DomCLIC Project, *United States of America v. José Luis Nazario Jr.*, available at http://www.haguejusticeportal.net/eCache/DEF/9/707.html.

[48] Elsworth 2008.

[49] Unreported (W.D. Ky. 2008) No. 5:06CR-19-R 2008 W.L. 4000868.

[50] CBS News 2009.

[51] *Id.*

[52] Interestingly, Green volunteered to reenlist in the military for the option to be prosecuted under the UCMJ. The military declined the option. Testimony had already developed in military court, because many of the co-conspirators, who were serving on active duty when the allegations arose and were already tried and convicted by court-martial. The UCMJ provides that convicted persons have a chance for parole after 10 years, while this option is not always available under federal law. Some military law scholars suggest that prosecuting Green in federal district court "undoubtedly reflects political pressure to ensure the most severe punishment for the crime's alleged ringleader." Zimmerman Miller 2010, at n. 118 (citing Professor Gary Solis, a former military prosecutor and law professor at the United States Military Academy at West Point). See also Associated Press 2007.

[53] 18 U.S.C. § 7(9) (as amended by the § 804 of the USA P.A.T.R.I.O.T. Act, P.L. 107-56, title VIII, October 26, 2001, 115 Stat. 377) (excluding persons covered by the Military Extraterritorial Jurisdiction Act, 18 U.S.C. § 3261).

[54] *Id.*

[55] 18 U.S.C. § 7; 18 U.S.C. §§ 3261-3267 (2000 & Supp. IV 2004). Indictment at 1, *United States v. Passaro*, No. 5:04-CR-211-1 (E.D.N.C. 2004).

a military base in Afghanistan, beat Abdul Wali, a suspected terrorist, to death.[56] In June 2004, prosecutors charged Passaro under SMTJ with assault with a dangerous weapon and assault resulting in bodily injury.[57] He was sentenced to 6 years and 7 months confinement in April of 2010, following correction of a sentencing error.[58] Passaro was never tried for murder, involuntary manslaughter, or torture due to evidentiary difficulties.[59] This case is perhaps of particular significance for what it does not say. Namely, there was no account of DoJ's failure to use the War Crimes Act to investigate and prosecute Passaro. Some scholars concluded that this was a policy choice, intended to avoid creating legal precedent and to avoid prosecuting United States personnel for war crimes generally, however, no conclusive evidence supports this position.[60]

Finally, it is foreseeable that U.S. government civilian employees' LOAC violations could be investigated and processed under the routine administrative systems governing their employment. Minor transgressions, or more serious actions for which inadequate evidence exists to support criminal prosecution, might be investigated and processed as violations of employment conditions. Typically such dispositions use streamlined administrative procedures and carry less significant consequences for employees than criminal prosecution, such as reprimand, reduction in grade, changes in duties or responsibilities, or dismissal.

3.2.2 United States Military Investigative Authority

Despite multiple sources of independent civilian authority, military investigations constitute the primary means for responding to LOAC violations by or against U.S. citizens. Military investigations of LOAC violations are commonly initiated on the basis of internal reporting. A DoD directive permits members of the armed forces to report suspected LOAC violations to military police in addition to or as an alternative to their chains of command.[61] DoD personnel may also report LOAC violations to a military lawyer (judge advocate) or an inspector general.[62] No policy or procedure prevents service members from reporting LOAC violations to civilian police or authorities. A few words about the specifics of the duty to report suspected LOAC violations are worthwhile to preface discussion of LOAC investigations specifically.

---

56 Indictment at 1–4, *United States v. Passaro* (2004).

57 *Id.* at 1–4.

58 Locke 2010.

59 Schmidt and Priest (2004); Shane (2006).

60 Giardino (2007), p. 725.

61 Department of Defense Directive 2311.01E, *DoD Law of War Program*, para 6.3, (9th May 2006) [hereinafter DoD Law of War Program].

62 *Id.* at para 6.3.

Rules for Court-Martial (RCMs), procedural elaborations on the U.S. military criminal law approved by the President, state, "any military authority who receives a report of an offense [including LOAC violations] shall forward as soon as practicable the report and any accompanying information to the immediate commander of the suspect."[63] A DoD directive provides further LOAC-specific reporting guidance.[64] All military and civilian DoD personnel, including contractors are required to report suspected LOAC violations through their chains of command.[65] All commanders must report suspected LOAC violations through their operational chain of command as well as to their respective service department.[66] Combatant Commanders are required to notify the Chairman of the Joints Chiefs of Staff, the Secretary of Defense, and the Secretary of the Army in his capacity as DoD Executive Agent for suspected war crimes.[67] Additionally, suspected LOAC violations must be reported to: the DoD General Counsel; the Assistant Secretary of Defense (ASD) for Public Affairs; Under Secretary of Defense (USD) for Policy; the USD for Intelligence; the ASD for Legislative Affairs; and the DoD Inspector General.[68]

Credible reports of suspected LOAC violations received by leaders must be forwarded "through the most expeditious means available."[69] The U.S. Army Special Assistant for Law of War Matters advises military lawyers that the reporting standard is intended to be over-inclusive.[70] Elaborating on the reporting standard, he advises:

> Information, although incomplete, is deemed credible when considering the source and nature of the information and totality of the circumstances the information leads a prudent person to suspect that a law of war violation may have occurred and investigate the allegation further. The severity of the alleged offense, the source of the information, and corroboration (if any) are all factors to consider in determining whether the allegation is credible. In case of doubt, the information must be presumed credible.[71]

The Special Assistant for Law of War Matters advises further, "when in doubt, report."[72] An instruction from the Chairman of the Joint Chiefs of Staff adds to the DoD directive, emphasizing that reports must be made through both criminal and command channels.[73]

---

[63] Manual of Courts-Martial, United States, R.C.M. 301(b) [hereinafter MCM].

[64] DoD Law of War Program, *supra* note 61,

[65] *Id.* at para 6.3.

[66] *Id.* at para 6.4.

[67] *Id.* at para 6.6.

[68] *Id.* at para 6.7.

[69] *Id.* at para 6.4.

[70] Jackson 2010, p. 98.

[71] *Id.*

[72] *Id.*

[73] Chairman of the Joint Chiefs of Staff, Instruction 5810.01D, *Implementation of the DoD Law of War Program*, para 6.f.(4)(a) [hereinafter Implementation of Law of War Program].

The U.S. Army provides additional investigative and law enforcement reporting requirements. A regulation categorizes war crimes as "Category 1 serious incidents," requiring reports through law enforcement channels with copies for commanders and legal advisors at each level, to Headquarters, Department of the Army.[74] The regulation specifically enumerates war crimes such as "mistreatment of enemy prisoners of war, detainees, displaced persons, retained persons, or civilian internees; violations of the Geneva Conventions; and atrocities."[75]

Finally with respect to reporting, operational debriefings, "hot washes," or after-action reviews (AARs) as they are frequently termed in DoD parlance, are conducted after nearly every military operation. The U.S. military relies heavily on the AAR process to capture tactical, technical and operational lessons. The AAR process does not constitute part of the military administrative or criminal investigative process. However, statements made or information discovered during AARs may trigger the requirement to report an incident or may form the basis for initiating either criminal or administrative investigations. Information revealed in AARs is not privileged or protected by any form of immunity like that occasionally granted to aviation and safety investigations.

Once a report has been received, the U.S. military relies on generally applicable procedures to investigate and prosecute breaches of LOAC. Very few procedures are specific to processing suspected breaches of LOAC.[76] A DoD directive establishes criteria for initiation of investigations. The directive states, "All reportable incidents committed by or against U.S. personnel, enemy persons, or any other individuals are reported promptly, investigated thoroughly, and where appropriate, remedied by corrective action."[77] The directive defines a "reportable incident" as a "possible, suspected, or alleged violation of the law of war, for which there is credible information, or conduct during military operations other than war that would constitute a violation of the law of war if it occurred during an armed conflict."[78] Guidance notwithstanding, it is clear the directive entrusts military commanders with a great deal of discretion regarding the ultimate direction of LOAC investigations and the disposition of potential LOAC violations.

The scope of activity the U.S. military regards as in violation of LOAC frames the scope of LOAC investigative authority and practice. A dated, though technically operative, definition of war crimes suggests that all LOAC breaches, no matter their significance, are subject to investigation and prosecution under U.S. military law. The U.S. Army Field Manual for the Law of Land Warfare states,

---

[74] Department of the Army, Regulation 190-45, *Law Enforcement Reporting* (20th March 2007) para 8-2*b*. [hereinafter Army Law Enforcement Reporting].

[75] *Id.*

[76] See Department of the Army Field Manual 3-19.13, Army Law Enforcement Investigations, (January 10, 2005) at para 18-7, [hereinafter Army Law Enforcement Investigations]; Army Law Enforcement Reporting, *supra* note 74, at para 8-2(b).

[77] DoD Law of War Program, *supra* note 61, at para 4.4.

[78] *Id.* at para 3.2.

"Every violation of the law of war is a war crime."[79] Read in conjunction with the UCMJ's extremely broad jurisdiction concerning offenses triable under the law of war, it seems nearly any LOAC violation could be investigated and tried at court-martial.[80] The UCMJ includes procedures and charges capable of addressing all acts constituting breaches of LOAC. For instance, the UCMJ grants courts-martial jurisdiction "to try any person who by the law of war is subject to trial by a military tribunal and may adjudge any punishment authorized by the law of war."[81]

In practice, however, it is more common for breaches of LOAC to be investigated and prosecuted under military law according to severity or seriousness.[82] Minor or technical breaches are likely to be handled under administrative processes. All military leaders are empowered to prescribe retraining or corrective processes related to such deficiencies in conduct. Commanders may also initiate more formal administrative procedures resulting in reassignment, changes in duties, or reduction in rank of lower enlisted persons.

Serious breaches of LOAC may be investigated simultaneously through administrative and criminal processes. Administrative measures such as suspension from consideration for awards, military schooling, and promotion frequently accompany criminal investigation and court-martial charges.[83] If an operational inquiry or administrative investigation reveals possible criminal activity, commanders and investigating officers are instructed to consult a legal adviser.[84] Although such suspicion must be reported through required channels, a service-specific regulation on administrative investigations does not preclude concurrent administrative and criminal investigations into the same incident or activity.[85] However, criminal investigations enjoy primacy over administrative investigations when procedural or jurisdictional conflicts arise.[86]

Rules for Court-Martial direct military commanders to make a "preliminary inquiry" into all charges or suspected offenses against the UCMJ.[87] Preliminary

[79] Department of the Army, Field Manual 27-10, Law of Land Warfare, (July 18, 1956) at para 499 [hereinafter Law of Land Warfare].

[80] See 10 U.S.C. § 818.

[81] 10 U.S.C. § 818.

[82] For example, one might imagine circumstances in which a U.S. P.O.W. camp commander failed to post copies of the 1949 Third Geneva Convention in the language of the prisoners. Although a technical violation of Article 41 of the Third Convention, it is highly unlikely such a breach would be regarded as a war crime in the U.S. military justice system.

[83] Administrative measures such as suspension from consideration for awards, schooling, and promotion frequently accompany court-martial charges. See e.g. Department of the Army, Regulation 635-200, Active Duty Enlisted Separations (April 25, 2010), at para 1-8.

[84] See e.g. Department of the Army, Army Regulation 15-6, Procedures for Investigating Officers and Boards of Officers (October 2, 2006) at para 2-3b, [hereinafter Procedures for Investigating Officers].

[85] *Id.* at para 1-5d.

[86] Department of Defense, Instruction 5505.03, *Initiation of Investigations by Defense Criminal Investigative Organizations*, para 4.b. (March 24, 2011).

[87] MCM, *supra* n. 63, at R.C.M. 303 (2008).

inquiries are typically very informal investigations, conducted by the commander personally or by a member of the command. It is important to distinguish "preliminary inquiries" governed by R.C.M. 303 from "pre-trial investigations" required by UCMJ Article 32, implemented by R.C.M. 405 et seq., discussed below. Most U.S. military units do not have extensive resources for or experience in complex investigations. Commanders typically conduct preliminary inquiries through junior subordinates regularly assigned to their units. The R.C.M. cautions commanders to seek law enforcement assistance in serious or complex cases.[88] Thus, exclusive use of preliminary commander's inquiries to investigate suspected violations is ideally reserved for the simplest breaches of LOAC.

Within the DoD, Military Law Enforcement Organizations (MCIOs) conduct criminal investigations into serious war crimes. Typically, U.S. armed forces use MCIOs for U.S. felony-level offenses.[89] Investigative agents of MCIOs are members of the armed forces, recruited from the ranks of lower non-commissioned officers with advanced educational qualifications and often with extensive policing experience. The various MCIOs enjoy a level of investigative autonomy through separate reporting chains, usually to their respective service Chiefs of Staff and Secretaries. Decisions to investigate rest primarily with commanders of MCIOs.[90]

War crimes investigations by MCIOs employ a number of specialized procedures. Policies and regulations establish extensive coordination requirements for agents and commanders in such cases.[91] For instance, the U.S. Army Criminal Investigative Division (CID) is required to coordinate war crimes investigations with the theater level commander and staff, the theater Provost Marshal, and with the relevant U.S. embassy.[92] Furthermore, investigative teams must report regularly to the U.S. Criminal Investigation Command in Washington, D.C.[93] A field manual instructs war crimes investigators to be alert to circumstances requiring transfer of investigative jurisdiction based on comparative expertise or political considerations.[94]

Separate from MCIOs, Provost Marshals operate at most U.S. military installations and are frequently members of commanders' staffs. Provost Marshals and Military Police (MP) investigators are assets of the installation or commander to

---

[88] *Id.*

[89] Department of Defense, Instruction 5505.3, *Initiation of Investigations by Military Criminal Investigative Organizations* (June 21, 2002). The Instruction identifies three MCIOs: The U.S. Army Criminal Investigation Command; the Naval Criminal Investigative Service; and the Air Force Office of Special Investigations. *Id.* at para 3.2.

[90] *Id.* at para 6.1.

[91] See Army Law Enforcement Investigations, *supra* note 76, at para 18-7; Dep't of the Army, Army Regulation 190-45, Army Law Enforcement Reporting, supra note 74, para 8-2(b) (requiring reports of "serious incidents to Headquarters, Department of the Army").

[92] Army Law Enforcement Investigations, *supra* note 76, at paras 18-7, 18-8.

[93] *Id.* at para 18-10.

[94] *Id.* at para 18-18. The manual discusses transfer to international authorities such as the United Nations in cases of suspected genocide.

whom they are assigned.[95] Installation commanders may order initiation of MP criminal investigations.[96] Thus, Provost Marshals and their MP organizations are comparatively less insulated from commanders and prosecutors than MCIOs. Provost Marshals are responsible for active law enforcement operations and military facilities and thus may conduct investigations into crimes not rising in complexity or seriousness to warrant MCIO investigation.[97]

Although, as discussed above, U.S. law requires commanders to initiate preliminary investigations into all suspected violations of military law including LOAC, the same law cautions commanders to cease operational or administrative investigations in complex or especially serious cases.[98] Commanders are instructed to refer such cases to MCIOs to initiate criminal investigations.[99] Even MP assets are instructed to refer investigation of serious criminal activity to MCIOs.[100]

High-level requirements restrain command discretion with respect to some LOAC investigations. A Chairman of the Joints Chief of Staff instruction orders commanders to take the following steps with respect to suspected LOAC violations by DoD personnel:

1. Upon obtaining information about a reportable incident alleged to have been committed by its command personnel, the commander of the unit shall conduct a preliminary inquiry.

2. If it is determined that U.S. personnel may be involved in or responsible for a reportable incident, the commander shall initiate a formal investigation by command investigation in accordance with Service regulations, and shall at the same time notify the cognizant military criminal investigative organization (MCIO). The MCIO will be responsible for subsequent criminal incident reporting, as appropriate, under the provisions of reference (b) and service directives.

3. If warranted, the commander of the unit or superior commanders, as appropriate, shall take action in response to the results of the investigation(s), or refer the matter to a commander who can take action.[101]

Army Regulation 15-6 provides an example of the command investigative procedures referred to in para 2 of the above excerpt. The Regulation outlines the procedural requirements of formal investigations, also referred to as "Formal

[95] Department of the Army, Army Regulation 190-30, Military Police Investigations, (1st November 1995) para 4-1 [hereinafter Military Police Investigations].

[96] *See id.* at para 4-3.

[97] For an example of offenses investigated by Military Police rather than MCIOs see *id.* at Table 4-1.

[98] MCM, *supra* note 63, R.C.M. 303.

[99] *Id.*; DoD Law of War Program, *supra* n. 61.

[100] For a delineation of offenses investigated by Military Police rather than MCIOs see Military Police Investigations, *supra* n. 95, at Table 4-1.

[101] Implementation of Law of War Program, *supra* note 73, para 6.f.(4)(e)(1)—(3).

Boards of Officers." Entitlement to counsel is one of the important procedural protections afforded to respondents to formal investigations.[102] In practice, formal procedures might be used to precede or compliment parallel criminal investigations, although criminal investigations enjoy primacy over these administrative counterparts. The complex procedures and right to counsel attendant to formal investigations leads many commanders to favor the use of informal investigations.

Regulations limit the ability of commanders to impede ongoing investigations. Operational commanders may not impede or interfere with investigations initiated by MCIOs, nor do MCIOs require outside command approval to investigate.[103] Commanders may lodge objections to MCIO investigations with the Secretary of their respective service. Commanders may request that MCIOs initiate criminal investigations, but such requests are not binding upon MCIO commanders.[104]

MCIOs are not involved in decisions regarding the disposition of matters discovered in their investigations. MCIOs do not have jurisdiction to convene courts-martial or to initiate any other adverse action against the subjects of their investigations. Typically, U.S. military commanders consider the information gathered by MCIOs in their decisions whether to initiate military disciplinary measures or adverse administrative actions. U.S. commanders retain great discretion in their charging decisions. Although higher commanders may themselves initiate charges where lower commanders decline to, they may not direct subordinate commanders to initiate charges in any case. Nor may higher commanders establish policies regarding types of offenses, such as LOAC violations, that must be charged under the UCMJ.

The primary safeguard against undue manipulations of investigations and prosecutions in the military justice system is the doctrine of unlawful command influence (UCI).[105] Unlawful command influence is the improper use of authority to interfere with the military justice process.[106] The most common targets of UCI are subordinate commanders, panel (jury) members, and potential witnesses to offenses, although investigators may also be targets of UCI. The threshold for a UCI challenge is quite low. A challenge based on UCI need only present "some evidence" to succeed.[107] Military courts have found UCI in circumstances that merely "give the appearance" of improperly influencing proceedings.[108] With respect to subordinate commanders, the purpose of UCI doctrine is to preserve the independence and exercise of personal judgment in military disciplinary

---

[102] See Procedures for Investigating Officers, *supra* note 84, para 5-6.a.

[103] Department of Defense, Instruction 5505.03, *Initiation of Investigations by Defense Criminal Investigative Organizations* (March 24, 2011), paras 4.a. & Enclosure 2, para 3.a.

[104] *Id.* at Enclosure 2, para 1.a.

[105] See 10 U.S.C. § 37(a).

[106] See Army Criminal Law Deskbook, *supra* note 41, at C-1 (citing 2 Francis A. Gilligan & Fredric I. Lederer, Court-Martial Procedure, §18-28.00 (2nd ed. 1999).

[107] *See United States v. Biagase*, 50 M.J. 143(1999).

[108] *United States v. Hawthorne*, 22 C.M.R. 83, 87 (C.M.A. 1956).

proceedings. Thus, commanders may not order subordinates to adopt specific dispositions of cases.[109] The doctrine of UCI also prevents commanders from establishing blanket policies with respect to offenses or punishment.

A recent case demonstrates that UCI may extend to actions of staff members and to steps taken during investigations of war crimes. In *United States v. Chessani*, a service Court of Criminal Appeals affirmed dismissal of charges of failure to accurately report and investigate alleged murders committed by marines at Haditha, Iraq.[110] The court found that a military lawyer's involvement in both investigation of the incident and later advice on charges to the convening authority tainted the proceedings against the accused battalion commander.[111] UCI doctrine may not always have its intended effect. Although no evidence indicates *Chessani* involved such a plan, the episode curiously demonstrates the ironic possibility that UCI doctrine could be used to deliberately thwart investigation and prosecution of a LOAC violation.

U.S. law further insulates participants in court-martial from influence or retribution for performing their assigned roles. By statute, supervisors of military personnel may not use the panel (jury) members' participation in that capacity in any fitness evaluation or efficiency report.[112] Such protection extends by logic, if not by law, to LOAC investigating officers especially those assigned temporary investigative duties. Military judges and defense counsel are evaluated by the respective Chiefs of their internal divisions and are insulated from influence of local commanders and supervising military attorneys.[113]

The U.S. system prescribes more elaborate investigative procedures for charges destined for courts-marital. The UCMJ requires that a "pre-trial investigation," commonly referred to as "Article 32 investigations," precede all charges referred to a general court-martial, including war crimes.[114] The purpose of the investigation is to inquire into the truth of the charges and gather information to assist the commander's determination of disposition of the case.[115] Investigating officers are usually commissioned officers in the grade of Major or higher, appointed by a court-martial convening authority.[116] Although the investigating officer need not have legal training, military lawyers may be used in serious or sensitive cases.

These pre-trial investigations resemble trials in many respects. Accused are entitled to counsel, to be present for witness testimony, and to cross-examine and call reasonably available witnesses.[117] Investigating officers make recommendations on

---

109 See Army Criminal Law Deskbook, *supra* n. 41, at C-26.

110 NMCCA 200800299 (March 17, 2009).

111 *Id.* at 19-21.

112 10 U.S.C. § 836(b).

113 See Department of the Army, Army Regulation 27-10, Military Justice (November 16, 2005).

114 10 U.S.C. § 832.

115 MCM, *supra* note 63, at R.C.M. 405(a), discussion.

116 *Id.* at 405(d)(1) and discussion.

117 10 U.S.C. § 832(b).

each charge, however, recommendations do not bind courts-martial convening authorities. Convening authorities retain complete discretion in the referral of charges to courts-martial.[118] The only significant limitations on referral to court-martial are superior commanders' power to withhold authority to themselves and the prohibition on commanders referring cases in which they are an "accuser," meaning they have either signed or sworn to the charges.[119]

The UCMJ also authorizes court-martial convening authorities to initiate courts of inquiry.[120] Courts of inquiry consist of three or more commissioned officers assisted by military legal counsel. Courts of inquiry investigating suspected offenses enjoy subpoena power similar to that of courts-martial.[121] Courts of inquiry make findings of fact but typically do not express opinions or make recommendations unless required by their convening orders. Despite clear statutory authority, the U.S. military does not use courts of inquiry widely.

Apart from criminal and pre-trial investigations, military procedures exist for both formal and informal administrative investigation of LOAC violations. Administrative investigations are common for incidents involving losses or destruction of property. There is no joint publication governing U.S. DoD investigations. Instead, service-specific regulations generally prescribe procedures for administrative investigations.[122] Investigating officers are to operate impartially.[123] Procedures and appointing authorities vary by service. For example, the U.S. Army reserves authority to investigate hostile fire incidents resulting in death to general court-martial convening authorities who may delegate such authority no lower than the equivalent of a Brigade Commander.[124] Administrative investigations are often used to gather information for preliminary decisions on criminal charging or administrative corrective measures. Administrative boards convened to separate soldiers from active duty may use Army investigations conducted in compliance with regulated procedures.[125]

Civilians may be subjects of the investigations described above. For instance, civilians subject to the *in personam* jurisdiction of the UCMJ may be the subjects of military criminal investigations. A U.S. statute, however, prevents the military from performing law enforcement functions on non-federal property within the

---

118 MCM, *supra* n. 63, at R.C.M. 601(b).

119 *Id.* at R.C.M. 601(c).

120 10 U.S.C. § 935.

121 MCM, *supra* n. 63, at R.C.M. 703(3)(2)(C).

122 See e.g. Procedures for Investigating Officers, supra note 84; Dep't of the Navy, JAGINST 5800.7C, The Manual of the Judge Advocate General (June20 2007) with change 2 (September 16, 2008). The U.S. Air Force has no general regulation or instruction governing command-directed administrative investigations. The Air Force relies on commanders' inherent authority to conduct investigations. See The Judge Advocate General's School, Administrative and Civil Law Dep't, (2010) *Administrative Law Deskbook Volume 1*, p. 4.

123 See *id.* at para 1-8.

124 Procedures for Investigating Officers, *supra* note 84, at para 2-1a(3).

125 See *id.* at para 1-9a.

United States, likely limiting the capacity of the armed forces to investigate civilians more broadly.[126] An executive order also strictly limits U.S. forces' authority to collect intelligence on U.S. citizens, potentially restricting investigative authority over civilians as well.[127] However, regulations governing military administrative investigations clearly anticipate as subjects civilians with connections to the military such as employment.[128]

A final consideration relates most immediately to prosecution but surely affects the nature of potential LOAC violations. Military legal policy discourages charging U.S. service members with war crimes at court-martial.[129] Instead, policy instructs prosecutors and commanders to charge service members with the underlying conduct of the war crime.[130] Thus, a U.S. soldier suspected of murdering prisoners of war ordinarily would not be charged with a grave breach of the Third Geneva Convention. Instead, the soldier would be charged with a standard homicide charge. With respect to investigative practice, the U.S. policy likely excuses investigators from collecting information necessary to prove a war crimes charge such as the legal status of the armed conflict in question or the protected status of victims under LOAC.

While the policy streamlines investigations and trials, it greatly frustrates efforts to track U.S. military prosecution of war crimes and investigation of LOAC violations. Offenses that would constitute war crimes or even grave breaches meld easily into the stream of routine criminal offenses processed by the military justice system. The U.S. DoD does not make routinely available comprehensive data on investigations and prosecutions of LOAC violations. Although the various services report annual court-martial data to the Congressional Armed Services Committees, these reports do not delineate prosecutions by charge nor do they indicate LOAC violations or investigations not brought to trial.[131] Moreover, the U.S. practice of

---

[126] 18 U.S.C. § 1385, *Posse Comitatus* Act. Exceptions and exclusions are available in emergency situations.

[127] Executive Order 12333, *United States Intelligence Activities*, 46 Fed. Reg. 59941 (December 4, 1981).

[128] See e.g. Procedures for Investigating Officers, supra note 84, at para 1-5.b.(5). (noting procedural requirements for investigating members of the Army civilian senior executive service).

[129] Law of Land Warfare, supra note 79, at para 507 (stating, "The United States normally punishes war crimes as such only if they are committed by enemy nations or persons serving the interests of the enemy State.").

[130] *Id.* (stating, "Violations of the law of war committed by persons subject to the military law of the United States will usually constitute violations of the Uniform Code of Military Justice and, if so, will be prosecuted under that Code.").

[131] Annual Report Submitted to the Committees on Armed Services United States Senate and United States House of Representatives and to the Secretary of Defense, Secretary of Homeland Security, and Secretaries of the Army, Navy, and Air Force Pursuant to the Uniform Code of Military Justice for the Period October 1, 2009 to September 30, 2010, available at http://www.armfor.uscourts.gov/newcaaf/ann_reports.htm.

charging service members with underlying offenses rather than war crimes greatly frustrates tracking data on LOAC prosecutions.

3.3 Concluding Thoughts

Ultimately, one finds in U.S. law, policy, and practice a LOAC investigative system that emphasizes and gives priority to internal, military command-focused processes. Neither the U.S. civil nor military systems reveal strong evidence of international influence. Satisfaction of perceived international obligations with respect to LOAC investigative processes appears to be largely coincidental rather than intentional or calculated. Particularly with respect to the U.S. military system, one finds a process focused largely on concerns of efficiency and necessity. Military LOAC investigations are likely best understood primarily as tools to ensure good order and discipline as means to the end of military mission accomplishment rather than as means to justice, humane warfare, or even international legal compliance.

U.S. LOAC investigations remain greatly subject to the perceived needs of military commanders. Outside observers will likely regard military procedures as susceptible to interruption, suspension, or sidetracking by leaders with competing priorities or even personal stakes. High-level reporting and investigative mandates appear to mitigate low-level disruptions but still leave a great deal of discretion to leaders. Moreover, these reporting and investigative requirements themselves remain in some sense hostage to their own efficacy. Reporting requirements are enforceable only by virtue of reporting or leaks of failed reporting. And even professional investigations protected from command influence, such as those initiated by MCIOs, eventually return to military command channels for decisions on disposition, publication, and prosecution. Overall, the U.S. system appears susceptible to many of the criticisms leveled at recent Israeli investigations.

Most significant may be the U.S. apparent intolerance for international investigations by multinational organizations or regional human rights organizations. Again, comprehensive analysis of these critiques remains beyond the scope of this comment. Yet surely the merits of these critiques depend to a great extent on their legal grounding. If such claims are understood to highlight failure of state practice to conform to positive legal standards, the merits appear slim. The evidence that States have prescribed for themselves details concerning the processes of investigation through international law is thin. At present, the Article 90 optional international investigative procedures made available to States parties to Additional Protocol I appears to be the most deliberate effort to internationalize LOAC investigations. Yet fewer than half of Additional Protocol I parties have ratified or assented to Article 90 and even between these States, use remains subject to *ad hoc* consent.

On the other hand, if recent critiques are understood as normative in character or statements of *lex ferenda*, the case for minimum international standards of investigation appear to be growing. It may be easy to generate support for the normative claim that the law of armed conflict has become more than a system to ensure internal discipline and military effectiveness. Understandings of LOAC as part of a broader humanitarian pact between States and humanity clearly further such claims.

Whatever one's interpretive or normative predilections, surely thorough and accurate understandings of State practice are an important component of future efforts to discern or develop the international law governing LOAC investigations. Whatever the ultimate outcome, criticism of the Israeli response to the Gaza flotilla has highlighted an important area of burgeoning legal dispute. It is hoped this Comment has provided partial support for future developmental and normative work on LOAC investigations as well as inspiration for complimentary work on other States' policies, procedures, and practices in this important field.

References

Amnesty International (2010) Israel's response on Gaza investigations is 'totally inadequate.' Available at http://amnesty.org.uk/news_details.asp?NewsID=18605

Associated Press (2007) Iraq rape-slay case hits snags. CBS News (29 Dec 2007). Available at http://www.cbsnews.com/stories/2007/12/19/iraq/main3631048.shtml

Brenner C (2010) "I am a bit Sickened": examining archetypes of congressional war crimes oversight after my Lai and Abu Ghraib. Mil Law Rev 1:205

CBS News (2009) Ex-soldier gets 5 life sentences for Iraqi rape. CBS News (5 Sept 2009). Available at http://cbs5.com/national/steven.green.iraqi.2.1166196.html

Department of Justice (2008) Closing legal loopholes: prosecuting sexual assaults and other violent crimes committed overseas by American civilians in a combat environment. Available at http://www.justice.gov/criminal/hrsp/pr/testimony/2008/04-09-08nelson-hearing.pdf

Doyle C (2010) Off the hook: Israel's own Widgery Inquiry into Bloody Monday. The Guardian (16 June 2010). Available at http://www.guardian.co.uk/commentisfree/2010/jun/16/israel-gaza-flotilla-inquiry

Elsworth C (2008) U.S. marine acquitted of war crimes in ground-breaking trial. The Telegraph (29 August 2008). Available at http://www.telegraph.co.uk/news/worldnews/middleeast/iraq/2641186/US-marine-acquitted-of-war-crimes-in-ground-breaking-trial.html

Fowler LL, Hill S (2006) Presentation at the annual meeting of the American Political Science Association: Guarding the guardians—Senate Oversight Activity in Foreign Affairs, 1947–2006

Giardino A (2007) Using extraterritorial jurisdiction to prosecute violations of the law of war: looking beyond the war crimes act. Boston Coll Law Rev 48:699, 725

Jackson D (2010) Reporting and investigation of possible suspected, or alleged violations of the law of war. Army Lawyer 95:98

Kaiser FM (2006) Congressional oversight. Available at http://www.fas.org/sgp/crs/misc/97-936.pdf

Locke M (2010) Passaro sentence is cut. News & Observer (Raleigh, NC). Available at http://www.newsobserver.com/2010/04/07/425210/passaros-sentence-is-cut.html#storylink=misearch

Schmidt S, Priest D (2004) Civilian charged in beating of Afghan detainee. Washington Post. Available at http://www.washingtonpost.com/ac2/wp-dyn/A50792-2004Jun17?language=printer

Shane S (2006) C.I.A. Contractor guilty in beating of Afghan who later died. New York Times (18 August 2006)

Zimmerman Miller O (2010) Murder or authorized combat action: who decides? Why civilian court is the improper forum to prosecute former military service members accused of combat crimes. Loyola Law Rev 56:447

Chapter 4
Splendid Isolation: International Humanitarian Law, Legal Theory and the International Legal Order

Aoife O'Donoghue

Contents

4.1 Introduction

International humanitarian law (IHL), from both a historical and contemporary perspective, holds a unique position within the international legal order.[1] This distinctiveness is central to the main theme of this article: to assess the role of IHL, or *jus in bello*, in contemporary theoretical debates on the international legal order. IHL's presence in the legal theory literature is sparse. A partial explanation for this is to be found in a number of its unique characteristics that contribute to IHL's

I would like to thank Colin Murray and the reviewers for their insightful comments on earlier drafts of this piece. All errors are my own.

[1] International humanitarian law and *jus in bello* are used interchangeably and are intended to mean the law of armed conflict, though some argue there are differences between them. Greenwood 2008, p. 11.

A. O'Donoghue (✉)
Durham Law School, Durham, UK
e-mail: aoife.o'donoghue@durham.ac.uk

M.N. Schmitt and L. Arimatsu (eds.), *Yearbook of International Humanitarian Law Volume 14, 2011*, DOI: 10.1007/978-90-6704-855-2_4,

absence from this debate. These include its exceptional status within war and law, its historical development, its early codification and, most importantly for this analysis, its treatment within international legal theory.[2] In exploring these characteristics, this article seeks to further account for the near absence of IHL within current legal theory and to suggest that a more active engagement with IHL has the potential to enrich the debates on the future of the international legal order.

Contemporary debates on the nature and future of international law take several courses including, among others, fragmentation,[3] global legal pluralism,[4] cosmopolitanism,[5] and constitutionalisation.[6] These theories are innovative, albeit not entirely new understandings of the governance models between branches of international law. Several of these debates engage with the whole of public international law while others consider one particular field such as trade or human rights law. Nonetheless, even in sectoral theories the relationship between different fields of international law remains a core concern. These theories do not entirely depart from the theoretical questions which dominated the attention of the different schools of thought during the last century, but their contemporary character is important in understanding where IHL fits into the present debates on the future of international law.[7]

More specifically, this article considers the place of IHL in the fragmentation[8] and constitutionalisation debates.[9] These contrasting approaches, centring on questions of governance and the future workings of the international legal order, are prime examples of current academic exchanges. Fragmentation considers the relationships between general international law and its specialised areas. It also examines these specialised areas in the context of the process by which they are all becoming more inwardly focused and divergent from one another. In contrast, constitutionalisation considers the increasing move in the international legal order from a horizontal consent based system to a hierarchal order that maintains core constitutional norms in its operation. Depending on the form of fragmentation or constitutionalisation which is advocated, these are not mutually exclusive approaches. Nonetheless, their contrasting basic hypotheses allows for a broad

---

[2] Neff 2005.

[3] Koskenniemi and Leino 2002, Hafner 2003–2004, Simma 2003–2004, Buffard et al. 2008, Dupuy 1999, Benvenisti and Downs (2007–2008), ILC Fragmentation Report.

[4] Wheatley 2010, Wheatley and Berman 2007, Kirsch 2010.

[5] Domingo 2011, Kumm 2009, Pierik and Werner 2010, Feldman 2006, Benhabib 2006.

[6] Klabbers et al. 2009, Walker 2008, Macdonald and Johnston 2005, Dunoff and Trachtman 2009, Fassbender 2009.

[7] Positivism and the New Haven School are two such examples. McDougal 1953, McDougal et al. 1967–1968, 1987–1988, Hart 1965.

[8] Koskenniemi and Leino 2002, Hafner 2003–2004, Simma 2003–2004, Buffard et al. 2008, Dupuy 1999, Benvenisti and Downs 2007–2008, ILC Fragmentation Report.

[9] Klabbers et al. 2009, Walker 2008, Macdonald and Johnston 2005, Dunoff and Trachtman 2009, Fassbender 2009.

discussion of the role of international humanitarian law within them and, as such, within contemporary discourse.

Jus ad bellum dominates as a central concern irrespective of theoretical approach, in particular in discussions on the role of the Security Council or in the rise of multilateralism. By contrast, its counterpart, *jus in bello*, receives little attention.[10] An overview of the contemporary literature suggests that IHL is often either largely ignored or granted only a hasty examination. Since other specialised areas such as trade or human rights receive extensive analysis, the 'specialisation' argument cannot fully account for why IHL is so often side-lined.[11] This lack of interaction may derive from several sources. The aforementioned specialisation of IHL, to the extent that many public international lawyers do not feel comfortable delving into its inner depths, provides one possible, albeit partial, explanation. This specialisation is in part driven by the dominance of certain forms of legal expertise, in particular, the military and the International Committee of the Red Cross (ICRC). The military, for obvious reasons, has a particular perspective and focus on IHL and further, has the resource necessary to command a complete understanding of all its rules. Similarly, the ICRC, with its competence driven by IHL treaty law, maintains a complete expertise. While military and ICRC opinion may not always correlate, their knowledge and competence, which extends to understanding all the rules of IHL, makes it difficult for those outside this realm to compete without being dismissed as ignorant of the entirety of the law and therefore not competent to comment.

The resulting discomfort of those international lawyers who lack comprehensive knowledge and thus are less likely to engage in discussions pertaining to theory and IHL is compounded by the fact that within IHL circles there does not appear to be an obvious concern with the wider on-going debates in public international law. This lack of enthusiasm may be due to the perception that IHL has largely settled its relationship with other bodies of international law through the development, for example, of the doctrine of *lex specialis*.[12] Yet, the dearth of IHL discourse in these broader governance deliberations cannot be understood on that basis alone, particularly as certain questions, such as the relationship with human rights continues to ignite extensive discussions and disagreements.

This article considers several differing perspectives on international humanitarian law. Public international law evolves to cope with new challenges. For example, the rise in intra-state conflicts and transnational terrorism both required a reconsideration of some traditional understandings of law's operation. However, IHL remains largely static and within the confines that more traditional academic voices would recognise as Westphalian international law. Of course, IHL's isolation could simply mean that it is insignificant to these debates; however, this

10 Fassbender 2009, pp. 124–125, 145–146, Tzanakópoulos 2011, pp. 56–58.

11 Cass 2005, Petersmann 2008.

12 Dunoff 2000, p. 86.

particular position may be dismissed as an all too easy solution which, as this article will show, does not stand up to scrutiny.

This article seeks to confound comfortable claims regarding IHL's place in the international legal order and asks what contemporary debates tell us about this particular body of law in the twenty first century. As one of the originators of many of the core rules of public international law, from treaty interpretation to state responsibility, IHL is a prime example of how an area develops to become a fragmented sector of international law. On the other hand, it also appears to highlight the difficulties faced by a constitutionalisation process. Indeed, since it is staunchly traditional in its operation, it arguably provides an example of why public international law in the twenty first century is largely unchanged from its twentieth century form.

To consider the role played by IHL in contemporary legal debate, this paper will first give a brief account of how this body of law interacts with other aspects of international law. As with other specialist fields, IHL is not absolutely settled; nevertheless, it is possible to broadly outline its place within the international legal order. This article aims to set a firm basis for considering what current discussions on the future of public international law can tell us about IHL and vice versa. Following an examination of the interplay between IHL and international law, this piece will turn to two thematic approaches that dominate current international legal discourse, namely, fragmentation and constitutionalisation. A brief outline of the parameters of both approaches is followed by an assessment of how each has engaged with IHL. The article concludes with some thoughts on how IHL could make a contribution to these debates. Ultimately, this article will discuss and propose how engagement from both ends of the spectrum would benefit international law and suggest why such connections should be encouraged.

4.2 International Humanitarian Law and the Development of Public International Law

An examination of the historical evolution of public international law suggests that, for the great preponderance of its existence, IHL formed a core part of its content. This is perhaps only to be expected since IHL's origins can be traced to ancient times and to a period prior to the arrival of public *inter-national* law which evolved out of a need to regulate the relations between the emerging nation-States.[13] Grotius, Gentilli, even Blackstone, all considered IHL, or the laws of war, as central to the character of international law. Indeed, arguably for the majority of the international legal order's history *jus in bello* combined with *jus as bellum*

[13] Pictet 1985, pp. 5–25, see particularly, pp. 15–16 on chivalry and its influence on the development of international law, see also Grotius 1646, Gentili 1612, Blackstone 1758 Book IV Chapter V.

comprised the mass of international law. Some of the first international efforts to codify international law, such as the 1886 St. Petersburg Declaration, were entirely focused upon IHL.[14] Arguably, such codification was possible due to the body of customary law already in existence together with a willingness to negotiate on aspects that were considered vital but which had not, as yet, formed into customary law.[15] Yet, while just war theories and other elements of *jus ad bellum* waxed and waned, IHL remained steadfast, if not in its content, in its relevance and centrality to broader international law. Today, in contrast, IHL appears to be located on the periphery of public international law.

Contemporaneous to the codification of IHL, public international law began its ongoing exponential expansion.[16] The extent of the expansion of international law is evident in law school curriculums where public international law modules now merely introduce students to the basics of the system. Specialised courses on everything from trade, environment, human rights, international institutions and IHL provide the arena in which students learn the nuance of the practice which underpins the international legal order. This expansion inevitably has resulted in increased specialisation by both the academics and practitioners of international law. The role of both the military and the ICRC contribute greatly to this specialisation. These practitioners of IHL, entirely focused on this one area of law, are partially to blame for this trend, as their extensive knowledge, at times, prevents others occupied by international law to engage with the topic. Further, because IHL is only applicable in exceptional circumstances—in other words in times of armed conflict—it makes it safer for public international lawyers to ignore its existence, compared with other sectors which cannot be so easily by-passed. This specialisation has resulted in IHL becoming one of the most highly focused areas of public international law and has hastened its omission from contemporary debate. Indeed, most general public international lawyers (if any truly still exist) would only claim a basic understanding of humanitarian law and, as such, are slower to engage with it than perhaps other sub-genres within the international legal order.[17] While specialisation is also apparent in other areas of public international law, for example investment law, it is particularly acute within IHL. Specialisation also has the reverse effect as international humanitarian lawyers rarely engage with the wider contemporary debate and this has had a significant impact on the development of these debates. This is not intended as a criticism of expertise, which is necessary, but rather an observation which goes towards explaining the peripheral place that IHL occupies within contemporary debates.[18]

[14] Berman 2004–2005, pp. 15–16, *Legality of the Threat or Use of Nuclear Weapons*, Advisory Opinion (1996) ICJ Rep 226, para 82, Neff 2005.

[15] MacMahon 2010, pp. 496–497, International Committee of the Red Cross 2011.

[16] Lindroos 2005, p. 30.

[17] See as an example the relationship between human rights and IHL Provost 2002, pp. 2–3.

[18] Schachter 1995.

Within the international legal order, IHL is the only area whose operation must be triggered before coming into operation. This may occur due to the operation of *jus ad bellum*, the operation of the Security Council or the dissent into violent conflict within a state.[19] As with other specialised sectors within the international legal order, IHL relies on "general" public international law but, arguably, its unique status within international law sets it apart. Several factors, including the extent of its codification, its ancient pedigree and its general acceptance by all states, combine to distinguish it still further.[20] Although human rights law, the law of state responsibility, international criminal law, international environmental law *inter alia*, all have a baring upon IHL, the extent of its remit during armed conflict means that it dominates in a way that no other area of international law appears to do.[21] During periods of non-armed conflict these other areas clamour for room and authority; however during armed conflict humanitarian law comes to the fore and stands above, though not without the presence of, these other aspects of international law.[22]

Unlike other areas of international law, such as human rights or environmental law, the establishment of international law's institutions, whether in the form of the League of Nations, the United Nations, or even the international courts and tribunals, have been of secondary importance to the development of IHL. While the considerable case law of the *ad hoc* tribunals[23] and the International Court of Justice (ICJ) have contributed to the evolution of IHL, they are not the primary drivers behind the development of this body of law. Instead, they have had a major role in the cementing of international criminal law as part of the enforcement mechanisms for both IHL and human rights law.[24] While the role of the ICRC is considerable, states, not institutions, remain the primary promoters of IHL. Its absence from international institutions has meant that IHL is not at the centre of the debate on the international legal order's framework, particularly when institutions are considered central.

International humanitarian law's isolation manifests itself in several ways. For example, even though it is possibly the ideal candidate for exploring the evolution of self-contained regimes or *lex specialis* rarely, if ever, is it used as an example in general discussions on these topics.[25] Cassese argues that, '[t]he world community swarms with myriad legal orders.'[26] While IHL is clearly a very good example of such a legal order, it has largely remained outside these debates.

---

[19] Sloane 2009.

[20] Henckaerts and Doswald-Beck 2009.

[21] Dinstein 2005, p. 57, Berman 2004–2005.

[22] *Legality of the Threat or Use of Nuclear Weapons*, *supra* n. 14.

[23] The ICC will doubtless also contribute, though at this point at least, its case law is limited.

[24] Danner 2006, Kaul 2008.

[25] Simma and Pulkowski 2006, pp. 484–485, 529.

[26] Cassese 1990.

The role of IHL in the historical development of self contained regimes and *lex specialis* is rarely considered beyond specific occurrences or disputes. An explanation could be that that the sheer volume of IHL treaty law instils a sense of apprehension into many public international lawyers who do not feel comfortable engaging with a topic so heavily treaty-laden.[27] Second, there is no apparent eagerness to engage in such debates among IHL experts possibly because there is an assumption that IHL has largely settled its relationship with other areas of international law through the development of the doctrine of *lex specialis* and other mechanisms. International courts and tribunals as well as the vast majority of IHL scholars handle the interaction of IHL with other areas of public international law so adroitly that it is possible to argue that a clear, if not always definitive, understanding of their interactions subsists.[28] It might also be claimed that the on-going human rights versus IHL debate (which arguably is not as thorny as is sometimes suggested) takes away from a wider consideration of what the impact of a process of fragmentation or a movement towards constitutionalisation may have upon *lex specialis* or self-contained regimes.[29] This claim is not entirely persuasive since similar arguments apply equally to other genres of international law that are part of contemporary debates; it therefore follows that the justification that IHL constitutes a perfect working order is far from satisfactory.

The exceptionalism of international humanitarian law raises issues for any theory which seeks to outline the possible direction of the international legal order. Nonetheless, the opposite appears to be the case. Indeed, the proliferation of public international law has led to what could be described as the 'splendid isolation' of international humanitarian law as an area apart, but within the discourse of public international law.[30]

4.3 International Humanitarian Law and International Law

This section examines how the international legal order regulates the interaction of IHL with other areas of international law including general international law. The general rules applied by courts to reconcile differences between areas of law as well as the academic debate surrounding these rules are explored. The aim of this section is to set the broad terms by which IHL interacts with other areas of international law and thus it does not seek to settle when, and under what circumstances, general international law or other sub-genres of international law

[27] Dunoff 2000, pp. 87–88.

[28] Moreno-Ocampo 2010, Cassese 1998 and on the quality of Court's analysis Kretzmer 2005.

[29] Orakhelashvili 2008, p. 162 discusses the role of pre-conceived attitudes in the debate between human rights and IHL as does Cassimatis 2007, pp. 628–629, Draper 1979, Stephens 2001, pp. 9–14.

[30] Though this isolation is not related to IHL as a form of law.

triumph over IHL or vice versa. Three main methods of differentiating between areas of the law, *lex specialis*, self-contained regimes and the hierarchy of norms, are discussed.

The Fragmentation Report of the International Law Commission (ILC) lists four ways by which general international law settles the relationship between it and the various specialised international legal systems.[31] This taxonomy provides a useful foundation to examine how IHL interacts with the rest of the international legal order. The four methods identified by the ILC are: relations between special and general law, relations between prior and subsequent law, relations between laws at different hierarchical levels and relations of law to its normative environment more generally. The first and third group are the most common methods by which IHL interacts with other areas of international law. Given the controversy surrounding such interactions, they will form a focus herein. Although this article will not discuss these relational incidences in detail, the conflicts that do exist in the academic debate illuminate some of the reasons for the isolation of humanitarian law and further aids in discussing the place of humanitarian law within fragmentation and constitutionalisation.

The doctrine of *lex specialis* is probably the most commonly used and well-defined method of interpreting and understanding the relationship between IHL and general international law. As previously noted, IHL was at the core of the historical development of public international law. The well ploughed history of IHL is thoroughly discussed elsewhere and will not be the focus here, rather it is important to stress its historical place within public international law more generally and understand its development as a form of *lex specialis*.[32] The historical absolutist division of the laws of war and laws of peace has been abandoned so that while IHL takes precedence in armed conflicts, '[i]nternational humanitarian law must be applied in context with other principles and provisions of international law'[33] including the rules of treaty interpretation and the laws of state responsibility, as well as the more specific branches of international law.[34]

In circumstances of conflict the question of which law is applicable is resolved by the doctrine of *lex specialis*. Where two areas of law cover the same substantive facts the more specific law trumps its more general counterpart. Importantly, the

---

[31] ILC Fragmentation Report, p. 14.

[32] Greenwood 2008, pp. 105–124.

[33] Greenwood 2008, p. 72.

[34] *Lex Specialis* appears in Article 55 of the Draft Articles on State Responsibility and is defined as, 'These articles do not apply where and to the extent that the conditions for the existence of an internationally wrongful act or the content or implementation of the international responsibility of a State are governed by special rules of international law'—Draft Articles on State Responsibility, Official Records of the General Assembly, Fifty-third session Supplement No 10 a/56/10. These articles operate in a residual fashion, Commentary on Draft Articles pp. 140, 136. See also European Union Guidelines on promoting compliance with international humanitarian law at para 12—European Union Guidelines on promoting compliance with international humanitarian IHL law [2005] OJC327/04, UN Report Situation of Detainees at Guantanamo Bay E/CN.4/2006/120, p. 10.

specific law's application does not imply conflict between the two, both may require the same end, for example, the protection of human life, but if one is more specific on how to achieve this end or is most relevant to the circumstances it is applied. Alternatively, *lex specialis* maybe regarded as merely a tool of interpretation. However, knowing when to apply which law requires more than a mere requirement of detail.[35] Instead, understanding *lex specialis* as a method of exception enables a clearer view of its operation. Even if general public international law is also applicable, in situations of inconsistency or doubt between two areas of public international law, the area which possesses the more specific detail on the question at hand trumps the other. It is important to not consider this process as adversarial, *lex specialis* is part of the panoply of general international law.

The ILC Report examines several cases from the European Court of Human Rights, the Dispute Settlement Body of the WTO, the Permanent Court of Justice, the European Court of Justice, the International Court of Justice and the Iran-US Claims Tribunal to illustrate the use of *lex specialis*.[36] The application of *lex specialis* in other sectors of international law such as trade, investment and human rights law suggests that it is with regard to IHL that it has most traction as a point of controversy.[37] For example, the International Court of Justice considered the application of general public international law to IHL in several cases, including, most famously the *Nuclear Weapons* case, *The Wall* case and *DRC v Uganda*.[38] These cases illustrate how IHL applies within the structure of general international law and while the ILC Report argues that there are difficulties with it, as with most areas of law, these are not necessarily insurmountable.[39]

When *lex specialis* operates is not always obvious. The *Loewen* case states that a normative conflict arises when the express terms of a particular law 'are at variance with the continued operation of the relevant rules of international law.'[40] This variance, however, may not always be evident. The ILC Report suggests two specific difficulties with the application of *lex specialis*. First, it is not necessarily clear what is general and what is a special law and second, that the nature of the relationship of *lex specialis* with other principles of general public international law such as *lex posterior*, normative hierarchies or matters of relevance is not always apparent.[41] This illustrates the inherent problems in setting out *lex specialis* without considering other aspects of general international law, general

[35] Akehurst 1974–1975 '*lex specialis* is nothing more than a rule of interpretation' p. 273.

[36] ILC Fragmentation Report, pp. 33–39.

[37] Pauwelyn 2003, pp. 386–399.

[38] *Legality of the Threat or Use of Nuclear Weapons*, *supra* n. 14, *Legal Consequences of the Construction of a Wall in the Occupied Palestinian Territory,* Advisory Opinion [2004] ICJ Reports 136, *Armed Activities on the Territory of the Congo, Democratic Republic of the Congo v. Uganda* [2005] ICJ Reports 168.

[39] Greenwood 2008.

[40] *The Loewen Group, Inc. and Raymond L. Loewen and United States of America Award*, Case No ARB (AF/98/3, 26 June 2003, 42 ILM 2003 811, p. 837.

[41] ILC Fragmentation Report, p 29.

international law and its interaction with specialised areas as well as specialised areas themselves. Further, *lex specialis* is a necessary part of general international law, for example, in the interpretation of treaties. Arguably, when *lex specialis* is applicable, general international law always subsists, even if it is on the basis that *lex specialis* is itself a rule of general public international law.[42]

The first category in the ILC Report, identifying a special *lex*, is perhaps easier to divine with regard to IHL than in other parts of the international legal order. The effect of *jus ad bellum* and other triggers for its operation makes IHL's special nature more evident than in other areas of international law.[43] Unlike trade, environmental, investment and human rights law, which all exist concurrently, IHL must be triggered for the regime to be set in motion and the doctrine of *lex specialis* to be applied. IHL lies dormant until called into force. This differentiation between IHL and other self-contained regimes is significant and central to understanding contemporary debates and the isolation of IHL.

Self-contained regimes and *lex specialis*, though similar, are not interchangeable. The term 'self-contained regime' was first used by the Permanent Court of International Justice in the *S.S. Wimbledon* case to describe a substantive and self-reliant body of law.[44] In contrast, *lex specialis* requires only that a particular law be more detailed on a specific point, including a single treaty. Another difference between the two systems lies in their application. A self-contained regime, by its nature, can operate independent of other regimes. While self-contained regimes rely on general international law much of their operation is internal and particular to the specific legal regime, though not always in splendid isolation. *Lex specialis* operates in situations where both general and specific law, though not necessarily in conflict, deal with the same substantive question.[45] This is apart from situations of competing norms. It is possible for a body of law to be only *lex specialis* or both *lex specialis* and self-contained. Arguably IHL is the latter.

The second method highlighted in the ILC Report is the relationship between *lex specialis* and other norms of international law. Simma argues that, 'a certain degree of hierarchisation of international norms cannot be denied.'[46] If the character of the hierarchy is understood and operates effectively this is not in itself problematic, but herein lies the problem.[47] At first glance, normative hierarchies appear the most problematic issue in understanding the relationships between norms and are relevant to the debates on fragmentation, and constitutionalisation.

[42] Cassimatis 2007, p 631, Lindroos 2005, p. 31.

[43] Sandoz 2003, pp. 11–12.

[44] *S.S. Wimbledon*, PCIJ, Ser. A, No. 1, p. 23.

[45] Akehurst 1974–1975, p. 273.

[46] Simma and Pulkowski 2006, p. 496.

[47] Paulus 2005.

Their interaction is also important in understanding IHL's isolation and the operation of *jus cogens* norms is a prime example of the issues which arise.[48]

Certain *jus cogens* norms such as the prohibition of torture and genocide are also key aspects of IHL. Indeed, IHL uses core norms to maintain the minimum standards as much, if not more, than other areas of international law.[49] Nonetheless, conflicts arise regarding other norms such as immunity or the use of force.[50] This is an issue for IHL, which arguably is in line with *jus cogens* norms, and for other self-contained regimes such as international criminal law and *jus ad bellum*.[51] For example, targeted killings can lead to a conflict between IHL and particular rights, such as the right not to be arbitrarily deprived of life as a *jus cogens* norm.[52] Whilst, targeted killing is permissible under IHL, its boundaries are strictly defined as states must ensure their use of lethal force meets certain standards which keeps it within the bounds of *jus cogens*. While violations of these standards do occur, when this happens, theoretically at least, IHL combined with international criminal law ensures that enforcement mechanisms are in place. This is not to underplay potential tensions between aspects of IHL and *jus cogens* but rather suggests that international law has mechanisms for resolving these tensions in most situations and that the hierarchical value of *jus cogens* norms plays a key role in resolving such conflicts as they arise.

Questions regarding the interaction of IHL with *lex specialis* and *jus cogens* exist, but international law has developed mechanisms for settling these issues. Yet, such resolutions are dependent on the international legal order as presently understood and are not always successful in settling conflicts satisfactorily. The question remains whether, if a process of constitutionalisation is underway or if fragmentation is occurring, what impact do these processes have upon IHL and the operation of *lex specialis*, self-contained regimes and the hierarchisation of norms. If these are proved to be occurring what is the impact upon IHL? In a fragmentised or constitutionalised system would *lex specialis*, self-contained regimes or

48 Meron 2000, case law discussing *jus cogens* include, ICTY, *Prosecutor v Zejnil Delalić, Zdravko Mucić, Hazim Delić, and Esad Landžo* ('*Čelebići*'), Judgment of the Trial Chamber (IT-96-21-T) 16th November 1998, para 454, and *Al-Adsani v United Kingdom*, Judgment of 21 November 2001, no.35763/97 ECHR 2001. The ICJ's approach to *jus* cogens has been somewhat tortuous see, *Legality of the Threat or Use of Nuclear Weapons*, *supra* n. 14 at para 79, *Armed Activities on the Territory of the Congo* (Democratic Republic of Congo v. Rwanda) Jurisdiction and Admissibility [2006] ICJ Rep 1, paras 64 and 125. For a good overview of the development of *jus cogens* see Nieto-Navia 2003.

49 Hannikainen 1988, p. 606.

50 Gill and Fleck 2010, pp. 75–77, Linderfalk 2007, p. 866.

51 For a discussion on the relationship between international criminal law and IHL law see Kaul 2008.

52 Gill and Fleck 2010, p. 281, The Human Rights Committee in its General Comment No. 29 on the ICCPR, recognises the right to life as a *jus cogens* norm—see UN Human Rights Committee, 'General Comment No.29: State of Emergency (Article 4)', 31 August 2001, CCPR/C/21/Rev.1/Add.11.

hierarchy of norms suffice to rationalise the relationship between IHL and the rest of the international legal order?

4.4 New International Governance Theories

We now move to consider how IHL interacts with contemporary international legal theory with an emphasis on fragmentation and constitutionalisation. This analysis has two aims, first to understand how these debates deal with IHL and second to understand how IHL can add to and inform both these theories. The section also endeavours to clarify why IHL has all but been excluded from these discussions. Fragmentation and constitutionalisation are chosen as two, not necessarily opposing, but nonetheless divergent perspectives on the future shape of international law. As two distinct developments they should enlighten the varied perspectives on IHL's development within the global legal order. Fragmentation will be considered first, followed by constitutionalisation. They will then be compared in terms of their impact upon IHL.

4.5 Fragmentation

Fragmentation examines two processes within international law. The relationship between general international law and its various specialised areas and the interaction among these specialised areas. Generally, fragmentation centres upon the increasingly independent and ultimately stand-alone systems of international, regional and domestic law that have, particularly over the past 40 years, emerged. Fragmentation focuses on the process by which these sectors are becoming increasingly distinctive and, as such, more divergent from each other. The ILC Report defines fragmentation as 'the splitting up of the law into highly specialized "boxes" that claim relative autonomy from each other.'[53] This results in an increasing divergence among and volume of, self-contained regimes within international law.[54] The roots of fragmentation can be observed in the Pre-Charter era and therefore it is not a new development; however, debates regarding the impact of fragmentation upon international law have, of late, gained traction. The multiplicity of subsystems, be they trade, human rights, environmental or most importantly from our perspective, IHL suggest that international law is developing its own variety of *sui generis* systems.[55] The ILC's decision to commission a report on the concept emphasises the importance of giving consideration to the possible

[53] ILC Fragmentation Report, pp. 13–14.

[54] Simma 1985, p. 112.

[55] Mégret 2011, p 226.

ramifications of fragmentation.[56] Interestingly, IHL, though later given consideration, is marked by its absence from the ILC Report's initial list of areas which illustrate the fragmentation process.[57] This section questions whether fragmentation is manifest within IHL law and, if so, what impact IHL has upon fragmentation.

Fragmentation has several features. For example, fragmented sectors of international law are regarded as maintaining areas of overlap with both general international law and other fragmented sectors. Part of fragmentation describes the internal orders developing to meet the particular needs of these sectors of law. These fragmented sectors have an internal, though not necessarily external order and they develop and integrate at different speeds. Reaction to fragmentation is mixed. Observers tend to either see fragmentation positively as international law becoming ever more sophisticated or negatively as evidence of the disintegration of the international legal order.[58] According to its supporters fragmentation is a superior account of the present international legal orders than, for example, claiming the existence of a fully co-ordinated system. Fragmentation seeks to reflect international law as it presently operates; it recognises the complexities of a regime of law which is becoming more and not less intricate.

Lex specialis is often linked to fragmentation; indeed it is a central aspect of the ILC's Report. In the introduction to the Report fragmentation is described as a post World War II phenomena. Indeed, Jenks' key 1953 article on the topic appears to be a favourite starting point for many discussions on the process.[59] But was Jenks a visionary as suggested by Simma, Pulkowski and the ILC Report or, alternatively, could it be argued that IHL was already present as a prime example of a self-contained regime or *lex specialis* which substantiates a claim towards a trend of fragmentation?[60] Arguably, IHL is an early example of the increased specialisation of a particular area of international law which has since been replicated in, among others areas, trade, environmental, human rights and investment law.[61] Critically, the specialisation or fragmentation of IHL appears to have occurred earlier than in these other areas.

The ILC Report's analysis of the development and place of fragmentation within international law is highly detailed. The Report acknowledges that fragmentation is the continuation of an ongoing process of specialisation and therefore is not necessarily a negative process as it is sometimes presented elsewhere but

---

56 ILC Fragmentation Report.

57 ILC Fragmentation Report, pp. 9 and 11.

58 Koskenniemi and Leino 2002, Hafner 2003–2004, Simma 2003–2004, Buffard et al. 2008, Dupuy 1999, Benvenisti and Downs 2007–2008, ILC Fragmentation Report.

59 ILC Fragmentation Report, p. 8, Jenks 1953, p. 403, Klager 2011, p. 91, Simma and Pulkowski 2006, pp. 485–486, Tzanakópoulos 2011, p. 57.

60 Jenks 1953, p. 403, Simma and Pulkowski 2006, pp. 485–486, ILC Fragmentation Report, p. 8.

61 For a discussion of the role of fragmentation in investment law see, Klager 2011, pp. 89–112 and the interactions between trade, environment and human rights see Hafner 2003–2004, pp. 851–854.

part of the evolution of international law.[62] Yet, the Report's reflections on IHL are somewhat limited, its first direct reference is not until page 44.

The ILC Report discusses the *Nuclear Weapons* case and it is here that IHL is first discussed in detail.[63] Arguably, starting the discussion on IHL here automatically sets it as antagonistic to other fragmented sectors and general international law. The Report acknowledges that the ICJ decided that both human rights and IHL law applied in times of war. From a fragmentation perspective, the concurrent subsistence of both IHL and human rights law is crucial. The Report examines the Court's finding that in circumstances of armed conflict, where there is arbitrary deprivation of life, the *lex specialis* applicable is IHL, and suggests that an alternative interpretation is possible. The Report proposes that the judgement sets aside the established practice of the ICCPR which, in such circumstances, would regard human rights as applicable instead of IHL.[64] The Report subsequently suggests that the ICJ decided the case as it did because to have only applied human rights would have been idealistic so the 'Court created a systemic view of the law in which the two sets of rules related to each other as today's reality and tomorrow's promise, with a view to the overriding need to ensure the "survival of a State".'[65]

This interesting interpretation of the *Nuclear Weapons* case frankly puts IHL law in a strange position within the international legal order and arguably confuses it with *jus ad bellum*. It also highlights some of the reasons why IHL has not traditionally been part of the fragmentation debate. The 'scourge of war' is indeed a bad thing, but the rationales for war are the basis of *jus ad bellum* and it is its proper application that is 'tomorrow's promise.' Suggesting that the ICJ considered IHL to be the *lex specialis* and, as such, a choice resultant from cruel reality appears to ignore how IHL operates. IHL is not dependent upon reality or promise but rather operates to ensure the symmetrical treatment of those engaged in armed conflict. Also, arguing that the Court 'created a systemic view' of the law appears incorrect to the extent that they applied IHL correctly, as *lex specialis* during armed conflict. Besides the IHL reasoning, all law operates in 'reality', however much the promise of utopia might appeal.

Instead, the ICJ based their reasoning upon an interpretation of the law as it stands. The 'ideal' world with no war would be the product of *jus ad bellum*, among other political developments, and that issue was not before the ICJ. This suggests a bias against IHL, not based upon its content, but rather upon the uncomfortable actuality that requires its existence. This is perhaps part of the reason for its isolation.[66] Of course, the opposite, a prejudice against human rights

[62] ILC Fragmentation Report, p. 11.

[63] ILC Fragmentation Report, p. 44.

[64] ILC Fragmentation Report, p. 44.

[65] ILC Fragmentation Report, pp. 47–48.

[66] For a discussion of some of the complementary elements of human rights and IHL law see Zimmerman 2008, pp. 764–766, Orakhelashvili 2008, Cassimatis 2007 and on the case Lindroos, 2005, pp. 42–44.

law in favour of IHL, also exists in some quarters.[67] Nonetheless, in arguing that the ICJ was wrong, not on the basis of *lex specialis*, self-contained regimes, hierarchy of norms or indeed on fragmentation, but rather upon an idea of the Court being forced into a conclusion by reality, the Report perhaps missed an opportunity to engage with the possibility of IHL as an interesting example of fragmentation.

Klabbers argues that international and domestic law are quite similar in their approach to fragmentation.[68] Within domestic legal orders discrete areas such as intellectual property and family law rarely interact. Within international law, this is also the case. The converse is also true. In domestic law, there are areas such as contract and company law which frequently brush up against each other and, so too, aspects of international law. Arguably, these distinct areas of law are all specialised. Yet, within domestic law this specialisation does not inevitably lead to fragmentation and arguably this may also be the case within international law. Nonetheless, the need for a central governance order, an issue dealt with by constitutionalisation, becomes evident in taking account of the impact of fragmentation upon the international legal order which has only *lex specialis* and hierarchy of norms to settle any conflict.

An ongoing process of fragmentation, whether a positive or negative possibility, requires some reflection on the rules that already regulate the interactions of the various sections of international law. While, as suggested earlier, the very fact that IHL is triggered by very specific events makes it easier to pinpoint when it trumps other areas of international law, the lack of such a trigger in other sectors may create issues as further fragmentation occurs. In this respect, IHL may provide an example of how to regulate a fragmented legal order. The development of specific rules which establish an area of law's supremacy, be it trade or human rights, modelled upon the relationship between *jus ad bellum* and IHL, offers an additional tool to the international legal order in a fragmented future.

What does this brief overview of fragmentation tell us about IHL? First, IHL, despite potentially being a prime example of fragmentation, is infrequently discussed. Arguably, IHL is such a good example of fragmentation that it is a victim of its own success. As it has become more and more specialised, those involved in the fragmentation debate are less likely to be well versed in IHL. Alternatively, the lack of discussion of IHL could be because the development of self-contained regimes, *lex specialis* and hierarchy of norms combined with the *jus ad bellum* have resolved how IHL interacts with other areas of international law in a systemised fashion. Nonetheless, even though IHL is both self-contained and a *lex specialis*, it forms part of the panoply of international law as one legal order. This is evident in the existence of human rights alongside IHL. Consequently, while IHL is a good example of the issues raised by fragmentation, it also contradicts the notion that a process of fragmentation disrupts international governance and

---

[67] Petrasek 1998, p. 560, Draper 1979, Stephens 2001, pp. 9–14, Cassimatis 2007, p. 629.

[68] Klabbers et al. 2009, p. 11.

further indicates that fragmentation is a long-running process that perhaps increases the strength of the global legal order.

The dearth of IHL in discussions on fragmentation is a missed opportunity for both. From the IHL perspective, fragmentation presents an opportunity to understand IHL as part of the evolution of the global legal order. From the fragmentation perspective, IHL is an excellent example of the specialisation and operation of a self-contained regime which frequently interacts with other areas of international law. While this brief consideration has raised more issues than it has settled, it does suggest more consideration from both perspectives would be worthwhile.

4.6 Constitutionalisation

International constitutionalisation is a difficult theory to summarise. The many variants and strands within the theory and the lack of agreement within it as to what the constitutionalisation of international law entails makes a neat summation impossible.[69] Constitutionalisation, outside any international characterisation, is a process by which a legal order transitions from a consent based horizontal order to one which is hierarchal and maintains core constitutional norms in its operation. Generally, international constitutionalisation comes in two forms: the first maintains that the entirety of international law is becoming one constitutional order while the second asserts that particular sectors of international law such as trade, or human rights law are in a process of constitutionalisation. Should constitutionalisation proceed, these two variants would have differing effects on IHL. This section questions whether constitutionalisation, in either form would result in change in IHL, how this would be manifested and what impact IHL has or should have upon constitutionalisation.

As with fragmentation, thus far, IHL has not been a focus of international constitutionalisation. Given the dedication of some authors to arguing that sectors such as trade, human rights and most significantly *jus ad bellum* and Security Council's role within it, are going through a process of constitutionalisation, its omission is remarkable.[70] IHL has all but been forgotten, yet arguably it is an important aspect of any domestic or international constitutional order. Even those academics that suggest the entire international legal order is going through a process of constitutionalisation do not tackle the potential issues raised by IHL. Theorists arguing for sectoral constitutionalisation need to consider why IHL is or is not going through such a process and what sets it apart from other sectors which are suggested to be constitutionalising. This section considers what these issues are

[69] As an example of contrast see single sector constitutionalisation Cass 2005, Petersmann 1999 and world order constitutionalisation Peters 2005, De Wet 2006.

[70] Fassbender 2009.

and suggests some potential methods of understanding them from a constitutional perspective.

IHL already operates within domestic constitutional orders and therefore it is not much of a leap as may first be supposed to establish how IHL and an international constitutionalisation process would interact. Indeed, customary international law ensures that states are bound to follow IHL and therefore even where no formal system is established IHL already subsists within domestic legal orders. Though caution must be exercised, as has been argued by Walker, there is no reason to confine constitutionalism to the domestic realm, exact emulation or transposition is not recommended.[71]

Of central concern is whether IHL is in a process of sectoral constitutionalisation or alternatively does it fit into the pattern of the constitutionalisation of the entire international legal order? Arguably, it is more difficult with IHL (particularly due to its close ties to *jus ad bellum* and international criminal law) to argue for a standalone constitutional order and this is perhaps why, unlike trade or human rights law, there are not any advocates of a sole IHL constitutionalisation process. However, if it is accepted that constitutionalisation can occur in human rights or trade law, there must be robust reasons why this cannot be emulated in IHL. If contented that the entire international legal order is becoming constitutionalised the impact upon IHL should be manifest within these proposals.

Any form of international constitutionalisation requires a re-consideration of the relationship between IHL and other aspects of public international law. In domestic constitutional orders (where IHL law also applies in incidences of armed conflict) probably the closest equivalent are models of accommodation such as martial law or states of siege.[72] As exceptions to normal practice both impact on the normal operation of a constitutional order. Models of accommodation have a long history in domestic legal orders. Roman dictatorship is a very early example of the suspension of constitutional norms to accommodate the necessary means to deal with emergencies.[73] While a constitutional dictatorship may not be an ideal model and is not advocated here, the notion that a constitutional system enables the operation of other laws in times of crisis is important.[74] These crises trigger the suspension of some, though not all, constitutional norms. Arguably a similar model already subsists in international law. The trigger effect of armed conflict upon IHL and the displacement, though not suspension, of other sectors of international law such as human rights provides a comparable model of accommodation.

Generally speaking, for a model of accommodation to come into operation, a trigger is required. A set level of violence or conflict is required before constituted power holders are enabled to decide that martial law, a state of siege or emergency powers are necessary. In the case of martial law in the UK, whenever state

[71] Walker 2008.

[72] Gross and Ní Aolain 2006, p. 17.

[73] Gross and Ní Aolain 2006, pp. 17–26.

[74] Watkins 1940.

activities could no longer function due to a breakdown of order, martial law was imposed.[75] A similar, though not exactly comparable requirement is necessary for states of siege.[76] Other comparable triggers are necessary in domestic law based around declarations of war, which are perhaps closer to Security Council procedures.[77] IHL could develop a similar constitutional trigger mechanism.

Dicey maintained that the operation of 'martial law' under UK constitutional law maintained public order whatever the cost to property or blood yet this did not mean the total suspension of ordinary law.[78] With regard to IHL the idea that ordinary law persists under martial law is important in an international constitutionalisation process. The separation of the laws of war and of peace no longer survives as both the development of *lex specialis* and the case law of the ICJ suggests. An international constitutionalised order, developing from a basis which would enable the continuation of the current international constitutional order, including those constitutional norms directly linked to human rights once IHL was in operation, would therefore respect traditional constitutional tropes.

States of siege[79] or martial law[80] no longer operate in their original form and largely have been replaced by systems of emergency powers. Nonetheless, the underlying rationale, that in circumstances where conflict reaches a minimum level the constitutional system allows for the suspension of some, though not all, human rights law, is a recognisable re-occurring theme within constitutionalism. Not all domestic constitutional orders explicitly refer to emergency laws; such powers are often set out at other governance levels or within legislation while other states have dual systems for different forms of emergency.[81] Whilst there is no ideal constitutional model of accommodation these states of exception have bled into international human rights as, for example, the European Convention on Human Rights and other rights regimes maintain the possibility of emergencies.[82]

IHL can be rationalised as the equivalent of a model of accommodation in international law. While *jus ad bellum* falls outside the realm of IHL, it is directly linked to it and would also form part of an international model. The proposition that IHL is a model of accommodation has been made by Gross and Ní Aolain quoting Justice Scalia's judgement in the *Hamdi* case. 'Many think it not only inevitable but entirely proper that liberty give way to security in times of national

[75] Gross and Ní Aolain 2006, pp. 30–35.

[76] Gross and Ní Aolain 2006, pp. 26–30.

[77] Gross and Ní Aolain 2006, pp. 17–26.

[78] Dicey 1915, p. 280.

[79] Gross and Ní Aolain 2006, pp. 26–30.

[80] Martial law is, of the two, closest to the use of military law, though not necessarily IHL law, Gross and Ní Aolain 2006, pp. 30–35, see also for a historical overview Fairman 1943 and the work of Dicey, particularly the final 8th edition which was the last volume which Dicey edited.

[81] Gross and Ní Aolain refer to Japan, US and Belgium as three examples of constitutions which are silent on explicit powers during emergencies, Gross and Ní Aolain 2006, pp. 37, 41–43.

[82] McGoldrick 2004, p. 380 Gross and Ní Aolain.

crisis—that, at the extremes of military exigency, *inter arma silent leges*.'[83] What makes the proposal here somewhat different is that it is set within international as opposed to domestic constitutionalism. Domestic models of accommodation are not perfect paradigms.[84] Depending on the domestic regime, models of accommodation can continue indefinitely with very low levels violence or conflict which would not meet the 'armed conflict' threshold necessary for IHL. Also, from a domestic constitutional perspective, though perhaps more clear-cut in international law, in situations of intrastate conflict where the differences between emergency and IHL are not always evident, differing triggers would have to be maintained in tandem. For those that advocate an existent international constitutional order, this is already established through the monist/dualist system of incorporating international law into domestic legal orders. Nonetheless, in a process of international constitutionalisation with multiple governance levels, reform of the role of constituted powers holders would be required to fully constitutionalise the system already established by *jus ad bellum* and IHL.

Jus ad bellum and IHL are bound together. Other than in instances of Security Council sanctioned actions (which may have to be reformed in any putative constitutionalisation process), a level of armed conflict is required to enable the state to use force to repel an attack and trigger IHL.[85] Naturally, this requires change for both IHL and *jus ad bellum*, although reform of the substantive elements of the minimum threshold of armed conflict is probably unnecessary. The systems for establishing the threshold of armed conflict, by contrast, would probably require reform.

A process of constitutionalisation requires the re-configuration of IHL's interaction with general international law. Constitutionalisation would affect both *lex specialis* and the hierarchy of norms and would incorporate core norms of constitutionalism. This presents two options. First, incorporating what is already occurring into a constitutional regime and, as such, maintaining much of the *status quo*. This, however, presents a quandary. If there is no real need for change then the current order must already be constitutionalised or at the very least be far advanced in the process of constitutionalisation. The second possibility, which presents more complications, but is perhaps more accurate, is that an ongoing process of constitutionalisation will occur which incorporates constitutional norms and moves international law into a more centralised and hierarchical system. Part of this process would be the entrenchment of core constitutional norms such as the rule of law or democratic legitimacy.[86]

While the constitutionalisation debate does not regularly engage with the substantive and procedural differences within constitutionalism a process of constitutionalisation would require that, for example, *lex specialis* be re-configured in

---

[83] Gross and Ní Aolain 2006, p. 326, *Hamdi v Rumsfield* 542 US 507 (2004), p. 579.

[84] Walker 2008.

[85] Dinstein 2005, pp. 175–216, 278–290.

[86] Nollkaemper 2009, Wheatley 2010.

terms of constitutional norms or, at least, in terms of a constitutional order. This probably would not impact on the substantive content of IHL but it is quite possible that the conflict between it and other areas of the global constitutional regime would set the terms of settlement differently to the *lex specialis* principle, which currently fulfils this role. Such constitutional reforms could result in more clarity regarding IHL's interactions with other areas of international law, but it may also involve a rebalancing of these relationships.

IHL in an international constitutional order requires a model of accommodation to replace or, at least, alter the operation of *lex specialis* or self contained regimes. One possibility would be to constitutionalise the 'trigger' which already subsists but would, by necessity, require reform building upon the current role of *jus ad bellum* and the processes by which the level of armed conflict necessary for IHL to operate is established. Obviously, such changes to the trigger for IHL would have to be in tandem with the development of a broader constitutional regime within international law which would also establish a firmer rule of law, democratic legitimacy, and rights regime as without these other reforms any model of accommodation would be open to abuse by the holders of constituted power by a combination of militarism and *jus ad bellum*. For example, reform of the Charter to ensure its operation within constitutional norms would require reform of both the structure of UN organs and the legal regimes which underpin their decision-making processes.

How much change within the international legal order constitutionalisation requires depends on whether a form of thin or thick constitutionalism takes root.[87] At a minimum, a hierarchy of norms within the international legal order would have to be recognised. Further, all aspects of the inter-relationship between these norms and the various sectors of the international legal order would need to be fully rationalised. Take the hierarchy of norms; within a 'thick' constitutional order norms such as the rule of law, democratic legitimacy, human rights and the separation of powers are present and ensure that a hierarchical order is maintained and that the legal system operates on a constitutional basis. Most importantly a constitutional legal order regulates the activities of constituted power holders. Arguably, this falls within the remit of *jus ad bellum*. Nonetheless the scope of IHL's operation is effected by thick constitutionalisation in the same manner as trade, human rights or environmental law.

Some proponents of constitutionalisation argue that *jus cogens* are the core of the process.[88] As IHL already aligns itself with *jus cogens* norms this is not necessarily problematic.[89] If a thick constitutional order is established, containing the norms of constitutionalism such as the rule of law, human rights, democratic legitimacy, separation of powers and the acknowledgement of constituent and constituted power holders, this may require IHL to be better drawn into a

[87] Walker 2008, pp. 526, 537.

[88] De Wet 2006, Fassbender 2009, Peters 2006.

[89] Greenwood 2008, p. 39.

centralised international legal order. This may necessitate the establishment of a more consolidated system of control where the disparate domestic systems, international criminal law, the ICRC, among other bodies, are regulated by minimum constitutional standards such as the rule of law and democratic legitimacy. Arguably, at present, these relationships would not meet the standard of constitutional norms. For example, the operation of the ICRC and the International Criminal Court probably would not meet the standards of oversight required within domestic constitutional systems, though this is not necessarily an issue for IHL.

What does the constitutionalisation theory tell us about IHL? As the debate has largely not engaged with IHL, it is difficult to establish how it would fit into a new international constitutional order or indeed into a process of constitutionalisation. As discussed, there are several possible outcomes based around the trigger for IHL's operation and its place within a constitutional hierarchy of norms. IHL's operation points to the existence of a crisis which an international constitutional order must regulate. This makes IHL's omission from the constitutionalisation debate all the more surprising. Any international constitutional order that cannot effectively tackle armed conflict arguably does not possess the elements necessarily to truly be described as constitutional.

4.7 Conclusion

Contemporary debates on international law largely ignore IHL. This is to the detriment of both international legal theory and IHL. By tackling one of humanity's ever-present negative conditions, war, IHL is an essential aspect of international law, The ICJ recognised this in the *Nuclear Weapons* case;

> It is undoubtedly because a great many rules of humanitarian law applicable in armed conflict are so fundamental to the respect of the human person and 'elementary considerations of humanity' as the Court put it in its Judgment of 9 April 1949 in the *Corfu Channel* case (*I.C.J. Reports 1949*, p. 22), that The Hague and Geneva Conventions have enjoyed a broad accession. Further these fundamental rules are to be observed by all States whether or not they have ratified the conventions that contain them, because they constitute intransgressible principles of international customary law.[90]

No scholar or state contends that IHL is an entirely detached regime of law. General international law, human rights law, law of state responsibility, environmental law, diplomatic law, trade law all interact with IHL. As discussed at the outset, mechanisms such as *lex specialis* and hierarchy of norms enables IHL to subsist and interact with general and specific aspects of international law. Yet, IHL remains aloof from the debates on the future shape of public international law, in particular, fragmentation and constitutionalisation. This article has sought to

[90] *Legality of the Threat or Use of Nuclear Weapons*, *supra* n.14, para 79.

articulate why this is the case and further what implications both debates could have on IHL.

Its highly specialised character has meant that most general international lawyers are unwilling to engage with the complexities of IHL. In contrast to continuously operating sectors of international law, IHL is so closely associated with *jus ad bellum* that it is only in exceptional circumstances that non-specialists must deal with the field. The eternal debate between IHL and human rights law, which sets an antagonistic tone between IHL as exceptional and other aspects of international law also contributes to this isolation. It could be argued that neither fragmentation nor constitutionalisation processes cause difficulties for IHL. Since IHL is perhaps a prime example of fragmentation its parameters are already understood and set. If IHL is not affected beyond the hierarchical value of *jus cogens* norms, the constitutionalisation debate is irrelevant. Yet, these claims do not stand up to examination. Fragmentation will probably lead to a further entrenchment of law as it is presently understood but not without the further development of *lex specialis*, self contained regimes and a hierarchy of norms to further optimise its operation. Constitutionalisation may not change the substantive content of IHL but it will require fundamental shifts in our broader understanding of the international legal order's operation. The need for a discussion of a model of accommodation further emphasises the need to reconsider the relationship of IHL to the trigger for its operation in a constitutional system.

Both fragmentation and constitutionalisation deal with the entire international legal order. As such, IHL's absence raises questions. Arguably, until both theories address these issues, neither can be wholly endorsed. While IHL's specialisation has made its isolation more acute, this makes its inclusion in these debates all the more pressing. If the international legal order is evolving beyond its traditional parameters then understanding the role of IHL amidst these changes is important. To allow IHL to remain in splendid isolation prevents these contemporary debates from fully realising their potential to shape the future development of international law.

References

Akehurst M (1974–1975) The hierarchy of the sources of international law. British Yearb Int Law 47:273

Benhabib S (2006) Another cosmopolitanism. Oxford University Press, Oxford

Benvenisti E, Downs GW (2007–2008) The Empire's new clothes: political economy and the fragmentation of international law. Stanford Law Rev 60:595

Berman N (2004–2005) Privileging combat—contemporary conflict and the legal construction of war. Columbia J Transnatl Law 43:2

Blackstone W (1758) Commentaries on the laws of England. Clarendon Press, Oxford

Buffard I, Crawford J, Hafner G, Pellet A (2008) International law between universalism and fragmentation: Festschrift in honour of Gerhard Hafner. Martinus Nijhoff, Leiden

Cass DZ (2005) The constitutionalization of the World Trade Organization. Oxford University Press, Oxford

Cassese A (1998) On the current trends towards criminal prosecution and punishment of breaches of international humanitarian law. European J Int Law 9:2–17
Cassese A (1990) Remarks on Scelle's theory of 'role splitting' (dédoublement fonctionnel) in international law. European J Int Law 2:210
Cassimatis AE (2007) International humanitarian law, international human rights law, and fragmentation of international law. Int Comp Law Q 56:623
Danner AM (2006) When courts make law: how the international criminal tribunals recast the laws of war. Vanderbilt Law Rev 59:2
De Wet E (2006) The international constitutional order. Int Comp Law Q 55:51
Dicey AV (1915) Introduction to the study of the law of the constitution. MacMillian, London
Dinstein Y (2005) War, aggression and self-defence. Cambridge University Press, Cambridge
Domingo R (2011) Gaius, Vattel, and the new global law paradigm. European J Int Law 22:627
Draper G (1979) Humanitarian law and human rights. Acta Juridica 193:205
Dunoff JL (2000) International legal scholarship at the millennium. Chic J Int Law 1:85
Dunoff JL, Trachtman JP (eds) (2009) Ruling the world? Constitutionalism, international law, and global governance. Cambridge University Press, Cambridge
Dupuy P (1999) The danger of fragmentation or unification in the international legal system and the international court of justice. N Y J Law Policy 31:791
Fairman C (1943) The law of martial rule. Callaghan, Chicago
Fassbender B (2009) The United Nations Charter as the constitution of the international community. Brill, Leiden
Feldman N (2006) Cosmopolitan law? Yale Law J 116:101
Gentili A (1612) De iure belli libri tres. (Rolfe JC Translator). Clarendon Press, London
Gill TD, Fleck D (2010) The handbook of the international law of military operations. Oxford University Press, Oxford
Greenwood C (2008) Scope of application of humanitarian law. In: Fleck D (ed) International law. Oxford University Press, Oxford
Gross O, Ní Aolain F (2006) Law in times of crisis emergency powers in theory and practice. Cambridge University Press, Cambridge
Grotius H (1646) De jure belli ac pacis libri tres. (Kelsey, FW Translator). Clarendon Press, Oxford
Hafner G (2003–2004) Pros and cons ensuing from fragmentation of international law. Mich J Int Law 225:849
Hannikainen L (1988) Peremptory norms in international humanitarian law. Finnish Lawyers' Publishing, Helsinki
Hart HLA (1965) The concept of law. Clarendon Press, Oxford
Henckaerts J, Doswald-Beck L (2009) Customary international humanitarian law. Cambridge University Press, Cambridge
ILC Fragmentation Report, International Law Commission (2006) Fragmentation of international law: difficulties arising from the diversification and expansion of international law. Yearbook of the international law commission, vol II, Part 2
International Committee of the Red Cross (2011) Customary International Humanitarian Law Database. http://www.icrc.org/customary-ihl/eng/docs/home. Accessed 22 Nov 2011
Jenks W (1953) The Conflict of Law-Making Treaties. British Yearb Int Law 30:401
Kaul H (2008) International criminal court—international humanitarian law at work. In: Buffard I, Crawford J, Hafner G, Pellet A (eds) International law between universalism and fragmentation: festschrift in honour of Gerhard Hafner. Martinus Nijhoff, Leiden
Kirsch N (2010) Beyond constitutionalism: the pluralist structure of postnational law. Oxford University Press, Oxford
Klabbers J, Peters A, Ulfstein G (2009) The constitutionalisation of international law. Oxford University Press, Oxford
Klager R (2011) Fair and equitable treatment in international investment law. Cambridge University Press, Cambridge
Koskenniemi M, Leino P (2002) Fragmentation of international law? Postmodern anxieties. Leiden J Int Law 15:553

Kretzmer D (2005) The advisory opinion: the light treatment of international humanitarian law. Am J Int Law 99:88
Kumm M (2009) The Cosmopolitan turn in constitutionalism: on the relationship between constitutionalism in and beyond the state. In: Dunoff JL, Trachtman JP (eds) Ruling the world? Constitutionalism, international law, and global governance. Cambridge University Press, Cambridge
Linderfalk U (2007) The effect of *Jus Cogens* norms: whoever opened Pandora's Box, did you ever think about the consequences? European J Int Law 18:853
Lindroos A (2005) Addressing norm conflicts in a fragmented legal system: the doctrine of lex specialis. Nordic J Int Law 74:27
Macdonald R, Johnston DM (eds) (2005) Towards world constitutionalism, issues in the legal ordering of the world community. Martinus Nijhoff, Leiden
McDougal MS (1953) International law, power and policy: a contemporary conception. Recueil des Cours 82:137
McDougal MS, Lasswell HD, Reisman WM (1967–1968) Theories about international law: prologue to a configurative jurisprudence. Vanderbilt J Int Law 8:188
McDougal MS, Reissman WM, Willard AR (1987–1988) The world community: a planetary social process. UC Davis Law Rev 21:807
MacMahon J (2010) Laws of war. In: Besson S, Tasioulas J (eds) The philosophy of international law. Oxford University Press, Oxford
McGoldrick D (2004) The Interface between public emergency powers and international law. Int J Const Law 2:380
Mégret F (2011) International human rights law theory. In: Orakhelashvili A (ed) Research handbook on theory and history of international law. Edward Elgar, Cheltenham
Meron T (2000) The humanization of humanitarian law. Am J Int Law 94:239
Moreno-Ocampo L (2010) The international criminal court—some reflections. Yearb Int Humanit Law 12:3
Neff SC (2005) War and the law of nations: a general history. Cambridge University Press, Cambridge
Nieto-Navia R (2003) International pre-emptory norms and international humanitarian law. In: Cassese A, Vohrah L (eds) Man's inhumanity to man: essays on international law in honour of Antonio Cassese. Martinus Nijhoff, Leiden
Nollkaemper A (2009) The internationalized rule of law. Hague J Rule Law 1:74
Orakhelashvili A (2008) The interaction between human rights and humanitarian law, fragmentation, conflict, parallelism or convergence? Eur J Int Law 19:161
Paulus A (2005) Jus Cogens in a time of hegemony and fragmentation. Nordic J Int Law 74:297
Pauwelyn J (2003) Conflict of norms in public international law: how WTO law relates to other rules of international law. Cambridge University Press, Cambridge
Pierik R, Werner WG (eds) (2010) Cosmopolitanism in context: perspectives from international law and political theory. Cambridge University Press, Cambridge
Peters A (2005) Global constitutionalism revisited. Int Legal Theory 11:39
Peters A (2006) Compensatory constitutionalism: the function and potential of fundamental international norms and structures. Leiden J Int Law 19:579
Petersmann E (1999) Constitutionalism and international adjudication: how to constitutionalize the UN dispute settlement system? N Y University J Int Law Policy 31:75
Petersmann E (2008) Human rights, international economic law and 'constitutional justice'. European J Int Law 19:769
Petrasek D (1998) Current developments—moving forward on the development of minimum humanitarian standards. Am J Int Law 92:557
Pictet J (1985) Development and principles of international humanitarian law. Martinus Nijhoff, Dordect
Provost R (2002) International human rights and humanitarian law. Cambridge University Press, Cambridge

Sandoz Y (2003) International humanitarian law in the twenty-first century. Yearb Int Humani Law 6:3
Schachter O (1995) International law in theory and practice. Martinus Nijhoff, Leiden
Simma B (1985) Self contained regimes. Neth Yearb Int Law 16:112
Simma B (2003–2004) Fragmentation in a positive light. Michigan J Int Law 25:845
Simma B, Pulkowski D (2006) Of planets and the universe: self-contained regimes in international law. European J Int Law 17:483–529
Sloane RD (2009) The cost of conflation: preserving the dualism of jus ad bellum and jus in bello in the contemporary law of war. Yale J Int Law 34:47
Stephens D (2001) Human rights and armed conflict—the advisory opinion of the international court of justice in the nuclear weapons case. Yale Human Rights Dev Law J 1
Tzanakópoulos A (2011) Disobeying the Security Council: countermeasures against wrongful sanctions. Oxford University Press, Oxford
Walker N (2008) Taking constitutionalism beyond the state. Political Studies 56:519
Watkins FM (1940) The problem of constitutional dictatorship. Public Policy 1:324
Wheatley S (2010) The democratic legitimacy of international law. Hart, Oxford
Wheatley S, Berman PS (2007) A pluralist approach to international law. Yale J Int Law 32:301
Zimmerman A (2008) Extraterritorial application of human rights. In: Buffard I, Crawford J, Hafner G, Pellet A (eds) International law between universalism and fragmentation: Festschrift in honour of Gerhard Hafner. Martinus Nijhoff, Leiden

Chapter 5
The Rules Governing the Conduct of Hostilities in Additional Protocol I to the Geneva Conventions of 1949: A Review of Relevant United States References

George Cadwalader Jr.

Contents

Lieutenant Colonel, U.S. Marine Corps. Lieutenant Colonel Cadwalader is assigned to the faculty of the United States Naval War College International Law Department. He is writing in his personal capacity and the opinions expressed herein do not necessarily reflect those of the United States Government, the Department of Defense, or any agency thereof. The author would like to thank Professor Mike Schmitt, Professor Ken Watkin, Colonel Rick Rousseau, and Dr. Louise Arimatsu for their invaluable assistance.

G. Cadwalader Jr. (✉)
International Law Department, U.S. Naval War College, Newport, RI, USA
e-mail: gcadjr@yahoo.com

M.N. Schmitt and L. Arimatsu (eds.), *Yearbook of International Humanitarian Law Volume 14, 2011*, DOI: 10.1007/978-90-6704-855-2_5,

5.1 Introduction

Unlike 171 other nations,[1] the United States is not a party to Additional Protocol I to the Geneva Conventions of 1949 (hereinafter AP I).[2] AP I complements and expands upon the 1949 Geneva Conventions.[3] It is comprised of supplemental rules governing means and methods of warfare, combatant and prisoner of war status, treatment of detainees, and protections of civilians and civilian objects among other important matters within the law of armed conflict.[4] The decision of the United States not to join AP I has resulted in what one prominent commentator describes as a "Great Schism" between the majority of nations bound by its provision and a "determined minority" who are not.[5]

As the world's preeminent military power, and one that has been involved in continuous armed conflict for more than a decade, the United States' interpretation and implementation of LOAC have significant ramifications for the international

[1] See International Committee of the Red Cross database of State Parties to International Humanitarian Law and Other Related Treaties (hereinafter ICRC database)at: http://www.icrc.org/IHL.nsf/(SPF)/party_main_treaties/$File/IHL_and_other_related_Treaties.pdf.

[2] Protocol Additional to the Geneva Conventions of 12 August 1949, and Relating to the Protection of Victims of International Armed Conflicts (Protocol I) Dec. 12, 1977, June 8, 1977, 1125 U.N.T.S. 3 [hereinafter AP I]. A companion Protocol pertains to non-international armed conflict. *See* Protocol Additional to the Geneva Conventions of 12 August 1949, and Relating to the Protection of Victims of Non-International Armed Conflicts (Protocol II), June 8, 1977, 1125 U.N.T.S. 609 [hereinafter AP II].

[3] Geneva Convention for the Amelioration of the Condition of the Wounded and Sick in Armed Forces in the Field, Aug. 12, 1949, 6 U.S.T. 3114, 75 U.N.T.S. 31 [hereinafter GCI]; Geneva Convention for the Amelioration of the Condition of Wounded, Sick, and Shipwrecked Members at Sea, Aug. 12, 1949, 6 U.S.T. 3217, 75 U.N.T.S. 85 [hereinafter GCII]; Geneva Convention Relative to the Treatment of Prisoners of War, Aug. 12, 1949, 6 U.S.T. 3316, 75 U.N.T.S. 135 [hereinafter GCIII]; Geneva Convention Relative to the Treatment of Civilian Persons in Time of War, Aug. 12, 1949, 6 U.S.T. 3516, 75 U.N.T.S. 287 [hereinafter GCIV].

[4] The U.S. Department of Defense uses "Law of Armed Conflict" and "Law of War" interchangeably in official publications; however, "Law of War" is the official term, see para 5.C. of Chairman of the Joint Chiefs of Staff Instruction 5810.01D, "Implementation of the DOD Law of War Program" (30 April 2010).The Department of Defense specifically rejects the term "international humanitarian law." Ibid. at p. 2, n. 1. The author will use the term "Law of Armed Conflict" in this article.

[5] Dinstein 2010, at p. 16. There are 193 Member States of the United Nations (see http://www.un.org/depts/dhl/unms/whatisms.shtml).

community.[6] Operationally, because most of the US' key allies and partners are party to the Protocol,[7] differing legal obligations between coalition partners affect interoperability in multinational operations.[8] More broadly, the manner in which the United States conducts hostilities constitutes significant state practice that may, depending on the extent it converges or diverges with the practice of other nations, shape or frustrate the development of customary international law.[9]

Unfortunately, there is no single authoritative reference detailing those provisions of AP I the US accepts as an accurate restatement of customary international law or other legal obligations, or that it follows as a matter of policy during armed conflict. This paper seeks to partially address that lacuna through a systematic review of official US policies, directives, publications, treaty obligations, laws, and proclamations pertinent to those provisions of AP I governing the conduct of hostilities.[10] This paper will not opine whether any of these official materials are conclusive proof that the US accepts any specific provision of AP I as customary

---

[6] The Legal Adviser for the International Committee of the Red Cross has observed that the "failure to ratify by a major power such as the United States would deprive the world of a common framework for the humanitarian rules governing armed conflicts. It would hinder the development and acceptance of universal standards in a field where they are particularly needed: armed conflict." Gasser 1987, at p. 924.

[7] For example, see the following ratification/accession dates: Australia—21 June 1991; Belgium—20 May 1996; Canada—20 November 1990; France—11 April 2001; Germany—14 February 1991; Italy—27 February 1986; Japan—31 August 2004; Republic of Korea—15 January 1982; Netherlands; 26 June 1987; Spain—21 April 1989; United Kingdom—28 January 1998.

States that have not become Parties to AP I include, *inter alia*, India, Iran, Israel, Pakistan, and Turkey. See ICRC database, *supra* n. 1.

[8] The United States Army Center for Law and Military Operations (CLAMO) compiles After Action Reports (AAR) of lessons learned from judge advocates (uniformed military attorneys) deployed in support of overseas military operations. These volumes devote significant attention to the importance of understanding and integrating the legal constrains and restraints of coalition partners into the planning process. In particular, see CLAMO 2008, at p. 331."

[9] The International Court of Justice held that in the formation of customary international law, "[s]tate practice, including that of *States whose interests are specially affected*, should have been both extensive and virtually uniform in the sense of the provision invoked and should moreover have occurred in such a way as to show a general recognition that a rule of law or lègal obligation is involved." *North Sea Continental Shelf Cases Federal Republic of Germany v. Denmark; Federal Republic of Germany v. Netherlands* (1969) I.C.J. Reports, pp. 4,43 as quoted in Bellinger and Haynes 2007, at p. 445, n. 4.(emphasis in original). This article, containing the aforementioned quote from the International Court of Justice, is the published version of a letter submitted by John B. Bellinger, III, Legal Adviser US Department of State and William J. Haynes, General Counsel US Department of Defense to Dr. Jacob Kellenberger, President, International Committee of the Red Cross of 3 November 2006. The letter describes the initial reaction of the United States Government to the International Committee of the Red Cross study on customary international humanitarian law—see Henckaerts and Doswald-Beck 2005.

[10] These provisions are included in Articles 35 through 60 of AP I, *supra* n. 2.

international law.[11] Nor will it evaluate the merits of the US position with regard to the instrument. Rather, it will furnish a consolidated resource for the researcher who contemplates these questions. More practically, it will provide military operational law practitioners with US references that embrace, modify, or contradict provisions of AP I as they pertain to the conduct of hostilities.[12]

5.2 Background

On 29 January 1987, President Ronald Reagan informed the Senate that he would not submit AP I for its advice and consent to ratification declaring the treaty to be "fundamentally and irreconcilably flawed."[13] As will be discussed below, this decision constituted an about face for the United States. The US had signed the Protocol on the first day it was open for signature and its ratification seemed all but certain to those who had negotiated the treaty. A review of the US assessment of AP I during negotiations and thereafter provides useful background on the United States understanding of certain provisions, the scope of AP I, and its legal and policy implications.

5.2.1 United States Involvement in AP I Negotiations and Initial Decision to Sign AP I

The United States played an active role in the negotiations of AP I.[14] Ambassador George H. Aldrich, who served as head of the US delegation, noted that "[w]hen the Geneva Diplomatic Convention finished its four years of work in 1977 with

---

[11] The degree to which official publications evince the existence of customary international law is disputed. Bellinger and Haynes 2007, at p. 445 reads "the United States is troubled by the type of practice on which the [ICRC study on customary international humanitarian law] has, in too many placed relied. The initial U.S. review of the State practice volumes suggest that the study places too much emphasis on written materials, such as military manuals and other guidelines published by States, as opposed to the actual operational practice by States during armed conflict. Although manuals provide important indications of State behavior and *opinio juris* they cannot be a replacement for a meaningful assessment of operational state practice in connection with actual military operations."

[12] Paragraph 4.1 of Department of Defense Directive 2311.01E, "DOD Law of War Program" (9 May 2006 w/Change 1 of 15 Nov 2010)[hereinafter DOD Law of War Program], states that is Department of Defense Policy that "DOD components comply with the law of war during all armed conflicts, however such conflicts are characterized, and in all other military operations." Accordingly, although AP I is only applicable to international armed conflict, the extent to which the United States follows its rules will also have bearing in how the United States conducts hostilities in non-international armed conflict.

[13] Letter of Transmittal from President Ronald Reagan, Protocol II Additional to the 1949 Geneva Conventions, and Relating to the Protections of Victims of Non International Armed Conflicts, S. Treaty Doc. No. 2, 100th Cong., 1st Sess., at III (1987) [hereinafter Letter of Transmittal]. The Letter of Transmittal recommends ratification of AP II, but states the United States should not ratify AP I.

[14] The Diplomatic Conference on the Reaffirmation and Development of International Humanitarian Law Applicable in Armed Conflict [hereinafter "CDDH"] drafted AP I and AP

adoption of Protocols I and II, I stated the following on behalf of my Government: 'The United States welcomes the adoption of Protocol I. We are satisfied this Protocol represents a major advance in international humanitarian law, an advance of which this Conference can be proud. We hope that it will be signed and ratified by all the States represented in this conference.'"[15]

Aldrich's report of the Convention to the Department of State lauded AP I for its provisions protecting military medical aircraft, requiring better accounting for the missing of the dead, refining eligibility for prisoner of war status, and protecting civilians from the effects of war. However, he recommended that upon signature or ratification the US consider a statement of understanding concerning the application of AP I to nuclear weapons and a reservation preserving rights of reprisal.[16]

With regard to nuclear weapons, Aldrich advised there were provisions in AP I that would appear to have application to the use of nuclear weapons, such as Article 55 regarding protection of the natural environment against widespread, long-term, and severe damage. However, it was the understanding of the US delegation that the Protocol only applied to the effects of conventional weapons.[17]

He also reported that a number of Articles in AP I had the effect of unduly curtailing the right of reprisal, to include the provision in Article 51 that prohibits

---

(Footnote 14 continued)
II, *supra* n. 2, over four sessions held between 1974 and 1977. The Final Act of the CDDH provides the dates the Conference was in session, the States and organizations represented, and the names and nationalities of the key officials. The Final Act is reprinted in Schindler and Toman 2004, at p. 699 *et. seq*. The Official Records of the CDDH are comprised of seventeen volumes [hereinafter 'Official Records']. Electronic copies of these volumes may be obtained at http://www.loc.gov/rr/frd/Military_Law/RC-dipl-conference-records.html.

15 Aldrich 1991.

16 Report of the U.S. Delegation to the Diplomatic Conference on the Reaffirmation and Development of International Humanitarian Law in Armed Conflicts—Fourth Session—March 17-June 10,1977 submitted to the Secretary of States by George H. Aldrich, Chairman of the Delegation on Sept 8, 1977, 30–31.[hereinafter Delegation Report].

17 Ibid. at 919. The Official Records of the CCDH summarized Aldrich's statement on the applicability of AP I to nuclear weapons as "[i]t was his Government's understanding that the rules established by the Protocol were not intended to have any effect on, and did not regulate or prohibit the use of, nuclear weapons." Official Records, *supra* n. 14, at Vol. II, p. 285 [CDDH/SR. 58/Para 82]. Upon ratification of AP I, several nations expressed similar understandings. See reservations and declarations of Canada, France, Germany, Italy, The Netherlands, Spain, and the United Kingdom reprinted in Schindler and Toman 2004 at pp. 797, 800, 802, 807, 809, 813, and 816 respectively.

Paragraphs 1838 to 1862 of the *Commentary on the Additional Protocols of 8 June 1977 to the Geneva Conventions of 12 August 1949* discuss the applicability of AP 1 to nuclear weapons. The AP I Commentary concluded that during negotiations an agreement was reached not discuss nuclear weapons. Moreover, it determined the use of nuclear weapons is not specifically prohibited by AP I or other sources of international law. Rather, AP I reaffirmed existing principles and rules of international humanitarian law that "severely restrict" the use of nuclear weapons to include the prohibition against employment of weapons that cause superfluous injury or unnecessary suffering, the prohibition against indiscriminate attacks, and the obligation to distinguish between the civilian population and combatants. Sandoz et al. 1987, at paras 1852 and 1859.

reprisals against the civilian population of the enemy. He wrote, "It is unreasonable to think that massive and continuing attacks directed against a nation's civilian population could be absorbed without a response in kind. By denying the possibility of response and not offering any workable substitute, Article 51 is unrealistic and cannot be expected to withstand the test of future conflicts."[18]

In a 1991 article calling for the ratification of AP I, Aldrich described official statements made by the US delegation during negotiations reflecting the delegation's understanding of certain important provisions in AP I.[19] Given the historical context they provide, they are reproduced below. The accompanying footnotes explain the AP I provisions to which the understandings pertain.

(1) "[T]he rules established by the Protocol were not intended to have any effect on, and do not regulate or prohibit, the use of nuclear weapons."[20]
(2) "[T]he situations in which combatants could not distinguish themselves throughout their military operations, as stated in Article 44, para 3, could exist only in the exceptional circumstances of territory occupied by an adversary or in those armed conflicts described in Article 1, para 4."[21]
(3) "[T]he phrase 'military deployment preceding the launching of an attack,' in Article 44, para 3, means any movement toward a place from which an attack is to be launched."[22]
(4) "[A] specific area of land may be a military objective if, because of its location or other reasons specified in Article 52, its total or partial destruction,

[18] Delegation Report, *supra* n. 16, at p. 919. This concern was shared by other nations. For instance, in its reservations and declarations made upon ratification of AP I, the United Kingdom stated it would be entitled to take reprisals against the civilian population, civilians, or civilian objects of an adversary for the sole purpose of compelling the adverse power to cease serious and deliberate violations of Articles 51 to 55. Such reprisals require approval by the highest level of government, are only authorized after formal warnings have been disregarded, and must not be disproportionate to the violations of the adversary. Moreover, no reprisal may be taken in violation of the Geneva Conventions of 1949 and the right of reprisal terminates after the enemy discontinues their violations. See Schindler and Toman 2004, at p. 817.

[19] Aldrich 1991.

[20] Ibid. at p. 18.

[21] Ibid. This understanding pertains to two of the most controversial provisions of Additional Protocol I (discussed in more detail *infra* in the text accompanying notes 30–36), namely Articles 1(4) and 44(3). Aldrich argued that these rules have the salutary effect of protecting irregular forces fighting against occupying powers, for whom blending in with the civilian population when not engaged in hostilities is essential to their survival. Aldrich 1991 at p. 8. The full statement of the US delegation regarding this understanding can be found at Official Records, *supra* n. 14, at Vol. VI p. 150 [CDDH/SR. 41/Para 45].

[22] Aldrich 1991 at p. 18. This understanding pertains to the provision in Article 44(3)(b) that allows irregular fighters to maintain their combatant status so long as they carry their arms openly "during such time that he is visible to the enemy while he is engaged in a military deployment proceeding the launching of an attack in which he is to participate."

The full statement of the US delegation regarding this understanding can be found at Official Records, *supra* n. 14, at Vol. VI, p. 150 [CDDH/SR. 41/Para 46].

capture or neutralization, in the circumstances ruling at the time, offers definite military advantage."[23]

(5) "[T]he first sentence of para 2 of Article 52 prohibits only such attacks as may be directed against nonmilitary objectives and does not deal with the question of collateral damage."[24]

(6) "[I]f the cultural objects and places of worship protected by Article 53 are used in support of the military effort, they lose the special protection of that article."[25]

(7) "[I]n relation to Articles 51 through 58, commanders and others responsible for planning, deciding upon, or executing attacks necessarily have to reach decisions on the basis of their assessment of the information from all sources that is available to them at the relevant time."[26]

(8) "[T]he reference in Articles 51 and 57 to "military advantage" means the advantage anticipated from the attack considered as a whole and not only from isolated or particular parts of that attack."[27]

The US signed AP I on 12 December 1977, the first day the Protocol was open for signature[28] subject to two understandings. These understandings were first, "the rules established by this protocol were not intended to have any effect on and do not regulate or prohibit the use of nuclear weapons;" and, second "the phrase

---

[23] Aldrich 1991, at p. 18. This understanding pertains to Article 52(2) that states, in pertinent part, "military objectives are limited to those objects which by their nature, location, purpose, or use make an effective contribution to military action and whose total or partial destruction, capture or neutralization, in the circumstances ruling at the time, offers a definite military advantage." The full statement of the US delegation regarding this understanding can be found at Official Records, *supra* n. 14, at Vol. VI, p. 204 [CDDH/SR. 41/Annex].

[24] Aldrich 1991, at p. 18. This understanding recognizes that striking military objectives may cause collateral or incidental damage to civilians or civilian objects and that collateral or incidental consequences are not prohibited by the rule. The full statement of the US delegation regarding this understanding can be found at Official Records, *supra* note 14, at Vol. VI p. 204 [CDDH/SR. 41/Annex].

[25] Aldrich 1991, at p. 18. This understanding clarifies that protected property may be attacked if the adversary has improperly employed the protected property for military purposes. The full statement of the US delegation regarding this understanding can be found at Official Records, *supra* n. 14, at Vol. VI, p. 240–41 [CDDH/SR. 42/Annex].

[26] Aldrich 1991, at p. 18. Articles 51 through 58 establish rules for the protection of civilians, civilian objects, and the natural environment during military operations. This understanding emphasizes that the propriety of decisions made by commanders and their staffs under these rules are evaluated based on the information known to them at the time, and not by *ex post facto* information. The full statement of the US delegation regarding this understanding can be found at Official Records, *supra* n. 14, at Vol. VI p. 241 [CDDH/SR. 42/Annex].

[27] This understanding pertains to the proportionality test articulated in Articles 51(5)(b) and 57(2)(a)(iii) which require combat leaders to refrain from attacks which "may be expected to cause incidental loss of civilian life, injury to civilians, damage to civilian objects, or a combination thereof, which would be excessive in relation to the concrete and direct military advantage anticipated." The full statement of the US delegation regarding this understanding can be found at Official Records, *supra* n. 14, at Vol. VI p. 241 [CDDH/SR. 42/Annex].

[28] Schindler and Toman 2004, at pp. 699 and 791.

'military deployment preceding the launching of an attack' in Article 44, Para 3, means any movement towards a place from which an attack will be launched."[29]

5.2.2 *The Decision Not to Seek Ratification of AP I by the Reagan Administration*

So what happened between signature in 1977 and President Reagan's decision in 1987 not submit AP I for ratification? President Reagan's letter of transmittal and the accompanying correspondence from his Secretary of State, George P. Schultz, highlight the concerns that arose during the hiatus that tipped the balance against submitting AP I to the Senate in any form. The concerns expressed therein included the following:

Applicability of AP I to Wars of National Liberation
Article 1(4) expands the applicability of the Protocol to include not only international armed conflicts as contemplated by Common Article 2 of the Geneva Conventions of 1949[30] but also "armed conflicts which people are fighting against colonial domination and alien occupation and against racist regimes in the exercise of their right of self-determination." President Reagan stated "to rest [applicability of AP I] on such subjective distinctions based on a war's alleged purposes would politicize humanitarian law and eliminate the distinction between international and non-international conflicts. It would give special status to 'wars of national liberation,' an ill-defined concept expressed in vague, subjective, politicized terminology."[31]

Protection for Irregular Forces
President Reagan noted that AP I "grant[s] combatant status to irregular forces even if they do not satisfy the traditional requirements to distinguish themselves from the civilian population and otherwise comply with the laws of war. This would endanger civilians among whom terrorists and other irregulars attempt to conceal themselves."[32] His comment pertains to Article 44, which modifies or eliminates three of the four traditional requirements necessary to qualify for combatant and prisoner of war status and modifies a third.[33] First, it does not require a combatant to wear a fixed

---

[29] Ibid. at 817–818.

[30] Common Article 2 states that the Conventions "shall apply to all cases of declared war or other armed conflict which may arise between two or more of the High Contracting Parties, even if the state of war is not recognized by one of them."

[31] Letter of Transmittal, *supra* n. 13, at IV.

[32] Ibid.

[33] For the traditional requirements, see Article 1 to the Annex of The Hague Convention (IV) of 1907, Hague Convention (IV) Respecting the Laws and Customs of War on Land and its Annex: Regulations Respecting the Laws and Customs of War on Land Oct. 18, 1907, 36 Stat. 2227. Similarly, see GC III, Article 4(A).

distinctive sign recognizable at a distance. Rather Article 44(3) states combatants are only "obliged to distinguish themselves from the civilian population while they are engaged in an attack or in a military operation preparatory to an attack."[34] Second, as it pertains to the traditional requirement that combatants carry their arms openly, Article 44(3) continues, "there are situations in which armed conflicts where, owing to the nature of the hostilities an armed combatant cannot so distinguish himself [from the civilian population], he shall retain his status as a combatant provided that, in such circumstances, he carries is arms openly: (a) during each military engagement, and (b) during such time he is visible to an adversary while he is engaged in a military deployment preceding the launching of an attack in which he is to participate." Third, with regard to the traditional requirement that combatants conduct their operations in accordance with laws and customs of war, Article 44(2) states that failure to do so shall not deprive a combatant of his right to be a combatant and, if captured, a prisoner of war.[35]

Secretary Schultz, in his accompanying letter of submittal, opined that "Article 44(3), in a single subordinate clause, sweeps away years of law by 'recognizing' that an armed irregular 'cannot' always distinguish himself from non-combatants; it would grant combatant status to such an irregular anyway. As the essence of terrorist criminality is the obliteration of the distinction between combatants and non- combatants, it would be hard to square ratification of this Protocol with the United States' announced policy of combatting terrorism."[36]

Military Objections

Finally, President Reagan noted "the Joint Chiefs of Staff have also concluded that a number of the provisions of the Protocol are militarily unacceptable."[37] Secretary Schultz provided some more detail: "The Joint Chiefs of Staff have conducted a detailed review of the Protocol, and have concluded that it is militarily unacceptable for many reasons. Among these are that the Protocol grants guerrillas a legal status that often is superior to that accorded to regular forces. It also unreasonably restricts attacks against certain objects that traditionally have been considered legitimate military targets. It fails to improve substantially the compliance and verification mechanisms of the 1949 Geneva Conventions and eliminates an important sanction against violations of those Conventions. Weighing all aspects of the Protocol, the Joint Chiefs of Staff found it to be too ambiguous and

[34] Article 44(7) makes it clear that this rule is limited in application to irregular forces.

[35] Read together, AP I Article 44(3), (4), & (5) provide that an irregular fighter who falls into the hands of the enemy while failing to carry his arms openly during a deployment preceding an attack (in which he is visible to the enemy) or during a military engagement, forfeits his right to be a combatant and a prisoner of war. However, the adverse Party must nevertheless provide "protections equivalent in all respects to those accorded prisoners of war by the Third Convention and by this Protocol," rendering the distinction to be mostly academic regarding treatment in captivity since he would enjoy protections equivalent to a *bona fide* prisoners of war. However, he would be susceptible to criminal penalty for his actions.

[36] Letter of Transmittal, *supra* n. 13 at IX.

[37] Ibid. at IV.

complicated to use as a practical guide for military operations, and recommended against ratification by the United States."[38]

President Reagan acknowledged that there were meritorious elements to AP I and informed the Senate that the United States was in consultation with its allies to "develop appropriate methods for incorporating these positive provisions into the rules that govern our military operations, and as customary international law. I will advise the Senate of the results of this initiative as soon as it possible to do so."[39] This report to the Senate never transpired.

5.2.3 Reagan Administration Criticism of AP I Provisions Governing the Conduct of Hostilities

Although the Joint Chiefs of Staff review was not released to the public, subsequent comments by officials in the Reagan administration detailed military concerns. In remarks presented to the Sixth Annual American Red Cross-Washington College of Law Conference on International, Humanitarian Law held on 22 January 1987, the State Department's Legal Adviser, Judge Abraham Sofaer, listed provisions within AP I that, among others, were objectionable to the military. His remarks were subsequently published in the American University Journal of International Law and Policy.[40] These provisions included Article 47, Article 51, and Article 56 and they are outlined below. According to Sofaer, these examples were not meant to be an exhaustive list of all the provisions found unacceptable by the JCS, but rather provisions whose flaws were emblematic of problems that permeated the Protocol.

Prohibition against Mercenaries. Article 47(1) states that a "mercenary shall not have the right to be a combatant or prisoner of war" and defines a mercenary, in part, as one who is motivated to participate in hostilities for private gain.[41] Sofaer opined that "[t]his article was included in the Protocol not for humanitarian reasons, but purely to make the political point that mercenary activity in the Third

[38] Ibid. at IX. Aldrich dismissed the assertion that the impact on military operations militated against ratification. He stated that the Department of Defense was very involved in the negotiations of AP I and concurred with the decision to sign. The only real controversial issue was whether or not to reserve rights of reprisal. He concluded that "references to military considerations were made simply to buttress the decision to reject the protocol—a decision that had already been made on different, political grounds." Aldrich 1991, at p. 11. W. Hays Parks, who took part in the Joint Chiefs of Staff review that ultimately recommended against ratification, states that such assertions are misleading. Parks 1990, at p. 76 n. 259. He said the Joint Chiefs of Staff had insufficient time to review AP I and voted in favor of signature subject to the condition of a "full military review prior to any decision as to ratification by the United States." Ibid. at 88.

[39] Letter of Transmittal, *supra* n. 13 at IV.

[40] Sofaer 1987. Judge Sofaer served as Legal Adviser to the Department of State from 1985 to 1990.

[41] For the definition of a mercenary for the purpose of Article 47(1), see Article 47(2).

World is unwelcome. In doing so, this article disregards one of the fundamental principles of international humanitarian law by defining the right to combatant status, at least in part, on the basis of the personal or political motivations of the individual in question. This politicizing of the rules of warfare is contrary to Western interests and the interests of humanitarian law itself."[42]

Prohibition against Reprisals. Article 51(6) prohibits reprisals against civilians.[43] Sofaer asserted that this blanket prohibition had unacceptable consequences. Specifically, he noted that "[h]istorically, reciprocity has been the major sanction underlying the laws of war. If Article 51 were to come into force for the United States, an enemy could deliberately carry out attacks against friendly civilian populations, and the United States would be legally forbidden to reply in kind. As a practical matter, the United States might, for political or humanitarian reasons, decide in a particular case not to carry out retaliatory or reprisal attacks involving unfriendly civilian populations. To formally renounce even the option of such attacks, however, removes a significant deterrent that presently protects civilians and other war victims on all sides of a conflict."[44]

Prohibition against Attacks on Traditional Military Objectives. Article 56 prohibits attacks on "[w]orks or installations containing dangerous forces, namely dams, dykes, and nuclear engineering stations... even where these objects are military objectives, if such attack may cause the release of dangerous forces and consequent severe losses among the civilian population," Sofaer asserted this constituted an unreasonable restriction on military targeting. He noted that the term "severe" had two flaws. First, the negotiations did not indicate what degree of civilian losses would qualify. Second, if the requisite quantity of casualties could result, the attack would be forbidden regardless of the military value of the target. In short, once civilian casualties reached a certain level, the target would be immune from attack. Although Article 56(2) removes immunity from attack in cases where the specially protected work or installation provides "regular, significant, and direct support of military operations," this limited exception did not redeem the overbroad application of the rule to "objects that would be considered legitimate military objectives under customary international law."[45]

5.2.4 Reagan Administration Comments on AP I and the Development of Customary International Law

At the same conference, Soafer's deputy at the State Department, Michael J. Matheson, articulated the United States position on the relationship between the Additional

---

[42] Sofaer 1987 at p. 469.

[43] Article 51(6) reads "[a]ttacks against the civilian population or civilians by way of reprisal is prohibited."

[44] Sofaer 1987, at p. 469.

[45] Sofaer 1987, at p. 468.

Protocols and customary international law. The remarks were also the substance of an article in the American University Journal of International Law and Policy.[46] This article is the only exhaustive public statement by a senior government official cataloguing the US view of specific provisions in AP I. Accordingly, it is often cited as expressing the US position on which provisions of AP I are customary international law. However, it is important to note that Matheson refrained from identifying those provisions which were exact expressions of customary international law.[47] Instead, he focused his remarks on the principles "we believe should be observed and in due course recognized as customary international law, even if they have not already achieved that status…."[48] While Matheson recognized that portions of AP I were customary international law, his remarks did not differentiate between principles the US believed to already be part of customary international law and those it hoped would ripen into customary international law in the future. Thus, his remarks cannot be seen as stating which provisions of AP I are legally binding in their own right. However, he provided greater clarity in listing the articles in AP I which the United States did *not* support as expressing customary international law and which should *not* be recognized as such in the future.

Whether Matheson's article was an authoritative expression of US policy has been disputed. For example, W. Hays Parks, a former senior Department of Defense attorney[49] maintains that Matheson's article reflected personal opinions.[50] The 2005 edition of the Operational Law Handbook published by the United States Army Judge Advocate General's Legal Center and School cited the Matheson article as authority for its list of the AP I articles that the US viewed as either "legally binding as customary international law or acceptable practice though not legally binding."[51] This echoed previous editions of the Handbook. However, an *errata* sheet to the 2005 Handbook stated the section should be disregarded because the Matheson article "takes an overly broad view of the US position."[52] Subsequent editions have made no reference to the article. Unfortunately, no explanation was given regarding where Matheson's remarks were seen as extending beyond official government policy. Of note, nothing in Matheson's article indicated he was speaking in a personal, rather than official, capacity. Moreover, in a 2006 article, Matheson said his public statement reflected the official position of the Reagan administration.[53]

---

[46] Matheson 1987.

[47] See Ibid. at pp. 421–422.

[48] Ibid. at p. 422.

[49] Parks served as the Special Assistant for Law of War Matters in the Army Office of the Judge Advocate General from 1979 to 2003 and as the Senior Associate Deputy Counsel in the Department of Defense Office of General Counsel International Law Division from 2003 until 2010. See biography in Parks 2010a, at p. 769.

[50] Parks 2003, at p. 519, n. 55.

[51] International & Operational Law Department, The Judge Advocate General's Legal Center & School, *Operational Law Handbook* (2005 ed.).

[52] Ibid. *errata* sheet dated 27 September 2004.

[53] Matheson 2006, at p. 546. Moreover, this Matheson article was cited as an authoritative reference in the Bellinger and Haynes 2007, at pp. 455–456.

Matheson's comments on the merits of those provisions of AP I governing the conduct of hostilities are provided in the following tables.[54] The first table reflects provisions cited with approval. The second, provisions rejected by the United States (Tables 5.1, 5.2).

Table 5.1 AP I provisions cited with approval

AP I Article	Matheson commentary
Methods and Means Article 35(1) & (2)	"[W]e support the principle that the permissible means of injuring the enemy are not unlimited and that parties to a conflict not use weapons, projectiles, and materials and methods of warfare of a nature to cause superfluous injury or unnecessary suffering."[55]
Perfidy Articles 37(1) & 38	"We support the principle that individual combatants not kill, injure, or capture enemy personnel by resort to perfidy and that internationally recognized protective emblems, such as the red cross, not be improperly used."[56]
Denial of Quarter Article 40	"We support the principle that no order be given that there shall be no survivors nor an adversary be threatened with such an order or hostilities be conducted-on that basis."[57]
Parachutists Article 42	"We... support the principle that persons, other than airborne troops, parachuting from an aircraft in distress, not be made the object of attack."[58]
Combatant/Prisoner of War Status Articles 44 & 45	"We support the principle that persons entitled to combatant status be treated as prisoners of war in accordance with the 1949 Geneva Conventions, as well as the principle that combatant personnel distinguish themselves from the civilian populations while engaged in military operations."[59]
	"We... support the principle that, should any doubt arise as to whether a person is entitled to combatant status, he be so treated until his status has been determined by a competent tribunal, as well as the principle that if a person who has fallen into the power of an adversary is not held as a prisoner of war and is to be tried for an offense arising out of the hostilities, he should have the right to assert his entitlement to prisoner-of-war status before a judicial tribunal and to have that question adjudicated."[60]

(continued)

[54] For a summary of all of Mr. Matheson's remarks, see International and Operational Law Department 2010, at p. 232. The Documentary Supplement also contains a memorandum from W. Hays Parks, LCDR Michael F. Lohr, JAGC, USN, LtCol Dennis Yoder, USAF, and William Anderson, to Assistant General Counsel (International), OSD, *Subject: 1977 Protocols Additional to the Geneva Conventions: Customary International Law Implications* (8 May 1986) that provides an advisory opinion regarding which provisions of AP I are recognized as customary international law and which should be supported "for eventual conclusion in that law." Regarding provisions governing the conduct of hostilities, this memorandum cites Articles 35(a) & (2); 40; 42; 45(3)(first sentence); 51(2); 52(1)&(2) (except the reference to "reprisals"); 57(1),2(c), &(4); 59; and, 60 as reflecting customary international law. Ibid. at 234.

[55] Matheson 1987, at p. 424.

[56] Ibid. at p. 425.

[57] Ibid.

[58] Ibid.

[59] Ibid.

[60] Ibid. at p. 425–426.

Table 5.1 (continued)

AP I Article	Matheson commentary
Protection of Civilians Article 51(2)	"We support the principle that the civilian population as such, as well as individual citizens, not be the object of acts or threats of violence the primary purpose of which is to spread terror among them."[61]
Proportionality Articles 51(5)(b) & 57(2)(a)(iii)	"We support the principle... that attacks not be carried out that would clearly result in collateral civilian casualties disproportionate to the expected military advantage."[62]
Civilians Participating in Hostilities Article 51(3)	"We... support the principle that immunity shall not be extended to civilians who are taking part in hostilities."[63]
Human Shields Article 51(7)	"We... support the principle that the civilian population not be used to shield military objectives or operations from attack."[64]
Starvation of Civilians Article 54(1)	"We support the principle that starvation of civilians not be used as a method of warfare."[65]
Precautions in Military Operations Article 57–60	"We support the principle that all practicable precautions, taking into account military and humanitarian considerations, be taken in the conduct of military operations to minimize incidental death, injury, and damage to civilians and civilian objects, and that effective advance warning be given of attacks which may affect the civilian population, unless circumstances do not permit. We also support the principle that attacks not be made against appropriately declared or agreed non-defended localities or agreed demilitarized zones. These various principles are reflected in Articles 57 through 60."[66]

Table 5.2 AP I provisions rejected by the United States

AP I Article	Matheson commentary
The Natural Environment Article 35(3) & Article 55(1)	"We... consider that another principle in Article 35, which also appears later in the Protocol, namely that the prohibition of methods or means of warfare intended or expected to cause widespread, long-term and severe damage to the environment, is too broad and ambiguous and is not a part of customary law."[67]

(continued)

[61] Ibid. at p. 426.
[62] Ibid.
[63] Ibid.
[64] Ibid.
[65] Ibid.
[66] Ibid. at p. 426–427.
[67] Ibid. at p. 424.

Table 5.2 (continued)

AP I Article	Matheson commentary
Enemy Uniforms Article 39(2)	"We do not support the prohibition in Article 39 of the use of enemy emblems and uniforms during military operations."[68]
Combatant/Prisoner of War Status Articles 44 & 45	"[A]rticles 44 and 45… relax the requirements of the [Third] Geneva Convention concerning prisoner-of-war treatment for irregulars, and, in particular, include a special dispensation allowing individuals who are said to be unable to observe this rule in some circumstances to retain combatant status, if they carry their arms openly during engagements and deployments preceding the launching of attacks….. [T]he executive branch regards this provision as highly undesirable and potentially dangerous to the civilian population and of course does not recognize it as customary law or deserving of such status…."[69]
Mercenaries Article 47	"We do not favor the provisions of Article 47 on mercenaries, which among other things introduce political factors that do not belong in international humanitarian law, and do not consider the provisions of Article 47 to be part of current customary law."[70]
Reprisals Articles 51(6), 52(2), 53(c), 54(4), 55(2), 56(4)	"[W]e do not support the prohibition on reprisals in Article 51 and subsequent articles… and do not consider it part of customary law."[71]
Works & Installations Containing Dangerous Forces Article 56	"We do not support the provisions… concerning dams, dykes, and nuclear power stations… nor do we consider them to be customary international law."[72]

[68] Ibid. at p. 425.

[69] Ibid.

[70] Ibid. at p. 426.

[71] Ibid. p. 426.

[72] Ibid. at p. 427.

5.3 Certain United States Treaty Obligations Concerning the Conduct of Hostilities with Provisions Analogous to AP I

The US is party to several treaties governing the conduct of hostilities that have provisions similar to or the same as those in AP I. The commonalities between these treaties will be outlined below since, to the extent these similar or identical provisions bind the United States, they reflect legal obligations shared with signatories to AP I.

5.3.1 Hague Convention (IV) of 1907

The US is a party to the Hague Convention (IV) respecting the Laws and Customs of War on Land and its Annex of Regulations October 18, 1907 [*hereinafter* "Hague IV"].[73] The Annexed Regulations to the instrument contain the substantive provisions. Of note, Hague IV is seen as having achieved the status as customary international law despite the general participation clause at Article 2 limiting its application to only those conflicts between contracting powers and only where all belligerents are parties to the Convention.[74]

The commonalities and, where applicable, the distinctions between the provisions of AP I governing the conduct of hostilities and Hague IV are outlined below for the purpose of illustrating the extent to which the obligations of the US under Hague IV match requirements in AP I.

Methods & Means. AP I Articles 35(1) and (2) declare "the right of the Parties to the conflict to choose methods or means of conflict is not unlimited" and "[i]t is prohibited to employ weapons, projectiles and Materials and methods of warfare of a nature to cause superfluous injury or unnecessary suffering" respectively. Article 22 to the Hague IV Annex states "the rights of belligerents to adopt means of injuring the enemy is not unlimited," whereas Article 23(e) forbids employment of "arms, projectiles, or material calculated to cause unnecessary suffering."

---

[73] See Hague IV 1097, *supra* n. 33.

[74] The International Court of Justice held the Hague Convention (IV) of 1907 is among the seminal Geneva and Hague conventions promulgating "fundamental rules [which] are to be observed by all States whether or not they have ratified the conventions that contain them, because they constitute intransgressible principles of international customary law." See *Legality of the Threat or Use of Nuclear Weapons Advisory Opinion* (1996) I.C.J. Rep 266 at pp. 256–57. This opinion noted that Nuremberg International Military Tribunal concluded that the regulations annexed to Hague (IV) "were recognized by all civilized nations and were regarded as being declaratory of the laws and customs of war." Ibid. at 258 (citing *Trial of the Major War Criminals, 14 November 1945–1 October 1946*, Nuremberg, 1947, Vol. 1, p. 254). See Dinstein 2010, at p. 15 and Roberts and Guelff 2005 at p. 68 for additional discussion on the incorporation of Hague Convention (IV) into the body of customary international law.

Perfidy and Treachery. AP I Article 37(1) states that "[i]t is prohibited to kill, injure or capture an adversary by resort to perfidy. Acts inviting the confidence of an adversary to lead him to believe that he is entitled to, or is obliged to accord, protection under the rules of international law applicable in armed conflict, with intent to betray that confidence, shall constitute perfidy." The Article lists examples of perfidy as feigning surrender; feigning incapacitation by wounds or sickness; feigning of civilian status, feigning non-combatant status; and feigning of protected status by the use of signs, emblem or uniforms of the United Nations or of neutral or other States not party to the conflict. This develops Article 23(b) to the Hague IV Annex, which forbids the treacherous killing or wounding of the enemy without further elaboration. AP I Article 37(1) is also distinguishable because it adds capture of the enemy to the list of actions which cannot be achieved by perfidious means.

Ruses. Article 24 to the Hague IV Annex reads "[r]uses of war and employment of measures necessary for obtaining information about the enemy and the country are considered permissible." AP I Article 37(2) also authorizes the use of ruses and defines them "as acts which are intended to mislead the an adversary and induce him to act recklessly but which infringe no rule of international law applicable in armed conflict and which are not perfidious because they do not invite the confidence of an adversary with respect to protection under the law." It cites "camouflage, decoys, mock operations, and misinformation" as examples of lawful ruses.

Improper Use of Emblems. AP I Article 38(1) prohibits "improper use of the distinctive emblem of the red cross, red crescent or red lion and sun or of other emblems, signs or signals provided for by the Conventions or by this Protocol. It is also prohibited to misuse deliberately in an armed conflict other internationally recognized protected emblems, signs or signals, including the flag of truce, and the protective emblem of cultural property." It also prohibits the use of the distinctive emblem of the United Nations unless authorized. These provisions expand upon Articles 23(f), 32, 33, and 34 to the Hague IV Annex which prohibit misuse of a flag of truce and the distinctive badges of the Geneva Convention.

Enemy Uniforms. AP I Article 39(2) prohibits the use of "the flags or military emblems of adverse Parties while engaging in attacks or in order to shield, favour, protect or impede military operations."[75] Article 23(f) to the Hague IV Annex forbids improper use of the military insignia and uniform of the enemy, without further amplification of what constitutes "improper."

Denial of Quarter. AP I Article 40 and Article 23(d) to the Hague IV Annex both prohibit the denial of quarter.

Persons Hors de Combat. AP I Articles 41(1) and (2) augment the rule in Article 23(c) to the Hague IV Annex that forbids killing or wounding "an enemy who, having laid down his arms, or having no longer means of defence, has surrendered at

---

[75] Article 39(3) states that the prohibitions listed in Article 39(1) and (2) do not affect the generally recognized rules in international law that pertain to espionage (that is gathering information about the enemy) or the use of flags in armed conflict at sea.

discretion."[76] Article 41(1) provides that a "person who is recognized or who, in the circumstances, should be recognized to be *hors de combat* shall not be made the object of attack." Under Article 42(2), a person is *hors de combat* "if he is in the power of an adverse party", "he clearly expresses an intent to surrender", or "he has been rendered unconscious or is otherwise incapacitated by wounds or sickness, and therefore is incapable of defending himself." The protection of this article is forfeited if that person engages in a hostile act or attempts to escape.

Irregular Combatants. As discussed above, AP I Article 44 significantly alters the requirements for members and militias and volunteer corps to qualify as combatants and prisoners of war established Article 1 to the Hague IV Annex as well as Article 4 to the Third Geneva Convention of 1949 for the protection of prisoners of war.[77]

Spies. AP I Article 46 and Articles 29–31 to the Hague IV Annex govern spies. Article 29 to the Hague IV Annex stipulates "[a] person can only be considered a spy when, acting clandestinely or on false pretenses, he obtains or endeavours to obtain information in the zone of operations of a belligerent, with the intention of communicating it to the hostile party. Thus, soldiers not wearing a disguise who have penetrated into the zone of operations of the hostile army, for the purposes of obtaining information, are not considered spies." Similarly, AP I Article 46(2) states "[a]member of the armed forces of a Party to the conflict who, on behalf of that Party and in territory controlled by an adverse Party, gathers or attempts to gather information shall not be considered as engaging in espionage if, while so acting, he is in the uniform of his armed forces." Both AP I and Hague IV recognize that a spy who is caught while engaged in espionage is not entitled to prisoner of war status.[78] However, they also acknowledge that if the spy rejoins his armed force after committing an act of espionage and is subsequently captured, his previous actions do not deprive him of a prisoner of war status.[79] AP I Article 46(3) has no analogous provision in Hague IV. It applies different criteria for what constitutes spying to members of armed forces who are resident of territory occupied by the adverse Party. Such individuals are only considered to have engaged in espionage if they gather or attempt to gather information of military value on behalf of their Party through false pretenses of in a deliberate clandestine manner. Moreover they may only be treated as a spy and deprived prisoner of war status if apprehended while engaged in espionage.[80]

---

[76] GC I, Article 12 also prohibits violence against the wounded and sick.

[77] See discussion accompanying notes 32–36, *supra*.

[78] AP I Article 46(1); Hague IV Regulations Article 31.

[79] AP I Article 46(4); Hague IV Regulations Article 31.

[80] This rule reflects the enhanced protection provided in AP 1 to irregular fighters, particularly when they are engaged in hostilities against an occupying power. "The basic premise underling [Article 46(3)] is that resident members of organized resistance movements in occupied territories are not practicing deception simply by appearing to be civilians even while engaged in such a military operation as gathering intelligence." Their information gathering would only arise to the level of espionage if they employed clandestine measures such as using a forged pass, concealed camera, or clandestine radio transmitter. See Bothe, Partsch, and Solf 1982, at pp. 265–266.

Undefended Locations. Article 25 to the Hague IV Annex prohibits "[t]he attack or bombardment, by whatever means of towns, villages, or buildings which are undefended." AP I Article 59(1) prohibits attacks against "non-defended localities." AP I Article 59(2) provides that a Party may declare a locality non-defended if it is an "inhabited place near or in a zone where armed forces are in contact which is open for occupation by an adverse Party."[81]

Warnings Prior to Attack. Article 26 to the Hague IV Annex requires that the "officer in command of an attacking force must, before commencing a bombardment, except in cases of assault, do all in his power to warn the authorities." AP I Article 57(c) provides "effective advance warning shall be given of attacks which may affect the civilian population, unless circumstances do not permit."

Protected Property. Article 27 to the Hague IV Annex requires that in "sieges or bombardments all necessary steps must be taken to taken to spare, as far as possible, buildings dedicated religion, art, science, or charitable purposes, historic monuments, hospitals, and places where the sick or wounded are collected, provided they are not being used for military purposes." AP I Article 53 states that "it is prohibited (a) to commit any acts of hostility directed against the historic monuments, works of art or places of worship which constitute the cultural or spiritual heritage of peoples; (b) to use such objects in support of the military effort; (c) to make such objects the object of reprisals."[82]

5.3.2 Convention on Certain Conventional Weapons of 1980

The United States is also party to the Convention on Prohibitions or Restrictions on the Use of Certain Conventional Weapons Which May be Deemed to be Excessively Injurious or to Have Indiscriminate Effects and its five Protocols and accompanying amendments (hereinafter CCW).[83] Portions of the CCW replicate language from AP I and as such suggest where the legal obligations of the US are the same or similar to Parties to AP I. The US' statements of understanding and reservations to these provisions are also instructive.

Protection of the Environment. The fourth paragraph to the preamble of the Convention reads in pertinent part that "it is prohibited to employ methods or means of warfare which are intended, or may be expected, to cause widespread, long term and severe damage to the natural environment." This is identical to the language of AP I Article 35(3) and Article 55(1). The United States signed the

[81] Article 59(2), API provides the necessary conditions to be fulfilled by a non-defended locality.

[82] Additionally, with regard to the provision in Hague IV Article 27 requiring the safeguarding of places where the sick or wounded are collected, GC 1 Article 19 and AP I Article 12 protect medical units and establishments from attack.

[83] Convention on Prohibitions or Restrictions on the Use of Certain Conventional Weapons Which May Be Deemed to Be Excessively Injurious or to Have Indiscriminate Effects, Oct. 10, 1980, 1342 U.N.T.S. 137 [hereinafter CCW].

Convention subject to the understanding this language in the Convention only applies to States who accepted the analogous provisions in AP I.[84]

Military Objectives. Amended Protocol II to the CCW regulates the use of mines, booby traps, and similar devices.[85] Protocol III to the CCW regulates the use of incendiary weapons.[86] Article 2(6) of Amended Protocol II and Article 3 of Protocol III define physical military objectives as "any object which by its nature, location, purpose, or use makes an effective contribution to military action and whose total or partial destruction, capture or neutralization, in the circumstances ruling at the time, offers a definite military advantage." This definition is identical to that set forth in AP I Article 52(2). Both of the aforementioned CCW Protocols define civilian objects as any object that is not a military objective.[87] This characterization likewise mirrors AP Article 52(1).

In a declaration accompanying its ratification of CCW Amended Protocol II, the US expressed its understanding that "an area of land itself can be a legitimate military objective for the purpose of the use of landmines, if its neutralization or denial, in the circumstances applicable at the time, offer a military advantage."[88]

Reprisals. CCW Amended Protocol II Article 3(7) prohibits the use of mines, booby-traps, and other similar devices in either offence or defense or as means of reprisal against the civilian population, individual civilians, or civilian objects. Although this language echoes the broader prohibitions in AP I prohibiting all attacks including reprisals against civilians and civilian objects, it is limited to the aforementioned weapons.[89]

Indiscriminate Attacks. CCW Amended Protocol II Article 3(8) also proscribes the indiscriminate use of mines, booby-traps, and other similar devices. It articulates three situations where the placement of such weapons would be indiscriminate.

---

[84] See United States Statement of Understanding reprinted in Schindler and Toman 2004, at p. 221.

[85] Protocol on Prohibitions or Restrictions on the Use of Mines, Booby-Traps and Other Devices (Amended Protocol II) as Amended on May 3, 1996, 2048 U.N.T.S. 133 [hereinafter CCW Amended Protocol II].

[86] Protocol on Prohibitions or Restrictions on the Use of Incendiary Weapons (Protocol III), October 10, 1980, 1342 U.N.T.S. 171 [hereinafter CCW Amended Protocol III].

[87] CCW Amended Protocol II, *supra* n. 85, Article 2(7); CCW Protocol III, *supra* n. 86, Article 4.

[88] See United States Statement of Understanding in Schindler and Toman 2004, at p. 232. Several Parties to AP I expressed their understanding that an area of land could qualify as a legitimate military objective. For example, the United Kingdom upon ratification of AP I stated "a specific area of land may be a military objective if, because of its location or other reasons specified in [AP I, Article 52], its total or partial destruction, capture or neutralisation in the circumstance ruling at the time offers a definite military advantage." Ibid. at 816. See also similar declarations made by Canada, France, Germany, Italy, and the Netherlands Ibid. at pp 798, 801, 802, 818, and 810 respectively.

[89] See AP I, *supra* n. 2, Articles 51(2), 51(6), & 52(1).

First, if the mine, booby trap, or similar device is not placed on, or directed against, a military objective then its employment would be indiscriminate. This language parallels the language in AP I Article 51(4)(a) that defines an indiscriminate attacks as "those which are not directed against a specific military object." CCW Amended Protocol II Article 3(8) stipulates that in the case of doubt whether an object normally used for civilian purposes, such as a place of worship, dwelling, or school, is being used to make an effective contribution to military action, the presumption is that it retains it civilian status. The presumption is also found in AP I Article 52(3).

The second situation arises where the method or means of delivery cannot be directed at a specific military objective. This corresponds with AP I Article 51(4)(b).

The third situation arises where the mine, booby-trap, or similar device is employed in a manner "which may be expected to cause incidental loss of civilian life, injury to civilians, damage to civilian objects, or a combination thereof, which would be excessive in relation to the concrete and direct military advantage to be gained." This balancing test is identical to the rule of proportionality codified in AP I Articles 51(5)(b) and 57(2)(b).

Protected Property. CCW Amended Protocol II Article 7(1)(i) prohibits affixing booby traps and similar devices to "historic monuments, works of art, or places of worship which constitute the cultural or spiritual heritage of peoples." This language is identical to the definition of protected property set out in AP I Article 53(a). The US expressed its understanding that objects described in CCW Amended Protocol II Article 7(1)(i) refer "only to a limited class of objects that, because of their clearly recognizable characteristics and because of their widely recognized importance, constitute a part of the cultural or spiritual heritage of peoples."[90]

Separate & Distinct Military Objectives. CCW Amended Protocol II Article 9, states "[s]everal clearly separate and distinct military objectives located in a city, town, village or other area containing a similar concentration of civilians are not be treated as a single military objective." AP I Article 51(5)(a) contains a similar admonishment. It provides that "an attack by bombardment by any methods or means which treats as a single military objective a number of clearly separated and distinct military objectives located in a city, town, village or other area containing a similar concentration of civilians or civilian objects" is considered indiscriminate and thus prohibited."[91]

Precautions. CCW Amended Protocol II Article 10 governs precautions to be taken when employing mines, booby-traps, and similar devices. It reads "[a]ll feasible precautions should be taken to protect civilians from the effects of

[90] Schindler and Toman 2004, at p. 232.

[91] During the AP I negotiations, the United States delegation stated they understood the language "clearly separated" to not only require an observable distinction but also "an element of significant distance [which] should be at least sufficiently large to permit the individual military objectives to be attacked separately." Official Records, *supra* note 14, at Vol. XIV, p. 307 [CDDH/III/SR. 31/Para 50].

weapons to which this Article applies. Feasible precautions are those precautions which are practicable or practically possible taking into account all circumstances ruling at the time, including humanitarian and military considerations." AP I uses the term "feasible" in a number of different contexts,[92] but unlike this portion of the CCW does further define exactly what standard of care the term entails.[93] Accordingly, it would appear that States used the CCW as an opportunity to define "feasible" in a manner that reflects the exigencies of military operations.

5.3.3 Hague Convention for the Protection of Cultural Property of 1954

In 2009, the United States ratified the Hague Convention for the Protection of Cultural Property in the Event of Armed Conflict of 1954 (*hereinafter* "1954 Hague Convention").[94] Thus, even though not bound by AP I Article 53, the US has affirmative obligations to protect cultural property during armed conflict with other Parties to the 1954 Hague Convention.[95] However, there are some important distinctions between AP I and the 1954 Hague Convention regarding what qualifies as protected property and the ability of military commanders to waive such protection.

---

[92] See AP I, *supra* note 2, Articles 41(3), 56(2), 57(2)(a), 58, 78(1), and 86(2).

[93] Of note, the more detailed definition of "feasible" in the text of CCW Amended Protocol II reflects the understanding of several Parties to AP I regarding the meaning of that term in the context of AP I. For example, the United Kingdom upon ratification of AP I stated "[t]he United Kingdom understands the term "feasible" as used in the Protocol to mean that which is practicable or practically possible, taking into account all circumstances ruling at the time, including humanitarian and military considerations." Schinder and Toman 2004 at p. 816. See also similar declarations made by Canada, Germany, Italy, the Netherlands, and Spain ibid. at pp. 797, 802, 807, 810, and 813 respectively.

A United States understanding accompanying ratification of CCW Amended Protocol II reads "any decision by any military commander, military personnel, or any other person responsible for planning, authorizing, or executing military action shall only be judged on the basis of that person's assessment of the information reasonably available to the person at the time the person planned, authorized, or executed the action under review, and shall not be judged on the basis of information that comes to light after the action under review was taken." Ibid. at 231.

This yardstick for evaluating of military decisions is shared by several Parties to AP I. Upon ratification of AP I the United Kingdom declared "[m]ilitray commanders and others responsible for planning, deciding upon, or executing attacks necessarily have to reach decisions on the basis of their assessment of the information from all sources which is reasonably available to them at the relevant time." Ibid. at 816. See also similar declarations of Australia, Austria, Belgium, Canada, Germany, Italy, the Netherlands, and New Zealand ibid. at pp. 793, 794, 796, 802, 807, 810, and 810 respectively.

[94] Convention for the Protection of Cultural Property in the Event of Armed Conflict, May 14, 1954, 249 U.N.T.S. 240 [hereinafter 1954 Hague Convention].

[95] Article 18(1) to the 1954 Hague Convention, ibid. limits the scope of the Convention to situations of declared war or other armed conflict between two or more High Contracting Parties.

"Cultural Property" as contemplated by the 1954 Hague Convection includes, *inter alia*, "movable or immovable property of great importance to the cultural heritage of every people."[96] Moreover, it authorizes special protection for a limited number of refuges intended to shelter movable cultural property and of centers containing "monuments and other immovable property of *very* great importance" (emphasis added) so long as certain conditions are met and the special protection is granted by entry of the property into the "International Register of Cultural Property under special protection."[97]

Unlike the express language in AP I Article 53,[98] the 1954 Hague Convention allows the protection accorded cultural property to be waived "where military necessity imperatively requires such a waiver."[99] With regard to cultural property that has been afforded "special protection," its immunity is withdrawn if the Party fails to abide by the conditions required for its special protection or in "exceptional cases of unavoidable military necessity."[100]

However, 1954 Hague Convention Article 4(4) and AP I Article 53(c) both prohibit reprisals against cultural property.

5.4 Department of Defense Publications Relevant to AP I

5.4.1 Department of Defense Law of War Manual

Unfortunately, there is no single Department of Defense (DoD) publication that offers a common, comprehensive exposition of the law of armed conflict applicable to all services, although such a volume, styled the "Department of Defense Law of War Manual," is being prepared under the auspices of the General Counsel of the DoD. When complete, it will serve "as the authoritative statement on the law of war" within the DoD.[101]

---

[96] For examples of cultural property provided by the Hague Convention 1954, see Article 1(a).

[97] Article 8 provides the prerequisite conditions for granting of special protection. Chapter II to the Regulations for the Execution of the Convention provides the mechanism by which a Party can apply for special protection from the Director-General of the United Nations Educational, Scientific, and Cultural Organization (UNESCO).

[98] AP 1 Article 53(b) prohibits the use of cultural property or places of worship in support of the military effort, but does not stipulate that its protected status is surrendered if it is so used. Nonetheless, given that Article 53 states that it is without prejudice to the Hague Convention of 1954, it follows that its protection is lost if it is used in support of the military effort. Thus, it may be attacked if it qualifies as a military objective per AP I Article 52 (and the attack meets the proportionality requirements of AP I Articles 51(5)(b) and 57(2)(a)(iii)). See New Rules, *supra* n. 80, at pp. 332–333.

[99] 1954 Hague Convention, *supra* n. 94, at Article 4(2).

[100] Ibid. at 11(1) & (2).

[101] DOD Law of War Program, *supra* n. 12, Para 5.1.3.

In a November 2010 speech to the American Bar Association, W. Hays Parks, the principal author of the Manual, provided insight into its contents.[102] According to Parks, the DOD Manual incorporates AP I provisions where they are deemed to be accurate expressions of the law or otherwise in accord with the practice of the United States.[103] He also stated that the manual exceeds 1100 pages and contains more than 3,000 footnotes.[104] Accordingly, those interested in researching the extent to which the United States has incorporated AP I into its application of the law of armed conflict would be well served to obtain a copy when the Manual is finally released. Although the speech indicated publication was forthcoming shortly, the author of this paper has been informed that the Manual remains under review and its release date is uncertain.

5.4.2 Department of Defense Joint Doctrinal Publications

Joint doctrine, published under the authority of the Chairman of the Joint Chiefs of Staff, pertains to all of the armed services within the DoD and governs the conduct of joint operations.[105] Although there is no doctrinal publication that exclusively or exhaustively addresses the law of armed conflict, some of the doctrine addresses legal issues and requirements pertinent to the conduct of DoD operations. These legal matters reflect areas of the law also contemplated in AP I.

Joint Publication 1, "Doctrine for the Armed Forces of the United States of America," requires commanders at every level of command to ensure their forces operate in compliance with the law of armed conflict.[106] In furtherance of this requirement, a separate doctrinal publication, Joint Publication 1-04 "Legal Support to Military Operations," specifically requires the integration of legal support into the planning and execution of military operations.[107] This publication addresses the roles and responsibilities of legal advisors at every level of command. Although it is not a legal manual, it provides definitions of the overarching law of armed conflict principles which must be considered by commanders, planners, and legal advisors. Given the importance of these principles in guiding the compliance of US military operations with the law of armed conflict, they are set forth below.

Military necessity. "The principle of military necessity justifies those measures not forbidden by international law that are indispensable for securing the complete

---

[102] The written version of this speech can be found at Parks 2010b.

[103] Ibid. at p. 7.

[104] Ibid. at p. 9.

[105] "Doctrine" is defined as "[f]undamental principles by which the military forces or elements thereof guide their actions in support of national objectives. It is authoritative but requires judgment in application." Joint Publication [hereinafter "JP"] 1-02, "Department of Defense Dictionary of Military and Associated Terms," (8 Nov 10 as amended through 15 Nov 11) at 104.

[106] JP 1, "Doctrine for the Armed Forces of the United States of America" (2 May 07 incorporating Change 1 of 20 Mar 09) at I-21.

[107] JP 1-04, "Legal Support of Military Operations,"(17 Aug 11) [hereinafter JP 1-04].

submission of the enemy as soon as possible. However, this principle is not applied in a vacuum. It must be applied in conjunction with other law of war principles. Military necessity generally prohibits the intentional targeting of protected persons (civilians, hostile personnel who have surrendered or are otherwise "out of combat," etc.) and places (objects or places that are used for purely civilian purposes, such as hospitals, schools, and cultural property that have not been converted to or for military/hostile use) because they do not constitute legitimate military objectives in furtherance of the accomplishment of the mission."[108]

The comparable provisions in AP I include Article 41 on safeguarding combatants who are *hors de combat*; Articles 51 and 52 prohibiting attacks against civilians and civilian objects; and Article 53 prohibiting attacks against cultural property and places of worship.

Unnecessary suffering. "The principle of unnecessary suffering forbids the employment of means and methods of warfare calculated to cause unnecessary suffering. This principle acknowledges that combatants' necessary suffering, which may include severe injury and loss of life, is lawful. This principle largely applies to the legality of weapons and ammunition. Generally, weapons and ammunition that have been issued by [the Department of Defense] have been reviewed to ensure compliance with the law of war and this principle. However, approved weapons and ammunition also may not be used in a way that will cause unnecessary suffering or injury. A weapon or munition would be deemed to cause unnecessary suffering if, in its normal use, the injury caused by it is disproportionate to the military necessity for it, that is, the military advantage to be gained from its use."[109]

The analogous AP I provision is Article 35(2).

Distinction. "This principle requires parties to a conflict to distinguish between combatants and noncombatants and to distinguish between military objectives and protected property and places. Parties to a conflict must direct their operations only against military objectives. Military objectives are combatants and those objects which by their nature, location, purpose, or use make an effective contribution to military action and whose total or partial destruction, capture or neutralization, in the circumstances ruling at the time, offer a definitive military advantage."[110]

This language is substantively identical to AP I Articles 48 and 52(2).

Proportionality. "The principle of proportionality prohibits attacks that may be expected to cause incidental loss of civilian life, injury to civilians, damage to civilian objects, or a combination thereof, which would be excessive in relation to the concrete and direct military advantage expected to be gained. As such, this principle is only applicable when an attack may possibly affect civilians or civilian objects, and thereby, may cause collateral damage."[111]

This language is substantively identical to AP I Articles 51(5)(b) and 57(2)(a)(iii).

---

[108] Ibid. at II-2.

[109] Ibid.

[110] Ibid.

[111] Ibid.

Joint Publication 3-60, "Joint Targeting," (hereinafter "JP 3-60") provides doctrinal guidance on the process of selecting, evaluating, and prosecuting targets across the range of military operations.[112] It is also not a legal manual. However, its annex on legal considerations in targeting reiterates the fundamental principles of the law of armed conflict expressed in JP 1-04, albeit in greater detail as to their practical application. Relevant provisions that implicate rules in AP I are outlined below. Of note, the publication charges targeting planners with consulting their legal adviser when considering law of armed conflict issues.

Proportionality. As described above, the US has incorporated the proportionality balancing test laid out in AP I Articles 51(5)(b) and 57(2)(a)(iii). When weighing military advantage against anticipated collateral damage during military operations, JP 3-60 provides that "military advantage… is intended to refer to the advantage anticipated from those actions considered as a whole, and not only from isolated or particular parts thereof. Generally, 'military advantage' is not restricted to tactical gains, but is linked to the full context of a strategy."[113] Thus the military value of a particular target is not evaluated independently, but rather by how supports the successful execution of an operation considered as a whole.[114]

Human Shields. JP 3-60 states "[a] defender may not use civilians as human shields in an attempt to protect, conceal, or render military objects immune from military operations or force them to leave their homes or shelters to disrupt the movement of an adversary. In these cases, the civilians have not lost their protected status and [the attacker's] responsibilities during such situations are driven by the principle of proportionality…. In such cases, otherwise lawful targets shielded with protected civilians may be attacked, and the protected civilians may be considered as collateral damage, provided that the collateral damage is not excessive compared to the concrete an direct military advantage anticipated by the attack."[115] These rules are also set out in AP I Articles 51(7) and (8).

Military Objectives. Military attacks will only be directed at military targets. In addition to intrinsically military targets such as military troops, installations, and armaments, JP 3-60 recognizes other objects also may be prosecuted. These include economic targets that effectively contribute to the enemy's military capability such as factories, workshops, and plants.[116] In addition "dual-use"

---

[112] JP 3-60, "Joint Targeting," (13 Apr 07) [hereinafter JP 3-60].

[113] Ibid. at E-1.

[114] Ibid. To illustrate this concept, the military advantage of an attack on a small, minimally fortified outpost overlooking a mountain pass is not judged simply on the military assets contained therein. If the attacking force intends to use that pass to infiltrate enemy territory, the military advantage is calculated based on the need to eliminate the outpost to accomplish the larger mission. The degree of acceptable collateral damage is judged accordingly.

[115] Ibid. at E-2.

[116] Ibid. at E-3. Additionally, United States Air Force doctrine states that targetable economic objects include those which make an effective (though not necessarily direct) contribution to the adversary's military capability. Air Force Doctrine Document 3-60, "Targeting," 8 June 2006, incorporating Change 1 of 28 Jul 2011) at p. 91.

objects which have both a civilian and military application may constitute legitimate targets subject to the principle of proportionality. These may include targets that "indirectly, but effectively, support and sustain the adversary's warfighting capability."[117] This definition casts a wider net than AP I Article 52(2) that limits military objectives to objects "which by their nature, location, purpose, or use make an effective contribution to military action."

Works & Installations Containing Dangerous Forces. Attacks on objects such as dams and dikes are prohibited if "their breach or destruction would result in the loss of civilian lives disproportionate to the military advantage to be gained."[118] By applying the proportionality test used in evaluating other legitimate targets, JP 3-60 provides a less rigid standard than that set forth in AP I Article 56, discussed in the analysis accompanying note 45 above.

Protection of the Environment. JP 3-60 also establishes a lower standard than that required by AP I with regard to protection of the environment. AP I Articles 35(3) prohibit the use of "methods or means of warfare that are either intended, or may be expected, to cause widespread, long-term, and severe damage to the environment." This provision brokers no exception. Accordingly, even a valid military objective of paramount importance could not be attacked if the only way to achieve its destruction or neutralization would require an attack that could be expected to have such consequences on the environment. JP 3-60 does not include a similar bright line test. It provides "[i]t is generally lawful under the [law of armed conflict] to cause collateral damage to the environment during an attack on a legitimate military target. However, the commander has an affirmative obligation to avoid unnecessary damage to the environment to the extent that it is practical to do so consistent with mission accomplishment. To that end and as far as military requirements dictate, methods and means of attack should be employed with due regard to the protection and preservation of the natural environment. Destruction of the environment not required by military necessity and carried out wantonly is prohibited."[119]

Warnings Prior to Attack. "Required precautionary measures are reinforced by traditional tenets of military doctrine, such as surprise, economy of force, and concentration of effort. Warnings must be given when circumstances permit (e.g., any degradation in attack effectiveness is outweighed by reduction in collateral damage, because advanced warning allows the adversary to get civilians out of the target area)."[120] This is consistent with AP I Article 57 (c) that requires that "effective advance warning shall be given of attacks which may affect the civilian population, unless circumstances do not permit."

---

[117] JP 3-60 at E-3.

[118] Ibid. at E-3.

[119] Ibid. at E-6. Of note, the United States has expressly rejected the assertion that the prohibition against methods or means of warfare that are intended, or may be expected to cause widespread, long-term, and severe damage to the natural environment is prohibited under customary international law. *See* Bellinger and Haynes Letter, *supra* note 9, at 455–460.

[120] JP 3-60 at E-4.

Cancellations of Attacks. JP 3-60 provides an additional rule for precautions in attack. It states that "[if] it becomes apparent that a target is no longer a lawful military objective, the attacks must be cancelled or suspended."[121] This comports with the requirement of AP I, Article 57(2)(b)(iii).[122]

5.4.3 Department of the Army Field Manual (FM) 27-10, The Law of Land Warfare[123]

The Department of the Army released FM 27-10 in 1956. It was updated in 1976. Despite its vintage, FM 27-10 serves as the primary legal reference manual within the DoD implementing the law of armed conflict as it pertains to the conduct of hostilities on land.[124] Of course, given its age, it must be read in conjunction with more recent developments in the law. Provisions of FM 27-10 addressing the conduct of hostilities are reviewed against comparable provisions in AP I below.

Parachutists. Paragraph 30 states "The law of war does not prohibit firing upon paratroops or other persons who are or appear to be bound upon hostile missions while such persons are descending by parachute. Persons other than those mentioned in the preceding sentence who are descending by parachute from disabled aircraft may not be fired upon." This comports with AP I Article 42 with the exception that it does not expressly require that a parachutist from a disabled aircraft be given the opportunity to surrender upon reaching the ground unless it is apparent he is engaging in a hostile act.

Means & Methods/Unnecessary Suffering. Paragraph 34 discusses the prohibition against the use of "arms, projectiles, or material calculated to cause unnecessary suffering." It states "[w]hat weapons cause 'unnecessary injury' can only be determined in light of the practice of States in refraining from the use of a given weapon because it is believed to have that effect. The prohibition certainly does not extend to the use of explosives contained in artillery projectiles, mines, rockets, or hand grenades. Usage has, however, established the illegality of the use of lances with barbed heads, irregular-shaped bullets, and projectiles filled with glass, the use

---

121 Ibid.

122 This rule leaves open the issue of who retains the authority to cancel an attack. If not reserved to certain level of command, then any military personnel charged with executing an attack would have the authority to supplant his judgment for that of the commander who ordered the attack. In its ratification of AP I, Switzerland made the following reservation: "The provisions of Article 57(2) are binding only on battalion or group commanders and higher echelons." Schindler and Toman 2004, *supra* n. 14, at p. 814.

123 Department of the Army Field Manual 27-10, The Law of Land Warfare (18 July 56 incorporating Change 1 of 15 July 76).

124 For example, para 3.e. of Secretary of the Navy Instruction 3300.1C, "Department of the Navy Law of War Program,"(28 May 09) references FM 27-10 as applicable law and policy. Marine Corps Reference Publication 5-12.1A, "The Law of Land Warfare", (undated) adopts FM 27-10 verbatim.

of any substance on bullets that would tend unnecessarily to inflame a wound inflicted by them, and the scoring of the surface or the filing off of the ends of the hard cases of bullets." AP I Article 35(2) prohibits the employment of "weapons, projectiles and Materials and methods of warfare of a nature to cause superfluous injury or unnecessary suffering" but provides no specific examples of unlawful weapons.

Military Objectives. The definition in paragraph 40(c) of legitimate military objectives is similar to that contained in AP I Article 52(2). It defines military objectives as "combatants, and those objects which by their nature, location, purpose, or use make an effective contribution to military action and whose total or partial destruction, capture or neutralization, in the circumstances ruling at the time, offers a definite military advantage.... Military objectives include, for example, factories producing munitions and military supplies, military camps, warehouses storing munitions and military supplies, ports and railroads being used for the transportation of military supplies, and other places that are for the accommodation of troops or the support of military operations." In addition, paragraph 40(b) states that defended places are permissible objects of attack or bombardment (as distinct from undefended towns, villages, dwellings, or buildings, which are excluded from attack).[125] Paragraph 40(b) provides three examples of what constitutes a defended place: "a fort or fortified place,"[126] "a place that is occupied by a combatant military force or through which such a force is passing,"[127]; and "a city or town surrounded by detached defense positions, if under the circumstances the city or town can be considered jointly with such defense positions as an indivisible whole."[128]

Proportionality. Paragraph 41 also sets forth a proportionality test similar to that contained in AP I Article 51(5)(b) and 57(2)(b). This paragraph requires that during attacks or bombardments "loss of life and damage to property incidental to attacks must not be excessive in relation to the concrete and direct military advantage expected to be gained." With regard to the standard of care expected of those who plan and order attacks, paragraph 41 requires these individuals "must take all *reasonable* steps to ensure not only that the objectives are identified as military objectives or defended places... but also that these objectives may be attacked without probable losses in life and damage to property disproportionate to the military advantage anticipated." (emphasis added). The use of the term "reasonable"

---

[125] FM 27-10 Paragraph 39(b) defines an undefended place as "any inhabited place near or in a zone where opposing armed forces are in contact which is open for occupation by the adverse party without resistance. In order to be considered undefended, the following conditions must be fulfilled: (1) Armed forces and other combatants, as well as mobile weapons and mobile military equipment, must have been evacuated, or otherwise neutralized; (2) no hostile use shall be made of fixed military installations or establishments; (3) no acts of warfare shall be committed by the authorities or by the population; and (4) no activities in support of military activities shall be undertaken." This definition is the same as that contained in AP I Article 59(2).

[126] Ibid. at Para 40(b)(1).

[127] Ibid. at Para 40(b)(2). This paragraph also stipulates that "the occupation of a place by medical units alone, however, is not sufficient to render it a permissible object of attack."

[128] Ibid. at Para 40(b)(3).

differentiates this standard of care from the AP I Article 57 which mandates those who plan and decide upon attacks take all "feasible" measures and precautions in evaluating targets and avoiding or minimizing civilian causalities.[129] Moreover, this reasonable test sets a lower standard of care than AP I Articles 50(1) and 52(3), which further require that in the case of doubt whether a person is a civilian or whether a typically civilian object has surrendered its protection by making an effective contribution to military action, that person or object shall be presumed to be civilian.[130]

Treachery & Perfidy. Paragraph 31 prohibits treachery such as putting a price on an enemy's head as well as offering a reward for an enemy "dead or alive." Paragraph 50 provides as examples of perfidious conduct feigning surrender in order to gain an advantage over an enemy or falsely broadcasting to the enemy that an armistice has been reached since both situations constitute lying "where there is a moral obligation to speak the truth." This definition of perfidious conduct is broader than that set forth in AP I Article 37(1) which prohibits perfidy to the extent it is employed to "kill, injure, or capture an adversary."

Ruses. Paragraphs 50 and 51 provide examples of legitimate ruses including, among others, tricking an enemy to surrender to an inferior force under the pretense that it is surrounded, sending misleading messages, sending messages purporting to be from an enemy commander, fabricating the existence of forces that do not exist, and using dummy weapons and installations. This comports with the guidance on ruses in AP I Article 37(2).

Enemy Flags/Insignia/Uniforms. With regard to using national flags, insignia, and uniforms as a ruse, Para 54 states "[i]n practice, it has been authorized to make use of [these items] as a ruse. [Article 23(f) to the Hague IV Annex] does not prohibit such employment, but does prohibit their *improper use*. It is certainly forbidden to employ them during combat, but their use at other times is not forbidden." (emphasis in original) This stands at odds with AP I Article 39(a)(2) which not only prohibits the use of enemy flags, military emblems, insignia, or uniforms during an attacks, but also if used to "shield, favour, protect or impede military operations." Under the AP I rule, military units would not be allowed to wear enemy uniforms while conduct covert operations behind enemy lines, such as intelligence gathering or reconnaissance.[131]

---

129 AP I, *supra* note 2, Article 57(2)(a)(i) & (ii).

130 The problem with this presumption was described in the Final Report to Congress on the Conduct of the Persian Gulf War (available at www.ndu.edu/library/epubs/cpgw.pdf) which stated the "language [in AP I Article 52(3)], which is not a codification of the customary practice of nations, causes several things to occur that are contrary to the traditional law of war. It shifts the burden for determining the precise use of an object from the party controlling that object (and therefore in possession of the facts as to its use) to the party lacking such control and facts, i.e., from defender to attacker. *This imbalance ignores the realities of war in demanding a degree of certainty of an attacker that seldom exists in combat*. It also encourages a defender to ignore its obligation to separate the civilian population, individual civilians and civilian objects from military objectives, as the Government of Iraq illustrated during the Persian Gulf War." (emphasis added).

131 For an excellent analysis of both state practice and the legal issues surrounding the wear of non-standard and enemy uniforms, see Parks, Special Forces 2003.

Qualifications of Members of Militias and Volunteer Corps. Paragraph 64 reiterates and explains the four criteria required for members of militias and volunteer corps to qualify as prisoners of war under Article 4(A)(2)(a)-(d) of the Third Geneva Convention governing treatment of prisoners of war.[132] As such, it is distinguishable from the relaxed requirements set forth in AP I Article 44.[133]

Spies. Paragraph 77 states there is a "well-established right of belligerents to employ spies and other secret agents for obtaining information of the enemy." Paragraph 78(c) states that a spy who rejoins the army to which he belongs, and is subsequently captured by the enemy, retains his right to prisoner of war status and may not be punished for his previous acts of espionage. This paragraph comports with AP I Article 46(4).

Neutralized/Demilitarized Zones. Paragraph 254 restates the rule in Article 15 of the Fourth Geneva Convention governing protection of civilians.[134] Parties to a conflict may agree to "neutralized zones" where wounded and sick combatants and non-combatants as well as civilians who are not taking part in hostilities and who perform no work of a military character may take shelter. AP I Article 60 provides more substance to this rule. However, both provisions make it clear that rules governing any such zone are only those contracted upon by the Parties.

Reprisals. Paragraph 497 authorizes reprisals where not specifically prohibited under the Geneva Conventions of 1949[135] so long as certain strict conditions are

---

[132] GC III, *supra* n. 3. Paragraph 64 provides that the requirements set forth in GC III, Article 4(A)(2)(a)–(d) "are satisfied in the following fashion":

a. *Command by a Responsible Person*. This condition is fulfilled if the commander of the corps is a commissioned officer of the armed forces or is a person of position and authority or if the members of the militia or volunteer corps are provided with documents, badges, or other means of identification to show that they are officers, non-commissioned officers, or soldiers so that there may be no doubt that they are not persons acting on their own responsibility. State recognition, however, is not essential, and an organization may be formed spontaneously and elect its own officers.

b. *Fixed Distinctive Sign*. The second condition, relative to the possession of a fixed distinctive sign recognizable at a distance is satisfied by the wearing of military uniform, but less than the complete uniform will suffice. A helmet or headdress which would make the silhouette of the individual readily distinguishable from that of an ordinary civilian would satisfy this requirement. It is also desirable that the individual member of the militia or volunteer corps wear a badge or brassard permanently affixed to his clothing. It is not necessary to inform the enemy of the distinctive sign, although it may be desirable to do so in order to avoid misunderstanding.

c. *Carrying Arms Openly*. This requirement is not satisfied by the carrying of weapons concealed about the person or if the individuals hide their weapons on the approach of the enemy.

d. *Compliance With Law of War*. This condition is fulfilled if most of the members of the body observe the laws and customs of war, notwithstanding the fact that the individual member concerned may have committed a war crime. Members of militias and volunteer corps should be especially warned against employment of treachery, denial of quarters, maltreatment of prisoners of war, wounded, and dead, improper conduct toward flags of truce, pillage, and unnecessary violence and destruction.

[133] See discussion accompanying notes 32–36, *supra*.

[134] GC IV, *supra* n. 3.

[135] GC I, *supra* n. 3, Article 46 forbids reprisals against "the wounded, sick, personnel, buildings or equipment protected by the Convention." GC II, *supra* n. 3, Article 47 forbids reprisals against "wounded, sick and shipwrecked persons, the personnel, the vessels or the equipment protected

met. It defines a reprisal as an act of "retaliation in the form of conduct which would otherwise be unlawful against enemy personnel or property for acts of warfare committed by the other belligerent in violation of the law of war." This paragraph only authorizes reprisals if used as an "unavoidable last resort" to induce the enemy to bring their behavior into compliance with the law. Other means of inducing compliance must be exhausted where practicable before resorting to reprisals. The reprisal need not take the same form as the unlawful act employed by the enemy. For example, the Paragraph states the aggrieved belligerent could use an unlawful weapon as a reprisal for the enemy's intentional maltreatment of prisoners of war. However, the reprisal should "not be excessive or exceed the violence committed by the enemy."[136] The remedy of reprisal is largely foreclosed under AP I Articles 51(6), 52(2), 54(4), 55(2), and 56(4).

5.4.4 Naval Warfare Publication (NWP) 1-14 M, The Commander's Handbook on the Law of Naval Operations[137]

NWP 1-14 M provides legal guidance on matters of international and operational law to the US Navy, Marine Corps, and Coast Guard. Although its focus is primarily on maritime operations, it also contains provisions relevant to operations ashore. Several, described below, contemplate legal issues addressed in AP I.

Legal Review of Weapons. Paragraph 5.3.4. states "before a new weapon or weapons system is acquired, an authorized attorney must conduct a legal review to ensure the new weapon is consistent with all applicable domestic laws and international agreements, treaties, customary international law, and the law of armed conflict." This is consistent with the requirement in AP I Article 36.[138]

(Footnote 135 continued)
by the Convention." GC III, *supra* n. 3, Article 13 forbids reprisals against prisoners of war. GC IV, *supra* n. 3, Article 33 forbids reprisals against civilians in occupied territory.

[136] FM 27-10 Paragraph 497 invests commanders with the authority to engage in reprisals. However, this authority has been superseded and the authority to order reprisals is retained at the national level. *See* International and Operational Law Department 2011, at p. 25.

[137] US Navy, US Marine Corps & US Coast Guard, NWP 1-14 M/MCWP 5-12.1/COMDTPUB P5800.7A, The Commander's Handbook on the Law of Naval Operations [hereinafter NWP 1-14 M].

[138] U.S. Department of Defense rules governing legal review of weapons and weapon systems are contained Department of Defense Directive 5000.01, "The Defense Acquisition System," (12 May 2003); Department of the Air Force Instruction 51-402, "Legal Reviews of Weapons and Cyber Capabilities," (27 Jul 2011); Department of the Army Regulation 27-53, "Review of Legality of Weapons Under International Law," (1 Jan 1979); and, Secretary of the Navy (SECNAV) Instruction 5000.2D, "Implementation and Operation of the Defense Acquisition System and the Joint Capabilities Integration and Development System," (16 Oct 2008).

Reprisals. The guidance on reprisals set forth in NWP 1-14 M[139] is similar to the provisions in FM 27-10 in most respects,[140] with the significant exception that it includes enemy civilians (other than those in occupied territory) as authorized targets of reprisals.

Military Objectives. Paragraph 8.1 requires that "all reasonable precautions must be taken to ensure that only military objectives are targeted...." This language again emphasizes the preference of the US for the "reasonable" instead of the "feasible" standard employed in AP I. As is the case in FM 27-10, it does not include the requirements that in case of doubt of whether a civilian or a civilian object has forfeited its protected status, the presumption is they have not. Thus it is also distinguishable from AP I Articles AP Articles 50(1) and 52(3).[141]

Military objectives are defined in para 8.2 as "combatants, military equipment and facilities (except medical and religious equipment and facilities), and those objects which, by their nature, location, purpose or use, effectively contribute to the enemy's war fighting or war-sustaining capability and whose total or partial destruction, capture, or neutralization would constitute a definite military advantage to the attacker under the circumstances at the time of the attack. Military advantage may involve a variety of considerations, including the security of the attacking force." Paragraph 8.2.5 explains that proper objects of attack include geographical features and "economic objects of the enemy that indirectly but effectively support and sustain the enemy's war fighting capability." This definition of what constitutes a proper military objective is more expansive than that expressed in AP I Article 52(2).

Parachutists. Paragraph 8.2.3.1 states "Parachutists descending from disabled aircraft may not be attacked while in the air unless they engage in combatant acts while descending. Upon reaching the ground, such parachutists must be provided an opportunity to surrender. Airborne troops, special warfare infiltrators, and intelligence agents parachuting into combat areas or behind enemy lines are not so protected and may be attacked in the air as well as on the ground. Such personnel may not be attacked, however, if they clearly indicate in a timely manner their intention to surrender." This provision comports with AP I Article 42.

Proportionality/Means and Methods of Attack. Paragraph 8.3.1 affirms that is not unlawful to cause collateral damage during an attack on a legitimate military objective. This paragraph provides a more comprehensive proportionality test than AP I Articles 51(5)(b) and 57(2)(a)(iii). It states "[t]he principle of proportionality requires that anticipated incidental injury or collateral damage must not... be excessive in light of the military advantage expected to be gained. Naval commanders must take all reasonable precautions, taking into account military and humanitarian considerations, to keep civilian casualties and damage to the minimum consistent with mission accomplishment and the security of the force. In each

139 See NWP 1-14 M, *supra* n. 137, Paragraphs 6.2.4; 6.2.4.1; 6.2.4.2; 6.2.4.3; & 6.2.5.

140 See discussion accompanying n. 135–136 *supra*.

141 See discussion accompanying n. 129–130 *supra*.

instance, the commander must determine whether the anticipated incidental injuries and collateral damage would be excessive, on the basis of an honest and reasonable estimate of the facts available to him. Similarly, the commander must decide, in light of all the facts known or reasonably available to him, including the need to conserve resources and complete the mission successfully, whether to adopt an alternative method of attack, if reasonably available, to reduce civilian casualties and damage."

The final sentence of the above paragraph concerns a Commander's responsibility to choose means and methods of attack that best avoids incidental injury and collateral damage. AP I Article 57(2)(a)(ii) requires taking "all feasible precautions in the choice of means and methods of attack with a view to avoiding, and in any case minimizing, incidental loss of civilian life, injury to civilians and damage to civilian objects."

Direct Participation in Hostilities. NWP 1-14 M Para 8.2.2 states that individuals "who are taking part in hostilities may be attacked while they are taking a direct part in hostilities, unless they are *hors de combat*." This is similar to the provision in AP I Articles 51(2) and (3) which, read together, protect civilians from attack "unless and for such time as they take a direct part of hostilities." AP I provides no further explanation of what constitutes direct participation in hostilities or the temporal scope of how long a civilian's protection is forfeited when he does engage in hostilities. NWP 1-14 M provides greater clarity. It explains that direct participation in hostilities "must be judged on a case-by-case basis. Examples include taking up arms or otherwise trying to kill, injure, or capture enemy personnel or destroy enemy property. Additionally, civilians serving as lookouts or guards, or intelligence agents for military forces may be considered to be directly participating in hostilities. Combatants in the field must make an honest determination as to whether a particular person is or is not taking a direct part in hostilities based on the person's behavior, location and attire, and other information available at the time."[142]

---

[142] This language in NWP 1-14 M is the only existing official definition of direct participation of hostilities within DoD literature. However, despite expanding on the definition in AP I, it still only provides broad outlines and leaves open the issue of how involved a civilian must be to qualify as taking a direct part in hostilities and for how long they lose their protected status if they do qualify. Recognizing the need for clarity in the field, the ICRC published an analysis in 2009. See Melzer 2009.

Addressing the Interpretive Guidance in detail is beyond the scope of this article; however, its conclusions regarding the scope of who qualifies as taking a direct participation in hostilities and how and when they could be targeted are controversial. For example, the Interpretive Guidance concludes that those who assemble or store improvised explosive devices do not qualify as taking a direct participation in hostilities. Ibid. at 54. Moreover, it concludes that civilians who take a direct part in hostilities are only susceptible to direct attack during "measures preparatory to the execution of a specific act of direct participation in hostilities, as well as the deployment to and return from the locations of its execution" thus enabling a civilian who regularly engages in hostilities to be immune from attack between his discrete belligerent acts. Ibid. at 65.

These conclusions, among others within the Interpretive Guidance, have been subject to serious criticism by prominent scholars with military experience. See e.g. Schmitt 2010; Boothby 2010; Parks 2010a; Watkin 2010.

Objects Indispensable to the Survival of the Civilian Population. Paragaph 8.3 echoes AP I Article 54(2) in that it prohibits "the intentional destruction of food, crops, livestock, drinking water, and other objects indispensable to the survival of the civilian population, for the specific purpose of denying the civilian population of their use."[143]

Human Shields. Paragraph 8.3.2 restates the rule in AP I that civilians shall not be used to shield attacks, but that the improper use of human shields by the adversary does not release the attacker from his responsibility to apply the principle of proportionality.[144] However, this paragraph takes a more aggressive stance regarding voluntary human shields. It provides "[c]ivilians who voluntarily place themselves in or on a military objective as 'human shields' in order to deter a lawful attack do not alter the status of the military objective. While the law of armed conflict is not fully developed in such cases, such persons may also be considered to be taking a direct part in hostilities or contributing directly to the enemy's warfighting/war-sustaining capability, and may be excluded from the proportionality analysis." Attacks under such circumstances likely raise political, strategic, and operational issues that commanders should identify and consider when making targeting decisions."

Protection of the Environment. Paragraph 8.4 addresses the impact of attacks on the natural environment in language similar to that in JP 3-60 and is thus also distinguishable from AP I Article 35(3) and Article 55(1).[145] It provides "[i]t is not unlawful to cause collateral damage to the natural environment during an attack upon a legitimate military objective. However, the commander has an affirmative obligation to avoid unnecessary damage to the environment to the extent that it is practicable to do so consistent with mission accomplishment. To that end, and as far as military requirements permit, methods or means of warfare should be employed with due regard to the protection and preservation of the natural environment. Destruction of the natural environment not necessitated by mission accomplishment and carried out wantonly is prohibited. Therefore, a commander should consider the environmental damage that will result from an attack on a legitimate military objective as one of the factors during targeting analysis."[146]

---

[143] Of note, neither FM 27-10 nor NWP 1-14 M contain a prohibition against the starvation of civilians as a method of warfare, as is prohibited in AP I, Article 54(1). This is perhaps because of the traditionally lawful use of sieges to compel the surrender of the enemy through starvation and other privation which will necessarily impact civilians caught in the besieged location. See Dinstein 2010, at pp. 218–223.

[144] See AP I, *supra* n. 2, Article 51(7) and (8).

[145] See discussion accompanying n. 119 *supra*.

[146] The United States has expressly rejected the assertion that the prohibition against methods or means of warfare that are intended, or may be expected to cause widespread, long-term, and severe damage to the natural environment is prohibited. See Bellinger and Haynes 2007, at pp. 455–460.

Means & Methods/Unnecessary Suffering. Paragraph 9.1.1 concerns the prohibition of weapons calculated to cause unnecessary suffering also found in AP I Article 35(2). It states "[a]ntipersonnel weapons are designed to kill or disable enemy combatants and are lawful notwithstanding the death, pain, and suffering they inflict. Weapons that are designed to cause unnecessary suffering or superfluous injury are, however, prohibited because the degree of pain or injury, or the certainty of death they produce is needlessly or clearly disproportionate to the military advantage to be gained by their use. Poisoned projectiles and small arms ammunition intended to cause superfluous injury or unnecessary suffering fall into this category. Similarly, using materials that are difficult to detect or undetectable by field x-ray equipment, such as glass or clear plastic, as the injuring mechanism in military ammunition is prohibited, since they unnecessarily inhibit the treatment of wounds. Use of such materials as incidental components in ammunition, e.g., as wadding or packing, is not prohibited. Use of .50-caliber weapons against individual enemy combatants does not constitute a violation of this proscription against unnecessary suffering or superfluous injury."

Perfidy. Paragraph 12.2 prohibits the perfidious use of protected signs, signals, and symbols to injure, kill, or capture an enemy. Similarly, Para 12.7 states "it is a violation of the law of war to kill injure, or capture the enemy by false indication of intent to surrender or by feigning shipwreck, sickness, wounds, or civilian status." These provisions are virtually identical to the perfidious acts forbidden in AP I Article 37(1).

Neutral Flags/Insignia/Uniforms. Paragraph 12.3.3 states "belligerents engaged in armed conflict on land are not permitted to use the flags, insignia, or uniforms of a neutral nation to deceive the enemy." This prohibition is mirrored in AP I Article 39(1) that bars "use in an armed conflict of the flags or military emblems, insignia or uniforms of a neutral or other States not Parties to the conflict."

Enemy Flags/Insignia/Uniforms. Paragraph 12.5.3 states the law of land warfare does not forbid a belligerent from using enemy indicia for the purposes of deception before or after an armed engagement. However, a belligerent must not use such deception during the engagement. This is contrary to AP I Article 39(2) that prohibits the use of these items to gain any advantage over the enemy.

5.4.5 2010 Manual for Military Commissions

The Military Commissions Act of 2009[147] (hereinafter 2009 MCA) established "procedures governing the use of military commissions to try alien unprivileged enemy belligerents for violations of the law of war and other offenses triable by

[147] Military Commissions Act of 2009, Pub. L. 111-84, 123 Stat. 2574 [hereinafter "2009 MCA"] The Act superseded the Military Commission Act of 2006, Pub. L. 109-366, 120 Stat. 2600. The 2009 MCA is available at http://www.mc.mil/LEGALRESOURCES/Military CommissionsDocuments/CurrentDocuments.aspx.

military commission."[148] The 2009 MCA authorized the Secretary of Defense to promulgate specific procedures for the conduct of the commissions, to include elements of the crimes set forth in the statute and the modes of proof.[149] To that end, the Secretary of Defense published the 2010 Manual for Military Commissions [hereinafter 2010 Manual] on 27 April 2010.[150] Since the 2009 MCA and 2010 Manual constitute an expression of what both the legislative and executive branches believe to constitute violations of the law of armed conflict, they represent valuable references.

The 2010 Manual list the crimes codified in the 2009 MCA and supplement them with supporting elements and commentary. These enumerated criminal offenses proscribe certain conduct in a manner largely consistent with comparable provisions in AP I. For instance the 2010 Manual prohibits, *inter alia*, denial of quarter; use of human shields; and, intentional attacks against the civilian population, civilians not taking a direct or active part in hostilities, civilian property, and property granted special protection by the law of armed conflict.[151]

There are two areas worthy of specific mention where the 2010 Manual overlaps provision of AP I. The 2010 Manual defines objects which qualify as military objectives as those "which by their nature, location, purpose, or use, effectively contribute to the opposing force's war fighting or war sustaining capability… the total or partial destruction, capture, or neutralization of which constitute a definite military advantage to the attacker under the circumstances at the time of the attack."[152] The notable distinction between this definition of military objective and that listed in AP I Article 52(2) is the inclusion of "war sustaining capability."[153] Article 52(2) only references objects which by their nature, location, purpose, or use make an effective contribution to *military action*" (emphasis added).

The Manual also delineates the crime of "treachery and perfidy." The text of the offense reads "[a]ny person subject to [the jurisdiction of the military commissions] who, after inviting the confidence or belief of one or more persons that they were entitled to, or obliged to accord, protection under the law of war,

---

[148] 2009 MCA, *supra* n. 147, at §948b(a). The Act defines an "unprivileged enemy belligerent" as one who does not belong to any of the categories enumerated in Article 4 of GC 3, *supra* note 3, and who has "engaged in hostilities against the United States or its coalition partners; has purposefully or materially supported hostilities against the United States or its coalition partners; or was part of al Qaeda at the time of the alleged offense." Ibid. at §948a(6)&(7). The Act further defines "hostilities" as "any conflict subject to the law of war." Ibid. at §948a(9). Thus, it confers jurisdiction over unprivileged enemy belligerents in both international and non-international armed conflict.

[149] Ibid at §949a(a).

[150] Department of Defense Manual for Military Commissions (2010 edition) [*hereinafter* "2010 Manual"]. The 2010 Manual is available at: http://www.mc.mil/LEGALRESOURCES/MilitaryCommissionsDocuments/CurrentDocuments.aspx.

[151] See ibid. at Part IV "Crimes and Elements" at pp. IV-1-26.

[152] Ibid. at Part IV, Para 1(a)(1)(B), p. IV-1.

[153] This is consistent with NWP 1-14 M, *supra* note 137, para 8.2 that also references "war sustaining capability" in its definition of military objectives.

intentionally makes use of that confidence or belief in killing, injuring, or capturing such person or persons shall be punished [as a commission may direct]."[154]

The crime is substantively similar to AP I Article 37(1). Although the text of the crime itself does not contain the examples of perfidy included in AP I Art 37(1)(a)–(d), they are included in the 2010 Manual's commentary regarding the offense. What makes the Commissions' use of the AP I definition notable is it incorporates "capture" as one of the ends that cannot be achieved by perfidious conduct. AP I added "capture" to the definition of perfidy where it had not existed before in treaty law.[155] The International Committee of the Red Cross believes the rule against capture by perfidy represents customary international law.[156] Not all agree that this rule has achieved such status.[157]

5.5 Conclusion

Since there is no single authoritative instrument specifying which AP I provisions the United States rejects or follows in whole or in part, those who seek answers to these questions must analyze a multitude of references. Given that the vast majority of States are Party to AP I, including almost all of the US' major allies, the importance of identifying which provisions are regarded by the US as binding—as a matter of law and/or policy—is not merely an academic exercise. For military commanders, planners, and operational law practitioners, understanding the different legal obligations of the respective States participating in, for example, multinational operations enhances interoperability.

In the process of collating existing documentation from treaty provisions to military manuals which together form the basis of current US practice in respect of conduct of hostilities, this note has aimed to draw attention to the commonalities and points of divergence between such practice and the provisions contained in AP I. Thus, it is envisaged that this study might provide others with a helpful point of departure from which to pursue further research. One caveat is in order. The law of armed conflict treaty obligations of the United States provide the framework for its legal obligations during the conduct of hostilities. They are not easily changed. However, to the extent the reader draws conclusion from legal manuals, doctrinal publications, policy statements, and domestic law included in this note, these are more susceptible to revision. They should be periodically reviewed for currency.

---

154 2010 Manual, *supra* note 150 at Para 5(17), pp. IV-14-15.

155 However, "capture" is included in the definitions of perfidious conduct set forth NWP 1-14 M, *supra* note 137, paras 12.3 & 12.7.

156 See Henckaerts and Doswald-Beck 2005, [Vol. 1] Rule 65.

157 Dinstein 2010, at p. 231.

References

Aldrich GH (1991) Prospects for United States ratification of additional protocol I to the 1949 Geneva Conventions. Am J Int Law 85:2

Bellinger JB, Haynes WJ (2007) A US Government response to the International Committee of the Red Cross Study Customary International Humanitarian Law. Int Rev Red Cross 89:443

Boothby W (2010) "And for such time as": the time dimension to direct participation in hostilities. N Y Univ J Int Law Policy 42:741

Bothe M, Partsch KJ, Solf WA (1982) New rules for victims of armed conflicts: commentary on the two 1977 protocols additional to the Geneva Conventions of 1949. Martinus Nijhoff, The Hague

CLAMO (2008) Forged in the fire: legal lessons learned during military operations 1994–2008. United States Army Center for Law and Military Operations

Dinstein Y (2010) The conduct of hostilities under the law of international armed conflict. Cambridge University Press, Cambridge

Gasser HP (1987) An appeal for ratification by the United States. Am J Int Law 81:912

Henckaerts JM, Doswald-Beck L (2005) Customary International Humanitarian Law, vols 1 and 2. Cambridge University Press, Cambridge

International and Operational Law Department (2010) The Judge Advocate General's Legal Center & School, Law of War Documentary Supplement (2010 ed.) available at http://www.loc.gov/rr/frd/Military_Law/pdf/law-of-war-documentary-supplement_2010.pdf

International & Operational Law Department (2011) The Judge Advocate General's Legal Center & School, Operational Law Handbook

Matheson MJ (1987) The United States position on the relation of customary international law to the 1977 protocols additional to the 1949 Geneva Conventions. Am Univ J Int Law Policy 2:419

Matheson MJ (2006) Continuity and change in the law of war: 1975 to 2005: Detainees and POWs. George Wash Int Law Rev 38:543

Melzer N (2009) Interpretive guidance on the notion of direct participation in hostilities under international humanitarian law. ICRC, Geneva

Parks WH (1990) Air war and the law of war. Air Force Law Rev 32:1

Parks WH (2003) Special forces' wear of non-standard uniforms. Chic J Int Law 4:493

Parks WH (2010a) Part IX of the ICRC "Direct participation in hostilities" study: no mandate, no expertise, and legally incorrect. N Y Univ J Int Law Policy 42:769

Parks WH (2010b) "National Security Law in Practice: The Department of Defense Law of War Manual" available at http://www.americanbar.org/content/dam/aba/migrated/2011_build/law_national_security/hays_parks_speech_2010.authcheckdam.pdf

Roberts A, Guelff R (2005) Documents on the law of war, 3rd edn. Oxford University Press, Oxford

Sandoz Y, Swinarski C, and Zimmerman B (eds) (1987) Commentary on the additional protocols of 8 June 1977 to the Geneva conventions of 12 August 1949, Martinus Nijhoff

Schindler D, Toman J (2004) The laws of armed conflict: a collection of conventions, resolutions, and other documents, 4th edn. Martinus Nijhoff, Boston

Schmitt MN (2010) The interpretive guidance on the notion of direct participation in hostilities: a critical analysis. Harv Nat Sec J 1:5

Sofaer A (1987) The position of the United States on current law of war agreements. Am Univ J Int Law Policy 2:460

Watkin K (2010) Opportunity lost: organized armed groups and the ICRC "Direct Participation in Hostilities" interpretive guidance. N Y Univ J Int Law Policy 42:641

Part II
Current Developments

Chapter 6
Year in Review 2011

Mohbuba Choudhury, Aleksandra Bojovic and Louise Arimatsu

Contents

L. Arimatsu (✉)
Chatham House, London, UK
e-mail: LArimatsu@chathamhouse.org

M. Choudhury
e-mail: mohbuba.c@gmail.com

A. Bojovic
LSE, London, UK
e-mail: A.Bojovic@lse.ac.uk

M.N. Schmitt and L. Arimatsu (eds.), *Yearbook of International Humanitarian Law Volume 14, 2011*, DOI: 10.1007/978-90-6704-855-2_6,

6.1 Major Events in IHL in 2011

2011 will be remembered for two defining series of events of a global dimension, each of which prompted debate and disagreement among IHL experts: the Arab Spring and the killing of Osama bin Laden and other high ranking terrorist suspects.

6.1.1 The Arab Spring

Even the most visionary expert commentators on the Middle East and North Africa could not have predicted on 1 January 2011 that by year end, three autocratic heads of state in the region would have been toppled and that hundreds of thousands of Syrian citizens would have taken to the streets in those final days of 2011 to demand the removal of President Bashar al-Assad. The history books will record 2011 as a year in which parts of the Arab world witnessed fundamental political change with the deposing of Zine el Abidine Ben Ali in Tunisia, Hosni Mubarak in Egypt and Muammar Gaddafi in Libya. But the history books will also note that 2011 marked the beginning of a new age when mass protest, revolution and armed conflict was not only facilitated by, but made possible through, digital communication networks and social networking sites. *Facebook*, *Twitter* and *YouTube* had transformed civil society's engagement with, and in, warfare.

The catalyst for the revolutions—some violent, some less so—that swept across the Arab world can be traced back to the single act of a young Tunisian man. On 17 December 2010, following the confiscation of his street stall by the local police, Mohamed Bouazizi set himself on fire as an act of protest sparking riots and demonstrations across the country. When Bouazizi died of his wounds on 5 January, the rioting intensified. Nine days later, Ben Ali, who had ruled Tunisia for 23 years, fled the country and was eventually granted asylum in Saudi Arabia. That a regime which had lasted decades would collapse within weeks under popular protest inspired others in the region to follow suit. Over the course of the year protestors took to the streets in Egypt, Yemen, Libya, Syria, Saudi Arabia, Bahrain, Morocco and Jordan.

By mid-January protestors in Egypt had clashed with riot police and the state's notorious security service. The regime's hard-line approach towards the protestors back-fired and, as the days progressed, the number of disaffected grew. Cairo's Tahrir Square became the symbolic site of protest, with tens of thousands gathering daily demanding the end of Mubarak's 29 year rule. At the end of January, Egypt's military formally declared that it would not use force against the protestors and on 11

February, after 18 days of mass protest, Mubarak's rule came to an unexpectedly swift end with the announcement that power was being transferred to the military. In May, Mubarak was charged, inter alia, with 'intentional murder, attempted killing of some demonstrators, misuse of influence and deliberately wasting public funds, and unlawfully making private financial gains and profits'; his trial opened on 3 August. Meanwhile, delays in handing over to a civilian government prompted demonstrators to return to Tahrir Square leading to clashes with the armed forces. On 28 November, Egyptians voted in record numbers in the first of a three stage electoral process to determine the composition of both houses of parliament; the event marked the first free ballot for over 80 years.

In late January thousands gathered in a public demonstration calling for the end of President Ali Abdullah Saleh's 32 year rule in Yemen. As the movement for change gathered momentum, on 2 February, President Saleh announced he would relinquish power in 2013. Demonstrations nevertheless continued throughout the spring and summer for the immediate removal of Saleh from office. Violent clashes with the security forces and government loyalists led to the killing of hundreds of protestors. On 3 June President Saleh was seriously wounded in an attack—initially attributed to anti-government loyalists and later to al Qaeda—and underwent medical treatment in Saudi Arabia. Throughout September and into early October the violence intensified as the Republican Guards deployed greater force in their confrontations with the pro-democracy campaigners who were joined by a division of renegade soldiers. On 23 November, after nine months of mass protest, Saleh agreed to step down in return for immunity from prosecution; but the growing insecurity within Yemen (evidenced by al Qaeda's continued presence) coupled with the lack of a united opposition enabled Saleh to continue to assert political power.

Despite the media blackout imposed by the Gaddafi regime, by mid-February, reports of violent clashes between protestors and the Libyan security forces began to surface. In Benghazi, in the east of Libya, the death toll rose to several hundred within a matter of days as the troops and mercenaries deployed by the regime exerted an unparalleled level of force against the demonstrators. With the violence intensifying, high-ranking Libyan diplomats and some members of the Libyan military began to defect in protest and, on 23 February, news emerged that Benghazi had fallen under rebel control. By early March the number of refugees fleeing from Libya to Tunisia had risen to over 85,000 and the heightened security situation across the country prompted foreign governments to arrange the mass evacuation of non-nationals. In the face of an escalating air campaign by the regime, the newly established Provisional Transitional National Council (TNC) called on the international community to impose a no-fly zone. On 18 March, the Security Council adopted a resolution authorising member states to use force to protect civilians under attack and to establish a no-fly zone.[1] Within 48 h, Operation Odyssey Dawn—later renamed Operation Unified Protector—was launched: more than 110 Tomahawk cruise missiles were fired from US and British ships and submarines in the

[1] See Sect. 6.3.1.5 for further details.

Mediterranean striking Libya's air-defence system and other military targets and around 20 French Mirage and Rafale fighter planes were deployed in the region of Benghazi.[2] Despite NATO's intervention, heavy fighting continued unabated throughout the spring and into summer; rebel advances towards Tripoli were met with resistance and the cities of Misrata and Sirte became synonymous with high levels of civilian casualties. On 27 June the ICC issued arrest warrants for Gadaffi, his son and Libya's chief of intelligence for crimes against humanity committed during the anti-regime protests.[3] As the summer progressed, the rebels made significant advances against Gaddafi's forces and, in late June, Britain formally recognised the TNC as the official government of Libya. By the third week in August Tripoli had fallen under rebel control but Gadaffi loyalists continued to put up strong resistance in Sirte where, on 20 October, Gadaffi was captured and killed bringing to an end the dictator's 42 years in power.

Reports of protests and unrest in Syria began to filter through in mid-March when the security forces opened fire on protesters in the southern city of Deraa killing several people. Over the following weeks unrest and violence spread across the country with demonstrators demanding 'freedom' and calling for President al-Assad, whose family has ruled Syria for nearly 40 years, to step down. By the end of April the violence had intensified with hundreds reported dead following wide-scale military operations prompting foreign governments to advise their nationals to leave the country. As the protests continued over the course of late spring into early summer, the Syrian authorities exerted increasing levels of force with the death toll soon reaching over 1,000. Although an EU arms embargo came into effect in early May, it was not until 3 August, that the Security Council agreed to issue a presidential statement condemning the on-going violence against the protesters by the Syrian forces. Four days later the Arab League called on Syria to stop the violence against civilians and, as international criticism of the regime mounted, Saudi Arabia recalled its Ambassador from Damascus in protest. Undeterred, the Syrian authorities continued to shell cities and detain hundreds of activists. On 4 October, China and Russia vetoed a draft Security Council resolution recommending measures under Article 41 of the Charter; several days later, the Russian president publicly urged al-Assad to reform or leave office and several days later China, too, called for swift reforms. On 8 November, the Office of the High Commissioner on Human Rights (OHCHR) estimated that at least 3,500 civilians had been killed and thousands of others detained, tortured and ill-treated; the highest number of casualties were in the cities of Homs, Hama and Daraa. In an emergency session on 12 November, the Arab League voted to suspend Syria's membership provoking further violence across the country in which nearly 300 more civilians were killed. On 23 November a report by the independent international commission of inquiry, established by the Human Rights Council, was

[2] On March 23 it was agreed that NATO would assume the day-to-day military command of the operation.

[3] See Sect. 6.3.2.

published documenting widespread human rights violations amounting to crimes against humanity.[4] Under increasing international pressure, on 19 December, Syria agreed to the terms of an Arab League proposal to withdraw its armed forces from cities and residential areas, release detained protesters, and allow monitors into the country to verify implementation of the accord. The mission began its visit on 26 December amidst continued violence across the country; as the year came to an end, OHCHR estimated that over 5,000 people have lost their lives since March 2011.

There is no shortage of evidence pointing to widespread human rights violations across the Arab world in response to protests by civil society. However, whether, and if so on what basis, such violations *also* breached international humanitarian law is another matter. Whether IHL applied to the armed violence in each of the Arab states is contingent on whether there was an armed conflict that requires consideration on a case by case basis. Nonetheless, human rights law continues to apply in armed conflict with IHL applying as the *lex specialis*.

It is now accepted that an armed conflict exists when there is a resort to armed force between states or protracted armed violence between governmental authorities and organized armed groups, or between such groups. The test to determine the existence of a non-international armed conflict—in contrast to situations of internal disturbances and tensions, such as riots and isolated and sporadic acts of violence—consists of two criteria: the intensity of the conflict and the organization of the parties to the conflict.

The number of casualties sustained as a consequence of the violence is *one* indicator, among others, to suggest that the intensity criterion has been met. Other criteria may include the mobilisation of troops by the government, the kind of weaponry utilised, the destruction of property and the displacement of local populations. Factors that indicate that the armed group is sufficiently organised include, for example, the command structure and exercise of leadership control, the provision of training, the organised acquisition of weapons, the recruitment of new members and the existence of a communication infrastructure. Although these criteria function to assist in reaching an objective assessment as to the existence of an armed conflict, there is no bright line rule. Consequently these and other factors must be considered in their totality.[5]

In Tunisia it is estimated that over 300 people were killed during the protests; crucially, what was not identifiable was an organized armed element with a defined command structure among the protesters. It is doubtful therefore that IHL applied in Tunisia. What is worthy of note is that much of the organised action was mediated through digital social networks that are intrinsically horizontal, rather than vertical, in nature. But even if Tunisia represents a new organisational model, the decisive factor is that such groups resort to resistance by every means except

[4] UN Human Rights Council, Report of the independent international commission of inquiry on the Syrian Arab Republic, A/HRC/S-17/2/Add.1, 23 November 2011, available at: http://www.ohchr.org/Documents/Countries/SY/A.HRC.S-17.2.Add.1_en.pdf.

[5] ICTY, *Prosecutor v Milosevic*, Trial Chamber Decision on motion for judgement of acquittal, 16 June 2004 (IT-02-54-T).

through *armed* violence; moreover the direct and immediate effect of the strategies adopted are not intended to be equivalent to the effect of armed violence.

Compared with Tunisia, the number of casualties in Egypt was higher with 900 killed and an estimated 6,400 injured. The Egyptian army's decision not to use force against the protesters was of critical significance in that a full scale civil war was averted. As with Tunisia, there was no clearly identifiable organized armed opposition grouping as such, and much of the protest movement was facilitated through digital social networks. The arbitrary killings and detentions as well as the abusive treatment of detainees by the state amounted to gross human rights violations, potentially to crimes against humanity, but it is unlikely that IHL applied.

The level of the violence in Yemen with over 1,500 killed and a further 1,000 injured would suggest that the intensity criteria of the NIAC test was met. Yemen, however, presents an ambiguous case.[6] A renegade division of the Yemeni armed forces which defected to the opposition in March as well as members of organized armed groups belonging to various tribal groups were involved in heavy fighting with the Yemeni authorities. Insofar as the hostilities between these groups and government forces are concerned, it is likely that, at a minimum, common Article 3 applies. Nevertheless, human rights law continues to apply to the armed forces in their engagement with the protesters, the vast majority of whom, it would appear, are not part of any organized command structure.

Most commentators are agreed that two concurrent armed conflicts were waged in Libya during 2011 to which IHL applied. With some estimates suggesting that as many as 30,000 were killed and a further 50,000 injured, it is clear that from the first days of unrest, the level of violence was severe. It is difficult to pinpoint the precise moment at which IHL became applicable to the fighting between the rebel forces and the Gadaffi loyalists. But at some point in late February (when the rebel forces took control of Benghazi) and early March (when the TNC was formally established with some command and control over the rebels) the two-fold test of a non-international armed conflict was satisfied.[7] The international armed conflict—between Gadaffi's armed forces and those states that were acting under SCR1973 to enforce the no fly zone and to 'protect civilians'—broke out at the point when Operation Odyssey Dawn was launched. What is less certain is the precise moment when the conflict became non-international in character. In other words, does the recognition of a rebel group as the legitimate representatives of the state by a single member state of a coalition force transform an IAC into a NIAC between the recognising state and the

---

[6] See for example, Security Council resolution 2014, para 5 which '[d]emands that the Yemeni authorities immediately ensure their actions comply with obligations under applicable international humanitarian and human rights law, allow the people of Yemen to exercise their human rights and fundamental freedoms, including their rights of peaceful assembly to demand redress of their grievances and freedom of expression, including for member of the media, and take action to end attacks against civilians and civilian targets by security forces'; S/RES/2014 (2011) of 21 October. See also Chap. 1 on concurrent non-international armed conflicts on Yemen's territory.

[7] As Libya was party to Additional Protocol II, the conflict was governed by both CA3 and APII.

armed forces of what was until then, the legitimate government? Or is recognition by a majority of states (at least those directly involved in the armed conflict) required? The IAC also prompted a string of supplementary legal questions over which experts divided including: (1) What precisely did SCR1973 authorise? (2) Could Gaddafi be targeted? (3) Could the rebels be trained and armed? (4) What rules governed the different parties to the conflict?[8]

As the year came to an end, there was a growing body of opinion that the situation in Syria had deteriorated to such a degree that IHL applied. With 5,000 dead and an estimated 14,000 detained (and many 'disappeared') the level of the violence wielded by the state authorities clearly satisfied the requisite intensity threshold. But was there an identifiable organised armed element? Since the start of the unrest, there have been numerous defections from the military and security forces that have joined the protesters and some have organized themselves into the 'Free Syrian Army' which has called for international intervention in much the same way as did the Libyan TNC. The shift in the Russian and Chinese positions towards the end of the year, together with the steps taken by the Arab League, suggest that unless the regime adopts a change of course within the first half of 2012, al-Assad may face the same fate as three heads of state did in 2011.

6.1.2 Targeted Killings and Al Qaeda[9]

On 2 May 2011 Osama bin Laden, the leader of al Qaeda, was killed in his compound in Abbottabad, Pakistan during a military operation carried out by American Special Forces. Following the operation President Obama, who authorized it, commented: 'The death of bin Laden marks the most significant achievement to date in our nation's effort to defeat al Qaeda, yet his death does not mark the end of our effort'.[10]

When the news broke, Pakistan publicly objected to the unauthorized unilateral use of force by the US on its territory and former President Musharraf criticized the operation on the grounds that Pakistan's sovereignty had been violated. This raised questions as to whether a state could invoke the right to self-defence against a non-state actor on the territory of another state without the consent of the territorial state. The operation also raised a host of other legal questions including, once more, whether an armed conflict exists between the US and al Qaeda and, if so, what type and whether international human rights law had been breached. The US administration has long maintained that it continues to be in an armed conflict with al Qaeda[11] and on that basis, it acted in full compliance with the principles of

---

[8] See Chap. 7.

[9] For a further discussion of the legal questions raised, see Chap. 9.

[10] US Department of Defense 2011.

[11] Koh 2010.

international humanitarian law.[12] US Attorney General Holder stated before the US Senate Judiciary Committee that bin Laden was a 'lawful military target' and equated killing him to the targeting of an enemy commander in the field.[13]

On 7 May 2011, the US launched a drone strike in Yemen against the leader of al Qaeda in the Arab Peninsula (AQAP), Anwar al-Awlaki, an American citizen. The strike was conducted by the US military with close cooperation of Yemeni officials, though al-Awlaki escaped.[14] On 30 September 2011, a further drone strike by the US in Yemen killed al-Awlaki. These drone strikes raise similar questions regarding the existence of an armed conflict and the appropriate legal framework to be applied to such situations. This particular killing has also prompted debate as to whether the Executive branch has the authority to execute US citizens outside of combat zones. A judicial review by the American Civil Liberties Union and the Center for Constitutional Rights challenging the US policy on targeted killings in the Federal Court was unsuccessful on procedural grounds.[15] The US administration has continued to justify the drone strikes under the laws of armed conflict and self defence.

6.1.3 Turkel Commission Report

Israel's public commission to examine the maritime incident of 31 May 2010[16]—the Turkel Commission—was set up by the Israeli government on 14 June 2010 and headed by a former Justice of the Supreme Court, Justice Emeritus Jacob Turkel. The other members of the Commission included Ambassador Reuven Merhav, a retired diplomat; Major-General Amos Horev, a former army general; Professor Miguel Deutch, a civil law expert; and Ambassador Professor Shabtai Rossene, an international law expert (who died prior to the release of the report). The Commission also included two international observers, Lord David Trimble and the former Judge Advocate General of the Canadian Forces, Brigadier General Kenneth Watkins.

On 23 January 2011 the Turkel Commission published the first of its two reports into the Maritime Incident of 31 May 2010.[17] The report addresses two

---

[12] Koh 2011.

[13] US Attorney General Holder 2011.

[14] Coker et al. 2011.

[15] *Al-Aulaqi v Obama* (US District Court for the district of Columbia) 7 December 2010, available at: http://www.aclu.org/files/assets/2010-12-7-AulaqivObama-Decision.pdf.

[16] For further details and analysis on the incident, see volume 12 Yearbook of International Humanitarian Law.

[17] Part two of the report will address the question of whether the mechanism for examining and investigating complaints and claims of violations of IHL as carried out by Israel in general (and in particular as implemented with regard to the Maritime Incident) complies with Israel's international law obligations. See also Chap. 2.

main legal questions surrounding the incident: (i) the legality of the naval blockade on Gaza; and (ii) whether the actions undertaken by the Israeli Defence Force (IDF) to enforce the naval blockade complied with international law. In arriving at its findings, the Commission relied on oral and written evidence and took legal advice from two independent international law experts, Professor Wolff Heintschel von Heinegg and Professor Dr Michael Schmitt.

Prior to determining the legality of the blockade, the Commission first considered the classification of the conflict between Israel and Hamas. This was because the rules governing naval blockades were generally developed within the framework of international armed conflicts; in other words, those fought between two or more states rather than between a state and a non-state armed group or between such groups. Although the Commission concludes that 'it is likely there will be a willingness on the part of courts and other bodies to recognize that the rules governing the imposition and enforcement of a naval blockade are applicable to non-international armed conflicts',[18] it nonetheless assumes for the purposes of the Report, that the conflict between Israel and Hamas is international in character.[19] This decision was reached on the basis of the case law of Israel's Supreme Court and the practice of various UN organizations, humanitarian organizations and human rights organizations. The Commission was therefore able to rely largely on the 1994 San Remo Manual on International Law applicable to Armed Conflicts at Sea in finding that the naval blockade was lawful and that Israel had complied with all conditions for imposing it.

IHL prohibits the imposition of a naval blockade if its sole purpose is to starve the civilian population or prevent the supply of other objects essential for its survival.[20] The Commission concluded that there was no evidence, in the considerable amount of material submitted to it, to the effect that Israel was 'trying to deprive the population of the Gaza Strip of food or to annihilate or weaken the population by means of starvation'.[21] Moreover, according to the Commission, humanitarian and human rights organizations had described the situation as one of 'food insecurity' rather than 'starvation'.[22] Article 102 of the San Remo Manual also prohibits a blockading party from depriving the civilian population of 'objects essential for its survival'. Basing its conclusions on the evidence before it, the Commission found no evidence that Israel was in violation of this rule.[23] Nor did the Commission find that Israel was in violation of the customary international humanitarian law rule that requires a state to allow the free passage of medical equipment, albeit subject to the right to prescribe technical arrangements under

[18] Para 42.
[19] Para 41.
[20] Article 102(a) San Remo Manual and Article 54(1) of Additional Protocol I.
[21] Turkel Committee Report, Part A, para 76.
[22] Para 77.
[23] Para 80.

which such passage is permitted.[24] Nevertheless, the Commission was not entirely uncritical of the provision and level of healthcare available to civilians in Gaza.

The Commission took very seriously the claims made by some critics that the naval blockade constituted a form of 'collective punishment' on the civilian population in Gaza. Such measures have long been prohibited under IHL and, in some instances, criminalised. The Commission rejected the proposition that imposing a naval blockade and adopting a method of economic warfare could be equated to 'collective punishment' as understood under international law. A broad interpretation of what constitutes 'collective punishment', according to the Commission, 'has to be reconciled with both the nature of a naval blockade as a lawful form of warfare and the specific customary law provisions regulating the conduct of such a blockade.'[25] While conceding that civilian population is likely to feel the adverse effects of a blockade or economic warfare, the critical issue is 'what that impact is and what mitigating humanitarian measures are put in place' by the blockading party. The Commission found no evidence to suggest that Israel was *intentionally* placing restrictions on goods for the sole or primary purpose of denying them to the population of Gaza.[26]

The Commission then examined the actions undertaken by the IDF aboard the Mavi Marmara which resulted in the death of nine Turkish nationals as well as the wounding of fifty-five passengers and nine IDF soldiers to assess whether they had been in conformity with international law. As the Commission noted, 'an attempt to breach a properly established blockade is a non-neutral act' and, as a result, a ship that attempts to do so becomes subject to the rules governing the conduct of hostilities.[27] Customary international law entitles a blockading party to intercept a vessel that is purposefully attempting to breach the blockade in international waters. The Commission therefore concluded that the Israeli armed forces were justified in boarding the flotilla vessels given the intention of the flotilla organizers to breach the blockade and the refusal of the ships' captains to alter their course after repeated warnings.[28]

Having found the interception to have been lawful under international law, the Commission then turned to the difficult question of the level of force that could be deployed against those on board the flotilla. In doing so, it distinguished between the vast majority of the passengers who, throughout the incident, retained the protections of their civilian status and a small minority of activists who, in taking a direct part in the hostilities by resorting to violence, lost that protection.[29] The test applied by the Commission to determine direct participation was that established in the *Targeted Killings* case although the same conclusion, in the Commission's

---

[24] Para 86.

[25] Para 103.

[26] Turkel Committee Report, Part A, para 106.

[27] Para 171.

[28] Para 175.

[29] Para 189.

view, would have been reached by applying the standards set out in the ICRC's *DPH Interpretive Guidance*.[30] According to IHL, 'the use of force against civilians who are not taking a direct part in the hostilities is governed by law enforcement norms, whereas direct participants can be targeted for such time they are taking part in hostilities.'[31] Applying this test to the facts at hand, the Commission declared that of the 133 incidents in which force was used, 127 cases appeared to be in conformity with international law. Insufficient evidence prevented the Commission from reaching a conclusion on the remaining six cases.[32] In five out of the 127 incidents, each of which involved individuals taking a direct part in the hostilities, there was insufficient evidence to conclude that the use of force was in accordance with law enforcement norms although IHL standards were satisfied.[33]

6.1.4 Report of the Secretary-General's Panel of Inquiry on the 31 May 2010 Flotilla Incident

On 2 August 2010, the UN Secretary-General established a Panel of Inquiry to examine the facts, circumstances and context of the flotilla incident which occurred on 31 May 2010 and to make recommendations to avoid similar situations in the future.[34] The panel was headed by Sir Geoffrey Palmer, former Prime Minister of New Zealand. The other panel members included Alvaro Uribe, former President of Columbia; Joseph Ciechanover Itzhar, a representative of Israel; and Süleyman Özdem Sanberk, a representative of Turkey.

The Report was released in September 2011 after the Panel had the opportunity to review the reports of the national investigations conducted by both Turkey (*Report of Turkish National Commission of Inquiry, February 2011*) and Israel (report of *The Turkel Commission*). In rejecting Turkey's arguments that the blockade itself was illegal (and therefore the interception of the flotilla was in breach of international law) the Panel accepted the Israeli report's reasoning that the blockade was adopted for the purpose of defending its territory and population. Accordingly, the Panel found that the blockade was not 'a disproportionate measure for Israel to have taken in response to the threat it faced.'[35] Turning to the characterization of the conflict between Israel and Hamas, the Panel concluded that the conflict should be treated as an international one for the purposes of the law of blockade.[36]

30 Para 201.

31 Para 234.

32 Para 239(e).

33 Para 255.

34 Para 3.

35 Para 72.

36 Para 73.

The Panel considered the conditions for a lawful blockade and noted that important humanitarian considerations constrain such measures. It nevertheless found no evidence that suggested the naval blockade was imposed by Israel other than as a legitimate security measure in order to prevent weapons from entering Gaza by sea; moreover, its implementation complied with the requirements of international law and was therefore found to be lawful.[37] In concluding that the blockade was neither disproportionate nor amounted to collective punishment on the civilians in Gaza, the Panel noted that its findings deviated from those of the Turkish report and the Human Rights Council's report of the international fact-finding mission.[38] This discrepancy in outcome was justified on the grounds that 'the reasoning of both reports rested on an analysis that the naval blockade formed an indivisible part of Israel's land restrictions policy'; this was a factual conclusion that the Panel did not share.[39]

The Panel turned to the question of the manner in which the blockade had been enforced by Israel and whether it was executed appropriately in the circumstances.[40] In the opinion of the Panel, Israel's decision to board the Mavi Marmara 'with such substantial force at a great distance from the blockade zone and with no final warning prior to the boarding was excessive and unreasonable'. In particular, the Panel was of the view that 'non-violent options should have been used in the first instance' and 'clear prior warning that the vessels were to be boarded and a demonstration of dissuading force should have been given to avoid the type of confrontation that occurred.'[41] Although the Panel recognised that the IDF faced 'significant, organized violent resistance' from a group aboard the Mavi Marmara which required the soldiers to use force, it also found the resulting loss of life and injuries by the IDF to be 'unacceptable'. Criticism was directed at Israel for failing to provide a satisfactory explanation for the nine deaths[42] but also for the significant mistreatment of passengers by Israeli authorities in the period between taking over the vessels and deportation. Passengers had been physically mistreated, harassed and intimidated, their belongings confiscated without justification and been denied timely consular assistance.[43]

The Panel then addressed the second part of its remit and directed its first recommendation to Israel: that it should keep the naval blockade under regular review in order to assess whether it continues to be necessary.[44] Insofar as naval blockades more generally are concerned, the Panel made the following recommendations[45]:

---

37 Paras 76–82.

38 UN Human Rights Council 2010, Report of the international fact-finding mission to investigate violations of international law, including international humanitarian law and human rights law, resulting from the Israeli attacks on the flotilla of ships carrying humanitarian assistance, A/HRC/15/21 (27 September 2010).

39 Turkel Commission, para 81.

40 Para 110.

41 Para 117.

42 Para 134.

43 Para 145.

44 Para 150.

45 Para 164.

- The imposition of a naval blockade as an action in self-defence should be reported to the Security Council under the procedures set out under Article 51 of the Charter;
- States maintaining a naval blockade must abide by their obligations with respect to the provision of humanitarian assistance. Humanitarian missions must act in accordance with the principles of neutrality, impartiality and humanity and respect any security measures in place. Humanitarian vessels should allow inspection and stop or change course when requested.
- Attempts to breach a lawfully imposed naval blockade place the vessel and those on board at risk. Where a State becomes aware that its citizens or flag vessels intend to breach a naval blockade, it has a responsibility to take pro-active steps compatible with democratic rights and freedoms to warn them of the risks involved and to endeavour to dissuade them from doing so.
- States enforcing a naval blockade against non-military vessels, especially where large numbers of civilian passengers are involved, should be cautious in the use of force. Efforts should first be made to stop the vessel by non-violent means. In particular, they should not use force except when absolutely necessary and then should only use the minimum level of force necessary to achieve the lawful objective of maintaining the blockade. They must provide clear and express warnings so that the vessels are aware if force is to be used against them.

6.1.5 Report of the Secretary General's Panel of Experts on Accountability in Sri Lanka[46]

On 22 June 2010, the Secretary General announced the appointment of a Panel of Experts to advise him on the 'modalities, applicable international standards and comparative experience relevant to an accountability process' to address violations of international human rights and humanitarian law committed during the final stages of the conflict in Sri Lanka.[47] More specifically, its temporal focus was on the period from September 2008 through May 2009 which encompassed the most intense and violent phase of the war culminating, in the words of the ICRC, in an 'unimaginable humanitarian catastrophe'.[48]

On 12 April, the three member Panel comprising Marzuki Darusman (chair), Yasmin Sooka and Steven Ratner delivered its report to the Secretary General. The key sections of the report deal with the nature and the scope of the alleged

[46] UNSG 2011, Report of the Secretary-General's Panel of Experts on Accountability in Sri Lanka, 31st March 2011, available at: http://www.un.org/News/dh/infocus/Sri_Lanka/POE_Report_Full.pdf. (Hereinafter 'Sri Lanka Panel of Experts').

[47] Executive summary and para 5.

[48] Para 123.

violations, legal evaluation of allegations, Sri Lanka's approach to accountability and further obstacles to accountability. The Panel examined a wide range of written sources, satellite images, photographs, video materials and conducted interviews with various individuals to arrive at its findings. Although its mandate precluded a fact-finding mission or investigation, it determined that there were credible allegations of serious violations of international humanitarian and human rights law (both treaty and customary international law) committed by both the Government of Sri Lanka and the Liberation Tigers of Tamil Eelam (LTTE) some of which would amount to war crimes and crimes against humanity.

On the evidence before it, the Panel identified 'five core categories of potential serious violations' committed by the Government of Sri Lanka which included[49]:

a. *Killing of civilians through widespread shelling*. The Sri Lanka Army (SLA) used 'large-scale and widespread shelling, at times with heavy weapons, causing large numbers of civilian deaths' in the Vanni region. It shelled in three No Fire Zones—where it had encouraged the civilian population to concentrate—and after it had indicated that it would stop using heavy weapons. Around 330,000 civilians were trapped into an ever decreasing area, fleeing the shelling but kept hostage by the LTTE. The SLA shelled in spite of its knowledge of the impact, provided through its own intelligence systems, including UAVs and through notification by various external actors, including the UN and ICRC. 'The majority of civilian casualties in the final phases were caused by Government shelling.' The Government sought to limit external criticism by excluding international organisations from the conflict zone.
b. *Shelling of hospitals and other humanitarian objects*. The Government 'systematically shelled hospitals on the frontlines, some of them repeatedly'. An unknown number of civilians were re-injured or killed due to the shelling; this was despite the fact that hospital locations were well-known to the Government.
c. *Denial of humanitarian assistance*. The Government 'systematically deprived those in the conflict zone of humanitarian aid in the form of food and medical supplies, particularly surgical supplies, adding to their suffering'. 'It deliberately underestimated the number of civilians who remained in the conflict zone.' Tens of thousands lost their lives between January and May 2009, many of whom died anonymously in the 'carnage of the final few days'.[50]
d. *Human rights violations suffered by victims and survivors of the conflict*. The Government 'subjected victims and survivors of the conflict to further deprivation and suffering after they left the conflict zone'. 'Suspected LTTE cadres were executed' and others 'disappeared'; compelling evidence indicated that the women were raped and sexually assaulted; and 'torture during interrogation continued'. IDPs were held in appalling conditions and prevented from speaking privately with humanitarian organizations.

---

[49] Para 176.

[50] Executive summary.

e. *Human rights violations outside the conflict zone*. The Government sought to intimidate and silence its critics through threats and abductions.

The Panel also identified six core categories of potential serious violations committed by the LTTE:

a. *Using civilians as a human buffer*. 'The LTTE refused civilians permission to leave the conflict zone and at times used them as a strategic human buffer between themselves and the advancing SLA'.
b. *Killing civilians attempting to flee LTTE control*. From February onwards, 'a policy of shooting civilians attempting to escape the conflict zone was instituted'.
c. *Using military equipment in the proximity of civilians*. 'The LTTE fired artillery from the NFZs in the knowledge that it would provoke a response from the SLA' putting civilians in harm's way.
d. *Forced recruitment of children*.
e. *Forced labour*.
f. *Killing of civilians through suicide attacks*.

Having documented the core potential violations, the Panel turned its attention to the applicable law. It found that at the material time, a non-international armed conflict was being waged between the LTTE and the Government; as such, IHL applied. Common Article 3 applied by virtue of treaty law supplemented by customary international law. In identifying the content of the latter, the Panel relied on various sources including the ICRC's 2005 *Customary International Humanitarian Law* Study (CIHL Study) and the jurisprudence of international criminal tribunals. While the Panel conceded that some disagreement among states exist over the customary status and scope of some restrictions on the conduct of parties involved in non-international armed conflicts, in its opinion, the rules on which it relied are 'beyond dispute' as to their binding status.[51] The Panel also noted that, 'as accepted by most states and confirmed by the International Court of Justice', IHR law also applied to the conflict. The Panel expressly rejected claims by both parties, albeit on different grounds, that the nature of the conflict affects the applicability of IHL obligations.[52]

For each of the five categories of credible allegations concerning the conduct by the Government, the Panel identified the following relevant legal rules[53]:

1. *The killing of civilians through widespread shelling*: CA3; the principle of distinction (Rule 1, *CIHL* study); the prohibition on attacking civilians and civilian objects (Rule 7 and 35); the prohibition on indiscriminate or disproportionate attacks on civilians (Rules 11-14); and the requirement to take precautions (Rules 15-20).

[51] Paras 181–183.

[52] Para 189.

[53] Paras 192–236.

2. *The shelling of hospitals and humanitarian objects*: CA3; the requirement to extend special protection to medical and humanitarian personnel and objects (Rules 25, 28, 30 31, 32); and the prohibition on attacking civilian and civilian objects (see above for Rules).
3. *The denial of humanitarian assistance*: CA3; the requirement to extend special protection to medical and humanitarian personnel and objects (as above); the prohibition on starvation as a method of warfare and denial of humanitarian relief (Rules 53, 55.
4. *Human rights violations suffered by victims and survivors of the conflict*: CA3; the prohibition on enforced disappearances (Rule 98); the requirement to ensure minimal levels of treatment for those deprived of liberty (Rule 118); the requirements regarding the dead and missing (Rules 112, 113, 115–117); the right to life and physical security and integrity (Articles 6 and 9, ICCPR and Article 7 CAT); the prohibition on arbitrary detention (Article 9, ICCPR); the right to food and water, clothing and shelter and health (Articles 11 and 12, ICESCR); freedoms of assembly and association (Articles 21 and 22 ICCPR). In addition, the Panel lists further human rights violations including provisions in CEDAW and the CRC; and the right to an effective remedy.
5. *Human rights violations outside the conflict zone*: ban on disappearances (Article 9, ICCPR); prohibition on torture (Article 7, ICCPR), right of detainees to be treated with respect (Article 10 ICCPR); freedom of opinion and expression (Article 19, ICCPR).

Insofar as the allegations involving the LTTE were concerned, the following rules were relevant:

1. *Using civilians as a human buffer:* CA 3.
2. *Killing civilians attempting to flee*: CA3.
3. *Using military equipment in the proximity of civilians*: the prohibition on locating military objectives near densely populated civilian areas (Rules 23-24).
4. *Forced recruitment of children*: the prohibition on recruiting children (Rules 136); and potentially violate CA3.
5. *Forced labour*: the prohibition on uncompensated or abusive force labour (Rule 95).
6. *Killing of civilians through suicide attacks*: CA3.

The Panel concluded that the allegations and violations by both parties point to the commission of war crimes and crimes against humanity[54]; moreover, that there are international obligations on states to investigate and prosecute such crimes irrespective of type of conflict.[55]

In the fifth section of the report, Sri Lanka's accountability mechanism is considered in some depth with the Panel concluding that the government's notion of

---

[54] Paras 246–252.

[55] Para 268.

accountability was 'not in accordance with international standards'.[56] In particular, the Panel found that the Government's *Lessons Learnt and Reconciliation Commission* (LLRC) failed to satisfy 'key international standards of independence and impartiality'. The LLRC was 'deeply flawed' because it had failed to conduct 'genuine truth-seeking' and had 'not sought to investigate systematically and impartially the allegations of serious violations'. The Panel's Report concluded with a set of recommendations including short and long term measures to advance accountability in Sri Lanka. It also recommended the Secretary-General to immediately establish an international mechanism to conduct independent investigations into the alleged violations of international humanitarian law and human rights law.

In November, the LLRC released its final report dealing with, inter alia, 'the facts and circumstances which led to the failure of the Ceasefire Agreement operationalized on 21st February 2002 and the sequence of events that followed thereafter until 19th May 2009'.[57] The report dedicates an entire chapter on 'Humanitarian Law Issues' (or 114 pages out of a total of 388) which is divided into a section listing relevant legal obligations followed by an application to the facts. On the principle of proportionality, the report emphasises the subjective element of the rule but, in doing so, fails to expressly acknowledge that the test also integrates an objective element. This is regrettable since the application of the rule to the facts fails to fully take into account the objective obligation, particularly in respect of the 'No Fire Zones' which had been unilaterally declared by the Sri Lankan Army.[58] The LLRC's report is striking for what is absent. Thus, while conceding that hospitals were repeatedly shelled, it draws no conclusion as to responsibility; moreover, it dismisses all allegations involving the denial of humanitarian assistance and the provision of medical care as either having been solely due to the actions the LTTE or that such measures were unavoidable given the level of hostilities existing at the material time.[59] By contrast, the commission encountered no difficulty in concluding that the LTTE were responsible for all the allegations referred to in the Panel's report.

Both reports are expected to be discussed at the next session of the UN Human Rights Council in March 2012.

6.1.6 In Brief

Many US citizens may look back at 2011 as marking the 'end' of the war in Iraq (2003-2011). The announcement on 21 October by President Obama that all US

---

56 Executive summary.

57 Report of the Commission of Enquiry on Lessons Learnt and Reconciliation, available at: http://www.priu.gov.lk/news_update/Current_Affairs/ca201112/FINAL%20LLRC%20REPORT.pdf. See LLRC section 1.5 for further details of its mandate.

58 Sections 4.278–4.284.

59 Sections 4.295–4.311.

troops would be pulling out of Iraq by year end was prompted by a failure on the part of the two Governments to reach agreement on the immunity of US armed personnel from criminal prosecution by Iraqi courts.

In October, a prisoner exchange agreement was reached between the government of Israel and Hamas. Under the terms of the agreement Corporal Gilad Shalit, who had been detained since the 2006 Gaza armed conflict between Israel and Hamas, was released in exchange for the transfer of 477 Palestinian prisoners held by Israel.[60] Repeated requests by the ICRC to Hamas over the five-year period for access to Corporal Shalit, to monitor his condition and to facilitate the exchange of news with his family, had been uniformly rejected. The right of the ICRC to visit detainees in international armed conflicts is found in the Third and Fourth Geneva Conventions.[61] There is no specific treaty provision requiring access by the ICRC to detainees in non-international armed conflict although common Article 3 expressly allows the ICRC to 'offer its services' to the parties to the conflict. Customary international law suggests that such requests must be examined in "good faith and may not be refused arbitrarily".[62] Thus, irrespective of the classification of the conflict, Hamas was in clear violation of, at the very least, this fundamental rule of IHL. In addition to ICRC access, the Third Geneva Convention provides a range of protection for prisoners of war (POW) and sets forth detailed rules for their treatment while in detention as well as rules pertaining to release. Israel's detention policy has also been subject to criticism with the ICRC stating its "regret that hundreds of families of Palestinians from Gaza held in Israeli places of detention were punished by being prevented from visiting their detained relatives".

6.2 Protected Persons

6.2.1 Women

In April, the Special Representative on Sexual Violence in Conflict, Margot Wallstrom, took the opportunity to remind the Security Council of their commitments under Resolution 1960[63] which had been unanimously adopted only four months earlier in December 2010.[64] Noting the slow progress in addressing sexual violence during armed conflict, SCR 1960 had created institutional mechanisms to combat impunity and outlined specific steps needed for both the prevention of and

60 ICRC 2011a.

61 Article 126, Geneva Convention III, Article 76 and 143 Geneva Convention IV.

62 Rule 124, Henckaerts and Doswald-Beck 2005.

63 UN Doc. S/RES/1960, 16 December 2010. The Resolution, negotiated under the US Presidency, covers the main recommendations in the Secretary-General's report (S/2010/604).

64 UN Doc. S/PV.6515, 14 April 2011.

protection from sexual violence in conflict. One such measure mandated the Secretary-General to introduce "a list of parties that are credibly suspected of committing or being responsible for patterns of rape and other forms of sexual violence in situations of armed conflict on the Security Council agenda".[65]

In her statement to the Council, the Special Representative pointed out that despite the ambitions articulated in SCR 1960, the resolutions subsequently adopted in relation to Libya[66] had made no mention of the risk of sexual violence in armed conflict, although other conflict related risks including, for example, arbitrary detention, enforced disappearance and torture had been listed. Sexual violence, the Special Representative urged, "should be automatically and systematically included in protection measures" adopted by the Security Council.

The Special Representative highlighted her concerns over the "shocking reports" of sexual violence in Cote d'Ivoire as well as the mass rapes perpetrated on 31 December 2010 and 1 January 2011 in the DRC allegedly by soldiers of the Congolese armed forces (FARDC/ex-CNDP) who were participating in a joint UN/MONUSCO operation. The latter incident had led to the trial and conviction by a Congolese military court of eleven FARDC officers. In March, another senior FARDC officer was convicted for crimes of sexual violence suggesting "a new awareness among the [Congolese] political leadership" that such measures are vital to the DRC's future. The Special Representative also drew the Council's attention to the mass rapes of Congolese women and girls in connection with expulsions from Angola implicating the Angolan armed forces. In addition, there were serious and legitimate concerns regarding sexual violence, trafficking and enforced labour of women and girls in the context of the illegal diamond-mining activities on the borders of Angola and the DRC.

The Special Representative informed the Council that her Office was developing a number of tools to accelerate the implementation of SCR 1960 including the establishment of monitoring, analysis and reporting arrangements; the compilation of a matrix of early warning signs to assist field personnel predict spikes in sexual violence; and the establishment of an accountability regime to fight against impunity.

In September, the Secretary General issued his annual Report (Women, Peace and Security) on the implementation of SCR 1325.[67] The Report provides an overview of progress made and actions taken by various actors in relation to the priorities identified in 2010 (the tenth anniversary of SCR 1325).[68] As in previous years, the Report addresses the four core topics: prevention, participation, protection and relief and recovery. The Report further notes that one of the most "significant institutional developments" with regard to women and peace and security was the creation of UN-Women with the mandate to improve coordination

---

[65] UN Doc. S/RES/1960, paras 3 and 18.

[66] UN Doc. S/Res. 1970, 26 February 2011, UN Doc. S/Res. 1973, 17 March 2011.

[67] UN Doc. S/2011/598, 29 September 2011.

[68] See 'Year in Review', 13 YIHL (2010) for further details.

and accountability in the UN system on women's empowerment and gender equality. In addition, it is envisaged to act as a major institutional resource for Member States in respect of efforts to implement the relevant resolutions on women, peace and security.

6.2.2 Children

In April, the Secretary-General issued the annual report on Children and Armed Conflict covering the period from January to December 2010.[69] The report provides an overview of the situation of children affected by conflict and action taken for their protection over the reporting period. The report highlights the fact that attacks on schools and hospitals are the most reoccurring violation; of the 22 country situations reported in the annual report, 15 make reference to such attacks. The report also provided an update on the progress made by particular countries in implementing measures to end the recruitment and use of child soldiers. Afghanistan and the Sudan were amongst the states that signed an action plan for the prevention of underage recruitment into security forces.

The Report lists[70] those parties to conflict who recruit and use, kill and maim or commit rape and other forms of sexual violence against children in conflict. Of the 59 parties included in the list last year, none were removed and a further four parties were added.[71] In his recommendations the Secretary General welcomed the universal ratification campaign by the Special Representative for Children and Armed Conflict, UNICEF and the Office of the United Nations High Commissioner for Human Rights to encourage Member States that have not done so to sign and ratify or accede to the Optional Protocol to the Convention on the Rights of the Child.

Having considered the annual report the Security Council also passed SCR 1998[72] on 12 July. The resolution reiterated its commitment to address the widespread impact of armed conflict on children and strongly condemned all violations of applicable international law involving the recruitment and use of children by parties to armed conflict as well as their re-recruitment, killing and maiming, rape and other sexual violence, abductions, attacks against schools or hospitals and all other violations of international law committed against children in situations of armed conflict. In its operative paragraph the resolution reaffirms that the monitoring and reporting mechanism will continue to be implemented. The resolution further expresses its readiness to adopt targeted and graduated measures against persistent perpetrators and calls upon those parties listed in the annexes of

[69] UN Doc. S/2011/250, 23 April 2011.

[70] UN Doc. S/2011/250, 23 April 2011, Annex I and Annex II.

[71] Two from Yemen and two from Iraq.

[72] UN Doc. S/Res. 1998, 12 July 2011.

the Secretary General's report to prepare, without delay, concrete time-bound action plans to halt those violations and abuses.

The Secretary General also issued five country specific reports on children and armed conflict concerning Chad,[73] Afghanistan,[74] Central African Republic,[75] Iraq[76] and Sudan.[77]

6.2.3 Medical Personnel[78]

In July, the International Committee of the Red Cross (ICRC) released a sixteen-country study which found that over 650 violent attacks had been committed against health care facilities, medical personnel and patients since 2008.[79] The report concludes that the right of the wounded and the sick to health care was not respected in the contexts studied. This lack of respect was attributed to both state and armed non-state actors. In finding that medical personnel and facilities face widespread and serious dangers during armed conflict and that special protection for the health-care community is currently lacking, the report calls for further action "in the domain of law and politics, in humanitarian dialogue and in the adoption of appropriate procedures by State armed forces".

In September, the ICRC issued a press release condemning the lack of respect for medical services in Syria following attacks on the Syrian Arab Red Crescent (SARC) personnel and vehicles during the violence.[80] This was followed by the release in October of an Amnesty International (A.I.) report into the provision of health care during the violence in Syria. The report catalogues systematic human rights abuses by the Syrian authorities directed at medical personnel, health care providers and those injured in the violence. More specifically, the report documents allegations of general intimidation and of verbal and physical abuse directed at clinicians; the denial of medical assistance to the injured; and of the detention and torture of protestors and, in particular, of medical staff who have treated the injured.[81] The British Medical Association (BMA) called on the Syrian authorities to investigate the allegations raised in the A.I. report and if necessary, to prosecute those responsible.[82] In December, Physicians for Human Rights also released a

73 UN Doc. S/2011/64, 9 February 2011.

74 UN Doc. S/2011/55, 3 February 2011.

75 UN Doc. S/2011/241, 12 April 2011.

76 UN Doc. S/2011/366, 15 June 2011.

77 UN Doc. S/2011/413, 5 July 2011.

78 See Chap. 10.

79 ICRC 2011b.

80 ICRC 2011c.

81 Amnesty International 2011.

82 British Medical Association 2011.

report detailing attacks against patients, doctors and medical facilities by the Syrian authorities.[83]

6.3 The United Nations

6.3.1 The Security Council[84]

6.3.1.1 Afghanistan

The Security Council passed two resolutions on Afghanistan in 2011. SCR 1974 extended the mandate of the United Nations Assistance Mission in Afghanistan (UNAMA) for another year until 23 March 2012.[85] The resolution condemned all attacks including the use of improvised explosive devices, suicide attacks, assassinations, abductions, the targeting of civilians, Afghan and international forces. The resolution also expressed its strong condemnation of the recruitment of child soldiers and the use of children in suicide attacks in violation of applicable international law. The Council welcomed the achievement to date of the implementation of the Mine Action Programme and the Government of Afghanistan's continued efforts towards the removal of anti-personnel landmines, anti-tank landmines and explosive remnants of war in order to reduce the threats posed to human life.

The second meeting on Afghanistan resulted in the adoption of SCR 2011.[86] The resolution in its preamble expressed serious concern with the high number of civilian casualties, and condemned the terrorist attacks against the Inter-Continental Hotel, British Council, International Security Assistance Force (ISAF) headquarters and the Embassy of the United States. The Council determined that the situation in Afghanistan still constitutes a threat to international peace and security; as a result it extended the mandate of ISAF for another year until 13 October 2012.[87]

6.3.1.2 Côte d'Ivoire

The Security Council met on several occasions to consider the deteriorating situation in Cote d'Ivoire. There were a total of seven Resolutions adopted during

---

[83] Physicians for Human Rights 2011.

[84] This year in review only discusses those situations where the Security Council refers to international humanitarian law.

[85] UN Doc. S/Res. 1974, 22 March 2011.

[86] UN Doc. S/Res. 2011, 12 October 2011.

[87] UN Doc. S/Res. 2011, 12 October 2011, para 1.

2011, which expressed concern about continued violations of international humanitarian law. SCR 1967 authorised the deployment of an additional 2,000 military personnel to the United Nations Operation in Cote d'Ivoire (UNOCI) until 30 June 2011.[88] The Council also authorised the immediate deployment of additional capacities and requested the support of troop and police contributing countries. The resolution makes unambiguous, the Council's readiness to impose targeted sanctions against persons who obstruct the work of UNOCI.

In its subsequent resolution of 16 February,[89] the Council, acting under Chapter VII, authorized the temporary redeployment of three infantry companies, one aviation unit and three armed helicopters from the United Nations Mission in Liberia (UNMIL) to UNOCI.

In SCR 1975 of 30 March, the Security Council repeated its concerns over the continued human rights violations against civilians and reiterated its firm condemnation of all violence committed, in particular enforced disappearances, extrajudicial killings, killing and maiming of children, rapes and other forms of sexual violence.[90] The resolution urged all the Ivorian parties and other stakeholders to respect the will of the people and the election of Alassane Dramane Ouattara as President of Cote d'Ivoire. In addition the resolution provided financial and travel sanctions[91] against those individuals[92] who obstruct peace and reconciliation in Cote d'Ivoire, obstruct the work of UNOCI and commit serious violations of human rights and international humanitarian law. These sanctions were renewed until 30 April 2012 by SCR 1980,[93] subject to a mid-term review with a view to modifying, lifting or maintaining all or part of the sanctions regime.

The subsequent resolutions adopted by the Security Council extended the mandate of UNOCI until 31 July 2011[94] and provided an additional 2,000 military personnel to the peacekeeping force.[95] The final resolution, adopted in July 2011,[96] welcomed in its preamble the progress made by the country in restoring peace and stability following the inauguration of President Alassane Dramane Ouattara. However the resolution expressed concern about the precarious and volatile security situation. The security challenges were also highlighted in the Secretary General's report[97] on UNOCI which recommended an extension of the mandate. As a result the Council extended the mandate of UNOCI until 31 July 2012, deciding that UNOCI's military component shall remain at 9,600 troops.

[88] UN Doc. S/Res. 1967, 19 January 2011.
[89] UN Doc. S/Res. 1968, 16 February 2011.
[90] UN Doc. S/Res. 1975, 30 March 2011.
[91] UN Doc. S/Res. 1572, 15 November 2004, paras 9–11.
[92] UN Doc. S/Res. 1975, 30 March 2011, Annex I.
[93] UN Doc. S/Res. 1980, 28 April 2011, para 1.
[94] UN Doc. S/Res. 1981, 13 May 2011.
[95] UN Doc. S/Res. 1992, 29 June 2011.
[96] UN Doc. S/Res. 2000, 27 July 2011.
[97] UN Doc. S/2011/387, 24 June 2011.

The resolution also defined a specific mandate for UNOCI during this period. The mandate requires UNOCI to: protect civilians; to address the remaining security threats and border challenges; to monitor the arms embargo; to collect weapons; to assist the government in the national programme for the disarmament, demobilization and reintegration of combatants; to contribute to the protection and promotion of human rights with special attention to grave violations and abuses against women and children; to provide support for humanitarian assistance; and to support the organisation of fair and transparent elections.

6.3.1.3 Democratic Republic of Congo

The Security Council passed one resolution in respect of the Democratic Republic of Congo (DRC) in 2011, though it met on a few occasions to consider the progress in the region. In February, the Special Representative and Head of United Nations Organization Stabilization Mission in the Democratic Republic of the Congo (MONUSCO), Roger Meece, briefed the Council on the progress made by the Mission. The greatest difficulty facing the Mission, according to Meece, were the foreign and domestic armed groups in eastern DRC as they continued to act as "predatory forces" often incorporating the use of rape and other violence as a weapon against civilians.[98]

In June, the Security Council adopted SCR 1991[99] and acknowledged in the preamble of the resolution that the overall peace and security situation in the DRC had improved in recent years. However, the Council stressed that significant security challenges remain. It reiterated concern over the humanitarian situation and the persistent levels of violence and human rights abuses against civilians. The resolution condemned in particular the targeted attacks against civilians, widespread sexual and gender-based violence, recruitment and use of children by parties to the conflict and extrajudicial executions. It stressed the urgent need for the Government of the DRC to end violations of human rights and humanitarian law and called for the swift prosecution of all perpetrators of such abuses. Taking note of recommendations of the report by the Secretary General on MONUSCO,[100] the Security Council extended the mandate[101] of the Mission until 30 June 2012.

6.3.1.4 Iraq

The Security Council adopted one resolution in respect of Iraq that referred to international humanitarian law. SCR 2001 extended the mandate of the United

[98] UN Doc. S/PV.6476, 7 February 2011.

[99] UN Doc. S/Res. 1991, 28 June 2011.

[100] UN Doc. S/2011/298, 12 May 2011.

[101] UN Doc. S/Res. 1925, 28 May 2010, paras 2, 11 and 12.

Nations Assistance Mission for Iraq (UNAMI) for a further twelve months.[102] The Council also urged all those concerned, as set forth in international humanitarian law, including the Geneva Conventions and the Hague Regulations, to allow full unimpeded access by humanitarian personnel to all people in need of assistance. Further, to make available, as far as possible, all necessary facilities for humanitarian operations, and to promote the safety, security and freedom of movement of humanitarian personnel.

6.3.1.5 Libya[103]

The Security Council met on several occasions to discuss the uprising against the Gaddafi government and subsequent civil war that erupted in Libya in early 2011. In the preamble of SCR 1970[104] the Security Council deplored the gross and systemic violation of human rights and considered that these widespread attacks against the civilian population may amount to crimes against humanity. In its operative paragraph the Council, acting under Chapter VII, urged the Libyan authorities to act with the utmost restraint, respect human rights and international humanitarian law and allow immediate access to international human rights monitors.[105] Furthermore the Security Council took measures under Article 41 imposing an arms embargo,[106] travel ban[107] and the freezing of Libyan assets.[108] The resolution also made a referral to the Prosecutor of the ICC,[109] inviting him to address the Security Council on the actions taken pursuant to the resolution.

In March 2011 the Council convened again and adopted SCR 1973.[110] The resolution demanded that the Libyan authorities comply with their obligations under international law, including international humanitarian law, human rights and refugee law and take all measures to protect civilians. The resolution authorized Member States to take all necessary measures to protect civilians and civilian populated areas under threat of attack in the Libyan Arab Jamahiriya, including Benghazi.[111] Acting under Chapter VII the Security Council established a no fly zone, banning all flights in Libya's airspace.[112] Importantly, SCR 1973 also

[102] UN Doc. S/Res.2001, 28 July 2011.

[103] See Chap. 7.

[104] UN Doc. S/Res. 1970, 26 February 2011.

[105] UN Doc. S/Res. 1970, 26 February 2011, para 2(a).

[106] UN Doc. S/Res. 1970, 26 February 2011, paras 9–13.

[107] UN Doc. S/Res. 1970, 26 February 2011, para 15, Annex I.

[108] UN Doc. S/Res. 1970, 26 February 2011, para 17, Annex II.

[109] UN Doc. S/Res. 1970, 26 February 2011, paras 4 and 7.

[110] UN Doc. S/Res. 1973, 17 March 2011, para 3.

[111] UN Doc. S/Res. 1973, 17 March 2011, para 4.

[112] UN Doc. S/Res. 1973, 17 March 2011, para 6.

explicitly excluded a foreign occupation force of any form on any part of the Libyan territory.[113]

A third resolution adopted by the Security Council in September 2011[114] welcomed the improved situation in Libya and repeated the obligation upon Libyan authorities to comply with international humanitarian law and human rights law. The resolution also established a United Nations Support Mission in Libya (UNSMIL) for an initial period of three months to assist and support Libyan national efforts to:

a. restore public security and order and promote the rule of law;
b. undertake inclusive political dialogue, promote national reconciliation, and embark upon the constitution-making and electoral process;
c. extend state authority, including through strengthening emerging accountable institutions and the restoration of public services;
d. promote and protect human rights, particularly for those belonging to vulnerable groups, and support transitional justice;
e. take the immediate steps required to initiate economic recovery; and
f. coordinate support that may be requested from other multilateral and bilateral actors as appropriate.[115]

In October the Council passed two resolutions as a result of further developments in Libya. In the preamble of SCR 2016,[116] it noted the National Transitional Council's 'Declaration of Liberation' on 23 October 2011 and welcomed the positive development. The resolution strongly urged Member States to cooperate closely with the Libyan authorities in their efforts to end impunity for violations of international human rights and international humanitarian law. In its closing paragraphs the resolution decided that certain provisions of SCR 1973[117] shall be terminated on 31st October 2011, including the no fly zone.[118]

In SCR 2017[119] the Council expressed its concern at the proliferation of all arms and related materials in Libya. It called upon the Libyan authorities to take all necessary steps to prevent the proliferation of all arms and to meet Libya's arms control, disarmament and non-proliferation obligations under international law. The resolution also called upon Libyan authorities to continue their close coordination with the Organisation for the Prohibition of Chemical Weapons, with the aim of destroying their stockpiles in accordance with their international obligations.[120]

---

[113] UN Doc. S/Res. 1973, 17 March 2011, para 4.
[114] UN Doc. S/Res. 2009, 16 September 2011.
[115] UN Doc. S/Res. 2009, 16 September 2011, para 12.
[116] UN Doc. S/Res. 2016, 27 October 2011.
[117] UN Doc. S/Res. 1973, 17 March 2011, paras 4 and 5.
[118] UN Doc. S/Res. 2016, 27 October 2011, para 6.
[119] UN Doc. S/Res. 2017, 31 October 2011.
[120] UN Doc. S/Res. 2017, 31 October 2011, para 2.

6.3.1.6 Liberia

The Security Council adopted two resolutions on Liberia in 2011. On 3 March SCR 1971 was adopted requesting the United Nations Mission in Liberia (UNMIL) to withdraw the military personnel providing security for the Special Court of Sierra Leone.[121] In a subsequent resolution, the Security Council determined that the situation in Liberia continues to constitute a threat to international peace and security in the region and decided to extend the mandate of UNMIL until 30 September 2012.[122] The resolution reiterated the Security Council's authorization to UNMIL to continue to assist the Liberian government with the 2011 presidential and legislative elections.

6.3.1.7 The Middle East

Given the continuing instability in certain parts of the Middle East, there was significant activity on the part of the Security Council. The first[123] of three resolutions was adopted on 30 June concerning the United Nations Disengagement Observer Force (UNDOF) which is mandated to monitor the ceasefire between Israel and Syria. In its preamble the resolution expressed grave concern at the serious events[124] on 15 May and 5 June in UNDOF's area of operation that put the long held ceasefire in jeopardy. The resolution recalled the obligation on both parties to fully respect the terms of the 1974 Disengagement of Forces Agreement and called upon the parties to exercise maximum restraint and prevent any breaches of the ceasefire. The Security Council decided to renew the mandate of UNDOF for a period of six months until 31 December 2011.

SCR 2004[125] concerned the United Nations Interim Force in Lebanon (UNIFIL) which is mandated[126] to monitor the cessation of hostilities between Israel and Lebanon. The resolution expressed deep concern at the latest grave violations on 15 May and 1 August 2011,[127] and condemned in the strongest terms the terrorist attacks against UNIFIL peacekeepers. In determining that the situation in Lebanon continues to constitute a threat to international peace and security, the resolution extended the mandate of UNIFIL until 31 August 2012.

The final resolution in relation to the Middle East concerned the security situation in Yemen. SCR 2014 expressed profound regret at the hundreds of deaths, mainly of civilians and strongly condemned the continued human rights violations

---

121 UN Doc. S/Res. 1971, 3 March 2011, para 1.

122 UN Doc. S/Res. 2008, 16 September 2011, para 1.

123 UN Doc. S/Res. 1994, 30 June 2011.

124 UN Doc. S/2011/359, 13 June 2011, paras 3 and 4.

125 UN Doc. S/Res. 2004, 30 August 2011.

126 UN Doc. S/Res. 1701, 11 August 2006.

127 UN Doc. S/2011/406, 1 July 2011, paras 7 and 8.

by the Yemeni authorities, such as the excessive use of force against peaceful protestors.[128] It demanded that the Yemeni authorities immediately ensure their actions comply with obligations under applicable international humanitarian and human rights law.

6.3.1.8 Somalia

The Security Council met several times to consider the long standing armed conflict taking place in Somalia. The first[129] of four resolutions, SCR 1972, was adopted on 17 March. In its operative paragraph, the resolution stressed the obligation of all states to fully comply with measures imposed by SCR 733[130] establishing an embargo on delivery of all weapons and military equipment to Somalia. A subsequent resolution[131] condemned the flow of weapons and ammunition supplies through Somalia and Eritrea in violation of the arms embargo. As a result the resolution re-established the Monitoring Group for a period of 12 months to monitor these measures.

In SCR 1976[132] the Security Council expressed its grave concern by the growing threat of piracy off the Somali coast. The resolution invited States and individual organizations to assist Somalia in strengthening their counter-piracy law enforcement capacities and stressed the need to support the investigation and prosecution of those who illicitly finance, plan, organize, or unlawfully profit from pirate attacks off the coast of Somalia. In addition, the resolution decided to urgently consider the establishment of specialized Somali courts including an extraterritorial Somali specialized anti-piracy court to try suspected pirates as recommended in the report[133] of the Special Adviser to the Secretary-General on Legal Issues related to Piracy off the Coast of Somalia.

A further resolution was adopted on 30 September.[134] SCR 2010 expressed grave concern at the dire and worsening humanitarian situation in Somalia and called on all parties to allow for safe and unhindered access to humanitarian agencies in accordance with humanitarian law. The resolution called for the cessation of all acts of violence including sexual and gender based violence committed against civilians in violation of international humanitarian law. The Security Council authorized the Member States of the African Union to maintain the deployment of the African Union Mission to Somalia (AMISOM) until 31 October 2012 and to take all necessary measures to carry out its existing mandate.

---

[128] UN Doc. S/Res. 2014, 21 October 2011.

[129] UN Doc. S/Res. 1972, 17 March 2011.

[130] UN Doc. S/Res. 733, 23 January 1992.

[131] UN Doc. S/Res. 2002, 29 July 2011.

[132] UN Doc. S/Res. 1976, 11 April 2011.

[133] UN Doc. S/2011/30, 25 January 2011, UN Doc. S/2011/360, 15 June 2011.

[134] UN Doc. S/Res. 2010, 30 September 2011.

6.3.1.9 Sudan

The Security Council adopted a total of six resolutions on Sudan in 2011, the majority relating to peacekeeping missions. On 27 April, SCR 1978[135] was adopted extending the mandate of the UN Mission in Sudan (UNMIS) until 9 July 2011 and announced its intention to establish a mission to succeed UNMIS. A further resolution[136] adopted on 17 May extended the mandate of the Panel of Experts until 19 February 2012 in order to continue monitoring the arms embargo and sanctions provided in SCR 1591.[137]

The Security Council convened again on 27 June and adopted SCR 1990.[138] The preamble expressed deep concern of the situation in the Abyei Area, particularly the acts of violence committed against civilians in violation of international humanitarian law and human rights law. Recognizing that the situation in Abyei demands an urgent response, the Council established the United Nations Interim Security Force for Abyei (UNISFA) for a period of six months with a maximum of 4,200 military personnel. The mandate of UNISFA includes the protection of civilians in the Abyei area under imminent threat of physical violence.[139]

In SCR 1996[140] the Security Council welcomed the establishment of the Republic of South Sudan upon its proclamation as an independent state. The resolution deplored the persistence of conflict and violence and its effect on civilians. Further, determining that the situation in South Sudan continues to constitute a threat to international peace and security the Council established the United Nations Mission in the Republic of South Sudan (UNMISS). The mission will consist of 7,000 military personnel with a mandate to consolidate peace and security in South Sudan. In particular UNMISS is required to monitor, investigate and report regularly on actual and potential violations of international humanitarian and human rights law.[141] UNMISS is also required to deter violence through proactive deployment and patrols in areas at high risk of conflict in order to protect civilians under imminent threat of physical violence.[142] In a subsequent resolution[143] the Security Council ordered the withdrawal of UNMIS following the termination of the Mission's mandate.

The final resolution in relation to Sudan was passed on 29 July. SCR 2003[144] expressed deep concern at the deteriorating security situation in some parts of Darfur, including ceasefire violations, attacks by rebel groups, aerial bombardment by the

---

135 UN Doc. S/Res. 1978, 27 April 2011.

136 UN Doc. S/Res. 1982, 17 May 2011.

137 UN Doc. S/Res. 1591, 29 March 2005.

138 UN Doc. S/Res. 1990, 27 June 2011.

139 UN Doc. S/Res. 1990, 27 June 2011, para 3(d).

140 UN Doc. S/Res. 1996, 8 July 2011.

141 UN Doc. S/Res. 1996, 8 July 2011, para 3(b)(iii).

142 UN Doc. S/Res. 1996, 8 July 2011, para 3(b)(v).

143 UN Doc. S/Res. 1997, 11 July 2011.

144 UN Doc. S/Res. 2003, 29 July 2011.

Government of Sudan, inter-tribal fighting and attacks on humanitarian personnel and peacekeepers. The resolution demanded that all parties to the conflict in Darfur immediately end violence, attacks on civilians, peacekeepers and humanitarian personnel and comply with their obligations under international human rights and humanitarian law. The resolution extended the mandate of the UN Assistance Mission in Darfur (UNAMID) for a further twelve months until 31 July 2012.

6.3.1.10 Peacekeeping Operations and Missions

There are currently 15 UN peacekeeping operations deployed across the world, the majority of which had their mandate extended by Security Council Resolutions in 2011. In July 2011 the General Assembly adopted a peacekeeping budget of more than $7 billion for the period of July 2011-June 2012.[145]

Peacekeeping operations have been on the agenda of both the Security Council and the General Assembly. In August 2011 the General Assembly passed a resolution[146] welcoming the report[147] by the Special Committee on Peacekeeping Operations endorsing its recommendations and conclusions. The report provides a comprehensive review of the whole question of peacekeeping operations and considers new proposals to enhance the capacity of the UN to fulfil its responsibilities in this field. At the conclusion of its 2011 substantive session the Special Committee on Peacekeeping Operations condemned the tragic rise in the killing of UN peacekeeping personnel.

In July the Security Council was briefed by force commanders from missions in Darfur, DRC, Lebanon and Liberia. The Force Commanders provided a survey of the development on their respective missions and discussed strategies for overcoming operational challenges, particularly the need to carry out complicated mandates on reduced budgets.[148]

6.3.2 International Criminal Court

The situation in Libya was referred to the ICC Prosecutor by the Security Council through the unanimous adoption of SCR 1970.[149] On 3 March after a preliminary examination of available information the Prosecutor announced that he had opened an investigation into the situation in Libya. On 16 May, the Prosecutor requested the issuance of arrest warrants against Muammar Gaddafi, Saif Al-Islam Gaddafi and Abdullah Al-Senussi under Article 58 of the Rome Statute. The warrants were in relation to their alleged criminal responsibility for the commission of murder

[145] GA, 65th Session, 106th Meeting, 1 July 2011.

[146] UN Doc. GA/Res 65/310, 26 August 2011.

[147] UN Doc. A/65/19.

[148] SC, 6592nd Meeting, 27 July 2011.

[149] UN Doc. S/Res. 1970, 26 February 2011.

and persecution as crimes against humanity from 15 February 2011 until at least 28 February across Libya, through the Libyan state apparatus and security forces. On 27 June, the Pre-Trial Chamber granted the Prosecutor's request and issued arrest warrants for these three individuals.[150] In addition, the Pre-Trial Chamber issued a request[151] to member states not party to the Rome Statute to arrest and surrender the suspects. In November, the Pre-Trial Chamber terminated the case against Muammar Gaddafi on receipt of a death certificate from the Libyan authorities.[152] The warrants of arrest remain outstanding for Saif Al-Islam Gaddafi and Abdullah Al-Senussi, both of whom were captured in Libya. Following their capture, the ICC reminded the Libyan authorities of their obligation to cooperate fully with the Court in accordance with SCR 1970; it expressly noted that should the Libyan authorities wish to conduct national prosecutions they are required to submit a challenge to the admissibility of the case before the Pre-Trial Chamber.[153]

On 3 October, Pre-Trial Chamber III granted the prosecutor's request[154] to commence an investigation into crimes against humanity allegedly committed by pro-Gbagbo forces following the elections in Cote d'Ivoire on 28 November 2010. The evidence presented to the Trial Chamber satisfied the requisite threshold—that it provides a 'reasonable basis' to believe that crimes against humanity have been committed on Ivorian territory. On 25 October the prosecution applied for a warrant of arrest for the former President of Cote d'Ivoire, Laurent Koudou Gbagbo. A warrant was issued on 23 November in relation to four counts of crimes against humanity (murder, rape and other sexual violence, persecution and other inhuman acts) committed in the context of post-electoral violence between 16 December 2010 and 12 April 2011. On 30 November the Ivorian authorities transferred Gbagbo to the ICC's custody.

6.4 Regional Organisations

6.4.1 Council of Europe

6.4.1.1 The European Court of Human Rights[155]

In July, the European Court of Human Rights (ECtHR) rendered two judgments involving the United Kingdom during the armed conflict in Iraq. *Al-Skeini v UK* concerned the killings of six Iraqi civilians by UK troops.[156] *Al-Jedda v UK* concerned the arrest and internment of an Iraqi civilian by UK troops at the

---

150 ICC-01/11-01/11-2, ICC-01/11-01/11-3, ICC-01/11-01/11-4, 27 June 2011.

151 ICC-01/11-01/11.

152 ICC-01/11-01/11-28, 22 November 2011.

153 ICC Press Release, 23 November 2011.

154 ICC-02/11-14, 3 October 2011.

155 See Chap. 8.

156 *Al-Skeini v. UK,* Grand Chamber, Judgment of 7 July 2011, no.55721/07 ECHR 2011, paras 8–88.

Sha'aibah Divisional Temporary Detention Facility in Basrah City.[157] Significantly, in both judgments, the Court found that the circumstances of these cases fell within the jurisdiction of the UK for purposes of Article 1 of the European Convention on Human Rights (ECHR).

In *Al-Skeini*, the Court reaffirmed its previous case law and held that the ECHR applied outside a state's territory only in exceptional circumstances: (i) when a state agent exercises authority and control over a person outside its territory[158]; and (ii) when a contracting state has control of an area.[159] The Court expanded on the former identifying three defining principles: (a) when diplomatic and consular agents present on foreign territory in accordance with international law exert authority and control over others; (b) when through consent, invitation or acquiescence, a state assumes all or some of the *public powers* normally exercised by the government of the territory; and (c) when agents of state exercise physical power and control over a person. The Court concluded that on the basis that between the removal from power of the Ba'ath regime and until the accession of the Interim Government, the UK (together with the US) assumed in Iraq the exercise of some of the *public powers* normally to be exercised by a sovereign government (namely, authority and responsibility for the maintenance of security in South East Iraq), a jurisdictional link between those killed in the course of security operations conducted by UK troops had been established for the purposes of Article 1 of the Convention.[160]

In *Al-Jedda*, the Court concluded that the applicant fell within the jurisdiction of the UK for the purposes of Article 1 because the internment had taken place within a detention facility controlled exclusively by the British forces. Throughout the material period, UK troops exercised physical power and control, or *authority and control* over the applicant.[161]

Insofar as the alleged breaches were concerned, the Court found that in the case of *Al-Skeini* the UK had violated its *procedural* obligation to investigate the deaths of the applicants under Article 2 (right to life).[162] In *Al-Jedda*, the Court found that the UK had violated Article 5(1) (the right to liberty and security).[163]

---

[157] *Al Jedda v. UK,* Grand Chamber, Judgment of 7 July 2011, no.27021/08 ECHR 2011, paras 8–77.

[158] *Al-Skeini*, paras 133–137.

[159] *Al-Skeini*, paras 138–140. Such control typically occurs as a consequence of occupation; significantly, the Court also added, "the importance of establishing the occupying State's jurisdiction in such cases does not imply, a contrario, that jurisdiction under Article 1 of the Convention can never exist outside the territory covered by the Council of Europe Member States."

[160] *Al-Skeini*, para 149.

[161] *Al Jedda v. UK*, paras 85–86. The Court referenced para 136 in *Al-Skeini*, namely the principle identified in (c) above.

[162] *Al-Skeini*, paras 168–177. The violation of the procedural duty under Article 2 applied to the first, second, third, fourth and fifth applicants. By contrast, the sixth applicant was no longer a victim of any procedural breach since a public inquiry into his death was on-going; para 176.

[163] *Al-Jedda*, para 86.

6.4.2 Organization of American States

On 7 June, the General Assembly of the Organization of American States (OAS) adopted four separate resolutions involving IHL.

In the first of these resolutions—*Support for the Work of the Inter-American Committee Against Terrorism*[164]—OAS member states reaffirmed their respect for international law, including international humanitarian law, international human rights law, and international refugee law, when preventing, combating and eliminating terrorism. In a second resolution—*The Americas as an Antipersonnel Land Mine-Free Zone*[165]—the General Assembly expressed its continued concern over the presence of thousands of antipersonnel land mines in the Americas. The resolution condemned 'in accordance with the principles and norms of international humanitarian law, the use, stockpiling, production, and transfer of antipersonnel mines by non-state actors, acts which put at grave risk the population of the affected countries'.[166] In the third resolution—*Promotion of and Respect for International Humanitarian Law*[167]—the General Assembly expressed its deep concern 'that in various parts of the world violations of international humanitarian law persist, causing suffering to victims of armed conflict, particularly the civilian population, and by the challenges posed by the new situations that arise in the context of armed conflicts'.[168] The resolution underscored the need to strengthen international humanitarian law and urges member states engaged in armed conflict to respect their obligations under international humanitarian law and to continue to support efforts to implement and strengthen international humanitarian law.

The final resolution—*Persons who have Disappeared and Assistance to Members of their Families*[169]—urges states to adopt national measures on the subject of missing persons. In particular, the resolution calls on member states 'to continue the progressive adoption of measures, including domestic regulatory and institutional provisions, to prevent the disappearance of persons in the context of armed conflict or other situations of armed violence, to clarify the fate and whereabouts of those who have disappeared, to strengthen technical capacity to deal with human remains, and to attend to the needs of the family members, using as a reference, among others, the Guiding Principles/Model Law on the Missing prepared by the Advisory Service on International Humanitarian Law of the International Committee of the Red Cross'.[170]

[164] Organization of American States, AG/RES. 2618 (XLI-O/11) 7 June 2011.
[165] Organization of American States, AG/RES. 2630 (XLI-O/11) 7 June 2011.
[166] Ibid.
[167] Organization of American States, AG/RES. 2650 (XLI-O/11) 7 June 2011.
[168] Ibid.
[169] Organization of American States, AG/RES. 2651 (XLI-O/11) 7 June 2011.
[170] Ibid.

6.5 Arms Control and Disarmament

6.5.1 Conventional Weapons

6.5.1.1 Small Arms and Light Weapons

The second and third sessions of the Arms Trade Treaty (ATT) Preparatory Committee (PrepCom) were held from 28 February to 4 March and 11–15 July respectively. The fourth and final session of the PrepCom is scheduled for February 2012, which will be followed by the United Nations Conference on the ATT.[171] At the third session member states were provided with a draft paper on small arms and light weapons, technology, parts and components, ammunition, victim assistance and international cooperation.[172] Although the paper has been described as 'ambitious', it forms the basis for the ATT negotiations during 2012.[173]

In April, the UN Secretary-General issued a report on small arms[174] that builds on the 2008 report.[175] The report provides a set of recommendations on the implementation of the UN Programme of Action (PoA) to Prevent, Combat and Eradicate the Illicit Trade in Small Arms and Lights Weapons in All Its Aspects.[176] The following month, at the first Open-ended Meeting of Governmental Experts on the Implementation of the Programme of Action to Prevent, Combat and Eradicate the Illicit Trade in Small Arms and Lights Weapons in All Its Aspects,[177] experts were given the opportunity to consider the International Tracing Instrument.[178]

In September, the Draft African Union Strategy on the Control of Illicit Proliferation, Circulation and Trafficking of Small Arms and Light Weapons was adopted.[179]

---

171 See Arms Trade Treaty Preparatory Committee, available at: http://www.un.org/disarmament/convarms/ATTPrepCom/.

172 United Nations Non-Governmental Liaison Service (UN-NGLS) 5 August 2011, available at: http://www.un-ngls.org/spip.php?article3532 and ATT Monitory 3 October 2011, available at: http://attmonitor.posterous.com/moving-forward-on-the-armstreaty-at-the-unga.

173 Ibid.

174 UN Doc. S/2011/255, 5 April 2011.

175 UN Doc. S/2008/258, 17 April 2008.

176 UN Doc. S/2011/255, 5 April 2011.

177 Open-ended Meeting of Governmental Experts, available at: http://www.poa-iss.org/MGE/.

178 International Instrument to Enable States to Identify and Trace, In a Timely and Reliable Manner, Illicit Small Arms and Light Weapons 8 December 2005, available at: http://www.poa-iss.org/InternationalTracing/ITI_English.pdf.

179 Meeting of Member States Experts of the African Union, Conclusions, available at: http://unrec.org/docs/Final%20Conclusions%20SALW.pdf.

6.5.1.2 Convention on Cluster Munitions

In June, an Intersessional Meeting was held on the Convention on Cluster Munitions (CCM) attended by 80 signatory and non-signatory states. The meeting allowed States to engage in discussions on the progress made to implement the Convention, and the challenges ahead.[180] In addition, a number of recommendations were provided for consideration by State Parties at the second meeting in relation to the implementation architecture and means to coordinate the work of the CCM.[181]

In September, the Second Meeting of state parties to the CCM took place. Member states provided progress updates on implementing their treaty obligations, including measures taken to destroy stockpiled cluster munitions,[182] risk reduction[183] and pledges on victim assistance.[184] Non-signatory states also provided updates on the steps taken towards joining the CCM. The meeting stressed the promotion of universal compliance with the norms of the CCM and encouraged states to make public statements to condemn the use of cluster munitions.[185] A Third Meeting of state parties is scheduled to take place in September 2012, in Norway.

6.5.2 Nuclear Weapons

6.5.2.1 New START Treaty and Protocol

The New START Treaty, signed by the US and Russia in April 2010, entered into force on 5 February 2011. Since entry into force, there have been reports indicating progress in respect of implementation and in October, the US State Department issued a report detailing the measures taken. Achievements listed include, on-site inspections conducted by both states at intercontinental ballistic missile, submarine-launched ballistic missile and heavy bomber bases, storage facilities,

[180] Sessions and Statements from the Intersessional Meeting is available at: http://www.clusterconvention.org/work-programme/intersessional-meeting-2011/.

[181] Convention on Cluster Munitions, Discussion Paper on Implementation Architecture and Intersessional Work, available at: http://www.clusterconvention.org/files/2011/08/Discussion-Paper-on-Impl-Architecture-and-Intersessional-Work.pdf.

[182] Statements by State parties available at: http://www.clusterconvention.org/msp/2msp/day-2-c-storage-and-stockpile-destruction/.

[183] Statements by State parties available at: http://www.clusterconvention.org/msp/2msp/day-2-d-clearance-and-risk-reduction/.

[184] Statements by State parties available at: http://www.clusterconvention.org/msp/2msp/day-2-e-victim-assistance/.

[185] Statement by Cluster Munitions Coalition available at: http://www.clusterconvention.org/files/2011/09/compl_cmc.pdf.

conversion or elimination facilities, and test sites. In addition, both states have also exchanged approximately 1,500 notifications via Nuclear Risk Reduction Centres detailing movements, launches and data changes.[186]

6.5.2.2 Iran's Nuclear Programme

On 9 June, the Security Council adopted Resolution 1984,[187] which extended the mandate of the Panel of Experts, as set out in Resolution 1929,[188] for an additional year and also requested the Panel to provide a midterm report on its work.

On 8 November, the International Atomic Energy Agency (IAEA) released its report into Iran's implementation of the Nuclear Non-Proliferation Treaty Safeguards Agreement and relevant provisions of successive Security Council resolutions.[189] Lack of cooperation on the part of Iran left the Agency with little choice but to summarise in its report that it was 'unable to provide credible assurance about the absence of undeclared nuclear material and activities in Iran, and therefore to conclude that all nuclear material in Iran is in peaceful activities'. The report continues, '[t]he Agency has serious concerns regarding possible military dimensions to Iran's nuclear programme. …Iran has carried out activities relevant to the development of a nuclear explosive device. The information also indicates that prior to the end of 2003, these activities took place under a structured programme, and that some activities may still be ongoing'.[190] On the basis of this information, the IAEA requested that Iran engage with it 'for the purpose of providing clarifications regarding possible military dimensions to Iran's nuclear programme as identified in the Annex to the report' and it further urged Iran to meet its international obligations.[191]

References

Amnesty International (2011) Health crisis: Syrian government targets the wounded and health workers. http://www.amnesty.org/en/library/asset/MDE24/059/2011/en/74190b0e-cbc4-4596-91fc-eb89863362d8/mde240592011en.pdf. Accessed Oct 2011

British Medical Association (2011) Letters to Syrian ministers on targeting of the wounded and health workers in Syria. http://www.bma.org.uk/images/letterstosyrianministers28october2011_tcm41-210357.pdf. Accessed 28 Oct 2011

[186] US Department of State, The New START Treaty 20 October 2011, available at: www.state.gov/t/avc/rls/175945.htm.

[187] UN Doc. S/Res/1984, 9 June 2011.

[188] UN Doc. S/Res/1929, 9 June 2010.

[189] IAEA Report GOV/2011/65, 8 November 2011.

[190] Ibid at 10.

[191] Ibid.

Coker M et al (2011) Drone targets Yemeni cleric, The Wall Street Journal. http://online.wsj.com/article/SB10001424052748703992704576307594129219756.html. Accessed 7 May 2011

Henckaerts JM, Doswald-Beck L (2005) Customary international humanitarian law, vol 1. Cambridge University Press, Cambridge

ICRC (2011a) News release—ICRC welcomes release of Israeli soldier Gilad Shalit and Palestinian detainees. http://www.icrc.org/eng/resources/documents/news-release/2011/israel-palestine-news-2011-10-18.htm. Accessed 18 Oct 2011

ICRC (2011b) A sixteen-country study: health care in danger. http://www.icrc.org/eng/assets/files/reports/report-hcid-16-country-study-2011-08-10.pdf. Accessed July 2011

ICRC (2011c) Press release—Syria: ICRC condemns lack of respect for medical services. http://www.icrc.org/eng/resources/documents/news-release/2011/syria-news-2011-09-16.htm. Accessed 16 Sept 2011

Koh HH (2010) Legal adviser, US Department of State, annual meeting of the American Society of International Law. http://www.state.gov/s/l/releases/remarks/139119.htm. Accessed 25 March 2010

Koh HH (2011) Legal adviser, US Department of State, addressing the lawfulness of the Bin Laden operation. http://opiniojuris.org/2011/05/19/the-lawfulness-of-the-us-operation-against-osama-bin-laden/. Accessed 19 May 2011

Physicians for Human Rights (2011) Syria: attacks on doctors, patients and hospitals. https://s3.amazonaws.com/PHR_Reports/syria-attacks-on-drs-patients-hospitals-final-2011.pdf. Accessed Dec 2011

US Department of Defense (2011) News article: U.S. kills Bin Laden in intelligence-driven operation. http://www.defense.gov/news/newsarticle.aspx?id=63764. Accessed 2 May 2011

US Attorney General Holder (2011) Webcast of hearing on 'Oversight of the U.S. Department of Justice'. http://judiciary.senate.gov/. Accessed 4 May 2011

Chapter 7
Operation Unified Protector and the Protection of Civilians in Libya

Chris De Cock

Contents

7.1 Introduction

In the aftermath of the events which took place in Egypt and Tunisia, riots against the autocratic regime of Colonel Gaddafi broke out on 15th February 2011. Two weeks later, the regime lost control of major parts of the country after violent clashes

The views expressed in this paper are those of the author in his personal capacity and do not intend to reflect the views of the DG or of the Ministry of Defense.

C. De Cock (✉)
International Law Section, DG Legal Support and Mediation,
Belgian Ministry of Defense, Belgium, Europe
e-mail: christian.decock@mil.be

M.N. Schmitt and L. Arimatsu (eds.), *Yearbook of International Humanitarian Law Volume 14, 2011*, DOI: 10.1007/978-90-6704-855-2_7,

between pro- and anti-Gaddafi supporters which led to a refugee crisis in the vicinity of its borders with Tunisia and Egypt.[1] On 26th February 2011, the United Nations Security Council [hereafter: the Council] unanimously adopted Security Council Resolution 1970 [hereafter: UNSCR 1970] in order to implement an arms embargo on Libya; in addition, the resolution required a travel ban be imposed on Gaddafi and senior regime members and called for their private assets to be frozen. In accordance with UNSCR 1970, the European Union imposed an arms embargo on Libya that was broader in scope than that provided for in the resolution.[2] Concerned by the deteriorating situation in Libya, the League of Arab States, as a regional organization, condemned Gaddafi and called on the UN to impose a No Fly Zone [hereafter: NFZ] over Libya to protect the civilian population. On 17th March 2011, the Council adopted UNSCR 1973. Acting under Chapter VII of the UN Charter, it authorized States to take 'all necessary measures' to protect civilians and civilian populated areas under threat of attack in Libya. It also decided to establish a ban on all flights in Libyan airspace in order to help protect civilians. Finally, it allowed States to inspect in their territory (including seaports and airports) and on the high seas, vessels and aircraft bound to or from Libya, if the State had information that provided reasonable grounds to believe that they carried prohibited items.

Soon after the adoption of UNSCR 1973, a coalition of the willing, including the United States, the United Kingdom and France, started air operations against Libya. Other nations, including Belgium, Canada, Denmark, Italy, Norway, Spain, as well as some Arab nations, joined the coalition. After taking control of all military operations for Libya pursuant to UNSCR 1970 and 1973 in April 2011, NATO ended successfully Operation Unified Protector on 31st October 2011. Operation Unified Protector [hereafter: OUP] was the 'second largest scale air operation' undertaken by NATO in its history.[3]

This paper will focus on the following issues: the mandate of the Security Council and its implications for the use of force under the *jus ad bellum* and current challenges in targeting under the *jus in bello*.[4] Under the *jus ad bellum* and in accordance with the Charter, the Council shall determine that a threat to international peace and security exists. Only then can the Council decide to take coercive measures to restore international peace and security. This raises three questions. Firstly, what were the factual circumstances giving rise to a determination by the Council that such a threat existed? Only then could the Security

---

[1] According to OCHA, as of 13th March 2011, over 270000 migrant workers (mainly from Egypt and Tunisia) had left Libya since 22nd February 2011. The International Organization of Migration estimated that at least 20000 foreigners, (mostly Bangladeshi) still needed evacuation.

[2] Council Decision 2011/137/CFSP concerning restrictive measures in view of the situation in Libya, implementing United Nations Security Council Resolution 1970, 28 February 2011, OJ L 58, 3.3.2011, p. 53.

[3] The first large scale military operation of NATO was undoubtedly Operation Allied Force. (Wedgwood 1999, p. 828).

[4] The aim of this paper is not to discuss the protection of civilians in the R2P context. For more details, see: Evans 2008, p. 349; Nasu 2009; Focarelli 2008; Thakur 2006, pp. 244–264.

Council impose decisions (or recommendations) to cope with the situation. Interestingly, no direct reference to a threat to international peace and security can be identified in UNSCR 1970. Secondly, how did UNSCR 1973 affect the applicable *jus in bello*? Did the Council restrict the use of force to the protection of the civilian population and the enforcement of the NFZ and the arms embargo? Thirdly, did the hostilities amount to an armed conflict triggering the applicability of the law of armed conflict? Some authors argued that the military operations carried out pursuant to UNSCR 1970 and 1973 did not amount to a situation of war. Others argued that the conflict in Libya was an 'internationalized' armed conflict due to the support provided by some States to the anti-Gaddafi forces.[5] From the above, it follows that the following issues need further clarification:

- Did the conflict between the pro-Gaddafi and the anti-Gaddafi-forces reach the threshold of an armed conflict?
- Was there a situation of armed conflict between Libya and the States participating in OUP?
- Did the support of individual States to the anti-Gaddafi forces 'internationalize' the non-international armed conflict between those rebels and the pro-Gaddafi forces?[6]

In the second part, some targeting issues will be covered briefly, more particularly the validity of military targets, such as the Tripoli broadcasting facility, mercenary staging points, and police stations as legitimate military objectives. The complexity of the decision making process, especially in the context of deliberate targeting and the necessity to adapt the targeting process in view of the rapidly changing situation on the ground will be assessed.

7.2 The Legal Framework of Operation Unified Protector

7.2.1 Libya: A Threat to Peace and International Security?

The authority to intervene with military means in Libya was granted by the Council when it adopted—by ten votes in favor and five abstentions—Resolution 1973 authorizing '*Member States [...] acting nationally or through regional*

[5] Koutroulis 2011.

[6] Internationalized armed conflicts are armed conflicts that start as internal armed conflict but transform into an international armed conflict (Crawford 2010, p. 15). According to David, if the internal strife can only subsist through external support, the conflict is internationalized: 'A partir du moment où l'intervention étrangère attaint un certain niveau, ce qui est le cas lorsqu'elle influence de manière decisive sur la poursuite du conflit [...], il devient artificiel de maintenir la distinction entre le conflit international et le conflit interne. [...]. Si, en effet, une partie à un conflit armé interne ne peut continuer la lutte que grâce à l'aide extérieure, il s'opère une sorte de *confusion* entre cette partie [...] et l'Etat étranger qui la soutient, ce qui justifie que les relations de cette partie avec son adversaire national deviennent internationales.' (David 2008, pp. 173–174).

organizations or arrangements, […] to protect civilians and civilian populated areas under threat of attack in the Libyan Arab Jamahariya. […]'.[7] This authorization was preceded by its earlier Resolution 1970 adopted at its 4691st meeting on 26 February 2011. Indeed, before the Council can adopt measures to enforce the peace, it must first determine 'the existence of any threat to the peace, breach of the peace or act of aggression'.[8] It is not unambiguously clear as to what triggered the Council to determine the existence of such a threat: the massive violations of human rights (R2P) or the potential spillover to neighboring countries? The implied determination that the internal situation in Libya amounted to a threat to the peace can be found in UNSCR 1973 when the Security Council determined '*that the situation in the Libyan Arab Jamahiriya continues to constitute a threat to international peace and security*'. The use of '*continues*' in UNSCR 1973 merely serves as a '*renvoi*' to a pre-existent threat to international peace and security, which is nowhere to be found in the text of UNSCR 1970. Nevertheless, neither the absence of any reference to Chapter VII of the UN Charter nor the lack of a determination as to the existence of a threat to international peace and security is a new development[9]; what matters is that no State displayed any opposition.[10]

One approach is to read the extreme violence by the regime forces against the civilian population as the real threat to peace and security.[11] In this respect, human rights should not be viewed in isolation from the maintenance of international peace and security.[12] Both UNSCR 1970 and 1973 strongly condemned '*those widespread and systematic attacks against the civilian population*'. This would be consistent with the practice of the Council in other cases of internal strife which it classified as threats to the peace.[13] As stated by the ICTY Appeals Chamber in Tadić: '*Indeed, the practice of the Security Council is rich with cases of civil war or internal strife which is classified as a 'threat to the peace' and dealt with under*

---

[7] UNSC Res 1973, S/RES/1973 (2011), OP 4.

[8] Article 39 of the UN Charter.

[9] UNSC Res 713, S/RES/713 (Yugoslavia, 1991), UNSC Res 794, S/RES/794 (Somalia, 1992), UNSC Res 841, S/RES/841 (Somalia, 1993), UNSC Res 917, S/RES/917 (Haiti, 1994).

[10] Simma 2002, p. 724.

[11] The other approach is to consider the spillover of the refugee problem to neighboring countries as a threat to peace and security caused by the widespread and systematic attacks on the civilian population. UNSCR 1973 which led to enforcement actions against Libya when the Security Council clearly stated its concern '*at the plight of refugees and foreign workers forced to flee the violence in the Libyan Arab Jamahariya, welcoming the response of neighbouring States, in particular Tunisia and Egypt, to address the needs of those refugees and foreign workers*'. According to Schmitt, the Security Council '*implicitly made this finding with regard to the Libyan crisis in Resolution 1970 […] by indicating that it was "[a]cting under Chapter VII"*'. (Schmitt 2011, p. 47).

[12] On the UN Charter as a basis for the contribution of human rights to peace and security within the United Nations, see: Breen 2007, pp. 263–271.

[13] For example : UNSC Res 771, S/RES/771 (1991) and UNSC Res 836, S/RES/836 (1993) (Former Yugoslavia); UNSC Res 794, S/RES/794 (1992) (Somalia); UNSC Res 918, S/RES/918 and Res 929, S/RES/929 (1994) (Rwanda); UNSC Res 1306, S/RES/1306 (2000) (Sierra Leone).

Chapter VII [...] It can thus be said that there is a common understanding, manifested by the 'subsequent practice' of the membership of the United Nations at large, that the 'threat to the peace' of Article 39 may include, as one of its species, internal armed conflicts'.[14] Although intervening in the internal affairs of a State is not prohibited by the Charter, it nevertheless remains an exceptional measure.[15] However, the practice of the Council shows that the violation of jus cogens norms may constitute a threat to international peace and security.[16]

7.2.2 Scope of the Enforcement Actions

Almost as soon as it was adopted, concerns were raised that the text of UNSCR 1973 which authorized Member States to take 'all necessary measures' to enforce the NFZ and 'to protect civilians and civilian populated areas under threat of attack' in Libya, while excluding a military occupation force, was too broadly worded[17] Subsequent events were to underscore the need for UNSC resolutions to be clear as to whether they are intended to authorize the use of force and, if so, in what circumstances. As Gary Wilson observes, the danger is that 'ambiguous resolutions might be invoked as the legal basis for the use of force when this was not the Council's intention'.[18]

UNSCR 1973 merits several observations.

Firstly, it authorized military action on Libya *only* for the purpose of protecting civilians and the civilian population in Libya. The international community was *not* mandated to support the rebels in their internal strife against the regime. Although easy to distinguish in theory, in practice there was a thin line between, on the one hand, the protection of civilians and civilian populated areas and, on the other, indirect support to the anti-Gaddafi forces. Insofar as NATO's attacks on the regime forces for the purpose of protecting the civilian population were concerned, it is unlikely that UNSCR 1973 was violated, even if the attacks indirectly advantaged the anti-Gaddafi forces in their non-international armed conflict with the pro-Gaddafi forces.

---

[14] ICTY, *Prosecutor v Dusko Tadić*, Decision on the Defence Motion for Interlocutory Appeal on Jurisdiction, Appeals Chamber I (IT-94-1-AR72) 2nd October 1995, paras 20–2. See also Lamb 1999, pp361–388; Forsythe 2006, pp. 59–61; Boustany and Dormoy 2002, pp. 15–33.

[15] Article 2(7) of the UN Charter clearly states that 'Nothing contained in the present Charter shall authorize the United Nations to intervene in matters which are essentially within the domestic jurisdiction of any State or shall require the Members to submit such matters to settlement under the present Charter; but the principle shall not prejudice the application of enforcement measures under Chapter VII'.

[16] Kolb 2003a, p. 69.

[17] On the *jus ad bellum/jus in bello* distinction in relation to assessing the scope of the powers of the Security Council, see: McLaughlin 2007; Gardem 1996; Orakhelashvili 2007.

[18] Wilson 2007.

Secondly, in the context of the mandate 'to protect the civilian population' the relationship between the *jus ad bellum* and the *jus in bello* came to the fore. The specific question raised was whether 'the protection of the civilian population' in operative para 4 referred to the aim of the military operation '*in se*' (*jus ad bellum*) or if there was a legal obligation to demonstrate a clear and unambiguous nexus with the civilian population in the conduct of hostilities (*jus in bello*). In the former case, military units of the regime could be attacked at any time of the conflict, based on the assumption that the neutralization or the destruction of those forces contributed to the protection of the civilian population, and thus to the strategic objectives of the operation. In the latter case, only those pro-Gaddafi forces which were actually threatening or attacking the civilian population could be engaged thereby necessitating a direct nexus between those forces and the attack on civilians. The former interpretation is more persuasive. The protection of the civilian population, as enshrined in UNSCR 1973, relates to the legitimate aim of the military operation as a whole ('necessary measures'). This can also be deduced from the express exclusion of a foreign occupation force as not being in conformity with the perceived end state. The exclusion of belligerent occupation, whether partial or total, did not however prohibit the sending of ground forces, such as special forces or forward air controllers for the purpose of intelligence or target acquisition.

Thirdly, UNSCR 1973 provided enough flexibility to engage all military forces which attacked or threatened to attack the civilian population. This was particularly relevant in regard to the use of mercenaries by the Libyan authorities. NATO forces were therefore authorized to attack mercenaries, including their material and staging points, whenever necessary to enforce the mandate. Additionally, the absence of any reference to the adverse party in UNSCR 1973 meant that military action against rebel forces was not excluded had they attacked or threatened to attack the civilian population. This underpinned the impartial way in which NATO forces implemented the mandate, namely, to protect the civilian population against attack or threat of attack irrespective of the aggressor.

Fourthly, operative para 6 established 'a ban on all flights in the airspace of Libya in order to help protect civilians'. In this context the term 'civilian' was read as being interchangeable with the term 'civilians and civilian populated areas' in operative para 4 which concerned protection related to attacks and threat of attacks emanating from enemy forces. Thus, the wording of UNSCR 1973 allowed for a robust enforcement of the NFZ. As mentioned, the NFZ was not restricted solely to military aircraft from the Libyan armed forces, but included aircraft operated by anti-Gaddafi forces and all civil aircraft. This reading is supported by the terms of operative para 7 enumerating exhaustively the exceptions to the general rule in para 6, namely, that the ban did not apply '*to flights whose sole purpose is humanitarian, such as delivering or facilitating the delivery of assistance, including medical supplies, food, humanitarian workers and related assistance, or evacuating foreign nationals [...]*'. Whereas the mandate *ratione materiae* left the commanders with enough flexibility, it restricted the *ratione loci* to only the airspace of Libya. Consequently, no authority was granted to enforce the NFZ in international airspace.

Finally, UNSCR 1973 authorized the enforcement of an arms embargo, including the right to inspect vessels and aircraft on the high seas bound to or from Libya if there was information providing reasonable grounds to believe that the cargo contained prohibited items, including the provision of mercenary armed personnel. This corroborates the interpretation of the term 'all necessary measures' as including the possibility to detain persons whenever necessary to successfully enforce the embargo and protect the civilian population. Had this operation involved ground forces, the mandate would have also allowed for the authority to detain. The specific provision in operative para 13 referring to 'mercenary armed personnel' authorized States to prevent mercenaries from entering and leaving Libya and thus implied the right to detain. *Ratione materiae*, the embargo was strictly limited to those items expressly covered by UNSCR 1970 and 1973: arms and related materiel of all types, including weapons and ammunition, military vehicles and equipment, paramilitary equipment, and spare parts for the aforementioned, and technical assistance, training, financial or other assistance, related to military activities or the provision, maintenance or use of any arms and related materiel.[19] The term 'other assistance' did not cover oil exports since the Council imposed an *arms* embargo rather than a trade embargo. The intent of the embargo provisions was clearly to stop the supply, trade or transfer of arms and related supplies and not to prevent oil exports. Finally, since the embargo could only be enforced on the high seas, it followed from this restriction that the transport of prohibited goods between seaports not leaving the territorial waters was not covered by the mandate.

7.3 Typology of Military Operations in Libya

Libya was the theatre of multiple conflicts, each of them regulated by a particular set of legal rules. Firstly, there was the conflict between the pro- and anti-Gaddafi forces. Secondly, multinational troops, operating under the NATO umbrella, were engaged in hostilities against the pro-Gaddafi forces in implementing their mandate in accordance with the applicable UNSC Resolutions. In such an environment, one needs to define the nature of the conflict(s) in order to apply the correct legal standards.

[19] UNSC Res 1970, S/RES/1970, OP 9.

7.3.1 From Internal Strife to Non-International Armed Conflict

7.3.1.1 January 2011–Mid February 2011

Following the events in Egypt and Tunisia, riots and protests broke out in Benghazi, in the eastern part of Libya. The clashes between protesters and governmental forces did not reach the threshold of armed conflict triggering the applicability of the law of armed conflict.[20]

According to the ICRC, what principally distinguishes situations of serious tension or internal disturbances from armed conflict is that the former are 'situations in which there is no non-international armed conflict as such, but there exists a confrontation within a country, which is characterized by a certain seriousness or duration and which involves acts of violence… In these situations, which do not necessarily degenerate into open struggle, the authorities in power call upon extensive police forces, or even armed forces, to restore internal order'.[21] According to Gasser, the following three criteria are helpful in distinguishing situations of internal disturbances from armed conflict: the violence exceeds the normal duration; the violence is overt and the situation is characterized by general violations of the fundamental rights of the individual.[22] In this particular case, it is not easy to establish at what point the situation became a non-international armed conflict. As stated by the Inter-American Commission on Human Rights: 'The most difficult problem regarding the application of common Article 3 is not at the upper end of the spectrum of domestic violence, but rather at the lower end. The line separating an especially violent situation of internal disturbances from the lowest level Article 3 armed conflict may sometimes be blurred and thus, not easily determined. When faced with making such a determination, what is required in the final analysis, is a good faith and objective analysis of the facts in each particular case.'[23]

---

[20] The law of armed conflict does not apply in situations when the armed forces are engaged within their own borders in situations of internal disturbances and tensions, such as riots, isolated and sporadic acts of violence and other acts of a similar nature, as not being armed conflicts. If the law of international armed conflict does not apply in those situations, we need to distinguish situations of internal disturbances and tensions from (non-international) armed conflicts.

[21] *See also* Dahl and Sandbu 2006. The International Committee of the Red Cross [ICRC] defined, albeit not exhaustively, situations of internal disturbances and tensions by way of the following examples: riots, that is to say, all disturbances which from the start are not directed by a leader and have no concerted intent; isolated and sporadic acts of violence, as distinct from military operations carried out by armed forces or organized armed groups; other acts of a similar nature which incur, in particular, mass arrests of persons because of their behavior or political opinion. ICRC (1973), Commentary on the Draft Additional Protocols to the Geneva Conventions. ICRC, Geneva.

[22] H. Gasser, 'A Measure of Humanity in Internal Disturbances and Tensions', 262 *IRRC* 38 (1988).

[23] The Tablada Case, *Inter-American Comm'n Hum. Rts.*, Rep. No. 55/97, Case No. 11.127: Argentina, OEA/Ser/L/V/II.97, Doc. 38, 18 Nov. 1997, paras 619–620.

7.3.1.2 Mid February 2011–September 2011

By the end of February 2011, the anti-Gaddafi forces controlled parts of the territory allowing them to conduct sustained operations against the regime forces. At the same time, the National Transitional Council (NTC) was created with the authority to take quasi-governmental powers in the 'liberated' areas. But when did the situation shift from internal disturbances to non-international armed conflict?

The distinction between situations of internal unrest and non-international armed conflict, triggering the applicability of Common Article 3 of Geneva Convention, was analyzed by the Inter-American Commission on Human Rights in relation to the attack and the recovery of the Tablada military base in Argentina on the 23rd and 24th of January 1989.[24] For approximately 30 h, an armed confrontation took place between attackers and Argentine armed forces. The Inter-American Commission found that the events at the Tablada base could *not* be characterized merely as a situation of internal disturbance.[25] The intensity of the violence and the degree of organization of the Parties involved seemed to be decisive in distinguishing situations of internal disturbances from non-international armed conflicts.[26]

In *Tadić*, the International Criminal Tribunal for the former Yugoslavia (ICTY) stated that 'the test applied by the Appeals Chamber to the existence of an armed conflict for the purposes of the rules contained in Common Article 3 focuses on two aspects of a conflict: *the intensity of the conflict and the organization of the parties to the conflict*.[27] In an armed conflict of an internal or mixed character, these closely related criteria are used solely for the purpose, as a minimum, of distinguishing an armed conflict from banditry, unorganized and short-lived insurrections, or terrorist activities, which are not subject to international humanitarian law' [Emphasis added].[28] According to D. Schindler,

---

[24] The American Convention on Human Rights, 1969, (also known as the "Pact of San José") (1144 *U.N.T.S.* 123) sets forth the human rights protected. It empowers two bodies, the already established Inter-American Commission on Human Rights and the Inter-American Court of Human Rights. For a more comprehensive study of this Convention, see Pasqualucci 2003.

[25] The Tablada Case, *Inter-American Comm'n Hum. Rts.*, Rep. No. 55/97, Case No. 11.127: Argentina, OEA/Ser/L/V/II.97, Doc. 38, 18 Nov. 1997, paras 154–55: 'What happened there was not equivalent to large scale violent demonstrations, students throwing stones at the police, bandits holding persons hostage for ransom, or the assassination of government officials for political reasons—all forms of domestic violence not qualifying as armed conflicts. What differentiates the events at the Tablada base from these situations are *the concerted nature of the hostile acts* undertaken by the attackers, the direct involvement of governmental armed forces, *and the nature and level of the violence* attending the events in question. More particularly, the attackers involved carefully planned, coordinated and executed an armed attack …'. (Emphasis added.).

[26] ICTY, *Prosecutor v Dusko Tadić*, Judgment, Trial Chamber (IT-94-1-T) 7 May 1997, para 562.

[27] See also ICTY, *Prosecutor* v *Ljube Boškoski and Johan Tarčulovski*, Judgment, Trial Chamber II (IT-04-82-T) 10 July 2008, paras 175–292.

[28] ICTY, *Prosecutor* v *Tadić*, n. 24, para 562. See also *Prosecutor v Zejnil Delalić, Zdravko Mucić, Hazim Delić, and Esad Landžo*, Judgment, Trial Chamber (IT-96-21-T) 16th November 1998 ("*Čelebići*"), para 184.

> the hostilities have to be conducted by force of arms and exhibit such intensity that, as a rule, the government is compelled to employ its armed forces against the insurgents instead of mere police forces. Secondly, as to the insurgents, the hostilities are meant to be of a collective character, i.e. they have to be carried out not only by single groups. In addition, the insurgents have to exhibit a minimum amount of organization. Their armed forces should be under a responsible command and be capable of meeting minimal humanitarian requirements.[29]

In 1978 Libya acceded to the Additional Protocols, including AP II which applies to armed conflicts taking place 'in the territory of a High Contracting Party between its armed forces and dissident armed forces or other organized armed groups which, under responsible command, exercise such control over a part of its territory as to enable them to carry out sustained and concerted military operations and to implement this Protocol.'[30] In such case both AP II and common Article 3 GC apply simultaneously. Although it remains difficult to indicate precisely at what point in time the rebels effectively controlled (substantial) parts of the Libyan territory, it is fair to say that when NATO assumed command of the military operations, the internal armed conflict in Libya was governed by Common Article 3 GC and Protocol II.

Some commentators argued that the support given to the rebels 'internationalized' the existing non-international armed conflict.[31] As a result, the entire conflict in Libya would have been subject to the law governing international armed conflict (LOIAC). In its decision on the merits in the *Tadić* case, the Appeals Chamber of the ICTY noted that '*It is indisputable that an armed conflict is international if it takes place between two or more States. In addition, in case of an internal armed conflict breaking out on the territory of a State, it may become international (or, depending upon the circumstances, be international in character alongside an internal armed conflict) if (i) another State intervenes in that conflict with its troops, or alternatively if (ii) some of the participants in the internal armed conflict act on behalf of that other State*.'[32] Dinstein convincingly argues that whereas 'the mere supply of arms to the rebels does not qualify as an actual use of armed force, there comes a point-for instance, when the weapons are accompanied by instructors training the rebels-at which the foreign country is deemed to be waging warfare.[33]

In *Tadić*, the ICTY noted that the belligerent parties may use paramilitary units or other irregulars in the conduct of hostilities only on condition that those belligerents are prepared to take responsibility for any infringements committed by such forces. In order for such irregulars to qualify as combatants, control over them by a party to the conflict was required and thus a relationship of dependence and allegiance. Accordingly, the term '*belonging to a party to the conflict*' used in

---

[29] Schindler 1979, p. 147.

[30] AP I, Article 1.

[31] This view was expressed by Koutroulis 2011. See also Schindler 1982; Gasser 1983–1984.

[32] *Prosecutor* v *Dusko Tadić,* Judgment, Appeal Chamber (IT-94-1-A) 15 July 1999, para 84.

[33] Dinstein 2005, p. 10. See also Solis 2010, p. 155.

Article 4 GCIII implicitly refers to a control test.[34] However, whether the applicable test is one of effective or overall control remains unclear.[35]

Although it cannot be excluded that individual States provided support to the rebels in their internal struggle against the regime, it should be recalled that in the conduct of OUP, NATO did not provide material support to the rebel forces. In sum, this resulted in the coexistence of two armed conflicts:

- An international armed conflict between the NATO-led nations and Libya;
- A non-international armed conflict in Libya between the pro- and anti-Gaddafi forces.

7.3.2 Operation Unified Protector

7.3.2.1 March 2011–September 2011

The military intervention pursuant to UNSCR 1973 clearly amounted to an international armed conflict between the States participating in the coalition and Libya, regulated by Common Article 2 to the Geneva Conventions.[36] According to the Commentaries on the Geneva Conventions 'any hostile act—no matter how minor—against another [State] makes applicable all of international humanitarian

[34] Ibid, paras 94–95.

[35] *Case Concerning Military and Paramilitary Activities in and Against Nicaragua* (Nicaragua v United States of America), Merits Judgment (1986) I.C.J. Reports 14 para 115: 'For this conduct to give rise to legal responsibility of the United States, it would in principle have to be proved that that State had effective control of the military or paramilitary operations in the course of which the alleged violations were committed.'. This high threshold was confirmed by the ICJ in the *Armed Activities on the Territory of the* Congo (DRC v Uganda) Merits Judgment (2005) ICJ Rep 168, paras 160–161) and in the *Case Concerning the Application of the Convention on the Prevention and Punishment of the Crime of Genocide* (Bosnia and Herzegovina v Serbia and Montenegro), Merits Judgment (2007) I.C.J. Rep. 43, para 413). See also Article 8 of the ILC Draft Articles on State Responsibility (Crawford 2001). In *Tadić*, the Appeals Chamber of the ICTY took a totally different approach than the ICJ when it stated that 'in order to attribute the acts of a military or paramilitary group to a State, it must be proved that the State wields overall control over the group, not only by equipping and financing the group, but also by coordinating or helping in the general planning of its military activity. Only then can the State be held internationally accountable for any misconduct of the group. However, it is not necessary that, in addition, the State should also issue, either to the head or to members of the group, instructions for the commission of specific acts contrary to international law' (*Tadić,* n. 29, para 131. See also Meron 1998, pp. 236–242).

[36] Article 2 common to the 1949 Geneva Conventions: 'In addition to the provisions which shall be implemented in peacetime, the present Convention shall apply to all cases of declared war or any other armed conflict which may arise between two or more of the High Contracting Parties, even if the state of war is not recognized by one of them'. As far as coalition operations were concerned, one should distinguish between the operations carried out by the coalition of the willing (19th March–31st March 2011) and the operations conducted under the umbrella of NATO (1st April–31st October 2011).

law'.[37] In enforcement operations authorizing the use of force against a State and provided the threshold of an armed conflict is reached, the full body of the law of international armed conflict applies.[38] Whether a particular intervention reaches the threshold of armed conflict will depend upon the circumstances,[39] and is not dependent on the characterization by the parties involved.[40]

From the above, it is clear that the coalition operations conducted prior to NATO assuming responsibility for the operations on Libya amounted to an international armed conflict, regulated by the law of international armed conflict. When NATO assumed responsibility for the operations in Libya pursuant to UNSCR 1973, the applicable legal framework remained unchanged and the law of international armed conflict applied.[41]

7.3.2.2 September 2011–30 October 2011

With the fall of the Gaddafi regime and the NTC assuming governmental authority over Libya, the conflict between NATO-led forces and pro-Gaddafi forces was transformed into a non-international armed conflict. Indeed, an initially international armed conflict can be 'internalized' when the regular armed forces become opposing forces following the fall of the governmental authorities.[42] In that sense, the Libyan

---

[37] Sandoz 2003, pp. 11–12.; Pictet 1956, pp. 28 et seq.

[38] Garraway 2010, para 5.26.

[39] UK Ministry of Defence 2004, para 3.3.1.

[40] See Judgment of the IMTFE in relation to the Mukden incident in the Chinese-Japanese war. The Tokyo Tribunal held that: 'From the outbreak of the Mukden incident till the end of the war the successive Japanese Governments refused to acknowledge that the hostilities in China constituted a war. They persistently called them "an incident". With this as an excuse the military authorities persistently asserted that the rules of war did not apply in the conduct of the hostilities.[…]" (*International Military Tribunal for the Far East*, Judgment of 4 November 1948, p. 386). On the other hand, see Solis 2010 stating that 'the way in which the two states choose to characterize the action (incident or war) can make the difference'—Solis 2010, p. 152. In non-international armed conflicts, see ICTR, *The Prosecutor v Jean-Paul Akayesu*, Judgment, Trial Chamber (ICTR-96-4-T) 2 September 1998, paras 619–620 and 622–626: 'It should be stressed that the ascertainment of the intensity of a non-international armed conflict does not depend on the subjective judgment of the parties to the conflict […]. If the application of International Humanitarian Law depended solely on the discretionary judgment of the parties to the conflict, in most cases there would be a tendency for the conflict to be minimized by the parties thereto. Thus, on the basis of objective criteria, both common Article 3 and Additional Protocol II apply once it has been established there exists an internal armed conflict, which fulfils their respective predetermined criteria'.

[41] It should be noted that at least one nation considered that the law of international armed conflict was not the applicable law, arguing that it acted under Chapter VII of the UN Charter. On a similar argument by some States during operation Allied Force, see the critical comments by Sassoli 2007, p. 260 and Okimoto 2003, p. 211.

[42] See also Naert asserting that in situations where the opponent is a non-State actor, the better view is that 'this kind of conflict is not of an international character in the sense of the LOAC'. (Naert 2010, p. 492). Others advocate the applicability of the LOIAC: see Kolb 2003b, p. 92: 'S'il

case is not fundamentally different from the Afghan scenario when the Taliban were forced to flee and president Karzai was sworn in as president.[43]

For the purpose of this paper, it suffices to state that the conflict was 'internalized' when the NTC effectively controlled the country.[44]

7.4 The Conduct of Hostilities

7.4.1 Targeting Process[45]

Based on the applicable UNSC Resolutions, OUP was authorized to take '*all necessary measures*' to fulfill its mandate. In military terms, this mandate is translated in an operational plan in which the precise rules of engagement are detailed. The authorization to use force in order to implement the mandate follows from the formulation '*all necessary measures*', including the use of force in self-defense, mission accomplishment and force protection.

Once the war began, the key missions for coalition air forces were essentially to enforce the NFZ in order to gain and maintain air superiority, prevent (artillery and armored) attacks on civilian areas and enable humanitarian assistance missions to enter Libya.[46] NATO-led air forces had an unprecedented ability to execute these missions and the ability to paralyze the Libyan air force; the systematic

(Footnote 42 continued)
s'agit de factions internes (parfois criminelles), on peut admettre que c'est le droit des armés non-internationaux qui s'appliquera; mais on peut aussi estimer dans ce cas *que c'est le droit des conflits armés internationaux par voie de réciprocité et en vertu du principe de l'égalité des belligérants'* [Emphasis added].

43 The question was raised to what extent the unilateral recognition of the National Transitional Council by participating OUP States impacted on the classification of the conflict in times when governmental authority was still exercised by the regime of Gaddafi. In principle, such unilateral recognition remains without effect on the classification of the conflict. As stated in the commentaries of Article 2 GC 'the danger arising in such situations is obvious. There had been too many cases where the contested legitimacy of the enemy Government, or the temporary disappearance of sovereign States as a result of annexation or capitulation, had been invoked as pretexts for not observing one or other of the Conventions. The need for a remedy to this state of affairs had become urgent' (Pictet 1956, p. 28).

44 As stated by Shaw: 'The effective control of a new government over the territory of the state is thus an important guideline to the problem of whether to extend recognition or not, providing such control appears well established and likely to continue' [Emphasis added]. Shaw 2003, pp. 377–378.

45 Targeting is the process of selecting targets and matching the appropriate response to them taking account of operational requirements and capabilities (NATO Glossary of Terms – AAP-6).

46 See the statement on Libya of 14th April 2011 following the working lunch of NATO Ministers of Foreign Affairs with non-NATO contributors to Operation Unified Protector (available at http://www.nato.int/cps/en/natolive/official_texts_72544.htm).

suppression of Libyan air defense systems allowed NATO to achieve air superiority shortly after the first days of the operation.[47]

The ability to rapidly target and re-target proved to be crucial in achieving the mission objectives, especially when regime forces changed their fighting behavior from regular to irregular warfare.[48] One of the major concerns was that the 72-h deliberate targeting process could not (always) keep pace with the dynamics of the battlefield. The key reason was due to the fact that the planning to execution cycle was too long and the process did not react quickly enough to changes in the scheme of maneuver. Shortening the 72-h targeting cycle and pushing the targeting planning cycle closer to execution helped to keep the Prioritized Target List more current (and relevant) during Air Task Order execution.[49] A guiding principle of the air campaign was to achieve maximum effect with minimum force. The use of precision guided munitions was key to this. This helped NATO achieve its objectives more quickly, while minimizing civilian casualties. Precision weapons were used against targets in (densely) populated areas where the aim was to destroy single targets while leaving neighboring buildings intact. Because no ground troops were deployed during OUP, unmanned aerial vehicles (UAV) were of utmost importance. Its ability to loiter on station not only meant that it provided real time battle damage assessment but the ability to adjust fire in real time ensured the desired effect was satisfied in respect to specific targets.

7.4.2 Military Objectives

Planning for the air campaign included the development of a list of potential targets that would help NATO to achieve its overall objectives. Targets were derived from the campaign plan and were selected to achieve a particular (military) effect. All feasible precautions were taken in order to positively identify the targets prior to prosecution.[50] Operating within the parameters agreed by the North

---

[47] DCA was used to enforce the arms embargo and the NFZ and has proven to be very effective. The weight of effort shifted heavily from DCA ("Defensive counter Air") to OCA ("Offensive Counter Air") operations in order to protect the civilian population against attack. Accordingly, air power was used effectively to destroy armor and artillery, C2 nodes and logistic nodes supporting the attack on civilians and populated areas.

[48] Rasmussen 2011.

[49] This concept was commonly referred to as the "DDT" process ("Dynamic Deliberate Targeting") using already planned air assets on the ATO and reroll them to prosecute targets that were cleared by the JTCB ("Joint Targeting Coordination Board").

[50] In the Final Report to the Prosecutor by the Committee Established to Review the NATO Bombing Campaign Against the Federal Republic of Yugoslavia (2000), available at http://icty.org/x/file/Press/nato061300.pdf [hereafter: OTP Report], this obligation was formulated in the following terms: 'A military commander must set up an effective intelligence gathering system to collect and evaluate information concerning potential targets. The commander must also direct his forces to use available technical means to properly identify targets during operations. Both the

Atlantic Council, the operational commanders had legal advisers available to them at all times during the air operations. All were aware of the need to comply with the law of armed conflict, the core principles of which are that only military objectives may be attacked, and that no attack should be carried out if any expected civilian damage (incidental loss of life, injury or damage) would be excessive in relation to the concrete and direct military advantage expected from the attack. Characterizing the nature and size of asymmetric forces, particularly when sheltered in urban or build-up areas, remained a constant challenge.[51]

7.4.2.1 Broadcasting Facilities

At the end of July 2011, NATO airplanes bombed the Tripoli TV station.[52] According to the Alliance, the regime had used the station 'to intimidate the people and incite acts of violence against them'.[53] Like all objects, broadcasting stations can only be attacked insofar they are military objectives according to Article 52(2) Additional Protocol I; that is to say when by their nature, use, purpose or location they make an effective contribution to military action and its, total or partial destruction offers a definite military advantage, in the circumstances prevailing at the time. This is undoubtedly the case when they are integrated into the command and control structure of the enemy.[54] The media is not generally regarded as a legitimate military objective.[55] It is not a military target merely because it spreads propaganda, and attacking the media to undermine civilian morale is similarly impermissible.[56] However, it becomes a legitimate military target if a party to the conflict uses it to incite others to commit war crimes, crimes

(Footnote 50 continued)
commander and the aircrew actually engaged in operations must have some range of discretion to determine which available resources shall be used and how they shall be used.' (para 29).

51 As was the ability to identify dispersed weapon systems like military aircraft (fixed and rotary wing) and SAM-systems ("Surface-to-Air-systems").

52 Holland 2004, p. 63.

53 Huffington Post 2011.

54 Dinstein 2010, pp. 106–107.

55 Following some criticism of the NATO bombing campaign, the ICTY Prosecutor established a committee to assess some of the allegations. During Operation Allied Force in 1999, NATO aircraft bombed the Serb Radio and Television (RTS), thereby causing civilian casualties. In support of this strike, NATO argued that the Serbs used the RTS as a military command and control tool. OTP Report, n. 47, para 55. See also the position of Dinstein arguing that civilian TV and radio stations are military objectives, thereby referring to Article 8 of the Hague Cultural Property Convention (Dinstein 2010, p. 107). Contra: M. SASSOLI & L. CAMERON, 'The Protection of Civilian Objects—Current State of the Law and Issues *de lege feranda*', in N. Ronzitti & G. Venturini (Eds.), The Law of Air Warfare—Contemporary Issues, (Utrecht, Eleven International Publishing), 2006, p. 65.

56 OTP Report, n. 47, paras 47, 55, 74–76. See also Byron 2010, pp. 185–186.

against humanity or genocide.[57] In such cases, the proximate causation between the incitement to commit crimes and the carrying out of such conduct is sufficient to establish that the particular media outlet is making an effective contribution to military action and, therefore a legitimate target.[58] Thus, provided the facts support the allegations, NATO was justified in bombing the Libyan TV station on the basis that it had incited others to commit crimes against the civilian population, including crimes against humanity.[59]

7.4.2.2 Mercenaries

The use of mercenaries, recruited for waging war and taking a direct part in hostilities, is not a new phenomenon.[60] In UNSCR 1973, the Security Council

---

[57] OTP Report, n. 47, para 55.

[58] In the *Nahimana* case, the ICTR stated that 'The nature of media is such that causation of killing and other acts of genocide will necessarily be effected by an immediate proximity cause in addition to the communication itself. In the Chamber's view, this does not diminish the causation to be attributed to the media, or the criminal accountability of those responsible for the communication'. (ICTR, *Prosecutor v. Nahimana, Barayagwiza and Ngeze*, Judgment, Trial Chamber (ICTR-99-52-T) 3 December 2003, para 65). See also the OTP Report in relation to the Rwandan genocide and the role of Radio Milles Collines, stating that if the media is used to incite crimes, as in Rwanda, then it is a legitimate target'. (para 74).

[59] See OTP Report, n. 47, para 55. On the 27th June 2011, the Pre-trial Chamber of the ICC gave its decision on the prosecutor's application for the issuance of arrest warrants in respect of Muammar Gadaffi, Saif Al-Islam Gadaffi and Abdullah Al-Senussi, finding that there was sufficient evidence to issue the arrest warrants alleging murders and persecutions as crimes against humanity (ICC, *Situation in the Libyan Arab Jamahiriya*, Decision on the "Prosecutor's Application Pursuant to Article 58 as to Muammar Mohammed Abu Minya GADDAFI, Saif Al-Islam Gaddafi and Abdullah AL-SENUSSI" (ICC-01/11–12) 27 June 2011). On the broader implications of targeting media, see Pokemper, Garlasco and Docherty 2003, pp. 121–122.

[60] As observed by the Special Rapporteur on the question of the use of mercenaries: 'Whether acting individually, or in the employ of contemporary multi-purpose security companies, the mercenary is generally present as a violator of human rights. On occasions, he acts as a professional agent in terrorist operations; he takes part in illicit trafficking; he commits acts of sabotage, among others. The mercenary is an element in all kinds of covert operation. In comparison with the cost of mobilizing armed forces, the mercenary offers an inexpensive means of conducting operations, organizations, sects and groups, simply for payment. The mercenary is hired because he has no scruples in riding roughshod over the norms of international humanitarian law or even in committing serious crimes and human rights violations (UN Commission on Human Rights, Report on the Use of Mercenaries as a Means of Violating Human Rights and Impeding the Exercise of the right of Peoples to Self-Determination submitted by Mr Enrique Bernales Ballesteros, Special Rapporteur, UN Doc. E/CN.4/2004/15, 24 December 2003, para 30). According to Article 47 AP I, a mercenary is a person who: (a) is specially recruited locally or abroad in order to fight in an armed conflict; (b) dos, in fact, take a direct part in the hostilities; (c) is motivated to take part in the hostilities essentially by the desire for private gain and, in fact, is promised, by or on behalf of a Party to the conflict, material compensation substantially in excess of that promised or paid to combatants of similar ranks and functions in the armed forces of that Party; (d) is neither a national of a Party to the conflict nor a

censured the Libyan authorities for the continuing use of mercenaries. It goes without saying that the mandate given to enforce the NFZ and to protect the civilian population included the authority to attack mercenaries involved in such attacks. For targeting purposes, the situation was clear: they were not combatants and could be attacked for taking a direct part in the hostilities.[61] Given the fact that mercenaries were actively and systematically involved in attacks on the civilian population, they undoubtedly constituted legitimate military objectives.

7.4.2.3 Human Shields

During the conduct of OUP, pro-Gaddafi forces used human shields in order to shield legitimate military objectives from attack, despite the prohibition contained in Article 51 (7) of AP I.[62] From a targeting perspective, a distinction must be made between voluntary and involuntary human shields. In the latter case, they retain their civilian status and may not be attacked. That is not to say that by virtue of their presence the military objective they are shielding may not be attacked. It only means that in the proportionality analysis, planners and executors must satisfy themselves that the incidental damage is not excessive compared to the military advantage to be gained from the attack.[63] Having said that and even assuming all parameters were met (positive identification, Rules of Engagement, collateral damage), it is clear that it would have been illogical and contrary to the 'spirit' of UNSCR 1973 to attack legitimate military targets shielded by involuntary human shields having regard to the purpose of the operation: to protect civilians and civilian populated areas.

Whereas the situation is clear in relation to involuntary human shields, the controversy surrounding the legality of targeting voluntary human shields still

(Footnote 60 continued)
resident of territory controlled by a Party to the conflict; (e) is not a member of the armed forces of a Party to the conflict; and (f) has not been sent by a state which is not a Party to the conflict on official duty as a member of its armed forces. See also Article 1 of the 1989 International Convention against the Recruitment, Use, Financing, and Training of Mercenaries that broadens the scope of the definition of mercenaries and Article 1.2 of the OAU Convention for the Elimination of Mercenarism in Africa.

[61] The notion of DPH is controversial and what this practically means is subject of debate. For a comprehensive critique of the DPH Study, see in particular Watkin 2010, 642–693. Other contributions include Schmitt 2010; Boothby 2010; Parks 2010; Rogers 2009.

[62] The presence or movements of the civilian population or individual civilians shall not be used to render certain points or areas immune from military operations, in particular to shield military objectives from attack or to shield, favor or impede military operations: Article 28 GC IV; Article 23 GC III. See also Article 8(2)(b)(xxiii) of the ICC Statute.

[63] Article 57 API. UK Ministry of Defence 2004, paras 2.7.2–2.7.3. It should be recalled that the prohibition relates to the excessiveness thereof, even if the damage is extensive.

exists.[64] Some authors argue that voluntary human shields lose their civilian protection because 'they are deemed civilians who take a direct part in hostilities'[65] while others claim that even then they continue to enjoy civilian protection. A third view is that civilians retain their civilian status, but should not be included in the proportionality analysis.[66]

7.4.2.4 Police Stations

In general, police officers remain civilians and are thus protected against enemy attack, unless they directly participate in the hostilities or when law enforcement agencies are incorporated into the armed forces.[67] On a practical level, a distinction operated between the interior security forces which were engaged in repressing and attacking the civilian population, and the municipal police agents who were acting as law enforcement officers. The former constituted legitimate military objectives, the latter not. Additionally, special precautions should be taken in respect of police stations which are being used as recruitment stations but managed by civilians who had been coerced into assisting. Attacking these recruitment stations risks killing the very civilian population that NATO was mandated to protect.

7.4.2.5 Retreating Troops

Images of the retreating Iraqi army convoy from Kuwait City during the Iraq campaign, led some commentators to assert that these troops cannot be attacked.[68] However, as stated by Dinstein, 'the only way for members of the armed forces to immunize themselves from attack is to surrender, thereby becoming hors de combat.'[69] In the context of OUP, there was a possibility that pro-Gaddafi forces might comply with the UNSC Resolutions and halt all attacks on the civilian population by returning to their military barracks. Had such a situation materialized and, provided there was no intention of repositioning into new

---

[64] On human shields, see Dinstein 2008, pp. 13–16; Schmitt 2008, pp. 17–59; De Cock 2008, p. 95.

[65] Dinstein 2010, pp. 152–155; Schmitt 2006. See also Solis 2010, p. 321.

[66] De Cock 2008, p. 95; See also Rogers 2006, p. 128: 'There is, inevitably, the question of the significance in those calculations that the military planners attach to likely civilian casualties in different situations. They, and the public, will be very concerned about civilians who happen to be in the vicinity of objects that have been selected for attack, *but perhaps less so for civilians who aid the war effort by, for example, working in an armaments factory, and hardly at all for those who have volunteered to act as 'human shield'*". [Emphasis added].

[67] Article 43, (3) AP I. See also Dinstein 2010, p. 104.

[68] David 2008, p. 313.

[69] Dinstein 2010, pp. 102–103; Holland 2004, p. 67.

fighting positions, these troops would have been granted immunity from attack. Insofar as the pro-regime forces which were taking part *solely* in the non-international armed conflict were concerned, to the extent that they could be identified as not involved in the attacks against civilian, attacking them would constitute a material breach of the mandate.

7.4.3 Collateral Damage

Although collateral damage remains one of the main concerns for planners and decision makers in any military operation, it should be emphasized that the concern of hitting civilians unintentionally was one of the major priorities during the execution of OUP, especially having regard to the aim of the operation, namely to protect the civilian population against attack and threat of attack from regime forces. In targeting military objectives, authority to strike is excluded if the following parameters are not met: positive identification (PID), collateral damage (CD), and rules of engagement (ROE). PID is the reasonable certainty that a given object is a valid military objective.[70] Assuming PID and (implemented) ROE are met, a valid target can be prosecuted if the incidental losses or injury to civilians and/or the collateral damage to civilian objects is not excessive in relation to the concrete and direct military advantage to be gained from the attack.[71]

As stated previously, NATO forces were confronted with opposing military forces who intentionally disregarded their obligations under the law of armed conflict by using civilian cars to transport troops and material to combat zones and, in particular, to use civilian dwellings as staging points, logistic nodes, and even as command and control posts. In such a setting, the proportionality analysis is of paramount importance. It is for this reason that pilots in many cases refrained from striking valid military targets, despite some allegations of unintended high civilian casualties.[72] Consequently, all feasible precautions were taken to avoid or to minimize collateral damage, including *inter alia*: the use of precision guided munitions, the use of a detailed collateral damage estimation methodology prior to any deliberate strike, and the use of delay fuses. This can be illustrated by the following examples. Firstly, targets that were scheduled to be attacked in the deliberate targeting process were subject to a pattern of life assessment (PoL). Only in those cases where PoL assessment conclusively supported the facts of the case, that is to say PID and CD, were targets eligible for further analysis in the targeting process and prosecution by aircrew. Secondly, NATO procedures

[70] Article 57, (2), (a) AP I.

[71] Article 51, (5), (b) AP I.

[72] See in particular 'In Strikes on Libya by NATO, an Unspoken Civilian Toll, New York Times, 17 December 2011. It should also be noted that the UN Human Rights Council decided to establish an Independent Commission of Inquiry on Libya to investigate alleged violations of international human rights law in Libya.

described the conditions under which pilots were authorized to release ordinance on military targets. If targets did not meet the required proofs of PID and CD or in case of doubt, both in the deliberate and the dynamic targeting mode, attacks were cancelled or postponed.

Although it is not disputed that air strikes on a number of legitimate military targets might have caused some collateral damage, only 'excessive' collateral damage is prohibited. In that sense, it should be recalled that even extensive collateral damage is not *in se* illegal insofar it is not 'excessive'.[73] Finally, it should be noted that the UN Human Rights Council decided to establish an Independent Commission of Inquiry on Libya to investigate alleged violations of international human rights law in Libya.[74]According to Judge Kirsch, the Commission is not limited to investigate serious violations of human rights, but also of international humanitarian law by other forces in the conflict, including NATO.[75] Whereas international investigation mechanisms on possible violations of the law of armed conflict should not be ruled out, it seems that the Human Rights Council in this particular case is having regard to its mandate, namely to solely address '*situations of violations of human rights*' in contrast to violations of international humanitarian law.[76]

7.5 Conclusion

It is submitted that different legal regimes applied in the context of the operations in Libya. Until the take-over by the TNC there existed:

- An international armed conflict between the NATO-led countries and the pro-Gaddafi forces;
- A situation of internal disturbances until mid February 2011 between the protesters and the pro-Gaddafi forces;
- A non-international armed conflict between the pro- and anti-Gaddafi forces from mid February 2011.

Following the take-over by the TNC:

- A non-international armed conflict between the NATO-led countries and the pro-Gaddafi forces;
- A non-international armed conflict between the anti- and the pro-Gaddafi forces.

---

[73] Dinstein 2010, pp. 130–133.

[74] Human Rights Council, Report of the Human Rights Council on its fifteenth special session, A/HRC/S-15/1, 25 February 2011, para 11.

[75] Conclusion of the first part of investigations in Libya by the Commission of Inquiry (available at http://www.ohchr.org/en/NewsEvents/Pages/DisplayNews.aspx?NewsID=11735&LangID=E).

[76] GA Resolution A/RES/60251, 3 April 2006, para 3.

Over 260 air assets (fighter aircraft, ISR and AAR aircraft, UAV and attack helicopters) and 21 naval assets (supply ships, frigates, destroyers, submarines, amphibious assault ships and aircraft carriers) took part in the mission.[77] Over 26,500 sorties (including over 9700 strike sorties) were flown destroying over 5900 military objectives, including 400 artillery or rocket launchers and over 600 tanks or armored vehicles.[78] The main focus of the operation was to prevent the attacks and the threat of attacks on civilians. OUP has undoubtedly been the most intense NATO air campaign since Operation Allied Force during the Kosovo conflict in 1999. It has proved that air assets are critical parts of every modern operation and can contribute to the success of a military campaign. In all phases of OUP, constant care was taken to comply strictly with the Security Council mandate and the imperatives of the law of armed conflict. When requirements changed and pro-Gaddafi forces shifted their tactics from regular to irregular warfare, NATO-led forces proved to be capable of responding rapidly and adequately to these changing circumstances. The use of precision guided weapons, coupled with high tech ISR assets was crucial for mission accomplishment. Using precision laser-guided and satellite-guided munitions made every strike count. With a minimum of collateral damage, the air strikes enabled NATO to enforce the mandate. Operation Unified Protector offered convincing proof that airpower is flexible enough to take the lead in many different types of conflict. In targeting enemy forces, NATO forces strictly adhered to their obligations under the law of armed conflict. Targets were positively identified prior to prosecution and all feasible precautions were taken in order to minimize damage to civilian property and the civilian population.

References

Boothby B (2010) "And for such time as": the time dimension to direct participation in hostilities. N Y Univ Int Law Policy 42:741

Boustany K and Dormoy D (2002) Rapport de Synthèse. L'intervention de l'OTAN au Kosovo. L'humanitaire aux Confins du Politique, de la Force Armée et du Droit'. In: Boustany K, Dormoy D (eds) Collection de Droit International, Perspectives Humanitaires. Entre Conflits, droit(s) et action. Bruylant, Bruxelles

Breen C (2007) The necessity of a role for the ecosoc in the maintenance of international peace and security. J Confl Secur Law 12(2) 261

Byron C (2010) International humanitarian law and bombing campaigns: legitimate military objectives and excessive collateral damage. Yearb Int Humanit Law 13:175

Crawford E (2010) The treatment of combatants and insurgents under the law of armed conflict. Oxford University Press, Oxford

Crawford J (2001) ILC draft articles on state responsibility. Yearb Intl Law Comm 2(2)

---

[77] ISR: Intelligence, surveillance and reconnaissance. AAR: air-to-air refueling.

[78] NATO Fact Sheet, Operation UNIFIED PROTECTOR, Final Mission Stats, 02 November 2011.

Dahl AW, Sandbu M (2006) The threshold of armed conflict. Rev Droit Mil Droit de la Guerre 3–4:369–88

David E (2008) Principes de Droit des Conflits Armés, 4ième edn. Bruylant, Bruxelles

De Cock C (2008) The use of air assets and military operations in urban terrain: legal constraints. Israel Yearb Hum Rights 38:95

Dinstein Y (2005) War, aggression and self defence, 4th edn. Cambridge University Press, Cambridge

Dinstein Y (2008) Distinction and loss of civilian protection in international armed conflicts. Israel Yearb Hum Rights 38:1

Dinstein Y (2010) The conduct of hostilities under the law of international armed conflict, 2nd edn. Cambridge University Press, Cambridge

Evans G (2008) The responsibility to protect ending mass atrocity once and for all. Brookings Institute Press, Washington

Focarelli C (2008) The responsibility to protect doctrine and humanitarian intervention: too many ambiguities for a working doctrine. J Confl Secur Law 13(2):191

Forsythe DP (2006) Human rights in international relations, 2nd edn. Cambridge University Press, Cambridge

Gardam JG (1996) Legal restraints on security council military enforcement action. Mich J Int Law 285

Garraway CHB (2010) Applicability and application of international humanitarian law to enforcement and peace enforcement operations.In: Gill TD, Fleck D (2010) The handbook of international law of military operations. Oxford University Press, Oxford

Gasser HP (1983–1984) internationalized non-international armed conflicts: case studies of Afghanistan, Kampuchea, and Lebanon. Am Univ Law Rev 33:145

Holland J (2004) Military objective and collateral damage: their relationship and dynamics. Yearb Intl Humanit Law 7:35

Huffington Post (2011), NATO Planes target tripoli tv stations in fresh bombing attacks. Huffington Post (29 September 2011). http://www.huffingtonpost.co.uk/2011/07/30/nato-planes-target-tripol_n_913900.html. Accessed 19 Dec 2011

Kolb R (2003a) Ius contra bellum. Le Droit International Relatif au Maintien de la Paix. Bruylant, Bruxelles

Kolb (2003b) Ius in bello. Le Droit International des Conflits Armés. Bruylant, Bruxelles

Koutroulis V (2011) 12th Bruges colloquium of the college of Europe (20–21 October 2011) on "international organizations' involvement in peace operations: applicable legal framework and the issue of responsibility". Bruges

Lamb S (1999) Legal limits to United Nations security council powers'. In: Goodwin-Gill, Talmon S (eds) The reality of international law: essays in honour of Ian Brownlie. Clarendon Press, Oxford

Meron T (1998) Classification of armed conflicts in the former Yugoslavia: Nicaragua's fallout. AJIL 236

McLaughlin R (2007) The legal regime applicable to use of lethal force when operating under a United Nations Security Council chapter VII mandate authorizing 'all necessary means'. J Confl Secur Law 12(3):389

Naert F (2010) International law aspects of the eu's security and defence policy with particular focus on the law of armed conflict and human rights. Antwerp-Oxford-Portland, Intersentia

Nasu H (2009) Operationalizing the 'responsibility to protect' and conflict prevention: dilemmas of civilian protection in armed conflict'. J Confl Secur Law 14(2): 209

Okimoto K (2003) Violations of international humanitarian law by United Nations Forces and their legal consequences. Yearb Int Humanit Law 6:199

Orakhelashvili A (2007) Overlap and convergence: the interaction between Jus ad Bellum and Jus in Bello. J Confl Secur Law 12(2):157

Parks WH (2010) Part IX of the ICRC "direct participation in hostilities" study: no mandate, no expertise, and legally incorrect. N Y Univ Int Law Policy 42:770

Pasqualucci JM (2003) The practice and procedure of the Inter-American court of human rights. Cambridge University Press, Cambridge

Pictet J (1956) Commentary of the Geneva convention of 12 August 1949 for the amelioration of the condition of the wounded and sick in armed forces in the field. ICRC, Geneva

Pokemper D, Garlasco M, Docherty B (2003) Off target on the Iraq Campaign: a response to Professor Schmitt. Yearb Int Humanit Law 6:111

Rasmussen AF (2011) NATO after Libya, the atlantic alliance in austere times. foreign affairs, July/August 2011. Available at https://www.foreignaffairs.com/articles/67915/anders-fogh-rasmussen/nato-after-libya. Accessed 19 Dec 2011

Rogers APV (2006) Law on the battlefield, 2nd edn. Manchester University Press, Manchester

Rogers APV (2009) Direct participation in hostilities: some personal reflections. Mil Law Law War Rev 48 (1–2):143

Sassoli M (2007) Ius ad Bellum and Ius in Bello—the separation between the legality of the use of force and humanitarian rules to be respected in warfare: crucial or outdated? In: Schmitt MN and Pejic J (2007) International law and armed conflict: exploring the faultlines, essays in honour of Yoram Dinstein. Martinus Nijhoff, Leiden-Boston

Sandoz Y (2003) International humanitarian law in the twenty-first century. Yearb Int Humanit Law 6:3

Schindler D (1982) International humanitarian law and internationalized internal armed conflicts. Int Rev Red Cross 230:255

Schindler D (1979) The different types of armed conflicts according to the Geneva conventions and protocols. RCADI 163:147

Schmitt MN (2006) War, technology and the law of armed conflict, the law of war in the 21st century: weaponry and the use of force. Int Law Stud 82:137

Schmitt MN (2008) human shields in international humanitarian law. Israel Yearb Hum Rights 38:17

Schmitt MN (2010) Deconstructing direct participation in hostilities: the constitutive elements. N Y Univ Int Law Policy 42:697

Schmitt MN (2011) Wings over Libya: the no-fly zone in legal perspective. Yale J Int Law Online 36:45

Shaw MN (2003) International law, 5th edn. Cambridge University Press, Cambridge

Simma B (2002) The charter of the United Nations, a commentary, vol 1, 2nd edn. Oxford University Press, Oxford

Solis GD (2010) The law of armed conflict international humanitarian law in action. Cambridge University Press, Cambridge

Thakur R (2006) The United Nations peace and security. Cambridge University Press, Cambridge

UK Ministry of Defence (2004) The manual of the law of armed conflict. Oxford University Press, Oxford

Watkin K (2010) Opportunity lost: organized armed groups and the ICRC "direct participation in hostilities" interpretive guidance. N Y U Int Policy 42:697

Wedgwood R. (1999) NATO's campaign in Yugoslavia. AJIL 93:828

Wilson G (2007) The legal, military and political consequences of the 'coalition of the willing' approach to UN military enforcement action. J Confl Secur Law 12(2):304

Chapter 8
The ECtHR's *Al-Jedda* Judgment: Implications for IHL

Jelena Pejic

Contents

8.1 Introduction

In July 2011, the European Court of Human Rights (ECtHR) handed down two long-awaited and momentous judgments involving the conduct of the United Kingdom's armed forces during the occupation and armed conflict in Iraq.[1] In both cases, the Court found against the UK government. The first decision, in the *Al-Skeini* case,[2] essentially clarified and revised the Court's position on the extraterritorial application of the European Convention on Human Rights (ECHR)

This article was written in a personal capacity and does not necessarily reflect the views of the ICRC.

[1] Both cases were decided by the Grand Chamber of the European Court of Human Rights and were almost unanimous.
[2] *Al Skeini v. UK*, Grand Chamber, Judgment of 7 July 2011, no.55721/07 ECHR 2011.

J. Pejic (✉)
Legal Division, International Committee of the Red Cross (ICRC), Geneva, Switzerland
e-mail: jdpejic@gmail.com

M.N. Schmitt and L. Arimatsu (eds.), *Yearbook of International Humanitarian Law Volume 14, 2011*, DOI: 10.1007/978-90-6704-855-2_8,

and attracted the most attention. The second case, *Al-Jedda*,[3] received less focus even though its legal and practical consequences are just as significant. The purpose of this note is to outline some of the ramifications of the *Al-Jedda* case that have not been picked up in other commentaries, in particular its implications for detention operations carried out by ECHR member states abroad. As will be argued, the Court's approach to and interpretation of international humanitarian law (IHL) do not comport with the spirit or letter of this body of rules.

8.2 The Facts of the Case

The case was lodged by a dual Iraqi/British national, Mr. Hilal Abdul-Razzaq Ali Al-Jedda, who had been interned for imperative reasons of security by UK forces at the Sha'aibah Divisional Temporary Detention Facility in Basrah City between October 2004 and December 2007. Al-Jedda was believed by the British authorities to have been "personally responsible for recruiting terrorists outside Iraq with a view to the commission of atrocities there; for facilitating the travel into Iraq of an identified terrorist explosives expert; for conspiring with that explosives expert to conduct attacks with improvised explosive devices against coalition forces in the areas around Fallujah and Baghdad; and for conspiring with the explosives expert and members of an Islamist terrorist cell in the Gulf to smuggle high tech detonation equipment into Iraq for use in attacks against coalition forces."[4] Al-Jedda's internment was subject to a review process that was conducted by UK forces and later involved Iraqi representatives as well. The Court's description of the review process is provided below:

1. The applicant's internment was initially authorised by the senior officer in the detention facility. Reviews were conducted seven days and twenty-eight days later by the Divisional Internment Review Committee ("the DIRC"). This comprised the senior officer in the detention facility and Army legal and military personnel. Owing to the sensitivity of the intelligence material upon which the applicant's arrest and detention had been based, only two members of the DIRC were permitted to examine it. Their recommendations were passed to the Commander of the Coalition's Multinational Division (South East) ("the Commander"), who himself examined the intelligence file on the applicant and took the decision to continue the internment. Between January and July 2005 a monthly review was carried out by the Commander, on the basis of the recommendations of the DIRC. Between July 2005 and December 2007 the decision to intern was taken by the DIRC itself, which during this period included as members the Commander together with members of the legal, intelligence and other staffs. There was no procedure for disclosure of evidence nor for an oral hearing, but representations could be made by the internee in writing which were considered by the legal branch and put before the DIRC for

[3] *Al Jedda v. UK,* Grand Chamber, Judgment of 7 July 2011, no.27021/08 ECHR 2011. (Hereinafter '*Al-Jedda* Judgment').

[4] *Al-Jedda* Judgment, *supra* n. 3, para 11.

consideration. The two Commanders who authorised the applicant's internment in 2005 and 2006 gave evidence to the domestic courts that there was a substantial weight of intelligence material indicating that there were reasonable grounds for suspecting the applicant of the matters alleged against him.

2. When the applicant had been detained 18 months, the internment fell to be reviewed by the Joint Detention Committee (JDC). This body included senior representatives of the Multi-National Force, the Iraqi Interim Government and the Ambassador for the United Kingdom. It met once and thereafter delegated powers to a Joint Detention Review Committee, which comprised Iraqi representatives and officers from the Multi-National Force.[5]

Al-Jedda was released from internment on December 30, 2007. He lost an appeal against an order depriving him of British citizenship in 2009. The Special Immigrations Appeal Commission held—for reasons set out in detail in a closed judgment—that on the balance of probabilities the Secretary of State [for Defence] had proved that Al-Jedda had facilitated the travel to Iraq of a terrorist explosives expert and conspired with him to smuggle explosives into Iraq and to conduct improvised explosives device attacks against coalition forces around Fallujah and Baghdad.[6] Al-Jedda did not appeal against that judgment.

8.3 The Legal Proceedings and the Grand Chamber's Decision

Al-Jedda's complaint before the European Court of Human Rights alleged that his internment by UK forces in Iraq was in breach of Article 5(1) of the European Convention on Human Rights. The relevant paragraph guarantees the right to liberty and security of person, and exhaustively lists six permitted reasons based on which a deprivation of liberty may lawfully occur.[7] Needless

---

[5] *Al-Jedda* Judgment, *supra* n. 3, paras 12 and 13.

[6] *Al-Jedda* Judgment, para 15.

[7] Article 5(1) of the Convention provides:

> 1. Everyone has the right to liberty and security of person. No one shall be deprived of his liberty save in the following cases and in accordance with a procedure prescribed by law: (a) the lawful detention of a person after conviction by a competent court; (b) the lawful arrest or detention of a person for non- compliance with the lawful order of a court or in order to secure the fulfilment of any obligation prescribed by law; (c) the lawful arrest or detention of a person effected for the purpose of bringing him before the competent legal authority on reasonable suspicion of having committed an offence or when it is reasonably considered necessary to prevent his committing an offence or fleeing after having done so; (d) the detention of a minor by lawful order for the purpose of educational supervision or his lawful detention for the purpose of bringing him before the competent legal authority; (e) the lawful detention of persons for the prevention of the spreading of infectious diseases, of persons of unsound mind, alcoholics or drug addicts or vagrants; (f) the lawful arrest or detention of a person to prevent his effecting an unauthorised entry into the country or of a person against whom action is being taken with a view to deportation or extradition.

to say, detention/internment for imperative reasons of security, a quintessentially war-time ground for detention is not among them. It should be noted that Al-Jedda did not complain of a violation of Article 5(4) of the European Convention concerning the lack of judicial review of the detention, as proceedings on this issue were still pending before UK courts at the time his application was lodged.

The domestic proceedings will not be mentioned here except to note that, for different reasons, the three instances that examined the case, ending with the House of Lords, ruled in the Government's favour. In its submissions to the European Court, the UK posited two arguments: first, that the internment was attributable to the United Nations and not to the United Kingdom, and that Al-Jedda was therefore not within UK jurisdiction under Article 1 of the European Convention. Second, and in the alternative, the Government argued that Al-Jedda's internment was carried out pursuant to United Nations Security Council Resolution 1546 which created an obligation on the UK to detain him and which, pursuant to Article 103 of the United Nations Charter, overrode obligations under the European Convention on Human Rights.[8]

The first contention was rejected by the European Court, as it had been by the House of Lords before it. The Court determined that Al-Jedda's detention could not be attributable to the United Nations after, *inter alia*, analyzing relevant UN Security Council resolutions which authorized the multinational force of which the UK was a part. The Court considered that the UN Security Council had neither effective control nor ultimate authority and control over the acts and omissions of troops within the Multinational Force and that Al-Jedda's detention was therefore not attributable to the United Nations.[9]

The Government's second argument was essentially that the relevant UN Security Council resolutions authorized the Multinational Force to take "all necessary measures" to contribute to the maintenance of security and stability in Iraq, and that such measures comprised the use of preventive detention "where necessary for imperative reasons of security". The latter wording—on detention—was not included in UN Security Council resolution 1546 itself,[10] but was provided for in letters exchanged between the then Iraqi Prime Minister and the then US Secretary of State that were annexed to the resolution and were believed to constitute its integral part. In the Government's view, the UK's obligations under

[8] *Al-Jedda* Judgment, *supra* n. 3, para 60.

[9] *Al-Jedda* Judgment, *supra* n. 3, para 84.

[10] S/RES/1546 (2004), 8 June 2004.

Article 5 of the European Convention were displaced by the legal regime established by resolution 1546 due to the operation of Articles 25 and 103 of the UN Charter. Pursuant to the latter, states' obligations under the Charter prevail over their obligations under any other international agreement in the event of a conflict. The Government argued, based on practice and prevailing international law doctrine, that the language of Article 103 cannot be limited to Security Council resolutions *obliging* states to act in a particular way, but also to decisions *authorizing* them to do so (as resolution 1546 and the appended letters had done).

The European Court did not explicitly opine on this issue, but addressed it indirectly by positing that the "key question" was "whether resolution 1546 placed the UK under an obligation to hold the applicant in internment."[11] The Court then adopted an interpretive "presumption" that the UN Security Council does not intend to impose "any obligation" on member states to breach fundamental human rights, and that in the event of ambiguity in the text of a resolution the Court must choose the interpretation most in harmony with the European Convention.[12] The Court added that, in light of the UN's role in promoting and encouraging respect for human rights, it is to be expected that "clear and explicit language would be used were the Security Council to intend States to take particular measures that would conflict with their obligations under human rights law". The Court concluded that due to the ambiguity of resolution 1546 (it rejected the legal significance of the appended letters mentioned above),[13] it could not be held that the Security Council intended to oblige the Multinational Force to resort to internment in breach of international human rights instruments, including the European Convention.

The most relevant part of the *Al-Jedda* Judgment for the purposes of this note is the section in which the Court examines IHL. It is of particular significance, as it would appear to be a first in terms of the Court's direct interpretation of specific IHL treaties, the Fourth Geneva Convention in particular, some

[11] *Al-Jedda* Judgment, *supra* n. 3, para 101.

[12] *Al-Jedda* Judgment, *supra* n. 3, para 102.

[13] "However, such an agreement could not override the binding obligations under the Convention. In this respect, the Court recalls its case-law to the effect that a Contracting State is considered to retain Convention liability in respect of treaty commitments and other agreements between States subsequent to the entry into force of the Convention"[...]. *Al-Jedda* Judgment, *supra* n. 3, para 108.

articles of which are included in the Judgment's section on relevant law.[14] The paragraph of the Judgment dealing with IHL is reproduced in full[15]:

[14] These are laid out in paras 42–44 of the Judgment entitled "Relevant provisions of international humanitarian law". Fourth Geneva Convention, Article 27: Protected persons are entitled, in all circumstances, to respect for their persons, their honour, their family rights, their religious convictions and practices, and their manners and customs. They shall at all times be humanely treated, and shall be protected especially against all acts of violence or threats thereof and against insults and public curiosity.

Women shall be especially protected against any attack on their honour, in particular against rape, enforced prostitution, or any form of indecent assault.

Without prejudice to the provisions relating to their state of health, age and sex, all protected persons shall be treated with the same consideration by the Party to the conflict in whose power they are, without any adverse distinction based, in particular, on race, religion or political opinion.

However, the Parties to the conflict may take such measures of control and security in regard to protected persons as may be necessary as a result of the war.

Fourth Geneva Convention, Article 41: Should the Power, in whose hands protected persons may be, consider the measures of control mentioned in the present Convention to be inadequate, it may not have recourse to any other measure of control more severe than that of assigned residence or internment, in accordance with the provisions of Articles 42 and 43.

Fourth Geneva Convention, Article 42: Article 42. The internment or placing in assigned residence of protected persons may be ordered only if the security of the Detaining Power makes it absolutely necessary.

If any person, acting through the representatives of the Protecting Power, voluntarily demands internment, and if his situation renders this step necessary, he shall be interned by the Power in whose hands he may be.

Fourth Geneva Convention, Article 43: Article 43. Any protected person who has been interned or placed in assigned residence shall be entitled to have such action reconsidered as soon as possible by an appropriate court or administrative board designated by the Detaining Power for that purpose. If the internment or placing in assigned residence is maintained, the court or administrative board shall periodically, and at least twice yearly, give consideration to his or her case, with a view to the favourable amendment of the initial decision, if circumstances permit.

Unless the protected persons concerned object, the Detaining Power shall, as rapidly as possible, give the Protecting Power the names of any protected persons who have been interned or subjected to assigned residence, or who have been released from internment or assigned residence. The decisions of the courts or boards mentioned in the first paragraph of the present Article shall also, subject to the same conditions, be notified as rapidly as possible to the Protecting Power.

Fourth Geneva Convention, Article 78: Article 78. If the Occupying Power considers it necessary, for imperative reasons of security, to take safety measures concerning protected persons, it may, at the most, subject them to assigned residence or to internment.Decisions regarding such assigned residence or internment shall be made according to a regular procedure to be prescribed by the Occupying Power in accordance with the provisions of the present Convention. This procedure shall include the right of appeal for the parties concerned. Appeals shall be decided with the least possible delay. In the event of the decision being upheld, it shall be subject to periodical review, if possible every six months, by a competent body set up by the said Power.

Protected persons made subject to assigned residence and thus required to leave their homes shall enjoy the full benefit of Article 39 of the present Convention.

[15] Only references to other paragraphs in the Judgment have been omitted.

> 107. The Court has considered whether, in the absence of express provision in Resolution 1546, there was *any other legal basis for the applicant's detention which could operate to disapply the requirements of Article 5 § 1* [emphasis added]. The Government have argued that the effect of the authorisations in paras 9 and 10 of Resolution 1546 was that the Multi-National Force continued to exercise the "specific authorities, responsibilities and obligations" that had vested in the United States and the United Kingdom as Occupying Powers under international humanitarian law and that these "obligations" included the obligation to use internment where necessary to protect the inhabitants of the occupied territory against acts of violence. Some support for this submission can be derived from the findings of the domestic courts (...). The Court notes in this respect that para 2 of the Resolution clearly stated that the occupation was to end by 30 June 2004. However, even assuming that the effect of Resolution 1546 was to maintain, after the transfer of authority from the Coalition Provisional Authority to the Interim Government of Iraq, the position under international humanitarian law which had previously applied, *the Court does not find it established that international humanitarian law places an obligation on an Occupying Power to use indefinite internment without trial.* [emphasis added.] Article 43 of the Hague Regulations requires an Occupying Power to take "all the measures in his power to restore, and ensure, as far as possible, public order and safety, while respecting, unless absolutely prevented, the laws in force in the country" (...). While the International Court of Justice in its judgment *Armed Activities on the Territory of the Congo* interpreted this obligation to include the duty to protect the inhabitants of the occupied territory from violence, including violence by third parties, it did not rule that this placed an obligation on the Occupying Power to use internment; indeed, it also found that Uganda, as an Occupying Power, was under a duty to secure respect for the applicable rules of international human rights law, including the provisions of the International Covenant for the Protection of Civil and Political Rights, to which it was a signatory (...). *In the Court's view it would appear from the provisions of the Fourth Geneva Convention that under international humanitarian law internment is to be viewed not as an obligation on the Occupying Power but as a measure of last resort (see para 43 above)*[16] [emphasis added.]

The Court holding in the case, based on the reasoning outlined above, was that there was no conflict between the UK's obligations under the UN Charter and its obligations under the European Convention. It held that Al-Jedda's detention was in breach of ECHR Article 5(1) as its provisions were not displaced and none of the permissible grounds for detention exhaustively listed in the article applied.

8.4 Implications of the *Al-Jedda* Case

As may be deducted from the above, a principal consequence of the Court's decision is that ECHR member states will in future have to secure "clear and explicit language" on detention/internment in a Chapter VII UN Security Council resolution in order to avoid a conflict with the European Convention. The Court did not indicate what level of specificity would be desired. An appropriate resolution would presumably need to provide both the grounds for internment, as well as outline the process that must be followed. Leaving aside whether the Security

[16] *Al-Jedda* Judgment, *supra* n. 3, para 107.

Council could reach a political agreement on the requisite standards, the more important question is whether the Council is the right body to legislate on detention matters, a task implicitly put to it by the European Court. It is not clear why the Council, composed of 15 member states, should be better placed to regulate detention in armed conflict than the 194 States parties to the Geneva Conventions, each of which have already agreed to be bound by the provisions regulating internment.

If the Security Council were to rely on the relevant provisions of the 1949 Conventions the main result would be one of duplication, in which case the question is why duplication is necessary. If, on the other hand, the Council chose to draft new rules on detention in armed conflict, i.e. provisions that departed from IHL, it would introduce unwelcome uncertainty into the conduct of military operations and effectively create two sets of rules for states taking part in multinational forces, whether under UN auspices or otherwise. One set would presumably apply when detention is regulated by a binding Security Council resolution, while another would apply in situations of armed conflict in which the Council has not opined on detention under Chapter VII. The resulting fragmentation of the law would be of great concern from both a legal and protection point of view.[17]

The second consequence of the European Court's ruling in *Al-Jedda* is a dismissal of the Fourth Geneva Convention as a legal basis that "could operate to disapply" the requirements of Article 5(1) of the European Convention on Human Rights.[18] The Court explained this conclusion by stating that it "did not find established that international humanitarian law places an obligation on an Occupying Power to use indefinite internment without trial".[19] It further added that, in its view, "it would appear from the provisions of the Fourth Geneva Convention that under international humanitarian law internment is to be viewed not as an obligation on the Occupying Power but as a measure of last resort".[20] In between these two statements is included a brief reference to the Judgment of the International Court of Justice in the *DRC v. Uganda* Case. Each point will be

[17] It should also be noted that the *Al-Jedda* Judgment only determined that the relevant article of the European Convention on Human Rights was not displaced by UN Security Council resolution 1546 because the language of the latter was not sufficiently clear and precise. The Court did not pronounce on whether the resolution could have prevailed over the ECHR even if those requirements had been met, which is by no means a given. As already mentioned, the Court also did not explicitly opine on whether Article 103 of the UN Charter is triggered only when a state's conflicting *obligations* under another international instrument are in conflict with its obligations under the Charter (i.e. a Chapter VII resolution), or whether *authorizations* are also covered by the operation of Article 103. See Milanovic 2012.

[18] *Al-Jedda* Judgment, *supra* n. 3, para 107. Even though Al-Jedda was in fact interned when the armed conflict in Iraq was non-international in character, the legal regime applied to his detention by the UK as a result of UN Security Council Resolution 1546 was that prescribed by the Fourth Geneva Convention, an issue which the Court did not contest in para 107.

[19] Idem.

[20] Idem.

addressed in turn. Before that a brief reminder of the relevant IHL provisions on detention and internment seems to be warranted. Both the Fourth Geneva Convention on the protection of civilians and of the Third Geneva Convention on prisoner of war will be summarized as the reasons for the Court's disavowal of IHL as a legal basis for internment would equally apply. Based on the Court's arguments it would appear irrelevant whether Al-Jedda was detained as a civilian (which was the case), or as a prisoner of war (POW), as explained below.

In international armed conflict, IHL permits the internment of prisoners of war and, under certain conditions, of civilians.

8.4.1 POW Internment

POWs[21] are essentially combatants captured by the adverse party in an international armed conflict. As a term of art, "combatant" denotes a legal status that, as such, exists only in this type of conflict. Under IHL rules on the conduct of hostilities, a combatant is a member of the armed forces of a party to an international armed conflict who has "the right to participate directly in hostilities".[22] This means that he or she may use force against, i.e. target and kill or injure other persons taking a direct part in hostilities and destroy other enemy military objectives. Because such activity is obviously prejudicial to the security of the adverse party, the Third Geneva Convention provides that a detaining State "may subject prisoners of war to internment".[23] It is not obliged to provide review, judicial or otherwise, of the lawfulness of POW internment as long as active hostilities are ongoing, because enemy combatant status denotes that a person is *ipso facto* a security threat.[24] However, a POW may not be prosecuted by the detaining state for lawful acts of violence committed in the course of hostilities ("combatant privilege"), but only for violations of IHL, in particular war crimes, or other crimes under international law such as genocide or crimes against humanity.

In case of doubt about the entitlement to POW status of a captured belligerent, Article 5 of the Third Convention provides that such person shall be protected by the Convention until his or her status has been determined by a competent tribunal.[25] This provision is often misunderstood as requiring judicial review.

[21] Third Geneva Convention, Article 4.

[22] AP I, Article 43 (2).

[23] Third Geneva Convention, Article 21.

[24] Judicial review under the domestic law of the detaining State could be sought to obtain the release of a POW who is detained despite the end of active hostilities. As mentioned further below, that is a grave breach of IHL.

[25] Third Geneva Convention, Article 5.

That is not the case, as Article 5 tribunals are meant to operate in or near the zone of combat; they only determine status, not criminal or any other responsibility.[26]

POW internment must end and POWs must be released at the cessation of active hostilities,[27] unless they are subject to criminal proceedings or are serving a criminal sentence.[28] They may also be released earlier on medical grounds[29] or on their own cognizance.[30] Unjustifiable delay in the repatriation of prisoners of war at the close of active hostilities is a grave breach of Additional Protocol I.[31]

8.4.2 Internment of Civilians

Under the Fourth Geneva Convention, internment—and assigned residence—are the most severe "measures of control"[32] that may be taken by a state with respect to civilians whose activity is deemed to pose a serious threat to its security. It is uncontroversial that civilian direct participation in hostilities falls into that category. Despite the fact that only combatants are explicitly authorized under IHL to participate directly in hostilities,[33] the reality is that civilians often do so as well, in both international and non-international armed conflicts. (In such cases they are colloquially referred to as "unprivileged belligerents" or, wrongly referred to as "unlawful combatants"). Civilian direct participation in hostilities modifies the basic IHL rules under which civilians are entitled to protection against the dangers arising from military operations[34] and may not be made the object of attack.[35] IHL expressly provides that civilians are protected from direct attack "unless and for such time as they take a direct part in hostilities".[36]

Apart from direct participation in hostilities other civilian behaviour may also meet the threshold of posing a serious security threat to the detaining power[37] (Al-Jedda's alleged activity being a case in point). The Fourth Convention provides

---

[26] See commentary to Article 45 (1) of AP I on the nature of a 'competent tribunal' under Article 5 of the Third Geneva Convention in: Sandoz, Swinarski and Zimmermann 1987, para 1745.

[27] Third Geneva Convention, Article 118.

[28] Third Geneva Convention, Article 119.

[29] Third Geneva Convention, Articles 109 (1) and 110.

[30] Third Geneva Convention, Article 21.

[31] AP I, Article 85 (4) (b).

[32] Fourth Geneva Convention, Article 27; Articles 41 and 78.

[33] The only exception is the relatively rare occurrence of a *levée en masse*, provided for in Article 4 (6) of the Third Geneva Convention.

[34] AP I, Article 51 (1). Given the consequences of civilian direct participation in hostilities it is clearly crucial to avoid broad interpretations. The ICRC's view on this issue is outlined in Melzer 2009.

[35] AP I, Article 51 (2).

[36] AP I, Article 51 (3) and AP II, Article 13 (3).

[37] Examples of activities that are not direct participation in hostilities but would constitute a serious security threat are the financing of combat operations, general recruitment for combat etc.

different wording in terms of permissible grounds for internment depending on whether an internee is detained in a state party's own territory ("if the security of the Detaining Power makes it absolutely necessary")[38] or is held in occupied territory ("imperative reasons of security").[39] It has been suggested that the difference in language is irrelevant and aims to indicate that internment in occupied territory should in practice be more exceptional than in the territory of a party to the conflict.[40]

The internment review process in a state party's territory would also appear to differ somewhat from that in occupied territory. In a state's own territory internment review is to be carried out by an "appropriate court or administrative board",[41] while in occupied territory, the Convention refers to a "regular procedure" that is to be administered by a "competent body".[42] Despite these and other textual differences the rules are in essence the same. A person interned in IAC has the right to submit a request for review of the decision on internment (to challenge it), the review must be expeditiously[43] conducted either by a court or an administrative board, and periodic review is thereafter to be automatic, at least on a six-monthly basis.[44] The Fourth Convention does not specify the right to legal assistance, but does not bar it either.

It is sometimes asked why IHL provides procedural safeguards for civilians interned in international armed conflict and not to POWs.[45] The simple answer is that, in reality, there is far less certainty as to the threat a captured enemy civilian actually poses than is the case with a combatant who is, after all, a member of the adversary's armed forces. In contemporary warfare civilians are, for example, often detained not in combat, but on the basis of intelligence information suggesting that they represent a security threat. The purpose of the review process is to enable a determination of whether such information is reliable and whether the person's activity meets the high legal standard that would justify internment.

Unlike combatants, who may not be prosecuted by a capturing state for direct participation in hostilities (combatant privilege), civilians who do so can be prosecuted for having taken up arms and for all acts of violence committed during such participation, as well as for war crimes or other crimes under international law that might have been committed. This rule is the same in international and non-international armed conflict. Contrary to certain assertions,[46] civilian direct

[38] Fourth Geneva Convention, Article 42 (1).

[39] Fourth Geneva Convention, Article 78 (1).

[40] Pictet 1958, p. 367.

[41] Fourth Geneva Convention, Article 43 (1).

[42] Fourth Geneva Convention, Article 78 (2).

[43] Fourth Geneva Convention, Articles 41 and 78.

[44] Pictet 1958, p. 261 and pp. 368–369.

[45] See Garraway 2007, at p. 330.

[46] See, for example, Office of the Judge Advocate General (Canada), *Law of Armed Conflict at the Operational and Tactical Levels*, National Defence Joint Doctrine Manual, B-GJ-005-104/FP-021, 13 August 2001, pp. 16-4, para 1609 (3)(g), available at: http://www.forces.gc.ca/jag/training-formation/index-eng.asp.

participation is not a violation of IHL and is not a war crime *per se* under either treaty or customary IHL.[47]

Civilian internment must cease as soon as the reasons which necessitated it no longer exist.[48] It must in any event end "as soon as possible after the close of hostilities".[49] Unjustifiable delay in the repatriation of civilians is also a grave breach of Additional Protocol I.[50]

The European Court's implicit finding in relation to IHL in the *Al-Jedda* case was that the provisions of the Fourth Geneva Convention did not constitute an independent legal basis for detention. It is not clear from the Judgment why this conclusion was reached given that, according to the principle of legality, a deprivation of liberty is permissible when it transpires on grounds and in accordance with procedures that are established by law (a statute in the case of domestic law,[51] a treaty or customary law in the case of IHL). As has been explained above, the Fourth Geneva Convention provides both the grounds for the internment of civilians in a state party's own territory, as well as in occupied territory, and in each case outlines the procedure to be followed. The level of detail of the relevant provisions, when read in conjunction with Article 75 (3) of Additional Protocol I, is no less than the provisions of general human rights law related to non-criminal detention, i.e. Article 9 (1) and (4) of the International Covenant on Civil and Political Rights, to which the Court also referred.

Furthermore, it is almost uniformly recognized and accepted in state practice, that IHL governing international armed conflict provides a sufficient legal basis for detention. There is, admittedly, some debate among legal scholars as to whether the Fourth Geneva Convention must be accompanied by domestic legislation. It is unclear why this question, where posed, is posed only in relation to the Fourth Convention and not the Third, for there is no indication that the treaties differ in the legal authority provided or in the level of elaboration of rights granted. It is submitted that the Fourth Convention constitutes, on its own, a sufficient legal basis for internment.

The Court's expressed argument as to why the Fourth Convention does not provide a legal basis for detention was that there is no "obligation" on the detaining state/Occupying Power, "to use indefinite internment" "without trial".[52] It must be said that that the Court's approach to and understanding of IHL merits review in relation to all the elements put forward.

First, as demonstrated by the language of the Fourth Convention summarized above, the notion of internment as an *obligation* on the parties to an international armed conflict is absent from IHL. Under the Convention, states are authorized to

---

47 See, for example, the list of War Crimes under Article 8 of the ICC Statute.

48 Fourth Geneva Convention Article 132; AP I, Article 75 (3).

49 Fourth Geneva Convention, Article 46 and 133 (1).

50 AP I, Article 85 (4) (b).

51 Nowak 2005, para 27.

52 *Al-Jedda* Judgment, *supra* n. 3, para 107.

("may") intern a person whose activity represents a serious security threat, whether to their forces and/or to the security of others, such as civilians. However, parties to an armed conflict are also free not to intern a person—despite an obvious potential security risk to themselves or the accomplishment of their mission—based on other considerations inherent to succeeding in an armed conflict (e.g. the prevailing military circumstances, logistical impediments, the need to foster trust, or win the hearts and minds of the local population, etc.). The logic of armed conflict differs in this respect from the logic of peace-time, as a result of which the respective rules on detention in the relevant bodies of law also diverge. It would thus be not only legally incorrect, but also operationally counterproductive if IHL were read to oblige states to intern in military operations, rather than authorize them to do so. By leaving states no possibility but to apply internment, a disservice would also be done to persons who would as a result "have to be" interned, but could be released if it were not for the legal obligation, hardly a human rights-friendly outcome.

Second, it is unfortunate that the European Court used the term "indefinite detention". Its recent adoption in some of the legal literature, as well as in the media, may serve to create a perception of acceptability where none should exist. As already noted, IHL is clear on the duration of internment for imperative reasons of security: it must end as soon as the reasons justifying it cease to exist.[53] The initial and periodic review processes described above were designed precisely because there is no assumption that a person will automatically constitute an imperative security threat until the end of an armed conflict. Each case has to be examined initially on the merits, and periodically thereafter, to assess whether the threat level posed remains the same. In view of the rapid progression of events in armed conflict, the assessment may, and in most cases does, change. The outer temporal limit of internment, according to which it must in all cases end at the close of active hostilities, may thus be called the "default" position. The close of hostilities is a factual matter that is also determined on a case-by-case basis.

Third, by implying that criminal trial is the only lawful and desired outcome of detention the Court is overlooking the fact that IHL rules on detention differ from human rights provisions, under which criminal trial is the norm. The former are specific to the reality they govern, which is armed conflict, not peace-time. By way of reminder the ultimate aim of military operations is to prevail over the enemy's armed forces. IHL attempts to humanize war by providing rules regulating the conduct of hostilities, and rules permitting the detention of persons—either because they take a direct part in hostilities or because of other activity that represents a serious security threat. If parties to a conflict are allowed to use force, i.e. to target and kill persons who constitute military objectives because they take a direct part in hostilities, then they are clearly also authorized to detain persons who fall into their power while doing so.

---

[53] Fourth Geneva Convention, Article 132, and AP I, Article 75 (3).

Internment is not conceived as a punishment, but a measure aimed at removing combatants, as well as other persons seriously harmful to the detaining authority, off the "battlefield" for such time as they pose a security threat.[54] The notion of a criminal trial for persons who have merely taken up arms and inflicted violence against the adversary is not part of the "fabric" of IHL because such activity is not a war crime *per se* under this body of rules. Rather, it is up to the domestic law of the detaining state to determine whether a captured person (the exception being POWs, as explained above) will be prosecuted for unprivileged belligerency. In the vast majority of cases, and unless they are tried for war crimes, internees are spared prosecution under domestic law in international armed conflict and are simply released when they no longer pose a security threat, and in any case must be released when hostilities cease. In this context, strange as it may sound, internment can actually be preferable to criminal trial from an internee's standpoint. It is likely to last for a shorter duration than if the activity that led to internment was the subject of domestic criminal proceedings. The release of Al-Jedda is a case in point. Had he been criminally tried under UK or Iraqi law, it is quite possible that he would still be in prison today.

The European Court's other express argument for rejecting IHL as basis for Al-Jedda's deprivation of liberty is that "internment is to be viewed not" as an "obligation" on the detaining state, but as a "measure of last resort". The fact that IHL does not provide an obligation to intern, which the Court would have seemingly required to find that Al-Jedda could be detained under IHL, has been explained above. Two brief remarks may be made as regard its conclusion that it must be a measure of last resort.

The first is that the Court did not rely on the wording of IHL, for reasons that remain unclear. The language of the relevant articles of the Fourth Convention are different[55] and do not convey that precise meaning. Rather, they indicate that internment is the most "severe" measure of control that a state may apply with respect to a person who represents a serious security threat. It is submitted that the quality of a measure, suggested by the word "severe", does not necessarily imply sequence, i.e. that other options must be exhausted before it is undertaken. Moreover, given that this standard is not generally part of human rights rules or jurisprudence governing detention, but is relevant to the use of force, it is likewise unclear why the Court chose to introduce this concept in relation to deprivation of liberty in armed conflict. The second remark is that, despite enunciating the requirement, the Court did not opine on whether Al-Jedda's internment could, under the circumstances, have been a justified as "a measure of last resort".

Finally, as regards the IHL-related aspects of the *Al-Jedda* Judgment, it may be noted that the way in which the European Court relied on the ICJ's

---

[54] Because internment is not akin to trial-related detention, internment conditions, as well as other aspects of internment provided for in the Fourth Convention, are not modelled on the rules governing detention for criminal purposes.

[55] Fourth Geneva Convention, Articles 41 and 78.

DRC v. Uganda case is curious. It was cited in order to illustrate that IHL does not contain an obligation to intern (dealt with above), and to indicate that an Occupying Power has a duty to secure respect for the applicable provisions of human rights law, including the ICCPR.[56] This is certainly a well-established proposition. However, beyond the general statement on the parallel application of IHL and human rights law, the ICJ made no comment in that case on the specific interplay of the two legal frameworks, as a result of which no conclusion can be drawn with respect to the detention issue examined in *Al-Jedda*. In addition, there are other cases in which the ICJ outlined its views in more detail, not referred to in the European Court's Judgment. For example, the ICJ stated in the 1996 Nuclear Weapons Advisory Opinion that what constituted an arbitrary deprivation of life in armed conflict was to be determined by the applicable *lex specialis*, namely IHL.[57] Given that this conclusion was reached in relation to the non-derogable right to life under human rights law, there would seem to be room to believe that a similar conclusion could be reached when a derogable right, such as liberty, is involved.[58]

According to the *Al-Jedda* Judgment—aside from securing a Chapter VII Security Council resolution—the only other way in which ECHR member states could possibly intern in an armed conflict without falling afoul of their obligations under the European Convention would be to lawfully derogate under Article 15 of that treaty. It is interesting to note that the Court devotes a mere half a sentence to this option.[59] Under Article 15 states may take measures, "in time of war or other public emergency threatening the life of the nation", derogating from some of their obligations under the Convention—including Article 5—"to the extent strictly required by the exigencies of the situation".[60]

It is unclear, however, whether an ECHR member state could successfully invoke Article 15 based on the plain language of the text. First, the wording requires that the war in which the state might be involved "threaten the life of the nation". It would appear that recent armed conflicts involving ECHR countries in the territory of a third "host" state could not be deemed to have reached the requisite threat level to them. A second and overlapping issue is which country should in fact derogate: the intervening or the "host" state? It has on occasion been posited in expert debates that the host country should derogate from its obligations under the international human rights law treaties to which it is a

---

56 *Al-Jedda* Judgment, *supra* n. 3, para 107.

57 *Legality of the Threat or Use of Nuclear Weapons*, Advisory Opinion (1996) I.C.J. Rep. 9, para 25.

58 In its Advisory Opinion on the Legal Consequences of the Construction of a Wall in the Occupied Palestinian Territory the Court made a broader statement about the interplay of human rights law and IHL, reiterating that IHL is the lex specialis to the general law of human rights. *Legal Consequences of the Construction of a Wall in the Occupied Palestinian Territory*, Advisory Opinion (2004) ICJ Rep. 136, para 106.

59 *Al-Jedda* Judgment, *supra* n. 3, para 99.

60 ECHR, Article 15.

party.[61] But in cases where internees in a multinational military operation are under the effective control of an intervening ECHR state, it remains unclear how a "host" state's derogation of its own obligations could suffice.

Given that no ECHR country has ever derogated with respect to military action taken abroad, these and other legal issues have never been tested. The reasons are presumably not only legal, as it must be acknowledged that there would likely be formidable political obstacles as well. An alternative would be for states to base arguments in detention-related cases on the *lex specialis* nature of IHL governing international armed conflict, which the UK Government did not do in *Al-Jedda*. It is to be hoped that this course of action, which should be considered preferable, might be attempted in the future.

8.5 Concluding Remarks

The importance of the *Al-Jedda* Judgment for detention operations carried out by ECHR member states abroad can hardly be overstated. The import of the Court's decision is that states parties to the European Convention may not intern civilians—even though non-criminal detention for imperative reasons of security may be necessary and is allowed under IHL in international armed conflict—unless there is a binding and explicit UN Security Council mandate or a derogation to Article 5 has been entered.

By implying that a Chapter VII UN Security Council resolution could possibly displace the operation of the relevant detention provisions of the ECHR, the Court has effectively invited the Security Council to legislate on matters of detention. The wisdom or feasibility of the Court's suggestion to this effect may be deemed questionable.

The Court also reminded ECHR member states, however briefly, that derogation is another avenue by which they could avoid a conflict with their obligations under the European Convention when engaged in detention abroad. Whether this option will be resorted to by member states in the future remains to be seen.

What the Court did not do is accept that IHL constitutes a valid legal basis for detention in international armed conflict, based on its conclusion that the Fourth Geneva Convention does not impose an obligation of internment on parties to such conflicts. In so doing, the Court seems not to have grasped the logic of IHL, and thus, it is submitted, erroneously interpreted the plain language of that treaty. Importantly, the Court's conclusion about why the Fourth Geneva Convention could not be a basis for civilian internment may be read to equally apply to POW internment (like the Fourth, the POW Convention only authorizes, but does not explicitly "oblige" internment). This may be deemed a potential and serious revision of a legal regime—IHL—agreed to by all states in the world and one

[61] See Chatham House and ICRC 2008.

generally considered to constitute the applicable *lex specialis* in international armed conflicts.

It is thus also submitted that ECHR member states should seriously consider arguing similar cases in the future, where they arise, on the IHL *lex specialis* ground.

Whatever course is chosen, it is clear that, for the moment, *Al-Jedda* casts a chilling shadow on the current and future lawfulness of detention operations carried out by ECHR states abroad. In addition, their ability to engage with other non-ECHR countries in multination military forces with a detention mandate currently remains, at best, uncertain.

References

Chatham House and ICRC (2008) Report of expert meeting on procedural safeguards for security detention in non-international armed conflict (September 2008), pp 22–23 . Available at http://www.icrc.org/eng/assets/files/other/security-detention-chatham-icrc-report-091209.pdf.

Garraway C (2007) "Combatants"—substance or semantics? In: Schmitt MN, Pejic J (eds) International law and armed conflict: exploring the faultlines. Martinus Nijhoff Publishers, The Hague

Melzer N (2009) ICRC interpretive guidance on the notion of direct participation in hostilities under IHL, ICRC. http://www.icrc.org/eng/assets/files/other/icrc-002-0990.pdf

Milanovic M (2012) Al-Skeini and Al-Jedda in Strasbourg 23. Eur J Int L (forthcoming)

Nowak M (2005) U.N. covenant on civil and political rights, 2nd rev edn. Engel, Germany

Pictet J (ed) (1958) Commentary: Geneva convention IV. ICRC, Geneva

Sandoz Y, Swinarski C, Zimmermann B (eds) (1987) Commentary on the additional protocols of June 8, 1977 to the Geneva conventions of 12 August, 1949. Martinus Nijhoff Publishers, Geneva

Chapter 9
The Killing of Osama Bin Laden and Anwar Al-Aulaqi: Uncharted Legal Territory

Beth Van Schaack

Contents

Professor of Law, Santa Clara University School of Law. This article benefited from the excellent comments of Sasha Greenawalt and the other attendees of the American Society of International Law International Criminal Law Interest Group Workshop at John Marshall Law School. Diane Marie Amann, Andy Gillman, and David Glazier were incredibly generous in their comments, suggestions and criticisms. I am grateful to the U.S. Department of State for inviting me to present this paper as a Martins Fellow and for the constructive feedback I received. In addition, Louise Arimatsu and Michael Schmitt provided valuable comments during the editorial stage. The author is indebted to John Engers, Paul Keating, and Mary Sexton for their research assistance.

B. Van Schaack (✉)
Santa Clara University School of Law, Santa Clara, CA 95053, USA
e-mail: bvanschaack@scu.edu

M.N. Schmitt and L. Arimatsu (eds.), *Yearbook of International Humanitarian Law Volume 14, 2011*, DOI: 10.1007/978-90-6704-855-2_9,

9.1 Introduction

The killing of Osama bin Laden in Pakistan in May 2011 and Anwar al-Aulaqi in Yemen in September 2011 both raise the question of when the killing of an identified individual posing a threat to a nation-state is lawful.[1] Although it has not yet been forced to publicly defend either killing in any great detail, the Obama Administration has insisted on the legality of both operations by deploying an amalgam of legal and rhetorical arguments that explicitly or implicitly invoke multiple bodies of law. As an administration spokesperson stated in connection with the Bin Laden operation:

> The operation was conducted in a manner fully consistent with the laws of war. ... There is simply no question that this operation was lawful. Bin Laden was the head of al Qaeda, the organization that conducted the attacks of September 11, 2001. And al Qaeda and bin Laden himself had continued to plot attacks against the US. We acted in the nation's self-defense. The operation was conducted in a way designed to minimize and avoid altogether, if possible, civilian casualties.[2]

In litigation brought by al-Aulaqi's father in 2010, the Administration likewise argued both that Congress authorized the President to use force overseas to protect the U.S. from threats of attack and that additional legal authority comes from, *inter alia*, the inherent right of national self-defense recognized by international law.[3]

These statements reveal that the legality of such targeted operations can be evaluated along a number of dimensions—under public international law devoted to the *jus ad bellum*, under international humanitarian law and the *jus in bello*, under international human rights law, and under the applicable domestic legal regimes. Of particular relevance in U.S. law are two instruments: the long-standing Executive Order proscribing resort to assassination and the 2001 Authorization to Use Military Force. Common law prohibitions against murder may also apply in Pakistan and Yemen.

Notwithstanding these multiple legal regimes, there is little positive law that speaks definitively to the legality *vel non* of the Bin Laden and al-Aulaqi operations. In particular, the law is not entirely clear with respect to: the legality of the United States' use of force in these foreign territories; the United States' use of lethal force

---

[1] To a certain extent, the attack on Col. Muammar el-Qaddafi's compound in Tripoli in May 2011, days before the Bin Laden raid, also engages these questions. Schaack 2011a, b.

[2] White House Press Secretary 2011.

[3] *Al-Aulaqi v. Obama*, Opposition to Plaintiff's Motion for Preliminary Injunction and Memorandum in Support of Defendants' Motion to Dismiss, Case Civ. A. No. 10-cv-1469, at pp. 4–5 (Sept. 25, 2010) [hereinafter '*Al-Aulaqi*, Obama brief'], available at http://www.aclu.org/files/assets/Al-Aulaqi_USG_PI_Opp__MTD_Brief_FILED.pdf.

against these two individuals; the reach of the *jus in bello* beyond active theaters of war; and the question of whether the U.S. was under a duty to endeavor to capture either Bin Laden or al-Aulaqi rather than kill them outright. In light of the gaps in the law on these fundamental questions, a legal analysis of these operations threatens to yield a situation of *non liquet*—"it is not clear."

Although the relevant legal regimes developed along different historical, doctrinal, and philosophical trajectories, they increasingly collide and even overlap in contemporary counterterrorism and counterinsurgency operations. With only rudimentary choice of law tools to draw upon, it is not yet clear which body of law is authoritative in the event of tensions and contradictions between them. Because the doctrinal and conflicts of law questions are difficult to sort out in a vacuum, the definitive legality of such events may turn on which domestic or international legal forum—if any—ultimately asserts jurisdiction. Judicial review, however, is not likely to be forthcoming, given that there are limited fora in which to raise any sort of formal legal challenge, there is no obvious sovereign or individual complainant, there is only limited personal jurisdiction over potential sovereign and individual respondents, and there are vast disparities of power between the U.S. and other involved states. As such, where the law is incomplete or indeterminate, a form of jurisprudential relativity sets in, by which states are free to make policy choices, subject only to the constraints—none trivial, to be sure—imposed by military strategy, diplomatic relations, and the political process.[4] The multiplicity of legal regimes also invites a "mixing and matching" of doctrinal elements that blurs the distinctions between the various paradigms and can lead to doctrinal imbalances.

In the light of the legal indeterminacy surrounding these two operations, this article will endeavor to systematically tease out the various arguments advanced in their defense and to map the contiguous and overlapping legal regimes that speak to the killing of these two men. I compare the legality of the two operations primarily under international law, leaving to others to develop whatever domestic constitutional limitations may exist by virtue of the 4th and 5th Amendments to the U.S. Constitution. The paper outlines several doctrinal pathways within international law that lead to the conclusion that both operations were legal. Along the way, I identify established landmarks in positive law. Reaching the ultimate destination, however, requires one to traverse uncertain terrain by deploying legal theories that remain under-developed, in flux, and contested. At these crossroads, the necessary arguments often do not enjoy textual support in the relevant treaties or reflect consistent state practice or *opinio juris.* Nor are there authoritative judicial pronouncements that provide validation. Furthermore, our expedition requires us to navigate between overlapping legal regimes with no compass to help resolve potential conflicts of law that arise. In my accounting of this journey, I provide a rather cursory treatment of established law and linger more at those junctures that could lead to a conclusion of illegality because there is a diversity of viewpoints in the literature. All told, the law can be made to work in defense of the

[4] Corn and Jenson 2008, at pp. 827–828.

United States' actions, but there are points along the way at which an authoritative decision-maker might reach a defensible contrary conclusion.

Although this paper is primarily about law, the policy implications of these operations are momentous.[5] And, the "should we" question is often as compelling as the "can we" question. The U.S. may enjoy a technological monopoly on certain means and methods of warfare for the moment. Like the proverbial pocket calculator, however, it is only a matter of time before other states and entities have access to the same tools and techniques, given the dizzying pace of technological diffusion in war fighting. Any legal claims now employed will be up for grabs for other states and entities to appropriate.[6] And, because polynormativity is unsustainable in any system of law, the U.S. precedent will be cited as influential state practice and its legal claims as authoritative *opinio juris*, notwithstanding claims of U.S. exceptionalism. From a policy perspective, this suggests prudential grounds for caution when operating at the edge of the law.

9.2 The Operations and Their Justifications

Although the complete details of how Osama bin Laden and Anwar al-Aulaqi met their demise may never be fully known, it is possible to piece together a composite account by drawing on press coverage, government legal briefs, and statements from the Obama Administration. The following narratives assume the accuracy of such public records, bearing in mind that much relevant information remains classified.

9.2.1 Operation Neptune Spear: Osama Bin Laden

It has been reported that, in the early hours of May 2, 2011, about two dozen Navy SEALs departed by helicopter from a base in Jalalabad, Afghanistan, and entered Pakistani sovereign territory.[7] The SEALs were part of the Naval Special Warfare Development Group ("DEVGRU") under the Joint Special Operations Command (JSOC), a subunified component of the U.S. Special Operations Command (USSOCOM) dedicated to conducting antiterrorism operations.[8] In two helicopters (MH-60 Black Hawks),[9] the team entered the garrison town of Abbottabad and

---

[5] See Blum and Heymann 2010.

[6] Reisman and Armstrong 2006, at pp. 525–526 (noting the mimetic tendency of customary international law arguments).

[7] Schmidle 2011 (on an apparently "insider" account). See also New York Times 2011a; BBC News 2011.

[8] See generally Feickert 2011. Reports of the Bin Laden raid indicate that while the Pentagon implemented the operation, it was carried out under CIA authority. Ambinger 2011.

[9] It has been surmised that the Pentagon may have developed a stealth helicopter for such missions. Hennigan and Vartabedian 2011. See also Shalal-Esa 2011.

approached a compound that had been under surveillance for months.[10] The original plan was for members of the team to rappel out of the helicopters and raid the compound from the roof.[11] The plan did not unroll as planned, however, when the high temperatures, tall security walls, and the thin air of the compound caused one helicopter to "settle with power" and crash.[12] The other helicopter landed, and the SEALs moved toward the buildings in the compound after blasting through several internal walls with C-4 explosives. Some accounts tell it that the team immediately took fire from a peripheral building. The source was Abu Ahmed al-Kuwaiti, the courier who inadvertently revealed Bin Laden's whereabouts after a 10-year manhunt.[13] Other accounts suggest that the team was not fired upon until they entered the main house and confronted Bin Laden's son, Khalid, who was armed with an AK-47.[14] It now appears that these were the only shots fired against the Americans.[15]

Upon entering the structure where Bin Laden was thought to be residing, the SEAL team proceeded to the upper floors, killing Bin Laden's son on the way up.[16] Bin Laden was visually identified on an upper floor. Although reports originally suggested that Bin Laden had used one of his wives as a human shield,[17] later accounts suggested that she, her daughter, and/or another wife may have tried to position themselves in front of him or even rushed at the SEALs.[18] Versions of the story were also conflicting as to whether Bin Laden fired at the U.S. troops when he confronted them;[19] now it appears that he resisted capture,[20] or seemed ready to resist,[21] and that there were weapons within reach although he was unarmed.[22] One of the SEALs shot Bin Laden in the chest and then the head. All told, four other people were killed in the raid: the courier, Bin Laden's son Khalid, the courier's brother (who was armed), and the latter's wife (who was not).[23] One of Bin Laden's wives was later treated for a bullet wound in her leg.[24]

---

10 Mazzetti 2011.

11 BBC News 2011.

12 Shalal-Esa 2011.

13 Wilson et al. 2011.

14 Schmidle 2011.

15 Landler and Mazzetti 2011.

16 New York Times 2011a, b.

17 Wilson et al. 2011.

18 Drogin et al. 2011.

19 The White House Blog 2011 (After a firefight, they killed Osama bin Laden and took custody of his body).

20 Drogin et al. 2011.

21 Waraich 2011.

22 Williams 2011.

23 Worldwatch 2011.

24 Wilson et al. 2011.

Accounts suggest that Bin Laden made no effort at surrender.[25] That said, some narratives have suggested that the order was made to kill not capture Bin Laden, perhaps due to the spectacle that would no doubt have ensued were he captured.[26] This view has been vociferously contradicted by official spokespersons, who insist that "consistent with the laws of war, bin Laden's surrender would have been accepted if feasible."[27]

Meanwhile, a rescue MH-47 Chinook helicopter was dispatched. The SEALs destroyed the downed helicopter and the troops departed, carrying Bin Laden's corpse and a voluminous amount of intelligence with them. After DNA testing confirmed Bin Laden's identity, his remains were given Islamic funeral rites and were wrapped in a burial shroud. After the Saudi government indicated that it did not want the body, Bin Laden's corpse was dumped into the Arabian Sea from the aircraft carrier, USS *Carl Vinson*.[28]

9.2.2 Anwar Al-Aulaqi

Al-Aulaqi, a dual U.S.-Yemeni citizen whose parents left the U.S. when he was seven, was an al Qaida cleric, ideologue, and propagandist.[29] Although once a seemingly moderate voice, Al-Aulaqi's lectures had increasingly been linked to attacks around the world, such as the violent rampage by Major Nidal Malik Hasan in Texas, and the attempted Northwest Airlines bombing by Umar Farouk Abdulmutallab, both in 2009.[30] Originally the editor of *Inspire*, al Qaida's jihadist magazine, al-Aulaqi was alleged to have increasingly assumed an operational role in al Qaida in the Arabian Peninsula (AQAP)[31] by, for example, recruiting members, facilitating training camps, fundraising, and planning attacks on the U.S.[32]

Al-Aulaqi had been in U.S. sights for some time. It was reported that he had been placed on a list of individuals whom the Joint Special Operations Command,

---

[25] Williams 2011 (quoting Attorney General Eric Holder to the effect that "'If he had attempted to surrender, I think we should obviously have accepted that, but there was no indication that he wanted to do that. And therefore his killing was appropriate.'").

[26] See Robertson 2011.

[27] White House Press Secretary 2011. See also Drogin et al. 2011; Brennan 2011.

[28] Drogin et al. 2011.

[29] New York Times 2011b.

[30] Mazzetti et al. 2011a.

[31] On January 19, 2010, Secretary of State Clinton designated AQAP as a Foreign Terrorist Organization pursuant to the Antiterrorism and Effective Death Penalty Act, 9 U.S.C. §1189.

[32] Shane 2010. See also *Al-Aulaqi*, Obama brief, *supra* n. 3 at pp. 1, 6, 21 (arguing that al-Aulaqi assumed an "operational leadership role" in AQAP); *Al Aulaqi v. Obama* et al., Unclassified Declaration in Support of Formal Claim of State Secrets Privilege by James R. Clapper, Director of National Intelligence, at paras 13–17 (Sept. 24, 2010), available at http://www.fas.org/sgp/jud/statesec/aulaqi-clapper-092510.pdf.

tasked with tracking suspected terrorists, was specifically authorized to kill.[33] This list is colloquially called the "kill or capture list."[34] Since at least April 2010, al-Aulaqi was on a separate list of suspected terrorists whom the CIA was authorized to kill.[35] The Treasury Department also included him on a list of Specially Designated Global Terrorists suspected of "supporting acts of terrorism and for acting for or on behalf of AQAP."[36] Pursuant to U.N. Security Council Resolution 1267, he was identified as an individual associated with al Qaida and thus subjected to a global asset freeze and travel ban.[37] The revelation that the National Security Council had authorized al-Aulaqi's killing provoked a lawsuit by al-Aulaqi's father and the American Civil Liberties Union (ACLU) seeking injunctive relief,[38] which failed on standing and political question grounds.[39]

Al-Aulaqi had apparently evaded drone attacks in December 2009 and May 2011.[40] He was finally killed in a remote area of Northern Yemen on September 30, 2011, by a Hellfire missile fired from a Remotely Piloted Vehicle (RPV) deployed from a base somewhere in the Arabian Peninsula. The drone was likely operated by the CIA, although some reports suggest involvement by JSOC.[41] Killed along with him was another U.S. citizen, Samir Khan, who also edited *Inspire*. There is no indication that the U.S. was aware of Khan's presence in the convoy in question, but his death has not been treated solely as collateral damage.[42] This was not the first such operation outside of Afghanistan or a recognized theater of war.[43] That distinction goes to the November 2002 drone attack in Yemen that killed another U.S. citizen, Kamal Derwish (a.k.a. Ahmed Hijazi). In that attack, CIA operatives based in Djibouti killed six alleged al Qaida members, including the individual then considered the head of al Qaida in

---

33 Priest 2010.

34 Hosenball 2011.

35 Miller 2010. For a discussion of the legal and policy implications of generating secret "kill or capture" lists, particularly given the lack of transparency and accountability, see Alston 2011.

36 Designation of Anwar Al-Aulaqi Pursuant to Executive Order 13224 and the Global Terrorism Sanctions Regulations, 31 C.F.R. Part 594, 75 Fed. Reg. 43233, 43234 (July 23, 2010). See Fox News 2010.

37 Security Council Resolution 1267, 15 October 1999, S/Res/1267, para 4.

38 *Al-Aulaqi v. Obama*, Case 1:10-cv-01469, Complaint for Declaratory and Injunctive Relief (Aug. 30, 2010), available at http://www.aclu.org/national-security/al-aulaqi-v-obama-complaint [hereinafter '*Al-Aulaqi* Complaint'].

39 *Al-Aulaqi v. Obama*, 727 F.Supp.2d 1 (D.D.C. 2010).

40 Mazzetti et al. 2011a.

41 Mazzetti et al. 2011a.

42 Hosenball 2011. But see Finn 2011. Collateral damage is defined as "incidental loss of civilian life, injury to civilians and damage to civilian objects." Protocol Additional to the Geneva Conventions of 12 August 1949, and Relating to the Protection of Victims of International Armed Conflicts, June 8, 1977, 1125 U.N.T.S. 3 [hereinafter 'API'], art 57(2) (a) (ii).

43 The theater of war, also known as the area of operations, encompasses locations where actual military operations are taking place. Greenwood 2008, at para 53.

Yemen.[44] These operations have continued. In October 2011, al-Aulaqi's teen-aged son, Abdul Rahman Al-Aulaqi (also an American citizen), and Ibrahim al-Banna, another AQAP media chief, were killed by a drone.[45]

9.2.3 Evolving Narratives and Appraisals

In the evolving narratives of what happened during these two incidents, an amalgam of different bodies of law, legal rules, and moral principles have been invoked. Official and unofficial statements by Obama Administration officials concerning these and related operations engage complex public international law principles concerned with: the legality of the sovereign use of force extraterritorially; the concept of combatant status and combat function within international humanitarian law (IHL); the principles of self-defense, distinction, and proportionality; and the applicability of human rights obligations extraterritorially. In these accounts, it is not clear whether a single theory of legality is being advanced, or if there are multiple legal claims that provide alternative, or perhaps even mutually reinforcing, legal bases. Moreover, where multiple legal paradigms are invoked, there is a risk of taking the sugar without the salt: relying on permissive doctrinal elements while over-looking limitations or restrictions that exist to protect against excesses or abuse.

A primary articulated justification for both operations is "national self-defense."[46] The self-defense imperative operates to justify both the incursion into Pakistani territory without Pakistan's consent (assuming Yemen's consent to the presence of the drone in question) as well as the use of lethal force against the two men.[47] Even absent any territorial breach, self-defense has been invoked to provide a continuous targeting authority against individuals associated with al Qaida who pose a threat to the U.S. and its interests.[48] Appealing to self-defense as a public international law principle, however, requires a more lenient conception of what constitutes an imminent threat than would be acceptable under classic articulations of the doctrine. This doctrinal expansion is justified, according to the Administration, because "the threats posed by non-state actors do not present themselves in the ways that evidenced imminence in more traditional conflicts."[49] While self-defense has historically been cited in connection with attacks on hostile governments or military installations, invoking it in connection with these types of individualized operations outside of a law enforcement context is novel.

---

[44] Abu Ali Al-Harithi had been associated with the attack on the USS *The Sullivans* and USS *Cole* in 2000 in Yemen. Derwish was suspected of being the ringleader of the Lackawanna Six terrorist cell. McManus 2003.

[45] Kasinof 2011.

[46] Brennan 2011. See also Koh 2010.

[47] Williams 2011.

[48] Brennan 2011. But in contrast, see Janin 2007, at p. 98.

[49] Brennan 2011.

A separate rationale also appears in government statements: that both men were lawful military objectives according to the principle of distinction who were engaged in an armed conflict against the U.S. that is governed by IHL. In a blog post after the Bin Laden operation, State Department Legal Adviser Harold Koh stated,

> Given bin Laden's unquestioned leadership position within al Qaeda and his clear continuing operational role, there can be no question that he was the leader of an enemy force and a legitimate target in our armed conflict with al Qaeda.[50]

The accounts of the Bin Laden mission also emphasize that the IHL principles of distinction and proportionality were strictly adhered to,[51] and that American lives were at risk.[52] This latter observation implies that the U.S. did not prioritize force protection over the principle of proportionality, which protects civilians from harm. This comment implicitly differentiates this operation from those involving the use of drones, such as the al-Aulaqi operation, which lack the element of reciprocity of risk.

Other statements, however, go beyond self-defense and the law of armed conflict and sound more of revenge and reprisal.[53] For example, in the first appearance by an Obama administration Cabinet official following the Bin Laden operation, Attorney General Eric Holder stated that Bin Laden:

> was the head of al-Qaida, an organization that had conducted the attacks of September 11th. He admitted his involvement and he indicated that he would not be taken alive.[54]

President Obama himself simply noted that "justice has been done."[55]

Fewer official details have emerged about the al-Aulaqi operation, as it is still deemed a covert action. A government spokesperson did describe al-Aulaqi as a leader of, and recruiter for, AQAP, which has been deemed a threat to the U.S.[56] The Justice Department reportedly produced a detailed memorandum *ex ante* setting forth the legal bases for placing al-Aulaqi on the JSOC list of potential targets, but this reasoning has not been publicly released (or acknowledged).[57] The memo apparently grapples with the question of whether the law-of-war rationale so prominent in the Bin Laden case is equally applicable when dealing with someone affiliated with an organization formed well after 9/11 with uncertain connections to al Qaida proper.[58] The fact that al-Aulaqi was a U.S. citizen evidently problematized, but did not alter, the memo's ultimate conclusion of legality.[59]

---

50 Koh 2011.

51 Williams 2011.

52 White House Press Secretary 2011.

53 Amnesty International 2011a.

54 Williams 2011.

55 The White House Blog 2011.

56 Tapper 2011.

57 See Finn 2011. As this article was going to press, it was announced that the Obama Administration would reveal publicly the legal reasoning behind the decision to kill al-Aulaqi. See Klaidman (2012).

58 Cole 2011.

59 Johnson 2011.

In the most comprehensive articulation of the Obama Administration's counterterrorism policy to date, John Brennan, Assistant to the President for Homeland Security and Counterterrorism, reiterated that the U.S. was engaged in a global armed conflict with al Qaida that is not restricted to "hot" battlefields, like Afghanistan.[60] He emphasized that the "Administration's counterterrorism efforts outside of Afghanistan and Iraq are focused on those individuals who are a threat to the U.S., whose removal would cause a significant—even if only temporary—disruption of the plans and capabilities of al-Qa'ida and its associated forces."[61] This statement embodies twin justifications for resorting to lethal force—national defense and the IHL principle of distinction. It is unclear if these are alternative, or mutually reinforcing, rationales for such operations.[62] If the killings are lawful under IHL, no separate self-defense rationale seems necessary, except to justify the breach of Pakistani territory.[63] Indeed, if IHL is applicable, it is unclear if a self-defense rationale remains viable or if IHL targeting rules occupy the field under a theory of *lex specialis* just as international human rights may be subordinated to IHL in situations of armed conflict. If IHL is not applicable, the two individuals retained the full force of their international human rights not to be arbitrarily killed.

Notwithstanding these arguments in favor of the operations' legality, the attacks raised distinct international law concerns from other perspectives.[64] Some voices from the right and left—including those from major civil rights organizations—invoked international human rights law exclusively and went so far as to characterize the operations as extrajudicial killings[65] or targeted assassinations.[66] Indeed, Christof Heyns, the U.N. Special Rapporteur on Extrajudicial, Summary or Arbitrary Executions, and Martin Sheinin, the then-Special Rapporteur on the Promotion and Protection of Human Rights and Fundamental Freedoms while Countering Terrorism, requested more details about the Bin Laden operation. In particular, they sought clarification about whether capture was genuinely contemplated in order to address questions about whether the attack was legally justifiable and consistent with the United States' international human rights obligations.[67] The al-Aulaqi killing has raised even more dissension in light of his

---

60 Brennan 2011.

61 Brennan 2011.

62 Koh 2010 ("[S]ome have argued that the use of lethal force against specific individuals fails to provide adequate process and thus constitutes unlawful extrajudicial killing. But a state that is engaged in armed conflict or in legitimate self-defense is not required to provide targets with legal process before the state may use lethal force.").

63 Brennan in his Harvard speech reasoned that, "[b]ecause we are engaged in an armed conflict with al-Qa'ida, the US takes the legal position that—in accordance with international law—we have the authority to take action against al-Qa'ida and its associated forces without doing a separate self-defense analysis each time." Brennan 2011.

64 See Lewis 2011.

65 Cohn 2011.

66 Centre for Constitutional Rights 2011.

67 UN Office of the High Commissioner for Human Rights (OHCHR)—Geneva 2011.

U.S. citizenship, the lack of certainty about his role in al Qaida and the group's links to AQAP, and the loose nexus between the operation and any extant armed conflict.[68] Heyns in particular has been quoted as saying, "the current use of drones and raids into countries where there is not a recognised armed conflict to kill an opponent, such as in Pakistan or Yemen, is highly problematic."[69]

Although academics and human rights organizations voiced these concerns, neither operation generated full-throated opprobrium from other states.[70] Several legal and non-legal explanations for this apparent sovereign acceptance (or at least acquiescence) suggest themselves. These include: the realist recognition of the United States' position in the world as a global superpower, the feeling of many that both operations reached desirable outcomes, and the attitude that there may be certain individuals whose conduct is so heinous that they are—in a sense—outside the law.[71] Government elites may feel these actions are either legal, or—if not legal—then legitimate.[72] We may never know, however, whether U.S. officials received a diplomatic scolding—or more congratulations—outside the public eye.[73] Subtle public references, however, suggest that not all of the United States' actions have garnered unwavering support from other nations, even from the country's closest allies. The former Legal Adviser of the U.K. Foreign and Commonwealth Office has, for example, written that the U.S. "sees the conflict against Al Qaeda as without geographic limit.... Key allies see it differently, as a conflict geographically limited to 'hot battlefields.'"[74] In any case, there can be no doubt that the complexity of the international legal questions raised, and the persistent uncertainty about the relevant law, contributed to the muting of potential critical responses. It is to these issues that I now turn.

9.3 Adherence to the *Jus Ad Bellum*

Turning to the operative international law, two bodies of public international law directly regulate a state's use of armed force: the *jus ad bellum* and *jus in bello*, which govern the right to use force and the type and degree of force used in an armed conflict, respectively. The consequences of violating the *jus ad bellum* are different than those of violating the *jus in bello*. The former protects sovereign

---

[68] Ito 2011.

[69] OHCHR—New York 2011.

[70] See Wikipedia 2011 (noting that only Hamas, the Taliban, and Venezuela, publicly objected to the killing). See also Amnesty International 2011b.

[71] Ratner 2002.

[72] Roberts 2008.

[73] In response to the Bin Laden operation, Pakistan insisted that an air base within Pakistan be vacated, although it later relented. Masood 2011.

[74] Bethlehem 2011.

values, and violations for the moment give rise only to state responsibility.[75] The latter protects individuals and may lead to individual responsibility in addition to state responsibility.

Starting with the *jus ad bellum*, both operations prompt a preliminary inquiry into the question of whether the U.S. was entitled—under international law and domestic law—to employ force in Pakistan and Yemen, two sovereign countries with which the U.S. is not at war. While regulating the use of force is a central feature of international law, elements of U.S. domestic law—including the 1973 War Powers Resolution,[76] the 2001 Authorization to Use Force,[77] and other constitutional and statutory provisions allocating the country's war powers—are also authoritative.

As discussed below, the *jus ad bellum* provokes a more searching inquiry with respect to the Bin Laden operation, given the apparent lack of Pakistani consent to the SEALs' incursion. By contrast, the al-Aulaqi operation appears to have had the benefit of Yemen's consent and perhaps its involvement. As such, the U.N. Charter-based *jus ad bellum* is largely silent in this latter context.[78] By contrast, one reaches crisscrossing conclusions with respect to the legality of the operation under domestic law. While the Bin Laden operation seems to fall squarely within the AUMF enacted following the September 11th attacks, the al-Aulaqi operation has a more uncertain domestic-law footing. Even assuming no violation of either territorial state's sovereignty, the *jus ad bellum* provides an uncertain justification for the use of deadly force against these two men absent a more imminent threat.

9.3.1 International Law Aspects of the Jus Ad Bellum

The U.N. Charter framework dictates that Article 2(4)'s use of force prohibition is an obligation *erga omnes*. The threat of transnational terrorism, however, has given rise to security imperatives—and concomitant legal arguments—that strain the classic *jus ad bellum*. This section recaps the basic tenets of this body of law and evaluates several theories that have been, or may be, employed to justify the United States' uses of force in these instances, including consent, self-defense, and

[75] This will change once the International Criminal Court can exercise jurisdiction over the crime of aggression.

[76] 18 U.S.C. §§ 1541–1548.

[77] Authorization to Use Military Force, Public Law 107-40, 115 Stat. 224 (Sept. 18, 2001).

[78] "[W]hen the use of force is authorized by the territorial state (in accordance with the limits pertaining to 'intervention by invitation,' the *Ius ad Bellum* does not come into play. … For this reason, the US strike against a number of Al Qaeda suspects in Yemen in November 2002, and carried out in cooperation with Yemeni authorities, could not be justified on the basis of Article 51 UN Charter." Ruys 2010, at p. 377 n. 39. See Naert 2004, at p. 151.

a state of necessity.[79] Although a self-defense rationale is ultimately the most defensible *jus-ad-bellum* justification for the breach of Pakistan's territorial integrity occasioned by the Bin Laden operation, it is not unassailable. By contrast, consent provides an easy answer to the question of the legality of the American incursion into Yemen. A free-standing self-defense doctrine, independent of any territorial breach, also offers a justification for both killings, although the availability of this defense as articulated remains open to debate given the standard formulation of the doctrine.

9.3.1.1 Consent

Article 2(4) is not implicated where the territorial state consents to foreign intervention.[80] There is little indication that Pakistan was aware of the Bin Laden operation, let alone that it consented to it. This lack of consent potentially distinguishes the Bin Laden operation from the so-called "drone wars"[81] in Waziristan and the other Federally Administered Tribal Areas (FATA) in northwest Pakistan. These latter operations likely enjoy at least some tacit diplomatic acquiescence, even though Pakistani officials occasionally publicly criticize them for domestic political consumption.[82] Consent to action in FATA would not necessarily extend to the Bin Laden raid, however.[83] All that said, we may never know for sure whether Pakistan had at some time offered its open-ended consent to an operation of this kind notwithstanding the domestic unpalatability of such an authorization. In addition, it could be argued that Pakistan consented to the operation *ex post*, thus forgoing any claims based on the territorial breach.[84] In any case, the ensuing analysis assumes a lack of Pakistani consent at the time of the operation.

The viability of a consent defense to a breach of Article 2(4) is a major distinction between the Bin Laden and al-Aulaqi attacks, the latter of which was implemented with Yemen's consent and, to a certain extent, assistance.[85] The only potential impediment to this conclusion turns on whether any offer of consent from

[79] One can imagine a doctrine of hot pursuit also being invoked, given that Bin Laden was subject to a 10-year manhunt, but the facts do not bear this theory out. See Ago 1980, at §56 (suggesting that the principle of necessity may countenance "incursions into foreign territory … in pursuit of an armed band or gang of criminals who had crossed the frontier and perhaps had their basis in the foreign country."); Beehner 2007.

[80] Article 20, International Law Commission, Draft Articles on Responsibility of States for Internationally Wrongful Acts (2001), available at http://untreaty.un.org/ilc/texts/instruments/english/commentaries/9_6_2001.pdf [hereinafter 'ILC Draft Articles'].

[81] Wall Street Journal—Editorial 2010. Bergen and Tiedemann 2009; Mayer 2009.

[82] Blank 2010, at p. 183; Shane and Schmitt 2010.

[83] See *Armed Activities on the Territory of the Congo* (DRC v. Uganda) (2005) ICJ Rep. 168, paras 52–53 [hereinafter '*Armed Activities*'].

[84] O'Connell 2011.

[85] Indeed, Yemen apparently assisted with identifying al-Aulaqi's remains. Mazzetti 2011.

the territorial state must be explicit and public to satisfy Article 2(4). This position is not strongly supported in the law; even if good policy, it may also be unreasonable.[86] While Yemen can consent to another state entering its territory, however, it cannot consent to that state violating IHL or human rights law while there. Thus, some lawful justification for the use of deadly force must still be identified.

9.3.1.2 Self-Defense

The doctrine of self-defense appears in multiple incarnations in this analysis. The first is as a U.N. Charter-based exception to Article 2(4)'s principle of sovereign inviolability. This permutation of self-defense governs inter-state relations and has been employed to justify the violation of Pakistani territory and Article 2(4) in light of the threat posed by Bin Laden and his organization. A second form of the defense, not likely applicable under the facts as we know them, derives from standard criminal law doctrine and operates to justify an individual's use of deadly force in a face-to-face confrontation with another individual posing a distinct threat to the actor or to third parties.[87] A third version is the most unsettled in the law. This variant operates as a free-standing justification for a nation to employ deadly force against particular individuals who pose a national threat, but not necessarily an immediate threat at the time they are targeted. As articulated, this justification for deadly force exists even absent any territorial breach, state of armed conflict, or imminent threat as required in the criminal law context and provides continuous targeting authority with respect to individuals deemed dangerous to a particular nation. The two relevant versions of the self-defense doctrine will be considered in turn.

Self-Defense as a Defense to the Article 2(4) Breach

Absent Pakistan's consent, the Bin Laden raid resulted in a *prima facie* breach of that country's sovereignty within the meaning of Article 2(4) of the Charter. The primary argument advanced to justify this use of force is that the U.S. was exercising its inherent right—and sovereign duty—of self-defense,[88] a codified exception to the general prohibition on the use of force in the U.N. Charter.[89] The Charter-based theory of self-defense is that since at least September 11, if not earlier, the U.S. has been subjected to a continuous armed attack and an ongoing risk of further attacks

---

[86] Chesney 2011a, b.

[87] Corn and Jensen 2008, at pp. 813–815 (discussing standing rules of engagement authorizing the use of force in self-defense in war and peacetime conditions). See Chairman of the Joint Chiefs of Staff 2005, at p. 82.

[88] Murphy 2009, at p. 123.

[89] Article 51 states "Nothing in this Charter shall impair the inherent right of individual or collective self-defense if an armed attack occurs against a Member of the United Nations".

from al Qaida, with Bin Laden at the helm. This risk of future attacks is cited to justify the incursion into Pakistani territory. Notwithstanding this apparent Charter-based justification, a number of legal and factual hurdles exist to a smooth application of established self-defense doctrine in these circumstances.

For one, Article 51 by its terms is triggered by the commission of an "armed attack." Although the precise definition of "armed attack" remains the subject of dispute,[90] there was virtual international unanimity that the attacks of September 11th satisfied any necessary gravity threshold (from the perspective of scale and effect) to constitute such an attack. There is no precise formula for evaluating the temporal relationship and the degree of immediacy between the armed attack and the defensive response. At the moment, however, these tragic events might be deemed too long-passed to provide the predicate legal foundation for the operation under consideration absent some theory of extended or open-ended self-defense.[91]

It may be possible to accumulate effectuated and attempted attacks (starting with the embassy bombings through the failed Christmas bombing) against the U.S. both prior and subsequent to September 11th to justify a sustained invocation of self-defense. According to this so-called pinprick theory, such a chain of events indicates a strong likelihood of future attacks and gives rise to a potentially indefinite, but certainly protracted, right to engage in defensive action,[92] even when no particular attack is in progress that would, on its own, support a right to respond.[93] A state might then maintain a defensive response for some time in order to neutralize the ongoing threat. While it is possible to identify multiple armed attacks against the U.S. emanating from al Qaida proper, it is harder to do so with respect to AQAP if that is the relevant entity for analyzing the Al-Aulaqi operation. Although certain attempted attacks have been publicly attributed to AQAP, it remains uncertain whether any one act, or the acts taken together, has reached the necessary intensity to constitute an "armed attack" against the U.S. within the meaning of Article 51.

---

[90] It is clear that an armed attack is something short of a full-scale armed conflict or an act of aggression as envisioned by G.A. Resolution 3314, which the General Assembly promulgated to guide the Security Council in applying Article 39 of the Charter. The ICJ has opined that Article 2(4) and Article 51 are not co-extensive, which is to say not every act that violates Article 2(4) necessarily constitutes an "armed attack" that would trigger the inherent right of self-defense. See, e.g., *Case Concerning Military and Paramilitary Activities in and Against Nicaragua* (Nicaragua v. USA) (Merits) (1986) ICJ Rep. 14, paras 191, 195 [hereinafter '*Nicaragua*']; *Case Concerning Oil Platforms* (Islamic Republic of Iran v. USA) (2003) ICJ Rep. 161, para 64 [hereinafter '*Oil Platforms*'].

[91] *Nicaragua*, *supra* n. 90, at para 237 (noting that U.S. response "continued long after the period in which any presumed armed attack by Nicaragua could reasonably be contemplated."). By contrast, see Murphy 2009, at p. 124.

[92] Blum 1976, at p. 233. Indeed, the U.S. invoked this theory to justify its attacks on Libya in 1986 following the bombing of a German discotheque frequented by U.S. service members. Ruys 2010, at p. 171 n. 228.

[93] On the accumulation of events doctrine see, for instance, Ago 1980, at p. 70; Tams 2009, at pp. 388–390; and *Armed Activities*, *supra* n. 83, at para 146.

It is widely held that, notwithstanding the textual formulation of Article 51, international law continues to recognize some notion of anticipatory (as opposed to reactive) self-defense, such that a state need not await the launching of an attack in order to respond defensively.[94] Historically, as articulated in the exchange of notes generated in connection with the 1837 *Caroline* incident, any notion of preemptive self-defense required proof that the attack be imminent, such that the defensive imperative is "instant, overwhelming and leaving no choice of means and no moment for deliberation."[95] By this formulation, a state enjoys no privilege to act in the face of mere threats, remote risks, or inchoate dangers.[96]

This high barrier to action remains controversial and would render unlawful many efforts at anticipatory self-defense. The so-called Bush Doctrine, embodied in the President's 2002 National Security Strategy, endeavored to augment the right of anticipatory self-defense by relaxing the immediacy standard to allow for preventative attacks where there is a serious threat to American security but no concrete attack in progress.[97] Although compelling and influential,[98] it is doubtful whether this approach has been fully accepted by other members of the international community[99] such that it can be said with confidence that a new customary norm has developed.[100] Nonetheless, a self-defense rationale for the use of force in Pakistan requires the acceptance of some notion of anticipatory—indeed preventative—self-defense. This is because there is no suggestion that the U.S. was aware of any impending attacks being orchestrated by Bin Laden, although intelligence gleaned from seized materials suggests that future attacks were indeed contemplated.[101]

The risk of relaxing the immediacy requirement is that the self-defense exception could be invoked to mask unlawful aggressive acts or punitive measures taken in reprisal or retaliation. Although there are sources of international law that categorically prohibit reprisals,[102] military operations such as Operation Infinite

---

[94] See generally Van den Hole 2003 arguing in favor of the doctrine; but see Ruys 2010, at pp. 258–259 arguing that the Charter modified prior customary international law in this area.

[95] Letter from Daniel Webster to Mr. Fox (April 24, 1841), available in Webster and Everett 1851.

[96] See generally O'Connell 2002.

[97] The White House 2002, National Security Strategy of the US of America (Sept. 2002), available at http://georgewbush-whitehouse.archives.gov/nsc/nss/2002/. See generally Murphy 2003.

[98] Reisman and Armstrong 2006.

[99] See, e.g., Paul 2004. But see UN Secretary General, High-Level Panel on Threats, Challenges and Change, A More Secure World: Our Shared Responsibility, 2 December 2004, A/59/565, at p. 54 available at http://www.un.org/secureworld/report.pdf.

[100] O'Connell 2002, at pp. 12–13.

[101] Mazzetti and Shane 2011.

[102] UN General Assembly, Declaration on Principles of International Law Concerning Friendly Relations and Co-operation Among States in Accordance with the Charter of the United Nations. General Assembly Resolution 2625 (XXV), 24 October 1970, A/2625.

Reach launched in response to the 1998 embassy bombings may suggest enduring support, and a continuing utility, for such a concept.[103] This is especially compelling given the difficulty of distinguishing between self-help actions taken in reprisal and those taken in genuine self-defense.

Another challenge to positioning the raid within the archetypical self-defense framework is that, by some accounts, the right of self-defense applies only in response to an armed attack by another sovereign entity, even though no such limitation appears in Article 51 itself. The International Court of Justice has adopted this position, even following the attacks of September 11th.[104] By this rationale, measures in self-defense may only be exercised against the state legally responsible for the initial attack. Because Pakistan did not engage in an armed attack against the U.S., and no one is arguing that Bin Laden's actions may be attributed to that country, Article 51 would thus be inapplicable to justify the United States' use of force on Pakistani territory. There are indications, however, that the classically statist interpretation of Article 51 has given way to a more expansive and realistic view in light of the increasing threat posed by non-state actors in international relations.[105] Both the Security Council[106] and the North Atlantic Treaty Alliance (NATO)[107] invoked the right of self-defense following the attacks of September 11th, recognizing a more fulsome range of potential sovereign threats. This suggests that the Court's majority approach fails to fully correspond with state practice.[108] This may also signal either the emergence of a new custom[109] or the survival or revival of pre-Charter customary law.[110]

At a minimum, the right to use force in self-defense against non-state actors may extend to situations in which the target state is advertently or even inadvertently harboring militants,[111] given that the due diligence principle obliges states to prevent their territory from being used to the detriment of other states.[112] This

---

103 For support for the lawfulness of reprisals under international law, see Bowett 1972, at p. 233, and O'Brien 1990.

104 *Legal Consequences of the Construction of a Wall in the Occupied Palestinian Territory*, Advisory Opinion (2004) ICJ Rep. 136, para 139 [hereinafter '*Legal Consequences*'] and *Armed Activities*, *supra* n. 83, at para 147. But see Separate Opinion of Judge Higgins, *Legal Consequences,* at para 33.

105 Murphy 2002; Stahn 2003.

106 S/RES/1368, 12 September 2001. See also S/PV.5489 (July 14, 2006) and S/PV.5493 (July 21, 2006).

107 Statement by NATO Secretary-General, Lord Robertson (Oct. 2, 2001), available at http://www.nato.int/docu/speech/2001/s011002a.htm. The European Union also expressed support for Operation Enduring Freedom as an exercise of self-defense. Letter from the Representative of Belgium to the Secretary General, S/2001/967 (Oct. 8, 2001).

108 See, e.g., *Armed Activities*, *supra* n. 83, Separate Opinion of Judge Simma at paras 10–12.

109 Ruys 2010, at p. 455. Some scholars have adopted a middle position to the effect that a right of self-defense exists only against large-scale attacks by non-state actors. Wilmshurst 2005.

110 Janin 2007, at p. 89.

111 Gray 2004, at pp. 161, 165–167, 172–175.

112 *Corfu Channel Case (United Kingdom v. Albania)*, 1949 ICJ Rep. 4, at p. 22.

obligation—which finds affinity in doctrines of neutrality originating in the law of armed conflict[113]—exists even when the acts of such non-state actors cannot be formally attributed to the territorial state under the *Nicaragua* effective control threshold[114] or other tests of state responsibility.[115] As former Secretary of State George Shultz argued, this position is based on the proposition that international law does not prohibit a state from "attacking [terrorists] on the soil of other nations ... or from using force against States that support, train, and harbor terrorists or guerrillas."[116] Similar operations in the past, however, have provoked condemnation as violations of the territorial state's sovereignty. For example, in 1988, the Security Council considered Israel's "assassination" in Tunisia of an alleged Palestine Liberation Organization leader, Khalil El Wazir, to be an act of aggression[117]—one of the few instances in which the Council employed that term to describe the unlawful use of force by a state.[118] Likewise, states objected to Operation Phoenix, launched by Colombia into Ecuador to pursue Raul Reyes and other Revolutionary Armed Forces of Colombia guerrillas, although ultimately Colombia was not sanctioned in any meaningful way for its actions.[119] In a post-9/11 world, however, the international community (or at least powerful states) may evince greater tolerance for states taking defensive action within the territories of other states that are unwilling or unable to repress irregular fighters in their midst, even if the territorial state could not be held legally responsible for the acts of those militants. The theory is that such states forfeit their right to noninterference when they fail to deal with such transnational security threats.[120]

---

[113] Hague Convention Respecting the Rights and Duties of Neutral Powers and Persons in Case of War on Land of 1907 (Hague V), Oct. 18, 1907, 36 Stat. 2310. The principle of neutrality dictates that no hostilities are allowed on the territory of neutral states and that neutral states must not offer an advantage to any side in the conflict.

[114] *Nicaragua, supra* n. 90, at para 115; Ratner 2002, at p. 908.

[115] For example, Article 8 of the ILC's Principle of State Responsibility states that it is appropriate to attribute private action to a state only if non-state actors are "in fact acting on the instructions of, or under the direction or control of, that State in carrying out the conduct." ILC Draft Articles, *supra* n. 80.

[116] See U.S. Secretary of State George Shultz 1986. The Shultz Doctrine was at play in Operation Infinite Reach, which involved attacks by the US on Sudan and Afghanistan following the 1998 embassy bombings. See UN Doc. S/1998/780 (Aug. 20, 1998).

[117] Security Council Resolution 611, 25 April 1988, S/RES/611. On the assassination, for which Israel did not claim responsibility, see Smolowe 1988; O'Brien 1990.

[118] Van Schaack 2011b, at pp. 565–567.

[119] When Colombia invoked the doctrine of self-defense (and hot pursuit) in connection with these killings, neighbouring states denounced the action as a violation of Ecuador's sovereignty, notwithstanding Ecuador's lack of control over its porous border region. Organization of American States, Convocation of the Meeting of Consultation of Ministers of Foreign Affairs and Appointment of a Commission, Doc. OEA/Ser.G, CP.Res.930 (1632/08) (March 5, 2008), available at http://www.oas.org/council/resolutions/res930.asp. Nagle 2008, at pp. 360–361; Reinold 2011, at p. 274.

[120] Reinold 2011, at p. 285.

The case at bar presents some special considerations because the government of Pakistan has been under a continuing Security Council-imposed duty[121] since before September 11th to refrain from, and ensure that its nationals refrain from, harboring or assisting in any way Bin Laden and those who associate with him.[122] The most robust obligations in this regard are contained in Resolution 1373, which obliged all states to "deny safe haven to those who finance, plan, support, or commit terrorist acts" and "prevent those who finance, plan, facilitate or commit terrorist acts from using their respective territories for those purposes against other states or their citizens."[123] Indeed, one wonders how Bin Laden's whereabouts in a fortified compound in the vicinity of an elite military academy for the past 5 years could possibly have been unknown to the Pakistani government.[124] This suggests that elements of the Pakistani government are incompetent, implicated, or woefully ignorant about events in their own territory. Regardless of which portrait is accurate, Pakistan's unwillingness or inability to act against Bin Laden offers a partial justification for the United States' resort to defensive self-help in its territory.[125]

By some accounts, if the territorial state is making a good faith effort to address the presence of armed groups in its midst, there is no right to use force in self-defense.[126] Others argue that the right to intervene with force exists only so long as some level of prior notice to, and consultation with, the implicated territorial state is undertaken absent evidence of collusion.[127] According to Abe Sofaer, a former State Department Legal Adviser:

> While the U.S. regards attacks on terrorists being protected in the sovereign territory of other States as potentially justifiable when undertaken in self-defense, a State's ability to establish the legality of such an action depends on its willingness openly to accept responsibility for the attack, to explain the basis for its action, and to demonstrate that reasonable efforts were made prior to the attack to convince the State whose territorial sovereignty was violated to prevent the offender's unlawful activities from occurring.[128]

---

[121] See S/RES/1363 (30 July 2001) and S/RES/1368 (12 September 2001).

[122] See S/RES/1566 (8 October 2004), S/RES/1617 (29 July 2005), S/RES/1735 (22 December 2006) and S/RES/1822 (30 June 2008).

[123] See S/RES/1373 (28 September 2001).

[124] It has been suggested that some elements of the Pakistani military or security services may have known of Bin Laden's existence. Brulliard and DeYoung 2011; Perlez and Rhode 2011. But see *Armed Activities*, *supra* n. 83, at para 300 (finding the DRC had not violated its due diligence duties vis-à-vis rebels operating in the eastern regions of the country given the remoteness of the area and absence of a central government presence there).

[125] Brennan 2011.

[126] O'Connell 2009a; Murphy 2009, at p. 129 (arguing that "the unilateral use of force to strike at Al Qaeda in Pakistan in response to the 9/11 attacks would be found disproportionate, in that the spatial and temporal displacement of the threat of Al Qaeda to a different country introduces competing values, to wit the territorial integrity and political independence of a country that did not knowingly support, sponsor, or tolerate Al Qaeda in the years preceding 9/11.").

[127] Lubell 2010, at p. 46.

[128] Sofaer 1989, at p. 121.

In addition, assuming it applies in one of the forms discussed above, the inherent right of sovereign self-defense is limited as a matter of customary international law by the twin principles of necessity and proportionality.[129] These principles place a check on each use of force after the outbreak of armed violence.[130] The principle of necessity mandates that any response in self-defense be strictly and objectively essential to protect core interests of the defending state and be a last resort after more peaceful means (such as diplomacy) are exhausted or deemed futile.[131] Proportionality in the *jus ad bellum* requires that any response to an armed attack be calibrated to repel the original attack and prevent future attacks.[132] Although no strict one-to-one force ratio is required, the operation as a whole should be proportionate to the original transgression in terms of scale of the response, the targets chosen, the type and degree of force employed, and the results to be achieved.[133] The principle of proportionality might thus bar a state from widening the scope of the conflict, for example to new territories.[134] To the extent that non-state actors are the source of the threat, any right to engage in acts in self-defense would normally be confined to terrorist targets as contrasted to the infrastructure or installations of the territorial state,[135] except potentially in situations in which there is a high degree of symbiosis between the group and the host state.[136]

As a final constraint on invoking self-defense, Article 51 contains several procedural requirements, namely notification to the Security Council. These were adhered to in the immediate aftermath of 9/11, although not since.[137] These requirements are not generally deemed an absolute precondition for invoking the defense, although they are relevant to evaluating the authenticity of a state's claim of self-defense.[138]

---

[129] *Nicaragua*, *supra* n. 90, at para 194; *Legality of the Threat or Use of Nuclear Weapons*, Advisory Opinion (1996) I.C.J. Rep. 9, para 41 [hereinafter '*Nuclear Weapons*']; Naert 2004, at pp. 147, 155.

[130] Greenwood 2003, at p. 16.

[131] *Oil Platforms*, *supra* n. 90, paras 73 and 76 (noting that the U.S. did not complain to Iran about military activities on the platforms before the attacks).

[132] The principle of proportionality is also a feature of IHL, although the concept plays a different role in each paradigm. Nonetheless, the two concepts are often conflated in evaluations of a state's resort to forcible measures. Within IHL, the proportionality unit of analysis is the particular attack, rather than the military response as a whole. Each attack necessitates a proportionality analysis that measures the level and kind of force used against the risk to civilians, so-called collateral damage, in light of the military objectives to be achieved. Moussa 2008, at p. 977. The *jus ad bellum* do not address the risk to non-combatants directly; this is rather the province of other sources of law, such as international human rights law.

[133] *Oil Platforms*, *supra* n. 90, at para 77.

[134] *Armed Activities*, *supra* n. 83, at para 147; Greenwood 2003, at p. 17.

[135] Paust 2002, at p. 540.

[136] Stahn 2002, at pp. 225–226.

[137] Letter Dated 7 October 2001 from the Permanent Representative of the US of American to the United Nations addressed to the President of the Security Council, S/2001/946 (Oct. 7, 2001) [hereinafter 'U.S. Letter to the Security Council']. See also *Oil Platforms*, *supra* n. 90, at paras 37, 48.

[138] *Armed Activities*, *supra* n. 83, at para 145.

Any requirement to cooperate with the host state was clearly not satisfied in the Bin Laden killing.[139] Accounts indicate that although the U.S. contemplated involving Pakistani authorities in the operation, it ultimately resolved to act unilaterally.[140] It is clear, however, that little to no harm was done to Pakistani territory, which speaks to proportionality of response. In both cases, targeting a particular individual is a smaller-scale response than might be tolerated in light of the risks posed to the U.S. by al Qaida writ large and even by AQAP. In terms of necessity, decapitating a non-state group may result in its dissolution, disbanding, or considerable weakening, especially when the group is dominated by a messianic figure such as Bin Laden or al-Aulaqi.[141] Indeed, the Bin Laden plan was surgical by design to avoid confrontation with Pakistani authorities and damage to public infrastructure.[142] That said, the U.S. government has admitted that there were contingency plans in place in the event that the team was confronted by Pakistani military or police forces and had to fight their way out of the country.[143] Nonetheless, because there was no clear predicate armed attack and no imminent threat in the scenarios under consideration, neither operation fully complies with standard self-defense doctrine.

A Free-Standing Right of Self-Defense

The doctrine of self-defense has historically applied to national decisions to deploy military might on a macro scale against a threat to the nation. In the two scenarios under review, the unit of analysis is much smaller—the target is a single dangerous individual rather than a foreign regime or even a military asset or installation. This micro-level self-defense rationale does not seek to justify a violation of Article 2(4) by virtue of the use of force by a state in another sovereign's territory. Nor does it seek to justify individual action (i.e., by any one SEAL member) in the face of an imminent personal threat. Rather, the second relevant self-defense rationale is more in the nature of a hybrid of the classic *jus ad bellum* and criminal law versions of self-defense.[144] It also finds affinity in status-based targeting doctrines contained in IHL, although it is applied in situations outside of armed conflict when IHL is silent.

Presumably, this rationale is still bottomed on Article 51, which articulates a right to engage in defensive action absent any actual or anticipated breach of Article 2(4). If so, however, the textual necessity of a predicate armed attack and the debate over

---

[139] But see Deeks 2011 (noting that the U.S. was absolved of the need to consult with Pakistan given the risk that Bin Laden would be tipped off and the limitations of Pakistan's capacity to respond appropriately in any case).

[140] Calabresi 2011.

[141] Ruys 2010, at p. 377.

[142] Calabresi 2011 (noting that airstrikes were ruled out for fear of collateral damage).

[143] Walsh and Jones 2011.

[144] Obama Brief, *supra* n. 3, at pp. 4–5.

anticipatory self-defense remain paramount. All told, it is difficult to rely upon Article 51 for a continuous targeting authority against individuals posing a more diffuse threat to the nation. If the Article 51-based requirements for self-defense cannot be met, this rationale must find expression in customary international law that either pre-dates or coexists alongside the U.N. Charter. The most applicable state practice may be the Israeli action in Tunisia, which was not well-received internationally.[145] That said, the Tunisia episode was pre-9/11 and did not involve an individual of Bin Laden's infamy, so a blanket rule may no longer be valid.

Assuming such a continuous targeting authority exists, necessity remains to be established: that each man posed a sufficient enough threat to justify the use of lethal force and that there were no other operational means to suppress this threat. Certainly, if Bin Laden still had operational or financial control over al Qaida activities, his killing would eliminate a serious and continuing threat to the U.S., but that does not fully answer the question of necessity. The targetability of al-Aulaqi under such a self-defense rationale may be more contestable. This is where it becomes important to establish his actions and role beyond the vituperative propaganda that is available in the public record, unless such calls to jihad constitute a sufficient threat to the U.S.—a proposition that is difficult to endorse in light of the United States' constitutional devotion to free speech principles. However, the U.S. has never had to fully establish al-Aulaqi's role in AQAP or provide solid evidence of his conduct beyond his ideological rants. In either case, invoking a self-defense rationale for the killing of a single individual is very far from the original paradigm, which is addressed to neutralizing a more macro sovereign threat. Indeed, it operates more like a conflation of *jus ad bellum* self-defense concepts with *jus in bello* targeting rules.

9.3.1.3 A State of Necessity

A final argument that might have been invoked to preclude any wrongfulness of the United States' conduct is the existence of a general state of necessity not presenting a case of self-defense *stricto sensu*.[146] The freeform principle of necessity finds expression in Article 25 of the International Law Commission's Articles on Responsibility of States for Internationally Wrongful Acts; it also finds resonance in general principles of criminal law.[147] The Articles state that necessity may not be invoked unless the otherwise unlawful act:

(a) is the only means for the State to safeguard an essential interest against a grave and imminent peril; and
(b) does not seriously impair an essential interest of the State or States towards which the obligation exists, or of the international community as a whole.[148]

[145] See supra text accompanying note 117.
[146] See generally Boed 2000.
[147] Model Penal Code, § 3.02(1).
[148] Article 35, ILC Draft Articles, *supra* n. 80. Ago 1980, at pp. 14–51.

This defense cannot, however, be invoked to justify or excuse the impairment of an essential interest of another state or to breach a peremptory rule of international law,[149] such as Article 2(4) of the Charter,[150] limitations on the use of deadly force in IHL, or human rights law.[151]

In his discussion of the circumstances negating the wrongfulness of a state's conduct, Roberto Ago as the ILC's Special Rapporteur on State Responsibility opined that a state of necessity might, as a standalone imperative, preclude the wrongfulness of limited (in terms of duration and the means employed) sorties into sovereign territory falling short of acts of aggression. Ago specifically mentions the example of "incursions into foreign territory to forestall harmful operations by an armed groups which was preparing to attack the territory of the State."[152] The ICJ has made clear, however, that although such a defense may exist in customary international law, it is circumscribed such that it may only be invoked on an "exceptional basis" and under "strictly confined conditions."[153] In particular, the impugned conduct must be responsive to an imminent peril and be the sole means available to the responding state to safeguard an essential interest against such a danger.[154]

The high threshold for invoking the defense as formulated by the ILC and the ICJ means that it is difficult to apply to the incidents under consideration—which involve territorial intervention and the application of deadly force—notwithstanding that Bin Laden and al-Aulaqi had eluded capture in the past and that Pakistan and Yemen are undependable allies. A more micro application of the doctrine of necessity may, however, be useful in tandem with the self-defense doctrine to justify not informing Pakistan of the impending raid and other departures from the strict requirements of standard self-defense doctrine.

9.3.2 *Domestic Law Aspects of the* **Jus Ad Bellum**

Although the two operations prompt an immediate consideration of the international *jus ad bellum*, domestic law is implicated as well. The attack on Bin Laden had unequivocal authorization under U.S. law in the form of the 2001 AUMF,

149 Article 26, ILC Draft Articles, *supra* n. 80.

150 See UN General Assembly, Declaration on the Enhancement of the Effectiveness of the Principle of Refraining from the Threat or Use of Force in International Relations, 18 November 1987, G.A. Res. 42/22; Stahn 2002.

151 Ago 1980, at pp. 20–21, 36–37.

152 Ago 1980, at p. 39.

153 *Case Concerning the Gabčíkovo-Nagymaros Project* (Hungary v. Slovakia) (1997) I.C. J. Rep. 92 at para 51.

154 *Legal Consequences*, *supra* n. 104, at para 140.

which remains extant.[155] The AUMF, whose preamble invokes the right of self-defense,[156] authorized the President to

> use all necessary and appropriate force against those nations, organizations, or persons he determines planned, authorized, committed, or aided the terrorist attacks that occurred on September 11, 2001...[157]

In this way, the AUMF explicitly sanctions uses of force against the plotters of the attacks of September 11th and was drafted with Bin Laden in mind. Indeed, the operation arguably accomplished exactly what Congress had in mind upon passage of the AUMF, albeit a decade later. The only wrinkle concerns whether members of the CIA are covered by this legislation or if some additional authority is required.

The AUMF provides a less stable foundation for military activities against groups and individuals with more tenuous connections to 9/11,[158] such as AQAP, which was not in existence in 2001, or Tehrik-e-Taliban and the Haqqani Network in Pakistan, which only emerged later as distinct threats to the U.S.[159] Various pieces of legislation have been proposed to expand the existing AUMF to authorize force against emerging hostile groups and terrorist suspects globally.[160] None of these efforts has yet borne fruit, and the Obama Administration has resisted such Congressional re-authorization.[161] Indeed, the National Defense Authorization Act for Fiscal Year 2012 expressly reaffirms the original scope of the AUMF.[162]

To date, few facts have emerged specifically linking al-Aulaqi to the attacks of September 11th, although he apparently knew some of the plotters.[163] As such, the

---

155 The armed conflict in Afghanistan ostensibly presents no issue with the War Powers Resolution, because the AUMF states that it is intended to "constitute specific statutory authorization within the meaning of section 5(b) of the War Powers Resolution." AUMF, *supra* n. 77, at para 2(b)(1). This conflict can thus be contrasted with the situation in Libya, in which the continued involvement of the US past the War Powers Resolution's statutory 60 days without Congressional authorization was deemed by some to run afoul of the War Powers Resolution. See generally Chesney 2011b.

156 AUMF, *supra* n. 77, at Preamble, clause 3.

157 AUMF, supra n. 77. The AUMF marks the first time a joint resolution has authorized military force against organizations and persons rather than nations. Grimmett 2007.

158 Bellinger 2010. Indeed, President Bush's proposed post-9/11 resolution would have granted an authorization to use force to "deter and pre-empt any future acts of terrorism or aggression against the U.S." Grimmett 2007, at pp. 2–3, 5–6. Congress, however, removed this clause in the final resolution.

159 See generally Rassler and Brown 2011.

160 Pearlstein 2011. Presidential candidate Mitt Romney has proposed an expanded AUMF "to authorize the use of military force against any foreign terrorist entity that is waging war against the US." Romney 2011.

161 Pearlstein 2011.

162 NDAA, para 1021(d) (providing that "[n]othing in this section is intended to limit or expand the authority of the President or the scope of the Authorization for Use of Military Force.").

163 See The 9/11 Commission Report 221, 229–30 (July 22, 2004), available at http://www.911commission.gov/report/911Report.pdf.

AUMF provides an uncertain foundation for operations in Yemen against individuals such as al-Aulaqi. That said, theories of co-belligerency divorced from the law of neutrality[164] have been advanced to bring groups such as AQAP into the AUMF's folds.[165] Co-belligerency historically refers to a relationship among states that are engaged cooperatively in an international armed conflict against another state or other states. The theory is that an armed conflict between two parties automatically creates a state of armed conflict with the opposing state(s)' allies.[166] Although a feature of past international armed conflicts, it is not difficult to make the conceptual leap from states as co-belligerents to armed groups engaged in non-international armed conflicts as co-belligerents.[167] As one U.S. district court noted, "'co-belligerents' as that term is understood under the law of war" means "fully fledged belligerent fighting in association with one or more belligerent powers" but does not include organizations that "merely share an abstract philosophy or even a common purpose with al Qaeda—there must be an actual association in the current conflict with al Qaeda or the Taliban."[168] In the litigation brought by al-Aulaqi's father, the Obama Administration argued that by virtue of making common cause with al Qaida, AQAP "is a part of al-Qaeda—or at a minimum an organized, associated force or co-belligerent of al-Qaeda in the non-international armed conflict between the U.S. and al-Qaeda."[169] Even a notion of NIAC co-belligerency, however, may not be enough to satisfy the terms of the AUMF, which ultimately requires a link to 9/11.[170]

Some would argue that this discussion is moot. It is not settled whether domestic law is even necessary to authorize discrete drone attacks like the al-Aulaqi operation. The Obama Administration is on record stating that using drones in foreign countries does not require congressional approval unless some threshold of force is reached and the lives of U.S. solders are at risk. State Department Legal Adviser Harold Hongju Koh testified before the Senate Foreign Relations Committee in connection with the Libya intervention that U.S. involvement, including "limited strikes by Predator unmanned aerial vehicles against discrete targets,"[171] would not constitute participation in "hostilities" as understood by the War Powers Resolution, primarily because such operations do not involve the deployment of U.S. armed forces into

[164] Bothe (2008), at p. 485.

[165] Obama brief, *supra* n. 3, at p. 1; Bradley and Goldsmith 2005, at p. 2112.

[166] ICTY, *Prosecutor v. Blaškić*, Judgment of the Trial Chamber, IT-95-14-T, 3 March 2000, paras 137–143.

[167] *But see Al-Bihani v. Obama*, 590 F.3d 866, 873 (D.C. Cir. 2010) (refuting the availability of theories of non-state co-belligerency in NIACs).

[168] *Hamlily v. Obama*, 616 F. Supp. 2d 63, 74–75, n. 17 (D.D.C. 2009).

[169] *Al-Aulaqi*, Obama brief, *supra* n. 3, at p. 33. See also *Hamlily v. Obama*, 616 F.Supp.2d 63, 75 (D.D.C. 2009) (interpreting the term "associated forces" to mean "'co-belligerents' as that term is understood under the law of war.").

[170] Grimmett 2007, at p. 3.

[171] Testimony by Legal Adviser Harold Hongju Koh, U.S. Department of State, on Libya and War Powers Before the Senate Foreign Relations Committee, (June 28, 2011), available at http://foreign.senate.gov/imo/media/doc/Koh_Testimony.pdf, at p. 11.

situations that will expose them to exchanges of fire with hostile forces.[172] With no need for domestic legal authority, the al-Aulaqi operation would be evaluated under the international *jus ad bellum* only. This position has been, however, hotly contested within and without the U.S. government.[173]

9.3.3 *Conclusion:* Jus Ad Bellum

Absent Pakistan's consent, it is clear that Pakistan's territorial integrity was violated in the Bin Laden operation, although this infraction can be reasonably justified on expanded self-defense grounds. Complaints about breaches of the *jus ad bellum* and Article 2(4) are for Pakistan to raise against the U.S.[174] Although Pakistan has grumbled about the violation of its sovereignty, no formal claims have been pursued to date.[175] Nor are they likely to be forthcoming given the lack of actual damage to Pakistani property or interests[176] and the embarrassment factor stemming from the fact that Bin Laden was living in relative comfort in Abbottabad for so long. The al-Aulaqi operation does not run afoul of Article 2(4) in light of Yemen's consent to U.S. territorial engagement. That said, the employment of deadly force by a state even absent a territorial breach still requires justification. For this, a more expanded form of self-defense is required that hinges on a showing of the risk posed by the individual being targeted and his or her amenability to continuous targeting.[177] All told, relying on self-defense to justify these operations requires a number of controversial doctrinal leaps. These include: that a terrorist act can constitute an "armed attack;" that in the face of multiple attacks, self-defense applies on a continuous basis and not only in the immediate aftermath of any one attack; that self-defense can be exercised in the territory of a state that is not acting in collusion with the menace; that self-defense can be exercised against a single individual in keeping with the principle of necessity; and—most importantly—that the law supports a form of anticipatory self-defense that can be exercised in the absence of a concrete threat of future attack.

---

[172] *Id.* at p. 8.

[173] Huffington Post 2011.

[174] Compare ICTY, *Prosecutor v. Nikolić*, Decision On Defence Motion Challenging The Exercise Of Jurisdiction By The Tribunal, IT-94-2-Pt, 9 October 2002, at para 97 ("Traditionally, such breaches were considered a possible dispute between States with no role as such for the person involved. Much therefore depends on the reaction of the injured State itself.") with ICTY, *Prosecutor v. Tadić*, Decision on the Defence Motion for Interlocutory Appeal on Jurisdiction, IT-94-1-AR72, 2 October 1995, at para 55 ("an accused, being entitled to a full defence, cannot be deprived of a plea so intimately connected with, and grounded in, international law as a defence based on a violation of State sovereignty.").

[175] Perlez and Rhode 2011.

[176] But see *Corfu Channel*, *supra* n. 112, at pp. 35–36.

[177] Kretzmer (2005), at p.193.

Even if these international law *jus ad bellum* arguments prove satisfactory, our inquiry cannot end here. Domestic law governing the United States' war powers also have a say. Although the Bin Laden operation falls within the text and purpose of the AUMF, the domestic law foundation for the al-Aulaqi killing remains uncertain if al-Aulaqi cannot reasonably be connected to the September 11th attacks. In any case, it is difficult to imagine how any claims under domestic law would be raised, given the historical reticence of courts to challenge executive decisions about exercising the war powers.[178] This is all assuming that domestic authorization is needed at all. Yemen's consent coupled with the argument that there is no need for domestic authorization for discrete drone attacks means that the *jus ad bellum* may offer little resistance to the al-Aulaqi operation.

If the *jus ad bellum* authorizes these operations, the *jus in bello* may further constrain the way in which they were implemented. This depends on whether or not IHL applies to these events. If it does, the U.S. government cannot exclusively rely on a *jus ad bellum* framework to justify both killings to the exclusion of IHL. With this in mind, the next Section addresses the *jus in bello* implications of the two operations after considering the preliminary question of whether this body of law applies at all. A subsequent Section discusses the human rights implications under either a *jus ad bellum* or a *jus in bello* framework bearing in mind that Bin Laden and Al-Aulaqi, no matter how odious, still enjoy the protection of human rights law.

9.4 Adherence to the *Jus in Bello*

The *jus ad bellum* and *jus in bello* are often conceived of as applying sequentially, with the latter assuming greater salience once a party has resorted to armed force.[179] With the initiation of the *jus in bello*, however, the *jus ad bellum* does not recede entirely, as certain aspects (such as the principle of proportionality) continue to regulate the use of force once initiated. Moreover, not every use of force triggers the applicability of the law of war; it is only when a use of force rises to the level of an armed conflict, or has a sufficient nexus to an existing armed conflict, that international humanitarian law (IHL) is implicated. Assuming IHL is applicable, however, the *jus in bello* applies to all parties to the armed conflict pursuant to the equal application principle,[180] regardless of the outcome of any *jus ad bellum* analysis.[181] The law insists on this acoustic separation for pragmatic as

[178] See *Saltany v. Reagan*, 886 F.2d 438 (D.C. Cir. 1989) (rejecting case by Libyan nationals arguing for the illegality of U.S. and British airstrikes on Libya).

[179] Greenwood 2006, at pp. 13, 28.

[180] Roberts (Adam) 2008.

[181] API, *supra* n. 42, Preamble, Clause 5. The U.S. has not ratified API, although in public statements it has accepted the binding nature of certain provisions. See The White House—Fact Sheet (2011).

well as philosophical reasons.[182] The point is to ensure the application of the regulatory *jus in bello* no matter the cause or legality of the underlying conflict so that both the aggressor and the aggressed—as well as the privileged and the unprivileged—are bound by the same rules of conduct. The justness of one side's cause thus does not modify the application of the *jus in bello* between the parties. As such, the question of whether the U.S. was entitled to use force *vel non* in Pakistan and Yemen does not resolve questions about whether these particular applications of force were in compliance with the *jus in bello*.

It is natural to assume that IHL is the appropriate body of law to resolve questions of this nature, given the use of combat power as well as ongoing military operations in Afghanistan and elsewhere against elements of al Qaida. However, it is worth considering more closely the a priori question of whether IHL applied in Abbottabad, Pakistan, and in Khashef, Yemen, which are far from any active battlefield in Afghanistan and even from the border region between Afghanistan and Pakistan where a spillover conflict is under way.[183] If IHL is not applicable, then the deaths of Bin Laden and al-Aulaqi could not be characterized as the kind of wartime killing sanctioned as a normal—indeed expected—incident of war. The killings would then be evaluated under other bodies of law to dramatically different conclusions, as discussed in the next Section.

9.4.1 Is International Humanitarian Law the Operative Body of Law?

The law governing armed conflicts—IHL or the law of armed conflict—exhibits a Janus-like character. On the one hand, IHL is protective toward certain classes of persons who are considered *hors de combat*—detainees, surrendering combatants, civilians, the shipwrecked, the sick, and the wounded. It is unlawful to deliberately target such individuals. At the same time, IHL is permissive with respect to other classes of persons, namely active combatants and those who engage in hostilities. In contrast to the immunities afforded to protected persons, this latter class of persons may be lawfully targeted and killed. In situations in which it applies, IHL thus tolerates—and indeed anticipates—many forms of violence that would be unlawful outside of the context of war.[184] In particular, IHL countenances the use of deadly force against the adversary as a first resort as compared with peacetime law enforcement scenarios, in which the use of such force is allowed only to

182 Moussa 2008.

183 Blank 2010, at pp. 165, 178.

184 Report of the Special Rapporteur on Extrajudicial, Summary or Arbitrary Executions, A/HRC/14/24/Sdd.6 (28 May 2010), available at http://www2.ohchr.org/english/bodies/hrcouncil/docs/14session/A.HRC.14.24.Add6.pdf [hereinafter 'Alston Report'] at para 47; Blank 2010, at p. 15.

respond to the exigencies of self-defense, the defense of others, and halting a fleeing felon.[185] In this way, IHL challenges default rules premised on the right to life, such as the prohibitions against intentionally killing another human being.

The triggering of IHL is no longer dependent on a declaration of war but rather turns pragmatically on empirical facts on the ground, most saliently the presence of an armed conflict or situation of occupation. It is widely accepted that an armed conflict is deemed to exist when "there is resort to armed force between States or protracted armed violence between governmental authorities and organized armed groups or between such groups within a State."[186] The triggering conditions of IHL differ depending on whether the conflict is an international (IAC) or non-international armed conflict (NIAC).[187] Common Article 2 of the 1949 Geneva Conventions indicates that those treaties apply in all cases of "declared war or any other armed conflict which may arise between two or more of the High Contracting Parties." The law of armed conflict thus would apply wherever the armed forces of at least two states are embattled. Indeed, Pictet's authoritative commentary suggests that those treaties become activated upon a very low threshold of inter-state violence,[188] although this view has been qualified in several modern sources to effectively exclude border incidents and other small-scale military confrontations between states.[189] Indeed, the U.S. has argued that military responses undertaken pursuant to the inherent right of self-defense as set forth in Article 51 of the Charter do not under all circumstances rise to the level of an armed conflict.[190]

By contrast, a higher threshold exists for establishing the existence of a NIAC that is premised on two factors: the scale or intensity of the violence[191] and the degree of organization of the parties.[192] This higher threshold exists to distinguish such conflicts from a number of situations that do not trigger IHL, even if such events provoke a military response by the state. These include: small scale operations involving military assets that cannot be deemed to be part of a larger armed conflict; situations of "internal disturbances and tensions, such as riots,

---

[185] Blank 2010, at p. 187.

[186] *Tadić* 1995, *supra* n. 174, at para 70.

[187] *Tadić* 1995, *supra* n. 174, at para 67.

[188] Pictet 1960. Pictet indicates that an armed conflict exists between states when "any difference arising between two States and leading to the intervention of members of the armed forces." See also ICTY, *Prosecutor v. Mucić*, Judgment of the Trial Chamber, IT-96-21-T, 16 November 1998, at para 184.

[189] O'Connell 2009b, at p. 397; Greenwood 2008, at pp. 39, 42.

[190] Report of the Working Group on the Universal Periodic Review: United States of America, A/HRC/16/11, 4 January 2011, available at http://www2.ohchr.org/english/bodies/hrcouncil/docs/16session/A-HRC-16-11-Add1.pdf, at para 54.

[191] ICTY, *Prosecutor v. Boškoski*, Judgment of Trial Chamber, IT-04-82-T, 10 July 2008, at para 177.

[192] ICTY, *Prosecutor v. Limaj*, Judgment of Trial Chamber, IT-03-66-T, 30 November 2005, at para 84; *Boškoski*, *supra* n. 191, para 173–186.

isolated and sporadic acts of violence, and other acts of a similar nature;"[193] and acts of "banditry, unorganised and short-lived insurrections, or terrorist activities."[194]

All NIACs are governed by Article 3, which is common to the four Geneva Conventions and applies to all conflicts "occurring in the territory of one of the High Contracting Parties."[195] The International Committee of the Red Cross (ICRC) commentary offers several criteria for triggering common Article 3 (CA3) that turn on whether the party in revolt manifests a sufficient degree of organization and hierarchy, the legal government is obliged to have recourse to its military forces, the dissident group has popular support, the dispute has been placed on a U.N. agenda, and the insurgents exercise some level of control over territory.[196] The international tribunals, in turn, have identified a number of additional factors relevant to evaluating whether the intensity of the violence is sufficient to pass through the IHL gateway. These include: the number and duration of individual confrontations, the types of weaponry and equipment employed, the degree of physical destruction, the number of embattled individuals and casualties, the geographical and temporal breadth of clashes, the number of civilians displaced or otherwise impacted by fighting, and the involvement of the United Nations (particularly the Security Council).[197] This same case law employs criteria for identifying what constitutes an organized armed group. These mirror the characteristics of a formal national army and include: a hierarchical structure and rules of engagement, infrastructure to enlist and train recruits, the ability to launch military operations, a central authority empowered to negotiate with governmental representatives, and a leadership corps capable of being held

---

[193] Article 1(2), Convention on Prohibitions on Restrictions on the Use of Certain Conventional Weapons Which May Be Deemed to be Excessively Injurious or to have Indiscriminate Effects (as amended December 21, 2001), 2260 U.N.T.S. 82.

[194] ICTY, *Prosecutor v. Tadić*, Judgment of Trial Chamber, IT-94-1-T, 7 May 1997, para 562.

[195] Although not applicable to the events under consideration, Additional Protocol II to the Geneva Conventions applies to a subset of NIACs that.

> take place in the territory of a High Contracting Party between its armed forces and dissident armed forces or other organized armed groups which, under responsible command, exercise such control over a part of its territory as to enable them to carry out sustained and concerted military operations and to implement this Protocol.

Protocol Additional to the Geneva Conventions of 12 August 1949, and Relating to the Protections of Victims of Non-International Armed Conflicts of 8 June 1977, Article 1(1), 1125 U.N.T.S. 609 (1979) [hereinafter 'APII']. This threshold excludes "internal disturbances and tensions such as riots and isolated and sporadic acts of violence." *Id.* at Article 1(2). CA3 governs those NIACs that do not meet APII's standards of organization or territorial control. Because many rebel groups do not satisfy the high bar set forth in APII—often by design—CA3 provides important protections for a broader range armed conflicts.

[196] Pictet 1960, at pp. 35–36. See also *Juan Carlos Abella v. Argentina*, Case 11.137, Report No. 55/97, Inter-Am. C.H.R., OEA/Ser.L/V/II.98, Doc. 6 rev., 18th November 1997, at para 155.

[197] *Prosecutor v. Haradinaj*, Judgment of the Trial Chamber, Case No. IT-04-84-T, Judgment, 3 April 2008, para 49; *Limaj*, *supra* n. 192, at paras 84–90.

responsible for the group's acts.[198] It has been argued that in light of Article 3's reference to the "territory" of a High Contracting Party, CA3 is meant to govern classic civil wars and does not apply to situations in which a state is engaged in an armed conflict with a non-state actor outside its own borders and on the territory of another High Contracting Party.[199] Most commentators agree, however, that CA3 provides a floor of protection for all conflicts not of an international character.[200] Notwithstanding these treaty-based triggers for IHL, an emerging customary IHL applies across the conflict spectrum and is less dependent on the increasingly artificial classification dichotomy[201] that frames the Geneva Conventions and their Protocols.[202]

Situations of terrorism and counterterrorism do not constitute "armed conflicts" until a certain threshold of intensity, continuity,[203] group organization,[204] and military reciprocity is reached.[205] For example, the Council of Europe's Venice Commission—an advisory body on constitutional matters—determined in 2006 that

> sporadic bombings and other violent acts which terrorist networks perpetrate in different places around the globe and the ensuing counter-terrorism measures, even if they are occasionally undertaken by military units, cannot be said to amount to an 'armed conflict' in the sense that they trigger the applicability of International Humanitarian Law.[206]

Some commentators have gone further and resisted the application of IHL to terrorist (and criminal) organizations altogether, on the putative ground that to do so would give the members of such groups the status and legitimacy of belligerents.[207] Instead, they have urged the adoption of a pure law enforcement model for counterterrorism operations, acknowledging the occasional necessity to deploy military might in this context.[208]

---

198 *Haradinaj*, *supra* n. 197, paras 63–88; ICTY, *Prosecutor v. Lukic*, Judgment of Trial Chamber, IT-98-32/1-T, 20 July 2009, paras 879–888.

199 *Hamdan v. Rumsfeld*, 548 U.S. 557, 718-20 (2006) (Scalia, J., dissenting).

200 See, e.g., Pejic 2011.

201 Corn 2007.

202 International Law Association 2010. Henchaerts 2005, at p. 189. Many states apply the same norms regardless of classification as a policy matter. See, e.g., U.S. Dep't of Defence (2006) *Department of Defense Directive No. 2311.01E*, para 4.1, available at http://www.dtic.mil/whs/directives/corres/pdf/231101p.pdf.

203 ICTY, *Prosecutor v. Kordić & Cerkez*, Judgment of the Appeals Chamber, IT-95-14/2-A, 17 December 2004, at para 341.

204 International Law Association 2010, at p. 28.

205 *Public Committee Against Torture in Israel v. Israel*, HCJ 769/02 [2005] Isr.SC 57(6), para 16 [hereinafter '*Pub. Committee Ag. Torture*'].

206 Opinion on the International Legal Obligations of Council of Europe Member States in Respect of Secret Detention Facilities and Inter-State Transport of Prisoners, 17 March 2006, Op. No. 363/2005, CDL-AD (2006)009, para 78, available at http://www.venice.coe.int/docs/2006/CDL-AD(2006)009-e.asp [hereinafter 'Venice Commission']. See also Paust 2007, at p. 760.

207 Greenwood 2004, at p. 529; Rona 2003, at p. 61.

208 See generally Roth 2004.

Notwithstanding the distinction often drawn between armed conflicts and acts of terrorism, the international tribunals regularly consider acts that would be described as "terroristic" in determining whether the required intensity of violence has been reached for the purpose of applying IHL.[209] Indeed, a blanket rejection of the application of IHL to terrorism fails to acknowledge the evolution of modern threats to peace and security, the way in which classic terrorist attacks can be strategically employed in armed conflict situations, the ease of access to advanced and destructive weaponry by a slew of non-state actors, the reach and degree of organization of modern terrorist groups, the necessity of resorting to military assets in counterterrorism efforts, and the potency of ideology in the absence of territorial ambitions. Moreover, conceding that a situation amounts to a NIAC that is governed by IHL does not accord any legitimation or privilege to use force to non-state actors, be they rebels, insurgents, paramilitaries, drug-traffickers, insurrectionists, pirates, or terrorists. Such fighters remain unprivileged belligerents who enjoy neither combat immunity nor prisoner-of-war (POW) status and who can be prosecuted domestically for their acts of violence.

Accepting that IHL does apply in principle to terrorist groups and to conflicts pitting sovereign forces against such armed groups, the U.S. has been involved in an armed conflict with al Qaida since at least September 11th and the ensuing invasion of Afghanistan on October 7, 2001.[210] Prior to this point, the U.S. had responded to acts of terrorism attributable to al Qaida (such as the first World Trade Center attack in 1993[211] or even the U.S.S. *Cole* attack in Yemen in 2000[212]) primarily within a law enforcement framework.[213] Since September 2011, however, the U.S. has assumed a war footing by enacting an authorization to use military force, deploying troops abroad, and establishing military

[209] See, e.g., *Boškoski, supra* n. 191, at paras 187–190.

[210] This conflict is now characterized a one with "al-Qaeda, as well as the Taliban and associated forces, in response to the horrific 9/11 attacks." Koh 2010. See also G.W. Bush, President's Address to the Nation on the Terrorist Attacks, 37 Weekly Comp. Pres. Doc. 1301 (Sept. 11, 2001); G.W. Bush, President's Address to Joint Session of Congress on the US Response to the Terrorist Attacks of September 11, 37 Weekly Comp. Pres. Doc. 1347 at 1348 (Sept. 20, 2001). See U.S. Letter to Security Council, *supra* n. 137. Although this date provides an obvious starting point for any armed conflict involving the U.S., military commissions—which may only prosecute offenses "committed in the context of and associated with hostilities"—have twice convicted Guantánamo detainees for acts committed prior to September 11th. See § 950p(c), Military Commission Act of 2009 ("An offense specified in this sub-chapter is triable by military commission under this chapter only if the offense is committed in the context of and associated with hostilities."). One theory is that the armed conflict started as far back as 1996 or 1998, when Bin Laden purported to issue *fatwas* against the U.S. See PBS 1996 and PBS 1998.

[211] *U.S. v. Rahman,* 189 F.3d 88 (2d Cir. 1999) (per curiam).

[212] Soufan 2011 (describing FBI investigation in Yemen).

[213] The U.S. did respond militarily under a self-defense rationale to the 1998 attacks on U.S. embassies. See Letter Dated 20 August 1998 from the Permanent Representative of the United States to the United Nations Addressed to the President of the Security Council, S/1998/780 (1998). These uses of force were controversial, although primarily on account of the choice of targets rather than the decision to respond militarily. Bennet 1998.

commissions. In so doing, it has eschewed, or at least de-emphasized, the criminal law framework. In terms of the customary factors for finding the existence of an armed conflict, the level of intensity of violence in Afghanistan and in certain spillover regions obviously continues to exceed that necessary to signal the existence of an armed conflict. It is clear that al Qaida manifests a sufficient degree of organization to launch effective attacks against a range of military objectives and civilian objects. Although not necessary to trigger IHL, al Qaida exercises some control over territory in parts of Afghanistan, in pockets of the Af-Pak border region, and perhaps even in enclaves within the Arabian Peninsula, although territorial dominion is not really its *modus operandi*. The Security Council has described the situation as a threat to international peace and security[214] and expanded its counterterrorism agenda considerably in response, but—as is customary—it has never declared the existence of an armed conflict *per se*.

As a matter of U.S. law, the conflict originating in Afghanistan has been deemed a NIAC to which at least CA3 applies.[215] In an IAC, military operations can—at a minimum—be carried out throughout the sovereign territory of the parties at war.[216] However, it is unclear how to apply this concept to conflicts and to organized armed groups that are not confined to discrete territory. Thus, the precise temporal span, geographic boundaries, and spatial reach of the NIAC with al Qaida—and concomitantly of IHL—remains uncertain and variable.[217] If the killings of Bin Laden and al-Aulaqi are to be evaluated according to IHL, it is necessary to develop and defend a theory that IHL, and especially its targeting rules, applies to these extra-battlefield events.[218] This requires the extension of IHL to areas well beyond the territory where IHL's predicate requirements of intensity and organization have been met, far from those locations where a "hot" conflict is being waged, and even beyond areas where terrorist attacks are being planned or launched.

Several theories exist for applying IHL to both events. Adopting a territorial perspective reminiscent of the law governing IACs and the concept of neutrality, one can argue that IHL extends to any territory where combat activities between warring parties are under way.[219] Thus, IHL will apply to spillover conflicts that do not respect sovereign boundaries such that "the situation in the neighbouring country [is] immediately qualified as a non-international armed conflict."[220] At the moment, the conflict against al Qaida proper has leaked through the porous borders

214 See *supra* text accompanying note 106.

215 *Hamdan*, 548 U.S. at 628-30. See also *Hamdi v. Rumsfeld*, 542 U.S. 507, 521 (2004) (plurality).

216 The trend in the caselaw has been to extend the reach of IHL in an effort to maximize its protective potential. *Tadić* 1995, supra n. 174, at paras 67–70. This has consequences, however, because where IHL's protections go, so too do its permissions.

217 *Tadić* 1995, *supra* n. 174, at para 69 ("the rules contained in Article 3 also apply outside the narrow geographical context of the actual theatre of combat operations").

218 Aldrich 2002, at p. 893.

219 International Law Association 2010, at p. 32. See Venice Commission, *supra* n. 206, at para 80.

220 Geiß 2009, at p. 138.

of Afghanistan and into the FATA regions of Pakistan, although it is unclear to what extent the U.S. has troops on the ground there. How much farther IHL extends—to Abbottabad (roughly 120 miles from the Afghan border), to the Arabian Peninsula, or even to the U.S. itself—remains open to argumentation. In any case, from a territorial or combat activity perspective, the contention that the armed conflict with al Qaida extended at a minimum to the events in Abbottabad is defensible given the degree of cross-border hostilities already.

An alternative perspective premised on the identity of the parties would provide that so long as IHL has been triggered, it can be deemed to regulate the relationship between adversaries wherever they engage each other, regardless of the location of combat activities *stricto sensu*. By this more expansive, and more controversial, account,[221] IHL essentially follows the warring parties wherever they go,[222] and geographic borders are largely irrelevant to the application of IHL rights and duties.[223] The theater of war is thus non-static and potentially global when dealing with violent groups that are motivated by ideology rather than territorial aspirations or political ambitions and that spurn international borders. Out-of-theater attacks by and on members of an opposition force are thus automatically subject to IHL, regardless of where the predicate conflict is being waged geographically.[224] This approach finds some indirect support in the Geneva Conventions, which envisage the protective aspects of IHL extending anywhere that a protected person is "in the hands of" a party to an IAC.[225] So, in a NIAC, IHL may be deemed to apply any time a state uses forcible measures against a non-state fighter, whether on the state's own territory or extraterritorially and regardless of the proximity to hostilities. Thus, IHL would apply to any confrontation between U.S. forces and an al Qaida member, be it in the Near East or the Eastern Seaboard. A consequence of this approach, however, is an increased threat to civilians who are at risk of becoming "collateral damage" even when far from any battlefield.

In addition to needing a theory of IHL applicability writ large, it is also necessary to show that any use of force has a nexus to the predicate armed conflict. Although hostilities within Pakistan are part of the pre-existing conflict with al

---

[221] Thorp 2011.

[222] Anderson 2010. But in contrast, see Lubell 2010, at p. 255.

[223] President George W. Bush signaled this idea in the immediate aftermath of September 11th when he stated "Our war on terror will be much broader than the battlefields and beachheads of the past. The war will be fought wherever terrorists hide, or run, or plan." President George W. Bush, Radio Address of the President to the Nation (September 29, 2011) available at http://avalon.law.yale.edu/sept11/president_031.asp; see also Schmitt and Mazzetti 2008 (noting secret order issued by then Secretary of Defense Donald Rumsfeld authorizing attacks on Al Qaida members anywhere in the world, even in countries without ongoing hostilities).

[224] Chesney 2011a, b, at pp. 47–49.

[225] See, e.g., Article 19, Convention Relative to the Treatment of Prisoners of War, Aug. 12, 1949, 6 U.S.T. 3316, T.I.A.S. No. 3364 [hereinafter 'Geneva III']; International Law Association 2010, at p. 32.

Qaida, it is more difficult to argue that events in the Arabian Peninsula are connected to this particular conflict given the identity of the parties. Indeed, central to al-Aulaqi's father's lawsuit was that the U.S. was "not at war with Yemen, or within it."[226] Satisfying the requirement that operations in Yemen have a nexus to the larger al Qaida conflict would depend on the relationship between AQAP and al Qaida proper, an inquiry central to satisfying the AUMF as well.[227] In the alternative, it could be argued that IHL was activated by a different, parallel NIAC being waged in Yemen. This conflict pits AQAP against the government of Yemen,[228] with the U.S. occasionally intervening on the side of Yemen, but not a full party to the conflict.[229] The United States' actions would be governed by IHL under these circumstances, although arguably the nexus requirement would dictate that only attacks against unprivileged combatants waging war against Yemen (as opposed to against the U.S.) would be governed by IHL targeting rules.

If the United States' forcible measures in Yemen are not perforce part of the original conflict with al Qaida or part of the internal conflict being waged by Yemen, then a separate IHL trigger analysis is necessary in order to invoke IHL's permissive targeting rules for the al-Aulaqi killing. This would require the existence of an armed conflict between the U.S. and AQAP itself. In terms of the two criteria developed by the ICTY for determining the existence of an armed conflict—the existence of organized groups engaged in hostilities of a sufficient intensity—AQAP is now probably sufficiently coherent to satisfy the first criterion.[230] However, notwithstanding that the U.S. has engaged in a number of drone strikes against terrorist targets in Yemen since 2002, it is doubtful whether the required intensity of violence has been reached for the hostilities between the U.S. and AQAP on their own to have passed through the IHL gateway.[231] If they have, of course, then there would be domestic law implications in light of the War Powers Resolution.[232]

---

[226] *Al-Aulaqi* Complaint, *supra* n. 38, at 2.

[227] *Hamdi*, 542 U.S. at 518.

[228] Gerges 2011.

[229] Terrill 2011; Shane et al. 2010; Farley 2011.

[230] *Limaj*, *supra* n. 192, at para 89 ("This degree [of organization] need not be the same as that required for establishing the responsibility of superiors for the acts of their subordinates within the organization"). *But see Al-Awlaki v. Obama*, No. 10-cv-01469 (D.D.C. Oct. 7, 2010) (Declaration of Prof. Bernard Haykel), available at http://ccrjustice.org/files/Declaration%20of%20Bernard%20Haykel%2010-08-2010.pdf.

[231] Rona 2003, at p. 62.

[232] See Letter from the President Regarding the Consolidated War Powers Report (Dec. 15, 2010), available at http://www.whitehouse.gov/the-press-office/2010/12/15/letter-president-regarding-consolidated-war-powers-report (noting that "consistent with" the War Powers Resolution, the President "has deployed US combat-equipped forces to assist in enhancing counterterrorism capabilities of our friends and allies, including special operations and other forces for sensitive operations in various locations around the world" (but not mentioning Yemen in the unclassified portion of the submission)).

Assuming that IHL applies to these events because this body of law follows warring parties wherever they engage each other with force, the legality of both operations can be established, although it still remains necessary to make several crucial doctrinal leaps to do so. As discussed in the next section, these leaps turn on the fact that the positive law governing NIACs does not fully recognize the concept of combatancy or continuous status-based targeting, which is central to the principle of distinction in, and thus the targeting rules of, IHL.[233]

9.4.2 *Bin Laden and Al-Aulaqi as Lawful Targets*

Combatants engaged in an IAC are considered to be lawful military objectives; as such, they are vulnerable to continuous targeting, notwithstanding their conduct or role at the time they are engaged. There is no duty to endeavor to capture such individuals, unless they offer their surrender. While these permissive rules clearly apply to uniformed members of a state's armed forces, they also apply to officials occupying political positions so long as such individuals play a role within the military's chain of command. Civilians, by contrast, enjoy immunity from direct targeting unless and until they directly participate in hostilities. Individuals who offer indirect assistance to hostilities—by way of financing, training, or inspiration—retain their immunity from direct attack (although they may be prosecuted for their actions). In NIACs, according to APII, members of non-state groups employing military force are civilians directly participating in hostilities subject to conduct-based targeting rather than combatants subject to status-based targeting. States that have engaged in NIACs contest this view. Although the ICRC has accepted the notion that individuals may be targeted on the basis of their undertaking a continuous combat function within an organized armed groups, there is no consensus on whether the notion of combatancy and true status-based targeting exists in NIACs. Because neither Bin Laden nor al-Aulaqi were directly participating in hostilities at the time they were killed, this debate is central to confirming the legality of both operations.

9.4.2.1 The Right to Target Enemy Combatants as Military Objectives

If we are satisfied that IHL applies to these operations at all, the legal analysis goes rather smoothly—to a point.[234] The principle of distinction—foundational to the

[233] The law governing NIACs recognizes no generalized notion of privileged combatancy; as such, there is no requirement that non-state fighters be granted POW status, privileges, or immunities. See Rule 3, Henckaerts and Doswald-Beck 2005 (noting that "combatant status … exists only in international armed conflicts").

[234] In this analysis, it is often necessary to invoke customary international law, because the U.S. has ratified neither Protocol to the Geneva Conventions. Customary international law is also important because most IHL treaty rules—especially those regulating the means and methods of

law of war—dictates that only military objectives may be the target of direct attack.[235] Military objectives are defined, "in so far as objects are concerned" as "those objects which by their nature, location, purpose or use make an effective contribution to military action and whose total or partial destruction, capture or neutralization, in the circumstances ruling at the time, offers a definite military advantage."[236] Although enemy combatants are deemed military objectives under IHL, the text is unclear as to whether such persons are targetable only if their "destruction, capture or neutralization" offers "a definite military advantage."[237] The text implies otherwise by defining only military "objects" with reference to these limitations. Even with such a limitation, it can be argued that there is target engagement authority for all enemy combatants, because their elimination will inexorably offer a military advantage to the other side.[238] Indeed, the sole objective of hostilities is to "weaken the military forces of the enemy."[239]

The principle of distinction also embodies an "inward-looking responsibility:"[240] in exchange for the privilege of engaging in hostilities, combatants must distinguish themselves from the civilian population in order to signal their targetability.[241] Combatants are targetable as such by virtue of their status rather than their conduct.[242] Vulnerability to status-based targeting follows them wherever they go such that they may be attacked even when not directly engaged in hostilities.[243]

NIACs, by definition, involve the participation of non-state organized armed groups whose members are not accorded the status of combatants *per se*.[244] Violations of the principle of distinction are often the hallmark of NIACs, in which rebels and insurrectionists strategically use the civilian population for cover. In so doing, these fighters may exploit the principle of distinction—and the presumption that their opponents will respect it—to compensate for asymmetries in military might. Because these armed groups act independently of any state, their members

(Footnote 234 continued)
warfare—govern IACs, and only extend to NIACs as a matter of customary international law. Henckaerts and Doswald-Beck 2005.

235 Article 48, API. The same rule applies in NIACs governed by APII. Article 13(2), APII. See also Rule 1, Henckaerts and Doswald-Beck 2005, at p. 3.

236 Article 52(2), API. See Rule 8, Henckaerts and Doswald-Beck 2005.

237 Compare Melzer 2008, at pp. 288–290, with Parks 2010, at pp. 803–804.

238 Blum 1976.

239 St. Petersburg Declaration Renouncing the Use, in Time of War, of Explosive Projectiles Under 400 Grammes Weight, Dec. 11, 1868.

240 Gasser 1987, at p. 919.

241 Article 44(3), API.

242 ICRC 2008b, at p. 1005.

243 Parks 2010, at p. 778. See also Corn and Jensen 2008, at p. 812.

244 See *supra* note 233. Although members of armed groups are not considered "combatants" in NIACs, the treaties governing such conflicts do envision the existence of non-state armed groups. See, e.g., CA3(1), Geneva III (referring to "members of armed forces" of all parties to the conflict); APII (referring to "organized armed groups," "dissident armed forces," and "other armed groups.").

do not have the right to participate in hostilities; nor do they enjoy the privileges and immunities that are accorded to members of a state's armed forces, such as POW status or combat immunity.[245] As such, every act of violence committed by members of such militia in the context of an armed conflict is unlawful under the operative domestic law. Participating in an armed conflict without the privilege of doing so, however, does not violate humanitarian law *per se* unless particular acts rise to the level of a punishable war crime.[246]

9.4.2.2 No Express Duty to Capture Combatants

As a matter of established IHL doctrine, there is no express duty to capture privileged combatants in IACs in lieu of killing them[247] in the absence of an unambiguous offer of unconditional surrender.[248] Assuming no risk to civilians or civilian objects, the standard doctrine dictates that the right to kill combatants is only limited by rules prohibiting perfidy and proscribing the use of means and methods that cause *maux superflus*—"unnecessary suffering and superfluous injury."[249] The ability to make combatants the object of attack terminates once a combatant is *hors de combat* through illness, injury, surrender, capture, or other incapacitation.[250]

This categorical principle—that combatants may be targeted at any time regardless of their conduct—developed when troops confronted each other primarily on formal battlefields, far from civilian society. Arguably, it applies in full force to the soldier taking his family to the cinema, subject to the proportionality and precautionary principles. While doctrinally and operationally valid, this principle has rarely been fully tested in such non-theater-of-war contexts and is not without controversy. The weak form of the critique would countenance the killing of combatants only if there is no reasonable chance of apprehension,[251] with some allowance provided for considerations of force protection.[252] Thus, this continuous targeting authority may be lessened by the principle of military necessity where targets pose no threat to opposing forces or where any potential threat can be neutralized through lesser means.[253] The strong form of this revisionism rejects the premise of the "dispensability" of combatants altogether and would require the resort to non-lethal force whenever the military objective can be still be accomplished, even if military effectiveness, efficiency, or force protection may be

245 Baxter 1951.
246 ICRC 2008b, at p. 1045.
247 Parks 1989 and Corn 2009, at p. 29.
248 Article 41(2)(b), API.
249 Article 35(2), API.
250 Article 41(1), API.
251 Pictet 1985, at p. 75.
252 Solis 2010, at p. 538. Kasher and Yadlin 2005, at p. 51.
253 ICRC 2008b, at p. 1041. Lieber 1863, Article 14.

compromised.[254] Neither of these critiques, however, finds full expression in standard doctrine. All that said, there may be tactical, strategic, pragmatic, and moral reasons—including the imperatives of intelligence gathering, public relations, and mercy—for offering to accept the surrender of, or capturing, someone posing a threat rather than killing the person outright.

Although there may be no duty to capture fighters in lieu of killing them, especially in a theater of war, the right to kill the adversary is limited by the duty to accept surrender if genuinely offered.[255] Since ancient times,[256] it has been unlawful to declare *ex ante* that no quarter shall be given,[257] which includes the issuance of orders to not accept surrender.[258] Individuals who offer to surrender are deemed *hors de combat* and enjoy immunity from direct attack. As a general proposition, however, combatants need not be given an opportunity to surrender before they may be engaged. Moreover, a fighting force need not immediately take surrendering fighters into custody if it is not safe to do so; however, such individuals may no longer be the object of attack unless they resume hostilities.[259]

9.4.2.3 Targeting Heads of State, Commanders-in-Chief, and Political Leaders

Military officers, as well as the rank and file, operating on a battlefield within a chain of command are clear military objectives under IHL. By contrast, a blanket authorization to kill political leaders in their capitals, even in a time of armed conflict, may give pause.[260] Indeed, some early international law commentators expressed concern about targeting a sovereign leader outside the field of battle.[261] Many modern commentators still assume that IHL prohibits such acts of assassination. For support, they cite Article 23(b) of the 1907 Hague Regulations, which proscribes "assassination, proscription, or outlawry of an enemy, or putting a price upon an enemy's head, as well as offering a reward for an enemy 'dead or alive.'"[262] This prohibition, however, is now-a-days interpreted to address acts of

[254] Blum 2010.

[255] Feigning surrender constitutes the war crime of perfidy. Article 37(1)(a), API.

[256] Lieber 1863.

[257] Article 23(d), Hague Land Warfare Regulations (1907); Article 40, AP I; Article 4(1), APII. The ICC Statute penalizes declaring that no quarter will be given in NIACs in addition to IACs. Rome Statute of the International Criminal Court, A/CONF.183/9, at Article 8(2)(e)(x). See also Rule 46, Henckaerts and Doswald-Beck 2005, at p. 161; Section (c)(2), War Crimes Act of 1996, 18 U.S.C. § 2441.

[258] Parks 2010, at p. 778.

[259] Dinstein 2004, at p. 202.

[260] Wingfield 1998–1999, at p. 314.

[261] Zengel 1991, at p. 126.

[262] Regulations Respecting the Laws and Customs of War on Land, Article 23, annexed to Convention No. IV Respecting the Laws and Customs of War on Land (Oct. 18, 1907).

treachery or perfidy,[263] and modern IHL contains no specific rules[264] governing the targetability of heads of state or other political individuals *per se*.[265]

Evaluating the legality of attacks on political, rather than military, leaders thus proceeds according to default IHL targeting principles. What ultimately matters is the combat role played by the political leader and the manner and circumstances of the operation. A logical application of the military objective construct suggests that lawful targets would include any political leader (including a Minister of Defense or head of state) within a chain of command who ultimately designs or directs military operations as well as the civilian commander-in-chief of a national army.[266] Nonetheless, the rhetoric surrounding scenarios in which the targeting of heads of state is contemplated suggests lingering discomfort with this conclusion.[267] As a result, *post hoc* attack justifications often focus on the less troubling objective of targeting an army's command and control apparatus, which is often difficult to separate from the leader him- or herself. In light of the principle of distinction, IHL offers little to justify the killing of political leaders whose roles are purely civilian (e.g., a Minister of Education) or who are mere figureheads.

9.4.2.4 Targeting Civilians

Although the principle of distinction provides that civilians normally enjoy full immunity from direct attack, the Protocols provide that civilians can be targeted when and for such time as they take a direct part in hostilities (DPH).[268] These

263 The Department of the Army's Law of Land Warfare makes a distinction between assassination and outlawry on the one hand and a lawful wartime killing on the other. The prohibition against treacherous killing, assassination, and bounties "does not … preclude attacks on individual soldiers or officers of the enemy whether in the zone of hostilities, occupied territory, or elsewhere." *Field Manual 27-10: The Law of Land Warfare*, para 31 (1956), available at http://www.aschq.army.mil/gc/files/fm27-10.pdf; Dinstein 2004, at p. 199.

264 The British law of war manual states this explicitly: "Whether or not the killing of a selected enemy individual is lawful depends on the circumstances of the case. There is no rule dealing specifically with assassination." The Joint Service Manual of the Law of Armed Conflict, JSP 383 (2004), at para 513, available at http://www.mod.uk/NR/rdonlyres/82702E75-9A14-4EF5-B414-49B0D7A27816/0/JSP3832004Edition.pdf.

265 Heads of state are designated as "protected persons" by the Convention on the Prevention and Punishment of Crimes Against Internationally Protected Persons, Including Diplomatic Agents, although this treaty limits protection to when such a person is in a foreign state. Convention on the Prevention and Punishment of Crimes Against Internationally Protected Persons, Including Diplomatic Agents, Dec. 14, 1973, Article 1(1), 28 U.S.T. 1975, T.I.A.S. No. 8532, 1035 U.N.T.S. 167.

266 Solis 2010, at p. 539; Zengel 1991, at p. 148.

267 For example, during Operation Odyssey Dawn, Libyan government officials accused NATO coalition powers of launching "a direct operation to assassinate the leader" of Libya in violation of international law. Fahim and Mazzetti 2011. NATO commander Lt-General Charles Bouchard, however, stated that the intention was not to kill Qaddafi, but rather to immobilize his military apparatus and in particular the command and control nodes in Qaddafi's residence. Romero 2011.

268 Article 51(3), API. Article 13(3), APII.

provisions are premised on the idea that civilians lose their immunity from attack when they behave like combatants. The DPH doctrine applies in both IACs and NIACs.[269] That said, in today's armed conflicts, it is most salient in the NIAC context in which armed non-state actors are not considered "combatants" even when they do battle with governmental authorities or each other. The Protocols thus consider militants linked to non-state groups to be civilians who are targetable only when directly participating in hostilities.[270]

The ICRC Interpretive Guidance has set forth a three-part test for determining when an individual can be considered to be directly participating in hostilities.[271] This includes consideration of the threshold of harm posed by his or her actions, the causal link between his or her actions and potential harm to the opponent, and a nexus to hostilities.[272] Under this framework, it is not enough to contribute to the war-fighting capabilities of an armed group; rather, the potential target must be in a position to bring about the harm in question in "one causal step."[273] In this way, the DPH construct offers a conduct-based, rather than status-based, targeting doctrine.

Persons posing an immediate danger, such as an insurrectionist sniper or someone laying an improvised explosive device (IED), or persons providing direct assistance to such endeavors, easily satisfy the three-step DPH test.[274] The ICRC also accepts that direct participation in hostilities includes more than involvement in the physical attack itself; rather, a penumbra of preparatory and concluding activities may also qualify so long as the proximate causality criterion is met. By contrast, the test would tend to exclude from targetability persons planning a belligerent act, recruiting others to participate in such an act, financing violence, formulating ideology, or engaging in strategic decision-making about hostile activities.[275] That said, most thinking in this area has been in the nature of the hypothetical, so there is little positive law to draw on.

One jurisprudential source is the Israeli Supreme Court's opinion in the so-called *Targeted Killing* opinion. Here, the Court was asked to consider the Israeli policy in the context of an occupation and IAC and in the absence of concrete facts.[276] Rather than reaching a blanket conclusion, the Court mandated a

---

[269] ICRC 2008b, at p. 1015. CA3 makes no mention of DPH, but it does prohibit the commission of violence to life and person against "persons taking no active part in the hostilities." Presumably, if a conduct-of-hostilities rule applies in conflicts meeting the stricter requirements of APII, it also applies in CA3 conflicts. Article 1(1), APII.

[270] *Pub. Comm. Against Torture*, *supra* n. 205, at para 31. See also Henckaerts and Doswald-Beck 2005, at pp. 12–13. See also *Pub. Committee Ag. Torture*, Opinion of Rivlin, *supra* n. 205, at para 2.

[271] See ICRC 2008b, at p. 991; see also Melzer 2008, and Watkin 2010, at pp. 643–644.

[272] ICRC 2008b, at p. 1016.

[273] ICRC 2008b, at p. 1021.

[274] ICRC 2008b, at pp. 1017–1018. War-sustaining activities do not generally qualify. *Id.* at p. 1020.

[275] Kasher and Yadlin 2005, at p. 48. See also *Pub. Committee Ag. Torture*, *supra* n. 205, at paras 33, 35; Fleck (1995), at p. 232.

[276] *Pub. Committee Ag. Torture*, *supra* n. 205, at para 2. See also, Melzer 2008, at p. 5.

case-by-case approach.[277] Nonetheless, it signaled that it would find that "a person who aids the unlawful combatants by general strategic analysis, and grants them logistical, general support, including monetary aid" is taking only an *indirect* part in hostilities.[278] Likewise, an individual engaged in creating or distributing propaganda would not be targetable under this view.[279] The Court considers the person deploying others to take a direct part in hostilities or otherwise planning operations, however, to be lawfully subject to direct attack.[280] This latter conclusion is contestable as it reads "direct" more broadly than would the ICRC, which considers the generalized recruitment and training of fighters to be "indirect" participation because of a lack of an immediate causal link between the conduct and harm to the enemy.[281] According to the ICRC, in cases of doubt, the potential target must be presumed to be a civilian who is immune from direct attack.[282] The Israeli Supreme Court, by contrast, seems to flip this presumption in order to encourage civilians to avoid hostilities in order to protect them.[283]

The treaty language governing the DPH doctrine suggests that civilians are targetable only "for such time as" they are directly participating in hostilities.[284] This implies that the concept governs targeting decisions by state actors based on observing the commission of hostile acts *in flagrante* rather than on exterior manifestations of combatant status, such as a uniform or fixed distinctive sign. Armed forces are expected to internalize and employ the test to respond to targets of opportunity on the basis of incomplete information in an operational environment. The DPH doctrine also provides a criminal defense in the context of a prosecution for the unlawful killing of a civilian.[285] In light of its complexity, the multi-factor DPH test is perhaps more amenable to such an *ex post* application than to *ex ante* targeting decisions that may require virtually instantaneous decision-making. This temporal limitation also raises the specter of a revolving door, whereby individuals regain civilian status—which accords protection against direct attack—every time they suspend their participation in hostilities. As a result

[277] *Pub. Committee Ag. Torture*, *supra* n. 205, at para 60.

[278] *Pub. Committee Ag. Torture*, *supra* n. 205, at para 35. See also ICRC 2008b, at pp. 1020–1021.

[279] *Pub. Committee Ag. Torture*, *supra* n. 205, at para 35. See also ICRC 2008b, at p. 1020.

[280] *Pub. Committee Ag. Torture*, *supra* n. 205, at para 37.

[281] ICRC 2008b, at p. 1022. Training for a specific mission, however, is considered sufficiently direct to remove civilian immunity. *Id.*

[282] ICRC 2008b, at p. 1037. The treaties create a presumption of civilian status. Article 50(1), API. They do not, however, create a presumption that a civilian is not directly participating in hostilities. See Boothby 2010, at p. 766.

[283] See also Schmitt 2004, at pp. 505 and 509.

[284] ICRC 2008b, at p. 1034.

[285] ICTY, *Prosecutor v. Strugar*, Judgment of Appeals Chamber, Case No. IT-01-42-A, 17 July 2008, at paras 164–186.

of this textual limitation, unprivileged combatants in NIACs are able to evade direct attack more easily than are privileged combatants in IACs.[286]

To respond to the operational realities of NIACs and pressure from states seeking greater targeting authority vis-à-vis the members of organized armed groups engaged in NIACs, the ICRC proposed the "continuous combat function" concept, which envisions a notion of quasi-combatancy in NIACs[287] and a concomitant function-based (rather than merely conduct-based) targeting doctrine.[288] As the theory goes, when an individual's participation in hostilities is not "spontaneous, sporadic, or unorganized" but rather continuous, he or she may be deemed to be a member of an organized armed group belonging to a party to the conflict.[289] Individuals who take up such a continuous combat function within an organized armed group lose their civilian status "for so long as they assume their continuous combat function."[290] As such, so long as such individuals carry out a combat function, they may be targeted at any time, even when not directly participating in hostilities.[291] It is only once individuals disengage from the group or cease to perform a continuous combat function—however defined—that they regain their civilian status and their immunity from direct attack (but not from prosecution for war crimes or their acts of belligerency that violate domestic law).[292]

This concept hinges on what constitutes a "combat function." Logically, this could apply to those individuals who do not participate directly in tactical combat activities in the sense of regularly discharging weapons. Thus, it would encompass individuals who organize, equip, provide intelligence for, or otherwise direct the hostile activities of subordinates and collaborators on a continuous basis.[293] From this point, it may be difficult to draw the line to exclude those who, on a continuous basis, inspire and fund hostile activities in a collective operation; these activities, however, are not uniformly accepted as "combat functions."[294] In any case, within the continuous combat function framework, it is crucial to develop reliable, objectively verifiable, and current intelligence of a potential target's conduct and role because that individual will be targetable at any time or place by virtue of his

---

[286] *Pub. Committee Ag. Torture*, Opinion of Rivlin, *supra* n. 205, at para 2. Henckaerts and Doswald-Beck 2005, at p. 21 (noting imbalance in the law). Scholars have also criticized the ICRC's "narrow" interpretation of direct participation, particularly when it comes to preparation, deployment, and return. See Boothby 2010.

[287] Chesney notes that the three elements of combatancy are "disaggregated" in NIACs. Chesney 2011a, b, at 41.

[288] ICRC 2008b, at p. 995.

[289] *Pub. Committee Ag. Torture*, *supra* n. 205, at para 39.

[290] ICRC 2008b, at pp. 996, 1036.

[291] Solis 2010, at p. 544.

[292] ICRC 2008b, at pp. 996 and 1045. Relevant crimes include treason, perfidy, and murder as well as the full panoply of war crimes.

[293] Solis 2010, at p. 546.

[294] See Watkin 2010, at pp. 57, 660; but see Melzer 2008, at pp. 320–321.

or her function rather than contemporaneous conduct.[295] The strength of this evidence will be debated *ex ante* when target lists are drawn up; it may also be tested—in accordance with penal burdens of proof—in the event of a criminal prosecution for potential breaches of the principle of distinction.

The ICRC has also proposed additional restraints on the right of a state to target unprivileged combatants who are directly participating in hostilities, or who assume a continuous combat function in an organized armed group, that derive from the principles of military necessity and humanity.[296] These principles prohibit "the infliction of suffering, injury or destruction not actually necessary for the accomplishment of legitimate military purposes."[297] The ICRC notes that in certain circumstances—especially in NIACs in which the national force exercises plenary or at least partial control over territory—these limitations may require the capture of, or the offering of surrender to, a civilian directly participating in hostilities, rather than his or her outright killing.[298] In this way, the ICRC would accord civilians who are directly participating or assuming a continuous combat function in hostilities a measure of protection that is not accorded to privileged combatants in an IAC. This position finds resonance in the Israeli decision, which held that a civilian taking a direct part in hostilities "cannot be attacked at such time as he is doing so, if a less harmful means can be employed."[299] The Court traced this sequential least-injurious-means approach to a general principle of proportionality found in Israeli domestic law (and perhaps also to the state of occupation), rather than to IHL *stricto sensu*.[300]

The ICRC's guidance has not been universally accepted. In particular, the ICRC has been criticized by some governments and academics for aligning members of organized armed forces closer to civilians than to regular state armed forces and for unreasonably circumscribing the targetability of those who join organized armed groups.[301] In particular, the continuous combat function construct disallows the direct targeting of individuals who undertake many non-combat support functions that are regularly performed by uniformed service members and that are integral to a fighting force, but that are not combat functions *per se*.[302] The counter-argument is that civilians who join an organized armed group unaffiliated with a state should be equally as targetable as privileged combatants engaged in an IAC, regardless of their assumption of a combat versus support function. Indeed,

---

295 ICRC 2008b, at p. 1008. See also *Pub. Committee Ag. Torture*, *supra* n. 205, at para 40.

296 ICRC 2008b, at p. 996.

297 ICRC 2008b, at p. 1042. The ICRC Study distinguishes such situations from IACs involving well-equipped armed forces where there are no restrictions on "the use of force against legitimate military targets beyond what is already required by specific provisions of IHL." *Id.* at p. 1043.

298 ICRC 2008b, at p. 1043. See also *Pub. Committee Ag. Torture*, *supra* n. 205, at para 40; Melzer 2008, at p. 108.

299 *Pub. Committee Ag. Torture*, *supra* n. 205, at para 40.

300 Ibid.

301 Watkin 2010, at p. 686; Boothby 2010, at p. 758.

302 Watkin 2010, at pp. 672–673.

there is state practice in NIACs asserting a continuous targeting authority that does not hinge upon a showing that the individual was participating in hostilities or even engaged in a continuous combat function but rather that the target was a member of an organized armed group that is engaged in hostilities.[303] In addition, the continuous combat function concept unrealistically assumes that militants occupy a permanent functional role in any fighting force, which may not be the case with non-state groups whose members may occupy roles that are more fluid than in a national army.[304] There is also objection to the purported obligation to employ least injurious means in NIACs on the ground that militants should be targetable regardless of whether capture is possible, as is the rule in IACs. This latter criticism hinges in part on the fact that it is difficult to come up with defensible reasons to limit the proposed sequential approach to NIACs and to unprivileged belligerents.[305] Such limitations, whether applicable in NIACs or IACs, would constrain the use of lethal force in ways that the dissenters are unwilling to countenance. These perceived problems with the ICRC's guidance gave rise to intense controversy and caused several of the experts involved to recuse themselves from mention in the final report.[306]

9.4.2.5 The Events in Question

Turning to the events at issue, al Qaida has manifested an enduring intention to engage in hostilities against the U.S. and other states. Determining the targetability of particular members of al Qaida within the IHL targeting schema and the ICRC's DPH guidance nonetheless raises a number of ambiguities. Al Qaida has been characterized as a loosely-organized and internationally-dispersed organization whose subunits share an overarching ideology, but enjoy a high degree of autonomy in terms of tactics and objectives.[307] Perhaps by design, individual units may not meet the criteria employed in IHL for an organized armed group, which assume such groups are objectively identifiable and sufficiently organized to launch military operations of a particular intensity and duration. It is unclear to what extent al Qaida cells operating outside of Afghanistan take orders from any central authority in the sense of their being a "terrorism franchise."[308]

Not surprisingly, the U.S. took the position that both individuals were military objectives, equated to enemy commanders in the field. In statements following their deaths, U.S. spokespersons stressed the two men's continuing or growing (in the case of al-Aulaqi) operational roles.[309] If al Qaida satisfies the organized armed

303 Chesney 2011a, b, at p. 41.
304 Boothby 2010, at p. 754.
305 Parks 2010, at p. 797 n. 82.
306 Parks 2010, at pp. 784–785.
307 Hoffman 2006, at pp. 285–288.
308 Paulus and Vashakmadze 2009, at p. 119.
309 Williams 2011.

group criterion, Bin Laden—separate and apart from his command and control apparatus—as the head of an organized armed group involved in the conflict can be conceptualized as a lawful military objective. Of course, it is fair to query whether he still exercised any operational leadership at the time he was killed. In the alternative, his role may have become purely symbolic or ceremonial, especially given the apparent decentralization and compartmentalization of al Qaida and Bin Laden's relative isolation in Pakistan.[310] Likewise, al-Aulaqi has been described as a propagandist and media personality rather than a tactician. An argument could thus be made that both Bin Laden and al-Aulaqi were akin to political leaders, rather than military personnel, which would place them in the grey area surrounding the right to target civilian leaders. This may be a distinction without a difference when it comes to terrorist groups. Although "many of the world's most sophisticated non-state warring parties have distinct political and military wings,"[311] in terrorist groups, there may be little division between the political and military leadership.[312]

None of the reports of the incidents reveals evidence that either individual was directly participating in hostilities at the time he was killed; hence the importance of the continuing combat function concept for legalizing both attacks. That concept provides cover, however, only if both men in fact occupied *combat* roles on a continuous basis, which might be more difficult to prove if the two men were ideologues or financiers. These distinctions lose their force if continuous targeting authority exists vis-à-vis members of organized armed groups in NIACs on the basis of mere membership alone, as contended by many states. By this approach, both men were fully assimilated to combatants engaged in an IAC for targeting purposes who could be engaged at any time based on their status rather than their conduct or functional role without running afoul of the principle of distinction.

In terms of the United States' adherence to IHL proportionality in Operation Neptune Spear, collateral damage was minimal, especially when assessed against the high value of the target.[313] The raid resulted in the death or injury of two colorable civilians (excluding the courier and Bin Laden's son). This is an impressive result in light of the fact that upwards of thirty people, including potentially thirteen children, were thought to have been present or residing in the compound.[314] Apparently, there was some dissension among President Obama's inner national security circle about how to respond to the intelligence of Bin Laden's whereabouts. It has been reported that President Obama ultimately "vetoed a plan to obliterate the compound with an airstrike."[315] One concern with this plan was that Bin Laden's presence in the compound may have been impossible to verify. Given Bin Laden's residence in a

---

310 Mazzetti 2011; Schmidle 2011.

311 Mahnad 2011.

312 Kasher and Yadlin 2005, at p. 55.

313 Koh 2011.

314 Gall 2011; see also WorldWatch 2011.

315 Drogin et al. 2011.

civilian neighborhood, the risk of collateral damage would also no doubt have been higher with an air strike than a ground raid. That said, IHL tolerates a higher degree of collateral damage with high value targets.

Because accomplished face-to-face, the Bin Laden operation does not raise many of the concerns inherent to the use of RPVs as in the al-Aulaqi operation.[316] The use of drones in modern warfare has raised discomfort on a number of grounds, including the lack of reciprocity of risk, the concern that their use stems from an excessive preoccupation with force protection,[317] the inability to precisely calibrate the level of force employed, and the fact that their use precludes the ability to capture suspects or to accept their surrender[318] (which, of course, is true of all aerial attacks).[319] From a *jus in bello* perspective, there is nothing about using continuous surveillance and precision-guided missiles *per se* that runs afoul of the principle of proportionality so long as the object of the attack is a lawful one and precautions against incidental harm are implemented. Indeed, we might ultimately prefer a decapitation strike in which key individuals are targeted with precision, after detailed pattern-of-life analyses, rather than eliminated in large-scale clashes between armed forces or following airstrikes using heavier munitions.[320] In terms of collateral damage, there appears to have been no prior knowledge that Samir Khan, the other American citizen killed, was in the vehicle with al-Aulaqi that day.[321] Without an expressly operational role, it is unclear if Khan himself would have been considered a military objective. According to reports, he too played a central role in al Qaida's propaganda machine, but whether such machinery is a military objective remains controversial.[322] We have little insight into the identities of the other individuals in the car that day, although one of the dead may have been Ibrahim Hassan al-Asiri, an alleged bomb maker.[323]

Even if Bin Laden is a legitimate military objective, his death could still constitute a war crime if he was *hors de combat* (i.e., if he was surrendering, sick, or injured so as to pose no further threat) or killed treacherously or perfidiously (i.e., if he could have reasonably thought the SEALs were civilians). Accounts do not bear these scenarios out,[324] but we may never know for sure whether a genuine surrender was offered. Even if the attack was lawfully executed by the immediate actors, a war crime could have been committed by their superiors in the event that an order to take

---

316 Bergen and Tiedemann 2011; c.f. Alston 2011, at pp. 35–36.

317 Kahn 2002.

318 There are reports of soldiers attempting to surrender to drones. Shelsby 1991.

319 Alston 2011, at p. 31. This is, of course, unlikely given the remote-control nature of drone strikes and the asymmetries of power between the US and other involved states.

320 See, e.g., Gross 2011.

321 The U.S. government eventually offered its "condolences" to the family of Khan. Funk 2011.

322 In the Final Report to the Prosecutor by the Committee Established to Review the NATO Bombing Campaign Against the Federal Republic of Yugoslavia (2000), available at http://icty.org/x/file/Press/nato061300.pdf, at p. 74.

323 Mazzetti 2011.

324 But see The Telegraph 2011.

no prisoners was issued. The Administration insists, however, that contingency plans were in place for the team to accept Bin Laden's surrender if it was offered, implying that there was no order to take no quarter. A spokesperson stated:

> The team had the authority to kill Osama bin Laden unless he offered to surrender; in which case the team was required to accept his surrender if the team could do so safely. … Consistent with the laws of war, bin Laden's surrender would have been accepted if feasible.[325]

Even if surrender was offered, it may not have been safe for the SEAL team to immediately take Bin Laden into custody given the presence of weapons and other threatening individuals in the compound. That said, so long as he did not take up arms or attempt to flee, Bin Laden had he surrendered would have remained immune from direct attack until the hostile situation was defused. One final lingering objection to the way in which the operation was implemented concerns the two shots fired at Bin Laden. This invokes the controversial phenomenon of "double-tapping," which involves using a second shot to "finish off" a combatant who has been fully disabled by a first shot.[326]

In evaluating the legality of these operations, it is not enough to examine the status of the target; the status of the attacker may also be relevant. Navy SEALs—who would be deemed privileged combatants in an IAC—carried out the Bin Laden operation. By contrast, the drone program in Yemen is run largely by civilians in the CIA's Counterterrorism Center, thus signaling the evolution of the intelligence agency into a paramilitary force.[327] This actuality raises the question of whether these state actors are entitled to engage in hostilities under IHL. If members of the CIA involved in such an operation in an IAC were to be captured or extradited by the territorial or nationality state, they may not be entitled to assert the defense of combatant immunity, even if the operation were conducted lawfully under the law of war.[328] According to the Special Rapporteur on Extrajudicial Killings, Summary or Arbitrary Executions:

> [I]ntelligence personnel do not have immunity from prosecution under domestic law for their conduct. They are thus unlike State armed forces which would generally be immune from prosecution for the same conduct (assuming they complied with IHL requirements). Thus, CIA personnel could be prosecuted for murder under the domestic law of any country in which they conduct targeted drone killings, and could also be prosecuted for violations of applicable US law.[329]

---

325 White house Press Secretary 2011. See also Koh 2011 and Brennan 2011 for similar remarks. But c.f. Schmidle 2011 (quoting one of the team members indicating that there was no intention to capture Bin Laden: "'There was never any question of detaining or capturing him—it wasn't a split-second decision. No one wanted detainees.'").

326 Simpson 2006.

327 Alston 2011.

328 Davis 2011.

329 Alston Report, *supra* n. 184, at para 71. This ambiguity of status has given rise to the practice of double-hatting. Alston 2011, at p. 7. See also Feickert and Livingston 2010 (noting the increased fluidity between the CIA and Special Forces in terms of intelligence gathering and the use of kinetic force).

The ICRC's study of customary IHL takes a pragmatic approach to the question of the involvement of law enforcement and intelligence personnel in hostilities: "[w]hen these units take part in hostilities and fulfil the criteria of armed forces, they are considered combatants."[330] The incorporation of armed law enforcement agencies into the armed forces is normally accomplished through a formal legislative act.[331] Likewise, the ICC Statute reflects the diversity of state actors who may engage in hostilities by discussing armed conflicts involving "governmental authorities" rather than designating such participants as members of the "armed forces" *stricto sensu*.[332]

As a matter of established doctrine, combat immunity is a feature of the law governing IACs that protects privileged combatants from prosecution for lawful acts of war by another state. It does not exist as a formal matter in the law governing NIACs, where rebels and other non-state fighters are not privileged to use force and can be prosecuted for any acts of violence they commit or even for mere participation in an insurrection if domestic law penalizes such conduct.[333] This asymmetry stems from the fact that NIACs historically occurred on the territory of a single state, as in the classic civil war scenario, such that there was little risk that the state's own armed forces would be prosecuted for lawful acts of war. It bears consideration, however, of whether a doctrine of combat immunity should be developed to protect privileged combatants from being prosecuted for lawful acts of war committed in an extraterritorial NIAC. As it stands, international law would not constrain either Pakistan or Yemen from prosecuting a U.S. soldier or member of the CIA for committing a violent act on their territory.

9.4.3 Conclusion: Jus in Bello

The contention that both Bin Laden and al-Aulaqi were lawful military objectives subject to continuous targeting authority on the basis of their status, as opposed to their activities at the moment of their deathes, emerges as a central justification for both operations. A priori, this position requires a theory for the applicability of IHL to the events in question. If IHL follows our protagonists wherever they engage with each other—as opposed to applying only to territory where combat activities regularly occur—then IHL offers support for these operations. Legal certainty in the Yemen context requires a theory for why the conflict with AQAP is either part of the conflict against al Qaida writ large or triggers IHL on its own or in connection with some other armed conflict being waged on the Arabian Peninsula. The conclusion of legality also requires, at a minimum, acceptance of the ICRC's continuous combat

330 Henckaerts and Doswald-Beck 2005, at p. 17.

331 ICRC 2008a, at p. 1011 n. 71.

332 Zimmerman 1999, at p. 286.

333 Henckaerts and Doswald-Beck 2005, at pp. 11 and 384.

function concept, with a rejection of the least-injurious-means limitation that the ICRC proposes on such targeting authority. If the two men did not occupy a combat role, however, then a more robust targeting authority is required premised exclusively on their membership in an organized armed group.

All this analysis presumes the applicability of IHL. Outside of this framework, these events become more suspect given non-derogable prohibitions against summary execution[334] set forth in many human rights instruments, not to mention prohibitions against murder and assassination under relevant domestic law and the constitutional imperative of due process. The applicability of these latter bodies of law depends, in part, on complex and contested questions of choice of law and extraterritoriality. Indeed, even if IHL is applicable, it is not entirely settled that these other legal regimes do not also apply in parallel. There are conflicting views on whether IHL as the *lex specialis*, within the meaning of the adage *lex specialis derogate legi generali* ("the special rule overrides the general law"),[335] fully displaces or merely qualifies other otherwise applicable bodies of international law, such as human rights law, in a state of armed conflict. The next Section explores this choice of law dilemma.

9.5 Alternative Bodies of Law

All of the foregoing analysis assumes that IHL is the right framework from which to evaluate the two operations. If IHL is not applicable at all, then other bodies of law rise to the fore, including U.S. domestic law and international human rights law (IHRL) (presuming their extraterritorial application) alongside the *lex fori*, Pakistani and Yemeni domestic law.[336] Even if IHL has been triggered and regulates these events, IHRL may still apply in parallel as a source of rules to fill gaps in IHL, to interpret undefined or imprecise concepts in IHL, or even to mitigate certain more permissive aspects of IHL.[337] IHRL may be particularly relevant in regulating the conduct of states engaged in NIACs, where rules are less developed as compared to IACs. Likewise, elements of the relevant domestic law will continue to regulate aspects of these events in parallel with these bodies of international law. This Section will focus primarily on the international choice of law question, but will identify points of intersection and tension between international

[334] Alston Report, *supra* n. 184, at p. 9.

[335] See, e.g., International Law Commission, Conclusions of the Work of the Study Group on the Fragmentation of International Law: Difficulties Arising from the Diversification and Expansion of International Law, *available at*: http://untreaty.un.org/ilc/texts/instruments/english/draft%20articles/1_9_2006.pdf [hereinafter 'Fragmentation Study'], at 2(5).

[336] In any case, the existence of an armed conflict does not mean that every law enforcement exercise is governed by IHL; a nexus to the conflict is required. Geiß 2009, at p. 141.

[337] Melzer 2008, at p. 176.

and domestic law. Taken as a whole, this inquiry reveals the existence of overlapping regimes without clear rules on resolving conflicts of law that arise.

9.5.1 International Human Rights

Starting with human rights law, even if IHL does apply to these events, it is not entirely clear that IHRL is silent.[338] This query invokes the vexing issue in contemporary international law of how to resolve the normative tensions that exist at the intersection of these two bodies of law. Many theories have been espoused in the literature and jurisprudence to resolve potential conflicts of law that may arise at this interface. The first theory is one of *lex specialis*, which comes in a strong and a weak form.[339] The strong form envisions a total displacement of IHRL upon the commencement of armed conflict.[340] By this view, humanitarian law and human rights law are self-contained, mutually exclusive regimes. Where IHL does not speak to a situation, actors are free to choose a course of action, unfettered by legal rules drawn from elsewhere.[341] Gaps in the law are deemed purposeful in a sense such that they should not be filled from other sources.

The weak form of the *lex specialis* theory does not envision the total displacement of international human rights norms in armed conflict situations except where the rules of IHL and IHRL are in direct contradiction. Where the applicable rules are not directly opposed to each other, this approach would dictate that the two bodies of law should be harmonized[342] through interpretive techniques[343] and formal declarations of derogation.[344] As such, where there are gaps in IHL, there may be other rules—including human rights norms and domestic law—that are applicable.[345] Human rights law can thus be employed as an interpretive aid to add content to undefined terms in IHL, such as "judicial guarantees" and "humane

---

338 ICRC 2008b, at p. 993.

339 *Coard* et al. *v. U.S.*, Case 10.951, Inter-Am. C.H.R., Rep. No. 109/00, para 42 (1999); Watkin 2004, at pp. 2–9.

340 Greenwood 2008, at p. 39.

341 Parks 2010, at p. 806.

342 U.N. Human Rights Committee, General Comment No. 31 on the Nature of the General Legal Obligation Imposed on States Parties to the Covenant, adopted March 29, 2004, CCPR/C/21/Rev.1/Add.13 (May 26, 2004), para 11; *Legal Consequences*, *supra* n. 104, at para 106. Greenwood 2008, at p. 40; Lubell 2010, at pp. 193–235.

343 See Fragmentation Study, *supra* n. 335, at para 4.

344 Article 4 of the ICCPR, for example, allows for states to derogate from certain of its provisions in times of national emergency. See Human Rights Committee, General Comment No. 29 of 31 August 2001 (States of Emergency), CCPR/C/21/Rev.1/Add.1, available at http://www.unhchr.ch/tbs/doc.nsf/(Symbol)/71eba4be3974b4f7c1256ae200517361?Opendocument.

345 *Nuclear Weapons*, *supra* n. 129, at para 26; *Legal Consequences*, *supra* n. 104, at para 106.

treatment," or to expound upon treaty obligations, as in situations of occupation when the occupying state exercises plenary power over territory.[346] In a recent submission to the Human Rights Committee, the U.S. acknowledged that IHL and IHRL are "complementary and mutually reinforcing."[347] This is a departure from prior statements that adopted a more robust *lex specialis* position.[348]

While many adherents to a *lex specialis* approach consider human rights to be an invasive species vis-à-vis IHL, it cannot be gainsaid that positive IHL invites in these very norms. Thus, many IHL treaties create space for a consideration of, or even interlineations with, human rights norms and concerns. The Martens Clause is the precursor to this phenomenon,[349] and Articles 72 and 75 of API are more modern and fulsome manifestations of this tendency. These textual portals go far toward debunking the *lex specialis maximus* approach to the humanitarian law/human rights interface. By the same measure, there are IHRL treaties that specifically make allowances for situations governed by IHL. The European Convention on Human Rights, for example, specifically exempts from censure "deaths resulting from lawful acts of war."[350] This formulation necessarily imports elements of IHL into the human rights analysis such that in a situation of armed conflict, IHL defines what constitutes an "extrajudicial" killing.

A third approach to managing this interface rejects the idea of *lex specialis* and of a hierarchy of rules altogether. Instead, it presumes that the most appropriate rule or body of law should be applied in any particular scenario to promote "systemic integration."[351] This may result in a sliding scale between the two bodies of law depending on the circumstances. So, activities on the battlefield or in an active theater of hostilities may be governed almost exclusively by IHL, but human rights law may have more to say vis-à-vis detention practices in light of its detailed rules on conditions of confinement and judicial protections. Thus, the applicability of IHL is not necessarily binary, in the sense that the corpus of IHL either applies in its entirety to an incident, territory, or individual, or not at all. Finally, one can envision a reverse *lex specialis* prioritization, whereby international human rights norms temper elements of classic IHL. This may be due to the fact that many human rights norms constitute later in time legal

[346] *Armed Activities*, *supra* n. 83, at para 178.

[347] Fourth Periodic Report of the United States of American to the United Nations Committee on Human Rights Concerning the International Covenant on Civil and Political Rights (Dec. 20, 2011), para 507, available at http://www.state.gov/g/drl/rls/179781.htm [hereinafter 'Fourth Periodic Report'].

[348] See Inter-American Commission on Human Rights, Response of the US to Request for Precautionary Measures—Detainees in Guantánamo Bay (April 15, 2002), available at http://www.derechos.org/nizkor/excep/usresp1.html.

[349] Article 1(2), API.

[350] Article 15(2), Convention for the Protection of Human Rights and Fundamental Freedoms, November 4, 1950, 213 U.N.T.S. 221, 222.

[351] Fragmentation Study, *supra* n. 335, at para 17.

pronouncements.[352] Or, it may be by virtue of human rights rules' strong normative force.[353] This latter approach might demand the additive application of applicable rules to ensure maximum protection to the individual.[354]

Most courts and commentators have adopted a harmonizing approach to this question. The ICJ, for example, stated that IHL as the *lex specialis* would determine whether a particular killing was "arbitrary":

> The test of what is arbitrary deprivation of life, however, ... falls to be determined by the applicable *lex specialis*, namely, the law applicable in armed conflict is which designed to regulate the conduct of hostilities. Thus whether a particular loss of life ... is to be considered an arbitrary deprivation of life contrary to Article 6 of the Covenant [on Civil and Political Rights], can only be decided by reference to the law applicable in armed conflict and not deduced from the terms of the Covenant itself.[355]

Even the former Special Rapporteur on Extrajudicial Killing, Summary on Arbitrary Executions conceded that targeted killing can be lawful in the context of IHL: "[A]though in most circumstances targeted killings violate the right to life, in the exceptional circumstances of armed conflict, they may be legal."[356] This conclusion reveals the importance of the antecedent question of the applicability of IHL and the existence of a predicate armed conflict.

Resolving the conflict of law question is not the only impediment to applying human rights norms to these events. In many of today's conflict situations—especially transnational conflicts involving the U.S.—theories for the pertinence of human rights law also presume the extraterritorial application of states' IHR obligations.[357] This remains contested, especially by the U.S., which until recently could have been described as a persistent objector to the proposition that such extraterritorial obligations exist. This position, however, is increasingly out of step with the caselaw.[358] At a minimum, the current state of the law would dictate that human rights norms apply wherever a state exercises *de facto* control over territory (including in the sense of undertaking governmental functions)[359] or

---

352 Fragmentation Study, *supra* n. 335, at para 24.

353 Fragmentation Study, *supra* n. 335, at paras 31–32 (discussing *jus cogens* and other fundamental norms expressing "elementary considerations of humanity").

354 Schabas 2007, at p. 593.

355 *Nuclear Weapons*, *supra* n. 129, at para 25. See also *Legal Consequences*, *supra* n. 104, at para 106, *Armed Activities*, *supra* n. 83, at para 216 (noting that human rights protections continue to apply in armed conflicts).

356 Alston 2011, at p. 12.

357 General Comment 31, *supra* n. 342, at para 10.

358 U.N. Hum. Rts. Comm., *Consideration of Reports Submitted by States Parties Under Article 40 of the Covenant, Comments of the Human Rights Committee: United States of America*, CCPR/C/79/Add 50 (1995), available at http://www1.umn.edu/humanrts/hrcommittee/US-ADD1.htm, at para 19. But see Fourth Periodic Report, *supra* n. 347 (softening stance).

359 *Al Skeini & Others v. United Kingdom*, Judgment of 7 July 2011, No.55721/07 ECHR 2011, at para 141.

individuals.[360] An argument could be made that Bin Laden was in—or could easily have been brought into—the effective control of the SEAL team. It is more difficult to argue that al-Aulaqi was within the effective control of the U.S. since he was killed from a distance, without actually being physically in the hands of state agents.[361] If this distinction is valid, state responsibility under IHRL could turn on the way in which an individual was killed, rather than the question of whether state exercised control over the individual's life. Any requirement of physical custody for showing effective control, however, offers a perverse loophole for states to avoid their human rights violations by operating remotely.[362]

Turning to the content of IHRL, most human rights instruments contain a broad articulation of the right to life,[363] although some treaties qualify the formulation of this right by prohibiting only the "arbitrary" deprivation of life.[364] Furthermore, this right is considered non-derogable except when a sovereign employs deadly force in situations of self-defense, to otherwise protect life, or to prevent the escape of a dangerous suspect.[365] State actors can thus employ deadly force in law enforcement actions only when the target poses an immediate danger to the arresting officer.[366] The European Court of Human Rights has mandated a strict test of necessity be employed to determine if lethal force is warranted; there must also be proportionality between the state's response and the perceived threat, and alternatives to lethal force must be considered.[367] Generally, law enforcement personnel are expected to offer warnings and attempt apprehension before resorting to deadly force.[368]

---

[360] *Ocalan v. Turkey*, Judgment of 12 May 2005, No. 46221/99 ECHR 2005 at para 91 (finding that applicant was under the effective authority of Turkey, thus within the "jurisdiction" of the state within the meaning of the Convention). See also *Boumediene v. Bush,* 553 U.S. 723 (2008).

[361] *Bankovic & others v. Belgium & others*, Judgment of 19 December 2001, No. 52207/99 ECHR.

[362] *Alejandre v. Cuba* ("Brothers to the Rescue"), Case 11.589, Report No. 86/99, OEA/Ser.L/V/II.106, Doc. 3 rev. at 586 (1999) at paras 25, 53 (holding that victims were within the "authority and control" of Cuba when they were shot down by a military aircraft in international airspace).

[363] See, e.g., Article 3, Universal Declaration of Human Rights, G.A. Res. 217A (Dec. 10, 1948); Article 6, International Covenant on Civil and Political Rights, G.A. Res 2200A (XXI), 21 U.N. GAOR Supp. (No. 16) at 52, U.N. Doc. A/6316 (1966), 999 U.N.T.S. 171 [hereinafter 'ICCPR'].

[364] See, e.g., Article 4, African Charter on Human and People's Rights (Oct. 23, 1986); Article 4, American Convention on Human Rights (July 18, 1978).

[365] Principle 9, U.N. Basic Principles on the Use of Force and Firearms by Law Enforcement Officials, G.A. Res. 45/166 (Dec. 18, 1999).

[366] *McCann v. United Kingdom*, Judgment of 27 September 1995, No. 324 Ser.A ECHR 1995, at paras 146–214. See *Public Committee Against Torture, supra* n. 205, at para 40 (citing *McCann* for the proposition that capture should be effectuated where possible).

[367] *Isayeva v. Russia*, Judgment of 24 February 2005, No.57950/00 ECHR 2005, at para 191; Paulus 2006; Abresch 2005; Doswald-Beck 2006.

[368] UN Human Rights Committee, *Husband of Maria Fanny Suarez de Guerrero v. Colombia*, Decision on Admissibility, 37th Sess., No. R.11/45, Supp. No. 40 (A/37/40) (1982), at para 13.2.

Theoretically, the right to life adheres even in situations of armed conflict. Indeed, the former U.N. Special Rapporteur on Extrajudicial, Summary or Arbitrary Executions concluded that "extrajudicial executions can never be justified under any circumstances, not even in time of war."[369] Accordingly, the Rapporteur decried the first airstrike in Yemen in 2002 as "a clear case of extrajudicial killing."[370] Nonetheless, assuming the applicability of both bodies of law, the human right regime may cede regulatory authority to the *jus in bello*, which—as discussed above—can be interpreted to characterize the two killings as lawful wartime killings of the enemy.[371]

This analysis reaches a contrary conclusion if IHL is removed from consideration. If there is no armed conflict, and the *jus ad bellum* self-defense justification governs the decision to use military force, international human rights law continues to protect individuals from arbitrary deprivations of life. The *lex specialis* debate is less conceptually salient in the literature when only the *jus ad bellum* is applicable. In the operations under consideration, the degree of force employed exceeded that which would be acceptable under a law enforcement framework (although the Bin Laden raid is a closer call in light of the inherent dangerousness of the situation that day[372]). It is unclear, however, if *jus-ad-bellum* operations targeting a single dangerous individual should be analyzed as law enforcement operations or if some other harmonization of IHR and the *jus ad bellum* is necessary. Certainly there is some role for IHRL to play here, particularly to protect civilians from harm in light in the absence of a concept of collateral damage outside of situations of armed conflict.

There are multiple theories for how the law governing the use of force and human rights law interact. In particular, there will be situations in counterterrorism operations, such as the events in question, when the *jus ad bellum*, the *jus in bello*, and IHRL simply cannot be perfectly harmonized because the two bodies of law permit forms of action or impose obligations and restraints that are inherently

[369] UN Commission On Human Rights, Question Of The Violation Of Human Rights And Fundamental Freedoms In Any Part Of The World, With Particular Reference To Colonial And Other Dependent Countries And Territories, Extrajudicial, Summary Or Arbitrary Executions, Report Of The Special Rapporteur, Mr. Bacre Waly Ndiaye Submitted Pursuant To Commission On Human Rights Resolution 1997/61, E/Cn.4/1998/68/Add.2 (Mar. 12, 2998), at III.B.1.

[370] Report of the Special Rapporteur, Asma Jahangir, submitted pursuant to Commission on Human Rights resolution 2002/36, E/CN.4/2003.3, (January 13, 2003), at paras 37–39. In response, the U.S. argued that the events fell outside the Special Rapporteur's mandate and that the killing of an enemy combatant in a legitimate military operation could not constitute an extrajudicial killing. See Response of the Government of the United States of America to the letter from Special Rapporteur on Extrajudicial, Summary or Arbitrary Executions Asma Jahangir's letter to the Secretary of State dated November 15, 2002 and to the Findings of the Special Rapporteur contained in her report to the Commission on Human Rights (E/CN.4/2003/3), E/CN.4/2003/G/80 (April 22, 2003), at pp. 4–5, available at http://daccess-dds-ny.un.org/doc/UNDOC/GEN/G03/138/04/PDF/G0313804.pdf?OpenElement.

[371] But see *Isayeva*, supra n. 367, at para 191.

[372] O'Connell 2011.

incompatible. In such situations, it comes down to a pragmatic policy choice by the state as to which body of rules to follow. This choice is, of course, subject to the recognition that the state will have to accept any consequences, even if just reputational, for having breached an equally applicable legal obligation.

9.5.2 *Domestic Law*

As this article is primarily focused on international law, a full treatment of the domestic law implications of these operations is beyond its scope. It is worth simply highlighting several considerations that would be relevant to synchronizing the *jus in bello* considerations discussed above with U.S. statutory and constitutional law and with the *lex fori*.

9.5.2.1 U.S. Domestic Law

There are several elements of U.S. domestic law that might govern the events in question. Most saliently, the U.S. has banned assassination as a matter of national policy through an iterative series of executive orders, the last of which remains extant.[373] In the wake of alleged peacetime assassination plots against foreign leaders in the 1960 and 1970s,[374] U.S. Presidents Gerald Ford, Jimmy Carter, and Ronald Reagan issued executive orders (E.O. 11905 (1976),[375] E.O. 12036 (1978),[376] and E.O. 12333 (1981),[377] respectively) banning assassination without Presidential approval. E.O. 12333, for example, provides:

> No person employed by or acting on behalf of the United States Government shall engage in, or conspire to engage in, assassination.

Over the years, legislation has been introduced to fortify[378] or limit[379] the express prohibition against assassination in these decrees, but nothing has been enacted to date. Indeed, the Executive Order was likely passed originally in order to head off a legislative ban.

---

[373] For more on this topic, see Bazan 2002.

[374] Senate Select Committee to Study Government Operations with Respect to Intelligence Activities, S. Rep. No. 465, 94th Cong., 1st Sess. (1975).

[375] President Gerald R. Ford, Executive Order 11905, US Foreign Intelligence Activities, §5(g) (Feb. 18, 1976).

[376] President Jimmy Carter, Executive Order 12036, US Foreign Intelligence Activities, §2-305 (Jan. 24, 1978).

[377] President Ronald Reagan, § 2.11, Executive Order 12333, 3 C.F.R. 200 (1982) (Dec. 4, 1981).

[378] See Senate Report, *supra* n. 374, at 281-84; see also Brandenburg 1987, at pp. 685–686.

[379] Brandenburg 1987, at p. 686 n. 196.

In an exercise of concerted ambiguity, none of the E.O.s actually defines assassination, although "the context in which [the first order] was promulgated suggests that it was understood to apply to circumstances similar to those that recently had been the subject of investigation."[380] Colloquially, the concept of assassination—which carries a distinctly negative connotation—encompasses the intentional and premeditated killing of a particular individual (often a government official, influential civilian, or other prominent figure) for political purposes. To many, it embodies a notion of treachery[381] as in death by poison cigar or exploding umbrella.[382] This element of a betrayal of trust is not, however, inherent to the concept. The full reach of the Order has been the subject of speculation given recent events, such as with respect to the bombing of Libya in 1986[383] or calls to eliminate Saddam Hussein in the first Gulf War.[384]

For our purposes, the ban on assassination must be reconciled with the use of lethal force in the context of armed conflicts, counterinsurgency operations, and counterterrorism measures taken in self-defense. In its broadest terms, the Executive Order could be interpreted to mean that the U.S. cannot kill a pre-selected individual under any circumstances. In the alternative, the ban may remain applicable unless there is a valid authorization to use force emanating from Congress.[385] Another interpretation would exclude the Order's applicability in wartime altogether on the basis of the argument that it applies to intelligence rather than military activities.[386] To this end, the U.S. executive orders have been interpreted to apply only in peacetime or, at a minimum, to embody implicit exceptions in conventional military, counterinsurgency, and counterterrorism operations.[387] Col. W. Hays Parks, when he was Special Assistant for Law of War Matters to the Judge Advocate General of the Army, concluded that

> clandestine, low visibility or overt use of military force against legitimate targets in time of war, or against similar targets in time of peace where such individuals or groups pose an immediate threat to US citizens or the national security of the US, as determined by competent authority, does not constitute assassination or conspiracy to engage in assassination, and would not be prohibited by the proscription in EO 12333 or by international law.[388]

---

380 Zengel 1991, at p. 145.

381 See generally Kasher and Yadlin 2005.

382 Vattel for example, defined assassination as treacherous murder perpetrated "by the hand of any other an emissary, introducing himself as a suppliant, a refugee, a deserter, or, in fine, a stranger." Vattel 1758, at p. 359. See also Zengel 1991, at pp. 131–132 (noting that assassination is understood to mean the selected killing of an individual by treacherous means).

383 O'Brien 1990, at pp. 463–467.

384 Zengel 1991, at p. 124.

385 Chesney 2011a, b, at p. 52 n. 218; Lubell 2010, at p. 175.

386 Zengel 1991, at pp. 147, 150.

387 Janin 2007, at p. 96.

388 Parks 1989, at p. 8.

The classic historical example cited is the downing of the aircraft carrying Japanese Admiral Yamamoto Isoroku in 1943 far from any battlefield.[389] By this reasoning, the killing of the head of an organized armed force, even in a NIAC, would be governed by IHL as a form of *lex specialis* rather than the assassination ban. Even if some ban on assassination exists in IHL, it likely covers the killing of senior officers by treachery or trickery, which would not be the case where uniformed SEALs and remote attacks are involved.

Although outside the scope of this study, there is no question that other foundational elements of domestic law, such as the 4th and 5th Amendments to the U.S. Constitution, may speak to these events. Indeed, it is also worth considering whether these protections may be more robust vis-à-vis al-Aulaqi as a U.S. citizen, even though the 5th Amendment clearly applies to all persons and not just citizens. There is early precedent suggesting that citizenship might be relevant to determining the sliding scale between the law of war and domestic law (at least when it comes to the reach of military jurisdiction), but the issue of the rights of non-citizens was not squarely presented.[390] A devotion to universal human rights principles, however, might counsel against asserting any distinction between the two operations based on citizenship alone. The strength of constitutional protections may also turn on whether these events are perceived to have occurred on a battlefield. Indeed, in *Hamdi*, the Supreme Court specifically distinguished between actions "on the battlefield" against a U.S. citizen and the detention of that citizen, which "meddles little, if at all, in the strategy or conduct of war."[391] At the same time, prudential doctrines—such as the political question doctrine—may intrude to neutralize any potential constitutional claims arising out of these events.[392] All this said, assuming the parallel applicability of IHL, a robust *lex specialis* conclusion could theoretically override any limitations imposed by the 5th Amendment due process clause.[393] Absent a strong theory of *lex specialis*, the due process clause may mitigate the more permissive aspects of IHL, particularly outside of a "hot" conflict situation, which will be discussed in greater detail in the next Section.

9.5.2.2 Pakistani and Yemeni Law

It must not be forgotten that the law of the territorial state continues to apply to the actions of foreign states within its borders. Standard penal prohibitions against murder and mayhem would govern the events in question absent displacement by

---

389 Parks 1989, at p. 4.

390 *Ex Parte Milligan*, 71 U.S. 1, 119 (1866).

391 *Hamdi*, 542 U.S. at 534.

392 See, e.g., *El-Shifa Pharmaceutical Industries Co. v. U.S.*, 378 F.3d 1346 (D.C. Cir. 2004).

393 *Ex Parte Quirin*, 317 U.S. 1 (1942). In *Quirin*, one of the saboteurs, Haupt, may have been a U.S. citizen who was treated identically to his co-conspirators. See also In re *Territo*, 156 F.2d 142, 145 (9th Cir. 1946) (treating U.S. citizen who fought with the Italian army as a prisoner of war). But see Ex parte *Milligan*, 71 U.S. 2, 120-1 (1866).

the *jus ad bellum* or IHL as the *lex specialis*. One can imagine a counter-factual scenario in which one of the SEALs was captured by Pakistani forces and prosecuted for murder. That defendant would no doubt invoke combat immunity as a defense (along with individual self-defense perhaps). Pakistani jurists, however, would be under no international law obligation to recognize the defense in this NIAC context, especially given that the U.S. was employing forcible measures without Pakistan's consent. Because it was launched remotely, the Al-Aulaqi operation would not likely yield a prosecutable defendant, unless the base itself were located in Yemen. In any case, these contingencies are all extremely unlikely, given the state of the United States' relations with these two countries and the high profile nature of the targets.[394]

9.5.2.3 Conclusion: Domestic Law

It is, of course, unlikely that the U.S. would ever actually apply the assassination ban to the events in question, even if it were applicable. In any case, there is an authoritative interpretation of the Executive Order that suggests it is meant to govern peacetime killings of public figures rather than wartime killings of military objectives. Pakistani and Yemeni law continue to apply to these events. Even though the operations might be lawful under international law, there would be no bar to Pakistan or Yemen prosecuting one of the actors involved if custody could be obtained absent a doctrine of combatant immunity in the law governing NIACs.

9.6 Locating a Duty to Capture in International or Domestic Law

These operations have given rise to the claim that the U.S. was under a duty to endeavor to capture Bin Laden and/or al-Aulaqi in lieu of killing them outright, especially given that neither was confronted on a "hot" battlefield. There are a number of places in this international law schema where one might locate such an obligation, especially given the fuzziness of the interfaces between the relevant legal regimes and the potential for normative overlap. Within the *jus ad bellum*, the proportionality requirement inherent to the customary doctrine of self-defense may demand capture in certain circumstances when a state is addressing a threat posed by a single individual rather than by a sovereign entity, military installment, hostile force, or combat asset. This may especially be the case when the individual is found outside of an established battlefield. Similarly, the necessity requirement might place limits on the robustness of defensive action where capture is feasible.

[394] But see Mazzetti et al. 2011b (noting American arrested by Pakistanis after a robbery attempt).

Relevant considerations may include the strength of the relationship between the targeting state and the territorial state, the dependability of the territorial state as a partner in effectuating capture, and the sophistication of the intelligence, technology, and military assets that the targeting state has at its disposal (bearing in mind the debate over whether international law creates relative obligations among nations depending on their level of development). Indeed it could be argued that where the territorial state has consented to foreign intervention, there is a greater duty to attempt to capture rather than kill an individual, in light of the potential to gain cooperation and assistance from local law enforcement officials. At the same time, a state such as Yemen may be more willing to allow a remotely-piloted vehicle to enter its airspace than troops on its territory. Alternatively, it could be argued that where the exercise of self-defense is reactive (as in following a completed armed attack) or strictly preventative (as in the face of an inchoate threat, rather than imminent attack), international law—through the principles of necessity or proportionality—imposes heightened restrictions on the lethality of any defensive response.

Within the *jus in bello* and the rules governing NIACs, the ICRC's theory of least restrictive means might not countenance resort to lethal force unless the target is engaged while directly participating in hostilities, even if the individual is a member of an organized armed group who has assumed a continuous combat function in the group. In addition, the right to use lethal force might be limited by principles of military necessity, proportionality, or humanity in out-of-theater situations. Thus, while a state may be entitled to directly target a non-state fighter who is in the process of attacking national forces, armed forces may be limited to less injurious means when confronting an unarmed fighter who is not posing an immediate threat.

Human rights norms—and particularly the more robust version of proportionality governing law enforcement scenarios—might temper the *jus ad bellum* or IHL's targeting rules when an operation is undertaken outside of actual combat. In particular, the principle of military necessity might dictate the use of less than lethal means in such a scenario because it is difficult to argue that the killing (as opposed to capture) of fighters is "indispensable" under the circumstances.[395] Turning to domestic law, while the assassination ban is likely inapposite here, it remains to be fully explored whether the 5th Amendment due process clause, *a fortiori* with respect to al-Aulaqi, might impose any limits along the lines of the Israeli Supreme Court's conclusion in the *Targeted Killing* opinion.[396] This may be especially true when chargeable crimes—such as terrorism or treason—exist in domestic law. In short, there are places within this journey to legality where an

[395] Article 23(g), Hague IV. Indeed, the British Manual of the Law of Armed Conflict provides that "the use of force which is not necessary is unlawful, since it involves wanton killing or destruction." The Joint Service Manual, *supra* n. 264, at § 2.2.1.

[396] See *Pub. Committee Ag. Torture*, *supra* n. 205.

authoritative decision maker might impose heightened obligations on a state actor to endeavor to capture rather than kill an individual posing a threat to the nation.

The argument that members of such groups may be targeted wherever they are may be palatable when dealing with embattled foreign lands. It may be more problematic when applied to individuals found on U.S. soil—a scenario not presented by the two operations under consideration but logically foreseeable. Any arguments employed to justify unrestricted targeting of enemy combatants abroad with lethal force could be domesticated with little effort. And yet, the application of a pure law-of-war framework to alleged members of al Qaida apprehended in the U.S. has been controversial and remains the subject of litigation. In the face of legal challenge, the executive branch has eventually foregone detention and charged such individuals in Article III courts with violations of Title 18 of the U.S. Code.[397] As a result, whether or not the U.S. Constitution or any other source of law places limits on the application of IHL to exclusively domestic events in the absence of an armed conflict on U.S. territory has never been fully tested.

9.7 Conclusion

This epistemological journey has revealed multiple bodies of law under intense pressure from exogenous forces of globalization and the metastasis of transnational terrorism. The relevant law is unclear, indeterminate, or in flux at many key junctures along the way to a finding of legality vis-à-vis the two events in question. Thus, there is no definitive answer to the question of whether the doctrine of self-defense provides a justification for both the incursion into Pakistani sovereign territory and the use of deadly force against an individual posing an expected but inchoate threat to a nation. Likewise, assuming a self-defense rationale alone is insufficient or unavailable to justify both operations, IHL offers another source of potential authority. This, however, assumes that IHL follows militants wherever they may go, even if they journey far from the combat activities that activated this body of law in the first place. Nor is it certain that there is continuous targeting authority over individuals whom the core IHL treaties would classify as civilians, targetable only when directly participating in hostilities. The claim to legality requires an acceptance of the ICRC's continuous combat function construct—whose reach and limiting principles remain subject to debate—or a more robust targeting theory equating fighters in NIACs to privileged combatants in IACs. Finally, if there is an obligation to endeavor to capture a dangerous individual before killing him or her, from whence does such an obligation flow—the *jus ad bellum*, IHL, IHRL, or domestic law principles of proportionality and due process?

---

[397] See, e.g., *Al-Marri v. Spagone*, 555 U.S. 1220 (2009). In the context of cases involving the capture of enemy combatants, courts have characterized the US as "outside a zone of combat." *Padilla v. Rumsfeld*, 352 F.3d 695, 698 (2d Cir. 2003).

Determining the legality of these events also requires a consideration of the normative relationship between multiple potentially applicable bodies of law, including the *jus ad bellum,* the *jus in bello*, and human rights law. While it has been argued that IHL displaces IHRL, IHL may also displace other targeting theories, such as national self-defense, as independent rationales for these types of operations. Most of the debate on doctrinal hierarchies has focused on when and to what degree IHRL constrains actors engaged in armed conflicts governed by IHL; as such, there is little to suggest that IHRL does not apply in full force to pure self-defense operations absent a state of armed conflict.

This legal indeterminacy and doctrinal overlap has been lamented as a consequence of the "fragmentation" of international law.[398] This is, however, an inapt metaphor as it presumes a primordial whole that has since disintegrated. The fact that multiple conclusions on legality are possible is more likely due to the fact that modern conflicts and counterterrorism operations—which take place transnationally and outside of traditional theaters of war against non-state actors who countenance no limitations on their own actions whatsoever—generate novel legal questions that invoke multiple legal regimes. Secondary rules of recognition, interpretation, and choice of law have yet to catch up. Furthermore, notwithstanding the evolution of today's acute threats to world order, it has been decades since the existing IHL treaties were negotiated and drafted.

In all systems of law, regulatory gaps produce legal uncertainty but also a freedom to act. Thus, in the absence of clear legal rules, states are—in essence—free to choose a course of action. This suggests that while jurisprudentially discredited,[399] the legal legacy of the *Lotus* case—which set forth the proposition that what is not expressly forbidden by international law is permitted—continues to exert a strong gravitational pull.[400] There may, however, be consequences to acting along the edge of the law even in the absence of clear proscriptions, mandatory jurisdiction, and robust enforcement institutions. Negative repercussions may be diplomatic, reputational, and political. Furthermore, there remains the risk that where international reaction to controversial events is muted—for whatever reason—customary international law may evolve in ways that are ultimately undesirable.[401]

These observations also have implications for whether states should—as a matter of legal obligation or prudence—justify their actions when they choose to operate on the outer bounds of positive law.[402] On the one hand, it could be argued

---

[398] See Fragmentation Study, *supra* n. 335.

[399] *Arrest Warrant of 11 April 2000* (Democratic Republic of Congo v Belgium), 2002 I.C.J. Rep. 3, at para 51 (Joint and Separate Opinion of Higgins, Kooijmans, and Buergenthal) ("the [*Lotus*] dictum represents the high water mark of *laissez-faire* in international relations, and an era that has been significantly overtaken by other tendencies.").

[400] *S.S. Lotus* (France v Turkey), 1927 P.C.I.J. (ser. A), No. 10, at paras 18–19.

[401] Roberts 1993/4, at p. 198 (noting that where states acquiesce in breaches of the law, new law may be formed).

[402] Rona 2003, at p. 54.

that legal indeterminacy behooves governments to provide insight into the relevant facts, legal theories, and analyses—consistent with national security concerns—so that the international community can evaluate the state's claims to legality and shape the development of law with their reaction. The remarks by Brennan[403] and Koh[404] reflect this approach, although the reported withholding of the justificatory al-Aulaqi memorandum suggests a contrary impulse.[405] On the other hand, of course, enabling such scrutiny may aid the enemy by revealing means and methods of war; it may also generate statements against interest in the event that a judicial forum does eventually assert jurisdiction over some aspect of a controversial operation. Moreover, states are not monolithic entities, and it may be impossible to formulate a definitive legal theory justifying actions of this nature.[406] Articulating the legal, factual, and political basis for engaging in controversial conduct, however, will go far toward ensuring that such actions are treated as exceptional rather than precedential.

References

Abresch W (2005) A human rights law of internal armed conflict: The European court of human rights in Chechnya. Eur J Int Law 16:741

Ago R (1980) Addendum to the 8th report on state responsibility. Year B Int Law Commun 32

Aldrich GH (2002) The Taliban, Al Qaeda, and the determination of illegal combatants. Am J Int Law 96:891

Alston P (2011) The CIA and targeted killings beyond borders. New York university public law and legal theory working papers (1 Sep 2011). Available at http://lsr.nellco.org/cgi/viewcontent.cgi?article=1304&context=nyu_plltwp

Ambinger M (2011) The secret team that killed Bin Laden. Nat J (3 May 2011). Available at http://www.nationaljournal.com/whitehouse/the-secret-team-that-killed-bin-laden-20110502

Amnesty International (2011a) USA: a reflection on justice (17 May 2011). Available at http://www.amnesty.org/en/news-and-updates/reflection-justice-2011-05-17

Amnesty International (2011b) Questions around operation against Osama Bin Laden (4 May 2011). Available at http://www.amnesty.org/en/news-and-updates/questions-around-operation-against-osama-bin-laden-2011-05-04

Anderson K (2010) The Washington Post on targeting killing and US citizens. Volokh conspiracy (6 Sep 2010). Available at http://volokh.com/2010/09/06/the-washington-post-on-targeting-killing-and-us-citizens/

Baxter R (1951) So-called 'unprivileged belligerency': spies, guerrillas, and saboteurs. Br Year B Int L 28:328

Bazan EB (2002) Assassination Ban and E.O. 12333: a brief summary. Congressional Research Service RS21037 (Jan 2002). Available at http://www.fas.org/irp/crs/RS21037.pdf

BBC News (2011) Osama Bin Laden's death: how it happened. BBC News, vol 7 (June 2011). Available at http://www.bbc.co.uk/news/world-south-asia-13257330

403 Brennan 2011.

404 Koh 2010, 2011.

405 Finn 2011; DeYoung 2011. But see Klaidman 2012.

406 Aldrich 2002, at p. 892.

Beehner L (2007) Can states invoke 'hot pursuit' to hunt rebels? Council on Foreign Relations (7 June 2007). Available at http://www.cfr.org/publication/13440/

Bellinger J (2010) A counterterrorism law in need of updating. Wash Post, vol 26 (Nov 2010). Available at http://www.washingtonpost.com/wp-dyn/content/article/2010/11/25/AR2010112503116_pf.html

Bennet J (1998) U.S. Cruise missiles strike Sudan and Afghan targets tied to terrorist networks. New York Times, 21 Aug 1998

Bethlehem D (2011) Mopping up the last war or stumbling into the next? Harv Nat Secur J (7 Oct 2011). Available at http://harvardnsj.com/2011/10/mopping-up-the-last-war-or-stumbling-into-the-next/

Bergen P, Tiedemann K (2009) The drone war. New Republic (3 June 2009) Available at http://www.newamerica.net/publications/articles/2009/drone_war_13672

Bergen P, Tiedmann T (2011) year of the drone: an analysis of U.S. drone strikes in Pakistan, 2004–2010. New American Foundation, Last updated 10 Jan 2011. Available at http://counterterrorism.newamerica.net/drones

Blank L (2010) Defining the battlefield in contemporary conflict and counterterrorism: understanding the parameters of the zone of conflict. Georgia J Int Comp L 1:39

Blum G (2010) The dispensable lives of soldiers. J Leg Anal 2:69

Blum G, Heymann P (2010) Law and policy of targeted killing. Harv Nat Secur J 1:145

Blum YZ (1976) State response to acts of terrorism. Germ Year B Int Law 19:223

Boothby W (2010) "And for such time as": the time dimension to direct participation in hostilities. N Y Univ J Int Law Politics 42:741

Bothe M (2008) The law of neutrality. In: Fleck D (ed) Handbook of international humanitarian law in armed conflicts. Oxford University Press, Oxford

Brandenburg B (1987) The legality of assassination as an aspect of foreign policy. Va J Int Law 27:656

Bradley CA, Goldsmith JL (2005) Congressional authorization and the war on terrorism. Harv L Rev 118:2047

Brennan JO (2011) Strengthening our security by adhering to our values and laws. Harvard Law School (16 Sept 2011). Available at http://www.whitehouse.gov/the-press-office/2011/09/16/remarks-john-o-brennan-strengthening-our-security-adhering-our-values-an

Boed R (2000) State of necessity as a justification for internationally wrongful conduct. Yale Hum Rights Dev Law J 3:1

Bowett D (1972) Reprisals involving recourse to armed force. Am J Int Law 66:1

Brulliard K, DeYoung K (2011) Failure to discover Bin Laden's refuge stirs suspicion over Pakistan's role. Wash Post, 2 May 2011

Calabresi M (2011) CIA Chief: Pakistan would have jeopardized operation. Time (3 May 2011). Available at http://swampland.time.com/2011/05/03/cia-chief-breaks-silence-u-s-ruled-out-involving-pakistan-in-bin-laden-raid-early-on/

Chairman of the Joint Chiefs of Staff (2005) Standing rules of engagement/standing rules for the use of force for US forces, No. CJCSI 3121.01B (13 June 2005). Available in Condron S (ed) (2011) Operational law handbook

Chesney R (2011a) Who may be killed? Anwar Al-Awlaki as a case study on the international legal regulation of lethal force. Year B Int Human Law 13:3

Chesney R (2011b) A primer on the Libya/war powers resolution compliance debate. Brookings Institute (17 June 2011). Available at http://www.brookings.edu/opinions/2011/0617_war_powers_chesney.aspx

Centre for Constitutional Rights (2011) CCR Condemned targeted assassination of U.S. citizen Anwar Al-Awlaki. Centre for Constitutional Rights, 30 Sept 2011. Available at http://ccrjustice.org/newsroom/press-releases/ccr-condemns-targeted-assassination-of-u.s.-citizen-anwar-al-awlaki

Cohn M (2011) The targeted assassination of Osama Bin Laden. Truthout, 10 May 2011

Cole D (2011) Killing our citizens without trial. New York Review of Books Blog (9 Oct 2011). Available at http://www.nybooks.com/articles/archives/2011/nov/24/killing-our-citizens-without-trial/
Corn GS (2007) Hamdan, Lebanon, and the regulation of hostilities: the need to recognize a hybrid category of armed conflict. Vand J Trans Law 40:295
Corn GS (2009) What law applies to the war on terror? In: Lewis M et al (eds) The war on terror and the laws of war: a military perspective. Oxford University Press, Oxford
Corn GS, Jensen ET (2008) Untying the Gordian Knot: a proposal for determining applicability of the laws of war to the war on terror. Temp Law Rev 81:787
Davis M (2011) Combatant immunity and the death of Anwar al-Awlaqi, Jurist (17 Oct 2011). Available at http://jurist.org/forum/2011/10/morris-davis-anwar-al-awlaqi.php
Deeks AS (2011) Pakistan's sovereignty and the killing of Osama Bin Laden. ASIL Insights (5 May 2011) Available at http://www.asil.org/insights110505.cfm
DeYoung K (2011) Secrecy defines Obama's drone war. Wash Post (19 Dec 2011) Available at http://www.washingtonpost.com/world/national-security/secrecy-defines-obamas-drone-war/2011/10/28/gIQAPKNR5O_story.html
Dinstein Y (2004) The conduct of hostilities under the law of international armed conflict. Cambridge University Press, Cambridge
Doswald-Beck L (2006) The right to life in armed conflict: does international humanitarian law provide all the answers? Int Rev Red Cross 88:881
Drogin B, Parsons C, Dilanian K (2011) How Bin Laden met his end. LA Times (3 May 2011). Available at http://www.latimes.com/news/nationworld/world/la-fg-bin-laden-raid-20110503,0,7245803.story
Fahim K, Mazzetti M (2011) Allies defending actions in Libya after airstrike. NY Times (2 May 2011). Available at http://www.nytimes.com/2011/05/02/world/africa/02libya.html?_r=1&ref=africa
Farley BR (2011) Targeting Anwar Al-Aulaqi: a case study in U.S. drone strikes and targeted killings. II National Security Law Brief. Available at http://nationalsecuritylawbrief.com/wp-content/uploads/2011/12/AmerUnivNatlSecurityLawBrief_Winter2011.pdf
Feickert A (2011) U.S. Special Operations Forces (SOF): background and issues for congress. Congressional Research Service (15 July 2011). Available at http://www.fas.org/sgp/crs/natsec/RS21048.pdf
Feickert A, Livingston TK (2010) U.S. Special Operations Forces (SOF): background and issues for congress. Congressional Research Services (3 Dec 2010). Available at http://www.au.af.mil/au/awc/awcgate/crs/rs21048.pdf
Finn P (2011) Secret U.S. memo sanctioned killing of Aulaqi. Wash Post (20 Sept 2011). Available at http://www.washingtonpost.com/world/national-security/aulaqi-killing-reignites-debate-on-limits-of-executive-power/2011/09/30/gIQAx1bUAL_story.html
Fleck D (1995) The handbook of humanitarian law in armed conflicts. Oxford University Press, Oxford
Fox News (2010) U.S.-born radical cleric added to terror blacklist. Fox News.com (16 July 2010). Available at http://www.foxnews.com/us/2010/07/16/born-radical-cleric-added-terror-blacklist/
Funk T (2011) U.S. state dept. contacts Khan family. Charlotte Observer (13 Oct 2011) Available at http://www.charlotteobserver.com/2011/10/07/2673163/us-state-dept-contacts-khan-family.html
Gall C (2011) Pakistani military investigates how Bin Laden was able to hide in plain view. NY Times (4 May 2011) Available at http://www.nytimes.com/2011/05/05/world/asia/05compound.html?ref=abuahmedalkuwaiti
Gasser HP (1987) An appeal for ratification by the United States. Am J Int Law 81:912
Geiß R (2009) Armed violence in fragile states: low-intensity conflicts, spillover conflicts, and sporadic law enforcement operations by third parties. Int Rev Red Cross 91:127
Gerges FA (2011) Al-Qa'eda in the Arabian peninsula: does it pose a threat to Yemen and the West? Institute for Social Policy and Understanding (Feb 2011). Available at http://ispu.org/pdfs/514_ISPU_Report_al-Qaeda_Yemen_Gerges_WEB.pdf

Gray C (2004) International law and the use of force (2nd edn). Oxford University Press, Oxford

Greenwood C (2003) International law and the pre-emptive use of force: Afghanistan, Al-Qaida, and Iraq. San Diego Int Law J 4:7

Greenwood C (2004) War, terrorism and international law. Curr Leg Prob 56:505

Greenwood C (2006) The relationship between *Ius Ad Bellum* and *Ius in Bello*. In: Greenwood C (ed) Essays on war in international law. Cameron May, London

Greenwood C (2008) Scope of application of humanitarian law. In: Fleck D (ed) Handbook of international humanitarian law in armed conflicts. Oxford University Press, Oxford

Grimmett RF (2007), Authorization for use of military force in response to the 9/11 attacks (P.L. 107-40): legislative history. CRS report for congress (16 Jan 2007). Available at http://www.fas.org/sgp/crs/natsec/RS22357.pdf

Gross M (2011) Response to "Notes on asymmetrical war". Current Intelligence.net (15 Feb 2011). Available at http://www.currentintelligence.net/reviews/2011/2/15/notes-on-asymmetric-war.html

Hague Land Warfare Regulations (1907) Regulations respecting the laws and customs of war on land, Art. 23, annexed to Convention No. IV respecting the laws and custom of war on land (Oct. 10, 1907)

Henckaerts J-M, Doswald-Beck L (2005) Customary international humanitarian law, vol I. Cambridge University Press, Cambridge

Hennigan WJ, Vartabedian R (2011) Bin Laden raid reveals another elusive target: a stealth helicopter. LA Times, 7 May 2011

Hoffman B (2006) Inside terrorism. Columbia University Press, Columbia

Hosenball M (2011) Secret panel can put Americans on kill list. Reuters (5 Oct 2011). Available at http://www.reuters.com/article/2011/10/05/us-cia-killlist-idUSTRE79475C20111005

Huffington Post (2011) Libya advice from Justice department, Pentagon lawyers reportedly was overruled by Obama. HuffPost (17 June 2011). Available at http://www.huffingtonpost.com/2011/06/17/libya-advice-lawyers-obama_n_879644.html

ICRC (2008a) How is the term "armed conflict" defined in international humanitarian law. ICRC (March 2008). Available at http://www.icrc.org/eng/resources/documents/article/other/armed-conflict-article-170308.htm

ICRC (2008b) Interpretive guidance on the notion of direct participation in hostilities under international humanitarian law. Int Rev Red Cross 90:991

International Law Association (2010) Final report on the meaning of armed conflict in international law. ILA Committee on the use of force. Available at http://www.ila-hq.org/en/committees/index.cfm/cid/1022

Ito S (2011) American citizen Anwar Al-Aulaqi killed without judicial process. ACLU blog of rights. Available at http://www.aclu.org/blog/national-security/aclu-lens-american-citizen-anwar-al-aulaqi-killed-without-judicial-process

Janin AS (2007) Engaging civilian-belligerents leads to self-defense/protocol I marriage. Army Lawyer 82

Johnson C (2011) Debate erupts over legality of Awlaki's killing. NPR (30 Sept 2011). Available at http://www.npr.org/2011/09/30/140959250/debate-erupts-over-legality-of-al-awlakis-killing

Kahn P (2002) The paradox of riskless warfare. Phil Public Policy Q 22(3):2

Kasher A, Yadlin A (2005) Assassination and preventative killing. 25 SAIS Rev 41–57

Kasinof L (2011) Strikes hit Yemen as violence escalates in capital. NY Times (15 Oct 2011) Available at http://www.nytimes.com/2011/10/16/world/middleeast/yemeni-security-forces-fire-on-protesters-in-sana.html?_r=1&scp=1&sq=drone%20Yemen&st=cse

Klaidman D (2012) Obama team to break silence on al-Awlaki killing. Newsweek (23 Jan 2012). Available at http://www.thedailybeast.com/newsweek/2012/01/22/obama-team-to-break-silence-on-al-awlaki-killing.html?cid=newsletter;email;cheatsheet_morning

Koh HH (2010) U.S. Department of state. The Obama administration and international law. Annual meeting of the american society of international law (25 March 2010). Available at http://www.state.gov/s/releases-/remarks/139119.htm

Koh HH (2011) The lawfulness of the U.S. operation against Osama bin Laden. Opinio Juris (19 May 2011). Available at http://opiniojuris.org/2011/05/19/the-lawfulness-of-the-us-operation-against-osama-bin-laden/

Kretzmer D (2005) Targeted killing of suspected terrorists: extra-judicial executions or legitimate means of defense? Eur J Int Law 16:171

Landler M, Mazzetti M (2011) Account tells of one-sided battle in Bin Laden raid. NY Times (4 May 2011). Available at http://www.nytimes.com/2011/05/05/us/politics/05binladen.html?_r=1&adxnnl=1&ref=world&adxnnlx=1322504337-TPWyDXxa/ESPepIj6Gp9mg

Lewis A (2011) Osama Bin Laden: legality of killing questioned. BBC News (12 May 2011). Available at http://www.bbc.co.uk/news/world-south-asia-13318372

Lieber F (1863) War department, Instructions for the government of armies of the US in the field. Available at http://www.icrc.org/ihl.nsf/FULL/110?OpenDocument

Lubell N (2010) Extraterritorial use of force against non-state actors. Oxford University Press, Oxford

Mahnad R (2011) Targeting versus deprivation of liberty under the international law of armed conflict. ASIL Insights (1 Nov 2011). Available at http://www.asil.org/pdfs/insights/insight111101.pdf

Mayer J (2009) The predator war. The New Yorker (26 Oct 2009). Available at http://www.newyorker.com/reporting/2009/10/26/091026f_fact_mayer

Masood S (2011) C.I.A. leaves base in Pakistan used for drone strikes. New York Times (11 Dec 2011). Available at http://www.nytimes.com/2011/12/12/world/asia/cia-leaves-pakistan-base-used-for-drone-strikes.html?scp=3&sq=Pakistan%20anger%20drone%20attacks&st=cse

Mazzetti M (2011) Obama applauds C.I.A. for Bin Laden raid. New York Times (20 May 2011)

Mazzetti M, Shane S (2011) Data show Bin Laden plots; C.I.A. hid near raided house. New York Times. Available at http://www.nytimes.com/2011/05/06/world/asia/06intel.html?scp=1&sq=materials%20seized%20in%20bin%20laden%20raid&st=cse

Mazzetti M, Schmitt E, Worth AF (2011a) Two-year manhunt led to killing of Awlaki in Yemen. New York Times (30 Sept 2011) Available at http://www.nytimes.com/2011/10/01/world/middleeast/anwar-al-awlaki-is-killed-in-yemen.html?_r=1

Mazzetti M et al. (2011b) American held in Pakistan worked with C.I.A., New York Times (21 Feb 2011). Available at http://www.nytimes.com/2011/02/22/World/Asia/22pakistan.html?pagewanted=all

McManus D (2003) A U.S. license to kill. LA Times (11 Jan 2003). Available at http://articles.latimes.com/2003/jan/11/world/fg-predator11

Melzer N (2008) The ICRC's clarification process on the notion of direct participation in hostilities under international humanitarian law. Available at http://www.oas.org/DIL/esp/XXXVI_curso_The_ICRC_Clarification_Process_Nils_Melzer.pdf

Miller G (2010) Muslim cleric Aulaqi is 1st U.S. citizen on list of those CIA is allowed to kill. Wash Post (7 April 2010). Available at http://www.washingtonpost.com/wp-dyn/content/article/2010/04/06/AR2010040604121.html

Moussa J (2008) Can *Jus Ad Bellum* Override *Jus In Bello*? Reaffirming the separation of the two bodies of law. Int Rev Red Cross 90:963

Murphy SD (2002) Terrorism and the concept of 'armed attack' in Article 51 of the UN Charter. Harv Int Law J 43:41

Murphy SD (2003) Contemporary practice of the United States: U.S. adoption of new doctrine on the use of force. Am J Int Law 97:203

Murphy SD (2009) The international legality of U.S. military cross-border operations from Afghanistan into Pakistan. Int Law Stud Ser US Naval War Col 85:109

Naert F (2004) The impact of the fight against terrorism on the *Ius ad Bellum*. Ethical Perspect 11:144

Nagle LE (2008) Colombia's incursion into ecuadorian territory: justified hot pursuit or pugnacious error? J Trans Law Policy 17:359

New York Times (2011a) How the raid unfolded. New York Times. Available at http://www.nytimes.com/interactive/2011/05/02/world/asia/abbottabad-map-of-where-osama-bin-laden-was-killed.html

New York Times (2011b) Anwar Al-Awlaki. New York Times (13 Oct 2011). Available at http://topics.nytimes.com/top/reference/timestopics/people/a/anwar_al_awlaki/index.html

O'Brien WV (1990) Reprisals, deterrence and self-defense in counterterror operations. Va J Int Law 30:421

O'Connell ME (2002) The myth of preemptive self defense. ASIL task force on terrorism (Aug 2002). Available at http://www.asil.org/taskforce/oconnell.pdf

O'Connell ME (2009a) International law and the use of force. Oxford University Press, Oxford

O'Connell ME (2009b) Defining armed conflict. J Confl Secur Law 3913:3

O'Connell ME (2011) The Bin Laden aftermath: abbottabad and international law. Foreign Policy, 4 May 2011

Parks WH (2010) Part IX of the ICRC "Direct participation in hostilities" study: no mandate, no expertise, and legally incorrect. NY Univ J Int Law Politics 42:769

Parks WH (1989) Memorandum on executive order 12233 and assassination (2 Nov 1989). Available at http://www.hks.harvard.edu/cchrp/Use%20of%20Force/October%202002/Parks_final.pdf

Paul JR (2004) The Bush doctrine: making or breaking customary international law? Hastings Int Comp Law Rev 27:457

Paulus A (2006) The European court of human rights. Uppsala Year B East Eur Law 61

Paulus A, Vashakmadze M (2009) Asymmetrical war and the notion of armed conflict—a tentative conceptualization. Int Rev Red Cross 92:96

Paust JJ (2007) Responding lawfully to Al Qaeda. Cath Univ Law Rev 56:759

Paust JJ (2002) Use of armed force against terrorists in Afghanistan, Iraq, and Beyond. Cornell Int Law J 35:533

PBS (1996) Bin Laden's Fatwa. PBS News (August 1996). Available at http://www.pbs.org/newshour/terrorism/international/fatwa_1996.html

PBS (1998) Al Qaeda's Fatwa. PBS News (23 Feb 1998). Available at http://www.pbs.org/newshour/terrorism/international/fatwa_1998.html

Pejic J (2011) The protective scope of common Article 3: more than meets the eye. Int Rev Red Cross 93:189

Perlez J, Rhode D (2011) Pakistan pushes back against U.S. criticism on Bin Laden. New York Times (3 May 2011). Available at http://www.nytimes.com/2011/05/04/world/asia/04pakistan.html?_r=1

Pearlstein D (2011) New AUMF in the Senate. Opinio Juris (15 June 2011). Available at http://opiniojuris.org/2011/06/15/new-aumf-in-the-senate/

Pictet J (1960) III Commentary to the 1949 Geneva conventions relative to the treatment of prisoners of War. vol 23. ICRC, Geneva.

Pictet J (1985) Development and principles of international humanitarian law. International Institute of Human Rights, Martinus Nijhoff

Priest D (2010) U.S. Military teams, intelligence deeply involved in aiding yemen on strikes. Wash Post (27 Jan 2010). Available at http://www.washingtonpost.com/wp-dyn/content/article/2010/01/26/AR2010012604239.html

Rassler D, Brown V (2011) The Haqqani nexus and the evolution of al-Qa'ida. Combating Terrorism Center, Westpoint (14 July 2011). Available at http://www.ctc.usma.edu/wp-content/uploads/2011/07/CTC-Haqqani-Report_Rassler-Brown-Final_Web.pdf

Ratner S (2002) *Jus ad Bellum* and *Jus in Bello* after September 11. Am J Int Law 96:905

Reinold T (2011) State weakness, irregular warfare, and the right to self-defense post-9/11. Am J Int Law 105:244

Reisman WM, Armstrong A (2006) The past and future of the claim of preemptive self-defense. Am J Int L 100:525

Roberts A (1993/4) The laws of war in the 1990-91 Gulf conflict. Int Secur 18:171

Roberts (Adam) (2008) The equal application of the laws of war: a principle under pressure. Int Rev Red Cross 90:931

Roberts A (2008) Legality versus legitimacy: can uses of force be illegal but justified? In: Alston P, MacDonald E (eds) Human rights, intervention, the use of force. Oxford University Press, Oxford

Robertson G (2011) Why it's absurd to claim that justice has been done. The Independent (3 May 2011). Available at http://www.independent.co.uk/opinion/commentators/geoffrey-robertson-why-its-absurd-to-claim-that-justice-has-been-done-2278041.html

Romero C (2011) NATO Press Briefing on Libya. NATO (26 April 2011). Available at http://www.nato.int/cps/en/natolive/opinions_72902.htm

Romney M (2011) An American century: a strategy to secure America's enduring interests and ideals (7 Oct 2011). Available at http://mittromney.com/sites/default/files/shared/AnAmericanCentury-WhitePaper-10.7.11.pdf

Rona G (2003) Interesting times for international humanitarian law: challenges in the "war on terror". Fletcher Forum of World Affairs 27:55

Roth K (2004) The law of war in the war on terror. Foreign Affairs (Jan 2004). Available at http://www.foreignaffairs.com/articles/59524/kenneth-roth/the-law-of-war-in-the-war-on-terror

Ruys T (2010) 'Armed attack' and Article 51 of the UN Charter. Cambridge University Press, Cambridge

Schabas W (2007) *Lex Specialis*? Belt and suspenders? The parallel operation of human rights and the law of armed conflict, and the conundrum of *Jus Ad Bellum*. Israel Law Rev 40:592

Schmidle N (2011) Getting Bin Laden. The New Yorker (8 Aug 2011). Available at http://www.newyorker.com/reporting/2011/08/08/110808fa_fact_schmidle

Schmitt E, Mazzetti M (2008) Order lets U.S. strike Al Qaeda worldwide. Int Herald Trib, 11 Nov 2008

Schmitt MN (2004) Direct participation in hostilities and the 21st century armed conflict. In: Fischer H et al (eds) Crisis management and humanitarian protection: Festshrift Fur Dieter Fleck. BWV, Berlin

Shalal-Esa A (2011) Helicopter loss in Bin Laden raid highlights risk. Reuters (3 May 2011). Available at http://www.reuters.com/article/2011/05/03/us-binladen-helicopter-idUSTRE7427G420110503

Shane S (2010) U.S. approved targeted killing of American Cleric. New York Times (6 April 2010). Available at http://www.nytimes.com/2010/04/07/world/middleeast/07yemen.html

Shane S, Schmitt E (2010) CIA deaths surge in U.S. drone strikes. New York Times, 22 Jan 2010

Shane S, Mazzetti M, Worth RF (2010) Secret assault on terrorism widens on two continents. New York Times (14 Aug 2010). Available at http://www.nytimes.com/2010/08/15/world/15shadowwar.html?pagewanted=all

Shelsby T (1991) Iraqi soldiers surrender to AAI's drones. Balt Sun (2 March 1991). Available at http://articles.baltimoresun.com/1991-03-02/business/1991061100_1_rpv-aai-drones

Simpson SW (2006) Shoot first, ask questions later: double-tapping under the laws of war. West Va Law Rev 108:751

Smolowe J (1988) Gunned down in Tunis. Time (25 April 1988). Available at http://www.time.com/time/magazine/article/0,9171,967236,00.html

Sofaer AD (1989) Terrorism, the law and the national defense. Mil Law Rev 126:89

Solis GD (2010) The law of armed conflict: international humanitarian law in war. Cambridge University Press, Cambridge

Soufan A (2011) The black banners. WW Norton and Co, New York

Stahn C (2002) International law at crossroads? The impact of September 11, Zeitschrift für Ausländisches Öffentliches Recht und Völkerrecht 62:183

Stahn C (2003) Terrorist Acts as "armed attack": the right to self-defense, Article 51(1/2) of the U.N. Charter, and international terrorism. Fletcher Forum of World Affairs 27:35

Tams CJ (2009) The use of force against terrorists. Eur J Int Law 20: 359

Tapper J (2011) Today's Qs for O's WH—9/30/2011. ABC News (20 Sept 2011). Available at http://abcnews.go.com/blogs/politics/2011/09/todays-qs-for-os-wh-9302011/

The Telegraph (2011) Osama Bin Laden, "would have to be naked for surrender". The Telegraph (4 May 2011). Available at http://www.telegraph.co.uk/news/worldnews/al-qaeda/8491768/Osama-bin-laden-would-have-to-be-naked-for-surrender.html

Terrill WA (2011) The conflict in Yemen and U.S. National Security. Strategic Studies Institute, Available at http://www.strategicstudiesinstitute.army.mil/pdffiles/PUB1040.pdf

Thorp A (2011) Drone attacks and the killing of Anwar al-Awlaqi: legal issues. House of Commons

UN Office of the High Commissioner for Human Rights—Geneva (2011) Osama Bin Laden: statement by the UN Special Rapporteurs on summary executions and on human rights and counter-terrorism. OHCHR (6 May 2011). Available at http://www.ohchr.org/en/NewsEvents/Pages/DisplayNews.aspx?NewsID=10987&LangID=E

UN Office of the High Commissioner for Human Rights—New York (2011) U.N. human rights expert challenges 'targeted killing' policies. OHCHR (20 Oct 2011). Available at http://www.ohchr.org/EN/NewsEvents/Pages/DisplayNews.aspx?NewsID=11516&LangID=E

U.S. Secretary of State George Shultz (1986) Low-intensity warfare: the challenge of ambiguity (15 Jan 1986). Available at http://findarticles.com/p/articles/mi_m1079/is_v86/ai_4150055/

Van den Hole L (2003) Anticipatory self-defense under international law. Am Univ Int Law Rev 19:69

Van Schaack B (2011a) The legality of assassination under international and domestic law. IntLawGrrls (2 May 2011). Available at http://intlawgrrls.blogspot.com/2011/05/assassination-under-international.html

Van Schaack B (2011b) Negotiating at the interface of power and law: the crime of aggression. Columbia J Trans Law 49:505

De Vattel E (1758) Law of nations. Chitty J (ed.)/trans, T & JW Johnson, Philadelphia

Wall Street Journal—Editorial (2010) The drone wars. Wall Str J (9 Jan 2010). Available at http://online.wsj.com/article/SB10001424052748704130904574644632368664254.html

Walsh D, Jones S (2011) Osama Bin Laden raid team was prepared to fight Pakistani forces. The Guardian (10 May 2011). Aavailable at http://www.guardian.co.uk/world/2011/may/10/bin-laden-fight-hostile-pakistan

Waraich O (2011) Pakistan's military tries to explain itself. Time (6 May 2011). Available at http://www.time.com/time/magazine/article/0,9171,2069571-1,00.html

Watkin K (2004) Controlling the use of force: a role for human rights norms in contemporary armed conflict. Am J Int Law 98:1

Watkin K (2010) Opportunity lost: organized Armed Groups and the ICRC "direct participation in hostilities" interpretive guidance. NY Univ J Int Law Politics 42:641

Webster D, Everett E (1851) The works of Daniel Webster: legal arguments and speeches to the Jury Boston, C.C. Little and J. Brown

The White House (2002) The national security strategy of the United States of America 2002. http://merln.ndu.edu/whitepapers/USnss2002.pdf

The White House Blog (2011) Remarks by the president on Osama Bin Laden. (2 May 2011). Available at http://www.whitehouse.gov/blog/2011/05/02/osama-bin-laden-dead

The White House—Fact Sheet (2011) New actions on Guantanamo and detainee Policy. 7 March 2011

White House Press Secretary (2011) Press briefing by press secretary Jay Carney (4 May 2011). Available at http://www.whitehouse.gov/the-press-office/2011/05/04/press-briefing-press-secretary-jay-carney-542011

Wilmhurst E (2005) Principles of international law on the use of force by states in self-defense. Chatham House (Oct 2005). Available at http://www.chathamhouse.org/publications/papers/view/108106

Wikipedia (2011) Reactions to the death of Osama Bin Laden. Available at http://www.//en.wikipedia.org/wiki/Reactions_to_the_death_of_Osama_Bin_Laden

Williams P (2011) Bin Laden killing was legally justified, holder says. msnbc.com (4 May 2011). Available at http://www.msnbc.msn.com/id/42900659/ns/world_news-south_and_central_asia/t/bin-laden-killing-was-legally-justified-holder-says/

Wilson S, Whitlock C, Branigan W (2011) Osama Bin Laden killed in U.S. raid, Buried at Sea. Wash Post (2 May 2011). Available at http://www.washingtonpost.com/national/osama-bin-laden-killed-in-us-raid-buried-at-sea/2011/05/02/AFx0yAZF_story.html?wpisrc=emailtoafriend

Wingfield T (1998-9) Taking aim at regime elites. Md J Int Law Trade 22:287

Worldwatch (2011) Photos show some killed in bin laden raid. CBS News (4 May 2011). Available at http://www.cbsnews.com/8301-503543_162-20059828-503543.html

Zengel P (1991) Assassination and the law of armed conflict. Mil Law Rev 134:123

Zimmerman A (1999) Preliminary remarks on para. 2(c)-(f) and Para. 3: War crimes committed in an armed conflict not of an International Character. In Triffterer O (ed) Commentary on the Rome Statute of the International Criminal Court. Hart Publishing

Chapter 10
Protecting the 'Helpers': Humanitarians and Health Care Workers During Times of Armed Conflict

Helen Durham and Phoebe Wynn-Pope

Contents

10.1 Introduction

In recent years a gradual understanding has developed on the need to take a broader view of the concept of 'protection' during times of armed conflict. Whilst destruction and suffering caused directly by warring parties continues to be a

Helen Durham is a Senior Fellow at Melbourne Law School and Head of International Law at Australian Red Cross. Phoebe Wynn-Pope is a Fellow at the Asia Pacific Centre of Military Law and a Humanitarian Advisor. The views expressed in this article are exclusively those of the authors' and do not represent any institutional positions. The authors would like to acknowledge the significant assistance of Tim McFarland in preparing this article.

H. Durham (✉)
Melbourne Law School, Melbourne, Australia
e-mail: hdurham@redcross.org.au

H. Durham
Head of International Law and Principles, Australian Red Cross, Melbourne, Australia

P. Wynn-Pope
Asia Pacific Centre of Military Law, Melbourne, Australia
e-mail: p.wynnpope@bigpond.com

M.N. Schmitt and L. Arimatsu (eds.), *Yearbook of International Humanitarian Law Volume 14, 2011*, DOI: 10.1007/978-90-6704-855-2_10,

matter of deep concern, focus has started to also turn to an examination of the indirect impact armed conflict has on civilian populations. In particular, the large number of deaths caused by disruption to medical and humanitarian assistance is gaining attention. The Harvard Burden of Disease Unit has recently called for more reliable data on the health effects of armed conflict.[1] The Small Arms Survey of the Graduate Institute of International and Development Studies, Geneva, has stated that armed conflict is a major cause of ill health and mortality not just from obvious injuries and death on the battlefield but also due to factors such as loss of access to basic health care.[2] They estimate that in contemporary conflicts there is a ratio of four indirect to one direct death due to armed conflict.[3] The scale of the problem can be seen, for example, in the Democratic Republic of the Congo where it is estimated that 38,000 excess deaths per month are caused mostly by easily treatable diseases which go untreated due to insecurity arising from armed conflict.[4] The conflict in Iraq has had similar effects; between 2003 and 2007, 18,000 of the country's 34,000 doctors fled and many other were killed, with a catastrophic impact on the health care system.[5]

Adding to the calls for more work to be done in this area, on the 10th August 2011, the International Committee of the Red Cross (ICRC) launched a 4 year project entitled 'Health Care in Danger' (HCiD) which 'aims to address the widespread and severe impact of illegal and sometimes violent acts that obstruct the delivery of health care'[6] and '[strengthen] protection for the sick and wounded in these situations through the adoption of specific measures designed to help ensure that they have safe access to effective and impartial health care.'[7] Measures put forward by the ICRC include States enacting legislation to safeguard health care, sharing of best practices, regular and methodical information gathering, improving the physical protection of medical facilities and building a community of concern.[8]

With these issues in mind, this article aims to examine the existing rules and principles contained within the international humanitarian law (IHL) legal framework, in particular the protections afforded to humanitarian workers and health care workers under the 1949 Geneva Conventions and their 1977 Additional Protocols. It commences with an examination of the definition of relief workers, moves to discuss the implications of the increased political use of humanitarian aid and then reviews the legal framework within which this sector is located. The multi-dimensional nature of current conflicts, in particular as they pertain to health

[1] Murray et al. 2002, p. 346.

[2] Graduate Institute of International and Development Studies: Small Arms Study 2011.

[3] Ibid.

[4] Coghlan et al 2006, p. 44.

[5] International Committee of the Red Cross 2011a, p. 3; Oxfam International 2007, pp. 11–12.

[6] International Committee of the Red Cross 2011b.

[7] Ibid.

[8] The 31st International Conference of the Red Cross and Red Crescent 2011.

care workers, requires an examination of both human rights and IHL. In conclusion this paper argues that for the effective protection of affected communities much more should be done by all those engaged in conflict including ending impunity for attacks on humanitarian relief workers and material, and medical personnel, supplies and facilities, as well as the encouragement of further debate and discussion on the topic.

10.2 Origins of Protection for Civilians and the Provision of Relief to Protected Persons

In the context of legal developments in the latter part of the 1940s, the fourth Geneva Convention[9] was remarkable due to the fact that for the first time a binding international instrument was put in place specifically addressing the protection of civilians in conflict zones. However, protection was not offered to all civilians but only to those caught up in occupied territory or those who found themselves in the territory of the enemy. In 1949, any attempt to codify protection for citizens in territory controlled by their own government or military forces could have been seen to be an imposition on national sovereignty and, even to some degree, a challenge to the principle of territorial integrity. The international community, at that time, had a smaller appetite than today for making legally binding treaties protecting a State's citizens from the State itself.

The development of an active human rights regime and the changing nature of warfare, however, lead to a dramatic change in attitude by the time the Additional Protocols[10] were drafted in 1977. These Protocols concerned themselves not only with international and non-international armed conflict, but with the protection of all civilians affected by armed conflict regardless of in whose territory they could be found. The Additional Protocols expanded protection offered not only to civilians but also recognised those whose work and duty it is to assist and protect those civilians—humanitarian relief workers.

Demonstrating an understanding of the need to more broadly protect civilians, both the Geneva Conventions and the Additional Protocols provide a clear requirement for the delivery of relief to protected persons. This relief takes the form of medical, health, food, water and other basic needs. Implicit in the recognition of the need for relief, is the fact that personnel dedicated to the

[9] Geneva Convention Relative to the Protection of Civilian Persons in Time of War, opened for signature 12 August 1949, 75 UNTS 287 (entered into force 21 October 1950) (GC IV).

[10] Protocol Additional to the Geneva Conventions of 12 August 1949, and relating to the Protection of Victims of International Armed Conflicts (Protocol 1), opened for signature 8 June 1977, 1125 UNTS 3 (entered into force 7 December 1978) (AP I); Protocol Additional to the Geneva Conventions of 12 August 1949, and Relating to the Protection of Victims of Non-International Armed Conflicts (Protocol II), opened for signature 8 June 1977, 1125 UNTS 609 (entered into force 7 December 1978) (AP II).

implementation of relief operations are a crucial part of ensuring the survival and dignity of those 'protected' be they the wider community, prisoners of war or injured combatants.

As such the validity of a humanitarian relief worker's role in conflict zones is entrenched, not only by the precepts of humanity and basic human rights, but also under IHL. Three questions rise out of this basic understanding. First, who is to be considered a 'humanitarian relief worker'? Second, what constitutes 'humanitarian assistance'? Finally, what guiding principles exist for the relief workers under the law that assist this category of civilians to fulfil their humanitarian task?

For the purposes of this article 'humanitarian relief workers' are defined as both international and national personnel who strive to deliver relief in an impartial and humanitarian manner, to people *hors de combat* and to civilians in need. The words 'impartial' and 'humanitarian' appear consistently throughout the Geneva Conventions and Additional Protocols when referring to such assistance. Humanitarian personnel are generally employed by local civil society organisations, non-governmental organisations, or international organisations such as the UN. Personnel of the ICRC and National Red Cross and Red Crescent Societies are not included in the broad definition of 'humanitarian relief workers' as protection offered to Red Cross workers under the Geneva Conventions differs due to the specific international legal personality of these institutions.[11]

Humanitarian assistance is distinctly defined in the Geneva Conventions and refers to consignments of food and medical supplies[12] and 'clothing, bedding, means of shelter and other supplies essential to the survival of the civilian population'.[13] The idea of humanitarian assistance being 'essential to the survival of the civilian population' is critically important as many organisations working in situations of armed conflict also undertake development-type projects which may not be considered 'humanitarian' under IHL.[14]

Where the Geneva Conventions offer protections, they also bestow obligations not only on the parties to the conflict but also to third parties. This means that actors, such as international and non-governmental organisations, are required to comply with certain key principles in IHL. These principles, namely, impartiality, humanity, and independence,[15] form the basic obligations on humanitarian relief organisations and are important to the effective implementation of relief actions in conflict zones. Neutrality is often mentioned within this debate and whilst it is a main element of the work of the ICRC, National Societies, and used by a number of other humanitarian organisations, it is not specifically required under IHL.

---

[11] On the legal personality of the components of the Red Cross movement see: Mosler 1984, p. 455; Bugnion 2004, p. 204 n 52; Koenig 1991.

[12] GC IV Article 55.

[13] AP I Article 69.

[14] For example longer term projects such as income generation and the re-building of the judiciary.

[15] International Committee of the Red Cross 1998a, b, c.

As noted, references to humanitarian organisations or 'relief societies' in the Geneva Conventions refer to 'humanitarian and impartial' organisations. Impartiality may be defined as the 'absence of any discrimination based on race, nationality, religion, political opinions or any other similar criterion, with priority given to those in most urgent need.'[16] Impartiality is important in order to maintain the trust and respect of the parties to the conflict and is crucial in terms of gaining consent to relief activities and access to populations in need. Impartiality is also an obligation on individual relief workers as, without their adherence to this and other key principles of humanitarian relief under IHL, an organisation may be at risk of losing its 'impartial' status thereby jeopardising the relief operation and ultimately the protection of affected populations. Furthermore, a relief operation which is implemented exclusively for the benefit of one of the warring parties could be seen to be contributing to the armed conflict rather than addressing humanitarian needs.

Independence is a principle that is increasingly challenged in modern humanitarian operations. Many relief organisations are closely tied to government funding and are therefore often perceived to be 'State agents' even where this may not necessarily be true. In recent years States have been establishing humanitarian 'arms' to function as a separate aspect of any governmental engagement in armed conflict. For example the Australian Government has established the Australian Civilian Corp (ACC) which is intended to be a register of up to 500 civilian experts who are able to provide the Government with additional capability to rapidly deploy assistance teams to countries affected by natural disaster or conflict. ACC specialists will be posted to work 'with and within the governments of countries affected by crisis to rebuild state functions, to reinstate the rule of law and to restore essential services'.[17] The potential for a lack of clarity between the roles of these government 'agents' and the independent humanitarian community is a topic requiring further examination.

The principle of neutrality is a part of this debate and often referenced in documents and resolutions relating to the provision of humanitarian assistance. Neutrality means 'never taking part in hostilities or engaging in the political, religious or ideological controversies which underlie armed conflicts.'[18] Neutrality does not mean that one has to accept the root causes of a conflict; however it is not the role of a neutral humanitarian organisation to take sides in the conflict and adopt either a critical or supportive stance with regard to the specific strategies of a warring party. Neutrality is not a requirement of IHL and many humanitarian agencies will claim impartiality but not neutrality. The capacity for an organisation to be impartial in the face of conflict (and provide assistance based on need rather than political, ethnic grouping or other determining factors) is substantially different from the neutral approach which often relates specifically to advocacy or public statements. Furthermore within the humanitarian sector there are substantial

[16] Ibid.

[17] Australian Civilian Corp 2011.

[18] International Committee of the Red Cross 1998a, b, c.

debates on the meaning and usefulness of taking a neutral approach to those engaged in armed conflict. At times there appears confusion between the concepts of impartiality and neutrality that leads to a less focused and less useful debate.

10.3 Political Use of Humanitarian Aid in Current Conflicts

In recent times humanitarian action has been politicised in a way that could be seen as adversely affecting the security of relief workers and therefore threatening the perceived neutrality, impartiality and independence of aid operations. There are several reasons for the increasingly complex politicisation of aid, all of which contribute to the insecurity faced by relief workers.[19]

First, politicisation may be partly due to the changing nature of relief agencies that increasingly see a role for themselves in strategy and policy development through field based experiential public advocacy. However, advocacy by its very nature requires comment and opinion on situations that may be highly volatile, sensitive and complex, in particular during the timeframe of the conflict itself. To maintain either the reality or the perception of neutrality while advocating for a change in the political system, or a change in the status quo, is well nigh impossible. As noted this is why many agencies have declared themselves as impartial, but not neutral. However this declaration, in itself, may jeopardise a humanitarian organisation's ability to work with all sides in a conflict and indeed fulfil their obligations under IHL that help to allow for continued access to affected populations during times of armed conflict. In current complex conflicts it appears that those organisations which use the tools of both impartiality and neutrality gain far greater access to those in need. Yet it is important for the sector to have a range of diverse actors to cover all situations including the necessity of public advocacy as well as direct humanitarian assistance.

Secondly, the increasing threat to relief workers may also be in part due to a chronic overuse of the term 'humanitarian'. It is now a term that is used not only in relation to providing the basic needs of civilian populations, but also to justify military intervention on sovereign territory (humanitarian intervention).[20] Military actors also use the provision of humanitarian assistance as conditional on a certain level of cooperation by occupied civilian populations, or as a tool to 'win the hearts of minds' of the local population. Such declarations could be interpreted as infringements of the meaning and intent of humanitarian relief as defined by the Geneva Conventions. The risk to humanitarian workers presented by military use of the term 'humanitarian' was recognised by the International Commission on Intervention and State Sovereignty (ICISS) which suggested that it is an 'anathema

---

[19] For further discussion on this topic see Fishstein and Wilder 2012.

[20] International Committee of the Red Cross 1998b.

for the humanitarian relief and assistance sector to have this word appropriated to describe any kind of military action'.[21]

A third development that is inadvertently undermining the perceived neutrality and impartiality of humanitarian agencies and their personnel is the rising participation of humanitarian organisations in stabilisation and peace-building, or nation-building operations. These are most obvious in countries such as Afghanistan and Iraq where the independence and impartiality of humanitarian organisations is severely threatened by their role in the development and support of state services and infrastructure. Terry has written in a reflective and comprehensive manner on the continuing importance of neutrality in complex contexts such as Afghanistan and highlights the needs for a more detailed and robust debate on the topic.[22]

The need for protection is uppermost for the humanitarian practitioner placing his or herself on the front line to provide life-saving relief material and assistance. But it is equally critical for those vulnerable communities who are dependent on assistance. Historically legal protection for humanitarian practitioners has not been adequate. In the following section this article traces the protection offered to humanitarian practitioners by the Geneva Conventions and the Additional Protocols and then reviews other mechanisms that have been established in the last 20 years to reinforce the protections offered in IHL.

10.4 Protection for Humanitarian Relief Workers

Rule 31 of the ICRC's *Customary International Humanitarian Law Volume I: Rules* (CIHL) states that 'Humanitarian relief personnel must be respected and protected'[23] while Rule 32 provides that 'Objects used for humanitarian relief operations must be respected and protected.'[24] Although now regarded as customary in status, the explicit recognition that humanitarian practitioners as a particular group require special and specific protection in IHL is a relatively new practice.

The Geneva Conventions make express reference to and note that impartial humanitarian organisations are important for the provision of relief and services to the parties to the conflict, for the benefit of 'protected persons' under the Conventions.

Article 10 of the Fourth Geneva Convention (GC IV) common to all the conventions[25] states that:

---

[21] CISS 2001, para 1.40.

[22] Terry 2011.

[23] Henckaerts and Doswald-Beck 2009, p. 105.

[24] Ibid, p. 109.

[25] The equivalent provision is in article 9 of the other three 1949 Geneva Conventions.

> The provisions of the present Convention constitute no obstacle to the humanitarian activities which the International Committee of the Red Cross or any other impartial humanitarian organisation may, subject to the consent of the Parties to the conflict concerned, undertake for the protection of civilian persons and for their relief.

This is a clear statement of understanding that humanitarian activities are important and necessary and that they are constrained only by the requirement of consent of the Parties to the conflict, the nature of the organisation and the nature and objectives of the humanitarian activities. At the Diplomatic Conference little time was spent discussing this article and there was no dispute about the principle involved.[26]

However, while there was a recognised need for humanitarian assistance, there was no direct mention of humanitarian workers as a group in the 1949 Conventions. As civilians, humanitarian workers would receive the same level of protection offered to the general population under the fundamental principle of distinction. However, as we have noted above, relief workers are often in situations of greater risk and it is questionable as to whether such general protection would be adequate.

GC IV Article 23 relates to consignments of medical supplies, food and clothing and provides that such consignments should have free passage. This article was derived from the experience of the Second World War blockades, when humanitarian relief was prevented from reaching the civilian populations in need thereby causing the deaths of thousands. In the blockade on Stalingrad alone, it is estimated that one million civilians died of starvation. However, parties to the conflict may refuse free passage of relief supplies if there is either fear that a relief consignment may be diverted from its stated destination, fear that control over the consignment may not be effective, or be seen that there is a definite military advantage to the enemy. Nevertheless, these conditions may not be used to avoid the general prohibition on the use of starvation as a means of warfare.[27]

While Article 23 aims to guarantee the free passage of humanitarian assistance it is equally possible for the parties to the conflict to delay or block such assistance. Thus, although the spirit of the article is to impose an obligation for free passage of supplies, invoking military necessity does provide an opportunity *not* to co-operate. In addition, although the provision can be read as requiring the Protecting Powers to oversee the effective distribution of assistance, there is no mention of humanitarian relief workers and no protection for them is offered under the article. Certainly it was clear that while provisions for civilians was considered important there was less consideration about how those provisions would reach their final destination.

Two of the most important articles concerning humanitarian relief in the Geneva Conventions are Articles 30 and 142 of GC IV. The former guarantees that protected persons will have the right to contact the Protecting Powers, the ICRC,

---

[26] Pictet 1958, p. 95.

[27] AP I Article 54.

'as well as...any organisation that might assist them...within the bounds set by military or security considerations.' While the article relates to the two specifically mentioned entities, it also refers to any organisation whose object is to give spiritual or material aid. This would, therefore, include any impartial humanitarian organisation.

Where Article 30 establishes the right of *all protected persons* to have access to any organisation that may help them, Article 142 deals specifically with relief societies and other organisations and access to those in need. It is beneficial to read the two articles together in order to gain a true sense of their intention.

The history of Article 142 goes back to the Hague Conferences of 1899 where there was much debate around the right to relief for prisoners of war.[28] It is almost identical to Article 125 of Geneva Convention III[29] except for the last paragraph where there is greater specificity in Article 125 regarding receipt and notification of receipt of relief supplies by prisoners of war.

Article 142 outlines the main tasks of relief societies including the distribution of relief supplies and material. Importantly, the spirit of the article should be read to include protection of the personnel undertaking the approved tasks of relief societies—their 'duly accredited agents'[30] —although there is a lack of detail about such personnel. The article refers to the types of relief organisations that may undertake such work and they include 'societies or organisations... constituted in the territory of the Detaining Power, or in any other country, or they may have an international character'.

Article 142 is significant because it places an obligation on the Detaining Power to assist relief societies within the bounds set by military or security considerations. While permission must be applied for by both the relief organisation and the particular delegate, once granted the Detaining Power must provide all facilities within their means, for relief organisations to carry out their mission. This provides some protection to relief workers by creating clear legal requirements and validity to the humanitarian tasks they are undertaking.

Strong protective measures in respect of the civilian population in occupied territories exist in treaty law. The Occupying Power has an obligation to ensure '[t]o the fullest extent of the means available to it'[31] that food and medical supplies are available to the population. They should maintain medical and hospital establishments, public health and hygiene facilities and allow the continuation of religious practises.[32] Where there are insufficient supplies, the Occupying Power has an obligation to agree to, and facilitate relief operations and ensure free passage to relief consignments. This obligation on Occupying Powers to accept

[28] Pictet 1958, p. 557.

[29] Geneva Convention Relative to the Treatment of Prisoners of War, opened for signature 12 August 1949, 75 UNTS 135 (entered into force 21 October 1950).

[30] Pictet 1958, p. 560.

[31] GC IV Article 55.

[32] GC IV Articles 56, 58.

collective relief is unconditional.[33] In recognising the absolute obligation of the Occupying Power to care for the population under its control, Article 63 of GC IV contains some protection for relief workers and notes that the Occupying Power cannot change the structure or personnel of organisations in a way that would affect the delivery of relief. This is, however, conditional on the absence of 'temporary and exceptional measures imposed for urgent reasons of security by the Occupying Power.'[34]

There are many assurances regarding the obligations of the Parties to the conflict to ensure that the basic needs of the civilian population are met, and there are provisions allowing for relief consignments and the work of relief societies. Yet there is no direct reference to the relief workers themselves in the Conventions. All the important articles relating to relief are written from the perspective of protecting and ensuring the safety of the civilian population, not protecting relief workers.

At the same time all relief operations are subject to the sensitive and subjective judgments involving military objectives and the principle of necessity and are framed so as to ensure that relief operations will not interfere with the conflict itself. Therefore, while imposing an obligation on the Parties to the conflict to care for the civilian population, the conditional clauses actually enable the Occupying Power, or the Detaining Power, to refuse relief for the civilian population.

At the time of the Diplomatic Conferences leading up to the conclusion of the Additional Protocols it was seen that the Protocols should concentrate on those persons not already protected: in other words, on all civilians on the territory of a party to the conflict, and not only those on occupied or enemy territory. As previously discussed, this was a significant shift in position on the part of the international community. While the Conference did not consider it appropriate to make a provision obliging responsibility on each party to the conflict to secure supplies for its own population, it did impose an obligation on the parties to accept relief operations for any civilians without adequate supplies.[35] To some this was seen as a 'triumph of humanity over States' rights'.[36]

As is well known, Additional Protocol I (AP I) is an extension of the Fourth Geneva Convention, incorporating many of the obligations found in the 'Hague' legal regime and concentrates on the protection of civilians in international armed conflict. It increased significantly, not only the level of protection to civilians and the categories of civilians protected, but also the obligation on Parties to the conflict to ensure the provision, not only of food and medical supplies, but also clothing, shelter, bedding and 'other supplies'. Under Article 69, the obligation of an Occupying Power to accept relief actions is undisputed.[37]

---

33 Pictet 1958, p. 320.
34 GC IV Article 63.
35 ICRC 1987, p. 806.
36 Tchanile 1989, p. 403.
37 ICRC 1987, p. 806.

The Additional Protocols increased the scope of protected persons who would be guaranteed relief action (subject always to military necessity), and also, for the first time, recognised the personnel delivering that relief. In AP I, Article 71, despite the requirement of consent, there is specific reference to the right of relief personnel to form part of the assistance provided to populations in need. Paragraph 2 of Article 71 refers to such personnel being 'respected and protected'. This is highly significant and strong in legal terms as 'respect' and 'protect' are concepts that are found in conventions as early as 1906. In this regard, 'respect' is understood as meaning 'to spare, not to attack'[38] and 'protect' is interpreted as meaning 'to come to someone's defence, to lend help and support'.[39] This obligation provides relief workers with a more substantial footing and a specific status under IHL. This status is strengthened where there is an obligation for Parties to the conflict to defend and assist relief operations where possible. There are, however, qualifying clauses in para 3 of Article 71 which notes '[o]nly in case of imperative military necessity may the activities of the relief personnel be limited or their movements temporarily restricted'. The case for such exclusions is extremely subjective.

Importantly there are also obligations imposed on relief workers to adhere to the principles governing humanitarian assistance. They must not exceed their impartial humanitarian mission beyond the scope of the Protocol, and they must take account of security requirements of the Party in whose territory they are working.[40] If these requirements are not satisfied their mission may be terminated and permission to work in the territory withdrawn. Protection for relief workers in international armed conflict is substantial provided all conditions laid down by the Protocol are met.

In situations of non-international armed conflict, Common Article 3 of the Geneva Conventions provides for a humanitarian organisation to offer services to a party to the conflict, but makes no mention of relief activities for conflict affected populations. APII made some progress and specifically allows for relief societies and relief actions at Article 18; however there is no mention of humanitarian relief workers and their protection is inadequate. It is of concern that the majority of conflicts in the twenty-first century are non-international armed conflict in which relief workers are at greatest risk yet they have the least protection under the treaty law.

Following the end of the Cold War and the years of violent conflict throughout the 1990s (including, for example, in Somalia, Rwanda, Bosnia Herzegovina, Kosovo) there was an increasing awareness of the work of humanitarian workers, not least those mandated by the UN, and of the risks they sustained in conflict zones. By the early 1990s there had been a proliferation of UN peace-keeping missions: in the 42 years between 1945 and 1987 there had been only thirteen

---

[38] Pictet 1958, p. 146.

[39] Pictet 1958, p. 146.

[40] AP I Article 71(4).

missions but in the 5 year period between 1987 and 1993, 14 had been established.[41] During 1992–1993, 33 civilian UN personnel were killed, more than half of whom had been providing humanitarian assistance.[42] Although the Additional Protocols provided some protection for humanitarian workers as long as certain conditions were met, there was by no means universal agreement to the Additional Protocols. Consequently, there was an emerging feeling that the legal protections for humanitarian relief workers operating in complex humanitarian emergencies were simply not adequate and that further measures to provide particular protection for humanitarian and other personnel working in such situations was needed.

In 1992, the UN Secretary General drew attention to 'the pressing need to afford adequate protection to United Nations personnel engaged in life-endangering circumstances'.[43] Momentum gathered in support of further action, and on 9 December 1994, the UN General Assembly adopted,[44] by consensus, the Convention on the Safety of United Nations and Associated Personnel (CSUNAP).[45]

This convention is significant because it was born from an appreciation that UN workers in extraordinary circumstances (both peace-keepers and associated personnel) did not receive adequate protection under international law and that a new and specific instrument of protection was necessary. Those protected by the CSUNAP include peace-keepers, including military and civilian components of any peace-keeping operation, as well as other experts of the United Nations or any of the UN specialised agencies who are present in an official capacity where the UN operation is being conducted. 'Associated Personnel', which is significant for humanitarian relief workers, includes among others:

> Persons deployed by a humanitarian non-governmental organisation or agency under an agreement with the Secretary-General of the United Nations or with a specialised agency...[46]

The debate about the need for increased protection for humanitarian workers was reinforced again by the 1996 Protocol II[47] which revised the *Convention on Prohibitions or Restrictions on the Use of Certain Conventional Weapons which may be Deemed to be Excessively Injurious or to Have Indiscriminate Effects* (CCW).[48] One important change led to the scope of the CCW expanding to include both international and non-international conflicts.[49] Article 12 was also

---

[41] Palwankar 1993, p. 231.

[42] Ibid.

[43] Boutros-Ghali 1992, para 68.

[44] GA Resolution 49/59 December 9, 1994.

[45] Opened for signature 15 December 1994, 2051 UNTS 363 (entered into force 15 January 1999).

[46] CSUNAP Article 1(b)(iii).

[47] Protocol on Prohibitions or Restrictions on the Use of Mines, Booby-Traps and Other Devices as amended on 3 May 1996, 2048 UNTS 93 (entered into force 3 December 1998).

[48] Opened for signature 10 April 1981, 1342 UNTS 137 (entered into force 2 December 1983).

[49] Article 1 paras 2, 3.

strengthened and now requires parties to the conflict to ensure protection for peace-keeping forces, humanitarian and fact-finding missions of the UN system, missions of the ICRC, missions of national Red Cross or Red Crescent societies or of the International Federation of Red Cross and Red Crescent Societies and missions of other impartial humanitarian organisations. Each party under the Convention, is required to provide protection against the effects of mines, booby-traps and other devices to all these 'protected persons'.[50]

Again the mention of 'other impartial humanitarian organisations' reinforces the recognition of the special risks that humanitarian personnel take in the conduct of their operations, and the need for special protection for them before the law.

In addition, the numerous Security Council resolutions supporting the provision of humanitarian operations and safe access and protection for humanitarian relief operations began to contribute to a sense that there was emerging customary international law around the protection of relief operations and personnel.[51]

Finally, recognition of the important role of relief personnel was expressed in the explicit protection for them established by the *Rome Statute of the International Criminal Court*.[52] Accordingly, attacking relief personnel and material was criminalised for the first time under international law. Article 8(2)(b) states:

> Other serious violations of the laws and customs applicable in international armed conflict, within the established framework of international law ... (iii) Intentionally directing attacks against personnel, installations, material, units or vehicles involved in a humanitarian assistance or peacekeeping mission in accordance with the Charter of the United Nations, as long as they are entitled to the protection given to civilians or civilian objects under the international law of armed conflict.

Similarly Article 8(2)(e)(iii) is identical to the above but applies to situations of non-international armed conflict. Therefore, relief workers who maintain their civilian status according to the Geneva Conventions are better protected than ever before.

This volume of evidence together with changing state practise throughout the 1990s, led the ICRC in their landmark 2005 study on customary IHL to determine that there are two fundamental customary international law rules related to humanitarian relief operations that pertain to international as well as non-international armed conflict. As noted previously, Rules 31 and 32 respectively stipulate that:

---

50 International Committee of the Red Cross 1998a.

51 On respect for security and safety of humanitarian relief personnel see, for example, UN SC Res 733 (1992) on Somalia, UN SC Res 1001 (1995) on the mandate of the UN Observer mission in Liberia, and UN SC Res 1203 (1998) on the situation in Kosovo. On respect for objects used for humanitarian relief operations see for example UN SC resolution 1075 and 1087 (1996) when the UN Security council called on all parties to the conflict in Angola to guarantee the safety of humanitarian supplies throughout the country.

52 Opened for signature 17 July 1998, 2187 UNTS 3 (entered into force 1 July 2002) (Rome Statute).

> Humanitarian relief personnel must be respected and protected;

and

> Objects used for humanitarian relief operations must be respected and protected.

Despite the significant evolution of protection afforded to humanitarian relief personnel over the last 20 years and the emergence of their right to protection as part of customary international law, now, more than ever before, humanitarian workers are being targeted by belligerent forces. A study by the Humanitarian Practice Network shows that attacks on aid workers have increased from 27 incidents in 1998 affecting 69 personnel to 139 incidents in 2009 affecting 278 personnel.[53] However, protection for relief workers is not an end in itself but, rather, is about providing better protection to populations affected by conflict and other situations of violence and ensuring that as far as possible the basic needs of the affected community are satisfied. It appears that despite the strengthening of legal protection this has not translated into greater security and more effective delivery of humanitarian assistance, and this can be clearly seen in a recent study conducted by ICRC on the impact of violence on the delivery of health care.

10.5 Impact of Violence on the Delivery of Health Care

As with the expanded protections offered to humanitarian relief workers under AP I, protections that were originally offered under the Geneva Conventions I[54] (Articles 24 and 25) and II[55] (Article 15) for the protection of medical personnel of armed forces of a party to the conflict were also extended in Article 9 of AP I. The protection for medical personnel now extends to encompass staff of the ICRC and 'national voluntary aid societies' that have been recognised and authorised by a Party to the conflict.[56] The Commentary to the Protocol also notes that the protections include medical staff of international humanitarian organisations that are recognised by the parties. Protection also exists for medical staff made available to a State party from a neutral state but they must be exclusively assigned to medical tasks by a party to the conflict.[57] It is noteworthy that while the civilian populations have a right to assist with collecting the wounded and sick, this does not

---

[53] Humanitarian Practice Network 2010, p. 273.

[54] Geneva Convention for the Amelioration of the Condition of the Wounded and Sick in Armed Forces in the Field, opened for signature 12 August 1949, 75 UNTS 31 (entered into force 21 October 1950) (GC I).

[55] Geneva Convention for the Amelioration of the Condition of Wounded, Sick and Shipwrecked Members of Armed Forces at Sea, opened for signature 12 August 1949, 75 UNTS 85 (entered into force 21 October 1950) (GC II).

[56] AP I Article 8(c)(ii).

[57] ICRC Commentary, 125.

render them 'medical personnel' and such an activity, therefore, does not provide them with particular protection over and above being a civilian.[58] However civilian medical personnel[59] and staff of civilian hospitals[60] do receive specific protection.

There are general rules about preventing medical personnel from undertaking their work[61] and even more extensively regarding the assistance that should be provided to civilian medical personnel by occupying powers when services are disrupted by combat.[62] In situations of occupation, parties must be sure not to impede access or free passage to medical units and personnel and have an obligation to allow access to humanitarian relief agencies and aid consignments. Access is more limited in non-international armed conflict where the obligation to provide access to relief agencies is not as strong; however, an offer of assistance must not be rejected in cases of extreme need.[63]

International humanitarian law allows that health care must be provided without discrimination or adverse distinction[64] and that health personnel may not be required to treat with adverse distinction.[65] The Conventions clearly provide for the right to medical assistance which is unsurprising given the historical basis for the Conventions from the deserted wounded on the battlefield of Solferino.

In international human rights law there is also a strong legal basis for upholding the right to access medical attention and fundamental health care. The right to life is a basic non-derogable tenet of human rights law[66] and by inference, medical attention cannot be withheld in life threatening circumstances.[67] The provision of healthcare is fundamental to the maintenance of the right to life. States have an obligation to take action to fulfil their obligation to allow their people to enjoy the realisation of the highest attainable standard of health care.[68] This right is also enshrined in various regional instruments such as the African[69] Charter, and in

58 See AP I Article 17.

59 AP I Article 15.

60 GC IV Article 20.

61 GC I Article 18; AP I Articles 15,17; AP II Article 10.

62 AP I Article 15; AP II Article 9.

63 ICRC Commentary, 1478.

64 GC I Article 12; GC II Article 12; GC Common Article 3; AP I Articles 9–10(2); AP II Article 7; CIHL rule 110.

65 AP II Article 9(2).

66 Universal Declaration of Human Rights, GA Res 217A (III), UN GAOR, 3rd session, 183rd plenary meeting, UN Doc A/810 (10 December 1948) (UDHR) Article 3.

67 *Cyprus v Turkey*, Judgment 10 May 2001, No. 25781/94 ECHR 2001, paras 219–221.

68 International Covenant on Economic, Social and Cultural Rights, opened for signature 16 December 1966, 993 UNTS 3 (entered into force 3 November 1976) (ICESCR) Article 12.2.

69 Organization of African Unity, African Charter on the Rights and Welfare of the Child, 11 July 1990, CAB/LEG/24.9/49 (1990).

particular in the Convention on the Rights of the Child[70] (Article 24). The right to health care includes safe access to health care services[71] and should be provided without discrimination.[72]

Attacks on health care personnel may constitute an arbitrary deprivation of life as prohibited under Article 3 of the Universal Declaration of Human Rights (UDHR) and Article 6 of the International Covenant on Civil and Political Rights[73] and it is possible to argue that the above-mentioned rights to health care and the obligation on a State not to deny or limit access may be breached where attacks on medical personnel would deny citizens treatment.

Violence against the wounded, health care workers, or medical facilities will not always be targeted and intentional and in such cases may not violate principles of IHL. All medical personnel and objects should be clearly marked with the protective emblems although a failure to do so does not negate their protection. There is an obligation on warring parties to undertake all possible precaution to verify that the object of attack is not subject to special protection[74] and to minimise incidental damage and injury.[75] All attacks must comply with the general IHL principles and be assessed in this context. Even if an attack fulfils the requirement of distinction and does not specifically target protected persons, it must conform with all other IHL principles including proportionality,[76] military necessity[77] and unnecessary suffering.[78]

Protected persons can only lose their protected status if they directly participate in hostilities. This may include the use of medical units to shelter able-bodied combatants, to store arms or ammunition, as military observation posts, as a shield for military action, for the transport of healthy troops, arms or munitions and the collection or transmission of military intelligence. Acts that do not negate protected status of medical personnel include carrying light individual weapons for self-defence or defence of the wounded and sick; the presence of, or escort by, military personnel or protection by sentries, and possession of small arms and

---

[70] Opened for signature 20 November 1989, 1577 UNTS 3 (entered into force 2 September 1990).

[71] UNOHCHR/WHO 2008.

[72] UN Committee on Economic, Social and Cultural Rights, General Comment No. 14: The Right to the Highest Attainable Standard of Health (Art. 12 of the Covenant), 11 August 2000, E/C.12/2000/4, para 34; International Convention on the Elimination of All Forms of Racial Discrimination, opened for signature 21 December 1965, 660 UNTS 195 (entered into force 4 January 1969), Article 5(e)(iv).

[73] Opened for signature 16 December 1966, 999 UNTS 171 (entered into force 23 March 1976) (ICCPR).

[74] AP I Article 57(2).

[75] CIHL rule 17.

[76] AP I Articles 51(5)(b), 57(2)(a)(iii), CIHL rules 14, 18.

[77] AP I Article 51(4); CIHL rule 12.

[78] AP I Article 35(2); CIHL rule 70.

ammunition taken from the wounded and sick and not yet handed over to the proper authority.[79]

However, any wilful killing, inhumane treatment or the causing of serious injury to a protected person constitutes a war crime under the Rome Statute, Articles 8(2)(i)–(iii). Equally attacks against medical personnel and facilities displaying the emblem constitute war crimes[80] as do attacks against humanitarian personnel and material.

10.6 Conclusion

Today there is no doubt the IHL regime provides protection for both humanitarian workers and medical personnel. Yet increasingly these individuals and organisations are being targeted for attack fundamentally jeopardising relief operations and the provision of health care to populations affected by conflict and other situations of violence. States Parties to the Geneva Conventions have a responsibility under Common Article 1 to not only respect the law, but ensure respect for the law. Clearly, significantly more work needs to be done to promote and encourage respect for relief workers and medical personnel in conflict zones by all warring parties. Whilst increased prosecution of those accused of crimes such as attacking health care workers will not be the complete answer in itself, it would underscore the unacceptability of such crimes.

The ICRC 'Health Care in Danger' (HCiD) campaign offers an opportunity to further discuss, debate and identify additional measures that need to be taken in this area. Redressing some of the dangers faced by communities losing access to vital health care services is a topic worthy of further reflection as it currently remains a largely unrecognised humanitarian challenge. Recent images from Libya of desperate people in need of medical treatment and makeshift ambulances ferrying the wounded to often under-staffed and damaged hospitals may prompt more robust action by the international community. Health-care workers and volunteers who have striven in difficult and often dangerous circumstances to provide medical assistance to the wounded are sadly increasingly attacked. In a 4-day period alone, in May 2011, three Libyan Red Crescent ambulances were hit in three separate incidents, resulting in the death of a nurse and injuries to a patient and three volunteers.[81] In total, five volunteers of the Libyan Red Crescent were killed while performing their duty in 2011; such high levels of loss clearly have a large impact on the capacity to service the needs of the civilian population and other protected people.[82] The gravity of this issue was reflected in a resolution passed by the

79 GC I Article 22; GC II Article 5, GC IV Article19, AP I Article 13(2).

80 Rome Statute Articles 8(2)(b)(ix), (xxiv).

81 International Committee of the Red Cross 2011c.

82 International Committee of the Red Cross 2011d.

International Red Cross and Red Crescent Movement and all State parties to the Geneva Conventions at the 31st Conference in 2011.[83]

The ICRC recently launched a study into threats and violence affecting the delivery of health care in such situations.[84] Carried out in 16 countries over 30 months it found 1,834 individuals were killed or injured in 655 violent incidents and identified patterns of attacks ranging from direct attacks on patients, medical personnel and facilities, to looting, kidnapping, arrests and denial of access to health care. However the implications of these statistics are more sobering when the research demonstrates that one single act of violence that damages a hospital or kills health-care workers has a knock-on effect, depriving many patients of needed medical treatment. For example, the study concludes that the killing of six ICRC and Red Cross nurses in Chechnya in 1996 resulted in an estimated 2,000 war-wounded being deprived of a year of needed surgical care.[85] When such projections are multiplied, the reality can be disastrous with many thousands of people potentially deprived of essential medical care. This also includes basic services such as maternal and child care, access to specialist services for those suffering from chronic illnesses and the disruption of vital preventive programmes. These indirect implications of armed conflict require more attention.

Despite the significant advances made in the legal protection for humanitarian relief workers over the last 20 years and the existing protection for medical personnel in situations of armed conflict, there is much more that needs to be done. States Parties need to redress the impunity that surrounds attacks on relief personnel and material, as well as on medical personnel and facilities. To date, as far as the authors are aware, no criminal law cases have been brought against those who have launched attacks against humanitarian and medical personnel by either national or international justice systems. The HCiD programme established by the ICRC should be treated as a part of a broader effort to raise awareness and international mobilisation on this critical issue, with a particular focus on health as part of wider humanitarian assistance.

The capacity to deliver basic survival supplies and health care in situations of armed conflict and violence straddles the delicate balance between humanity and military necessity that is the essential aim of IHL. In the multi-dimensional conflicts witnessed today, the need to examine obligations found under human rights laws as well as IHL is crucial if the increased protection for humanitarian workers and their materials is to be achieved. Furthermore detailed evidence based studies, campaigns and academic discussion on the challenges faced by humanitarian workers and, in particular, the increased political nature of 'aid' is warranted. Prosecutions of those accused of breaching the existing rules pertaining to

---

[83] See http://www.icrc.org/eng/resources/documents/resolution/31-international-conference-resolution-5-2011.htm. The 31st International Conference of the Red Cross and Red Crescent 2011.

[84] International Committee of the Red Cross 2011a.

[85] International Committee of the Red Cross 2011b.

protections afforded to all humanitarian workers and their infrastructure could assist in highlighting the existing legal framework and the serious nature of such crimes. Protecting the 'helpers' needs to be an integral aspect of any discourse relating to protection during times of armed conflict—if not the repercussions for affected communities will be grave.

References

Australian Civilian Corp (2011) About ACC. 19 Dec 2011. Available at http://www.ausaid.gov.au/acc/about.cfm. Accessed 06 Jan 2012

Boutros-Ghali B (1992) An agenda for peace, UN Doc A/47/277S/24111

Bugnion F (2004) The International Committee of the Red Cross and the development of international humanitarian law. Chic J Int Law 5:191

Coghlan B et al. (2006) Mortality in the Democratic Republic of Congo: a nationwide survey. Lancet 367:44

Fishstein P, Wilder A (2012) Winning hearts and minds? Examining the relationship between aid and security in Afghanistan. Feinstein International Center. Available at https://wikis.uit.tufts.edu/confluence/pages/viewpage.action?pageId=48862164. Accessed 5 Jan 2012

Graduate Institute of International and Development Studies: Small Arms Study (2011) Indirect conflict deaths. http://www.smallarmssurvey.org/armed-violence/conflict-armed-violence/indirect-conflict-deaths.html. Accessed 3 Jan 2012

Henckaerts J-M, Doswald-Beck L (2009) Customary International Humanitarian Law volume 1: rules. Cambridge University Press, Cambridge

Humanitarian Practice Network (2010) Good Practice Review 8. Operational security in violent environments. Overseas Development Institute

International Commission on Intervention and State Sovereignty (2001) The responsibility to protect: report of the international commission on intervention and state sovereignty. International Development Research Centre, Ottawa

International Committee of the Red Cross (1987) Commentary on the additional protocols of 8 June 1977. ICRC, Geneva

International Committee of the Red Cross (1998a) 'Respect for and protection of the personnel of humanitarian organisations': preparatory document of ICRC for the first periodical meeting on international humanitarian law, Geneva 19–23 Jan 1998. Available at http://www.icrc.org/eng/resources/documents/misc/57jp85.htm Accessed 3 Jan 2012

International Committee of the Red Cross (1998b) Protecting the protector: statement. 29 Jan 1998. Available at http://www.icrc.org/eng/resources/documents/misc/57jp2c.htm (Accessed 06 Jan 2012)

International Committee of the Red Cross (1998c) Libya: red crescent volunteers and medical personnel in danger: operational update No 05/11, 17 May 2011. Available at http://www.icrc.org/eng/resources/documents/update/2011/libya-update-2011-05-17.htm (Accessed 06 Jan 2012)

International Committee of the Red Cross (2011a) Health care in danger: A sixteen-country study. Available at http://www.icrc.org/eng/assets/files/reports/4073-002-16-country-study.pdf. Accessed 4 Jan 2012

International Committee of the Red Cross (2011b) FAQ: healthcare in danger: questions and answers. 5 Aug 2011. Available at http://www.icrc.org/eng/resources/documents/faq/health-care-in-danger-faq-2011-08-05.htm. Accessed 06 Jan 2012)

International Committee of the Red Cross (2011d) Libya: humanitarian challenges six months on—interview. 12 Aug 2011. Available at http://www.icrc.org/eng/resources/documents/interview/2011/libya-interview-2011-08-12.htm. Accessed 06 Jan 2012

Koenig C (1991) Observer status for the International Committee of the Red Cross at the United Nations. Int Rev Red Cross 31:37

Mosler H (1984) Subjects of International Law. In: Bernhardt R (ed) Encyclopedia of International Law, vol 7. Amsterdam, Elsevier, p 455

Murray CJL et al (2002) Armed conflict as a public health problem. Br Med J 324:346–349

Oxfam International (2007) Rising to the humanitarian challenge in Iraq. http://www.oxfam.org/en/policy/briefingpapers/bp105_humanitarian_challenge_in_iraq_0707. Accessed 4 Jan 2012

Palwankar U (1993) Applicability of international humanitarian law to United Nations Peace-keeping forces. Int Rev Red Cross 294:227–240

Pictet J (ed) (1958) Commentary—IV Geneva convention, relative to the protection of civilian persons in time of war, ICRC

Tchanile T (1989) Actions de secours en faveur de la population civile dans les conflit armes internationaux et les conflit armes non internationaux' In: Kalshoven F, Sandoz Y (eds) Implementation of international humanitarian law'. Hague Academy of International Law, Dordrecht

Terry F (2011) The International Committee of the Red Cross in Afghanistan: reasserting the neutrality of humanitarian action. Int Rev Red Cross 93:173

The 31st International Conference of the Red Cross and Red Crescent (2011) Resolution 5—Health care in danger. http://www.icrc.org/eng/resources/documents/resolution/31-international-conference-resolution-5-2011.htm. Accessed 5 Jan 2012

UN Office of the High Commissioner for Human Rights (2008) Fact sheet No. 31. The right to health. http://www.unhcr.org/refworld/docid/48625a742.html. Accessed 5 Jan 2012

Part III
Forum: Reflections on 9/11 and IHL

Chapter 11
International Humanitarian Law a Decade after September 11: Developments and Perspectives

Dieter Fleck

Contents

Former Director International Agreements & Policy, Federal Ministry of Defence, Germany; Honorary President, *International Society for Military Law and the Law of War*, http://www.soc-mil-law.org; Member of the Advisory Board of the *Amsterdam Center for International Law (ACIL)*, http://www.jur.uva.nl/aciluk/home.cfm; Member of the Editorial Board of the *Journal of International Peacekeeping*, http://www.brill.nl/joup. All views and opinions are personal.

D. Fleck (✉)
International Agreements & Policy, Federal Ministry of Defence, Cologne, Germany
e-mail: DieterFleck@t-online.de

International Society for Military Law and the Law of War, Cologne, Germany

Amsterdam Center for International Law (ACIL), Amsterdam, The Netherlands

M.N. Schmitt and L. Arimatsu (eds.), *Yearbook of International Humanitarian Law Volume 14, 2011*, DOI: 10.1007/978-90-6704-855-2_11,

11.1 Introduction

The invitation to join this symposium provides an opportunity for critically reviewing opinions I had expressed years ago, in the immediate aftermath of 9/11.[1] Emphasizing the need for strict compliance with international humanitarian law, human rights law, national constitutional law and rules of due process, in order to convincingly meet the challenge terrorism poses to democratic societies, I had called for a culture of compliance in which incentives for faithful implementation of humanitarian law should be developed to make the expectation of reciprocity a realistic possibility rather than contemplating restraints of humanitarian protection and derogations of human rights. Developments went in a different direction: the world has witnessed an unlimited practice of operational detentions; *habeas corpus* was, and still is, denied in military operations; and prisoners have been tortured as part of deliberately planned activities. At the same time organized terrorist movements continue to plan and execute attacks while hiding among civilian populations; the number of suicide attacks has increased rather than decreased; and distinctive emblems protected under the Geneva Conventions are deliberately targeted by Taliban fighters.

An even wider spectrum of controversies becomes apparent within the *jus ad bellum*: here the dispute over whether the strictest reading of Article 51 of the Charter was 'inappropriate' in the case of terrorist attacks,[2] or the adaptation of the perceived threats concept, as occurred in the U.S. National Security Strategy 2002, had 'unacceptably' expanded the right of anticipatory self-defence,[3] is yet to be resolved in theory and practice.[4] While this larger controversy remains important to fully realise the challenges of 9/11 for international law as a law in transition, I will here focus on the *jus in bello*, starting with the applicability threshold of the principles and rules of international humanitarian law and their relevance in a wider sense (11.2). I will address differences and similarities in the legal paradigms of law enforcement and the conduct of hostilities (11.3), discuss their effects on peacebuilding (11.4), and consider the role of civil society in implementing relevant legal obligations (11.5). My conclusions will stress the need to concentrate on *jus post bellum* and to develop the proper structure, contents and implementation mechanisms of this evolving branch of international law (11.6).

11.2 The Notion of Armed Conflict

It is widely shared *opinio juris* today that the notion of armed conflict is based on two factual criteria, i.e. (a) the existence of organized armed groups which are (b) engaged in fighting of some intensity.[5] Given the nature of the attacks perpetrated

---

[1] Fleck 2003, at p. 70.

[2] Lietzau 2004, at p. 398.

[3] Bothe 2003, at pp. 227, 232–233, 236–239.

[4] See Gill in Gill and Fleck 2010, at 187 ff, 217 ff, 221 ff, 229 ff.

[5] ILA Committee on the Use of Force 2010, at p. 713.

in New York, Washington, D.C. and Pennsylvania on September 11, it was assumed that both these criteria were satisfied. Only one day thereafter, the Security Council condemned these 'horrifying terrorist attacks' in the strongest terms, regarding them 'like any act of international terrorism, as a threat to international peace and security',[6] and the North Atlantic Council agreed that 'if it is determined that this attack was directed from abroad against the United States, it shall be regarded as an action covered by Article 5 of the Washington Treaty, which states that an armed attack against one or more of the Allies in Europe or North America shall be considered an attack against them all'.[7] It may be noted that the term 'armed conflict' itself was not used in either of these political statements. A legal evaluation under international humanitarian law was made at a later stage and it led to distinct qualifications as regarding parties to the conflict, territories involved, and action to be taken.

In late 2001/early 2002 the conflict with Taliban-controlled Afghanistan was regarded as an international armed conflict; the character of the conflict changed subsequently when the *Loya Jirga* convened in June 2002 and a transitional Afghan Government was established on 19 June 2002. The ICRC stated, in an aide-mémoire submitted on 18 November 2002 to Permanent Missions in Geneva, that in view of the unanimous recognition of the new Afghan Government by the entire community of States and its broad-based recognition within the country through the *Loya Jirga* process the on-going military operations in Afghanistan directed against remnants of Taliban or al-Qaeda forces could no longer be viewed as an international armed conflict. Stressing the peace-building character of the Interim Security Assistance Force (ISAF),[8] many participating States had hesitated to qualify their military operations in support of the Afghan Government as part of an armed conflict altogether; yet, during the last years, due to the duration and intensity of fighting, the continuing existence of an armed conflict in Afghanistan became an undeniable phenomenon.

It should be recalled that any such qualification as to what body of law governs, must be fact-oriented. It does not depend on political will since the factual circumstances existing at the time determine the application of the relevant body of law whether it is the law of international armed conflict, the law of non-international armed conflict, or peacetime international law. Against this background it seems unconvincing to suggest that for the situation in Afghanistan 'a requalification of an armed conflict downwards to non-international' had been made that had led to

---

[6] SC Res 1368 (2001).

[7] Statement by the North Atlantic Council, 12 September 2001.

[8] For the ISAF mandate, its development and extensions over the years see SC Resolutions 1386 (2001), para 1; 1401 (2002), para 6; 1413 (2002); 1444 (2002); 1510 (2003); 1536 (2004), para 13; 1563 (2004); 1659 (2006), para 6; 1662 (2006), para 18; 1707 (2006); 1746 (2007), para 25; 1776 (2007); 1806 (2008), para 4 d; 1833 (2008); 1868 (2009), para 4 b; 1890 (2009); 1917 (2010), paras 5 b, 17; 1943 (2010); 1974 (2011), para 5 b; 2011 (2011); .

'a marked loss of protection for persons that were protected by the Geneva Conventions in the earlier stages of the conflict'.[9] Rather, it should be accepted that the proper qualification of a conflict is not contingent on a political choice but on an assessment of objective facts. As far as the legal protection of civilians in armed conflicts is concerned, Additional Protocol I (rather than Geneva Convention IV) sets forth obligations for Parties to international armed conflicts for which there are no treaty law counterparts with regard to opposition fighters in an internal war. It would, however, be wrong to conclude that the obligation to protect victims does not exist in the latter type of conflict, as such obligations are unambiguously enshrined in customary law today.

In 2008, the ICRC had reason to recall that in accordance with a strong and prevailing legal opinion

> 1. International armed conflicts exist whenever there is *resort to armed force between two or more States*.
> 2. Non-international armed conflicts are *protracted armed confrontations* occurring between governmental armed forces and the forces of one or more armed groups, or between such groups arising on the territory of a State [party to the Geneva Conventions]. The armed confrontation must reach *a minimum level of intensity* and the parties involved in the conflict must show *a minimum of organisation*.[10]

What has often rhetorically been referred to as 'war against terrorists' cannot then be legally considered an international armed conflict, as long as no State is fighting on the side of terrorist groups. For a legal qualification as non-international armed conflict the *level of intensity* and the degree of *organisation* of non-state parties must be examined, before any final assessment can be made. This assessment is necessary, not only because it triggers the application of international humanitarian law, but also for many other reasons which all make it essential to realise whether a state of peace or a state of armed conflict applies in an affected country.

States often refrain from making this assessment in an unequivocal manner. The present Legal Advisor to the U.S. Secretary of State, Harold Koh, has referred to 'armed conflicts' in Iraq and in Afghanistan and, in the same context, he stated that '[i]n the conflict occurring in Afghanistan and elsewhere, we continue to fight the perpetrators of 9/11: a non-state actor, al-Qaeda (as well as the Taliban forces that harbored al-Qaeda)'. He also referred to 'a war of self-defense against an enemy that attacked us on September 11, 2001, and before, and that continues to undertake armed attacks against the United States'.[11] Such language conveys an impression that it is no longer necessary to distinguish between 'conflicts' and 'armed conflicts' nor to differentiate between international and non-international armed conflicts. Moreover, rather than restraining conflicts, this reasoning widens

---

9 Wills 2011, at p. 173.

10 ICRC 2008.

11 Koh 2010.

them in a way that may potentially exclude identifying solutions at the political level within a foreseeable timeframe.

States are not alone in confusing political rhetoric with legal analysis. In a recent legal research project the question of whether fighters in non-international armed conflicts should be considered as actors in international law was addressed. That question was denied for Al-Qaeda as well as for all illegal bodies not organized 'in any recognized legal and identifiable manner',[12] but at the same time it was affirmed for 'organised armed opposition groups, rebel groups, insurgents, and belligerent groups, and parties to an armed conflict that reaches the applicability of international humanitarian law and its constraints'.[13] While this reveals an inconsistency that presumably will not stand as a final conclusion, it is difficult to establish parameters here that may be widely or even unanimously accepted.

At the last International Red Cross and Red Crescent Conference (Geneva, 2011), the ICRC focused on legal and policy effects of blurring armed conflict and terrorism, emphasizing the disadvantages caused by such blurring particularly for the protection of victims.[14] Branding fighters in non-international armed conflicts as 'terrorists', without any distinction whether or not they have committed any act prohibited under the laws of war (e.g. acts falling under Article 33 GC IV; Article 51, para 2 AP I; Article 4, para 2 lit. d, or 13, para 2, AP II), would deny them any incentive to fight according to the rules. It would create a situation unfavourable to non-state armed group compliance with international humanitarian law and reduce the likelihood of obtaining respect for its rules. This would also have the practical effect of proscribing such fighters as belonging to terrorist organizations; in addition, to provide support, services or assistance could be deemed a criminal offence, a particular problem to which I will come back below (Sect. 11.5).

It remains to be seen how States will cope with the phenomenon of terrorism in future: will solutions be sought and found under peacetime rules of international law or will States and societies let themselves be drawn into armed conflicts which must then be fought until the very end before a political settlement can be found? Armed conflicts can be forced upon States, but States do have full responsibility for avoiding military solutions wherever this is possible. And when a military battle has to be fought, strict application of the law of armed conflict will be an asset not only to provide humanitarian protection to the victims but also to treat the adversary in a way that includes incentives for compliance and may help to keep political solutions open. In that sense any branding of enemy fighters as 'terrorists' is counterproductive. At the same time, it remains vital that war crimes continue to be prosecuted and this is done by independent courts.

The legal difference between armed conflict and peacetime notwithstanding, it may be noted and appreciated that international humanitarian law is relevant in a wider sense also for acts committed outside armed conflicts. There are important

12 ILA Committee on Non-State Actors 2010, at p. 637.

13 Ibid., p. 638.

14 ICRC 2011, at pp. 48–53.

obligations for implementation, dissemination, instruction, and training of its rules which apply already in peacetime. Moreover, the respect for humanitarian principles requires full adherence to them in any situation in which victims are in need of protection. Decades ago, Jean Pictet held it important enough to stress: "What Government would dare to claim before the world, in a case of civil disturbances which could justly be described as mere acts of banditry, that, Article 3 not being applicable, it was entitled to leave the wounded uncared for, to torture and mutilate prisoners and take hostages?"[15] That statement is still relevant today. There are, indeed, standards of behaviour that need to be respected in any situation. The principles of distinction, avoidance of unnecessary suffering, and humanity are not confined to armed conflicts but they apply as well for law enforcement operations in peacetime, and this has consequences for many situations and their proper evaluation within the applicable legal order.

11.3 Law Enforcement and the Conduct of Hostilities

Terrorist attacks committed in the aftermath of 11 September 2001, such as those in London, Madrid, Bali, and Mumbai, have correctly been characterized as crimes, not as acts of armed conflict.[16] This underlines the very large extent to which anti-terrorist operations—both by the police and by armed forces—are to be qualified as law enforcement rather than conduct of hostilities. In law enforcement operations human rights obligations and rules of national law apply. These are less liberal than the *lex specialis* rules of international humanitarian law in armed conflicts, in which attacks are generally permitted in the conduct of hostilities against enemy fighters and military objectives. In law enforcement any use of force is limited to what is absolutely necessary to remove a particular threat to life or property, a decision to be made in the concrete circumstances.[17] Even during an armed conflict law enforcement activities will be necessary and they must remain distinct from the conduct of hostilities. International humanitarian law has specific *lex specialis* rules for that purpose, such as those regulating the treatment of prisoners of war, internees, and protected persons in occupied territory.[18]

Existing differences between law enforcement and the conduct of hostilities are, however, not a matter of principle but rather a matter of graduation.[19] This calls for more exchange between military and police lawyers to make an objective

[15] Pictet 1958, at pp. 35–36, with reference to the Final Record of the Diplomatic Conference of Geneva of 1949, Volume II, Section B, at 121.

[16] ILA Committee on the Use of Force 2010, at p. 705.

[17] Melzer in Gill and Fleck 2010, at 336 f, 281.

[18] Ibid., p. 37.

[19] Fleck 2008, p. 406; Gill and Fleck 2010, at p. 570.

comparison of applicable standards and procedures. The principles of proportionality and effectiveness as such remain a common feature, as they are inherent in all branches of law. Yet in law enforcement operations their application will be different from what would be appropriate in the conduct of hostilities, as the overall threat and prevailing conditions under which State organs have to act are not the same in these two situations. This will affect the relevance of various considerations in a given context, in particular concerning the degree of individual protection and the acceptability of collateral damage. The latter is generally much lower but not altogether excluded in law enforcement operations, when a perpetrator may be using human shields and cannot be prevented from committing a capital crime without exposing innocents to danger.

The different degrees of diligence to be observed in law enforcement and the conduct of hostilities do depend from the existing threat in the given situation. These differences will not only affect the use of force as such, but also the behaviour of State authorities and the procedures that must be observed. This will include the requirement to conduct formal investigations into any death/s resulting from the use of force which, under human rights law, is a strict obligation that may be considered as being generally lifted in the conduct of hostilities, unless there is excessive collateral damage, or allegedly war crimes or crimes against humanity have been committed.

Other relevant examples of *lex specialis* are not confined to the conduct of hostilities, but apply to military uses as such. A case in point is the ITU Constitution,[20] which *inter alia* prohibits any harmful interference in radio services or communications of other Member States or of recognized operating agencies and provides, in Article 48, that Member States retain their entire freedom with regard to military radio installations. This exemption applies also in peacetime and during peace operations. It would be worth investigating whether and to what extent police forces enjoy similar prerogatives for law enforcement. Also the control of communications in general, the transfer of personal data, and laws allowing a government to store personal data may be relevant in this context.

While not every governmental activity is clearly and fully regulated, certain agencies have, in recent times, tended to assume prerogatives that might not stand legal scrutiny. This applies to certain forms of operational detentions, their duration and review, and in particular to the practice of renditions. Where States refrain from extensive considerations of existing human rights obligations and existing legal gaps remain unregulated, at a minimum, the principles and rules of state responsibility apply, and that responsibility is sometimes even independent from the question whether or not a wrongful act has been committed.

---

20 Constitution of the International Telecommunication Union, http://www.itu.int/net/about/basic-texts/index.aspx.

11.4 Effects on Peacebuilding

What lessons might be learned from the experiences of the last decade for future peacebuilding efforts, not least in that transition period from armed conflict to peace? To begin with, clear accountability of Sending States and of international organizations is of particular importance to peace operations, as these actors should aim at institution building and the transfer of full governmental powers back to the Host State. This requires cooperation between these three categories of actors and a recognition among them that in this dynamic 'triangular' relationship the driving forces are subject to change; that competences will develop in a complex process; and that the distribution of responsibilities between the international organization, the particular Sending State, and the Host State may be less than clear. It is essential that each of the three entities concerned will, in any given situation, be able and willing to cooperate in exercising effective legal control of their operations and are aware of the applicable mode of action, be it general assistance, law enforcement, or conduct of hostilities. The responsibility for the outcome should in any event be shared and this idea is stressed here not so much for the preparation of an assessment *post factum*, but in the spirit of developing effective and lasting action in order to meet the agreed purpose.

Together with this triangle of forces a fourth and specifically incalculable entity is yet to be considered: non-state actors. This category of actors includes groups of different origin and potential, each with different aims and expectations. For example, there are civilians who should be given a share in peacebuilding activities; opposition groups who are to be disarmed, but must also be convinced of peacebuilding methods and goals; foreign and local workers engaged in humanitarian assistance or involved in enterprise. It may be difficult to exercise control over each from outside and to compound the challenge for the Sending State, Host State and international organizations, they not only operate at different distances but their various roles may change over time. Thus, for successful peacebuilding it is essential to provide transparency in operations, follow cooperative approaches, and constantly adapt as necessary. To reach these objectives an accepted legal order must be implemented and enforced, one that should offer everybody appropriate and clearly calculable perspectives.

The present detention practice followed by States and tolerated by the United Nations is a highly relevant example in this context. In many contemporary military operations the number of security detainees, uncertainties with respect to the concrete purpose of detention, and the absence of convincing and effective legal control have created problems that were neither contemplated by the planners of those operations nor solved by their executors. In the practice of States clear differences between criminal and security detainees are often not made or have turned out to be impossible. A deploringly large number of persons have been detained in recent years, without fully considering the purpose of detention, the applicable procedures and the duration of capture. No professional detention policy has been developed so far by the United Nations.[21] This problem should be taken up not only at executive level, but also at the political level. It poses a challenge for the United Nations and for national parliaments, whose approval to send military forces abroad should include a clear mandate for such forces under the rule of law. Receiving States should be encouraged to participate in cooperative solutions to secure the rule of law in peacebuilding processes.

The *Obama* Administration has expressly acknowledged that international law informs the scope of detention authority and it relies on legislative authority expressly granted to the President by Congress in the 2001 Authorization for Use of Military Force (AUMF).[22] Yet it appears less than convincing to draw the applicable rules of international law exclusively from the *jus in bello*,[23] as under current standards an amalgamation of international humanitarian law, human rights law, and good policy and practice is required.[24] This is more so since many security detentions are emanating from circumstances that do not amount to an armed conflict, transparent detention policy principles are widely missing, and criminal prosecution with clear perspectives for trial and release is not guaranteed in many cases. Excessive numbers of security detainees, without clear political perspectives for how and when to release them, may by themselves become a threat to peace and security, thus posing problems far beyond the category of individual human rights violations. Recent debates in the U.S. Senate on the National Defense Authorization Act for Fiscal Year 2012 with its several provisions dealing with the government's detention authority seem to have missed this important point: discussions had focused on mandating military custody and prosecution of alleged foreign terrorists and on the question whether this should apply to U.S. citizens as well. That the Supreme Court will have the last decision was admitted in these debates, but a responsible political decision-making should avoid any legal uncertainty for the armed forces in their operations and ensure that independent judges are available to examine detentions quickly and take responsible decisions as to their lawfulness and duration.

This problem is not limited to the United States. In most military operations that are conducted in foreign territories today *habeas corpus* rights are neglected or completely denied. The European Court of Human Rights has made it clear that Security Council resolutions cannot easily be used to escape liability for breaches of human rights obligations.[25] But appropriate action remains to be taken to specify operational mandates and ensure professional control under the rule of law. This should be seen as a challenge to the Security Council, to national Governments and national Parliaments likewise. Sending States and competent international

[21] Oswald 2011, at p. 123.

[22] Koh 2010.

[23] Ibid.

[24] Kleffner in Gill and Fleck 2010, at Chapter 25.

[25] European Court of Human Rights, Grand Chamber, *Al-Jedda v. United Kingdom*, no. 27021/08, 7 July 2011, available at http://www.icj.org/img/AL-JEDDA_v._UK.pdf, at paras 74–86.

organizations bear a clear responsibility together with Host States to ensure the lawfulness and effectiveness of their military operations.

A successful Security Sector Reform (SSR) should comprise effective security forces subordinate to civilian authorities and acting under parliamentary control. This should include judicial oversight by independent courts, the integration of structures and processes to engender full accountability, and a civil society, media, and individuals engaged in relevant debate and advocacy for the victims.

11.5 The Role of Civil Society

As discussed above (Sect. 11.2), branding armed individuals or groups as terrorists may criminalise assistance, protection and other activities rendered in support of such individuals or groups and even have chilling effects on activities of humanitarian organizations. Should even advice intended to be used for peaceful purposes be considered as material support for terrorism? This question is in the first place a matter of national law, but it has clearly international legal connotations.

The recent *Holder* judgment of the U.S. Supreme Court[26] is a case in point. The Supreme Court had to apply the provision of the United States Code according to which it is a federal crime to 'knowingly provid[e] material support or resources to a foreign terrorist organization'.[27] The plaintiffs had claimed that they wished to support the humanitarian activities of the *Kurdistan Workers' Party (Partiya Karkeran Kurdistan—PKK)* and the *Liberation Tigers of Tamil Eelam (LTTE)*, in particular by (1) training them on how to use humanitarian and international law to peacefully resolve disputes; (2) engaging in political advocacy on behalf of Kurds who live in Turkey; (3) teaching PKK members how to petition various representative bodies such as the United Nations for relief; and (4) engaging in political advocacy on behalf of the Tamils who live in Sri Lanka, activities they could not take for fear of prosecution. The Supreme Court, deciding in this case after 12 years of litigation, affirmed in part the judgment of the Court of Appeals of the Ninth Circuit and remanded it for further proceedings. It confirmed the criminalization of material support (including monetary contributions, other tangible aid, legal training, expert advice or assistance, and political advocacy) for organizations that are committed in both terrorist activities and activities of a humanitarian character, do not respect the line between humanitarian and violent

---

[26] Supreme Court of the United States, Nos. 08-1498 and 09-89, *Eric H. Holder, Attorney General, et al. v. Humanitarian Law Project et al.* and *Humanitarian Law Project et al. v. Eric H. Holder, Attorney General, et al.* (21 June 2010) available at http://www.supremecourt.gov/opinions/09pdf/08-1498.pdf.

[27] 18 U.S.C. §2339B(a)(1).

activities, and cannot be controlled by donors as to which activity will benefit from donations made.[28]

In his dissenting opinion Justice *Breyer*, joined by Justices *Ginsburg* and *Sotomayor*, argued that the U.S. Constitution does not permit the Government 'to prosecute the plaintiffs criminally for engaging in coordinated teaching and advocacy furthering the designated organizations' lawful political objectives' and that the Government had not met its burden of showing that 'an interpretation of the statute that would prohibit this speech- and association-related activity serves the Government's compelling interest in combating terrorism'. The Government had not explained in any detail 'how the plaintiffs' political-advocacy-related activities might actually be "fungible" and therefore capable of being diverted to terrorist use'. Consequently, the lower courts should be put in a position to consider more specifically the precise activities in which the plaintiffs still wish to engage. Activities relating to 'advocating' for the organizations' peaceful causes should not be excluded from such consideration.[29]

This case not only shows the negative long-term consequences such jurisprudence may have for humanitarian organizations, but also the inability of national courts to exercise legal control of the effectiveness of governmental acts in the fight against terrorism. The U.S. Supreme Court had focused on First Amendment rights rather than examining the necessity and appropriateness of government action under the rule of law. It thus enlarged the range of decision-making by the Administration with the negative effect of reducing that of citizens. International standards and obligations deriving from human rights protection were neglected despite the fact that the activities in question are transgressing national borders and many foreign actors are affected. The judgment has also cemented the legal assessment of this case within the spectrum and time-frame of on-going activities, as no *caveat* was made that would hint to a requirement of scrutinizing further developments. This limits civil society in taking activities that may be essential for post-conflict peacebuilding.

11.6 Conclusions

Negligence of international legal obligations and flawed policies in the fight against terrorism have not only led to a lack of consensus on relevant requirements under international law, but also proven to be counter-productive for long-term

[28] See Opinion of the Court, loc.cit., p. 2: 'We conclude that the material-support statute is constitutional as applied to the particular activities plaintiffs have told us they wish to pursue. We do not, however, address the resolution of more difficult cases that may arise under the statute in future.'

[29] See Breyer, J., dissenting, loc.cit., p. 23: '… the Court has failed to examine the Government's justifications with sufficient care. It has failed to insist on specific evidence, rather than general assertion. It has failed to require tailoring of means to fit compelling ends. And ultimately, it deprives the individuals before us of the protection that the First Amendment demands'.

settlements and stability post-conflict. A concentration on legal controversies in the interpretation of rules related to the conduct of hostilities rather than thinking of best practices has turned out to be as insufficient as continued attempts to provide security by military means alone. What is needed today is a renewal of efforts in developing a *jus post bellum*; consolidating its proper structure; expanding its contents as an evolving new legal framework in which certain rules may deviate from the *jus in bello*, but still influence the conduct of hostilities in a wider political context; and ensuring respect for its rules.

References

Bothe M (2003) Terrorism and the legality of pre-emptive force. Eur J Int L 14:227

Fleck D (2003) International humanitarian law after September 11: challenges and the need to respond. Yearb Int Humanit L 6:41

Fleck D (2008) Law enforcement and the conduct of hostilities: two supplementing or mutually excluding legal paradigms? In: Fischer-Lescano A, Gasser H-P, Marauhn T, Ronzitti N (eds) Frieden in Freiheit, Peace in liberty. Paix en liberté, Baden–Baden/Zürich

Gill TD, Fleck D (eds) (2010) The handbook of the international law of military operations. Oxford University Press, Oxford

ICRC (2008) How is the term “armed conflict” defined in international humanitarian law?, Opinion paper, March 2008. http://www.icrc.org/eng/resources/documents/article/other/armed-conflict-article-170308.htm

ICRC (2011) International humanitarian law and the challenges of contemporary armed conflicts, Report to the 31st conference of the red cross and red crescent, Geneva, 28 Nov–1 Dec 2011, 31/C/11/5.1.2

ILA Committee on Non-State Actors (2010) First report of the committee. Report of the Seventy-Fourth Conference, The Hague

ILA Committee on the Use of Force (2010) Final report on the meaning of armed conflict in international law. Report of the Seventy-Fourth Conference, The Hague

Koh HH, Legal Adviser, U.S. Department of State (2010) Speech at the annual meeting of the American Society of International Law (ASIL), Washington, DC, 25 Mar 2010. http://www.state.gov/s/l/releases/remarks/139119.htm

Lietzau WK (2004) Old laws, new wars: jus ad bellum in an age of terrorism. Max Planck Yearb U.N. Law 8:383

Oswald B (2011) Detention by United Nations peacekeepers: searching for definition and categorisation. J Int Peacekeeping 15 (1–2):119

Pictet JS (ed) (1958) The Geneva Conventions of 12 August 1949, Commentary. ICRC, Geneva.

The White House (2002) The national security strategy of the United States of America, Sept 2002. http://merln.ndu.edu/whitepapers/USnss2002.pdf

Wills S (2011) The legal characterization of the armed conflicts in Afghanistan and Iraq: implications for protection. Neth Int L Rev 58(2):173

Chapter 12
Perspective and the Importance of History

W. Hays Parks

Contents

12.1 Introduction

One day shy of the tenth anniversary of the al Qaeda attacks on the World Trade Center in New York City and the Pentagon in Washington, D.C. (commonly and hereinafter referred to as "9/11"), Professor Mike Schmitt invited me to join distinguished scholars in a forum containing "reflective pieces regarding the

---

Senior Associate Deputy General Counsel, International Affairs Division, Office of General Counsel, U.S. Department of Defense, 2003–2010; Special Assistant for Law of War Matters, Office of The Judge Advocate General of the Army, 1979–2003; Charles H. Stockton Chair of International Law, U.S. Naval War College, 1984–1985; Colonel, U.S. Marine Corps Reserve (Retired). This article is dedicated to the memory of Dr. Avril McDonald, Managing Editor, Yearbook of International Humanitarian Law, (1997–2007) respected colleague, wise counselor, and good friend.

W. H. Parks (✉)
International Affairs Division, Office of General Counsel, U.S. Department of Defense,
Butte, MT 59701, USA
e-mail: haysparks70@gmail.com

M.N. Schmitt and L. Arimatsu (eds.), *Yearbook of International Humanitarian Law Volume 14, 2011*, DOI: 10.1007/978-90-6704-855-2_12,

international humanitarian law implications of 9/11 to mark the tenth anniversary of the attacks". I accepted his invitation, honored to be included in such good company.

Rather than focus on a single implication or point, I thought it best to provide a bit of history, some of it based upon personal experience, to provide perspective for the topic identified by Professor Schmitt.

A personal anecdote is necessary in beginning.

Forty years ago it was my privilege to meet Brigadier General Edwin H. Simmons, U.S. Marine Corps, Director of Marine Corps History and Museums and an accomplished historian in his own right. In my subsequent association with him, I learned there are two words historians never use: "first", as in, "this is the *first* time this has happened"; and "never", as in, "this has *never* happened before".

In the wake of the al Qaeda 9/11 attacks and ensuing Coalition military operations in Afghanistan, Iraq, and Yemen, government officials, military members, academicians, and international lawyers referred to the "changing character of war" while characterizing the conflicts as "asymmetric" warfare, as if this was the first time in which opposing armed forces with dissimilar capabilities, strategic goals, and tactical choices faced one another[1]: that is, 9/11 was the first time the international community faced asymmetric threats or global acts of terror by armed non-State actors. History suggests otherwise.

12.2 Trans-national Terrorism

A longer view of history is necessary in order to consider the "international humanitarian law implications of 9/11". The history of modern trans-national terrorism began decades before 11 September 2001.

An Arab Summit Conference convened in Khartoum following Israel's defeat of the combined forces of Egypt, Syria, and Jordan in the June 1967 Six-Day War. Finding the destruction of Israel by conventional military forces unsuccessful, on 1 September 1967, the conference established Arab policy toward Israel that included its attack through other means. These included sponsorship of trans-national terrorism by armed non-State groups.

The pro-Palestinian terrorist group Black September executed a major (albeit not the first) act in its attack on the Olympic Village at the XX Summer Olympics in Munich on 5–6 September 1972. It resulted in the deaths of eleven members of the Israeli Olympic team. As one history reports, "The Munich attack was the

[1] See, e.g., Schmitt 2007, at pp. 11–48; Murphy 2011 and Heintschel von Heinegg 2011, at pp. 463–480. Reviewing "asymmetric warfare" on Google provided a list that ran into the hundreds of references. "Changing face of warfare" did not begin with 9/11: see Durham and McCormack 1999. It is not the author's intent to single out his respected colleagues in a negative way but to offer their works as representative of the level of discussion and use of the term "asymmetric" and phrase "changing character of war".

temporary culmination of a development the states aimed at had been caught to a great extent unawares".[2]

This incident led many nations to create dedicated, specially trained counter-terrorist forces and military or civilian law enforcement mechanisms to address the trans-national terrorist threat. For example, on 30 October 1972, the Federal Republic of Germany established its *Grenzschutzgruppe* Neun (Federal Border Guard Group Nine, or GSG9).[3] An incident 5 years later confirmed the need for such units. On 17 October 1977, in response to the hijacking of Lufthansa flight LH181 by members of the terrorist group Palestinian Front for the Liberation of Palestine (PFLP), a GSG9 team was deployed to the hijacked aircraft's location in Mogadishu, Somalia. The GSG9 team assaulted the aircraft, rescued the 87 surviving hostages (the aircraft's pilot having been murdered by the hijackers), and killed four of the five terrorists in the process. In contrast to overwhelming combined arms firepower employed by conventional military forces on a linear battlefield in an international armed conflict generally devoid of civilians, counterterrorist teams such as GSG9 depend on surprise, speed, and violence of action through highly discriminate shooting in order to eliminate the terrorist threat while protecting hostage lives.

This terrorist attack was not isolated. The hijacking and bombing of foreign flag aircraft, attack of Israeli and other foreign embassies, and assassination or attempted assassination of Israeli and foreign officials around the world preceded and followed the Munich Olympics massacre. Sponsored by the Soviet Union, financed by Libya, with each providing equipment and training, Palestinian and other terrorist operations of the 1970s through the 1980s were transnational.[4] For example:

- The Japanese Red Army (JRA), allegedly supported by the PFLP, attacked the Lod Airport in Tel Aviv on 30 May 1972, killing 28 civilians and injuring a dozen more. Two years later the JRA attacked a Shell Oil refinery in Singapore, taking five hostages, in an attack planned to coincide with the PFLP seizure of the Japanese Embassy in Kuwait. The JRA engaged in numerous other operations or attacks through the 1980s.
- The PFLP attacked or hijacked aircraft in Athens, Zurich, and Los Angeles before engaging in a single-day hijacking of four aircraft on 6 September 1970, en route to New York from Western European capitals.

---

[2] Tophoven 1985, at p. 8.

[3] GSG9 was created from an existing civilian law enforcement agency due to German constitutional restrictions on extraterritorial deployment of German military forces.

[4] State-sponsored transnational terrorism was detailed in Sterling 1981. In addition to supporting the Palestinian Liberation Organization and other Palestinian terrorist organizations, Libya's Muammar Qaddafi provided funding, weapons, and training to the JRA, the German Baader-Meinhof Gang, the Italian Red Brigades, Nicaragua's Sandanistas, the Moro National Liberation Front in the Philippines, Dhofario rebels in Oman, and the Provisional Wing of the Irish Republican Army (PIRA). Livingston 1982, at pp. 17–18.

- Between 1972–1976 and 1985–1986 Libyan dictator Moammar Ghadafi engaged in covert funding and shipment of arms to the Provisional Irish Republican Army in its fight against the government of the United Kingdom.
- On 7 October 1985, Palestinian Liberation Organization terrorist Abul Abbas hijacked the Italian cruise liner Achille Lauro. A 69-year-old wheelchair-bound American, Leon Klinghofer, was murdered by the hijackers in the process.
- On 27 December 1985, Palestinian terrorists launched attacks at Rome's Leonardo da Vinci-Fiumicino Airport and Vienna International Airport, killing sixteen and wounding ninety-nine at the former and killing three and wounding in excess of one hundred at the latter. Identifying Libyan support to the terrorists, these Rome and Vienna attacks led to a freedom-of-navigation operation by three U.S. Navy carrier battle groups in international waters off Libya from 23 to 27 March 1986. The objective of the exercise was not only to challenge Libya's excessive claim to the Gulf of Sidra but also to send a clear message to Libya's dictator Moammar Ghadafi that the United States would no longer tolerate Ghadafi's use of trans-national terrorism as a foreign policy option. This was followed by U.S. airstrikes against terrorist-related targets in Tripoli and Benghazi/Benina on the night of 14–15 April 1986, following a Libya-sponsored terrorist attack on a discotheque in Berlin that killed three and injured 229.[5]
- In turn, Ghadafi responded with the bombing of Pan American Airways flight 103 over Lockerbie, Scotland, on 21 December 1988, resulting in the deaths of 259 passengers and crew on the aircraft and eleven civilians on the ground.

The preceding examples are representative but far from exhaustive. The suggestion by some that the 11 September 2001 al Qaeda attacks on the World Trade Center and the Pentagon ushered in new era of Islamic terrorism neglects history, whether by pro-Palestinian or similar groups, or by al Qaeda.

During this same time, efforts were made by Third World delegations and others at the 1974–1977 Diplomatic Conference leading to the 1977 Additional Protocols I and II, to legitimize certain armed non-State actors and the manner in which they carried out their operations. In particular, Article 1, para 4 of Additional Protocol I states:

> The situations referred to in the preceding paragraph include armed conflicts in which peoples are fighting against colonial domination and alien occupation and against racist regimes in the exercise of their right of self-determination, as enshrined in the Charter of the United Nations and the Declaration on Principles of International Law concerning Friendly Relations and Cooperation among States in accordance with the Charter of the United Nations.

The words "colonial domination", "alien occupation" and "against racist regimes" referred respectively to Portugal in Angola (from which it withdrew in

---

[5] Parks, "Crossing the Line", U.S. Nav. Inst. Proc. (November 1986), pp. 40–52; and "Lessons from the 1986 Libya Airstrike", 36 New England Law Review (Summer 2002), 755–766. The author was the legal adviser for the military aspects of the airstrike.

1974), Israel in the Occupied Territories, and the apartheid governments of South Africa and Rhodesia (now Zimbabwe).

Governments were conscious of, if not entirely responsive to, the trans-national terrorist threat prior to 9/11. For example, in 1983 and 1984 this author served as a legal advisor in inter-agency meetings with military and domestic law enforcement agencies planning for responses to four possible trans-national terrorist group attacks within the United States: the XXIII Summer Olympics in Los Angeles; the New Orleans World's Fair; and the Democratic and Republican Party national conventions in San Francisco and Dallas, respectively. Typical of that time, responses to terrorist attacks were primarily reactive rather than proactive.

The suggestion by some that the 9/11 attacks ushered in a new era of terrorism by *al Qaeda* neglects history. The history of al Qaeda terrorist attacks prior to 11 September 2001, is more expansive in time and geography:

- On 20 November 1979, heavily-armed radical Islamists seized the Grand Mosque in Mecca, holding it and thousands of worshipers hostage for 2 weeks until the terrorists were defeated in a pitched battle by Saudi military forces trained and equipped by the French counterterrorist force Groupment D'Intervention De La Gendarmerie Nationale. The seizure of Mecca has been described as the birth of Al Qaeda.[6]
- World Trade Center, New York, 26 February 1993 (6 deaths).
- Hotel Aden, Aden, 29 December 1992 (3 deaths).
- Mogadishu, 3 October 1993 (18 U.S. deaths).
- Riyadh, 13 November 1995 (5 deaths).
- Khobar Towers, Saudia Arabia, 25 June 1996 (19 deaths).
- U.S. Embassies, Kenya and Tanzania, 7 August 1998 (301 deaths).
- USS Cole, Yemen, 12 October 1999 (17 deaths).
- The foiled "Millennium Plot" attack on Los Angeles International Airport, planned to occur on 31 December 1999.[7]

The world has faced the present "changing character of war" for more than four decades. Its military forces have faced or themselves employed "asymmetric" forms of warfare for centuries, as will be discussed infra.

12.3 Counterinsurgency and Conventional Military Forces

The post-9/11 conflicts in Afghanistan and Iraq evolved into counterinsurgency operations, prompting a second personal anecdote. In 1974 General Creighton Abrams, Chief of Staff of the U.S. Army, previously commander of U.S. forces in

---

[6] Trofimov 2007, at p. 7.

[7] Parks 2010, at p. 387. The December 29, 1992 attack on the Hotel Aden was directed against 100 U.S. military personnel billeted there, all of whom departed the previous day.

Viet Nam (1968–1972), traveled to Charlottesville, Virginia, to address students, staff and faculty of The Judge Advocate General's School, U.S. Army.[8] General Abrams described the way forward in the post-Vietnam War environment as the Army refocused on the North Atlantic Treaty Organization's (NATO) defense of Europe against the Warsaw Pact threat.

In the course of his visit I asked General Abrams what steps were being taken with regard to the lessons learned from the U.S. military's counterinsurgency experience in the Viet Nam War. General Abrams focused an ice-cold gaze on me and replied: "None. We've put Viet Nam behind us. We'll never again engage in counterinsurgency operations." The counterinsurgency mission was assigned to U.S. Army Special Forces which, at the time, were undergoing a significant force reduction. Counterinsurgency training for U.S. conventional forces ceased for more than three decades.

It is likely General Abrams was unaware of Brigadier General Simmons' admonition about use of the word "never", though in his case it was offered prospectively rather than in its historical sense. Dismissal of the many lessons learned by U.S. military forces in the Viet Nam War—in particular, an ineffective and unnecessarily destructive conventional-minded strategy of attrition of enemy forces through large unit "search-and-destroy" missions coupled with an embrace of massive firepower when protection of the civilian population should have been paramount—had to be relearned in Afghanistan and Iraq, often with considerable resistance by commanders and individual soldiers trained to fight Warsaw Pact conventional forces (notwithstanding the fact that the Cold War had ended more than a decade earlier).

When military operations began in Afghanistan in late 2001, U.S. Special Operations Forces (hereinafter "SOF") successfully executed the first phase in close coordination with the Central Intelligence Agency, employing highly discriminate force against al Qaeda and the Taliban.[9] U.S. and Coalition conventional forces subsequently joined the fray, prepared only for combat against enemy conventional forces on a linear battlefield, instead finding neither conventional enemy forces nor a linear battlefield.

Iraqi military forces were quickly defeated following the Coalition's March 2003 invasion of Iraq. As the insurgency began in late summer 2003 U.S. and other Coalition forces again found themselves unprepared for counterinsurgency operations. As the cover for the commercial version of the recent U.S.

---

[8] The JAG school is the principal military institution for education of judge advocates from each of the four U.S. military services and friendly governments.

[9] A contrast in discriminate force application between conventional military forces and SOF was not new. The precedent was established by SOF working with organized resistance movements in industrial espionage in Axis-occupied nations during World War II, where concern for civilian casualties was substantially greater than in attacks on Germany; see, e.g., Michel 1972, at pp. 212, 216–217. Attacks by organized resistance movements generally were more efficient in precision and effectiveness. See Parks 2003, at pp. 536–538, and (e.g.) Foot 1966, at p. 266, fn. 34, and pp. 505–517.

counterinsurgency manual (discussed infra) acknowledges, “in 2003, most Army officers knew more about the U.S. Civil War (1861–1865) than they did about counterinsurgency”. Mid- and senior-level U.S. military teaching institutions, in particular the U.S. Army War College, placed undue emphasis on examination of the conventional battles of the Civil War. The convenience of the geographic proximity of Civil War battlefields such as Gettysburg and Antietam took precedent over identification of the lessons learned from the most common form of conflict experienced through the nineteenth and twentieth centuries, as well as the terrorist threat faced in the decades preceding 9/11. The Civil War-focused curricula ignored the history of the guerrilla threat during that conflict and the Union Army’s difficulty in dealing with it.

Most of the U.S. military and virtually all of the senior civilian leadership denied the existence of an insurgency in Iraq. But as resistance movements grew on the ground, steps were taken to prepare for a new counterinsurgency operations doctrine. Field Manual 3-24, the U.S. Army and Marine Corps’ *Counterinsurgency Field Manual*, based upon an earlier Army manual but further supplemented by valuable private publications from or about the counterinsurgency era of the 1950 s and 1960 s,[10] was published in December 2007—more than 6 years after U.S. military forces entered Afghanistan and almost 5 years after the invasion of Iraq. To excuse their lack of preparation, the military and others began to speak in terms of “the changing character of war” and “asymmetric warfare”.

The U.S. military ignored military history in general and its own extensive experience in unconventional warfare, counterinsurgency, and counter-guerrilla operations in particular.[11] Confederate guerrilla operations and acts by armed non-State actors in the American Civil War were a principal reason for the Union Army’s General Orders No. 100. Prepared by Columbia College professor Francis Lieber and approved by President Abraham Lincoln in 1863, arguably it is the foundation document for the modern law of war. It distinguished between guerrilla forces acting under a government warrant—the historic “right authority”—and private armed bands, the latter commonly referred to today as armed non-State actors.[12] At the turn of the century, U.S. military forces had engaged in counterinsurgency operations inter alia in the Philippine War (1899–1902) and against the Moros, a Muslim armed non-State actor (1902–1913). U.S. Marines were involved

---

[10] A small but representative sample is Fall 1961; Galula 1964, and Trinquier 1961; Cluterbuck 1966; McCuen 1966; Kitson 1971; Horne 1977; and Marighella1985, as well as the writings of Mao Tse-Tung (discussed infra) and Lartéguy 1962 and Lartéguy 1963. All but the later books (Kitson 1971, Horne 1977) and the English-language edition of Marighella were virtually mandatory reading for serious students of counterinsurgency in the 1960s. Colonel Trinquier’s “modern warfare” is an equivalent to the present day’s use of “changing character of war” and “asymmetric warfare”, in particular in its arguments as to the obsolescence or inapplicability of the law of war.

[11] See, e.g., Birtle 1998. A belated sequel is U.S. Army Center of Military History 2010.

[12] General Orders No. 100 was preceded by Dr. Lieber’s essay, “Guerrilla Parties Considered with Reference to the Laws and Usages of War”, contained in Hartigan 1983, at pp. 31–44.

in counter-guerrilla/bandit operations in the island of Hispaniola (1915–1933) and Nicaragua (1916–1933), producing its *Small Wars Manual* in 1935—another source, even if outdated, to which the authors of the 2007 U.S. Counterinsurgency Manual turned for guidance. In the early 1950s, U.S. military forces had conducted counter-guerrilla operations in the Korean War. Yet, little more than a decade later, with the exception of Army Special Forces and Navy SEALs and, to a lesser degree, the Marines,[13] the U.S. military was unprepared for counterinsurgency operations in Vietnam. The overall U.S. commander, General William C. Westmoreland, remained steadfastly averse to considering, much less adopting, established counterinsurgency principles throughout his time in command (June 1964–May 1968).

Failure to study and understand the lessons of history is not limited to the U.S. military. The British Army has a longer history in "small wars", its term for guerrilla, counter-guerrilla, and counterinsurgency operations, through its colonial wars during the reign of Queen Victoria (1837–1901)[14] and, in particular, in the Anglo-Boer War (1898–1902). The unconventional warfare operations of T.E. Lawrence, commonly referred to as "Lawrence of Arabia", in the Arabian Peninsula in World War I is another such example of this type of operation. Reflecting on the experiences of the late nineteenth century, Colonel Charles E. Callwell's *Small Wars: Their Principles and Practice* was adopted by the British Army upon its publication in 1896, republished in 1899, and again in 1906 with updates from lessons learned in the Anglo-Boer War.[15]

Much credit for the success of Allied unconventional warfare (that is, guerrilla or resistance) operations in Axis-occupied territories in World War II is due to two British Army officers who, as that conflict loomed on the horizon, turned to the British counterinsurgency experience in its conflict against the Irish Republican Army in Ireland 1916–1921 to develop the idea for supporting, training, organizing, and equipping local resistance movements.[16] British Commonwealth and U.S military personnel, members of the Special Operations Executive (SOE) and the Office of Strategic Services (OSS), respectively, the forerunners of today's SOF, engaged in unconventional warfare operations in two dozen Axis-occupied nations during World War II.[17] U.S. Army personnel in The Philippines who

---

[13] Throughout the Viet Nam War the Marine Corps actively engaged in the full-time protection of the civilian population, placing a squad of volunteer Marines (Combined Action Platoons, or CAP), in virtually every village in its area of operations. The CAP program is described in West 1972.

[14] See, e.g., Farwell 1973.

[15] Callwell 1896. London: His Majesty's Stationery Office. The word "commando", subsequently embraced by the British in World War II in its designation of units specially organized, equipped, and trained for raids (today referred to as "direct action missions"), was derived from Boer commando units. A key publication from that conflict is Reitz 1930. Law of war principles relating to the conflict were delivered by Dr. Thomas Baty as lectures at Oxford and published in Baty 1900.

[16] Foot 1973, at pp. 57–69.

[17] Representative works in an area rich with materials are Foot 1977; Hæstrup 1978; and Stafford 1980.

refused to surrender independently organized armed resistance movements to oppose the Japanese occupation and to support conventional U.S. forces' operations when they returned.

Actions of State-sponsored organized resistance movements in World War II led to clarification of the law of war in article 4A, para 2 of the Geneva Convention (III) Relative to the Treatment of Prisoners of War of August 12, 1949 with respect to which insurgent or irregular armed groups are entitled to prisoner of war status.[18] Subsequently military forces of several Western European nations engaged in numerous and frequently protracted counterinsurgency operations in the decolonization era.[19]

"New" is not new just because someone says it is. In the 1980 Australian movie *Breaker Morant*, a fictional account based on an actual event involving the 1902 British court martial of three Australian Army officers for murder of a civilian and several captured Boer guerrillas, the defense counsel's closing argument offered that "this is a new kind of war".[20] Seventy years later and notwithstanding the numerous counterinsurgency operations in which U.S. and other nations' military forces had engaged, the U.S. Ambassador to the Republic of Viet Nam during the U.S. conflict observed "Because this kind of war was new to the American experience, it is clear we made mistakes [....] We did not in the beginning [...] fully understand the complexities of this kind of war".[21] A century after the Anglo-Boer War, the U.S. commission appointed to investigate the events of 11 September 2001, described the attack as a "new type of war", attributing the description to a U.S. air defense crewman.[22] The comments of each neglect the history of conflicts that preceded the Anglo-Boer War and the U.S. war in Viet Nam. The term guerrilla is said to have originated as "guerrillero" in the Spanish partisan resistance to Napoleon's campaign in Aragon during the Peninsular War (1808–1914). In addition to the previously-mentioned guerrilla-type operations

---

[18] Incorrect statements with respect to the law of war by Bush Administration officials in the period immediately following the September 11, 2001, al Qaeda attacks might have been avoided had these individuals taken the time to read and understand the contents and history of Article 4A(2), and seek advice and assistance from subject-matter experts provided, of course, that they were interested in using the law of war for anything other than a political tool. The author's personal experience is that they did not.

[19] See, e.g., Osanka 1962. British campaigns are described in Newsinger 2002 and, with respect to the 1948–1960 "Emergency" in Malaya (now Malaysia), the official history of that conflict by Short 1975. An excellent history of the beginning of the decolonialization period (1945–1949) is Bayly and Harper 2007.

[20] The movie was based upon Denton 1973. Denton subsequently authored a comprehensive non-fiction account—Denton 1983. The trial transcripts were destroyed, preventing confirmation of the defense counsel's closing statement. The movie version closely follows the 1907 account by the surviving co-defendant, Witton 1982, at pp. 118–130.

[21] Ambassador Bunker, Thayer Award Address, U.S. Military Academy, as printed in the Congressional Record (May 28, 1970), pp. E4731–4733, at 4732, and cited in Sorley 2011, at p. 1999.

[22] Leberman 2011, at p. 153.

during the U.S. Civil War, the concept of levee en masse and the legal status of the *franc-tireur* came to focus following experience gained during the Franco-Prussian War (1870–1871).[23] These were not the only examples of the guerrilla experience that preceded the Anglo-Boer War. Examples previously offered establish that neither guerrilla-type operations nor armed non-State actors are a recent phenomenon.

The problem is not a lack of history or experience but a failure to study history and use it properly, and to know when it is relevant and when it is not. In the case of the past decade, it is affected by and relates to the failure not only to read but to understand and relate history to later conflicts as they are being fought. British efforts to put forward their counterinsurgency experience in Malaya as the template for the U.S. conflict in Viet Nam and, decades later, in their own operations in Afghanistan and Iraq, ignored their shortfalls in as well as the unique characteristics of the Malaya conflict. Reliance upon 'the Malaya template' proved unsuitable in the conflicts of the past decade.[24] The situation and conditions in Malaya were markedly different from those in Viet Nam, Afghanistan, and Iraq. History is of value, but only when assessed in its proper context.

History plays an important part in understanding not only the way military forces engaged in military operations of the past decade but why, and how the traditional military view of use of or fighting against irregular forces has hindered application of the law of war outside traditional international armed conflict. In *Small Wars*, Colonel Callwell observed "It may be accepted as a general rule that guerrilla warfare is the most unfavorable shape which a campaign can take for the regular troops".[25] Democracies abhor large standing armies. Given the reduced size of peacetime armies, military leaders historically trained and prepared their forces for international armed conflict against the uniformed conventional forces of an enemy State, fighting on a linear battlefield. In the post-Viet Nam period, for many, the potential of an overt enemy invasion appeared to pose the greatest threat. Thus it was prudent for General Abrams, the Army leadership, and their counterparts in the other military services to rebuild the conventional military forces, acquiring new equipment to replace stocks destroyed, worn out, or otherwise depleted in Viet Nam, and return their focus to the Warsaw Pact threat. The error lay in ignoring contemporary history and emerging threats. The military placed all its eggs in a single basket, in this case entirely in a conventional warfare capability. It was necessary to prepare for battle against a conventional enemy on a linear battlefield, but Colonel Callwell's comment remained true in that the

[23] Moloney Spaight 1911, at pp. 41–72.

[24] With respect to Malaya, one failure was to properly investigate the alleged murder of twenty-four (possibly twenty-five) Chinese civilians at Batang Kali during the night of December 11–12, 1948, by soldiers of the Scots Guards. See Short 1975, at pp. 166–169, and Short 2010, at pp. 338–354); and Ward and Mirsflor 2009. A critical analysis of British operations in Iraq and Afghanistan is Ledwidge 2011.

[25] Callwell 1896, at p. 99.

military decided to prepare solely for the conflict it preferred to fight. As a popular adage states, "In combat, the enemy has a vote".

12.4 "Asymmetric Warfare"

This history leads to two closely inter-related questions: what is meant by "asymmetric warfare"? Are the conflicts that have been fought since 11 September 2001 distinguishable from previous armed conflict on the basis of "asymmetry"?

Consideration first must be given to a definition:

The Compact Edition of The Oxford English Dictionary declines to define asymmetric much less asymmetric warfare, referring the reader to asymmetrical, which is defined as "Not symmetrical; out of proportion, with the parts not arranged correspondingly".[26] In turn, it defines symmetrical as "Characterized by or exhibiting symmetry. Having the parts or elements regularly or harmoniously arranged; regular in form; well-proportioned; balanced."[27]

In contrast, asymmetrical warfare is a recent definition coined within military circles to include "threats outside the range of conventional warfare and difficult to respond to in kind (e.g., a suicide bomber)".[28]

Examination of the arguments of the past decade suggests that "asymmetric warfare" refers to unconventional warfare, guerrilla warfare, insurgency, counterinsurgency, terrorism, and counterterrorism, which are neither new nor a "changing character of war". A careful reading of history shows these to be some of the oldest forms of warfare.[29] Other than terrorism, which is prohibited by the law of war,[30] these are missions that, historically, have been pursued by special operations forces, discussed infra.

History shows that every military force prefers that an opponent fight the war for which that military force has planned. It also shows that few military forces choose to accommodate the desires or plans of its opponent. In particular, most prefer not to fight to its opponent's strong suit. Sun Tzu, in *The Art of War*, emphasizes fighting to the enemy's weaknesses rather than playing to its strengths,[31] an approach repeated by Mao Tse-Tung in his equally famous work.[32]

---

26 Oxford University Press 1979, at p. 132.

27 Ibid. at p. 3206.

28 Attributed to Joint Publication 1-02 2006. The current edition of JP 1-02 does not contain the term or definition of asymmetric warfare, having replaced it with irregular warfare, a topic beyond the author's remit for this volume.

29 For an overview, see Blacker 1954, and Laquer 1977.

30 Article 51(2) 1977 Additional Protocol I, which states in part "Acts or threats of violence for the primary purpose of which is to spread terror among the civilian population are prohibited".

31 Griffith 1963, at pp. 96–101.

32 Griffith 1961, at p. 100.

Few opposing military forces enjoy or seek symmetry. If a potential opponent enjoys military superiority, oftentimes a nation will pursue a different choice of forces or methods of warfare in an effort to counter or exploit its opponent's weaknesses. For example, the selection of types of naval forces (battleships, cruisers, submarines, etc.) in the arms race between the United States and Japan in the period between the world wars was based on relative geographic positions in the event of a Pacific war and known strengths and weaknesses of its potential opponent as, too, were their respective positions in international disarmament conferences.[33]

In other cases, strategy and tactics are developed with appreciation of an enemy's potential strengths and vulnerabilities. Germany's blitzkrieg approach, including its employment of a glider-borne assault force on 10 May 1940, to seize the Belgian strongpoint of Eben Emael in the opening hours of its invasion of France, were developed to flank and circumvent the French Maginot Line and France's emphasis on defensive warfare. Similarly, World War II resistance movements were ordered to limit their operations to intelligence collection and authorized sabotage until Allied forces were about to invade inasmuch as the resistance movements were not strong enough to defend against retaliatory or counter-offensive operations by Axis occupation forces.

Having experienced the rapid and decisive defeat of his conventional military forces in 1991 as Coalition forces liberated Kuwait from Iraq's occupation, in late 2001 and early 2003 Iraqi dictator Saddam Husayn developed a capability in his Fedayeen. This force was designed to undertake unconventional warfare operations in the event Iraq's rebuilt conventional warfare forces fared no better should the United States and its Coalition forces return, as they did in 2003. Saddam Husayn's decision did not differ from the planning of U.S. Army General Douglas MacArthur in the Philippines immediately prior to the beginning of World War II in the Pacific, nor that of the United Kingdom in its pre-war planning for organizing, funding, training, and supplying resistance in Axis occupied territories, or Swiss military preparations in the event Switzerland's neutrality was threatened. In the latter case, the Swiss would depend on their terrain to defend against invasion, an advantage Saddam did not enjoy. In the first examples, Saddam, MacArthur, and the British opted for a change in short-term strategy either to defeat invading forces or, failing that, engage in unconventional warfare against a superior enemy.

Whether in international negotiations, force development or combat, nations and their military forces seldom play to an opponent's strong suit. In so many words, battles seldom are fought symmetrically.

As Sun Tzu observed in 500 B.C.:

> Now an army may be likened to water, for just as flowing water avoids the heights and hastens to the lowlands, so an army avoids strength and strikes weakness.
>
> And as water shapes its flow in accordance with the ground, so an army manages its victory in accordance with the situation of the enemy.[34]

---

[33] See, e.g., Parks 2001, at pp. 339–385.

[34] Griffith 1963, at p. 101.

Almost 2000 years later, Mao Tse-Tung repeated Sun Tzu's points:

> The matter of initiative is especially serious for guerrilla forces, who must face critical situations unknown to regular troops. The superiority of the enemy and the lack of unity and experience within our own ranks may be cited. Guerrillas can, however, gain the initiative if they keep in mind the weak points of the enemy. Because of the enemy's [Japan in the Sino- Japanese War, 1937–1945] insufficient manpower, guerrillas can operate over vast territories; because he is a foreigner and a barbarian, guerrillas can gain full use of their own cleverness. Both guerrilla and regulars must exploit the enemy weaknesses [….] Some of our weaknesses are apparent only and are, in actuality, sources of strength. For example, the very fact that most guerrilla groups are small makes it desirable and advantageous for them to appear and disappear in the enemy's rear. With such activities, the enemy is simply unable to cope.[35]

From a law of war standpoint, there is no requirement for symmetry in fighting. Warfare is clearly not governed by a "fairness doctrine" or any requirement on the warring parties to fight with an equal number of players on the battlefield as, for example, in a football game. A historic rule of thumb for attack on a fortified emplacement is a three-to-one superiority by attacking forces over the defender. No umpire or referee was called upon to calculate whether the forces were 'symmetric' prior to the landing of Marines at Tarawa on 20 November 1943, Allied forces at Normandy on 6 June 1944, or by Marines at Iwo Jima on 19 February 1945, when, in each case, the attacking force faced heavily-entrenched and determined enemy forces. No "fairness" rule requires symmetry between attacker and defender. Indeed, the manpower superiority of the attacker is a response to the 'asymmetry' the defender has achieved or hoped to achieve with its fortified emplacement(s). No military person would refer to this as asymmetrical warfare; it is a historical given. Yet when an enemy force utilizes age-old tactics such as concealment and surprise, the surprise in this case being the result of the opposing force's failure to anticipate, plan, and train for the enemy's choice of means and methods, coining a term such as "asymmetric warfare" manifests an ignorance of history, as does characterization of the past decade as a "changing character of war". Governments and their military forces have no one to blame but themselves for their failure to adequately prepare for the attacks of 11 September 2001, given the substantial history of trans-national terrorist groups over the decades immediately preceding that memorable day.

In this respect the term "asymmetric warfare" appears to be more an excuse for ignorance of history and a lack of preparation than an accurate description of the post-9/11 experience.

12.5 The Emergence of Special Operations Forces

The post-9/11 conflicts included substantial—indeed, unprecedented—employment of U.S. and Coalition special operations forces. The history of their emergence is germane to the "changing character of war".

[35] Griffith 1961, at p. 100.

On 12 January 1954, Secretary of State John Foster Dulles announced a new U.S. deterrence strategy referred to as "massive retaliation". This strategy suggested the United States would consider reinforcing any conventional defense against an enemy attack (such as a Warsaw Pact attack on North Atlantic Treaty Organization nations, or a second North Korean invasion of the Republic of Korea, the latter a conflict that ended inconclusively only 6 months earlier) with nuclear weapons. An overt reply by the Soviet Union was not immediately forthcoming, but covert Soviet support for what became known as "wars of national liberation" was identified in the late 1950s –essentially insurgencies intended to stay beneath the trip wire posed by the Eisenhower Administration's "massive retaliation" deterrence policy. On 6 January 1961, 2 weeks before the inauguration of John F. Kennedy as President Eisenhower's successor, Soviet Premier Nikita Khrushchev publicly announced Soviet support for wars of national liberation. In response, President Kennedy quickly called for an addition of 3,000 soldiers to U.S. Army Special Forces.

Special Operations Forces (SOF) are "military forces specifically designated by higher authority and organized, trained, and equipped to conduct and support special operations".[36] SOF—the term used hereinafter in a generic sense rather than referring to U.S. forces only—have experienced a bumpy history in large measure owing to conventional forces leaders' opposition to facing a guerrilla threat or other non-traditional means of warfare, and what they often regard as "elite" forces within their respective military services. Notwithstanding the success of British Commonwealth and U.S. support for organized resistance movements and other special operations missions in World War II, the British Special Operations Executive, American Office of Strategic Studies, and other SOF of that day were quickly disbanded following that conflict, except for an immediate postwar mission given the British Special Air Service (SAS) to hunt down and capture suspected or known Nazi war criminals.[37] The SAS maintained a limited existence in supporting the government of Greece during its civil war (1946–1949) with the Popular National Liberation Army, commonly referred to as ELAS (for Ethnikos Laikos Apeleftherosis Stratos) and other irregulars supported by the Greek Communist Party, each among the several armed groups trained and equipped by the SOE to resist Nazi occupation during World War II. The SAS gained its footing as a regular Corps of the British Army in the 1950s through its

[36] Special Operations Forces missions or tasks are (1) Unconventional Warfare; (2) Direct Action; (3) Special Reconnaissance; (4) Foreign Internal Defense; (5) Counter-Terrorism; (6) Counter-Proliferation of weapons of mass destruction; (7) Civil Affairs Operations; (8) Psychological Operations; and (9) Information Operations. Historical SOF missions have been (1) through (4). Counterinsurgency is a subset of (1).

[37] Kemp 1986. This mission was the precedent for PIFWC (Persons Indicted for War Crimes) operations performed by NATO special operations forces on behalf of the International Criminal Tribunal for the Former Yugoslavia in the late 1990s pursuant to the Dayton Accords and UN Security Council Resolutions 1031 and 1088.

effective actions as a counter guerrilla force in Malaya and parallel or subsequent operations in Aden, Oman, Dhofar, Kenya, and elsewhere.[38]

The first U.S. Army Special Forces unit was formed on 11 June 1952. President Kennedy's 1961 emphasis on expanding the Army's Special Forces numbers in order to resist communist-sponsored insurgencies met strong resistance within the Army. Ultimately the Special Forces and its Navy counterpart SEALs (which stands for Sea Air Land, representing their broad operational capability) served well during the Viet Nam War, only to experience substantial force reductions in the post-Viet Nam era.

Several incidents spurred rebuilding and expansion of U.S. SOF. The 25 April 1980 failed SOF mission to rescue U.S. hostages seized following Iranian seizure of the U.S. Embassy in Tehran on 4 November 1979, was the first step. Progress remained slow. Notwithstanding President Kennedy's 1961 emphasis, Special Forces were not recognized as a separate branch of the Army until 9 April 1987, then only pursuant to a mandate given to each of the four military services by the Secretary of Defense. Following Congressional review of the October 1983 military operation to rescue U.S. citizens in the Caribbean nation of Grenada, Congress—over strong resistance from the Joint Chiefs of Staff and the leadership of the individual military services—established the United States Special Operations Command on 16 April 1987.

Overcoming initial command resistance to SOF employment in the 1991 Coalition war to liberate Kuwait, Coalition SOF performed invaluable services on strategic reconnaissance missions in that conflict, limiting Saddam Husayn's capability to widen the war and divide the Coalition with Scud missile attacks on Israel. Operations by U.S. and other Coalition SOF since 9/11 have been extensive. In addition to combat operations in Afghanistan and Iraq, SOF have engaged in numerous Foreign Internal Defense (FID) missions at the request of other nations faced with terrorist threats by franchised elements of the al Qaeda network. Notwithstanding substantial improvements in accuracy with precision guided munitions, SOF frequently were called upon where target validation (positive identification) and/or absolute minimization of risk of civilian casualties incidental to attack of an objective were necessary, repeating the actions during World War II attacks by organized movements in Axis-occupied territories.

SOF were charged with engagement of the al Qaeda networks in Iraq and Afghanistan through capture-or-kill missions, as well as the well-known killing of Osama bin Laden on 2 May 2010. In 2011, U.S. SOF were deployed in seventy-nine nations, in many cases on FID missions at the request of the host nation. President Obama's announcement on 5 January 2012, with regard to the postwar military force structure entails a reduction in the size of conventional ground forces together with a continued emphasis on special operations forces. This was a major difference from decades past, but as noted in these pages it began in the late 1980s.

---

[38] See Dewar 1984; Kemp 1994; Hoe and Morris 1994; and Jones 2005.

The lessons of the past 30 years prompted SOF commanders to identify four "SOF truths":

1. Humans are more important than hardware (that is, military equipment).
2. Quality is better than quantity.
3. Special Operations Forces cannot be mass produced.
4. Competent Special Operations Forces cannot be created after emergencies occur.

The "SOF truths", particularly the third and fourth, reflect the lessons and use of history.

12.6 The "Changing Character of War"

Certain characteristics have been identified in the battle against trans-national terrorism by non-State actors. These include: "advances in communication, transportation and global networking continue to make borders more transparent, economies more interconnected, and information available on an unprecedented scale".[39]

Awareness of characteristics of contemporary conflict necessitates an equal awareness of the historic balancing of measures and countermeasures. Revolutionary changes in warfare occurred with the development and fielding of smokeless gunpowder, aircraft, the tank, the submarine, and radar, each eventually countered by its acquisition by opposing forces, the latter in particular resulting in a continuous technological effort to improve or counter threats or opposing force capabilities.[40] At the lower end of the conflict spectrum, the Provisional Irish Republican Army's (PIRA) employment of various explosive devices during "The Troubles" (1969–1997) was addressed by British counter-measures, in turn met by PIRA counter–counter-measures. U.S. and Allied military forces faced similar threats from mines and booby traps in the Viet Nam War, as did Coalition Forces in Afghanistan and Iraq. The latter conflicts resulted in a new term—improvised explosive devices"—rather than the traditional terms "booby trap" and "mine", as well as development of advanced technical measures and improved vehicle and personal body armor to counter the threat. The regulation or prohibition of mines, booby traps, and similar explosive devices is addressed in the Amended Protocol II to the Convention on Prohibitions or Restrictions on the Use of Certain Conventional Weapons Which May Be Deemed to be Excessively Injurious or to Have Indiscriminate Effects of 10 October 1980. The term "improvised explosive device" likely appeared because some staff officer decided a different term was necessary to describe a historic form of weaponry employed by virtually every nation at one time or another.

---

[39] See, e.g., Olson 2009.

[40] For example, Hartcup 1988; Nissen 1987; and Pritchard 1989.

The purported changes may be new in some respects but not in others. As illustrated in this article, mobility of armed non-State actors existed well before 9/11, and governments had to pay attention to legal issues such as sovereign rights and the law of neutrality in considering responses to terrorist threats, just as they have since 9/11. Modern air transportation may facilitate transnational terrorist mobility. It has been countered substantially through post-9/11 passenger screening procedures and other security measures that were not enacted and emplaced by governments prior to 9/11 due to decisions against burdening the traveler and affecting airport budgets and airline income. "Advances in communication", such as the internet and cell phones, may bring advantages but also have disadvantages, such as interception of messages or the treasure trove of electronic information seized by U.S. Navy SEALs on 2 May 2011, in their attack on the hiding place of Usama Bin Laden in Abbottabad, Pakistan. International financing of terrorism faced new constraints as well as vulnerabilities after 9/11 as governments and international agencies established new restrictions. The age-old practice of measure, counter-measure, counter–counter-measure, etc., continues.

12.7 History and International Law

While it is not difficult to identify reasons to point fingers at the military for its neglect of history, the military is not alone. The determination of customary international law is based in part on the "practice of nations", a synonym for history. Yet it is a factor often ignored by many with the excuse that it is too hard to find. Thus, in *Prosecutor v Dusko Tadić* (a/k/a "Dule"), a case decided by the Appeals Chamber of the International Tribunal for the Prosecution of Persons Responsible for Serious Violations of International Humanitarian Law Committed in the Territory of the Former Yugoslavia Since 1991, the late Judge Antonio Cassese declared:

> Before pointing to some principles and rules of customary law that have emerged in the international community for the purpose of regulating civil strife, a word of caution on the law-making process in the law of armed conflict is necessary. When attempting to ascertain State practice with a view to establishing the existence of a customary rule or a general principle, it is difficult, if not impossible, to pinpoint the actual behavior of the troops in the field for the purpose of establishing whether they in fact comply with, or disregard, certain standards of behavior. This examination is rendered extremely difficult by the fact that not only is access to the theatre of military operations normally refused to independent observers (often even to the ICRC) but information on the actual conduct of hostilities is withheld by the parties to the conflict; what is worse, often recourse is had to misinformation with a view to misleading the enemy as well as public opinion and foreign Governments. In appraising the formation of customary rules or general principles one should therefore be aware that, on account of the inherent nature of this subject-matter, reliance must primarily be placed on such elements as official pronouncements of States, military manuals and judicial decisions.[41]

---

[41] ICTY, *Prosecutor v. Dusko Tadić*, Decision on the Defense Motion for Interlocutory Appeal on Jurisdiction, Case No. IT-94-I, 2 October 1995, Opinion of Judge Cassese, at para 99.

The International Committee of the Red Cross quotes the decision of the International Court of Justice in the *Continental Shelf Case*[42] that "It is of course axiomatic that the material of customary law is to be looked for primarily in the *actual practice* and opinion juris of States", yet cites no examples of physical practice, that is, actual battlefield actions. The ICRC's 2005 study of customary international law with respect to the law of war relied solely on what it represented to be official military manuals that in some cases were not regarded as such by the governments to which they were attributed.[43] The ICRC's failure to research history resulted in a cut-and-paste document that, while voluminous, is neither comprehensive nor authoritative. As this author has shown, examination of physical State practice is possible.[44] The ICRC's failure to research and consider actual history has been the object of official and other experts' criticism.[45]

One example illustrates the error in ignoring history. Much has been said of the practice of "targeted killing", an unfortunate euphemism for targeting particular individuals. Yet history is replete with examples of targeting specific combatants and armed non-State actors. Consider just a few examples of State practice that could have usefully informed the discussions:

- 9 March 1916: U.S. Army General John J. "Black Jack" Pershing conducted an unsuccessful 11-month military expedition into Mexico to capture or kill Mexican bandit leader Francisco "Pancho" Villa and his bandit gang for having attacked and murdered sixteen U.S. civilians and soldiers in Columbus, New Mexico.
- 16 November 1941: A direct action mission by No. 11 Scottish Commando went forward into Beda Littoria, Libya, to capture or kill German Field Marshal Erwin Rommel. The raid was unsuccessful as Rommel was not present.
- 7 December 1942: A composite British Army force commanded by then-Captain (later Brigadier) Fitzroy Maclean was dispatched to capture or kill General

---

[42] *Continental Shelf* (*Libyan Arab Jamahiryah v Malta*) Judgment (1985) ICJ Rep 13, at para 27 [emphasis provided], further citing the *North Sea Continental Shelf*, Judgment (1969) ICJ Rep 3 as the "'classic' approach" in determining customary international law. Henckaerts and Doswald-Beck 2005, at pp. xxxii. In his critique of the ICRC Study, Professor Ian Scobbie comments "In its account of methodology employed, the [ICRC] Study asserts that its approach in assessing whether a given proposition was customary law was a 'classic one', as delineated by the International Court in various cases but 'in particular in the North Sea Continental Shelf cases'. In reality, however, there appears to be a divergence between the rhetorical reaffirmation of views set out in the North Sea Continental Shelf and the less stringent methodology which actually appears to have been employed." Scobbie 2007, at p. 27.

[43] Denunciations have been expressed by officials of the United States, Belgium, and Canada, for example. Personal knowledge of the author.

[44] E.g., Parks 2003; and Parks 2009, at pp. 247–306.

[45] See, for example, Letter of William J. Haynes II, General Counsel, Department of Defense, and John B. Bellinger III, Legal Adviser, Department of State (November 3, 2006), to Dr. Jakob Kellenberger, President, International Committee of the Red Cross, reprinted at Bellinger and Haynes 2007. Non-official critique includes Parks 2005, at p. 211; Aldrich 2005, at p. 507; Turns 2006; and the very comprehensive Wilmshurst and Breau 2007.

Mohammad Fazlollah Zahedi, commander of Persian forces in the Isfahan area, fearing he had aligned his command with Germany and was planning an attack on Allied forces in southern Persia. His capture was successful. He remained in British custody until the end of the war, at which time he returned to Iran.

- 18 April 1943: Based on intercepted Japanese communications, U.S. Army Air Corps P38 Lightning fighters intercepted and shot down the aircraft carrying Admiral Isoroku Yamamoto, Imperial Japanese Navy, planner of the 7 December 1941, Japanese attack on the U.S. naval base at Pearl Harbor, killing him.
- 26 April 1944: Two British officers seconded to the Special Operations Executive engaged in a capture-or-kill mission on Crete, capturing Major General Karl Kreipe, Commander, 221nd Panzer Division.
- 30 October 1951: Eight U.S. Navy aircraft attacked a meeting of North Korean and Chinese military and Communist Party officials at a North Korean Army compound east of Kapsan, North Korea, killing 509 attendees.
- During the Viet Nam War, U.S. SOF engaged in the dismantlement of the North Vietnamese-sponsored Viet Cong (guerrilla) infrastructure through capture-or-kill missions. Notwithstanding allegations of "assassination" by those opposed to the U.S. role in Viet Nam, postwar historical investigation determined that the majority of individuals targeted either surrendered or were captured.[46]
- 2 December 1998: In the vicinity of Vlasenica, NATO SOF captured Lieutenant General Radislav Krstic, Deputy Commander, Drina Corps, Bosnian Serb Forces, indicted by the ICTY on charges of genocide, conspiracy to commit genocide, extermination, and mass murders during July 1995 mass in capture of Srebenica. Placed on trial before the ICTY on March 13, 2000, convicted August 2, 2001 in its first conviction for genocide, General Krstic was sentenced to 46 years in prison.[47]
- 13 December 2003: U.S. SOF captured Former Iraqi dictator Saddam Husayn in Ad Dawr.

As before, the examples are illustrative rather than exhaustive. They are provided to illustrate the importance of history in understanding or assessing contemporary military operations.

The problem—hopefully the lesson to be learned—is best summarized in the observation of an American nurse who joined the resistance against Japanese occupation of The Philippines during World War II, was captured and brutalized by her captors:

> Perhaps, after all, war has not changed so much—or people. We read history as though past things were dead things, with no relation to ourselves. And when the same things happen again, we are terribly surprised.[48]

---

[46] Andradé 1990, at Appendix 1.

[47] As previously noted, NATO SOF were operating pursuant to United Nations Security Council Resolutions 1032 and 1088. PIFWC operations are known to have resulted in the capture of 23 indicted individuals. Two died resisting capture attempts.

[48] Utinsky 1948, at p. 92.

The oft-quoted (frequently misquoted) statement of George Santana that "Those who cannot remember the past are condemned to repeat it" applies not only to the military or international law scholars. Knowing history is critical to understanding and applying it properly.

Ignorance of history has other dangers. An argument that there has been a change in the character of war has and may tempt military and civilian leaders to argue that the law of war does not apply, or cannot be applied. This was seen in Bush Administration reactions to the 11 September 2001 al Qaeda attacks on New York and Washington. Its mistakes were numerous. International lawyers, and others, owe it to their belief in the rule of law to study and understand history in understanding the law and its application over the past decade.

References

Aldrich GH (2005) Customary International Humanitarian Law—An interpretation on behalf of the International Committee of the Red Cross. Br Yearb Int Law 76:503

Andradé (1990) Ashes to ashes: the phoenix program and the Vietnam war. Lexington Books, Lexington

Baty T (1900) International Law of South Africa. Stevens and Haynes, London

Bayly C, Harper T (2007) Forgotten wars: freedom and revolution in Southeast Asia. Harvard University Press, Cambridge, MA

Bellinger JB, Haynes WJ (2007) A US Government response to the International Committee of the Red Cross Study Customary International Humanitarian Law. Int Rev Red Cross 89:443

Birtle AJ (1998) U.S. Army counterinsurgency and contingency operations doctrine 1860–1941. U.S. Army Center of Military History, Washington

Blacker Irwin R (1954) Irregulars, partisans, guerrillas. Simon and Schuster, New York

Callwell CE (1896) Small wars: their principles and practice. His Majesty's Stationery Office, London

Cluterbuck RL (1966) The Long long war: counterinsurgency in Malaya and Vietnam. Praeger, New York

Denton K (1973) The breaker. Angus and Robertson, London

Denton K (1983) Close file: The true story behind the execution of breaker Morant and Peter Handcock. Rigby Publishers, Sydney

Dewar M (1984) Brush fire wars: Campaigns of the British army since 1945. Robert Hale, London

Durham H, McCormack TLH (eds) (1999) The changing face of conflict and the efficacy of International Humanitarian Law. Martinus Nijhoff, The Hague

Fall B (1961) Street without joy. Stackpole, Harrisberg

Farwell B (1973) Queen Victoria's little wars. Allen Lane, London

Foot MRD (1966) SOE in France. HMSO, London

Foot MRD (1973) The IRA and the origins of SOE, In: Foot MRD (ed) war and society: historical essays in honour and memory of J. R. Western, 1928–1971. Paul Elek, London

Foot (1977) Resistance: European resistance to Nazism 1940–1945. McGraw-Hill, New York

Galula D (1964) Counterinsurgency warfare: theory and practice. Pall Mall Press, London

Griffith SB (1961) On guerrilla warfare. Frederick A, Praeger (Tr)

Griffith SB (1963) The art of war. Oxford University Press, Oxford (Tr)

Hæstrup J (1978) Europe ablaze: an analysis of the history of the European resistance movements, 1939–1945. Odense University Press, Odense

Hartcup G (1988) The War of invention: scientific developments, 1914–1918. Brassey's, London
Hartigan RS (1983) Lieber's code and the law of war. Precedent, Chicago
Heintschel von Heinegg W (2011) Asymmetric warfare: how to respond? International law and the changing character of war. US Navel War Coll Int Law Stud 87:463
Henckaerts JM, Doswald Beck L (2005) Customary International Humanitarian Law, vol 1. Cambridge University Press, Cambridge
Hoe A, Morris E (1994) Re-enter the SAS: the special air service and the Malayan emergency. Leo Cooper, London
Horne A (1977) A savage war of peace. Viking, New York
Joint Publication 1-02 (2006) Department of Defense Dictionary of Military and Associated Terms, in "Asymmetric Warfare". Available at http://www.au.af.mil/au/aul/bibs/asw.htm
Jones T (2005) SAS: the first secret wars: the unknown years of combat and counterinsurgency. I.B. Tauris, London
Kemp A (1986) The secret hunters. Michael O'Mara, London
Kemp A (1994) The SAS: savage wars of peace. John Murray, London
Kitson F (1971) Low intensity operations: subversive insurgency & peacekeeping. Faber & Faber, London
Laquer W (1977) Guerrilla: A historical and critical study. Weidenfeld and Nicolson, London
Lartéguy J (1962) The centurions. Dutton, New York
Lartéguy J (1963) The praetorians. Dutton, New York
Leberman G (2011) The 9/11 commission: 'this is a new type of war'. In: Zusman LK (ed) The law of counterterrorism. American Bar Association, Chicago
Ledwidge F (2011) Losing small wars: British failure in Iraq and Afghanistan. Yale University Press, London
Livingstone N (1982) The war against terrorism. Lexington Books, Landham
Marighella C (1985) Manual of the Urban Guerrilla. Documentary Publications, Chapel Hill
McCuen JJ (1966) The art of counter-revolutionary war. Stackpole, Harrisburg
Michel H (1972) The shadow war: European resistance, 1939–1945. Harper& Row, New York
Moloney Spaight J (1911) War rights on land. MacMillan, London
Murphy J (2011) Mission impossible? International Law and the Changing Character of War". US Naval War Coll Int Law Stud 87:14
Newsinger J (2002) British counterinsurgency from Palestine to Northern Ireland. Palgrave, Houndsmill
Nissen J (1987) Winning the radar war. St. Martin's Press, New York
Olson ET (2009) A balanced approach to irregular warfare. J Int Secur Aff, 16. available at http://www.securityaffairs.org/issues/2009/16/olson.php
Osanka FM (1962) Modern Guerrilla warfare: fighting communist Guerrillas, 1941–1961. The Free Press of Glencoe, Glencoe
Oxford University Press (1979) The compact edition of the Oxford English dictionary. Oxford University Press, Oxford
Parks WH (2001) Making law of war treaties: lessons from submarine warfare regulation In: Schmitt MN (ed) International law across the conflict spectrum: essays in honor of professor L. C. Green, vol 75. US Naval War College Int'l L Studies
Parks WH (2003) Special forces' wear of non-standard uniforms Chic J Int Law 4(3):495
Parks WH (2005) The ICRC customary law study: a preliminary assessment. Proc Am Soc Intl Law 99:208
Parks WH (2009) Combatants. In: Schmitt MN (ed) The war in Afghanistan: legal analysis, vol 85. Naval War College Int'l L Studies
Parks WH (2010) Jus in Bello in the struggle against terrorism. In: Norton Moore J, Turner RF (eds) Legal issues in the struggle against terror. Carolina Academic Press, Durham
Pritchard D (1989) The radar war: Germany's pioneering achievement, 1904–1945. Patrick Stevens, London
Reitz D (1930) Commando: A boer journal of the boer war. Faber and Faber, London

Schmitt MN (2007) Asymmetrical warfare and International Humanitarian Law. In: Heintschel von Heinegg W, Epping V (eds) International Humanitarian Law facing new challenges. Springer, Heidelberg
Scobbie I (2007) The approach to Customary International Law. In: Wilmshurst E, Breau S (eds) Perspectives on the ICRC study on International Humanitarian Law. British Institute of International and Comparative Law, London
Short A (1975) The communist insurrection in Malaya, 1948–1960. Frederick Muller, London
Short A (2010) The Malayan emergency and the Batang Kali incident, Asian Aff 3:XLI
Sorley L (2011) Westmoreland. Houghton Mifflin Harcourt, New York
Stafford D (1980) Britain and European resistance, 1940–1945: a survey of the special operations executive. University of Toronto Press, Toronto
Sterling C (1981) The terror network: the secret war of international terrorism. Holt, Rinehart and Winston, New York
Tophoven R (1985) GSG9: German response to terrorism. Bernard and Graefe, Verlag
Trinquier R (1961) Modern warfare: a French view of counterinsurgency. Frederick A, Praeger
Trofimov Y (2007) The Siege of mecca: the 1979 uprising at Islam's holiest shrine. Doubleday, New York
Turns D (2006) Weapons in the ICRC study on Customary International Law. *J Conf & Sec L* 11:201–237
U.S. Army Center of Military History (2010) U.S. Army counterinsurgency and contingency operations doctrine 1942–1976. U.S. Army Center of Military History, Washington
Utinsky M (1948) Miss U. The Naylor company, San Antonio
Ward I, Mirsflor N (2009) Slaughter and deception at Batang Kali. Media Masters, Singapore
West FJ (1972) The Village. Harper and Row, New York
Wilmshurst E, Breau S (eds) (2007) Perspectives on the ICRC study on International Humanitarian Law. British Institute of International and Comparative Law, London
Witton G (1982) Scapegoats of the empire. Angus & Robertson, London

Chapter 13
Can the Law of Armed Conflict Survive 9/11?

Charles Garraway

For those of my generation, the question always used to be, "Can you remember where you were when you heard of Kennedy's assassination?" I can, but that question has now been replaced by "Can you remember where you were when you heard about the Twin Towers?" Again I can. But such earth shattering events have different effects. Whilst the Kennedy assassination led to a plethora of conspiracy theories, books and films, it did not have any effect on the international legal structure. "9/11", on the other hand did. Although for many, the key issue is the strain placed on the laws of armed conflict, or international humanitarian law, to me "9/11" has challenged the very framework of international law itself, revealing a schism that has been there for some decades but which has been masked by other more demanding issues. I talk about the interrelationship between the law of war and the law of peace. Where does peace stop and war start and do the legal boundaries correspond?

For centuries, this was not a problem. Great writers such as Grotius and Oppenheim divided international law into the law of war and the law of peace. Despite an inevitable overlap, there was never any doubt as to which had primacy depending on the circumstances. This certainty all began to dissolve after the Second World War. The horrors of that conflict—and the civil and colonial wars that followed in the immediate aftermath—led the International Committee of the Red Cross to make a concerted effort to lower the threshold for the application of "Geneva law" protection below the traditional one of inter-State conflicts.

Charles Garraway is a former Stockton Professor, United States Naval War College. He is currently an Associate Fellow at Chatham House and a Fellow of the Human Rights Centre, University of Essex.

C. Garraway (✉)
University of Essex, Essex, UK
e-mail: charlesgarraway@hotmail.com

M.N. Schmitt and L. Arimatsu (eds.), *Yearbook of International Humanitarian Law Volume 14, 2011*, DOI: 10.1007/978-90-6704-855-2_13,

Although the result of this initiative was eventually limited to Common Article 3 to the 1949 Geneva Conventions, this was ground breaking as it was the first time that the law of war in treaty form had extended into non-international armed conflict. The mask of sovereignty which had protected States from external examination of their actions within their own borders was beginning to slip.

At the same time, the law of peace was being expanded through the growing influence of human rights law as led by the United Nations. Human rights law developed from a different philosophy to that of the classic law of war. The latter accepted the inevitable fact that in war there would be death—even of the innocent—and destruction but sought, in the words of the St Petersburg Declaration of 1868, to alleviate "as much as possible the calamities of war". The laws on the conduct of hostilities, "Hague law", had always been founded on this recognition of the reality of war. "Geneva law", the law protecting the victims of war, was more rights-orientated, but even that body of law recognised that the law of war is based on the balance between humanity and military necessity.

Human rights law, on the contrary, was designed to protect the individual from the power of the State. Whilst some rights were regarded as not absolute in that they had to take into account such matters as national security, public order, public health, morals or the rights and freedoms of others, others were considered so fundamental as to not be liable to any exception. The philosophy is to start with the "right" and require the State to justify—to a high standard—any deviation from that right.

For decades, the two legal systems developed side by side. Each influenced the other but neither saw itself in competition. In principle, one was the law of war and the other the law of peace and therefore they could not both apply together. However, this established wisdom was based more on historical theory rather than an examination of the texts.

I have already pointed out how, in 1949, the law of war—or at least part of it—was extended into internal conflicts, traditionally the preserve of domestic law. This was extended in 1977 with Additional Protocol II to the 1949 Geneva Conventions where again the ICRC sought to apply most of the then existing law of war to non-international armed conflict. Once more, the initiative failed though the provisions of Common Article 3 were expanded in language that bore great resemblance in some instances to that of human rights law. However, just as the law of war was extending downwards, so human rights law was extending upwards. Two key milestones should be noted. The first was as early as 1950 when the European Convention for the Protection of Human Rights was drafted. Its derogation clause, Article 15, expressly allowed certain derogations to take place "[i]n time of war or other public emergency threatening the life of the nation". The clear implication was that, without derogation, the Convention continued to apply in such situations, including "war". The second milestone was in relation to the 1966 International Covenant on Civil and Political Rights. Its jurisdiction clause required each State "to respect and to ensure to all individuals *within its territory and subject to its jurisdiction*" the Covenant rights. This gave a territorial limitation. However, the Human Rights Committee increasingly began interpreting the "and" as "or", culminating in General Comment 31 of 26 May 2004 which stated:

> States Parties are required by Article 2, para 1, to respect and to ensure the Covenant rights to all persons who may be within their territory and to all persons subject to their jurisdiction. This means that a State party must respect and ensure the rights laid down in the Covenant to anyone within the power or effective control of that State Party, even if not situated within the territory of the State Party. As indicated in General Comment 15 adopted at the twenty-seventh session (1986), the enjoyment of Covenant rights is not limited to citizens of States Parties but must also be available to all individuals, regardless of nationality or statelessness, such as asylum seekers, refugees, migrant workers and other persons, who may find themselves in the territory or subject to the jurisdiction of the State Party. This principle also applies to those within the power or effective control of the forces of a State Party acting outside its territory, regardless of the circumstances in which such power or effective control was obtained, such as forces constituting a national contingent of a State Party assigned to an international peace-keeping or peace-enforcement operation.

Clearly human rights were now seeking to impinge on the conduct of military operations extra-territorially.

At the same time, the reluctance of States to allow the international law of war to apply in any meaningful way in non-international armed conflict was itself being undermined by a combination of judicial intervention and the ICRC seeking to regain the ground that they had lost in the final negotiations on Additional Protocol II in 1977. The International Criminal Tribunal for the Former Yugoslavia in a series of judgements, starting with its very first case, Dusko Tadic, sought to apply, as a matter of customary law, the law relating to the conduct of hostilities in international armed conflict to non-international armed conflicts also. The Appeal Court stated in justification:

> What is inhumane, and consequently proscribed, in international wars, cannot but be inhumane and inadmissible in civil strife.

Following up on this, the ICRC in their seminal study into Customary International Humanitarian Law, published in 2005, developed 161 customary "Rules" of which no fewer than 147 were found to apply across the board in international and non-international armed conflict alike. What the ICRC had failed to achieve with States in the negotiating chamber, they had now introduced by a combination of judicial activism and interpretation of customary law.

It was thus inevitable that sooner or later the law of war and human rights law would come into juxtaposition and even conflict. The European Court of Human Rights had been called upon from the 1980s to deal with cases arising from conflict situations, both in relation to the Turkish invasion of Cyprus in 1974 (an international armed conflict) and the Kurdish insurgency in South East Turkey (a non-international armed conflict). "9/11" simply brought forward the clash in a manner that has created difficulties for both legal systems.

Terrorism is as old as the hills. So long as man has been in conflict with man, terror tactics have been employed. But there has always been a difference between terrorism *per se* and acts of terror. Acts of terror can be committed in time of peace or war and indeed are specifically prohibited as a method of warfare. However, terrorism as a phenomenon has always been treated as something within the sphere of law enforcement. The United Kingdom, in the latter part of the twentieth century, faced with a ruthless foe in the form of the Irish Republican Army and its splinter groups, consistently denied that there was an armed conflict in Northern Ireland. The matter was treated as an internal matter governed by domestic criminal law. A similar approach was adopted by the German Government in relation to the Red Army Faction and other terrorist groups and the Spanish Government in relation to Euskadi Ta Askatasuna (ETA). A clear distinction was drawn between terrorism and internal armed conflicts where terrorist acts were committed. Cross-border terrorism was far from unknown. Various Palestinian factions consistently carried out terrorist attacks outside the Middle East including the Munich Olympics massacre of 1972. Again this was treated by the German Government within a law enforcement paradigm though it is fair to say that the attack was not aimed directly at Germany.

Throughout the second half of the twentieth century, the United Nations was involved with the growing threat of terrorism. A range of Conventions was produced dealing with different aspects of the phenomenon but again all were based on increased international criminal cooperation. The United Kingdom summed up the position when, on ratification of the 1977 Additional Protocols to the Geneva Convention in 1998, a statement was made in the following terms:

> It is the understanding of the United Kingdom that the term 'armed conflict' of itself and in its context denotes a situation of a kind which is not constituted by the commission of ordinary crimes including acts of terrorism whether concerted or in isolation.

As late as 17 April 2000, Madeleine Albright, then the United States Secretary of State, said in a speech to the University of World Economy and Diplomacy at Tashkent in Uzbekistan:

> Terrorism is a criminal act and should be treated accordingly—and that means applying the law fairly and consistently. We have found, through experience around the world, that the best way to defeat terrorist threats is to increase law enforcement capabilities while at the same time promoting democracy and human rights.

"9/11" was to change all that.

The initial response to the attacks was to launch an attack on Afghanistan where Al Qaeda were sheltering under Taliban protection. In principle, this was supported by the international community and should have posed few problems to the existing legal framework. This was an international armed conflict within that framework, though running alongside an existing non-international armed conflict between the Taliban and the Northern Alliance. However, the rhetoric from the United States leadership seemed to go further, indicating that the United States was at war not merely with Afghanistan but with terrorism in general in a Global War on Terror. Supported by legal advice, though not unchallenged, President Bush drew a distinction between "our present conflict with the Taliban" to which the laws of war ("the provisions of Geneva") applied and "our conflict with al Qaeda in Afghanistan *or elsewhere throughout the world*" to which none of the "provisions of Geneva", including Common Article 3 applied.

In so far as Afghanistan was concerned, whilst the legal reasoning might have been faulty, the effects on the legal framework might not have been too bad. There was clearly an armed conflict underway and although it could indeed be argued that Al Qaeda were not entitled to combatant status in that conflict, there were still provisions within the legal framework that covered them. In an armed conflict, nobody is totally outside the protection of the law.

The problem lay with the words "or elsewhere throughout the world". The United States was now claiming to be involved in a global conflict—and furthermore one which was outside the traditional legal framework being neither an international armed conflict within the terms of Common Article 2 to the Geneva Conventions nor an "armed conflict not of an international character" governed by Common Article 3. It appeared that the United States was claiming the right to carry out military operations against Al Qaeda throughout the globe. The legal implications of this were huge. It could be argued that, because of the universal condemnation of international terrorism by the United Nations, the laws of neutrality in their classic form did not apply. Indeed, President Bush himself announced, in an address to a joint session of Congress on September 20, 2001, "Either you are with us, or you are with the terrorists." It was not long before the United States showed that it meant business when, in November 2002, a Hellfire missile attack on a convoy travelling in Yemen killed Abu Ali al-Harithi, supposedly the mastermind behind the bombing of the USS Cole in October 2000. Further strikes in Yemen have followed, as well as numerous attacks in Pakistan, culminating in the death of Osama Bin Laden himself.

But what law applies to these "targeted killings"? The United States maintains that it is at war and these matters are therefore governed by the laws and customs of war. As a result of the Supreme Court decision in Hamdan v Rumsfeld, the Administration have conceded that this "war" is governed by Common Article 3 of the 1949 Geneva Conventions but that article, in itself, says nothing on the rules governing the conduct of hostilities. It is unclear what rules the United States consider binding in that context although one thing is clear—targeting is based on status, as under the traditional law of war paradigm, and not immediate threat as under human rights law. Al-Harithi was posing no immediate threat to anyone at the time he was killed. Osama Bin Laden was, according to US sources, subject to lethal force because of his position as an enemy commander. The Navy Seals did not have to rely on any actions taken by him at the time of the attack.

In principle, there is no obstacle to the United States, on this reasoning, taking out an Al Qaeda leader on the streets of London or Paris. It is argued that, in practice, this would never happen because it would be left to the authorities in those countries to take action. But because Europe, and indeed much of the rest of the world, has not bought into this "Global War on Terror", the action would need to be taken under a law enforcement paradigm. What if domestic law did not provide the grounds for such action?

We seem to face here a dilemma. Do the laws of war extend down to cover all actions against Al Qaeda and affiliated organisations operating anywhere in the world, or are such actions covered by the law enforcement paradigm except where they take place within the bounds of a recognised armed conflict? If United States Navy Seals killed an unarmed Al Qaeda leader on the streets of London, would they be committing murder or could they claim combatant privilege? The boundaries between armed conflict and law enforcement now seem to have merged together in a way that there is no longer any clear dividing line. It can hardly be appropriate to say that the law governing the situation depends on the stability of the country in which the operation takes place.

This confusion is having a double effect. First, there is a fightback by those in the human rights community who argue that the events of the last 10 years have shown that the laws of war are inadequate to address modern day situations. Targeted killings are often accompanied by the deaths of other innocent people and this is seen as unacceptable. The danger here is that such a viewpoint will extend into more traditional armed conflicts. In Afghanistan, the McChrystal doctrine of "courageous restraint" led to a restriction on permitted collateral damage in planned attacks almost to the extent of zero tolerance. This is far more akin to a human rights standard than one emanating from the laws of war where the expected collateral damage must not be excessive to the anticipated military advantage. We have already seen how human rights bodies are becoming increasingly involved in situations of armed conflict. Whereas the United States continues to insist that human rights law and the laws of war are mutually exclusive, this is a position that is becoming increasingly untenable internationally. As has been pointed out above, the European Convention on Human Rights was always envisaged as applying to some extent in time of war and the Court has already considered cases arising from situations of armed conflict, most recently in relation to Chechnya and Iraq. There are a number of cases currently before it in relation to the Russia-Georgia conflict in 2008.

The International Court of Justice also has endorsed the continued application of human rights law in time of armed conflict. In the "Barrier" advisory opinion involving the Israeli security wall, it stated:

> As regards the relationship between international humanitarian law and human rights law, there are thus three possible situations: some rights may be exclusively matters of international humanitarian law; others may be exclusively matters of human rights law; yet others may be matters of both these branches of international law. In order to answer the question put to it, the Court will have to take into consideration both these branches of international law, namely human rights law and, as *lex specialis*, international humanitarian law.

Of course, the Court did not go on to outline where those situations can be found. There is a growing school that argues that human rights law is the foundation legal framework and that the law of war as the "*lex specialis*" should only apply where it is compatible with human rights law and can add to it. This is probably workable in relation to much "Geneva law", relating to the protection of victims of war, but it would play havoc with the traditional law of war relating to the conduct of hostilities, particularly in relation to the use of force where the standards are diametrically opposed.

There is a second and less obvious danger. There has been a tendency to look upon "terrorists" as modern day outlaws, beyond the pale. They should, like pirates, be subject to universal jurisdiction and "terrorism" should be an international crime. Attractive as this argument might be, it falls down on closer analogy. One of the reasons why pirates are subject to universal jurisdiction is because their crimes are committed on the high seas, territory beyond the jurisdiction of any one State. Acts which would amount to piracy if committed on the high seas but which are committed within the territorial sea of a State are classified as "armed robbery" and not subject to universal jurisdiction. Most acts of terrorism are committed within the territory of a State. Whilst I agree that there is a need for greater international cooperation in the justice sphere in dealing with acts of terrorism, and indeed the various United Nations Conventions were designed to do exactly that, there is a risk in making "terrorism" an international crime.

Apart from the difficulty in defining the term, it has become usual in recent years for Governments to describe all opponents who resort to arms as "terrorists". If such people were in theory committing an international crime subject to universal jurisdiction, it would completely undermine the application of the laws of war to non-international armed conflict. Already there is difficulty in persuading non-State actors that it is in their interests to apply the laws of war in a non-international armed conflict. Non-State actors remain subject to domestic jurisdiction and, if captured, can be tried and sentenced under that domestic law. However, provided that they comply with the laws of war, they will not be committing international crimes, war crimes, and thus, Additional Protocol II can urge the "authorities in power" at the end of hostilities to "endeavor to grant the broadest possible amnesty to persons who have participated in the armed conflict". This is not designed to protect those who have committed war crimes but those who have fought in accordance with the laws of war.

If "terrorism" is to become an international crime and all non-State actors in a non-international armed conflict are to be classed as terrorists, and thus international criminals, this provision of Additional Protocol II will become obsolete as it is generally accepted that amnesties should not apply to international crimes. There would then be no incentive at all for non-State actors to comply with the laws of war. If the laws of war were thus seen to be ineffectual, it would be a further argument for their subordination to human rights law.

It follows that the decision by the Bush Administration in the immediate aftermath of "9/11" to treat the fight against terrorism as a matter governed primarily by the laws of war rather than by a law enforcement paradigm may in fact have serious consequences for the laws of war themselves. The perceived underlying unsuitability of using the use of force provisions from the laws of war in counter-terrorist operations outside situations of armed conflict has given human rights lawyers a platform to attack some of the fundamental principles of the laws of war, such as the balance between humanity and military necessity, even in traditional conflict situations.

In addition, the extension of the definition of "terrorist", at least colloquially, and the wish to ensure that acts of terrorism are universally condemned and subject to the widest possible jurisdiction has cast doubt on the efficacy of the laws of war as they relate to non-international armed conflict and led to calls for a wider application of human rights standards, even where they conflict with the laws of war.

If the long term effect of this is to make it impossible to conduct military operations effectively in a legal manner, it could be disastrous. However much theorists may look forward to the days when war is no more, that utopian dream has never been achieved in past millennia. The laws of war were designed to recognize the sad reality of war but to seek to alleviate as far as possible the calamities of war. Human rights law does not recognize that reality, coming as it does from the law of peace. This clash of philosophies is already being seen in Afghanistan where there is increasing pressure on ISAF European contingents to refrain from handing detainees to the national authorities on human rights grounds. But such contingents have no legal authority themselves to hold the detainees for any length of time. The result is that they may have to be released. A soldier who captures an insurgent who has killed one of his colleagues on Monday only to find him back on the streets on Wednesday will not be impressed. If he captures him again and the same thing happens, he will wonder as to the point of what he is doing. The temptation will be to take the law into his own hands with fatal consequences.

The laws of war are there for a purpose, limited though it may be. The United States, in seeking to extend the scope of those laws into areas for which they were not designed have done the laws no service. Indeed, they may, in a worst case scenario, have struck a death knell for those laws. As wars unfortunately, like taxes, are not going to disappear in the foreseeable future, if the laws that regulate them no longer can be applied, then we are back to the law of the jungle. Henry Dunant would be turning in his grave.

Chapter 14
'Terrorism' as a Central Theme in the Evolution of Maritime Operations Law Since 11 September 2011

Rob McLaughlin

Contents

14.1 Introduction

As DP O'Connell noted in a seminal 1970 article ('International Law of Contemporary Naval Operations'[1]) and in his equally seminal 1975 book *The Influence of Law on Sea Power,* maritime operations law is a constantly evolving discipline in both theory and practice—with law often lagging practice by a noticeable margin.One consequence of the (then) '*Dreadnought* era' focus of much of the law of naval warfare was that '[I]f international law appears to the naval officer

[1] O'Connell 1970.

R. McLaughlin (✉)
Australian National University, Canberra, ACT, Australia
e-mail: mclaughlinr@law.anu.edu.au

M.N. Schmitt and L. Arimatsu (eds.), *Yearbook of International Humanitarian Law Volume 14, 2011*, DOI: 10.1007/978-90-6704-855-2_14,

a tangle of uncertainties in which he is likely to be ensnared, the technology of naval warfare induces in the legal theorists perplexity and dismay'.[2] However, for all of the sometimes haphazard and 'catch-up' nature of the relationship between law and practice in maritime operations, there are clearly a number of fundamental, normative, defining themes which have tended to play the dominant role in shaping and informing the evolution of maritime operations law over the last several decades (or, indeed, centuries). Pinpointing which themes come within this category is of course a matter for debate, but it would seem reasonably safe to assert that an indication as to their form and colour is evident in paradigmatic themes such as resource exploitation, maritime claims, technological advance, and freedom of navigation.

Periodically, however, a less traditional maritime theme achieves temporarily heightened influence over this process of evolution. I believe that the decade since 11 September 2001 is such a period—one in which the theme of 'terrorism' has played a significant and overt shaping and influencing role within this evolution. This is not to say that this decade's preoccupation with 'terrorism law' is something unique to the maritime operations sphere, for clearly, terrorism has functioned as a paradigm-defining factor in relation to a very broad legal spectrum—aviation, technology proliferation, and finance to cite but three. Nor is it to say that the more traditionally dominant themes have not also influenced evolution—indeed, the *ROKS Cheonan* incident,[3] and ongoing tensions related to resource security and maritime claims in the East China and South China Sea areas,[4] are stark reminders of the continuing claim of these long-term fundamental themes to normative influence. But it is very clear that the issue of terrorism has noticeably agitated the direction and development of maritime operations law over this last decade—or certainly as compared to its more staccato claim to influence within the maritime domain over the last 60 years as a whole.[5]

My aim in this short article is to briefly examine the ways in which I believe this focus upon terrorism has influenced, or is beginning to influence, the development of maritime operations law. To do this, I shall focus upon four sub-themes within the overall terrorism chapeau: terrorism from the sea; terrorism at sea; terrorism supported from the sea; and terrorist groups as subjects within the Law of Naval Warfare. Within each of the first three sections, I will briefly outline some examples of the types of threats emanating from this particular manifestation of terrorism, and then offer a short account of some (but by no means all) of the legal responses prompted by these threats. In relation to the last sub-theme, I will make some general comments only, as I believe that critical aspects of this debate are still in their infancy, making it difficult (at this stage) to sensibly point to a trending legal response.

---

[2] O'Connell 1975, at p. xiii.

[3] See, Joint Civilian-Military Investigation Group 2010.

[4] Such as the ongoing dispute between China and Japan over fisheries enforcement in the Senkaku Islands region—see, for example, the September 2010 incident reported in The Guardian 2010.

[5] See, for example, Greenberg et al. 2006.

14.2 Terrorism from the Sea

14.2.1 Threats

Terrorism from the sea is not a post-11 September 2001 phenomenon. The threat of terrorism from the sea is anchored in the simple fact that it has long been, and in many aspects still is, relatively easy to gain access to a State from the sea, or to import prohibited material (such as weapons or explosives) via the sea. Port, passenger, cargo, and container security is much improved over the last decade, but the ability to secrete material amongst bulk cargoes, and the ease of approach and access to ports or other landing points enjoyed by shipping, still far exceeds that available to aviation or land transport. Indeed, in many advanced ports, it is still the case that less than ten per cent of containers are examined upon unload—for example, by x-ray or opening and physical inspection. Terrorist threats from the sea include use of vessels as obstacles (e.g. sinking a vessel in a port chokepoint); as a kinetic force (such as a ram) to damage other vessels or port infrastructure; as (less achievably) 'floating bombs' aimed at igniting a flammable cargo; or as transport systems for other forms of explosive cargo (e.g. a 'dirty bomb' secreted within a shipping container).[6] Another manifestation of this phenomenon is shipborne improvised explosive devices used against stationary or navigationally constrained ships in port areas—the seminal example being the attack on *USS Cole* in Aden Harbour (Yemen) on 12 October 2000.[7]

A second—intricately related—type of threat posed by terrorism from the sea relates to the often porous nature of maritime borders and entry points. The Mumbai terrorist attack in November 2008, for example, was perpetrated by terrorists who entered Mumbai from the sea, utilising small dinghies to land from a mothership.[8] But again, this is a revived, as opposed to a new, threat: A decade prior to the Mumbai attacks, 150 Sri Lankan Tamil Tiger fighters conducted a sea-borne landing in the Maldives (in November 1988), defeated the local militia,

[6] See, for example: US Department of Homeland Security—Policy 2004; US General Accounting Office—Reports 2002; US General Accounting Office—Testimony 2002; US Government Accountability Office 2010; Fritelli 2003, 2005; Forbes 2003, pp. 27–28 (noting that it is no simple task to explode an LNG tanker, or to fire an oil cargo); Allison 2001; The Economist 2001; Council on Foreign Relations 2006; Schoen 2004; Richardson 2004; McNaught 2005.

[7] US Department of Defence 2001.

[8] Rahman 2008: 'Eyewitnesses have provided accounts of how the gunmen involved in yesterday's Mumbai massacre landed undetected in the heart of the port city's bustling downtown area. At least some of the terrorists, said to be in their early twenties and armed with AK-47 assault rifles and hand grenades, landed on the coast of Mumbai's commercial and entertainment neighbourhood in light and fast Gemini boats, powered by small outboard motors. These inflatable dinghies, according to Indian navy sources quoted by the Headlines Today TV news channel, were launched from a larger vessel, the MV Alfa, which arrived near Mumbai sometime yesterday and anchored offshore a distance from India's financial capital.'

and fled only after the Government of Maldives urgently sought, and gained, intervention by Indian forces (Operation Cactus).[9]

14.2.2 Some Legal Responses

Legal responses to the threat of terrorism from the sea have, in my view, been the most comprehensive and definitive sphere of advance in relation to terrorism and maritime operations law. The first, and primary, legal response has been the International Ship and Port Facility Security (ISPS) Code, negotiated under the auspices of the International Maritime Organisation (IMO). The IMO has long made the linkage between the ISPS Code and the terrorist attacks of 11 September 2001 explicit: 'The International Ship and Port Facility Security Code (ISPS Code—adopted 12 December 2002) is a comprehensive set of measures to enhance the security of ships and port facilities, developed in response to the perceived threats to ships and port facilities in the wake of the 9/11 attacks in the United States'.[10] The ISPS Code suite of measures (implemented as Chapter XI-2 of the SOLAS Convention 1974) are squarely aimed at enhancing port security, gathering and sharing information at an early stage—or at least early enough, hopefully, to allow for planning and response prior to a threat vessel entering port—and responding in a co-ordinated manner to security threats once threat vessels, cargoes, or people do enter a port. The *Australian Maritime Transport and Offshore Facilities Security Act* (2003) (as one example of national responses to and implementation of the ISPS Code) is explicit as to the priority for ensuring an adequate legal response to terrorism from the sea: s:3(4) provides that

The maritime security outcomes [expected of the Act] are as follows:

(a) Australia's obligations under Chapter XI 2 of the SOLAS Convention and the ISPS Code, including those with regard to the rights, freedoms and welfare of seafarers, are met;
(b) the vulnerability to terrorist attack of Australian ships, ports and other ships within Australia, and offshore facilities is reduced without undue disruption to trade;
(c) the risk that maritime transport or offshore facilities are used to facilitate terrorist or other unlawful activities is reduced;
(d) security information is communicated effectively among maritime industry participants and government agencies with security responsibilities for maritime transport and offshore facilities.

---

[9] Sakhuja 2002, at p. 3. On Operation Cactus, see, for example, Indian Navy (1988); Rakshak (2011).

[10] At http://www.imo.org/OurWork/Security/Instruments/Pages/ISPSCode.aspx. For a general background to, and analysis of, the key elements of the ISPS Code, see for example, Australian Government—Department of Infrastructure and Transport 2010.

Domestic implementation of the ISPS Code has been relatively high on the agenda of the Proliferation Security Initiative (PSI) (which has sponsored information sharing and capability development in the area) and has dovetailed closely with the associated Container Security Initiative (CSI).[11]

The ISPS Code has also generated or enhanced a range of subsidiary or related maritime security threat monitoring and assessment tools—from the Vessel Long Range Identification and Tracking System (LRIT),[12] through to Australia's own initially controversial declaration in December 2004 of an 'Australian Maritime Identification System' (AMIS)—originally described as a 'Maritime Identification Zone'.[13] The initial proclamation of the AMIS offers a case study in the potential for unwitting conceptual over-reach and associated misunderstanding when dealing with the highly sensitive juncture between port state security, terrorism, and perceived intrusions upon both High Seas freedoms and States' rights in EEZs. The initial confusion as to whether the Australian government had claimed an authority to interdict, for the purposes of identification, out to 1000 nautical miles from the Australian coast, was quickly clarified: As Klein records, the furore surrounding the initial MIZ/AMIS announcement quickly led to 'Australia reformulat[ing] the AMIS so that ships [would] now be requested to provide information on a wholly voluntary basis and the AMIS [would] be based on cooperative international arrangements, particularly with neighbouring states'.[14] Additionally, questions as to the legal capacity of Australia (or any State) to assert a right to collect information from vessels whilst transiting through other States' EEZs remain.[15] In my view, this nascent trend in terrorism-focussed, security-based outreach into international waters runs the risk of re-invigorating and re-casting ongoing debates as to the balances struck between coastal state security and freedom of navigation. It also presages a significant additional complication in so far as traditional proponents for freedom of navigation (and against the extension of additional security authorisations into international waters) may undermine the integrity of their long-held and principled positions by advocating such extensions in relation to the highly abused and contextually amorphous concept of terrorism.

A second legal response to the threat of terrorism from the sea—evident most particularly in evolving national legal regimes—has been to address the

---

[11] See, for example, Bateman 2007, at pp. 241–258.

[12] See, for example, IMO Circular, Guidance on the Implementation of the LRIT System, MSC.1/Circ. 1256 (5 June 2008) available at http://www.infrastructure.gov.au/transport/security/maritime/isps/circulars/pdf/1256.pdf (Last Accessed 30 December 2011).

[13] John Howard, Prime Minister of Australia, 'Strengthening Offshore Maritime Security' (Press Release, 15 December 2004) reported by the *ABC* at McGrath 2004.

[14] See, for example, Klein 2006.

[15] Rothwell and Stephens 2010, at p. 96.

challenge of force protection for warships in ports, or whilst transiting in the navigationally confined waters that generally attend entry and exit from ports and anchorages.[16] A perhaps little noticed, but increasingly important, legal response to this challenge is the concept of Controlled Access Zones (CAZ). Such zones—in essence bubbles of waterspace and airspace surrounding a warship alongside, at anchor, or on transit into/out of port, from which unauthorised vessels and aircraft are excluded—have been brought into effect, or are being considered, by a number of States. This is, in my view, a sound, sensible, and contextually sensitive response to the almost overwhelming attraction of a navigationally constrained warship as a target for terrorist attack. There are, of course, challenges: How big is the CAZ; how much interference with other shipping in a busy port is warranted; is there some built in discretion for the warship to threat assess and allow close transits, and so on. But each of these practical concerns is manageable. What is of greater concern—not because it is inherently problematic from either a legal or operational perspective, but because it will require much greater patience and precision in negotiation and explanation (given existing sensitivities regarding any perceived infringement of coastal State Territorial Sea sovereignty and High Seas freedoms)—is the transformation of extensive CAZs into permanent exclusion zones around warships underway. The US, for example, has extended authority for such security zones into their EEZ,[17] and a number of States claim the right to declare 'warning zones' around warships on the High Seas—ostensibly to discourage approach so as to de-clutter the surface and air picture in order to simplify the threat assessment process. But there is a fine line to be trod between such ubiquitous 'warning zones', and more geographically and jurisdictionally constrained CAZs or security zones.[18] The negotiating history of the INCSEA agreement perhaps offers some insight into the difficulties that will attend any attempt to universalise this particular force protection measure.

---

[16] For examples, see: (Canada) *Order Designating Controlled Access Zones (Halifax, Esquimalt and Nanoose Harbours)* 19 December 2002 at http://gazette.gc.ca/archives/p1/2003/2003-01-11/html/notice-avis-eng.html#i7; (Australia) *Maritime Transport and Offshore Facilities Security Act* 2003 (Commonwealth) available at http://www.comlaw.gov.au/Details/C2011C00831, and accompanying *Maritime Transport and Offshore Facilities Security Regulations* 2003 (Commonwealth), available at http://www.comlaw.gov.au/Details/F2005C00624; Explanatory Statement to the *Maritime Transport Security Regulations* 2003 (Commonwealth) at http://www.austlii.edu.au/au/legis/cth/num_reg_es/mtsr20032003n366481.html; (US) *Maritime Transportation Security Act* 2002, sec 101 'findings': '(7) Ports are often very open and exposed and are susceptible to large scale acts of terrorism that could cause a large loss of life or economic disruption', available at http://www.tsa.gov/assets/pdf/MTSA.pdf.

[17] Jacques et al. 2006, at Chap. 1.

[18] Jacques et al. 2006, at Chaps. 1 and 2.

14.3 Terrorism at Sea

14.3.1 Threats

Threats encompassed within the concept of 'terrorism at sea' include acts similar to those noted above in relation to terrorism from the sea—shipborne IEDs, ramming vessels, shooting at or into vessels, and so on. But they also include acts such as taking control a vessel from within (a Suppression of Unlawful Activities at Sea Convention (SUA) offence) or from another vessel (a SUA and/or piracy offence), for terrorism related purposes that do not necessarily involve using the ship as a weapon or a weapons platform. An example of the former is the 24 April 2004 shipborne IED attacks on Multinational Force (MNF) warships protecting oil platforms in the Iraqi Territorial Sea, which resulted in the deaths of two US Navy Sailors and a US Coast Guardsman.[19] Examples of the latter include the 'pirate attack' on the *Dewi Madrim*, in 2003 (reportedly involving 'terrorists learning how to drive a ship', and kidnapping the ship's officers 'in an effort to acquire expertise on conducting a maritime attack'[20]) and, of course, the *Achille Lauro* incident (itself one of the catalysts for the negotiation of the 1988 SUA).

14.3.2 Some Legal Responses

There are a range of legal responses which trace some provenance from the threat of terrorism at sea. I will focus upon two representative responses—one which I believe was, in legal terms, highly questionable and which did not appear to advance much beyond some initial discussion; the other a more logical, and legally sound, proposal. The first and more questionable 'legal' solution, which circulated in the earlier part of the decade, was to resurrect a form of 'privateering'—to authorise Private Military and Security Companies (PMSC) to conduct counter-terrorism at sea, leaving expensive 'high-end' equipped navies free to concentrate upon their core role of traditional warfighting.[21] Nicholas Gvosdev and Anthony Cipriano, for example, proposed that in the light of terrorist activity at sea

> Given the limits on the time and resources of U.S. intelligence agencies, Congress should revisit the power granted to it by Article I, Section 8 of the U.S. Constitution to 'grant letters of marque and reprisal, and make rules concerning captures on land and water.' In other words, it is time to consider reviving privateering—for 21st-century conditions.'[22]

[19] See, for example, Stephenson 2004; US Department of the Navy 2004.

[20] World Net Daily 2004.

[21] See, for example, Sechrest 2001.

[22] Gvosdev and Cipriano 2002.

Rightly, in my view, this proposal did not appear to garner widespread support at the time. Counter-terrorism at sea is, in certain select circumstances, a war-fighting task for navies (and coast guards to the extent that they can become combatants in accordance with LOAC), or it is a law enforcement operation for navies, coast guards, and maritime police forces. It is not a task for privateering. Customary International Law (drawing force from the 1856 Paris Declaration Respecting Maritime Law) certainly regards privateering as an unlawful trade for any mariner. Additionally, the development and domestication of associated international law since 1856 (such as in the fields of human rights, use of force in maritime law enforcement, and international criminal law) further assures that a revival of privateering as a legitimate and lawful trade is unrealisable. What is interesting about the future of this issue, however, is the inevitable—but misleading—correlations it seems to suggest in relation to PMSC ship protection teams as a response to piracy, and the debate over CIA management and authorisation of combat operations in the form of UAV strikes on targets ashore. Neither constitutes privateering, and neither should be employed by analogy to support any argument for its revival.

The second response—more substantial, useful, and legally sound—was the 2005 SUA Protocols in relation to terrorist offences and proliferation-related transport offences for ships, and for fixed platforms located on the continental shelf.[23] The 2005 ship protocol in particular is clearly a child of four related concerns which became more prominent after 11 September 2001—two as to scope, two as to functional operation. The *scope-broadening* requirements involved amending the SUA to more explicitly anticipate use of ships by terrorists as weapons or means of transport; and to take into account the potential exploitation of shipping to transport proliferation-controlled materials which could be used in terrorist threats or attacks. The animating *operational* concerns were the need to broaden the SUA's scope from its focus on 'prosecute or extradite' after the event—so as to enter more fully into the field of prevention (beyond the original SUA exhortation to information sharing and general co-operation); and to build into that preventive approach a formalised (and thus legally supported) process acknowledging and facilitating preventive boarding operations. The 2005 SUA Protocol remains only narrowly signed and even more narrowly ratified (having come into force on 28 July 2010 after ratification by Nauru). But its importance and value as a legal response to terrorism at sea lay less in this statistic than in the fact that it was drafted and settled in the first place. This Protocol emerged from very broad, detailed negotiations within the IMO Legal Committee, during which the overwhelming majority of States agreed that there was some

[23] See generally http://www.imo.org/About/Conventions/ListOfConventions/Pages/SUA-Treaties.aspx. For the text of the two 2005 Protocols (the Protocol on ships amending the SUA itself, and the Protocol on fixed platforms amending the original 1988 Protocol to the SUA concerning fixed platforms located on the continental shelf), see https://imo.amsa.gov.au/public/2005/sua-final-act.htm. For the consolidated text of the SUA and Protocol, see https://www.unodc.org/tldb/pdf/Convention&Protocol%20Maritime%20Navigation%20EN.pdf.

need to deal with gaps in the international legal regime relating to terrorism at sea—even if they were not ultimately able to carry this broad consensus across into a more widely ratified instrument. Regardless of its ratification status, discussions of the law applicable to terrorism at sea no longer take place without at least some analysis of the 2005 SUA Protocol, and thus of its underpinning propositions and its fundamental negotiating assumptions.

14.4 Terrorism Supported from the Sea

14.4.1 Threats

At first glance, distilling the influence of terrorism on maritime operations law over the last decade into a sub-theme of 'terrorism supported from the sea' may appear to give unwarranted prominence to a minor and essentially unrelated threat. However, it is worth briefly noting three indicative examples of this form of threat which clearly tie it into the broader narrative of terrorism and maritime operations law since 11 September 2001. The first in time was the threat of proliferation by sea as a mechanism for terrorist groups to acquire WMD, their precursor materials, or certain types of delivery systems. This threat underpinned a series of counter-proliferation interdictions at sea—most notably the *So San* interdiction on 9 December 2002 by the Spanish warship *Navarra*.[24] Such interdictions are neither rare nor routine—the *BBC China* in October 2003, is a further example. Nor have they been limited to WMD proliferation concerns—the January 2002 Israeli interdiction of a shipment of conventional weapons, in *Karine-A*, which were assessed to be bound for Hamas,[25] for example. But each generally shares with the *So San* interdiction a degree of imprecision in attribution and clear jurisdictional mandate. This is not, however, to read down the impact which proliferation by sea, and the potential for such materials to fall into the hands of terrorist groups, has had upon conceptualising and advancing maritime operations law since 2001. Indeed, then US President George W. Bush indicated in his 31 May 2003 'Krakow speech'—considered the genesis of the Proliferation Security Initiative (PSI)—that

> The greatest threat to peace is the spread of nuclear, chemical and biological weapons. And we must work together to stop proliferation. The countries of the G-8 committed last year to aiding Russia and others in securing and eliminating deadly weapons that remain from the Soviet era.... When weapons of mass destruction or their components are in transit, we must have the means and authority to seize them. So today I announce a new effort to fight proliferation called the Proliferation Security Initiative. The United States and a number of our close allies, including Poland, have begun working on new agreements to search planes and ships carrying suspect cargo and to seize illegal weapons or

[24] See, for example, Guilfoyle 2005.

[25] See, for example, Office of the Coordinator for Counter Terrorism Report 2002.

> missile technologies. Over time, we will extend this partnership as broadly as possible to keep the world's most destructive weapons away from our shores and out of the hands of our common enemies.[26]

The second aspect of terrorism supported from the sea was the alleged existence of an Al Qaeda 'phantom fleet' which provided equipment transport, funds generation, and platforms for terrorist acts.[27] This threat, if it was ever a significant one, appeared to have been localised to the early part of the decade.

It is, however, a third aspect of this relationship—the potential (either realised, or still only latent) for a linkage between piracy, and acts committed at sea by terrorist groups as a source of funds generation for terrorism ashore—that has become the more (most?) important question in relation to terrorism supported from the sea. This linkage is not unique to its current focal point of piracy off the coast of Somalia and Al Shabaab in Somalia. Indeed Singapore warned of similar links between South East Asian pirate groups and Jemaah Islamiyah in 2004.[28] Gal Luft and Anne Korin, writing in *Foreign Affairs* in 2004, argued that

> Most disturbingly, the scourges of piracy and terrorism are increasingly intertwined: piracy on the high seas is becoming a key tactic of terrorist groups. Unlike the pirates of old, whose sole objective was quick commercial gain, many of today's pirates are maritime terrorists with an ideological bent and a broad political agenda. This nexus of piracy and terrorism is especially dangerous for energy markets: most of the world's oil and gas is shipped through the world's most piracy-infested waters.[29]

Clearly, however, the current typology of this threat involves the actual, or anticipated, conduct of piracy by Al Shabaab affiliated Somalis, with a view to Al Shabaab profiting from ransoms and dedicating that income to financing other terrorist activities.[30]

14.4.2 Some Legal Responses

In my view, the legal response to an actual or potential piracy-terrorism linkage has taken two distinct forms. The first form of response—prior to the emergence of the Somali piracy issue as a specific concern—was informed by a general (and, I believe, misguided) desire to leverage the law of piracy in order to exploit its

---

[26] The text of the 'Krakow speech' is available at http://www.freerepublic.com/focus/f-news/920882/posts.

[27] See, for example, Bright et al 2001.

[28] This was the view of then Singapore Minister for Security, Tony Tan, 8 June 2004, as reported in World Net Daily 2004.

[29] See Luft and Korin 2004.

[30] See, for example, UN SC, *Report of the Special Adviser to the Secretary-General on Legal Issues Related to Piracy off the Coast of Somalia* (the 'Lang Report), UN DOC S/2011/30, 25 January 2011, para 24 available at http://www.securitycouncilreport.org/atf/cf/%7B65BFCF9B-6D27-4E9C-8CD3-CF6E4FF96FF9%7D/Somalia%20S%202011%2030.pdf.

attendant universal jurisdiction in dealing with terrorism. A number of commentators have argued that the best way to deal with the scourges of piracy and maritime terrorism is to 'couple' them and treat them similarly.[31] Tina Garmon was explicit (and in my view very honest) in her advocacy as to the reason this would be attractive to some:

> A reconciliation between conceptions of piracy and terrorism would enable more effective prevention and punishment of such acts. Under customary international law, piracy incurs greater jurisdiction. As the primary distinction between piracy and terrorism is a private versus a political motive, erasing the distinction would enable greater enforcement.[32]

My concern with this approach is two-fold. First, whilst many of the practical measures used to combat piracy and maritime terrorism are similar,[33] there remains a degree of definitional (and thus jurisdictional) uncertainty surrounding whether terrorism at sea (or at least that involving two ships) can be seamlessly collapsed into the concept of piracy.

> In some cases…in the charged political atmosphere, the mass media and governments have blurred the line between piracy and acts of terrorism. Such acts can appear similar, but it is important to understand that piracy and terrorism have different causes, objectives and tactics… Terrorism is distinct from piracy in a straightforward manner. Piracy is a crime motivated by greed, and thus predicated on immediate financial gain. Terrorism is motivated by political goals beyond the immediate act of attacking or hijacking a maritime target. The motivating factor for terrorists is generally political ideology stemming from perceived injustices, both historical and contemporary.[34]

Some analysts also draw a distinction between 'private ends' encompassing 'personally motivated hatred or sheer vengeance' and 'politically motivated acts'—with Judge Jose Luis Jesus of the International Tribunal for the Law of the Sea arguing that the 'adoption of the SUA Convention' has rendered it 'a lost cause to continue insisting on considering such a politically-motivated act as piracy'.[35] I am not as convinced of a clear, legally definable, separation between a 'private gain' motivation for piracy and an 'ideological' motivation for maritime terrorism. Sooner rather than later, however, piracy-maritime terrorism linkages off the Horn of Africa, off central West Africa, and in South-East Asia, will force deeper analysis of this question. But this specific concern, and—if we seek general coherence within international law—its analysis, must keep one eye upon analogous debates. Thus any resolution of this maritime specific question will need to exhibit some consistency with outcomes from the analogous current debate regarding the implications of a complex web of motivations and consequences evident in the spiralling 'drug war' in Mexico upon the applicability of NIAC LOAC in that conflict context.

---

[31] Ong 2004.

[32] Garmon 2002, at p. 275.

[33] Jesus 2003, at p. 371.

[34] Young and Valencia 2003.

[35] Jesus 2003, at pp. 377–378.

My second concern with any general and unmediated attempt to collapse maritime terrorism as a whole into piracy is one of legal and ethical hazard, in that there are clear indications that the international community is not currently in a position to endorse any broad extension of universal jurisdiction to terrorism as a crime generally. The fact that there is at least one separate and discrete instrument which deals explicitly with terrorism at sea (the 2005 SUA Protocol—which clearly does not anticipate traditional universal jurisdiction), coupled with the fact that there is no agreement on the application of universal jurisdiction to terrorism in other spheres of activity (save where the actual conduct constitutes certain war crimes or crimes against humanity), clearly indicates that terrorism is not currently considered to be a crime of universal jurisdiction. To collapse maritime terrorism into the concept of piracy in order to achieve precisely this consequence is (currently, at any rate) a highly contentious legal option.

The legal relationship between piracy and terrorism in terms of piracy being used to support terrorism, however, is of a different and more defined character than the broader debate over coupling the two concepts. This is a legal debate which is yet to be fully worked through—its practical importance hinging upon that moment when a clear linkage between piracy and terrorist financing is proved (most foreseeably in the Somalia context). At that point, any legal response will need to engage with the inter-relationship between laws which do not generally prohibit paying ransoms to pirates, and laws which generally do prohibit providing funds to terrorist groups. This is a much narrower, more nuanced, more practical, and more legitimate legal response to the piracy-terrorism nexus than any broad attempt to collapse one into the other in order to achieve a universal jurisdictional reach into terrorism—a step which the international community has not yet concluded to be appropriate or warranted.

The most significant response, in the last decade, to the terrorism-linked issue of proliferation by sea has been the PSI.[36] The PSI is not formally a legal response to the issue of proliferation support, via the sea, to terrorist groups—but it is a process with both maritime and legal dimensions, and thus requires attention. Originally established as an operationally focussed forum with a core membership of 11 likeminded States, the PSI as a process now claims more than 80 State interlocutors. The core of the PSI is the Statement of Interdiction Principles, which clearly indicates that PSI related activities are to be conducted 'to the extent [States'] national legal authorities permit and consistent with their obligations under international law and frameworks'.[37] The PSI operates as a mechanism for information sharing, capacity building, issue identification, and agenda setting, and has arguably been very successful—although deep suspicions remain, in some quarters, as to the validity of some PSI aims and processes. In its infancy, however, there was real potential for the PSI to have morphed into a narrow, very limited,

[36] See generally: Byers 2004; Song 2004; Ahlstrom 2005; Kaye 2005, 2007; Belcher 2011, at pp. 3–4; Klein 2011, at pp. 193–210.

[37] See US Department of State 2003.

and highly contested process. This is because the original Bush Administration vision appears to have been to push the boundaries of legal authority beyond where most of their core interlocutor States were comfortable. As was reported in the aftermath of the October 2003 London PSI meeting,

> Still, Undersecretary of State for Arms Control and International Security John Bolton holds out the hope that the initiative will lead countries to act more aggressively within current law and, in effect, change it. In comments published Oct. 21 by The Wall Street Journal, Bolton said, 'As state practice changes, customary international law changes.'[38]

Had the US maintained this push to stretch the law relating to WMD interdiction at sea beyond its generally accepted boundaries—in an attempt to create new state practice and thus CIL—it is doubtful that the other ten core States could or would have maintained as proactive an engagement with PSI as they ultimately did. It was only when the US vision for the PSI was scaled back to generally accord with their core interlocutors' understanding of the relevant law that it was able to shift aim and focus more directly upon the less contentious and more readily achievable aspects of the PSI endeavour—such as encouraging and facilitating implementation of existing law, and identifying issues for further legal development (a process which gave much impetus to the negotiation of the 2005 SUA Protocols).

14.5 Terrorist Groups as Subjects Within the Law of Naval Warfare

A final aspect of the last decade's preoccupation with terrorism, including terrorism at sea, requires some mention. This is the as yet unresolved, and very fraught, issue of terrorist groups as subjects within the Law of Naval Warfare (LoNW). Clearly, many of the same themes, pressures, and debates that have influenced advances in understanding the status of terrorist groups within LOAC—most particularly in terms of Organised Armed Groups (OAG)—are at play when seeking to understand the relationship between LoNW and terrorist groups. However, the nature of the maritime domain and some unique features of maritime operations law do illuminate a number of peculiarities. Some of the issues that fall under this chapeau are, I believe, relatively uncontroversial. I think it uncontentious, for example, that a State may impose a blockade (or a visit and search regime) against territory substantially controlled by a terrorist group which is also an OAG engaged in an armed conflict with that State—the Lebanon blockade in 2006,[39] and the Gaza blockade, are indicative, if imperfect and unsettled, examples.

---

[38] Arms Control Association 2003.

[39] See, for example, BBC News 2006.

Beyond this ray of clarity, however, lays a larger realm of opacity—some aspects of which have (re)arisen for further analysis. What can become difficult in such contexts, for example, is determining the status of people in interdicted vessels. With great respect to the Turkel Commission, I remain troubled by the finding that the 'hard core' of IHH activists resisting IDF boardings during the *Mavi Marmara*/'Gaza Freedom Flotilla' interdiction on 31 May 2010, were targetable under LOAC as civilians taking a direct part in hostilities (in the 'land-based' LOAC sense).[40] Crews of neutral merchant vessels which 'intentionally and clearly refuse to stop, or intentionally and clearly resist visit, search or capture'[41]—a clearly analogous situation—do not become civilians taking a direct part in hostilities in this sense. Indeed the actions of the crew, whilst they may render their vessel liable to attack, do not change their status once apprehended: They may be released or (because their vessel has engaged in acts of hostility) they are entitled to PW status[42] and should not be treated as other civilians taking a direct part in hostilities may be treated (that is, as criminals). On this issue, I am thus not as convinced as the Turkel Commission that the law is as clear cut as the Report seems to indicate. But I certainly agree that as a general matter of law, Israel could impose a blockade against territory controlled by an OAG—which includes the terrorist elements of Hamas—with which it was engaged in an armed conflict (be it IAC or NIAC). Of course, the ultimate lawfulness of the detailed implementation of any such blockade remains a separate assessment which can only be addressed on a case-by case basis.

Another issue upon which there has been hitherto little analysis concerns the access (or otherwise) of terrorist groups which are also OAGs engaged in a NIAC, to the LoNW, and the views of States as to whether the maritime conduct of such OAGs ought to be measured against the standards of LONW—much as States measure the conduct of OAGs such as the Taleban against NIAC LOAC. Maritime action by OAGs is not new. In the Sri Lankan context, the Liberation Tigers of Tamil Eelam (LTTE)—clearly both a terrorist group and an OAG engaged in a NIAC—conducted a number of maritime attacks against Sri Lankan Naval vessels. Clearly, States should hold the conduct of OAGs/terrorist groups accountable against LoNW in such situations—just as States do for OAGs/terrorist groups in relation to LOAC ashore. But opportunistic attacks—such as those by the LTTE upon *MV Cordiality* in September 1997, and *MV Princess Kash* in August 1998[43]—present more problematic cases. These attacks—depending upon one's perspective of the terrorist purpose versus private gain debate—may be most directly characterisable as simple piracy. But if we expect maritime OAGs to follow LoNW just as we expect land based OAGs to follow LOAC (the fundamental targeting rules are almost identical in both domains), the uncomfortable question becomes:

---

[40] The Turkel Commission 2011, paras 187–201.

[41] Doswald-Beck et al. 1995, Rule 67(a).

[42] For example, Doswald-Beck, Rule 166(c) and commentary para 166.4.

[43] Sakhuja 2002, at pp. 2–3.

Should we hold maritime OAGs, which are also terrorist groups, to account against all of LoNW—including, for example, rules on visit and search and blockade? Intuitively, I think this cannot be the case—surely the proper legal criteria against which to assess such acts is simple criminality (standfast, perhaps, the unique situation of formally recognised belligerency). Just as States require an OAG to act in accordance with LOAC (and thus not attack civilians, for example), but retain the option to prosecute OAG members for attacks upon combatants, in the maritime domain it is entirely congruous to hold OAGs to account against the LoNW (on visit and search, for example), whilst also retaining the option to prosecute OAG members for piracy. But the issue clearly requires sustained analysis in order that States do not inadvertently undermine the overall integrity of their position on the balance to be struck between demanding LOAC compliance by OAGs/terrorist groups engaged in armed conflicts, and maintaining the right to characterise all such conduct—including LOAC compliant conduct—as remaining fundamentally criminal in character.

14.6 Conclusion

It is, ultimately, no surprise that a decade long preoccupation with terrorism in its many dimensions has also influenced the focus and direction of maritime operations law. In this short piece, I have attempted to describe some ways in which concerns with terrorism rose to become primary animating factors in the development of maritime operations law after 11 September 2001. My list is far from exhaustive, but is, I hope, illustrative and indicative. All that remains, therefore, is to be frank about what I believe has been the underlying thread animating these developments. In my view, that thread is this: That the past decade has seen a perceptible cooling of passions and a reassertion of 'balance' within the maritime operations law domain—most particularly through a reversion to traditional norm creation mechanisms, and the weight given to the enduring concerns of freedom of navigation. In the raw first years after the atrocities of 11 September 2001, some States—the US, certainly, but others also—ran the risk (in their haste to achieve results) of trampling upon long held articles of faith in maritime operations law—most particularly the sanctity of ships' flags (evident still, I believe, in the 'master's consent' debate), and the need to constantly assert freedom of navigation in the face of encroaching and expanding claims to 'security' jurisdictions over oceanspace and security-based jurisdictions for boarding on the High Seas. The initially divided vision of the core PSI States as to the purpose and methods of that activity, attempts to collapse the concept of maritime terrorism into piracy as a means of backdoor access to universal jurisdiction over terrorists, and the assertion of expanding security based jurisdictions over EEZs, were examples of urgent, passionate, but—in terms of prior State practice and assertion—to some extent unprincipled departures from previously accepted norms. However the latter part of the decade—perhaps from 2004 onwards—witnessed the beginnings of a sustained return to relative normalcy and continuity. Any assessment as to why this re-balancing occurred is invariably subjective. It may have been that this return to the norm was born of a principled reassertion of traditional long-term views on the balances of interest implicit in maritime operations law. It may have been driven by a realist recognition that short-term departure from long held principles was giving succour to, and generating propaganda for, long term proponents of the 'other sides' of these debates. It may have simply been attributable to a pragmatic concession that there was not sufficient international weight behind any push to radically and rapidly evolve maritime operations law. Or it might equally have been underpinned by a re-emerging appreciation that the traditional methods (such as negotiating the 2005 SUA Protocols) could still deliver useful and relevant outcomes—even if more slowly than desired. I suspect the answer lays in a combination of all of these, and other, possible explanations. What is clear, however, is that the last decade's preoccupation with terrorism as a matter of maritime operational concern has indeed influenced the development of maritime operations law. What remains to be seen is whether 'terrorism' now joins that select group of issues which could be said to be constant themes underpinning the evolution of maritime operations law, or fades once more to become an issue of important, but secondary, concern.

References

Ahlstrom C (2005) The proliferation security initiative: international law aspects of the statement of interdiction principles SIPRI Yearbook 2005: armaments, disarmament and international security, p 741

Allison G (2001) Could worse be yet to come? The Economist (1 November 2001). Available at http://www.economist.com/node/842483. Accessed 30 Dec 2011

Arms Control Association (2003) Interdiction initiative participants agree on ends, differ on means, Arms Control Today (November 2003). Available at http://www.armscontrol.org/act/2003_11/PSI. Accessed 30 Dec 2011

Australian Government—Department of Infrastructure and Transport (2010) International Ship and Port Facility Security Code (ISPS Code), last updated 13 October 2010. Available at http://www.infrastructure.gov.au/transport/security/maritime/isps/index.aspx. Accessed 30 Dec 2011

Bateman S (2007) Outlook: the new threat of maritime terrorism. In: Lehr P (ed) Violence at sea—piracy in the age of global terrorism. Routledge, New York

BBC News (2006) Israel imposes Lebanon blockade, BBC News (13 July 2006). Available at http://news.bbc.co.uk/2/hi/5175160.stm. Accessed 30 Dec 2011

Belcher E (2011) The proliferation security initiative: lessons for using nonbinding agreements, international institutions and global governance program working paper No. 6, Council on Foreign Relations July 2011. Available at http://www.i.cfr.org/content/publications/.../IIGG_WorkingPaper6_PSI.pdf. Accessed 30 Dec 2011

Bright M et al (2001) Hunt for 20 terror ships: the armada of terror, The Observer (23 December 2001). Available at http://www.guardian.co.uk/world/2001/dec/23/september11.terrorism1. Accessed 30 Dec 2011

Byers M (2004) Policing the high seas: the proliferation security initiative. Am J Int Law 98(3):526

Council on Foreign Relations (2006) Backgrounder: targets for terrorism: ports (January 2006). Available at http://www.cfr.org/port-security/targets-terrorism-ports/p10215. Accessed 30 Dec 2011

Doswald-Beck L et al (1995) San Remo Manual on international law applicable to armed conflicts at sea. Cambridge University Press/International Institute of International Humanitarian Law, Cambridge

The Economist (2001) America the unready. The Economist, 20 December 2001. http://www.economist.com/node/917304. Accessed 30 Dec 2011

Forbes A (2003) International shipping trends and vulnerabilities. Maritime Studies 132:21

Frittelli JF (2003) CRS Report for Congress—Port and Maritime Security: Background and Issues for Congress (5 December 2003). Available at http://www.homelandsecurityus.net/ports%20and%20maritime%20terrorism/Maritime%20crs_report_for_congress.htm. Accessed 30 Dec 2011

Frittelli JF (2005) CRS Report for Congress—Port and Maritime Security: background and issues for Congress (27 May 2005). Available at http://www.fas.org/sgp/crs/homesec/RL31733.pdf. Accessed 30 Dec 2011

Garmon T (2002) International law of the sea: reconciling the law of piracy and terrorism in the wake of September 11th. Tulane Maritime Law J 27:257

Greenberg MD et al (2006) Maritime terrorism: risk and liability. RAND Centre for Terrorism Risk Management Policy, RAND Corporation. Available at http://www.rand.org/pubs/monographs/2006/RAND_MG520.pdf. Accessed 30 Dec 2011

The Guardian (2010) China-Japan sea dispute escalates as Beijing demands fisherman's release', The Guardian (10 September 2010). Available at http://www.guardian.co.uk/world/2010/sep/10/china-japan-diaoyu-senkaku-dispute. Accessed 30 Dec 2011

Guilfoyle D (2005) The proliferation security initiative: interdicting vessels in international waters to prevent the spread of weapons of mass destruction. Melb Univ Law Rev 29:733

Gvosdev NK, Cipriano AA (2002) Is privateering the answer to terrorism? History News Network (29 July 2002). Available at http://hnn.us/articles/881.html. Accessed 30 Dec 2011

Indian Navy, Operation Cactus—1988. Available at http://indiannavy.nic.in/cactus.htm. Accessed 30 Dec 2011

Jacques R et al (2006) Maritime operational zones. International Law Department, US Naval War College

Jesus JL (2003) Protection of foreign ships against piracy and terrorism at sea: legal aspects. Int J Marine Coastal Law 18(3):363

Joint Civilian-Military Investigation Group, Investigation Report on the Sinking of ROKS Cheonan (20 May 2010). Available at http://www.globalsecurity.org/jhtml/jframe.html#http://www.globalsecurity.org/military/library/report/2010/100520_jcmig-roks-cheonan/100520_jcmig-roks-cheonan.pdf. Accessed 30 Dec 2011

Kaye S (2005) The proliferation security initiative in the maritime domain. Israel Yearb Hum Rights 35:205

Kaye S (2007) Threats from the global commons: problems of jurisdiction and enforcement. Melb J Int Law 8:185

Klein N (2006) Legal limitations on ensuring Australia's maritime security. Melb J Int Law 7(2):306

Klein N (2011) Maritime security and the law of the sea. Oxford University Press, Oxford

Luft G, Korin A (2004) Terrorism goes to sea. Foreign Affairs, November/December 2004. Available at http://www.foreignaffairs.com/articles/60266/gal-luft-and-anne-korin/terrorism-goes-to-sea. Accessed 30 Dec 2011

McGrath C (2004) Government boosts maritime security, ABC News (15 December 2004). Available at http://www.abc.net.au/pm/content/2004/s1266082.htm. Accessed 30 Dec 2011

McNaught F (2005) Effectiveness of the International Ship and Port Facility Security (ISPS) Code in addressing the maritime security threat, Geddes Papers 2005. Available at http://www.defence.gov.au/ADC/docs/Publications/Geddes%20Papers%202005/89939%20Defence%209.pdf. Accessed 30 Dec 2011

O'Connell DP (1970) International law of contemporary naval operations. Br Yearb Int Law 44:20
O'Connell DP (1975) The influence of law on sea power. Naval Institute Press, Annapolis
Office of the Coordinator for Counter Terrorism Report (2002) Middle east overview: patterns of global terrorism (21 May 2002). http://www.state.gov/s/ct/rls/crt/2001/html/10247.htm. Accessed 30 Dec 2011
Ong GG (2004) Ships can be dangerous too: coupling piracy and maritime terrorism in Southeast Asia's maritime security framework, Institute of Southeast Asia studies working paper: International Politics and Security Issues Series No. 1. Available at http://www.asia-studies.com/ISEASips.html. Accessed 30 Dec 2011
Rahman M (2008) Witnesses describe mumbai attackers' arrival by sea. The Guardian (27 November 2008). Available at http://www.guardian.co.uk/world/2008/nov/27/mumbai-terror-attacks-terrorism-boats. Accessed 30 Dec 2011
Rakshak B (2011) Operation CACTUS: India's Airlift into the Indian Ocean. Available at http://www.bharat-rakshak.com/IAF/History/1988Cactus/index.html. Accessed 30 Dec 2011
Richardson M (2004) Growing vulnerability of seaports from terror attacks. Yale Global Online, 5 March 2004. http://yaleglobal.yale.edu/content/growing-vulnerability-seaports-terror-attacks. Accessed 30 Dec 2011
Sakhuja V (2002) Contemporary piracy, terrorism and disorder at sea: challenges for sea-lane security in the indian ocean. Marit Stud 127:1
Schoen JW (2004) Ships and ports are terrorism's new frontier. MSNBC News, 21 June 2004. http://www.msnbc.msn.com/id/5069435/ns/business-world_business/t/ships-ports-are-terrorisms-new-frontier/. Accessed 30 Dec 2011
Sechrest LJ (2001) Privateering and national defence: naval warfare for private profit, independent institute working paper no. 41 (September 2001). Available at http://www.independent.org/pdf/working_papers/41_privateering.pdf. Accessed 30 Dec 2011
Song Y-H (2004) An overview of regional responses in the Asia-Pacific to the PSI'. Marit Stud 135:1
Stephenson A (2004) This is not a drill: how a gulf crisis unfolded, Sydney Morning Herald (11 September 2004). Available at http://www.smh.com.au/articles/2004/09/10/1094789687650.html?from=moreStories. Accessed 30 Dec 2011
The Turkel Commission (2011) The public commission to examine the maritime incident of 31 May 2010 Report Part 1 (January 2011). Available at http://www.turkel-committee.gov.il/files/wordocs//8707200211english.pdf. Accessed 30 Dec 2011
Rothwell DR, Stephens T (2010) The international law of the sea. Hart Publishing, Oxford
US Department of Defence (2001) USS Cole Commission Report (Unclassified Version) (9 January 2001). http://www.fas.org/irp/threat/cole.pdf. Accessed 30 Dec 2011
US Department of Homeland Security—Policy (2004) Secure seas, open ports (21 June 2004). Available at http://www.dhs.gov/xlibrary/assets/DHSPortSecurityFactSheet-062104.pdf. Accessed 30 Dec 2011
US Department of the Navy (2004) Report on the 24 April 2004 attacks on Iraqi oil platforms in the Northern Arabian Gulf (16 July 2004). Available at http://www.history.navy.mil/shiphist/f/pc-10/2004.pdf. Accessed 30 Dec 2011
US Department of State (2003) Fact sheet—proliferation security initiative: Statement of Interdiction Principles (4 September 2003). Available at http://www.state.gov/t/isn/c27726.htm
US General Accounting Office—Reports (2002) Combating terrorism: actions needed to improve force protection for DOD deployments through domestic seaports, October 2002. Available at http://www.gao.gov/new.items/d0315.pdf. Accessed 30 Dec 2011
US General Accounting Office—Testimony (2002) Container security: current efforts to detect nuclear materials, new initiatives, and challenges (18 November 2002). Available at http://www.gao.gov/new.items/d03297t.pdf. Accessed 30 Dec 2011

US Government Accountability Office (2010) Maritime Security: DHS progress and challenges in key areas of port security (21 July 2010). Available at http://www.gao.gov/new.items/d10940t.pdf. Accessed 30 Dec 2011

World Net Daily (2004) Terror threat swells at sea. World Net Daily (8 June 2004). Available at http://www.wnd.com/?pageId=24966. Accessed 30 Dec 2011.

Young A, Valencia MJ (2003) Piracy, terrorism threats overlap, The Washington Times (7 July 2003). Available at http://www.washingtontimes.com/news/2003/jul/6/20030706-104801-9949r/?page=1. Accessed 30 Dec 2011

Chapter 15
Temporality and Terrorism in International Humanitarian Law

Matthew C. Waxman

Contents

It is widely agreed that the United States' armed conflict against al Qaida and its allies—if it is legally an armed conflict at all—does not fit neatly within contemporary *jus as bellum* and *jus in bello* (international humanitarian law, or IHL) regimes. The thinking goes that transnational conflicts with non-state terrorist groups and tactics do not correspond well to the categories comprising those regimes, and wide debate then proceeds about whether and how it is appropriate nevertheless to apply them.

Most of this discussion focuses on the nature of the actors, actions, and geography of this conflict—*who*, *how*, and *where* issues—because modern *jus ad bellum* and *jus in bello* regimes grew out of a long history of states or locally-confined armed groups waging violence in particular ways. In trying to apply those regimes to a conflict with a set of transnational terrorist groups, vexing questions include: Which individuals are sufficiently connected to the conflict that they may be detained or targeted? Do the specific practices of belligerent groups and members determine the treatment standards to which they are legally entitled, or open them to prosecution as law-of-war violations? Beyond the borders of Afghanistan, to what extent may the United States conduct operations based upon and regulated by IHL?

Associate Professor, Columbia Law School; Adjunct Senior Fellow for Law and Foreign Policy, Council on Foreign Relations; Member of the Hoover Institution Task Force on National Security and Law.

M. C. Waxman (✉)
Columbia Law School, New York, NY, USA
e-mail: matthew.waxman@gmail.com

M.N. Schmitt and L. Arimatsu (eds.), *Yearbook of International Humanitarian Law Volume 14, 2011*, DOI: 10.1007/978-90-6704-855-2_15,

Analysis and appraisal of such questions by states, courts, academics, and commentators focus attention not only on the particularities of this conflict but on the basic assumptions about conflict upon which armed conflict legal regimes are built—in particular, that most conflicts historically pitted states' military forces or clearly defined armed groups capable of sustained violence within geographically-limited areas.[1] A common refrain is that IHL and international law regulating use of force in self defense was not designed for conflicts involving widely-dispersed and shadowy networks of individuals sowing terrorist violence and fear across multiple continents.

In addition to resulting perplexities involving who, how, and where this conflict is waged, there are highly unusual temporal features of this conflict—and, therefore, *when* issues—that characterize it. It is difficult to discern when this conflict began (recognizing that it began at least as far back as the 9/11 attacks, though perhaps earlier than that), and even more difficult to assess even hypothetically its endpoint. Between those points in time, the tempo of the conflict, if one measures it in terms of intensity of violence, is erratic by design: groups like al Qaida exploit unpredictable timing of attacks, punctuating long periods of uncertainty, to produce terror; the United States, too, strikes episodically at the adversary in some places as actionable intelligence develops.

Like attributes of the actors, actions, and geography of this conflict, the temporal features also focus attention on some foundational assumptions upon which IHL is constructed. Indeed, the whole idea of IHL is that it applies on an exceptional basis, triggered by onset of conflict and untriggered by conclusion of that conflict—that is, IHL is a sort of emergency law, the application of which is bounded in time. The temporal aspects of the conflict have strained application of IHL, some would argue to the breaking point and others would argue necessitating legal or policy adaptation to meet the demands of 21st century warfare.

* * *

The temporal question that has attracted the most attention concerns the endpoint of the U.S. armed conflict with al Qaida and its allies, and the likely difficulty of ever marking it clearly and definitively.[2] Some political scientists have studied how terrorist movements end or lapse and tried to draw insights for a possible cessation of state-nonstate conflicts[3]; others might argue that the killing of Usama bin Laden, along with the killing or capturing of his key lieutenants and operational planners,[4] should mark the winding down of this particular conflict. However, it is widely recognized that the conflict with al Qaida—and especially if you include its regional franchises—will go on for a very long time and that a clear-cut endpoint akin to a surrender or peace agreement is implausible.

---

[1] For analysis of such issues, see, e.g., Chesney 2010; Waxman 2010.

[2] See Bellinger and Padmanabhan 2011, at pp. 228–229.

[3] See Klein 2010, at pp. 1887–1892.

[4] See Miller 2011.

The endpoint issue is important, among other reasons, because whatever detention authority exists pursuant to IHL would expire with conclusion of hostilities, as would other counter-terrorism legal powers premised on a state of armed conflict. For example, the Geneva Conventions envision that captured enemy fighters would be detained for the duration of hostilities, to prevent their return to the battlefield, and that they would be released upon cessation of hostilities. This easily-administered rule works well for temporally-bounded conflicts, but the balances it strikes may not seem so reasonable for conflicts that do not have a clear end in sight.

Since the 9/11 attacks, many have argued that the inability to articulate a plausible and foreseeable endpoint to this conflict is so problematic for application of IHL and states' reliance on wartime legal powers that it renders void the whole notion of a state of armed conflict with al Qaida. Instead, many dissenters from the US approach often argue that international human rights law—not IHL—should govern counterterrorism operations.[5] Whereas IHL is designed as a sort of emergency law, human rights law is designed to be baseline, everyday law; and if we are facing a perpetual threat, we need to look to perpetual law.

The United States and its legal defenders continue to point out that many previous wars lacked clear, discernible endings, and that during many past wars the foreseeable termination point was indefinite as well. In any event, they argue, the severe consequences of applying IHL to an indefinitely long-term conflict with a terrorist organization does not negate its international legal applicability (as explained below, instead it may require policy or domestic law adaptations).

In short, while everyone agrees that at a minimum the lack of foreseeable or definitive endpoint makes application of IHL rules and principles difficult and carries dire consequences, it is hotly debated whether the appropriate answer is to reject application of the armed conflict legal paradigm, apply it anyway, revise it, or supplement it with sound policy practices.

Besides the well-recognized difficulty of measuring and determining the temporal endpoint of the US armed conflict with al Qaida, it is also difficult to mark its starting point. For the past decade the United States has not had to resolve and defend much of a position on this, instead relying on the position that it has been engaged in armed conflict with al Qaida and its allies at least as far back as September 11, 2001, but possibly longer as a result of prior al Qaida threats, public declarations, and attacks. Ambiguity about the starting point of the armed conflict has not posed additional legal problems for the United States to the extent it has asserted powers pursuant to the laws of war since then. However, US prosecutions in Military Commissions charging war crimes that occurred prior to that date—such as allegations that Guantanamo detainees perpetrated the 2000 attack on the *U.S.S. Cole* in violation of the laws of war—are prompting new scrutiny of this issue.

---

5 See, for example, International Commission of Jurists 2009.

In addition to problems of delineating the beginning and end of hostilities, the temporal aspects of this conflict raise other difficulties in applying IHL, and fold back into questions about the conflict's geographic scope and delineations of individual belligerency. For example, some take the position that intensity of violence or belligerent activity defines the geographic reach of a conflict, and therefore the application of IHL to an area—that is, that at least with respect to non-international armed conflicts, merely sporadic violence or armed disturbances do not trigger application of IHL. Under this view, the United States might be engaged in armed conflict of one sort or another in Afghanistan and perhaps across its border in certain areas of Pakistan, but not beyond. If that is so, it begs the question of how to measure intensity of belligerent violence in this type of conflict—a concept that includes a substantive component or understanding of the type of violence or threat that characterizes warfare, as well as a temporal element: how often or episodic must it occur within an area to constitute sufficient intensity.

Alongside such questions tying the temporal features and geography of this conflict, a closely related issue concerns when force against particular individuals or targets might be justified in self-defense because a threat is sufficiently "imminent," a standard employed by some who do not accept that the conflict extends beyond the "hot battlefield." As President Barack Obama's top counterterrorism adviser explained in a speech commemorating the tenth anniversary of the 9/11 attacks, "We are finding increasing recognition in the international community that a more flexible understanding of 'imminence' may be appropriate when dealing with terrorist groups, in part because threats posed by non-state actors do not present themselves in the ways that evidenced imminence in more traditional conflicts." More specifically, al Qaida "possesses the demonstrated capability to strike with little notice."[6] Again, a reason why legal-translation difficulties arise is because the tempo, not just the mode, of terroristic conflict is conducted very differently than conventional warfare or even much guerrilla or insurgency warfare.

* * *

It is unlikely for several reasons that evolutionary consensus with regard to IHL and international law regulating force will evolve quickly to take account of the special temporal qualities of this conflict. All of the issues discussed above have contributed to a fragmentation and evolving debate rather than consensus among states and other international actors with respect to the appropriate legal framework for the US conflict with al Qaida. Within that context, US reforms to account for the mismatch between IHL and the temporal characteristics of the armed conflicts with al Qaida have largely taken place incrementally through domestic law and policy adaptation, and they will likely continue to do so for the foreseeable future.

Because IHL and its application to this conflict is being litigated through *habeas corpus* and other challenges to US government actions, US courts are

[6] Brennan 2011.

facing these conundrums and have expressed discomfort with the implications that flow from the conflict's temporal features.[7] Writing for a plurality of the Supreme Court in *Hamdi v. Rumsfeld*, which in 2004 held that a US citizen captured in Afghanistan fighting for al Qaida and the Taliban could be held as an enemy combatant but that he was entitled to some procedural review, Justice O'Connor expressed concern not with "the lack of certainty regarding the date on which the conflict will end," but with "the substantial prospect of perpetual detention."[8] Although at the time there was no debate that significant combat operations were ongoing, Justice O'Connor further observed that: "If the Government does not consider this unconventional war won for two generations, … then the position it has taken throughout the litigation of this case suggests that Hamdi's detention could last for the rest of his life."[9] Although persuaded at that time that Hamdi's detention without trial as an enemy belligerent was "based on longstanding law-of-war principles," Justice O'Connor cautioned that "[i]f the practical circumstances of a given conflict are entirely unlike those of the conflicts that informed the development of the law of war, that understanding may unravel."[10]

Writing for the Court four years later in *Boumediene v. Bush*, Justice Kennedy acknowledged that it was lawful to detain those who had fought against the United States for the duration the conflict. But, in holding that Guantanamo detainees had constitutional *habeas corpus* rights, he was moved in part because "the consequence of error may be detention of persons for the duration of hostilities that may last a generation or more."[11] So far, habeas courts have not seemed to come close to freeing a Guantanamo detainee on account of cessation of hostilities (and, accordingly, cessation of detention authority), though at some point events may raise new judicial doubts about its continuation—at least in understanding the president's continuing legal authority drawing upon the 2001 congressional Authorization of the Use of Military Force and IHL without further guidance from Congress.

In the absence of intervention so far from the courts on the temporal perplexities, the political branches of the US government have deliberated about how to account for them. Some members of Congress have pressed for new domestic legislation that would affirm that the United States remains in a state of armed conflict with al Qaida and its allies—that is, without providing any clarity on when the conflict might be deemed to have ended, such efforts would state that as a matter of domestic law armed conflict persists at this time—though the executive branch has opposed such a move as unnecessary.[12]

7 See Dudziak 2010, pp. 1698–1700.

8 *Hamdi v. Rumsfeld*, 542 U.S. 507, 520 (2004) (O'Connor, J. plurality).

9 *Id.*

10 *Id.* at 521.

11 *Boumediene v. Bush*, 553 U.S. 723, 785 (2008).

12 See Shanker and Savage 2011.

More significantly in a practical sense, the executive branch has developed an evolving set of policy practices designed to defer any need to resolve questions about the end of hostilities by focusing on the continuing threat of reengaging in belligerency posed or not posed by a particular detainee—a practice that some scholars view as an individualization of the cessation-of-hostilities concept.[13] For example, at Guantanamo the U.S. government has developed over recent years a set of increasingly robust periodic review procedures to determine whether individual detainees should be released because they no longer pose a significant threat or because their continuing threat could be mitigated through other means. These individualized review procedures are not viewed by the executive branch as legally required under IHL, though they resemble in some respects the sort of case-by-case continued necessity review that the Fourth Geneva Convention requires at least twice-annually with regard to civilian internees.[14]

These actions represent efforts to address problems of IHL through domestic lawmaking, whether judicial, statutory, or administrative practice. Over time these actions, and the international reactions to them, may contribute through state practice to an evolution of IHL or alternatives to it to account for such conflicts' temporal anomalies. However, clear resolution of neither this conflict nor the international legal regime governing it can be expected for the foreseeable future.

References

Bellinger JB III, Padmanabhan VM (2011) Detention operations in contemporary conflicts: four challenges for the Geneva Conventions and other existing law. Am J Int Law 105:201

Bradley CA, Goldsmith JL (2004–2005) Congressional authorization and the war on terrorism. Harv Law Rev 118:2047

Brennan JO (2011) "Strengthening our security by adhering to our values and laws", Harvard Law School, 16 September 2011. http://www.whitehouse.gov/the-press-office/2011/09/16/remarks-john-o-brennan-strengthening-our-security-adhering-our-values-an. Accessed 29 Dec 2011

Chesney R (2010) Who may be killed? Anwar al-Awlaki as a case study in the international regulations of lethal force. Yearb Int Humanit Law 13:3

Dudziak ML (2010) Law, war, and the history of time. Calif Law Rev 98:1669

International Commission of Jurists (2009) Assessing damage, urging action: report of the eminent jurists panel on terrorism, counter-terrorism and human rights. http://ejp.ijc.org/IMG/EJP-Report.pdf. Accessed 29 Dec 2011

Klein A (2010) The end of Al Qaeda? Rethinking the end of the war on terror. Colum Law Rev 110:1865

Miller G (2011) Al-Qaeda targets dwindle as group shrinks, Washington Post, 22 November 2011. http://www.washingtonpost.com/world/national-security/al-qaeda-targets-dwindle-as-group-shrinks/2011/11/22/gIQAbXJNmN_story.html. Accessed 29 Dec 2011

---

[13] See Bellinger and Padmanabhan 2011, pp. 231–232; Bradley and Goldsmith 2004–2005, pp. 2124–2125.

[14] See Articles 43, 78, Geneva Convention [IV] Relative to the Protection of Civilian Persons in Time of War art. 43, 78, Aug. 12, 1949, 6 U.S.T. 3516, 75 U.N.T.S. 287.

Shanker T, Savage C (2011) After Bin Laden, U.S. Reassesses Afghan Strategy, New York Times, 10 May 2011. http://www.nytimes.com/2011/05/11/world/middleeast/11military.html?pagewanted=all. Accessed 29 Dec 2011

Waxman MC (2010) The structure of terrorism threats and the laws of war. Duke J Comp Int Law 20:431

Chapter 16
Legacy of 9/11: Continuing the Humanization of Humanitarian Law

Vijay M. Padmanabhan

Contents

16.1 Introduction

In 2000 Theodor Meron published his landmark essay entitled *The Humanization of Humanitarian Law*.[1] Meron demonstrated that there is a gradual convergence in protections between human rights law and international humanitarian law (IHL) developing, which is fueled by a common commitment to human dignity. He explained that the shifting nature of conflicts away from traditional international armed conflict to non-international armed conflict "necessitated both new norms and reinterpretation of existing norms".[2] "Calamitous events and atrocities" during these contemporary conflicts pushes new IHL rules towards human rights principles, he explained.

Thank you to Ashley Deeks, Monica Hakimi, and Matthew Waxman whose thoughtful comments were helpful in preparation of this essay.

[1] Meron 2000.
[2] *Id.* at 243–44.

V. M. Padmanabhan (✉)
Vanderbilt University Law School, Nashville, USA
e-mail: vijay.padmanabhan@Law.Vanderbilt.Edu

M.N. Schmitt and L. Arimatsu (eds.), *Yearbook of International Humanitarian Law Volume 14, 2011*, DOI: 10.1007/978-90-6704-855-2_16,

The 9/11 attacks provide evidence for Meron's thesis. After the 9/11 attacks the United States launched three armed conflicts: international armed conflicts in Afghanistan and Iraq that quickly morphed into non-international conflicts against Islamist insurgents; and an unprecedented global war against al Qaida. These conflicts with non-State Islamist groups have three features that differentiate them from traditional international armed conflict, from which IHL emerged: a hard to identify enemy; sporadic, episodic fighting; and detention of individuals at unique risk of post-transfer mistreatment. These differences create unique problems in these conflicts that are either not addressed or addressed inadequately by IHL. And, as Meron predicted, the new norms created to resolve these problems draw heavily from human rights law.

Nowhere is this trend more evident than in detention operations. Even as U.S. officials continue to protest against application of human rights law to wartime settings,[3] the United States applied human rights concepts to detentions in Afghanistan, Iraq and Guantanamo Bay. The United States now provides procedural protections to detainees that match or approach the procedures human rights treaties require to justify detention. The government also provides detainees non-refoulement protection, a core human rights protection not expressly found in IHL. The introduction of human rights standards to these aspects of detention operations was necessary to prevent inequities inconsistent with today's understanding of human dignity.

The influence of human rights law on the war fighting domain—once thought solely the province of IHL—will continue to grow. Non-traditional conflicts appear to be on the rise. The human rights community, including many scholars, is committed to the application of human rights principles to warfare. And the lack of a clear boundary between IHL and human rights law means that the door is open to application of human rights to areas where it hitherto had no application. The controversy over the killing of Osama bin Laden and the U.S. drone campaign in Pakistan and Yemen suggests that targeting will be the next growth area for human rights.

16.2 Features of the Conflict

President Bush immediately characterized the 9/11 attacks as acts of war against the United States.[4] There is little question that the conflicts launched in

[3] See Reply of the Government of the United States of America to the Report of the Five UNHCR Special Rapporteurs on Detainees in Guantanamo (Mar. 10, 2006), available at http://www.asil.org/pdfs/ilib0603212.pdf (arguing that human rights rapporteurs erred in applying human rights standards to detentions at Guantanamo Bay).

[4] See President George W. Bush, Address to the U.S. Congress (Sep. 20, 2001) ("On September the eleventh, enemies of freedom committed an act of war against our country.")

Afghanistan or Iraq constituted an armed conflict. But the characterization of the global conflict with al Qaida as "war" is controversial.[5]

International law is underdeveloped on the question of when violence with a non-State group amounts to an armed conflict. The war crimes tribunals for the former Yugoslavia explained that an armed conflict with a non-State group exists where there is "protracted armed violence between governmental authorities and organized armed groups".[6] This violence must be of sufficient intensity to be characterized as an armed conflict, although the intensity threshold is undefined.[7] The non-State group must also be under "responsible command," and must be able to carry out "sustained and concerted military operations," terms which again are vague.[8]

The struggle between the United States and al Qaida appears to meet this vague test. There have been repeated episodes of violence of great intensity perpetrated by members of al Qaida, under the direction of its leadership, committed against U.S. interests. The United States has responded to these attacks with military force in Afghanistan, Sudan, and Yemen, among other places. While the conflict does not have to be characterized in this manner, successive U.S. administrations have opted to do so because of the greater operational flexibility found in IHL with respect to targeting and detention of enemy combatants.

But three features of the post 9/11 conflicts have rendered wholesale application of IHL targeting and detention rules problematic from a dignity perspective. First, IHL is premised on the concept of distinction: combatants must distinguish themselves from civilians, thereby easing targeting and detention decisions and protecting civilians. But members of al Qaida do not wear a uniform, carry their weapons openly, or even operate on a traditional battlefield where most persons present are likely to be combatants.[9] Instead, they use perfidy as a tool to perpetrate attacks without attracting attention from opposing forces. Because of this approach, among other reasons, captured members of al Qaida are not entitled

---

[5] See International Commission of Jurists 2009, p. 20 :"[H]uman rights law provides sufficient flexibility for States to adjust to security needs; States should rely upon this framework rather than seek to re-write the rule book."

[6] ICTY, *Prosecutor v Dusko Tadić*, Decision on the Defence Motion for Interlocutory Appeal on Jurisdiction, Appeals Chamber I (IT-94-1-AR72) 2nd October 1995.

[7] See ICTR, *The Prosecutor v Jean-Paul Akayesu*, Judgment, Trial Chamber (ICTR-96-4-T) 2 September 1998 (providing the criteria for finding the existence of an armed conflict with a non-State group).

[8] See Protocol Additional to the Geneva Conventions of 12 August 1949 and Relating to the Protection of Victims of Non-International Armed Conflict Article 1(1), June 8, 1977, 1125 U.N.T.S. 609 (defining the scope of application of the treaty).

[9] Matthew Waxman rightly notes that this characterization is an oversimplification because the combatant status of captured persons can be uncertain in international armed conflict as well. Waxman 2008, p. 1382 (describing the use of the 3rd Geneva Convention Article 5 tribunals in the first Gulf War to determine whether captured Iraqis were prisoners of war or civilians). But he agrees that the problem of misidentification is more acute in conflicts with non-State groups like al Qaida.

to prisoner of war privileges or combatant immunity, eliminating a strong incentive for admitting allegiance to the enemy organization. As a consequence, the United States has had to rely upon intelligence information or circumstantial indicators of involvement in enemy operations to guide detention and targeting decisions. This approach enhances the risk of misidentification compared to traditional international armed conflict.

Second, many of the IHL detention and targeting rules presume battlefield exigencies that reduce time for deliberation—the so called "fog of war." But unlike traditional armed conflicts, which feature continuous, intense fighting, the fighting against al Qaida has been sporadic and episodic. Al Qaida's operations against the United States involve large amounts of preparation for an attack, many or most of which do not come to fruition. Similarly, U.S. operations in the conflict consist of surveillance, intelligence gathering, and periodic efforts to neutralize an identified threat, either through capture or killing. Sporadic, episodic fighting reduces the fog of war, and thereby increases the potential range of procedures the State can undertake before targeting or after detaining a presumed enemy.

Third, IHL assumes that a detainee will be repatriated to his home country after the conflict, with little further consideration regarding what happens to returned prisoners. This rule reflects an understanding that most States welcome home their fighters after an armed conflict, and reward, not punish, those who fought for them. This description does not always hold true, as historical examples of post-repatriation detainee abuse has resulted in a developing consensus against forced repatriation in international armed conflict.[10] But here rather than detaining fighters from an enemy State, the United States had detained members of al Qaida, which often is also conducting attacks against the State of nationality of its members. Receiving states are more likely to mistreat members of al Qaida than their own returning troops.

These features create inequitable outcomes if IHL is applied wholesale, as is discussed below. The result, as Meron anticipated, is a shift in practice towards respecting human rights principles in these conflicts.

16.3 Human Rights and U.S. Detention Practices in the War with al Qaida

Human rights law has long influenced treatment of wartime detainees. The treatment protections afforded combatants and civilians in the Geneva Conventions and its Additional Protocols are similar to protections located in human rights instruments.[11] States, human rights organizations, and scholars invoked human rights principles alongside IHL in condemning enhanced interrogation tactics by the United States after 9/11.

---

[10] Meron 2000, pp. 254–255.

[11] Sandoz et al. (1987), pp. 861–89 (describing the relationship between the fundamental guarantees of Article 75 of Additional Protocol I and international human rights law).

But the conflict with al Qaida has opened the door for human rights standards to enter into new areas of detention operations. One such area is procedural protections provided to detainees. A recent report by the ICRC concluded that there is the need for new law guiding States on what procedural protections should be provided with respect to detention in conflicts with non-State actors.[12] The IHL instruments covering non-international armed conflict are silent on this question.

Mirroring IHL for international armed conflicts is not fruitful, because it provides very limited procedural protections for detained combatants. The reason is that the risk of misidentification in international armed conflict is limited, and the exigencies of the battlefield make elaborate procedures unrealistic.[13] By contrast, in the post-9/11 conflicts the risk of misidentification is great, and time and space exists to remedy that risk without impinging on battlefield operations, rendering application of traditional IHL rules inconsistent with human dignity.[14]

Nevertheless, the Bush administration provided the kind of limited review procedures typical to traditional armed conflicts to those it detained at Guantanamo Bay, in Afghanistan, and even at the naval prison in Charleston, South Carolina. These limited procedures led to widespread reporting that the United States was planning to detain for life persons who were in the "wrong place at the wrong time". Not surprisingly the U.S. courts responded to this inequity by pushing the military to adopt procedural protections with respect to detention that are similar to the more robust human rights protections attendant to detention in peacetime. The courts believed these robust procedures could ferret out misidentification and could be applied without undermining combat operations, especially where the locus of detention is separated from the battlefield, such as at Guantanamo Bay.

The U.S. Supreme Court plurality held in *Hamdi v. Rumsfeld* that a U.S. citizen detained as an enemy combatant in the United States has a due process right to "notice of the factual basis for his classification, and a fair opportunity to rebut the Government's factual assertions before a neutral decision maker," in this case the federal courts.[15] The plurality also held that citizen detainees are entitled to counsel in their *habeas* proceedings.[16] The Court's notice requirement is similar to the notice requirement found in Article 75(3) of Additional Protocol I, to which the

---

[12] See, ICRC, Draft Resolution & Report: Strengthening Legal Protection of Victims of Armed Conflicts 10 (Oct. 2011) ("A particular humanitarian concern related to detention is the lack of procedural safeguards for persons subject to internment in non-international armed conflicts.").

[13] See Bellinger and Padmanabhan (2011), pp. 222–24 (describing the procedural inadequacy of applying Third Geneva Convention Article 5 to the conflict with al Qaida).

[14] See Waxman 2008, p. 1384 (arguing the severity of consequences for misidentification in conflict with al Qaida merits departure from traditional IHL rules).

[15] *Hamdi v. Rumsfeld*, 542 U.S. 507, 533 (2004) (O'Connor, J. plurality).

[16] *Id.* at 539.

United States is not a party.[17] But a requirement of an opportunity to contest the lawfulness of detention before a court with counsel does not exist in IHL,[18] and instead reflects the influence of international human rights law.[19]

The Court then held in *Boumediene v. Bush* that those detained at Guantanamo Bay are protected by the Suspension Clause.[20] This ruling meant that detainees are entitled to the opportunity to demonstrate to a court that they are being held pursuant "to an erroneous application or interpretation of relevant law", and potentially to be released if so.[21] The Court found that the combined administrative review/federal court review system set up in the Detainee Treatment Act did not meet this standard because it did not provide detainees an adequate opportunity to present exculpatory evidence. Specifically, the absence of counsel during the administrative hearing and permissive rules regarding hearsay evidence undermined the ability of detainees to contest the lawfulness of their detention. While the Court declined to spell out what precise procedural protections must be provided to Guantanamo detainees, the opinion suggests the Court is skeptical of review procedures that do not provide a right of counsel or basic evidentiary protections, like hearsay rules, concepts foreign to IHL but recognized in human rights law.

---

[17] See Protocol Additional to the Geneva Conventions of 12 August 1949, and Relating to the Protection of Victims of International Armed Conflicts, June 8, 1977, 1125 U.N.T.S. 3, Article 75(3) ("Any person arrested, detained or interned for actions related to the armed conflict shall be informed promptly...of the reasons why these measures have been taken.") The United States does apply Article 75 as a matter of law in international armed conflicts today.

[18] The Fourth Geneva Convention grants civilian protected persons who the State wishes to detain initial review by a court or administrative body, the right of appeal to a court or administrative body, and twice annual status reviews. Geneva Convention [IV] Relative to the Protection of Civilian Persons in Time of War Articles 43, 78, Aug. 12, 1949, 6 U.S.T. 3516, 75 U.N.T.S. 287. Unlike *Hamdi*, the Fourth Geneva Convention permits administrative review in lieu of court review, and does not provide any right to counsel.

[19] The right of access to a court to review the lawfulness of detention is well-established in human rights treaties. See International Covenant on Civil and Political Rights Article 9(4), Mar. 23, 1976, 999 U.N.T.S. 171 ("Anyone who is deprived of his liberty by arrest or detention shall be entitled to take proceedings before a court, in order that that court may decide without delay on the lawfulness of his detention and order his release if the detention is not lawful."); American Convention on Human Rights Article 7(6), Nov. 22, 1969, 1144 U.N.T.S. 123 ("Anyone who is deprived of his liberty shall be entitled to recourse to a competent court, in order that the court may decide without delay on the lawfulness of his arrest or detention and order his release if the arrest or detention is unlawful."); Convention for the Protection of Human Rights and Fundamental Freedoms Article 5(4), Nov. 4, 1950, ETS No. 5, 213 U.N.T.S. 221 ("Everyone who is deprived of his liberty by arrest or detention shall be entitled to take proceedings by which the lawfulness of his detention shall be decided speedily by a court and his release ordered if the detention is not lawful."). The right to counsel does not appear in the treaties per se, but has been the strong recommendation of human rights bodies. See, e.g., U.N. Human Rights Comm., Concluding Observations: Israel, ¶ 13, U.N. Doc. CCPR/CO/78/Isr (2003) (recommending that Israel provide counsel to anyone it administratively detains within 48 hours).

[20] *Boumediene v. Bush*, 553 U.S. 723, 732 (2008).

[21] *Id.* at 779.

The federal courts have declined to extend the full set of these protections to those detained in places other than Guantanamo Bay,[22] a decision I have suggested is difficult.[23] Nevertheless, the government has chosen to implement elsewhere more robust review procedures that approach human rights standards. The Obama administration issued new regulations governing detentions by U.S. forces in Afghanistan that require providing detainees with notice of the reasons for their detention and a reasonable opportunity to contest,[24] albeit without federal court access.[25]

The regulations provide each detainee with a personal representative who, while not a lawyer, does have a fiduciary responsibility to the detainee. This personal representative is responsible for securing witnesses and other evidence for the detainee and representing the detainee's interests during the classified portions of hearings. The representative is also subject to a non-disclosure agreement prohibiting the disclosure of information adverse to the detainee's case garnered from discussions with the detainee. These procedures have increased the length of hearings, deepened the adversarial process, and ultimately resulted in a larger number of released detainees.[26]

Another area where human rights law has influenced U.S. conduct in these conflicts is the repatriation of detainees. The ICRC has identified the need for guidelines on repatriation of detained non-State fighters because of the absence of express protections for these fighters under IHL.[27] The Geneva Conventions did not include any such protections for combatants because States did not want to be legally obligated to accept detained enemy soldiers for resettlement,[28] and because they feared that the detaining State would pressure those detained to renounce their right to return home.[29] Even in the context of international armed conflict, there is

---

[22] See *Maqaleh v. Gates*, 605 F.3d 84, 87 (D.C. Cir. 2010) (holding that detainees picked up outside of Afghanistan and transported there for detention do not have *habeas corpus* rights).

[23] Bellinger and Padmanabhan 2011, pp. 227–28.

[24] Letter from Phillip Carter, Deputy Assistant Sec'y of Def. for Detainee Policy, to Senator Carl Levin, Chairman of the Senate Armed Services Comm. (July 14, 2010), available at http://www.wcl.american.edu/nimj/documents/addendum.pdf?rd=1.

[25] Arguably, the use of an administrative process rather than court review suggests a desire to comport with the IHL civilian standards found in the Fourth Geneva Convention rather than with human rights law. See *supra* n. 18 (describing the Fourth Geneva Convention protections for detained civilian protected persons). But the primary innovation of these tribunals, a personal representative with fiduciary duty to the detainees, well exceeds the requirement of the Fourth Convention, and is closer to the counsel requirement found in human rights law.

[26] See Bovarnick 2010, p. 24 (describing the net effects of new review procedures).

[27] See ICRC, n. 12, p. 12 ("[The] principle [of non-refoulement] is not…explicitly incorporated into international humanitarian law governing non-international armed conflict.") Article 45 of the Fourth Geneva Convention prohibits the transfer of civilian protected persons "to a country where he or she may have reason to fear persecution for his or her political opinions or religious beliefs."

[28] States rejected an Austrian proposal to give prisoners of war the right "to apply for their transfer to any other country which is ready to accept them: Pictet 1960, p. 542.

[29] Meron 2000, pp. 254–55.

a developing consensus against forced repatriation in the face of mistreatment risks. But the risk to human dignity posed by transfers in the post 9/11 conflicts is enhanced because of the identity of the detainees.[30]

Unlike IHL, human rights law speaks clearly on this issue. Article 3 of the Convention against Torture (CAT), a human rights treaty, prohibits the transfer of an individual to another State where there is substantial risk of torture. Under the U.S. interpretation of this provision, it has legal application only with respect to transfers originating out of the United States, and has no application during wartime.[31] Not feeling constrained by international law, the United States engaged in the practice of extraordinary rendition, or the transfer of a detainee from one State to another for purposes of interrogation using torture, early in the conflict with al Qaida.[32] There were also high profile cases of detainees repatriated from Guantanamo to their home country, where they were allegedly tortured.[33] These calamitous events led to international pressure on the United States to provide non-refoulement protection to all detainees.

At Guantanamo Bay, the United States abides by the CAT Article 3 principle as a matter of policy.[34] The United States negotiates diplomatic assurances with all States to which it sends detainees to ensure that they will not be tortured after repatriation. Sometimes this policy results in the transfer of detainees to States with poor human rights records pursuant to assurances. While this practice is controversial,[35] it matches U.S. practice in extradition and deportation. Other times the United States has decided not to repatriate detainees to their home

[30] Some scholars have found an implied non-refoulement obligation in the Geneva Conventions' prohibition on torture. See Byers M, Legal Opinion on the December 18 2005 "Arrangement for the Transfer of Detainees between the Canadian Forces and the Ministry of Defence of the Islamic Republic of Afghanistan," at 3 (Apr. 7, 2006), *Amnesty Int'l v. Canada* [2008] F.C. 336 (Can.). Such an approach would itself mirror human rights reasoning, as the Human Rights Committee and European Court of Human Rights have found non-refoulement obligations within their treaties under this theory. See Padmanabhan 2011, pp. 85–86 (describing history of non-refoulement protection). Nevertheless, the ICRC apparently rejects this approach, as does at least one respected IHL scholar. See Greenwood C, Report: International Law Framework for the Treatment of Persons Detained in Afghanistan by Canadian Forces, at 27, para 64, *Amnesty Int'l Can. v. Canada*.

[31] See United States Written Response to Questions Asked by the Committee Against Torture, at 32 (Apr. 28, 2006), available *at* http://www.state.gov/g/drl/rls/68554.htm ("[T]he United States…believes that CAT Article 3 does not impose obligations on the United States with respect to an individual who is outside the territory of the United States.")

[32] See Savage 2009 (describing the use of rendition).

[33] See Human Rights Watch 2005 (describing the torture of repatriated Russian detainees sent home from Guantanamo Bay).

[34] See Comm. Against Torture, Consideration of Reports Submitted by State Parties under Article 19 of the Convention: United States of America, annex 1, at 57, U.N. Doc. CAT/C/48.Add.3 (2005) ("U.S. policy is not to transfer a person to a country if it is determined that it is more likely than not the person will be tortured…").

[35] See Padmanabhan 2011, at 100–102 (describing instances where States have misused diplomatic assurances).

States—such as the Chinese-national, ethnic Uighurs—and has sought third country resettlement.

In Afghanistan and Iraq, the United States has stated that it does not believe that it is bound by the non-refoulement principle as a matter of law with respect to in-country transfers—for example, of Afghan citizens to the Afghan government. Such a policy seems to be driven at least in part by practical concerns about the alternatives should the United States conclude such transfers create a substantial risk of torture. In Iraq, from which the United States has now fully withdrawn, U.S. troops were protecting Camp Ashraf, which houses 3400 Iranian dissidents, from the Iraqi government, which wishes to close the camp. State Department officials have been open in their fear that the Iraqis may harm those in the camp, concerns bolstered by past violence perpetrated by Iraqi troops at Ashraf.[36] But the lack of options for the United States to protect the camp after withdrawal left those within largely at the mercy of the Government of Iraq.

Even with respect to in country transfers, however, the United States has sought to apply the non-refoulement principle where possible. It negotiated assurances from the Government of Afghanistan that any transferred individuals would not be tortured after transfer. And following a disturbing U.N. report finding systematic torture at Afghan-run detention facilities, NATO suspended transfers to several Afghan-run facilities and embarked on a plan to investigate and monitor the sites and better train Afghan interrogators.[37]

The reality then is that the United States, despite rejecting wartime application of human rights law, has in practice used its principles to regulate detention operations in the post 9/11 conflicts. Doing so allowed the United States to use wartime detention and targeting authorities, while addressing criticism that IHL applied wholesale to the conflict with al Qaida results in unjust outcomes.

16.4 To the Future: A Growing Role for Human Rights in War Fighting

There are at least three reasons to believe that human rights law will play an ever greater role in regulating armed conflict. First, it appears that at least the U.S. conflict with al Qaida will continue for the indefinite future. As it does, further situations will arise that fall uncomfortably between peacetime police action and wartime battle, leading to calls to apply human rights principles to reduce inequities resulting from application of IHL rules.

For example, the stepped up drone campaigns in Pakistan and Yemen, and the raid that killed Osama bin Laden are intensifying questions about whether the traditional IHL rule permitting targeting of combatants at any time unless they are

[36] See Shane 2011.

[37] See Rubin 2011 (describing the efforts of NATO commander General John Allen).

hors de combat should be applied to targeting in the conflict with al Qaida.[38] These operations involve time for deliberation, and arguably a great risk of misidentification, leading some scholars and human rights activists to question the equities of the traditional rule. The ICRC has proposed that deadly force be permitted against civilians directly participating in hostilities only where the target poses a threat of death and bodily injury that cannot be otherwise reasonably mitigated.[39] Such a rule would be consistent with human rights law. The United States and some IHL experts have resisted such a rule, fearing it would undermine the operational clarity needed in targeting.[40] But similar arguments were offered against the use of human rights concepts in detention operations, and were ultimately rejected.[41]

Second, human rights law exerts a dynamic influence on armed conflict because of the large number of human rights NGOs, scholars, and States that are invested in the project of the application of human rights norms to armed conflict situations. The voice of human rights advocates is much louder than that of IHL practitioners given their greater number. Even the ICRC, the world's preeminent IHL organization, has demonstrated openness to the use of human rights concepts to interpret IHL provisions. The drumbeat of voices from States, the human rights community and the ICRC were essential in shifting U.S. practice on treatment and process issues. And these groups will continue to exercise pressure on the United States to apply human rights principles in lieu of or as part of application of IHL where the traditional IHL rule produces inhumane outcomes.

Third, the absence of clear lines delimiting the respective domains of IHL and human rights law encourages further growth of the scope of application of human rights law. The International Court of Justice's (ICJ) famous statement that: "some rights may be exclusively matters of international humanitarian law; others may be exclusively matters of human rights law; yet others may be matters of both these branches of international law", has done little to clarify precisely when each of these three categories applies.[42]

---

[38] For an excellent critique of this rule, see Blum 2010 (arguing that necessity requires "a least-harmful-means test, mandating the capture or otherwise disabling of the enemy rather than direct targeting").

[39] See ICRC (2009) Interpretative Guidance on the Notion of Direct Participation in Hostilities under International Humanitarian Law. ICRC, Geneva (proposing change to traditional IHL rules in conflicts with non-State groups).

[40] See, for example, Corn 2010, p. 82.

[41] Professor Corn argues that human rights law appropriately influences detention operations, as a post-submission activity, but would be illegitimate in restricting use of force pre-submission. *Id.* Thus, he would accept the influence of human rights on the war with al Qaida to date, while making a principled stand against further encroachment. While this argument has some merit, it seems unlikely to gain sufficient traction to prevent expansion of the influence of human rights law.

[42] ICJ, *Legal Consequences of the Construction of a Wall in the Occupied Palestinian Territory*, Advisory Opinion, (2004) I.C.J. Rep. 136.

Lex specialis and complementarity only somewhat clarify the situation. *Lex specialis* provides that where there are conflicting international legal rules, the more specific rule should apply. Application of this rule means that IHL should trump conflicting human rights law in most armed conflict situations. Complementarity adds that international legal obligations should be read in light of one another. This means IHL should be read in light of relevant human rights law, and vice versa. Together these principles sometimes alleviate confusion about how to reconcile human rights law and IHL.

But where human rights law and IHL conflict, determining which rule to apply turns on a subjective characterization of the situation as peacetime or wartime. Such a methodology can be arbitrary.[43] For example, does *lex specialis* in the targeted killings context lead to application of the IHL rule or the human rights rule? The answer turns on the characterization of the situation as a wartime operation or a peacetime police raid, the very issue that is disputed in the conflict with al Qaida. Such slippery lines create room for the further application of human rights principles in these new conflicts.[44]

The continued humanization of IHL is thus inevitable as the conflict with al Qaida proceeds, particularly if and as al Qaida's pace and volume of attacks slows. The United States is certain to continue to claim wartime authority in the conflict because of the operational benefits of the wartime paradigm.[45] This authority will continue to raise questions to which IHL has inadequate or unsatisfactory answers, opening the door for human rights law to fill gaps or modify existing rules. While practitioners and scholars will disagree as to whether this is good or bad, the critical point is that there is no turning back. The influence of human rights law on war fighting will only grow over time.

References

Bellinger JB III and Padmanabhan VM (2011) Detention operations in contemporary conflicts: four challenges for the Geneva Conventions and other existing law. Am J Int Law 105:201

Blum G (2010) The dispensable lives of soldiers. J Law Anal 2:115

Bovarnick JA (2010) Detainee review boards in Afghanistan: from strategic liability to legitimacy. Army Lawyer 9

Corn G (2010) Mixing apples and hand grenades: the logical limit of applying human rights norms to armed conflict. J Int Humanit Law Stud 1:52

Hakimi M (2012) A functional approach to targeting and detention. Mich L Rev 110:1365

---

43 See Hakimi 2012 p. 2–3 (arguing that the distinction between armed conflict and non-armed conflict situations can be arbitrary leading to uncertainty).

44 Professor Hakimi argues for a shift from the traditional method that separates law of war and human rights domains to a functional approach to detention and targeting questions that creates a common inquiry in conflicts with non-State actors, whether characterized as war or not. *Id.* p. 5–6.

45 The 2011 National Defense Authorization Act reaffirms that wartime authorities should be used by the President in combating al Qaida, the Taliban and affiliated groups.

Human Rights Watch (2005) Still at risk: diplomatic assurances no safeguard against torture (14 April 2005). Available at http://www.hrw.org/sites/default/files/reports/eca0405.pdf. Accessed 21 Dec 2011

International Commission of Jurists (2009) 'Assessing damage, urging action: report of the eminent jurists panel on terrorism, counter-terrorism and human rights'. Available at http://ejp.ijc.org/IMG/EJP-Report.pdf. Accessed 21 Dec 2011

Meron T (2000) The humanization of humanitarian law. Am J Int Law 94:239

Padmanabhan VM (2011) To transfer or not to transfer: identifying and protecting relevant human rights interests in non-refoulement. Fordham Law Rev 780:3

Pictet J (ed) (1960) Commentary to the Geneva Convention (III) relative to the treatment of prisoners of war. ICRC, Geneva

Rubin AJ (2011) UN finds 'systematic' torture in Afghanistan. New York Times, 10 Oct 2011. Available at http://www.nytimes.com/2011/10/11/world/asia/un-report-finds-routine-abuse-of-afghan-detainees.html?pagewanted=all. Accessed 21 Dec 2011

Sandoz Y et al (eds) (1987) Commentary on the additional protocols of 8 June 1977 to the Geneva conventions of 12 August 1949. ICRC, Geneva

Savage C (2009) Obama's war on terror may resemble Bush's in some areas. New York Times, 17 Feb 2009. Available at http://www.nytimes.com/2009/02/18/us/politics/18policy.html?pagewanted=all. Accessed 21 Dec 2011

Shane S (2011) For obscure Iranian Exile Group, broad support in US. New York Times, 26 Nov 2011. Available at http://www.nytimes.com/2011/11/27/us/politics/lobbying-support-for-iranian-exile-group-crosses-party-lines.html?pagewanted=all. Accessed 21 Dec 2011

Waxman M (2008) Detention as targeting: standards of certainty and detention of suspected terrorists. Colum Law Rev 10:1365

Chapter 17
The Mottled Legacy of 9/11: A Few Reflections on the Evolution of the International Law of Armed Conflict

Charles J. Dunlap Jr.

Contents

17.1 Introduction

Has the way the law evolved since 9/11 been an unqualified good? Some might think so. Undoubtedly, there have been many positive developments in international law in general, and the international law of armed conflict (ILOAC)[1] in

[1] This essay will use the term "international law of armed conflict" (ILOAC) in lieu of the appellations "law of war" (LOAC) and "international humanitarian law" (IHL), both of which are, in this writer's view, too inexact and subject to misinterpretation. "Law of war" inevitably involves thorny questions of "what is 'war'?" variety even in situations where discussants agree that there is an "armed conflict." Like many Americans, this writer views the term "international humanitarian law" as one that dangerously seems to suggest that conflicts can somehow be made more humane that reality would permit. What is more is that it can too easily be conflated with "international human rights law" which is, of course, a very distinct legal regime.

C. J. Dunlap Jr. (✉)
USAF, Duke University Law School,
Durham, NC 27708-0358, USA
e-mail: dunlap@law.duke.edu

M.N. Schmitt and L. Arimatsu (eds.), *Yearbook of International Humanitarian Law Volume 14, 2011*, DOI: 10.1007/978-90-6704-855-2_17,

specific. Certainly those disposed towards the peaceful resolution of disputes and the efficacy of international law are heartened by recent studies that show, rather counterintuitively, that violence, and especially interstate violence, is actually declining.[2]

Yet it is just as important to understand that not every ILOAC-related development has been positive, even if one believes that overall the constructive advances outweigh the unhelpful ones. Indeed, this brief essay contends that while the increasing influence of law on armed conflict since 9/11 generally operates to diminish the human suffering that warfare traditionally occasions, there are nevertheless some disturbing trends that deserve considered attention.

Among the concerns are misplaced actions that encourage behaviors that may, over time, prove profoundly inimical to the fundamental purposes of ILOAC. In particular, this article contends that ILOACs efforts to grapple with the challenge of non-state actors engaged in armed conflict and terroristic acts is too often having the perverse effect of seeming to reward noncompliance with ILOAC, and thus—paradoxically—incentivizing further violations of the law.

All the same, this article will also point out positive evolutions such as the increasing importance of military lawyers, and their growing ability to influence military operations. Finally, the essay will offer some predictions as to the direction of the law in the next decade and beyond.

17.2 Law in Twenty-First Century Operations

9/11 coincided with several ongoing phenomena that while fully separate from the law, *qua* law, nonetheless have deeply affected ILOAC. Chief among these is the impact of globalization. Globalized commerce has stimulated the need not just for international law and international forums in order to conduct trade rationally and profitably, it has also internationalized a legal mindset among nations that heretofore have not needed to consider the impact of law. Today, their engagement with law is essential to their ability to function in the larger world. In short, countries wishing to profit—literally—from globalized trade need legal architectures that ensure agreed upon rights and responsibilities, as well as some means of enforcement.

Predictably, this market-driven trend caused a renaissance of sorts for international law. As has always been the case, whatever develops in the commercial sphere inevitably impacts the conduct of war. The development of the internal combustion engine, for example, led to the emergence of armored warfare and air warfare. More recently, the invention of the microchip has completely revolutionized warfare by permitting the development of highly-precise munitions, as well as unprecedented reconnaissance and surveillance technologies. Perhaps of equal importance with

[2] Goldstein 2011.

respect to ILOAC, the microchip spawned an array of communications technologies that enable the live (or near-instantaneous) broadcast of battlefield events across the globe.

These two phenomena—the rise of international law generally, and the changes wrought by microchip-based technologies—are among the leading causes of the emergence of what this author termed in 2001 as "lawfare".[3] Although it has often been given a nefarious interpretation as being the transformation of law into a weapon for terrorists to wage war against the law-abiding, it actually is a neutral concept. It conceptualizes the law much as a weapon that can be used for good or malevolent purposes.

The key, however, is that legal warfare—however bitter—is presumptively preferable to kinetic conflict. In this respect, lawfare carries the potential to achieve the aim of ILOAC generally, which is to mitigate the physical horror of war, if not eliminating it altogether. In other publications the author discusses in some detail how law might be used in just such an affirmative way to advance that laudable goal.[4] However, it is also true that adversaries—terrorists particularly—embrace a form of lawfare, one marked by the exploitation of actual violations of ILOAC by U.S. and other Western forces. Even more malevolently, they even try to orchestrate deadly incidents for the purpose of undermining the moral and political legitimacy of U.S. and other forces.

There is no question that events such as the detainee abuses at Abu Ghraib or, more recently, the videos of U.S. Marines urinating on the bodies of Taliban fighters, are the kind of illegalities that readily translate into battlefield advantages for adversaries.[5] In the years since 9/11 adversaries have internalized the concept that one of the best ways to unhinge U.S. and Western forces is via the civilian casualty issue. Professors Michael Riesman and Chris T. Antoniou presaged this in their 1994 book, *The Laws of War*:

> In modern popular democracies, even a limited armed conflict requires a substantial base of public support. That support can erode or even reverse itself rapidly, no matter how worthy the political objective, if people believe that the war is being conducted in an unfair, inhumane, or iniquitous way.[6]

Unsurprisingly, former Secretary of Defense Robert Gates believed that a "principal strategic tactic of the Taliban…is either provoking or exploiting civilian casualties."[7] This has been exacerbated by the disconcerting trend, it seems, to "improve" upon ILOAC by announcing presumably well-intended policies that can, perversely, operate to frustrate ILOAC goals.

A classic example is how NATO forces handled allegations of excessive civilian casualties in Afghanistan. In an apparent effort to sooth local outrage,

---

[3] Dunlap 2001.

[4] Dunlap 2010.

[5] Kudo 2012.

[6] Reisman and Antoniou 1994, p. xxiv.

[7] DoD 2009.

NATO announced in 2007 that if it "knew there were civilians nearby," it would not conduct airstrikes[8] A year later, NATO reiterated its stance—a stance demonstrably not dictated by legal imperatives—by asserting that no bombing would take place "[i]f there is the likelihood of even one civilian casualty... not even if we think Osama bin Laden is down there."[9]

This is exactly the kind of ILOAC development that, wholly counterproductively, encourages belligerents to burrow into civilian communities with the understandable expectation that they will thereby be shielded from air attack if they can manage to keep "one civilian" in the area. While efforts to protect civilians are admirable, as is restraint in the use of force, if the unintended consequences are not carefully thought out, they can have the effect of granting sanctuary to the forces most deadly to civilians in twenty-first century conflicts.

17.3 The Disappointing Performance of UN

Since 9/11, the UN has not been a particularly positive force in the evolution of ILOAC. Perhaps its most disastrous initiative was its now considered to be flawed investigation into *Operation Cast Lead*, Israel's 2009 military operation in Gaza against Hamas militants. In the aftermath of the bloody clash, both sides traded allegations of war crimes. The UN commissioned former South African jurist and legal scholar Richard Goldstone to lead the investigation. The final report was mainly critical of Israel, accusing it of intentionally targeting civilians.

In a rather astonishing 2011 op-ed in the *Washington Post* Goldstone, while complaining about the lack of Israeli cooperation for his report, nevertheless admitted that given what was discovered by Israel's independent investigations, if he "had known then what [he] know[s] now, [his] report have been a different document."[10] He expressed disappointment that Hamas did not conduct its own investigation as Israel had, but conceded that "asking Hamas to investigate may have been a mistaken enterprise."

Goldstone concluded by addressing the central conundrum of post-9/11 ILOAC jurisprudence:

> Simply put, the laws of armed conflict apply no less to non-state actors such as Hamas than they do to national armies. Ensuring that non-state actors respect these principles, and are investigated when they fail to do so, is one of the most significant challenges facing the law of armed conflict. Only if all parties to armed conflicts are held to these standards will we be able to protect civilians who, through no choice of their own, are caught up in war.

As important and as valuable as this admission is, it has too seldom been made a centerpiece of UN efforts as it should. Instead, the UN—and other governmental

[8] Associated Press 2007.

[9] Constable 2008, p. A12.

[10] Goldstone 2011.

and nongovernmental organizations—too often appears to focus on the failings of the U.S, and other nation-states. The rationale seems clear, nonstate actors may be happy to assert allegations of war crimes and other misconduct against the U.S. and others, but are indifferent—truly indifferent—to allegations against themselves. Regrettably, as Goldstone's own efforts suggest, the UN has yet to resolve how to address incidents in a way that does not make them vulnerable to post hoc critiques that raise serious questions of fairness and equity.

From a U.S. perspective, some elements of the UN seem to revel in criticizing the American military. Perhaps the most insensitive was the scorn that UN Special Rapporteur, Phillip Alston leveled against American airmen operating remotely piloted vehicles (RPVs or commonly but inaccurately called "drones"). In his official report about extrajudicial killings he speculated about the aviators "developing a 'Playstation' mentality to killing."[11] Exactly why this academic thought he was qualified to opine about the attitude of military professionals towards killing other human beings is unknown, but it is instructive that there is a plethora of evidence—apparently not considered by Alston—that demonstrates that the gravity of these duties causes many of the officers to suffer post-traumatic stress disorder (PTSD).[12]

The UN also seems fixated on airpower beyond just RPVs. A report issued by a UN agency in Afghanistan in 2011 misleadingly asserted that "Air strikes remained the leading cause of Afghan civilian deaths caused by Pro-Government Forces."[13] The UN arrived at this statistic by consolidating all airstrike deaths into one category, while dividing ground-based deaths into three different "causes." Specifically, the UN allocated 32% of the civilian deaths at the hands of "pro-government" forces to "ground combat". Inexplicably excluded from that category were the "escalation of force" deaths (12%) that refer to those killed at checkpoints and from fire from convoys. An additional 14% of the deaths were attributed to another ground activity: night raids. Collectively, ground operations were responsible for some 58% of the deaths, considerably more than the airstrikes that the UN characterized as the "leading cause" of civilian deaths.

Even the UN's own judicial arm has come under fire. Professor John Norton Moore, the respected international lawyer from the University of Virginia, gave a scathing assessment of the United Nations' International Court of Justice's performance in a series of *jus ad bellum* cases, accusing it of "shocking failure[s] of legal craftsmanship."[14] Such failings merit immediate and searching examination if international law related to security matters—to include ILOAC—is to continue to evolve as a legal construct worthy of respect and deference.

---

[11] Alston 2010, p. 25.

[12] Reuters 2011.

[13] United Nations Assistance Mission in Afghanistan 2011.

[14] Moore forthcoming 2012.

17.4 The Role of Military Legal Advisors

One of the most positive ILOAC trends of the post-9/11 era is the increased presence of lawyers, and especially military lawyers, in command centers and other venues where combat operations are being planned and carried out. Article 82 of Protocol I to the 1949 Geneva Conventions had long importuned state parties to ensure that legal advisers were "available," but exactly how effectively that was carried out prior to 9/11 was spotty, especially for nations other than the U.S. who either did not have large numbers of trained military lawyers, or who did not have any tradition of their involvement in matters other than military justice.

The rise of international law—and particularly "lawfare"—in the post-9/11 era did much to change that. Commanders, especially after the Abu Ghraib scandal, became keenly aware of the damage that illegalities could do to their operational objectives. As the *New York Times* reported, Air Force lawyers "vet" the targets to ensure the proposed bombing conforms "to a complex body of military law, including the Geneva Conventions, acts of Congress and court decisions."[15] Available to these military attorneys are sophisticated analytical tools to help them better evaluate targeting decisions.[16] As a result, Human Rights Watch conceded that "[i]n their deliberate targeting, the Air Force has all but eliminated civilian casualties in Afghanistan."[17]

General James Jones, the former commander of NATO, typified the new attitude of many senior commanders. While perhaps not especially evincing fondness for the legal profession, operational realities obliged him to admit that war in the twenty-first century had become "very legalistic and very complex" and now requires "a lawyer or a dozen."[18]

17.5 Accountability

Internationalized justice related to armed conflict has had a mixed record since 9/11. The apprehension of former Serb leader Slobodan Milošević in 2001 on a variety of war crimes led to real optimism about the feasibility of international tribunals. However, after 4 years of trial by the International Criminal Tribunal for the former Yugoslavia, the prosecution collapsed when Milošević died in 2006. The expensive and ultimately futile effort was hardly an endorsement of the global community's attempt to provide justice for war crimes' victims.

To be sure, there have been some successes, and the International Criminal Court (ICC) has made steady, albeit tortuously slow progress mainly by addressing

---

[15] Shanker 2008.

[16] Air Force 2009.

[17] Shanker 2008.

[18] Winik 2003.

horrendous allegations of crimes arising out of African wars. Still, convictions have been few. Many believe that the absence of ratification of the Rome Statue by such nations as China, Russia, India and, especially, the United States is hampering prospects for real success.

That opposition, at least insofar as the U.S. is concerned, seems to be formally rooted in concern about politicized prosecutions of American officials. To oversimplify the concerns, U.S. negotiators want to ensure that actions taken in self-defense, to include especially actions taken in anticipatory self-defense, do not become characterized as the war crime of "aggression." In that regard the Obama Administration seems to be taking steps toward reconciling U.S. concerns with the ICC by establishing a 7 year process with the real possibility of the U.S. becoming a party to the treaty.[19]

It is a mistake, however, to assume too much in this regard. Discussion surrounding the American Service-Members' Protection Act (a U.S. law which authorizes, among other things, the President to use "all necessary means" to free any U.S. person imprisoned or otherwise detained at the behest of the ICC[20]) suggests further issues. Specifically, the body politic of nation such as the U.S. that is dependent upon an all-volunteer force will not readily countenance the prospect of turning its soldiers over to a foreign entity for trial. It underestimates the importance to such volunteers of getting the benefit of the judicial system they are serving to protect.

No discussion of ILOAC accountability would be complete without some comment on the Haditha tragedy in Iraq in 2005. Twenty-four civilians, including children and elderly people, were killed by Marines, allegedly in retaliation for an improvised explosive device attack that killed a fellow Marine. While eight Marines were original accused of misconduct in the incident, only one was convicted—barely. In January of 2012 Staff Sergeant Frank D. Wuterich pled guilty to one minor charge of dereliction of duty.

The case and, indeed the handling of the entire incident, were rightly critiqued. The *New York Times* pointed out that although the military has convicted persons accused of unlawful killings in Iraq and Afghanistan, experts said that "the military and its justice system have repeatedly shown an unwillingness to second-guess the decisions made by fighters who said they believed they were in danger."[21]

Importantly, however, civilian courts are not demonstrably different. In acquitting a former soldier of allegations of killing four Iraqi prisoners in 2004 in Fallouja, Iraq, one juror explained the not guilty verdict by saying "I think you don't know what goes on in combat until you are in combat."[22] Another remarked "Who are we to decide what men in war are doing?"[23]

---

[19] Rapp and Koh 2010.

[20] Department of State 2003.

[21] Savage 2012.

[22] Associated Press 2008.

[23] Perry 2008.

Finally, one of the most daunting legal accountability issues faced by the international community in the post-9/11 era is not precisely an ILOAC matter. It is, however, a distinctly international security issue: pirates. Although the international community has enjoyed real success in dampening what had been a burgeoning threat, no real solution has been identified for the legal resolution of their case.[24]

17.6 Terrorist Detention

Few issues, save the use of coercive interrogation techniques, have been more controversial in the post-9/11 era than the detention of terrorists by the U.S. Many in the U.S. believe that the nation's political fortunes are at stake by the resolution of this issue. This belief may be misplaced as there is too often a rather na assumption in the U.S. that world opinion is more discerning than it really is.

For example, advocates of closing the detention facility at Guantanamo Bay seem to believe that once that is accomplished, peoples around the globe will suddenly embrace the American paradigm for addressing the long-term security threat posed by the relatively small but still potent number irreconcilable detainees committed to violence.

Underlying this issue are persisting misconceptions engendered by ill-advised U.S. policy pronouncements made shortly after 9/11. The announcement by then President Bush of his military commission order raised the expectation that all detainees would eventually face a trial. Many would understandably assume that such trials would take place in a timely manner and if the accused was acquitted, the detainee would be freed—as any other criminal suspect might.

Lost in this dialogue was the notion of law of war detention, that is, the well-established principle that belligerents who fall into the hands of their adversary may be held until the end of the conflict without trial and, in the case, of legitimate combatants, without criminal liability for their actions otherwise in compliance with ILOAC. Thus, the long-term detention of nonstate actors may well be necessary and, in any event, can be lawful.

Retreating from a well-established ILOAC principle in the hopes of gaining the global public's favor defies logic—and may produce unintended and unwanted consequences. Actually, the more realistic view would hold that so long as the United States continues to detain terror suspects—regardless of location—critics will persist. This is especially so since it is likely that any other facility would be as well-equipped or as well-staffed as Guantanamo is today. In short, it is a wiser approach to keep to the proven ILOAC procedures and avoid attempts to "improve" upon it in order to gain the approval of those who may not have the

24 Chivers 2012.

responsibility for the security of those innocents who may be jeopardized by the release of those committed to violence.

17.7 The Future

Where will the future of ILOAC take us? For all the focus in the post-9/11 era on radical Islamic terror organizations, too little attention has been paid to the rise of a permutation on the threat posed by nonstate actors, that is, the emergence of what is ever more frequently being called "criminal insurgencies." These are entities that, unlike more traditional insurgencies', are not primarily driven by political or social aims, but simply by a need to neutralize or replace the coercive power of the state in order to be free to conduct their self-aggrandizing criminal activities.

One might rightly point out that criminal gangs with a similar *raison d'être* have long existed. The difference today is that the most dangerous of them are super-empowered by enormous profits produced principally by illicit drug trade. So vast have been the monies flowing into these criminal enterprises that they have been able to arm their gangs with an array of military weaponry including crew-served weapons, armored vehicles, aircraft, and even submarines. All of this is supported by a sophisticated communications systems, tunnel complexes and, perhaps most importantly, battalions of corrupted government officials.

The classic example of this phenomenon is Mexico.[25] However, the Mexican government is loath to describe its security environment as any kind of insurgency even as it deploys its armed forces in a concerted effort to control its territory. While some might unhesitatingly characterize the situation as noninternational armed conflict and proceed accordingly, it may be that international law would be better served to evolve a model more suited to a situation where one of the belligerents has no agenda beyond an avowedly criminal one. In such circumstances there is no real possibility of a political settlement, yet at the same time norms which guarantee the protection of innocents might need further elaboration.

In any event, although many security experts believe that we are in an era of persistent, low-tech conflict against nonstate adversaries, it is also becoming increasing clear that the possibility of interstate warfare is not foregone. For the United States, disillusioned by costly wars in Iraq and Afghanistan against opponents who, for all their ruthlessness, do not—and cannot—pose an existential threat to the American homeland, there is increasing focus on the potential of selected nation-states to pose existential threats. Thus, the U.S. is engaged in a much–discussed "pivot" towards Asia, even as it recognizes conflicts in the Middle East and central Asia will be of continuing concern.

[25] Grillo 2011.

This Asia-focus may have interesting implications for ILOAC. In a 1999 interview, Col. Qia Liang and Col. Wang Xiangsui of the Chinese People's Liberation Army made this observation about ILOAC:

> War has rules, but those rules are set by the West…if you use those rules, then weak countries have no chance…We are a weak country, so do we need to fight according to your rules?[26]

Moreover, in 2003 the Chinese Communist Party formalized the concept of "three warfares" one of which was "legal warfare." As recently explained by the U.S. Department of Defense (2011) these three warfares are designed to "undermine the spirit and ideological commitment of the adversary." Specifically, "legal warfare"

> [U]ses international and domestic law to claim the legal high ground or assert Chinese interests. It can be employed to hamstring an adversary's operational freedom and shape the operational space. Legal warfare is also intended to build international support and manage possible political repercussions of China's military actions. China has attempted to employ legal warfare in the maritime domain and in international airspace in pursuit of a security buffer zone.[27]

Thus, although the term "lawfare" is not used, it seems clear that a form of it is intrinsic to Chinese planning. Accordingly, the international community must be ready to address not just the conundrums presented by a soon-to-be superpower's increasing military might, but also its obvious intent to leverage the law as a means and method of warfare. This is especially so under circumstances where the superpower itself may not feel particularly obliged to "fight according to..[the] rules."

17.8 Conclusion

This paper has only touched upon a few of the many ILOAC issues that have developed since 9/11. It was beyond the scope of this essay to address, for example, the merits of the profound and controversial issues raised, for example, by coercive interrogation techniques. Similarly, the complex issues of direct participation in hostilities by civilians were hardly mentioned. Likewise, although the issue of drones was mentioned, the far more challenging issue of fully autonomous weapons' systems was mentioned not at all, nor were the plethora of cyberwar matters eminently worthy of extended examination.

Clearly, there is no shortage of ILOAC subjects worthy of attention. Fortunately, there are an ever-expanding number of thoughtful lawyers around the globe who are engaging these concerns. It should be kept in mind that in this area of the

[26] Pomfret 1999, p. A-1.

[27] DoD 2011.

practice of law, competence demands far more than legal erudition. The practitioner must also be a student of the art of war, and all its many and varied aspects. It is an irreplaceable quality.

Finally, though the legacy of ILOAC in the post-9/11 era has been mottled—some bright spots marred by some very dark ones—one can still say that the evolution, as suggested in the beginning of this essay, has been far more beneficial than not. Perhaps the greatest legacy of this period is that law can—and does—evolve, so long as there are altruistic practitioners willing to devote themselves to its highest values and to the honorable profession which guides it.

References

Alston P (2010) Report of the special rapporteur on extrajudicial, summary or arbitrary execution: study on targeted killings, delivered to the Human Rights Council, U.N. Doc. A/HRC/14/24/Add.6. http://www2.ohchr.org/english/bodies/hrcouncil/docs/14session/A.HRC.14.24.Add6.pdf. Accessed 29 Jan 2012

Associated Press (2007) US Coalition Airstrikes Kill, Wound Civilians in Southern Afghanistan, official says. http://www.nydailynews.com/news/world/u-s-airstrikes-kill-wound-civilians-southern-afghanistan-article-1.224856. Accessed 29 Jan 2012

Associated Press (2008) Federal jury acquits ex-Marine in Iraqis' deaths http://www.msnbc.msn.com/id/26443458/ns/world_news-mideast_n_africa/t/federal-jury-acquits-ex-marine-iraqis-deaths/

Chivers C (2012) Seized Pirates in High-Seas Legal Limbo, with No Formula for Trials http://www.nytimes.com/2012/01/28/world/africa/seized-pirates-in-legal-limbo-with-no-formula-for-trials.html. Accessed 30 Jan 2012

Constable P (2008) NATO Hopes to Undercut Taliban with Surge of Projects. http://www.washingtonpost.com/wp-dyn/content/article/2008/09/26/AR2008092603452_pf.html. Accessed 29 Jan 2012

Dunlap C (2001) Law and Military Operations: Preserving Humanitarian Values in 21st Century Conflicts. http://www.hks.harvard.edu/cchrp/Web%20Working%20Papers/Use%20of%20Force/Dunlap2001.pdf. Accessed 29 Jan 2012

Dunlap C (2010) Does lawfare need an Apologia? 43 Case Western Reserve. J Int Law 43(1):121

Goldstein J (2011) Winning the War on War. Dutton

Goldstone R (2011) Reconsidering the Goldstone Report on Israel and war crimes. http://www.washingtonpost.com/opinions/reconsidering-the-goldstone-report-on-israel-and-war-crimes/2011/04/01/AFg111JC_story.html. Accessed 29 Jan 2012

Grillo I (2011) El Narco: inside Mexico's criminal insurgency. Bloomsbury Press, New York

Kudo T (2012) How the Marines video made the Afghan war even tougher. Washington Post http://www.washingtonpost.com/opinions/as-a-marine-and-afghan-war-vet-im-insulted-by-the-desecration-video/2012/01/12/gIQAswIrwP_story.html. Accessed 29 Jan 2012

Moore J (forthcoming) *Jus ad Bellum*: Before the International Court of Justice http://www.vjil.org/information/current/forthcoming. Accessed May 2012

Perry T (2008) IRAQ: For Jose Nazario, the trial and the war are over http://latimesblogs.latimes.com/babylonbeyond/2008/08/iraq-for-jose-n.html. Accessed 30 Jan 2012

Pomfret J (1999) China ponders new rules of 'Unrestricted War'. Washington Post, at A-1

Rapp S, Koh H (2010) Briefing on the International Criminal Court Conference in Kampala, Uganda. http://www.state.gov/j/gcj/us_releases/remarks/142585.htm. Accessed 30 Jan 2012

Reisman W, Antoniou C (1994) The laws of war. Random House, New York

Reuters (2011) Overstretched drone pilots face stress risk. http://www.reuters.com/article/2011/12/18/us-usa-drones-stress-idUSTRE7BH0VH20111218. Accessed 30 Jan 2012

Savage C (2012) An Iraqi Massacre, a Light Sentence and a Question of Military Justice. http://www.nytimes.com/2012/01/28/us/an-iraqi-massacre-a-light-sentence-and-a-question-of-military-justice.html?ref=world. Accessed 30 Jan 2012

Shanker T (2008) Civilian Risks Curb Strikes in Afghan War. http://www.nytimes.com/2008/07/23/world/asia/23military.html. Accessed 29 Jan 2012

United Nations Assistance Mission in Afghanistan (2011) Afghanistan Midyear Report 2011: Protection of Civilians in Armed Conflict. http://unama.unmissions.org/Portals/UNAMA/Documents/2011%20Midyear%20POC.pdf. Accessed 30 Jan 2012

U.S. Department of the Air Force (2009) Targeting and Weaponeering. http://www.afjag.af.mil/shared/media/document/AFD-100510-059.pdf. Accessed 30 Jan 2012

U.S. Department of Defense (2011) Military and Security Developments Involving the People's Republic of China. http://www.defense.gov/pubs/pdfs/2011_CMPR_Final.pdf. Accessed 29 Jan 2012

U.S. Department of Defense (2009) Press Conference with Secretary Gates and Adm. Mullen on Leadership Changes in Afghanistan from the Pentagon. http://www.defense.gov/transcripts/transcript.aspx?transcriptid=4424. Accessed 30 Jan 2012

U.S. Department of State (2003) American Service-Members' Protection Act. http://www.state.gov/t/pm/rls/othr/misc/23425.htm. Accessed 29 Jan 2012

Winik W (2003) A Marine's Toughest Mission (Gen. James L. Jones), http://www.parade.com/articles/editions/2003/edition_01-19-2003/General_Jones. Accessed 30 Jan 2012

Part IV
Documentation

Chapter 18
Classification Scheme

Part Zero	International humanitarian law in general
Part One	Sources and general principles
Part Two	Conflicts, armed forces and combatants
Part Three	Protected persons
Part Four	Methods, means and types of warfare
Part Five	Termination of armed conflicts
Part Six	International criminal law
Part Seven	Implementation of IHL
Part Eight	The law of neutrality
Part Nine	International organisations and international actions
Part Ten	Regional organisations and actions
Part Eleven	Arms control and disarmament
Part Twelve	Conflict prevention and resolution
Part Thirteen	Related fields

M.N. Schmitt and L. Arimatsu (eds.), *Yearbook of International Humanitarian Law Volume 14, 2011*, DOI: 10.1007/978-90-6704-855-2_18,

0.	**Zero:**	**International Humanitarian Law in General**
1.	**One:**	**Sources and General Principles**
1.1	I	Sources
1.11		A. Pre-Hague
1.12		B. Hague Law
1.13		C. Geneva Law
1.14		D. Post-1977 Developments
1.15		E. Customary Law
1.2	II	General Principles
1.21		A. Martens Clause
1.22		B. Superfluous Injury and Unnecessary Suffering
1.23		C. Principle of Distinction
1.24		D. Prohibition of Indiscriminate Attacks
1.25		E. Principle of Proportionality
1.26		F. Principle of Precaution
1.27		G. Military Necessity
2.	**Two:**	**Conflicts, Armed Forces and Combatants**
2.1	I	Types of Conflicts
2.11		A. International
2.12		B. Non-international
2.13		C. Other
2.2	II	Types of Actor(s)
2.21		A. Armed Forces and Combatant Status
2.22		B. Non-State Actors
2.23		C. Specific Groups
2.231		1. Mercenaries
2.232		2. Spies
2.233		3. Contractors/Private Military Companies
2.234		4. Other
3.	**Three:**	**Protected Persons**
3.1	I	Types of Protected Persons
3.11		A. Wounded, Sick and Shipwrecked
3.12		B. Prisoners of War
3.13		C. Civilian Population
3.131		1. Civilians Generally
3.132		2. Women and Children

3.133		3. Medical and Religious Personnel
3.134		4. Journalists
3.135		5. Other
3.2	II	Specific Situations and Prohibitions
3.21		A. Internment
3.22		B. Occupation
3.23		C. Prohibition of Collective Punishment
3.24		D. Prohibition of Deportation and Transfer
3.25		E. Reprisals

4.	**Four:**	**Methods, Means and Types of Warfare**
4.1	I	Methods and Means of Warfare
4.11		A. Basic Rules
4.111		1. Existing Weapons
4.1111		a. Conventional Weapons
4.11111		i. Mines
4.11112		ii. Small weapons and others
4.1112		b. Weapons of Mass Destruction
4.11121		i. Nuclear weapons
4.11122		ii. Chemical and biological weapons
4.112		2. New Weapons
4.113		3. Prohibition of Perfidy
4.114		4. Emblems and Safeguards of Persons hors de combat
4.12		B. Direct and Indiscriminate Attacks
4.13		C. Precautionary Measures
4.14		D. Protection of Civilian and Other Specified Objects
4.141		1. Specifically Protected Objects
4.142		2. Cultural Property and Places of Worship
4.143		3. Works and Installations Containing Dangerous Forces
4.144		4. The Natural Environment
4.145		5. Localities and Zones
4.146		6. Civil Defence
4.15		E. Medical Assistance

4.16		F. Humanitarian Assistance Operations
4.2	II	Specific Types of Warfare
4.21		A. Land Warfare
4.22		B. Air and Missile Warfare
4.23		C. Naval Warfare
5.	**Five:**	**Termination of Armed Conflicts**
5.1	I	Ceasefire, Armistices and Peace Agreements
5.2	II	War Crimes Commissions
5.3	III	Amnesties, Truth and Reconciliation Commissions
5.4	IV	Reparations/Compensation
5.5	V	Military Commissions and Tribunals
6.	**Six:**	**International Criminal Law**
6.1	I	The Crimes
6.11		A. War Crimes
6.12		B. Genocide
6.13		C. Crimes Against Humanity
6.14		D. Aggression
6.15		E. Terrorism
6.16		F. Other
6.2	II	General Principles, Including Defences
6.21		A. Nullum Crimen Sine Lege and Nulla Poena Sine Lege
6.22		B. Individual Criminal Responsibility
6.23		C. Superior/Command Responsibility
6.24		D. Irrelevance of Official Capacity
6.25		E. Non-Retroactivity of Criminal Law
6.26		F. Non-Applicability of Statutory Limitations
6.27		G. Grounds for Excluding Criminal Responsibility
6.3	III	Repression of Breaches
6.31		A. International and Internationalised Courts
6.311		1. Nuremberg and Tokyo
6.312		2. International Criminal Tribunal for the former Yugoslavia
6.313		3. International Criminal Tribunal for Rwanda
6.314		4. International Criminal Court
6.315		5. East Timor's Special Panels for Serious Crimes
6.316		6. Kosovo's Internationalised Courts
6.317		7. Special Court for Sierra Leone

6.318		8. Extraordinary Chambers for Cambodia
6.319		9. Iraqi Special Tribunal
6.320		10. Special Tribunal for Lebanon
6.32		B. National Courts
6.4	IV	Victims of Crimes
7.	**Seven:**	**Implementation of IHL**
7.1	I	National Policy Statements
7.2	II	National Law
7.21		A. Legislation to Implement IHL Treaties
7.22		B. Legislation to Implement Obligations vis-à-vis the International Criminal Court and International Criminal Tribunals
7.23		C. Military Manuals/National Instructions/Codes of Conduct
7.24		D. Role of Defence Force Legal Advisers
7.3	III	Protecting Powers
7.4	IV	ICRC
7.5	V	Fact-Finding, Including the International Fact-Finding Commission
7.6	VI	Dissemination
7.7	VII	Training and Education
8.	**Eight:**	**The Law of Neutrality**
8.1	I	The Rights and Duties of Nationals
8.2	II	War on Land
8.3	III	Naval Warfare
8.4	IV	Aerial Warfare
9.	**Nine:**	**International Organisations and International Actions**
9.1	I	International Organisations
9.11		A. United Nations Organisation
9.12		B. Other
9.2	II	International Actions
9.21		A. Peacekeeping
9.22		B. Peace Enforcement and Peace Building
9.23		C. Fact-Finding and Monitoring
9.24		D. Humanitarian and Other Interventions
9.25		E. Sanctions

10.	**Ten:**	**Regional Organisations and Actions**
10.1	I	European
10.2	II	American
10.3	III	Asian
10.4	IV	African
11.	**Eleven:**	**Arms Control and Disarmament**
11.1	I	Conventional Weapons
11.11		A. Mines
11.12		B. Small Weapons and Others
11.13		C. Production and Transfer
11.2	II	Weapons of Mass Destruction
11.21		A. Nuclear Weapons
11.22		B. Chemical and Biological Weapons
11.23		C. New Types
12.	**Twelve:**	**Conflict Prevention and Resolution**
12.1	I	Conflict Prevention
12.2	II	Conflict Resolution
12.3	III	The Peace Movement
13.	**Thirteen:**	**Related Fields**
13.1	I	Jus Ad Bellum
13.2	II	The Law Relating to Terrorism and Counter-Terrorism
13.3	III	Military Law
13.4	IV	Human Rights Law
13.5	V	Refugee Law

Chapter 19
Bibliography 2011

1 International Humanitarian Law in General

Books

- Banks, William, *New Battlefields/Old Laws: Critical Debates on Asymmetric Warfare* (New York, Columbia University Press 2011) 308 pp.
- Ben-Naftali, Orna, *International Humanitarian Law and International Human Rights Law: pas de deux* (Oxford, Oxford University Press 2011) 388 pp.
- Breitegger, Alexander, *Cluster Munitions and International Law Disarmament With a Human Face?* (UK, Routledge 2011) 274 pp.
- De Ruiter, D., *Humanitarian Law: Selected Documents* (Hague, International Courts Association 2011) 490 pp.
- Gillespie, Alexander, *History of the Laws of War: Volume 1: The Customs and Laws of War with Regards to Combatants and Captives* (Oxford, Hart Publishing 2011) 278 pp.
- Gillespie, Alexander, *History of the Laws of War: Volume 2: The Customs and Laws of War with Regards to Civilians in Times of Conflict* (Oxford, Hart Publishing 2011) 324 pp.
- Gillespie, Alexander, *History of the Laws of War: Volume 3: The Customs and Laws of War with Regards to Arms Control* (Oxford, Hart Publishing 2011) 180 pp.
- Jha, U.C., *International humanitarian law: the laws of war* (New Delhi, Vij Books 2011) 425 pp.

The bibliography was compiled by Aleksandra Bojovic, Mohbuba Choudhury, Manuela Melandri and Sarah Sadek. Aleksandra Bojovic holds an LLM in Public International Law from the London School of Economics and Political Science and is a Doctoral Candidate in International Economic Law at the London School of Economics and Political Science. Mohbuba Choudhury holds a BA (Hons) from the University of Oxford and an LLM in Public International Law from the London School of Economics and Political Science. Manuela Melandri is a Doctoral Candidate at the University College of London. Sarah Sadek holds an LLB from the University of Southampton and an LLM in Public International Law from the University College London.

M.N. Schmitt and L. Arimatsu (eds.), *Yearbook of International Humanitarian Law Volume 14, 2011,* DOI: 10.1007/978-90-6704-855-2_19,

- Kalshoven, Frits and Liesbeth Zegveld, eds., *Constraints on the Waging of War: An Introduction to International Humanitarian Law* (Cambridge, Cambridge University Press 2011) 312 pp.
- Otto, Roland, *Targeted Killings and International Law: With Special Regard to Human Rights and International Humanitarian Law* (London, Springer 2011) 679 pp.
- Schmitt, Michael N., *Essays on Law and War at the Fault Lines* (Hague, T.M.C. Asser Press 2011) 637 pp.
- Shah, Niaz A, *Islamic Law and the Law of Armed Conflict: The Conflict in Pakistan* (UK, Routledge 2011) 176 pp.
- Thurer, Daniel, *International Humanitarian Law: Theory, Practice, Context* (The Netherlands, Brill Academic Publishers 2011) 500 pp.

Articles

- Blum, Gabriella, 'On a Differential Law of War', 52 *Harvard International Law Journal* (2011) pp. 163-217
- Cohen, Amichai and Stuart A. Cohen, 'Israel and International Humanitarian Law: Between the Neo-Realism of State Security and the "Soft Power" of Legal Acceptability', 16(2) *Israel Studies* (2011) pp. 1-23
- Effron, Andrew S., 'United States v. Dubay and The Evolution of Military Law: The Fourth George S. Prugh Lecture in Military Legal History', 207 *Military Law Review* (2011) pp. 1-85
- Ford, Christopher M., 'From Nadir to Zenith: The Power to Detain in War', 207 *Military Law Review* (2011) pp. 203-252
- Geiss, Robin, and Michael Siegrist, 'Has the armed conflict in Afghanistan affected the rules on the conduct of hostilities?' 93 *International Review of the Red Cross* (2011) pp. 11-46
- Greenwood, Christopher, 'Human Rights and Humanitarian Law Conflict or Convergence', 43 *Case Western Reserve Journal of International Law* (2011) pp. 491-512
- Heintschel von Heinegg, Wolff, 'Asymmetric Warfare – How to Respond?', 41 *Israel Yearbook on Human Rights* (2011) pp. 327-358
- Lamp, Nicolas, 'Conceptions of War and Paradigms of Compliance: The 'New War' Challenge to International Humanitarian Law', 16(2) *Journal of Conflict and Security Law* (2011) pp. 225-262
- Mandel, Michael, 'Aggressors' Rights: The Doctrine of "Equality between Belligerents" and the Legacy of Nuremberg', 24 *Leiden Journal of International Law* (2011) pp. 627-650
- McLaughlin, Rob, 'The Law of Armed Conflict and International Human Rights Law: Some Paradigmatic Differences and Operational Implications', 13 *Yearbook of International Humanitarian Law* (2010) pp. 213-243
- Murphy, John F., 'Mission Impossible? International Law and the Changing Character of War', 41 *Israel Yearbook on Human Rights* (2011) pp. 13-42

- Ratner, Steven R., 'Law Promotion Beyond Law Talk: The Red Cross, Persuasion, and the Laws of War', 22 *European Journal of International Law* (2011) pp. 459-506
- Schmitt, Michael, 'Investigating Violations of International Law in Armed Conflict', 2 *Harvard National Security Journal* (2011) pp. 31-84
- Solis, Gary D., 'The Law of Armed Conflict: International Humanitarian Law in War' 80(1) *Nordic Journal of International Law* (2011) pp. 121-123
- Stephens, Dale, 'The Age of Lawfare', 41 *Israel Yearbook on Human Rights* (2011) pp. 1-30
- Tamura, Eriko, 'The Isayeva Cases of the European Court of Human Rights: The Application of International Humanitarian Law and Human Rights Law in Non-International Armed Conflicts', 10(1) *Chinese Journal of International Law* (2011) pp. 129-140
- Van den Herik, Larissa and Daniëlla Dam-De Jong, 'Revitalizing the Antique War Crime of Pillage: The Potential and Pitfalls of Using International Criminal Law to Address Illegal Resource Exploitation during Armed Conflict', 22(3) *Criminal Law Forum* (2011) pp. 237-273
- Von der Groeben, Constantin, 'The Conflict in Colombia and the Relationship between Humanitarian Law and Human Rights Law in Practice: Analysis of the New Operational Law of the Colombian Armed Forces', 16(1) *Journal of Conflict and Security Law* (2011) pp. 141-164
- Vuco, Ivana, 'Domestic, Legal or Other Proceedings Undertaken by Both the Government of Israel and the Palestinian Side', 13 *Yearbook of International Humanitarian Law* (2010) pp. 327-336

1.1 Hague Law

Books

- De Beer, L., ed., *Hague Conventions: A Compilation of Documents* (The Netherlands, Wolf Legal Publishers 2011) 800 pp.

1.2 Geneva Law

Articles

- Bellinger III, John B. and Vijay M. Padmanabhan, 'Detention Operations in Contemporary Conflicts: Four Challenges for the Geneva Conventions and Other Existing Law', 105 *American Journal of International Law* (2011) pp. 201-243
- Pejic, Jelena, 'The Protective Scope of Common Article 3: More than meets the Eye', 93 *International Review of the Red Cross* (2011) pp. 189-226

1.3 Principle of Distinction

Articles

- Kot, Jean-Philippe, 'Israeli Civilians versus Palestinian Combatants? Reading the Goldstone Report in Light of the Israeli Conception of the Principle of Distinction', 24 *Leiden Journal of International Law* (2011) pp. 961-988

1.4 Principle of Proportionality

Books

- Barak, Eitan, *Deadly Metal Rain: The Legality of Flechette Weapons in International Law: A Reappraisal Following Israel's Use of Flechettes in the Gaza Strip (2001-2009)* (Leiden, Martinus Nijhoff 2011) 262 pp.

Articles

- Blank, Laurie R., 'Finding Facts But Missing the Law: The Goldstone Report, Gaza, and Lawfare', 43 *Case Western Reserve Journal of International Law* (2011) pp. 279-305
- Chesney, Robert M., 'Who May be Held? Military Detention through the Habeas Lens' 41 *Israel Yearbook on Human Rights* (2011) pp. 113-177
- Newton, Michael A., 'Illustrating Illegitimate Lawfare', 43 *Case Western Reserve Journal of International Law* (2011) pp. 255-277
- Ochmannová, Petra, 'Unmanned Aerial Vehicles and Law of Armed Conflict implications', 2 *Czech Yearbook of Private & Public International* Law (2011) pp. 143-157
- Ondřej, Jan, 'Thirty Years since the Adoption of the Convention on Prohibitions or Restrictions on the Use of Certain Conventional Weapons especially the Protocol on Prohibitions or Restrictions on the Use of Mines, Booby-Traps and Other Devices', 2 *Czech Yearbook of Private & Public International* Law (2011) pp. 159-173
- Schabas, William A., 'Gaza, Goldstone, and Lawfare' 43 *Case Western Reserve Journal of International Law* (2011) pp. 307-313
- Sterio, Milena, 'The Gaza Strip: Israel, Its Foreign Policy, and the Goldstone Report', 43(1) *Case Western Reserve Journal of International Law* (2011) pp. 229-255
- Vogel, Ryan J., 'Drone Warfare and the Law of Armed Conflict', 39 *Denver Journal of International Law and Policy* (2011) pp. 101-138

2 Conflicts, Armed Forces and Combatants

Books

- Gill, Terry and Dieter Fleck, *The Handbook of the International Law of Military Operations* (Oxford, Oxford University Press 2011) 688 pp.
- Kalshoven, Frits, Zegveld, Liesbeth, *Constraints on the Waging of War* (Cambridge, Cambridge University Press 2011) 312 pp.
- Lubell, Noam, *Extraterritorial Use of Force against Non-State Actors* (Oxford, Oxford University Press 2011) 320 pp.

Articles

- Bellal, Annyssa, Giacca, Gilles and Casey-Maslen Stuart, 'International law and armed non-state actors in Afghanistan', 98 *International Review of the Red Cross* (2011) pp. 47-81
- Dinstein, Yoram, 'Concluding remarks: LOAC and attempts to abuse or subvert it', 87 *International Law Studies Series, US Naval War College* (2011) pp. 483-496
- Gadler, Alice, 'Armed Forces as carrying both the stick and the carrot – Humanitarian Aid in US Counterinsurgency Operations in Afghanistan and Iraq', 3 *Goettingen Journal of International Law* (2011) pp. 217-250
- Graham, David E, 'Law of Armed Conflict in Asymmetric Urban Armed Conflict', 87 *International Law Studies Series US Naval War* College (2011) pp. 301-314
- Lamp, Nicholas, 'Conceptions of war and paradigms of compliance; the 'new war' challenge to international humanitarian law', 16(2) *Journal of Conflict and Security Law* (2011) pp. 225-262
- Murphy, John F, 'Mission Impossible – International Law and the Changing Character of War', 87 *International Law Studies Series US Naval College* (2011) pp. 13-42
- Tabassum Sadia, 'Combatants, not bandits: the status of rebels in Islamic Law', 93 *International Review of the Red Cross* (2011) pp. 121-141

2.1 International Armed Conflicts

Articles

- Blank, Laurie R and Benjamin R. Farley, 'Characterizing US operations in Pakistan: Is the United States Engaged in an Armed Conflict', 34 *Fordham International Law Journal* (2011) pp. 151-189

2.2 *Non-international Armed Conflicts*

Articles

- Blum, Gabriella, 'Re-envisaging the international law of internal armed conflict; a reply to Sandesh Sivakumaran', 22(1) *European Journal of International Law* (2011) pp. 265-271
- Colassis, Laurent, 'The Role of the International Committee of the Red Cross in Stability Operations in Iraq', 40 *Israel Yearbook on Human Rights* (2010) pp. 183-202
- Lieblich, Eliav, 'Intervention and Consent; Consensual Forcible Interventions in Internal Armed Conflicts as International Agreements', 29 *Boston University International Law Journal* (2011) pp. 337-382
- Sivakumaran, Sandesh, 'Re-envisaging the international law of internal armed conflict', 22(1) *European Journal of International Law* (2011) pp. 219-264
- Sivakumaran, Sandesh, 'Re-envisaging the international law of internal armed conflict; A rejoinder to Gabriella Blum', 22(1) *European Journal of International Law* (2011) pp. 273-275
- Tamura, Eriko, 'The Isayeva cases of the European Court of Human Rights; the application of international humanitarian law and human rights law in non-international armed conflicts', 10(1) *Chinese Journal of International Law* (2011) pp. 129-140

2.3 *Occupation*

Books

- Akram, Susan et al., eds., *International law and the Israeli-Palestinian conflict: a rights-based approach to Middle East peace* (London, Routledge 2011) 342 pp.
- Ronen, Yael, *Transition from illegal regimes under international law* (Cambridge, Cambridge University Press 2011) 400 pp.

Articles

- Harpaz, Guy and Yuval Shany, 'The Israeli Supreme Court and the incremental expansion of the scope of discretion under belligerent occupation law', 43 *Israel Law Review* (2010) pp. 514-550
- Solomon, Solon, 'Occupied or not: the question of Gaza's legal status after the Israeli disengagement', 19(1) *Cardozo Journal of International and Comparative Law* (2011) pp. 59-90

2.4 Armed Forces and Combatant Status

Articles

- Creegan, Erin, 'Protocol Additional to the Geneva Conventions of 12 August 1949, and Relating to the Treatment of Terrorist Combatants (Protocol IV) – A Proposal', 41(2) *California Western International Law Journal* (2011) pp. 345-396
- Garraway, Charles, 'The Changing Character of the Participants in War: Civilization of Warfighting and the Concept of "Direct Participation in Hostilities"', 87 *International Law Studies Series US Naval War College* (2011) pp. 177-186
- Hampson, Françoise J., 'Direct Participation in Hostilities and the Interoperability of the Law of Armed Conflict and Human Rights Law', 87 *International Law Studies Series US Naval War College* (2011) pp. 187-216
- Rubinstein, Amnon and Yaniv Roznai, 'Human Shields in Modern Armed Conflicts: The need for a Proportionate Proportionality', 22(1) *Stanford Law & Policy Review* (2011) pp. 93-128

2.5 Private Military Companies/Mercenaries/Non-State Actors

Books

- Lubell, Noam, *Extraterritorial Use of Force Against Non-state Actors* (Oxford, Oxford University Press 2011) 320 pp.
- Francioni, Francesco, and Natalino Ronzitti, eds., *War by Contract: Human Rights, Humanitarian Law, and Private Contractors* (Oxford, Oxford University Press 2011) 576 pp.
- Tonkin, Hannah, *State Control Over Private Military and Security Companies in Armed Conflict* (Cambridge, Cambridge University Press 2011) 338 pp.

Articles

- Bellal, Annyssa and Stuart Casey-Maslen, 'Enhancing Compliance with International Law by Armed Non-State Actors', 3(1) *Goettingen Journal of International Law* (2011) pp. 175-198
- Corn, Geoffrey S., 'Thinking the Unthinkable: Has the Time Come to Offer Combatant Immunity to Non-State Actors', 22(1) Stanford Law & Policy Review (2011) pp. 253-294
- Hurst, Stephanie M., 'Trade in Force: The Need for Effective Regulation of Private Military and Security Companies', 84 *Southern California Law Review* (2011) pp. 447-486
- Kees, Alexander, 'Regulation of Private Military Companies', 3 *Goettingen Journal of International Law* (2011) pp. 199-216
- Nanda, Ved P., 'Maritime Piracy: How Can International Law and Policy Address This Growing Global Menace', 39 *Denver Journal of International Law and Policy* (2011) pp. 177-208

- Yasin, Huma T., 'Playing Catch-Up: Proposing the Creation of Status-Based Regulations to Bring Private Military Contractor Firms within the Purview of International and Domestic Law', 25 *Emory International Law Review* (2011) pp. 411-498

3 Protected Persons

3.1 Civilians

Articles

- Baruch, Sharvit Pnina, Newman, Noam, 'Warning civilians prior to attack under international law; Theory and Practice', 87 *International Law Studies Series US Naval War College* (2011) pp. 359-415
- Henderson, Christian, 'International measures for the protection of civilians in Libya and Cote d'Ivoire', 60(3) *International and Comparative Law Quarterly* (2011) pp. 767-778
- Schmitt, Michael N., 'Wings over Libya; the No Fly Zone in Legal Perspective', 36 *Yale Journal of International Law* (2011) pp. 45-58
- Welsh, Jennifer, 'Civilian Protection in Libya: Putting coercion and controversy back into responsibility to protect', 25 (3) *Ethics and International Affairs* (2011) pp. 255-262

3.2 Women and Children

Articles

- Cummings, Sara Kuipers, 'Liberia's New War: Post-Conflict Strategies for Confronting Rape and Sexual Violence', 43 *Arizona State Law Journal* (2011) pp. 223-262
- Desierto, Diane A., 'Leveraging international economic tools to confront child soldiering', 43 *New York University Journal of International Law and Politics* (2011) pp. 337-418
- Kamau, Evelyn W., 'Domestic Adjudication of Sexual and Gender-Based Violence in Armed Conflict: Considerations for Prosecutors and Judges', 4 *African Journal of Legal Studies* (2011) pp. 85-122
- Koenig, K. Alexa, Ryan Lincoln and Lauren E. Groth, 'Contextualizing Sexual Violence Committed during the War on Terror: A Historical Overview of International Accountability', 45 *University of San Francisco Law Review* (2011) pp. 911-958
- Nagle, Luz E., 'Child Soldiers and the Duty of Nations to Protect Children from Participation in Armed Conflict', 19 *Cardozo Journal of International and Comparative Law* (2011) pp. 1-58

4 Means and Methods of Warfare

Articles

- Pedrozo, Raul, 'Use of unmanned systems to combat terrorism', 87 *International Law Studies Series US Naval War College* (2011) pp. 217-271
- Stewart, Darren M, 'New technology and the law of armed conflict', 87 *International Law Studies Series US Naval War College* (2011) pp. 271-301
- Von Heinegg, Heintschel Wolff, 'Asymmetric Warfare; How to respond?', 87 *International Law Studies Series US Naval War College* (2011) pp. 463-483

4.1 Conventional Weapons

Article

- Coughlin, Timothy, 'The future of robotic weaponry and the law of armed conflict; irreconcilable differences', 17 *UCL Jurisprudence Review* (2011) pp. 67-99

4.2 Nuclear Weapons

Articles

- Joyner, Daniel H, 'Recent developments in international law regarding nuclear weapons', 60(1) *International and Comparative Law Quarterly* (2011) pp. 209-224
- Moxley, Charles J. Jr, John Burroughs and Jonathan Granoff, 'Nuclear Weapons and Compliance with International Humanitarian Law and the Nuclear Non-Proliferation Treaty', 34 *Fordham International Law Journal* (2011) pp. 595-696
- Moxley, Charles J. Jr, 'Obama's Nuclear Posture Review: An Ambitious Program for Nuclear Arms Control but a Retreat from the Objective of Nuclear Disarmament', 34 *Fordham International Law Journal* (2011) pp. 734-755

4.3 New Weapons

Articles

- Bradbury, Steven G., 'The developing legal framework for defensive and offensive cyber operations', 2 *Harvard National Security Journal* (2011) pp. 1-22
- Schmitt, Micheal N, 'Cyber operations and the Jus in Bello; Key Issues', 87 *International Law Studies Series US Naval War College* (2011) pp. 89-112
- Shackelford, Scott J, Andres, Richard B, 'State Responsibility for Cyber Attacks; competing Standards for a Growing Problem', 42 *Georgetown Journal of International Law* (2011) pp. 971-1016

- Vogel, Ryan J, 'Drone Warfare and the Law of Armed Conflict', 39 *Denver Journal of International Law and Policy* (2011) pp. 101-138
- Watts, Sean, 'Low intensity Computer Network Attack and self defense', 87 *International Law Studies Series US Naval War College* (2011) pp. 59-88

4.4 Cultural Property and Places of Worship

Articles

- Frulli, Micaela, 'The criminalisation of offences against cultural heritage in times of armed conflict; the quest for consistency', 22(1) *European Journal of International Law* (2011) pp. 203-217

4.5 Naval Warfare

Article

- Kraska, James, 'Rule selection in the Case of Israel's Naval Blockade of Gaza: Law of Naval Warfare or Law of the Sea?', 13 *Yearbook of International Humanitarian Law* (2010) pp. 367-396
- Sanger, Andrew, 'The Contemporary Law of Blockade and the Gaza Freedom Flotilla', 13 *Yearbook of International Humanitarian Law* (2010) pp. 397-448

5 Ceasfire, Armistices and Peace Agreements

Books

- Cunningham, David E., *Barriers to peace in civil wars* (Cambridge, Cambridge University Press 2011) 296 pp.

Articles

- Daase, Cindy, 'Redistribution of resources in internationalized intra-state peace processes by comprehensive peace agreements and Security Council resolutions', 43 *Goettingen Journal of International Law* (2011) pp. 59-84
- Sheeran, Scott P., 'International law, peace agreements and self-determination: the case of The Sudan', 60 *International and Comparative Law Quarterly* (2011) pp. 423-458

6 Amnesties

Books

– Sadat, Leyla, ed., *Forging a convention for crimes against humanity* (Cambridge, Cambridge University Press 2011) 584 pp.

Articles

– Allan, Kate, 'Prosecution and peace: a role for amnesty before the ICC?', 39 *Denver Journal of International Law and Policy* (2011) pp. 239-303
– Binder, Christina, 'The prohibition of amnesties by the Inter-American Court of Human Rights', 12 *German Law Journal* 05 (2011) pp. 1203-1230
– Tayeb, Beloudah, 'Amnesty as turning point for transitional justice in the light of democratic transitions – Algeria as a case', 1 *AGORA International Journal of Juridical Sciences* (2011) pp. 1-9
– Vandeginste, Stef, 'Bypassing the prohibition of amnesty for human rights crimes under international law: lessons learned from the Burundi peace process', 29(2) *Netherlands Quarterly of Human Rights* (2011) pp. 189-211

7 Reparation and Compensation

Books

– Payne, Cymie R. and Peter H. Sand, eds., *Gulf War reparations and the United Nations Commission: environmental liability* (Oxford, Oxford University Press 2011) 372 pp.

Articles

– Putorti, Matthew, 'International legal right to individual compensation in Nepal and the transitional justice context', 34 *Fordham International Law Journal* (2011) pp. 1131-1188
– Zyberi, Gentian, 'The International Court of Justice and applied forms of reparation for international human rights and humanitarian law violations', 7 *Utrecht Law Review* (2011) pp. 204-215

8 Military Commissions and Tribunals

Books

– Heller, Kevin J., *The Nuremberg military tribunals and the origins of international criminal law* (Oxford, Oxford University Press 2011) 509 pp.

Articles

- Chaffee, Devon, 'Military commissions revived: persisting problems of perception', 9 *University of New Hampshire Law Review* (2011) pp. 237-259
- Frakt, David J., 'Mohammed Jawad and the Military Commissions of Guantanamo', 60 *Duke Law Journal* (2011) 1367-1411
- McCaul, Michael and Ronald J. Sievert, 'Congress's consistent intent to utilize military commissions in the war against Al-Qaeda and its adoption of commission rules that fully comply with due process', 42 *St Mary's Law Journal* (2011) pp. 595-644
- Petty, Keith A., 'Beyond the court of public opinion: military commissions and the reputational pull of compliance theory', 42 *Georgetown Journal of International Law* (2011) pp. 303-374

9 Implementation of International Humanitarian Law

9.1 Fact-finding Commissions

Article

- Boutruche, Theo, 'Credible fact-finding and allegations of international humanitarian law violations; challenges in theory and practice', 16(1) *Journal of Conflict and Security Law* (2011) pp. 105-140
- Schmitt, Micheal N, 'Investigating violations of international law in armed conflict', 2(1) *Harvard National Security Journal* (2011) pp. 31-84

9.2 International Committee of the Red Cross

Books

- Wilmshurst, Elizabeth and Susan Breau, *Perspectives on the ICRC Study on Customary International Humanitarian Law* (Cambridge, Cambridge University Press 2011) 466 pp.

Articles

- Ratner, Steven R., 'Law promotion beyond law talk: The Red Cross, persuasion and the laws of war', 22(2) *European Journal of International Law* (2011) pp. 459-506
- Terry, Fiona, 'The International Committee of the Red Cross in Afghanistan; reasserting the neutrality of humanitarian action', 93 *International Review of the Red Cross* (2011) pp. 173-189

10 The Law of Neutrality

Articles

- Heller, Kevin J., 'The law of neutrality does not apply to the conflict with Al-Qaeda, and that's a good thing, too: a response to Chang', 47 *Texas International Law Journal* (2011)

10.1 United Nations

Books

- Simma, Bruno, et al., *The Charter of the United Nations: a commentary* (Oxford, Oxford University Press 2011) 2000 pp.
- Verdirame, Guglielmo, *The UN and human rights: who guards the guardians?* (Cambridge, Cambridge University Press 2011) 510 pp.

Articles

- Norton, Sebastian M., 'The United Nations Charter's collective security framework in the Twenty-First Century: a case-study of the United States' use of force in Pakistan', 57 *Loyola Law Review* (2011) pp. 157-206

10.2 Regional Organizations

10.2.1 African

Books

- Gumedze, Sabelo, *The Peace and Security Council of the African Union: its relationship with the United Nations, the African Union and sub-regional mechanisms* (Åbo, Åbo Akademi University Press 2011) 290 pp.
- Sriram, Chandra-Lekha, Olga Martin Ortega and Johanna Herman, eds., *Peacebuilding and the rule of law in Africa: just peace?* (London, Routledge 2011) 280 pp.

Articles

- Crane, David M., 'Take down: case studies regarding lawfare in international criminal justice: the West African experience', 43 *Case Western Reserve Journal of International Law* (2010) pp. 201-214
- Paliwal, Suyash, 'The primacy of regional organizations in international peacekeeping: the African example', 51 *Virginia Journal of International Law* (2011) pp. 26-47

10.3 Humanitarian and Other Interventions

Books

- Kuwali, Dan, *The Responsibility to protect: implementation of Article 4 (h) Intervention* (Cambridge, Cambridge University Press 2011) 527 pp.

Articles

- Allo, Awol K., 'Ethiopia's armed intervention in Somalia: the legality of self-defense in response to the threat of terrorism', 39 *Denver Journal of International Law and Policy* (2011) pp. 139-168
- Davis, JE, 'From ideology to pragmatism: China's position on humanitarian intervention in the post Cold-War era', 44 *Vanderbilt Journal of International Law* (2011) pp. 217-283
- Govern, Kevin H., 'Resigned to failure or committed to a resigned course of justice – the Matthew Hoh resignation, our current politico-military strategy in Afghanistan, and lessons learned from the Panama intervention of twenty years ago', 13 *Oregon Review of International Law* (2011) pp. 171-188
- Grimal, Francis and Graham Melling, 'British action in Libya 2011: the lawful protection of nationals abroad?', 23 *Denning Law Journal* (2011) pp. 165-177
- Hehir, Aidan, 'Pandora's box? Humanitarian intervention and international law', 7 *International Journal of Law in Context* (2011) pp. 87-94
- Hofmeister, Hannes, "Don't mess with Moscow' – Legal aspects of the 2008 Caucasus conflict', 12 *San Diego International Law Journal* (2010-2011) pp. 147-174
- Mazzochi, Sarah, 'Humanitarian intervention in a post-Iraq, post-Darfur world: is there a duty now to prevent genocide even without Security Council approval?', 17 *Annual Survey of International and Comparative Law* (2011) pp. 111-128
- Schmitt, Michael N., 'Wings over Libya: the no-fly zone in a legal perspective', 36 *The Yale Journal of International Law Online* (2011) pp. 45-58
- Tesòn, Fernando R., 'Humanitarian intervention: loose ends', 10 *Journal of Military Ethics* (2011) pp. 192-212
- Weiss, Robert H., 'China as peacekeeper: implications for the law and politics of humanitarian intervention', 6 *Yale Journal of International Affairs* (2011) pp. 137-139

10.4 Peacekeeping

Books

- Sloan, James, *The militarization of peacekeeping in the twenty-first century* (Oxford, Hart Publishing 2011) 336 pp.

Articles

- Ndulo, Muna, 'United Nations peacekeeping operations and security and reconstruction', 44 *Akron Law Review* (2011) pp. 769-808
- Weiner, Justus R.; Sharon Avinoam and Morrison, Michelle, 'Peacekeepers: will they advance any prospective Arab-Israeli peace agreement?', 34 *Fordham International Law Journal* (2010-2011) pp. 1-45

10.5 Peace Enforcement and Peace Building

Articles

- Jubilut, Liliana Lyra, 'Towards a new *jus post bellum:* The United Nations Peacebuilding Commission and the improvement of post-conflict efforts and accountability', 20 *Minnesota Journal of International Law* (2011) pp. 26-64
- Saul, Matthew, 'Local ownership of post-conflict reconstruction in international law: the initiation of international involvement', 16 *Journal of Conflict and Security Law* (2011) pp. 165-206
- Yoo, John, 'Fixing Failed States', 99 *California Law Review* (2011) 95-150

10.6 Sanctions

Books

- Charron, Andrea, *UN Sanctions and conflict: responding to peace and security threats* (London, Routledge 2011) 208 pp.
- Eirksson, Mikael, *Targeting peace: understanding UN and EU targeted sanctions* (Farnham, Ashgate 2011) 296 pp.
- Tzanakopoulos, Antonios, *Disobeying the Security Council: countermeasures against wrongful sanctions* (Oxford, Oxford University Press 2011) 243 pp.

Articles

- Addis, Adeno, 'Targeted sanctions as counterterrorism strategy', 19 *Tulane Journal of International and Comparative Law* (2011) pp. 187-2006
- Farrar, Quinton C., 'U.S. energy sanctions and the race to prevent Iran from acquiring weapons of mass destruction', 79 *Fordham Law Review* (2011) pp. 2347-2394
- White, Nigel D., 'UN sanctions: where public law meets public international law', 74 *The Modern Law Review* (2011) pp. 456-478
- Willis, Grant L. 'Security Council targeted sanctions: due process and the 1267 Ombudsperson', 42 *Georgetown Journal of International Law* (2011) pp. 673-746

11 Arms Control and Disarmament

11.1 Conventional Weapons

Articles

- Good, Rachel, 'Yes, we should: Why the US should change its policy toward the 1997 Mine Ban Treaty', 9 *Northwestern University Journal of International Human Rights* (2011) pp. 209-232
- Raccuia, Daniel Joseph, 'Convention on Cluster Munitions: An Incomplete Solution to the Cluster Munition Problem', 44 *Vanderbuilt Journal of Transnational Law* (2011) pp. 465-498

11.2 Weapons of Mass Destruction

Books

- Joyner, Daniel. H, *Interpreting the Nuclear Non-Proliferation Treaty*, (Oxford, Oxford University Press 2011) 200 pp.

Articles

- Asada, Masahiko, 'The Treaty on the Non-Proliferation of Nuclear Weapons and the universalisation of the Additional Protocol', 16(1) *Journal of Conflict and Security Law* (2011) pp. 3-34
- Mackby, Jenifer, 'Non-Proliferation Verification and the Nuclear Test Ban', 34(4) *Fordham International Law Journal* (2011) pp. 697-733
- Peloso, Chris, 'Crafting an Updated Nuclear Non-Proliferation Treaty; Applying the lessons learned from the success of similar International Treaties to the Nuclear Arms Problem', 9 *Santa Clara Journal of International Law* (2011) pp. 309-344
- Stransky, Steven G, 'Nuclear Non-proliferation Treaty and Pakistan: Interpreting Nuclear Security Assistance Prohibitions', 23 *Florida Journal of International Law* (2011) pp. 1-48
- Weiss, Peter, 'Taking the Law seriously: The imperative need for a Nuclear Weapons Convention', 34 *Fordham International Law Journal* (2011) pp. 776-787

12 Conflict Prevention

Books

- Gross, Eva, Juncos, Ana E., *EU Conflict Prevention and crisis management; roles institutions and policies* (London, New York, Routledge 2011) 192 pp.

Article

- Brosig, Malte, 'The emerging peace and security regime in Africa; the role of the EU', 16(1) *European Foreign Affairs Review* (2011) pp. 107-122
- Kennedy-Chouane, Megan Grace, 'Improving conflict prevention and peace building assistance through evaluation', *OECD Journal* (2011) pp. 99-107

13 Conflict Resolution

Books

- Feste, Karen A, *America responds to terrorism; Conflict resolution strategies of Clinton, Bush and Obama,* (New York, Palgrave MacMillan 2011) 286 pp.
- Gaub, Florence, *Military integration after civil wars; multi-ethnic armies, identity and post-conflict reconstruction,* (London, New York, Routledge 2011) 180 pp.

Articles

- Jubilut, Liliana Lyra, 'Towards a New Jus Post Bellum: The United Nations Peacebuilding Commission and the Improvement of Post-Conflict Efforts and Accountability', 20 *Minnesota Journal of International Law* (2011) pp. 26-64
- Nmaju, Mba Chidi, 'The role of judicial institutions in the restoration of post-conflict societies; The cases of Rwanda and Sierra Leone', 16(2) *Journal of Conflict and Security Law* (2011) pp. 357-384
- Saul, Matthew, 'Local ownership of post-conflict reconstruction in international law; the initiation of international involvement', 16(1) *Journal of Conflict and Security Law* (2011) pp. 165-206

14 Jus Ad Bellum

Books

- Moir, Lindsay, *Reappraising the Resort to Force: International Law, Jus ad Bellum and the War on Terror* (Oxford, Hart Publishing 2011) 194 pp.
- Okimoto, Keiichiro, *The Distinction and Relationship Between Jus Ad Bellum and Jus in Bello* (Oxford, Hart Publishing 2011) 411 pp.

Articles

- Martin, Craig, 'Taking War Seriously – A Model for Constitutional Constraints on the Use of Force in Compliance with International Law' 76 *Brooklyn Law Review* (2011) pp. 611-730
- Waxman, Matthew C, 'Cyber-Attacks and the Use of Force: Back to the Future of Article 2(4)', 2 *Yale Journal of International Law* (2011) pp. 421-460

15 Terrorism and Counter-Terrorism

Books

- Bianchi, Andrea and Yasmin Naqvi, *International Humanitarian Law and Terrorism* (Portland, Oregon, Hart Publishing 2011) 454 pp.
- Ford, Christopher and Amichai Cohen, eds., *Rethinking the Law of Armed Conflict in an Age of Terrorism* (Idaho Falls, Lexington Books 2011) 332 pp.

Articles

- Bianchi, Andrea, 'Terrorism and Armed Conflict: Insights from a Law & Literature Perspective', 24 *Leiden Journal of International Law* (2011) pp. 1-21
- Chesney, Robert, 'Who May Be Killed? Anwar al-Awlaki as a Case Study in the International Legal Regulation of Lethal Force', 13 *Yearbook of International Humanitarian Law* (2010) pp. 3-60
- Pistone, Michele R. and John J. Hoeffner, 'Unsettling Developments: Terrorism and the New Case for Enhancing Protection and Humanitarian Assistance for Refugees and Internally Displaced Persons, Including Victims of Natural Disasters', 42(3) *Columbia Human Rights Law Review* (2011) pp. 613-695
- Raguan, Galit, 'Adjudicating Armed Conflict in Domestic Courts: The Experience of Israel's Supreme Court', 13 *Yearbook of International Humanitarian Law* (2010) pp. 61-95
- Sabel, Robbie, 'The Legality of Reciprocity in the War Against Terrorism', 43 *Case Western Reserve Journal of International Law* (2011) pp. 473-482

16 International Human Rights Law

Books

- Ben-Naftali, Orna, *International Humanitarian Law and International Human Rights Law* (Oxford, Oxford University 2011) 424 pp.
- Doswald-Beck, Louise, *Human Rights in times of Conflict and Terrorism* (Oxford, Oxford University Press 2011) 600 pp.
- Martin Forrest, Francisco, Stephen J. Schnably, Richard Wilson, Jonathon Simon and Mark Tushnet, *International Human Rights and Humanitarian Law* (Cambridge, Cambridge University Press 2011) 1024 pp.

Articles

- Escorihuela, Alejandro Lorite, 'Humanitarian Law and Human Rights Law: The Politics of Distinction', 19 *Michigan State University College of Law Journal of International Law* (2011) pp. 299-408

17 Refugee Law

Articles

- Krever, Tor, 'Mopping Up: UNHCR neutrality and non-refoulement since the Cold War', 10(3) *Chinese Journal of International Law* (2011) pp. 587-608
- Leaning, Jennifer, 'Enforced displacement of civilian populations in war; a potential new element in crimes against humanity', 11(3) *International Criminal Law Review* (2011) pp. 445-462

Table of Cases*

INTERNATIONAL

African Commission on Human and People's Rights

European Court of Human Rights

* The Table of Cases was compiled by Mrs. C.C. Diepeveen, Middelburg, The Netherlands. e-mail: cdiep@zeelandnet.nl

M.N. Schmitt and L. Arimatsu (eds.), *Yearbook of International Humanitarian Law Volume 14, 2011*, DOI: 10.1007/978-90-6704-855-2,

Index*

* The Table of Cases was compiled by Mrs. C.C. Diepeveen, Middelburg, The Netherlands. e-mail: cdiep@zeelandnet.nl

M.N. Schmitt and L. Arimatsu (eds.), *Yearbook of International Humanitarian Law Volume 14, 2011*, DOI: 10.1007/978-90-6704-855-2,

I

T

MIX
Papier aus verantwortungsvollen Quellen
Paper from responsible sources
FSC® C105338

If you have any concerns about our products,
you can contact us on
ProductSafety@springernature.com

In case Publisher is established outside the EU,
the EU authorized representative is:
Springer Nature Customer Service Center GmbH
Europaplatz 3, 69115 Heidelberg, Germany

Printed by Libri Plureos GmbH
in Hamburg, Germany